DR. ANTHONY OSTRIC

D0161084

THE SOCIAL ORDER

THE SOCIAL ORDER
Fourth Edition

ROBERT BIERSTEDT
Professor of Sociology
University of Virginia

McGRAW-HILL BOOK COMPANY

New York   St. Louis   San Francisco
Düsseldorf   Johannesburg   Kuala Lumpur
London   Mexico   Montreal   New Delhi
Panama   Paris   São Paulo
Singapore   Sydney   Tokyo   Toronto

When we traverse the gallery of history, and observe its motley succession of fantastic paintings—when we examine in a cursory way the successive races of mankind, all different and constantly changing, our first impression is apt to be that the phenomena of social life are incapable of any general expression or scientific law, and that the attempt to found a system of sociology is wholly chimerical. But the first herdsmen who scanned the starry heavens, and the first tillers of the soil who essayed to discover the secrets of plant life, must have been impressed in much the same way by the sparkling disorder of the firmament, with its manifold meteors, as well as by the exuberant diversity of vegetable and animal forms. The idea of explaining sky or forest by a small number of logically concatenated notions, under the name of astronomy or biology, had it occurred to them, would have appeared in their eyes the height of extravagance. And there is no less complexity—no less real irregularity and apparent caprice—in the world of meteors and in the interior of the virgin forest, than in the recesses of human history.

Gabriel Tarde

THE SOCIAL ORDER

Copyright © 1957, 1963, 1970, 1974 by McGraw-Hill, Inc. All rights reserved. Printed in the United States of America. No part of this publication may be reproduced, stored in a retrieval system, or transmitted, in any form or by any means, electronic, mechanical, photocopying, recording, or otherwise, without the prior written permission of the publisher.

1234567890MAMM7987654

This book was set in Palatino by Black Dot, Inc. The editors were David Edwards, Ronald Kissack, and Phyllis T. Dulan; the designer was John Horton; and the production supervisor was John F. Harte. The Maple Press Company was printer and binder.

Library of Congress Cataloging in Publication Data

Bierstedt, Robert, date
 The social order.

 Includes bibliographical references.
 1. Sociology. I. Title.
HM51.B47 1974   301   73-11405
ISBN 0-07-005253-0

CONTENTS

PREFACE TO THE FOURTH EDITION

The Preface to the third edition carries several messages for the fourth as well, and I therefore reprint it here, with special attention invited to the first two paragraphs. In addition, however, I should like to follow the advice of several of my friendly critics and make explicit the systematic character of the sociological theory presented in this book.

A glance at the table of contents will disclose that the topics treated have a logical rather than a random order. Thus, after an introductory chapter, I discuss, in sequence, three kinds of conditions—geographic, biological, and demographic—that undergird human societies and give them, in effect, a natural foundation. In each case I have contrasted their contributions to contributions of a different kind—the contributions of culture. Since culture is so central a concept in sociology, I spend the space of three chapters explaining its meaning and significance, classifying its content, and indicating the role it plays in the socialization process. That part of culture most pertinent to sociology, of course, is not art or language or materiel but rather social organization, which then becomes the focus of detailed attention in a section of its own. I treat the organization of society—the social order in short—in terms of seven concepts—norms, statuses, groups, associations, institutions, authority, and power. Each of these is logically related to the others, as can be seen, for example, in the following series of propositions:

First, norms, as one of the three components of culture, are not "free floating" but are always attached to statuses. Second, an individual has exactly the same number of statuses as there are groups of which he is a member, a proposition that becomes clear in our classification of groups. Third, the classification of groups gives us, among others, one highly important kind of group that appears in complex societies, namely the organized group or association, every one of which has both a formal and an informal organization. Fourth, associations accompany and support orderly and recurrent procedures, which are called institutions. Fifth, authority, always present in associations and indeed a criterion of their organization, is institutionalized power. Sixth, power, which finds expression in society either as authority or as force, sustains the social order even as, in situations of conflict, opposing power threatens it. Thus, these seven concepts, as Gabriel Tarde's "small number of logically concatenated notions,"* give us a system of sociology.

The remainder of the book is less systematic. Inasmuch as any society exhibits different kinds of groups, in both horizontal and vertical juxtaposition, we look in the penultimate section at a number of them under the general rubric of social differentiation. They include such important pairs as women and men, city and suburb, class and caste, color and creed, and, treated second, the family. In a more philosophical mood we conclude the section with reflections on the relationship of individual and society. The final section, consisting of one brief chapter, is devoted to the problem of social change.

Deficiencies remain. I should perhaps attend in detail, rather than only incidentally, to economic, political, and religious institutions. But there is no end to this. Why not also educational, literary, and recreational institutions? And cocktail parties, festivals, and fairs? In spite of respect for my critics, I have not been

*See the remarkable quotation that precedes the contents.

beguiled into this expansion for three reasons: (1) the book has attained what I regard as an optimum size, and additional chapters would make it unwieldy; (2) treatment of particular institutions would inevitably produce an accent upon American society and thus generate a parochial sociology; and (3) (the obverse of the preceding reason) sociology is more concerned with the abstract and universal principles of the social order than it is with particular institutions and particular societies.

My debts to others are again too numerous to identify. They include all of those who have written about this book. I have an ineffable regard for the various editors and copy editors who have worked on it over a period of years. For this edition I owe an additional debt to my wife. And I am especially touched by the reader who assured me that if I ever needed "a sandwich or a couple of bucks" he would be glad to come around. I told him, in grateful response, that I would file his offer for future reference.

Robert Bierstedt

PREFACE TO THE THIRD EDITION

In all ages and human times, ever since our erect and restless species appeared upon the planet, men have been living with others of their kind in something called societies. Wherever these societies may be and whatever their chapter of history—whether primitive Polynesian or ancient Egyptian, classical Chinese or contemporary Russian, medieval English or modern American—they all exhibit common elements and constant features. These are the elements that give to society its form and shape, that constitute its structure, and that, in a word, comprise the social order. It is the first task of a general sociology to discover these constants, to describe them with an economy of concepts, and to delineate their interrelationships. This is the task to which the following pages are devoted.

If anyone should wonder why, when we have so many systems of sociology, it should seem desirable to bring forth yet another one, an answer can perhaps be found in terms of emphasis and approach. I have tried to focus the inquiry that follows upon society itself, upon its structure and its changes, and have avoided concerns that are psychological, economic, narrowly political, or even anthropological in character. Sociology has a scope and a grandeur of its own and it need not, in my opinion, assume in addition the problems of other disciplines. I hope that what I have written here will be construed, therefore, as an introduction to systematic sociology, an invitation to pursue for its own sake the reality that is society, and an effort to introduce into our knowledge of society the same centrality and significance that characterize the social order itself.

The preceding two paragraphs appeared as part of the preface to the first and second editions of this book. They continue to express my sentiments, and I hope therefore that they can sustain reiteration here. Although the basic plan remains intact, the third edition contains a number of changes and additions. I have endeavoured in this edition, as in the second, to bring all of the references and allusions up to date. Unfortunately, it is the task of a Sisyphus. Only authors of successive editions of the same book can fully appreciate how fleeting a current reference can be. What is current today, and in the forefront of everyone's awareness, is forgotten tomorrow, is medieval history the day after tomorrow, and ancient history the day after that. I speak of references, of course, and allusions, and not of facts and principles which, if they are "true," can escape the exigencies of the calendar.

Sociology, as we suggest in the introductory chapter, is a relatively abstract discipline. That is, as distinguished from ethnology and history, it attempts to set out principles of social organization that apply to all societies in all times and places. There are certain constants of the social order, persistent components of the social structure, which have to do with the nature of society itself, and which thus win an independence of the dimension of time. It is impossible, nevertheless, to provide illustrations of these constants, and these components, without reference to particular societies at particular times and places. These references should not always be contemporary, however great the temptation, because if they are they will tend to diminish the universality of sociological principles. Nor, for the same reason, should they be provincial. Every author, of course, is to some degree a captive of his own culture, whether he writes on sociology or on any other social subject, and it is inevitable therefore that the majority of the illustrations are drawn from the American society. We would ask the reader, however, to regard this situation as fortuitous rather than necessary, and to think of sociology as something that transcends the boundaries of nations and the limitations of time.

I have added to this third edition two new chapters to the section on social organization, one on authority and the other on power. Both of them are thoroughgoing revisions of articles on these subjects that I have previously published. The article on power especially, to my surprise and gratification, has been reprinted in more places than I can remember, and it occurred to me that I ought to utilize it myself. Power and authority, as I hope the sequences in this section will show, are both salient aspects of the social order and an essential part of social organization.

Another observation concerns the relationship between sociology and social psychology, and the clear separation between the two that receives continuing emphasis in these pages. Of two highly perceptive and penetrating persons who prepared critiques of the second edition, one regards the tendency to "psychologize" social phenomena as an unfortunate development in the history of the discipline and consequently views the separation to which I have referred as the greatest strength of the book. The other, in exact contradiction, wants much more about socialization and social interaction, including symbolic interaction, and regards the relative inattention to these subjects as the greatest weakness of the book.

It is clearly impossible to satisfy both these critics. Under the circumstances I have concluded, with a happy obstinacy, that the initial emphasis is the one to be preferred. This third edition therefore reaffirms this emphasis upon structure—upon norms, statuses, groups, associations, institutions, and authority—and continues to neglect "the people" and their personalities. I may say, in addition, that I have made no use of the category of "action," a concept that is basic in the sociological theory of two mentors of mine, Talcott Parsons and the late Florian Znaniecki. I would contend that no one who begins with action—either the stimulus-response of a behavioristic psychology or the means-end schema of a voluntaristic psychology—can easily arrive at a notion of the social order. The vagaries of response and the idiosyncrasies of choice preclude so desirable a termination of inquiry. The danger, even from such comprehensive efforts as those of Parsons and Znaniecki, which of course are voluntaristic rather than behavioristic, is that one will emerge with a supererogatory social psychology rather than a systematic sociology.

Emile Durkheim was surely guilty of exaggeration when he said that whenever we have a psychological explanation of a social phenomenon we can be sure the explanation is false. I would nevertheless insist with him that it is possible to explain social action in terms of social structure and exceedingly difficult if not impossible to explain social structure in terms of social action. This is especially the case if one conceives of sociology as an autonomous discipline, with its own focus, range, and responsibility, and not merely as one of the behavioral sciences.

Another complaint, unrelated to the preceding one, comes from a critic who believes that I should have given more attention to Durkheim and to Max Weber in this book. The complaint is muted perhaps by the fact that I attend in greater measure to both of them in this edition. I regard myself in many ways as a Durkheimian and even confess that I have produced an introduction to Durkheim, one written neither for colleagues nor for advanced students, but rather for the man on the Clapham bus, as the English call the man in the street. Weber on the Protestant ethic receives special attention in the concluding chapter. I also offer graduate seminars on both writers. Nevertheless, both of them addressed their work for the most part to special problems in sociology and not to the nature of society in general. In spite of the superiority of their separate essays, neither Durkheim nor Weber was a general theorist, neither constructed a systematic theory of the social order, and neither gave us a rounded and logical treatment of the structure of society.

The reader will therefore find more references to, and more reliance upon, such writers of another generation of sociologists as my own teachers, Pitirim A. Sorokin and Robert M. MacIver. They continue to influence my approach because, in their systematic works, they contributed above all a sense of the structure of society, a sense of society as a unique phenomenon, and of sociology as a challenging subject for intellectual inquiry. This preference will doubtless evoke a difference of opinion among those who adhere to other schools. Such differences, however, contribute animation and excitement to the life of a discipline.

It remains for me to acknowledge indebtedness to all those who have helped me, not only with the third edition, but with the first and second as well. A listing of their names—colleagues, students, and correspondents—would require several paragraphs. Instead of mentioning them I shall simply say that I am grateful to them all. To this general anonymity, however, I want to make one exception. The largest debt of all I owe to Janis M. Yates, who edited this book with grace, and patience, and distinction.

Robert Bierstedt

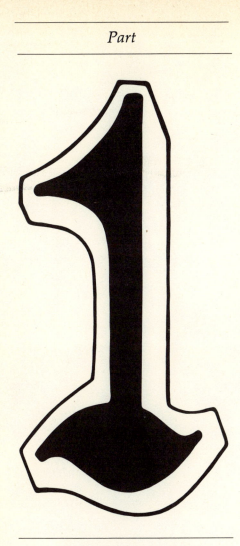

INTRODUCTION

Chapter 1

THE SCIENCE
OF SOCIOLOGY

LTHOUGH he may be approaching
the subject for the first time,
the reader of this book already
knows something about sociology.
He has been a member of society
for some time and has had continuous
personal experience with social
relationships. He knows that as a
civilized person he has inherited a
long tradition and that many of his
ideas and customs had their
origin in societies older than his own.
He knows also that in some
respects he is like all other
people, in certain respects
like some other people, and
in certain other respects like
no one except himself. All
this is sociological knowledge. His
participation in social relationships,
his possession of a social
heritage, and his awareness of the
likenesses and differences between
people all give him an insight
into the subject that now engages
his attention. But they do not,
of course, make him a sociologist, any
more than a walk through
the forest makes him a botanist
or a visit to the zoo a zoologist.
He may not yet know, in fact,
what sociology is, and so we
shall begin our discussion with an
answer to this first question.

1. The Story of Sociology

Sociology has a long past but only a short history. Since the dawn of civilization society has been a subject for speculation and inquiry, along with every other phenomenon that has agitated the restless and inquisitive mind of man. There is warrant, indeed, for saying that *The Republic* of Plato is the greatest of all sociological treatises in the West, and the *Analects* of Confucius in the East. But it is only within the last one hundred years or so that the study of society has become a separate subject and a separate science.

All inquiries were once a part of philosophy, that great mother of the sciences (*mater scientiarum*), and philosophy embraced them all in an undifferentiated and amorphous fashion. One by one, however, with the growth of Western civilization, the various sciences cut the apron strings, as it were, and began to pursue separate and independent courses. Astronomy and physics were among the first to break away, and were followed thereafter by chemistry, biology, and geology. In the nineteenth century two new sciences appeared: psychology, or the science of human behavior; and sociology, or the science of human society. Thus, what had once been cosmology, a subdivision of philosophy, became astronomy; what had once been natural philosophy became the science of physics; what had once been mental philosophy, or the philosophy of mind, became the science of psychology; and what had once been social philosophy, or the philosophy of history, became the science of sociology. To the ancient mother, philosophy, still belong several important kinds of inquiry—notably metaphysics, epistemology, logic, ethics, and aesthetics—but the sciences themselves are no longer studied as subdivisions of philosophy.

Various strains and tendencies, some intellectual and some ethical combined to form the science of sociology. Two of major importance are, on the one hand, an interest in social welfare and social reform and, on the other, an interest in the philosophy of history. How these together produced something called sociology is a fascinating story, but one that requires treatment in a book of its own. It will suffice to say that these separate and indeed somewhat disparate strains entered into the formation of this new science. In the United States particularly, in contrast to the European countries, sociology has been associated, especially in the public mind, with an effort to improve the social conditions of mankind and as an active agency in eradicating the problems of crime, delinquency, prostitution, unemployment, poverty, conflict, and war. That this identification is not currently correct, or is correct in only a very special and partial sense, will become clear as we proceed.

In the nineteenth century a French philosopher named Auguste Comte worked out, in a series of books, a general approach to the study of society. He believed that the sciences follow one another in a definite and logical order and that all inquiry goes through certain stages, arriving finally at the last, or positive, stage. He thought that it was time for inquiries into social problems and social phenomena to enter this last stage and so he recommended that the study of society become the science of society.

The name that Comte gave to his new science was "sociology," and this, from a number of points of view, was an unfortunate choice. "Sociology" is composed of two words: *socius*, meaning companion or associate; and *logos*, meaning word. Thus, the term formed from these two parts means talking about society, as geology (*geos*, earth) means talking about the earth; biology (*bios*, life), talking about life; and anthropology (*anthropos*, man), talking about man. Unfortunately, however, *socius* is a Latin word and *logos* is a Greek word, and the name of our discipline is thus an "illegitimate" offspring of two languages.[1] John Stuart Mill, another philosopher and social thinker of the nineteenth century, proposed the word "ethology" for some part of the new science. This term has the merit of being all Greek, but apparently it never appealed to other writers.[2] When, in the latter half of the century, Herbert Spencer developed his systematic study of society and frankly adopted the word "sociology" in the title of his work—on the ground that "the convenience and suggestiveness of our symbols are of more importance than the legitimacy of their derivation"[3]—it became the permanent name of the new science, and sociology, especially with Spencer's own contributions, was well launched on its career.

Sociology experienced a rapid development in the twentieth century, most notably in France, Germany, and the United States, although it advanced in somewhat different directions in the three countries. In spite of the fact that both Mill and Spencer were Englishmen, the development was nowhere near so rapid in the United Kingdom. In fact, there was little sociology in that country—except at The London School of Economics—until the 1960s, when a remarkable upsurge of interest resulted in the establishment of strong departments in almost all of the British universities. In this country Yale, Columbia, and Chicago, followed closely by the Middle Western universities, were in the vanguard of a vigorous sociological movement at the beginning of the century and today, of course, sociology is firmly established in American universities. All major universities, everywhere in the world, now offer instruction in the subject.

When it is recalled, however, that none of this American development

---

[1] Similarly, a large number of English words have a dual origin.
[2] Ethology now, curiously enough, means the study of animal behavior, especially animals in their normal habitats.
[3] "Preface," *Principles of Sociology*, vol. I.

significantly antedates the twentieth century, that Harvard, the oldest of American universities, had no department of sociology until 1930, that the department at Princeton became an independent one as late as 1960, and that Amherst waited until 1968 to appoint its first professor of sociology, it can be appreciated how new the science of sociology is. It is not yet in many respects a mature science, and one will find in it, therefore, more divergent points of view and rather less systematic agreement than in such older sciences as physics, astronomy, and biology.

2. Sociology and the Other Sciences

In order to acquire some understanding of the kind of science sociology is, it will be helpful to locate it in the scientific universe and to exhibit its relations with the other academic disciplines. Sociology is first of all a social science and not a natural science. One must exercise considerable caution, however, in interpreting this statement, for the phenomena that sociologists study, that is, social phenomena, are just as natural as are those, for example, that the physicist studies. There is nothing artificial, preternatural, or supernatural about social phenomena; if there were, they would elude investigation by the ordinary methods of inquiry. Social phenomena are as natural as the phenomena of magnetism, gravitation, and electricity, and a modern city is as natural as an anthill.

It was once believed, especially in one of the German schools of philosophy in the nineteenth century, that there are two distinct kinds of sciences—the natural sciences (*Naturwissenschaften*) on the one hand and the social sciences (*Kultur-, Sozial-,* or *Geisteswissenschaften*) on the other. It was further believed that in the first of these, the natural sciences, we *explain* the phenomena with which we are dealing, whereas in the second, the social sciences, we have the additional advantage of being able to *understand* them. We have all been members of a group, for example, and can therefore understand what a group is in a more intimate sense than we can understand a constellation, or a cloud. Thus the natural sciences are limited to the use of an *erklärende* (explaining) method, whereas the social sciences can use a *verstehende* (understanding) method.

This distinction, although it has its adherents, has not been popular in American sociology. Two principal arguments have been advanced against it. The first of these is that if we believe in it we are surrendering in advance any chance of making the study of society as scientific as the study of nature has become. This means that we are willing to consign society to the sphere of speculation and opinion and ultimately to deny that it can be brought into the realm of reliable knowledge. The second is that the more intimate knowledge we are presumed to have of phenomena in which we ourselves participate may not be an advantage. The intimacy may also help to introduce bias which would, in turn, detract from the objectivity of the knowledge to which we aspire. Thus, to adopt this distinction is to deny the possibility of dependable and objective knowledge about society and to exclude sociology from the domain of science.

Whatever the merit of these arguments—and we shall refer in another section to the method of sociology—it is a fact that for reasons of administrative convenience at least, the sciences are divided into two large areas: those that deal with the physical universe, including astronomy, physics, chemistry, geology, biology, and others; and those that deal with the social universe. In this division sociology clearly belongs with the social sciences, along with history, economics, political science, and juris-prudence (the science of law). That this division is more administrative than logical can be seen in the fact that some sciences do not clearly fit into one or the other of these categories, but rather cut across them—for example, psychology, geography, and anthropology, all three of which consider both physical and social facts. There are, for example, both physiological and social psychology, both physical and cultural geography, and both physical and cultural (or social) anthropology. But there is no physiological or physical sociology, so that in this sense sociology is clearly a social science.

It is more difficult to distinguish sociology from the various social sciences because here the distinction is frequently one that concerns not only differences in the content, or the area of investigation, but also differences in the degree of emphasis given certain aspects of the same content, or, more especially, the different ways in which the same content is approached and investigated. Furthermore, some of these relationships have been matters of controversy both within and without the sociological profession. There are those, for example, who would say that sociology is the basic social science, of which all the others are subdivisions. There are others who claim, with equal emphasis, that sociology is a specialized science of social phenomena, as specialized in its interests as are economics and political science. Again, some sociologists profess to see in their discipline the closest possible relations with psychology and anthropology, whereas others say that logically relations are just as close, if not closer, to history, economics, and government. We need, therefore, to caution the reader that the position outlined in the following preliminary pages may not find universal agreement among sociologists and that, if he continues to study sociology, he will inevitably expose himself to different points of view.

Let us consider first the relationship between history and sociology. Both are social disciplines and both are concerned with human activities and events. History is concerned primarily with the record of the past. The historian wants to describe, as accurately as possible, what actually happened to man during the long period he has lived on earth, and especially in that period since he began to live in cities and to have, in effect, a civilization. Thus the historian wants an accurate description of events, which he then relates to one another in a time sequence so that he can have a continuous story from the past to the present. He is not satisfied, however, with mere description; he seeks also to learn the causes of these events, to understand the past—not only how it has been (*wie es eigentlich gewesen ist*, in von Ranke's famous phrase) but also how it came to be. Nevertheless he is, in a sense, interested in events for their own sake. He wants to know everything there is to know about them and to describe them in all their unique individuality.

The sociologist, on the other hand, though using to all intents and purposes the same record of the past, is interested in events only in so far as they exemplify social processes resulting from the interaction and association of men in various situations and under various conditions; that is, he is not interested in events themselves but rather in the patterns that they exhibit. The historian, in other words, interests himself in the unique, the particular, and the individual; the sociologist, in the regular, the recurrent, and the universal. Although the statement is much too simple, it would not be too far wrong, as a working approximation, to say that history occupies itself with the differences in similar events, sociology with the similarities in different events.

To take a few examples, the historian is interested in the Peloponnesian War, the Norman Conquest, the Hundred Years' War, the Wars of the Roses, the Thirty Years' War, the Napoleonic Wars, the War between the States, the two world wars of the twentieth century, and all of the other wars within recorded time. The sociologist is interested in none of these wars as such, but in war itself as a social phenomenon, as one kind of conflict between social groups. Similarly, the sociologist is interested in neither the American Revolution, the French Revolution, nor the Russian Revolution, but in revolution in general as a social phenomenon, as another kind of conflict between social groups. Finally, as a third example, the historian and biographer are both interested in the lives and careers of famous men—military, political, religious, scientific, and other leaders— whereas the sociologist is interested not in the men themselves but in the phenomenon of leadership, because it is a phenomenon that appears in almost all social groups.

In summary, then, history and sociology may be distinguished most simply and clearly by the observation that the former is a particularizing or individualizing discipline, the latter a generalizing one. History is a descriptive discipline; sociology, an analytical one. History investigates the unique and the individual; sociology, the regular and the recurrent. An event that has occurred only once in the human past is of no sociological significance unless it can be related to a pattern of events that repeat themselves generation after generation, historical period after historical period, and human group after human group. If the past is conceived of as a continuous cloth unrolling through the centuries, history is interested in the individual threads and strands that make it up; sociology, in the patterns it exhibits.[4]

It is easier to distinguish sociology from such other social sciences as economics, political science (or government), and jurisprudence. Each of these sciences occupies itself with a special sector of human experience. Economics, for example, investigates all the phenomena that have to do with business, with getting and spending, with producing and consuming, and with distributing the resources of the world. Political science, similarly, investigates the ways in which men govern themselves—or are governed —and attempts to explain the intricacies and complexities of governments. Jurisprudence occupies itself with the law and investigates its origin, its nature, and its changes. And so on for the other social sciences of this kind. All of them may thus be called special social sciences inasmuch as they limit their focus of interest and their area of direct investigation to special kinds of events and experiences. Economic relationships, political relationships, and legal relationships, however, are also social relationships, and this circumstance has stimulated the controversy about whether sociology is a general or a special social science to which we referred above and to which we shall return in a following section.

Two other contemporary sciences that are closely related to sociology are psychology and anthropology. Indeed, the relationships here are so intimate that some writers would discourage any attempt to differentiate them and at one prominent university the three sciences appeared together in one department of social relations. Nevertheless, for the introductory student it is useful to recognize that the orientations and emphases of these sciences are somewhat different and that, although students of any one of them need to know as much as possible about the other two, the three are still separate sciences, with different origins and traditions and with somewhat different approaches to the general subject of man and society.

Psychology, as the science of behavior, occupies itself principally and primarily with the individual. It is interested in his intelligence and his learning, his motivations and his memory, his nervous system and his reaction time, his hopes and his fears, and the order and disorder of his mind. Social psychology, which serves as a bridge between psychology and

---

[4] For additional comparisons and contrasts see Robert Bierstedt, "Toynbee and Sociology," *The British Journal of Sociology*, vol. 10, no. 2, June, 1959, pp. 95–104.

sociology, maintains a primary interest in the individual but concerns itself with the way in which the individual behaves in his social groups, how he behaves collectively with other individuals, and how his personality is a function both of his basic physiological and temperamental equipment and of the social and cultural influences to which he is exposed.

Sociology, in contrast, has no primary interest in the individual, nor in his personality, nor in his behavior, but concerns itself rather with the nature of the groups to which individuals belong and the nature of the societies in which they live. If psychology and social psychology are primarily concerned with the behavior of individuals, sociology is interested in the social forms and structures within which this behavior takes place. This separation is difficult, and easy to oversimplify, but the reader will not be far wrong if he observes that psychology studies the individual, social psychology the individual in his social groups, and sociology the groups themselves and the larger social structures within which both individual and group processes occur.

Anthropology, which means literally the science of man, is another discipline so closely related to sociology that the two are frequently indistinguishable. In a number of universities anthropology and sociology are administratively organized into one department. Both sciences concern themselves with human societies. Anthropology, however, traditionally directs its attention to uncivilized societies, to societies whose members cannot read or write, to primitive or "folk" societies. And in studying these societies, the anthropologist investigates not only their forms of social organization and social relationship, which are of primary interest to the sociologist, but also their economics, religion, government, language, legends, and customs, as well as the personalities of their inhabitants.

Sociology, on the other hand, has limited its direct attention to historical societies, to societies that are complex rather than simple, to societies, in short, whose members can read and write. Since these societies are complex the sociologist does not study their economy as such, nor their religion, nor their government, nor their language and literature and science, but rather the social organization, the social structure, and the social matrix within which these various phenomena appear. The anthropologist has had to do the work with respect to nonliterate societies that all social scientists—sociologists, economists, political scientists, students of religion, law, science, philosophy, and so on—have done together with respect to modern civilized societies. There is thus a division of labor involved in the study of literate societies that would be neither practicable nor necessary in the study of the nonliterate.

In placing sociology in relation to these other social sciences, the reader is invited to observe several cautions. In the first place, as has often been said, every label is a kind of a libel, and what a scholar or scientist happens to call himself—psychologist, anthropologist, historian, sociologist, philosopher—may provide no adequate insight into the nature of the problems with which he wrestles and earnestly tries to solve. There are problems common to many disciplines and problems too that appear on the boundary lines between them. Furthermore, psychologists, philosophers, anthropologists, and historians have all made contributions to sociology. Mathematicians have written books on history, biologists on ethics, philosophers on law, and students of law on anthropology. And sociologists, in turn, have made contributions to other disciplines. The modern tendency is to break the barriers that separate the learned disciplines and sciences and to encourage specialists in various fields to concentrate their efforts upon common problems rather than upon isolated bodies of content.

In the second place, the present articulation of the sciences is attributable in some instances to history rather than to an intrinsic logic; that is, in the historical development of the disciplines, some of them became differentiated from philosophy at earlier stages than did others and thus have enjoyed a longer relative independence and an earlier recognition. In the third place, the sciences are frequently separated or put together for reasons of convenient administration in universities and colleges. In some universities, as has been said, sociology is closely associated with history, economics, and government; in others, with psychology and anthropology; in still others, with philosophy.

There is in the modern world, in short, a bewildering array of separate disciplines, many of them concerned with somewhat similar phenomena from somewhat different points of view. Sociology is one among many others. Having offered this brief account of its relations with its sister sciences—its external relations so to speak—we turn now to some observations about sociology itself and its internal structure.

3. The Nature of Sociology

If we look at sociology now from the point of view of its internal logical characteristics, we shall again be provided with clues that will help to locate the subject for us and to indicate what kind of science it is. We have already shown that sociology is a social and not a natural science. This, however, as will be elaborated further below, is a distinction in content and not in method. It serves to distinguish those sciences that deal with the physical universe from those that deal with the social universe. It particularly distinguishes sociology from astronomy, physics, chemistry, geology, biology, and all of their subdivisions.

In the second place, sociology is a categorical, not a normative, discipline; that is, it confines itself to statements about what is, not what should be or ought to be. As a science, sociology is necessarily silent about questions of value; it cannot decide the directions in which society ought to go, and it makes no recommendations on matters of social policy. This is not to say that sociological knowledge is useless for purposes of social and political judgment, but only that sociology cannot itself deal with problems of good and evil, right and wrong, better or worse, or any others that concern human values. Sociology can and does, in a categorical fashion, state that at a certain time and in a certain place a particular group of people adhered to certain values; but it cannot, in normative fashion, decide whether these people ought to have held these values in preference to others. There is no sociological warrant, nor indeed any other kind of scientific warrant, for preferences in values. It is this canon that distinguishes sociology, as a science, from social and political philosophy and from ethics and religion.

Closely related to the above point is a third canon, and one that it is sometimes difficult for the student to grasp. Sociology is a pure science, not an applied science. The immediate goal of sociology is the acquisition of knowledge about human society, not the utilization of that knowledge. Physicists do not build bridges, physiologists do not treat people afflicted with pneumonia, and chemists do not fill prescriptions at the corner drugstore.[5] Similarly, sociologists do not determine questions of public policy, do not tell legislators what laws should be passed or repealed, and do not dispense relief to the ill, the lame, the blind, or the poor. Sociology, as a pure science, is engaged in the acquisition of knowledge that will be useful to the administrator, the legislator, the diplomat, the teacher, the foreman, the supervisor, the social worker, and the citizen. But sociologists do not themselves—except, of course, in their own capacity as citizens—apply the knowledge that it is their duty and profession to acquire. Sociology thus stands in the same relation to administration, legislation, diplomacy, teaching, supervision, social work, and citizenship, as physics does to engineering, physiology to medicine, jurisprudence to law, astronomy to navigation, chemistry to pharmacy, and biology to plant and animal husbandry. Sociology is clearly and definitely concerned with acquiring the knowledge about society that can be used to solve some of the world's problems, but it is not itself an applied science. These comments mean neither that sociological knowledge is useless nor that it is impractical. They mean only that there is a division of labor involved and that the persons who acquire sociological knowledge are not always those who can use it best, and that those who use it are not usually those who have the time, the energy, and the training to acquire it.

[5] Except in England, where pharmacists are called chemists.

Men of action are sometimes impatient with men of thought and describe them as dreamers who live in ivory towers and who never come to grips with the harsh realities of the world. Even Einstein was once denounced as a "faker" by an ignorant columnist. It should not be forgotten, however, as the great teacher of philosophy Morris R. Cohen was fond of pointing out, that purely theoretical contributions to astronomy and mathematics, by increasing the precision of navigation, have saved more lives at sea than any possible improvements in the carpentry of lifeboats.

The relations between the pure and applied sciences can be seen more clearly, perhaps, if we juxtapose them in the following fashion:

Pure Sciences	Applied Sciences
Physics	Engineering
Astronomy	Navigation
Mathematics	Accounting
Chemistry	Pharmacy
Physiology	Medicine
Political science	Politics
Jurisprudence	Law
Zoology	Animal husbandry
Botany	Agriculture
Geology	Petroleum engineering
History	Journalism
Economics	Business
Sociology	Administration, diplomacy, social work

The relations between these two groups of sciences are not always as direct as the table indicates and not always quite the same in a logical sense.[6] In addition, each of the pure sciences has many more applications than are represented in the right-hand column and each applied discipline draws from more than one pure science on the left. Nevertheless, the table is useful in showing that sociology clearly belongs to one of these groups of sciences and not to the other. It is especially desirable to emphasize this point because sociology has often been associated in the public mind with social work, with social welfare, with the improvement of the conditions of the poor, and even, sometimes, with socialism.

A fourth characteristic of sociology is that it is a relatively abstract science and not a concrete one. This does not mean that it is unnecessarily

[6] History and journalism, for example, are not sciences in the sense of the others. Another difference between these two may be, as an English reviewer has facetiously expressed it, that "History is the art of using and revealing sources; journalism is the art of using and concealing them." John Vaizey in *The Listener*, 23 May 1968, p. 672.

complicated or unduly difficult. It means merely that sociology is not interested in the concrete manifestations of human events but rather in the form that they take and the patterns they assume. We said, for example, in distinguishing sociology from history, that sociology was concerned, not with particular wars and revolutions, but with war and revolution in general as social phenomena, as repeatable and recurrent processes in history, as types of social conflict. Similarly, sociology is not interested in any particular concrete organization, such as the United States Steel Corporation, New York University, the United States Navy, the Roman Catholic Church, the New York Yankees, Rotary International, Metro-Goldwyn-Mayer, or the American Philosophical Society, but rather in the fact that men organize themselves into associations of this kind in order to pursue certain interests and in the relations between such associations and social groups of various other types. Again, sociology is not interested in the Russians, the English, the Kwakiutl, the Spaniards, the Italians, the French, the Arabs, the Dobuans, the Eskimo, the Andaman Islanders—or the Texans—as such, but in the fact that all of these people, no matter how diverse their origins and no matter how disparate their beliefs and attitudes and ways of doing things, have nevertheless formed themselves into human societies that exhibit, in all places, the same general structural characteristics. It is in this simple sense that sociology is an abstract and not a concrete science.

A fifth characteristic of sociology, also mentioned above, is that it is a generalizing and not a particularizing or individualizing science. It seeks general laws or principles about human interaction and association, about the nature, form, content, and structure of human groups and societies, and not, as in the case of history, complete and comprehensive descriptions of particular societies or particular events. It is interested, not in the discrete historical fact that Italy under Mussolini once made war upon the Ethiopians, but in the sociological principle that external aggression is one way to intensify the internal solidarity of a group, a principle of which the Ethiopian conquest is only one of many thousands of examples.

A sixth characteristic of sociology is that it is both a rational and an empirical science. Since this is a methodological issue we shall ignore it here and consider it instead in the next section, which is devoted to the method of sociology.

Finally, a seventh characteristic of sociology is that it is a general and not a special social science. Although this distinction has been a matter of some controversy among sociologists themselves, as suggested above, it seems fairly clear that social relationships and social interactions between people occur in all the affairs of human life, whether these affairs are primarily economic or political or religious or recreational or legal or intellectual, and that there is no separate category of the social apart from all of these others, except those relations of "polite acquaintance" that are called social in a narrower sense. In other words, sociology studies those phenomena that are common to all human interaction. This point may be clarified by the following formula:[7]

Economic	*a, b, c, d, e, f*
Political	*a, b, c, g, h, i*
Religious	*a, b, c, j, k, l*
Legal	*a, b, c, m, n, o*
Recreational	*a, b, c, p, q, r*

In all of these phenomena, whether economic or political or religious, the same *a, b, c* occur. These are the social factors, the factors that they all have in common. It is on this level that sociology operates, and it does not, of course, investigate economic, political, religious, or any other special kind of phenomena as such. Note that we do not say that sociology is *the* basic social science—this is too large and imperialistic a claim—nor that it is *the* general social science—this claim can also be made by social psychology and anthropology—but only that it is *a* general rather than a special social science and is interested in social factors no matter what the context in which they occur. The focus of sociology may be a special one, as is the focus of every other science, but its area of inquiry is general.

We may now, for quick reference, arrange these categories or canons in a series of opposing pairs and italicize those logical characteristics that pertain to sociology:

Social	Natural
Categorical	Normative
Pure	Applied
Abstract	Concrete
Generalizing	Particularizing[8]
Rational	*Empirical*
General	Special

Sociology is thus a social, a categorical, a pure, an abstract, a generalizing, both a rational and an empirical, and a general science.

---

[7] This formula is taken, with modifications, from Pitirim A. Sorokin, *Society, Culture, and Personality*, Harper & Row, Publishers, New York, 1947, p. 7.
[8] These categories, generalizing and particularizing, are sometimes called "nomothetic" and "idiographic," respectively.

4. The Method of Sociology

There are many approaches to the human scene, ranging from philosophy to journalism. They include vast and abstract tomes on man and society in general; large and comprehensive volumes of history; miscellaneous compilations of statistics; magazines, newspapers, and periodicals of every description; and literature of many kinds, ranging from the poetry of Homer and Dante and Milton and Shakespeare to the latest novels on the best-seller lists. Indeed, in any age, and particularly perhaps in the present one, novelists contribute insights that are sometimes of profound sociological significance as they write about various human communities and sectors of society, and about the men and women who experience the trials and terrors, the hopes and fears, the joys and miseries that are all a part of our common human lot. One characteristic, among others, that distinguishes sociology from all of these other approaches is its method, the manner in which it approaches its problems.

As we noted above in talking about the story of sociology, the special sciences were once a part of philosophy. The moment in history—actually a time span of greater or less duration—at which they were able to declare their independence from the mother discipline was the moment when they adopted the method of science in the pursuit of their investigations. Sociology, as we have seen, did not achieve this independence until late in the nineteenth century. Since that time sociologists have tried, with ever-increasing diligence and care, to apply the scientific method to the study of society, in the hope that sociology could contribute its share to the sum total of human knowledge. What then is the scientific method and how is it used in the study of society?

Science has tremendous prestige in the modern world. In the popular imagination the scientist is a somewhat remote and obscure figure, a man who putters nearsightedly about a laboratory, who keeps irregular hours, and who is somewhat untidy in his personal habits. He is not, like "normal" people, trying to earn his first million dollars, and he spends his time delving into problems so "deep" and mysterious that they elude the comprehension of the common man—the man who nevertheless sees the results, for example, in the exploration of space. This stereotype, fostered largely by the movies and by the magazines, is as true and as false as most stereotypes.[9] Actually, a scientist, whatever his field of inquiry, is a man who is engaged in the use of rigorous method in the pursuit of knowledge.[10]

---

[9] In a later chapter we shall have something to say about the human tendency to indulge in stereotypes and the effect of these stereotypes upon social interaction.

[10] For an excellent discussion of research methods themselves, see Theodore Caplow, *Elementary Sociology*, Prentice-Hall, Inc., Englewood Cliffs, N. J., 1971, chap. 2.

Science is sometimes, though mistakenly, associated with a particular body of content. Thus, it is believed that in order to be a scientist a man must study protons, neutrons, electrons, atoms, molecules, microbes, viruses, plant molds, bodies, antibodies, stars, cells, rocks, rats, skeletons, or skulls. According to this view anyone who studies human beings and their social groupings, whether in the form of governments, business corporations, families, mobs, crowds, races, or religions, is not considered a scientist. This identification of science with particular kinds of content, particular areas of investigation, or special kinds of problems, however, is inaccurate. Science is not a body of content but a method of approach to any content—the only method, some would say, that results in the discovery of verifiable truth.

As a method of approach to the investigation of any phenomenon whatever, science implies primarily an attitude of mind, an attitude distinguished by adherence to several principles. Among these principles are objectivity, relativism, ethical neutrality, parsimony, skepticism, and humility, which we shall discuss in order.

Objectivity means that the conclusions arrived at as the result of inquiry and investigation are independent of the race, color, creed, occupation, nationality, religion, moral preferences, and political predispositions of the investigator. If his research is truly objective it is independent of any subjective elements, any personal desires, that he may have. This kind of objectivity is difficult to achieve, because factors of many varieties distort the processes of inquiry. The classic statement of the factors, or biases, that may enter into the pursuit of knowledge and prejudice its objectivity was made by the English philosopher Francis Bacon (1561–1626) in the first book of his *Novum Organum*. He called them "idols" and arranged them in four classes—Idols of the Tribe, Idols of the Cave, Idols of the Market Place, and Idols of the Theater. Although Bacon's choice of words sounds somewhat quaint in our day, his classification has never been excelled.

The Idols of the Tribe are the mistakes we make because we are human beings, belong to our own tribe or species, as it were, and have certain natural human tendencies. It is a human tendency, for example, to believe what we want to believe and to disbelieve what displeases us. In seeking to prove a proposition, we find it easy to look for confirming evidence and to disregard or to avoid any evidence that seems to disprove it. One of the greatest of modern scientists, the careful and patient Charles Darwin, was highly aware of this "idol," and he therefore took special pains to record in his notebook observations that did not at first fit into his theory. He knew that he would remember the confirming evidence and tend to forget the rest.

The second class of idols, the Idols of the Cave, are the mistakes we make, not simply because we are human beings, but because we are particular kinds of human beings. Each of us inhabits a kind of a cave, and when we peer timidly at the world outside its mouth, we see only what the experiences encountered in our own particular cave have conditioned us to see. Some of us are liberals and some conservatives, some prosperous and some poor, some Americans and some Russians, some Easterners and some Middle Westerners, and so on. This bias might be called the sociological idol, for it indicates the manner in which our social experiences and group affiliations influence the problems we choose to investigate, the evidence we select as probative, and the conclusions at which we arrive. Aware of this source of bias, officials of the Carnegie Foundation, when they wanted, some years ago, to support a definitive study of the Negro problem in America, chose a Swedish diplomat and sociologist, Gunnar Myrdal, to do the job, not because he was necessarily a better sociologist than the leading American sociologists, but because, being a foreigner, he could approach the problem without the initial biases that an American— Northern or Southern, black or white—would be likely to have.

   The third class of biases, the Idols of the Market Place, are, as Bacon himself said, the most troublesome of all. These are the errors that afflict us because of our choice and use of words. Words are like women—seductive, inconsistent, unpredictable, frequently faithless, and full of hidden meanings![11] We cannot think at all without words and often cannot think straight because of them. Since straight thinking is essential in science, contemporary scientists have become acutely conscious of the words they use and try in all possible ways to avoid the distortions that result from expression and communication by language. John Locke (1632–1704), another English philosopher and a master of English prose as well, had the following to say about this problem in his notable *Essay concerning Human Understanding:*

> For language being the great conduit, whereby men convey their discoveries, reasonings, and knowledge, from one to another, he that makes an ill use of it, though he does not corrupt the fountains of knowledge, which are in things themselves, yet he does, as much as in him lie, break or stop the pipes whereby it is distributed to the public use and advantage of mankind.

   The problem of language is so serious in sociology that we shall devote a few additional comments to it in a later section.
   The last of the idols, the Idols of the Theater, are the mistakes we make because of "received opinion," that is, because of the human tendency to assume that the older an idea is, or the more familiar, or the

[11] This, of course, would be an outrageously sexist statement if it were taken seriously.

larger the number of people who believe it, the greater chance it has of being true. It is hard to disabuse oneself of the notion that age and familiarity lend respectability or validity to a belief; and if millions of people accept a doctrine without question, it is difficult, even in the face of contrary evidence, to state that it is false. The popular saying "fifty million Frenchmen can't be wrong" is an example, in capsule form, of an Idol of the Theater. The greatest scientists in our Western tradition, men like Copernicus and Newton and Darwin and Einstein, were men who had the intellectual courage to question the beliefs of their predecessors and, even more important, to doubt the premises on which they were based. Scientific truth is not a matter of majority vote, and universally accepted premises are sometimes the most dangerous of all. Neither age nor universal acceptance nor self-evidence[12] nor yet indeed common sense suffices to validate a notion, doctrine, or idea for which evidence is lacking.

Although we shall have occasion to comment later on the difficulties associated with satisfying the criterion of objectivity in the study of social phenomena, we want nevertheless to say at this point that science knows no boundaries of nation or politics, of region or religion, of color or class. The law of gravitation works in San Francisco and Stalingrad, in Johannesburg and Montreal. Freely falling bodies fall with the same velocity in Spain and in Samoa, in Montenegro and Montana. The law of probability works equally well with people and with plants, with sand and stars, with bullets and ballots. Science is universal and international. There is therefore no such thing as a Russian genetics, an English mathematics, a Chinese chemistry, a Negro botany, a Republican physiology, a Socialist meteorology, a Catholic physics, or a Protestant sociology. Sociological principles, like all scientific principles, are true or false in independence of their origin and in independence of the race, religion, nationality, or politics of the scientists who happen to discover them.[13]

Relativism, the second of our characteristics of the scientific attitude, means merely that the conclusions the scientist arrives at are never considered permanent, universal, and absolute truths. He is never tempted to spell "truth" with a capital "T"; he knows that the propositions with which he operates today are subject to question tomorrow and that new evidence can wreck the most cherished notions. Because science, for this reason, is the only self-correcting discipline, it is the most reliable method

---

[12] Bertrand Russell once said in a statement which merits reflection, that "when self-evidence is alleged as a ground for belief, that implies that doubt has crept in, and that our self-evident proposition has not always resisted the assaults of scepticism." *Analysis of Mind*, George Allen & Unwin, Ltd., London, 1921, p. 263.

[13] This is not to say, of course, that different kinds of sociological problems and methods do not receive a differential emphasis in different countries.

of acquiring knowledge. Science, in other words, has no notions so sacred, no propositions so privileged, no truths so absolute that they are not subject to change when new evidence arises to challenge them. A scientific truth is true only until further notice.

Ethical neutrality, the third of the properties that belong to a scientific attitude of mind, means that the scientist, in his professional capacity, does not take sides on issues of moral or ethical significance. We suggested earlier in this chapter that sociology is a categorical science and not a normative one, and this distinction, in essence, is the same point that we wish to make here. The scientist, *as such*, has no ethical, religious, political, literary, philosophical, moral, or marital preferences. That he has these preferences as a citizen makes it all the more important that he dispense with them as a scientist. As a scientist he is interested not in what is right or wrong or good or evil, but only in what is true or false. Sociologists who are politically radical and imbued with a decent moral fervor often demand that we condemn certain doctrines which seem to them to have undesirable consequences. The task of science, however, is neither to approve nor to condemn, but only to confirm or to refute.

No science can tell a man whether to vote for a Republican or a Democrat, whether to join a Catholic or a Protestant church, whether to move to the country or remain in the city, whether to become a colonel or a conscientious objector, whether to make an atomic bomb or not to make it. Problems of this kind have nothing to do with the office and function of science. Science, and particularly sociological science, can of course indicate the consequences of alternative decisions. But it cannot itself decide. Science, on the contrary, attempts to accumulate the knowledge that will make decisions of personal and of public policy as sensible and as reasonable as possible in the circumstances in which the necessity for them arises. Failure to appreciate this property of science has resulted in much confusion. It is essential to recognize that, as important as it is, science is nevertheless a limited enterprise. It cannot legitimately answer all of the questions of the universe. It can, and does, attempt to answer certain categorical questions. On normative questions it necessarily preserves a silence.

Parsimony has something to do with simplicity. It means that when one explanation is adequate to explain a phenomenon, two or more are superfluous. When the movement of the branches of a tree in a windstorm can be explained by natural forces, it is unnecessary and undesirable to explain the movement also by supposing that a spirit or sprite lives in the trunk of the tree and agitates its branches when he is angry. This principle of parsimony was stated in the Middle Ages by William of Occam and, in the following form, is known as Occam's Razor: *Entia non multiplicanda sunt praeter necessitatem* (Entities ought not to be multiplied beyond necessity). As an example of this principle we may mention that in the seventeenth century two chemists named Stahl and Becher proposed a theory of combustion, according to which something called phlogiston is present in fire and makes it burn. After the discovery of oxygen by Priestley, the phlogiston theory was no longer needed and was consequently dropped from the explanation of combustion, though not without hesitation and reluctance by the chemists who had become accustomed to it. Occam's Razor, one might say, is used to shave the metaphysical stubble off the physiognomy of science.

A fifth characteristic of the scientific attitude of mind is *skepticism.* This does not mean skepticism for its own sake, which would lead to inaction and absurdity, but simply a willingness, if not indeed an eagerness, to question everything before accepting it and especially those things for which there is insufficient evidence. The scientist, in popular parlance, is always "a man from Missouri." He has to be shown. One of the most important questions that the scientist can ask is, "What is the evidence?" If there is none, or if it is inadequate, the theory is discarded or held in abeyance. Skepticism, in short, as George Santayana has so eloquently reminded us, is the chastity of the intellect and should be preserved through a long youth. It is an attitude of mind without which science cannot maintain its self-correcting features.

There is one final attitude that should be associated always and everywhere with the scientific method, and that is *humility*, a humility indeed that takes two forms. The first of these is humility before the limitations of the human mind, and the second, humility before the magnitude of that which is not yet known. What we know in fact is pitiable and frail in comparison with what we do not know. The greatest of the world's philosophers and scientists have recognized that arrogance and pride are incompatible with science and they have been wise with Socrates in the consciousness of their ignorance. It is Immanuel Kant who best exemplifies the first of these forms. The immortal introductory sentence to the first edition of *The Critique of Pure Reason* reads as follows: "Human reason has this peculiar fate that in one species of its knowledge it is burdened by questions which, as prescribed by the very nature of reason itself, it is not able to ignore, but which, as transcending all its powers, it is also not able to answer."[14] And it is "the incomparable Mr. Newton" who best exemplifies the second. Toward the end of his life Sir Isaac wrote, "I do not know what I may appear to the world, but to myself I seem to have been only a boy playing on the sea-shore, and diverting myself in now and then finding a smoother pebble or a prettier shell than ordinary, whilst the great ocean of truth lay all undiscovered before me."

---

[14] Preface to the First Edition, 1781, translated by Norman Kemp Smith.

5. Sociology and Science

Now sociology is obviously not an exact science. Special difficulties appear in attempts to apply the scientific method to the study of social phenomena. It is much more difficult, for example, for a scientist who studies the processes of society to maintain his objectivity than it is for a scientist who studies the processes of nature. For the sociologist stands in a peculiar relationship to his material, a relationship from whose constraints the astronomer, the physicist, the chemist, and the biologist are all relatively free.

Physical scientists are seldom a part of the problem they investigate. They begin their inquiries from a point of vantage that is wholly external to their data. The stars have no sentiments, the atoms no anxieties that have to be taken into account. Observation is objective with little effort on the part of the scientist to make it so. The binocular parallax may, of course, confound the observation of sidereal motions, the temperature of the chemist's body may introduce an extraneous variable into a precise experiment, and individual differences may produce constant errors in a series of detailed measurements. But these errors are known, their effects can be measured, and their influences can be subtracted from the total score. In addition, the variables in these observations and experiments can be limited and controlled. In few cases does the scientist himself become a factor in the inquiry. It is only when he has to use language to communicate the results of his investigations that there is an opportunity for social and subjective factors to intrude, and this opportunity is reduced by the use of a mathematical symbolism.

The sociologist, on the other hand, stands in no such fortunate relationship to his material. He is from the beginning completely immersed in his data. He is always in some sense a part of the phenomenon he is investigating. He is always, in the same sense, a participant observer of the processes he studies, never an external one. For him that extra-dimensionality that is synonymous with objectivity is a goal to be achieved, not a condition given in his initial situation. The spectacles through which he peers at the social process, the categories in which he arranges his manifold and complex data, and the language in which he announces his results are all products of a particular society at a particular time and place.[15] He himself is a product of his society, and conforms, consciously or unconsciously, to its folkways and mores, its institutions and laws, its customs and ideologies, its canons of evidence. This is one of the reasons

[15] That there are biases hidden in the very structure of the grammar sociologists are perforce required to use is argued in a quite sophisticated and lucid paper by Robert W. Friedrichs, "Choice and Commitment in Social Research," *The American Sociologist*, February, 1968, pp. 8–11. See also Friedrichs' distinguished book, *A Sociology of Sociology*, The Free Press, New York, 1970.

why not even the past is stable and why history needs continuously to be rewritten.

The sociologist has to strive, therefore, for an awareness of the biases and prejudices inherent in his own society, and in his own person, lest they interfere with his neutrality and color his conclusions. Without the constant diligence that alone can bring objectivity to his enterprise, the sociologist ceases to be an earnest seeker after truth and becomes only another variety of special pleader, susceptible to the patterns of his own cultural island and to the interests of the groups to which he happens to belong.

It is now necessary to introduce a certain discordant note into our discourse. The sentiments just expressed are not universally accepted and indeed invite dissent. Some sociologists reject the methodological ideals of objectivity, ethical neutrality, and *Wertfreiheit* (value-freedom), as Max Weber called it. They argue that the state of the world is too serious to permit such luxuries. Exhibiting all over again the reformist tendencies from which sociology once liberated itself, they call for action, not thought. They insist that sociology "take sides" on social issues. They call upon their colleagues to stand up and be counted as champions of the good and opponents of the evil that they detect in contemporary society. They want not an objective but a militant sociology.[16]

Respect for the canons of inquiry, however, and skepticism about particular remedies for social ills suggest that this may not be a wise course to pursue. Knowledge as such is unaffected by the contingencies of current events. To permit the search for knowledge to be contaminated by evanescent concerns is to alter the character of inquiry, to transform inquiry into advocacy. The German philosopher Hegel once observed that nothing great is ever accomplished without passion; surely he who insulates himself from the actions and passions of his time does so at the price of not having lived. It is desirable to recognize, however, that social action and sociological inquiry are two different enterprises. One can indulge in both but not at the same time. Social and political actions require commitment, but scholarship and science, on the contrary, require detachment. For the latter, one must appeal to Spinoza and consider, as he did, all things *sub specie aeternitatis*, in terms of eternity.[17]

A more subtle and sophisticated view of the methodological situation

---

[16] See, for example, Alvin W. Gouldner, *The Coming Crisis of Western Sociology*, Basic Books, New York, 1970.

[17] Durkheim had a word on this which applies as well to those who consider themselves "Marxist" rather than "academic" sociologists: "Socialism is not a science, a sociology in miniature—it is a cry of grief, sometimes of anger, uttered by men who feel most keenly our collective *malaise*. Socialism is to the facts which produce it what the groans of a sick man are to the illness with which he is afflicted, to the needs that torment him. But what would one say of a doctor who accepted the replies or desires of his patient as scientific truths?" Emile Durkheim, *Socialism*, Alvin W. Gouldner (ed.), Collier Books, The Macmillan Company, New York, 1962, p. 41.

in sociology regards the discipline, precisely because it is a social science, as resting upon shifting sands. The very knowledge it acquires alters conditions in society and history and thus, paradoxically, turns back upon that knowledge and falsifies it. We thus have the self-falsifying prophecy to correspond to Robert K. Merton's self-fulfilling prophecy and Robert M. MacIver's self-fulfilling postulate.[18] Attend to Robert W. Friedrichs who, in a brilliant article, tells us that sociology is susceptible to the trials of Jonah:[19]

> Jonah, we are told, prophesied the destruction of Nineveh due to its multiple transgressions; but the Ninevites are reported to have heeded the import of the prophecy and sought Yahweh's forgiveness through a return to his ways. And since the glory of the biblical God lay not in his justice but in his grace, they were indeed saved. In the process, Jonah's prophecy of their destruction was of course falsified; hence a demoralized and indignant Jonah, for his claim to omniscience had clearly been denied.[20]

The moral of the tale is that although the natural sciences are able to extricate order from experience, the social sciences cannot do so because the order changes in the process of discovering it. The search for basic laws in society is thus a snare and a delusion. The problem can be avoided only by granting to the physical sciences what is theirs—namely, the quest for order[21]—and accepting for the social sciences a new imagery in which the dimension of time reassumes its pristine significance. Only in this way can sociology avoid the destruction of its own predictions and understand the dialectical character of its own knowledge.

Somewhat similar views have been advanced by Karl R. Popper. In his opinion, the fact that knowledge is acquired at all in the social sciences renders a knowledge of the social order impossible for the simple reason that the original knowledge alters the order that it would capture, and so on in an infinite progression, every item falsifying anew an "established" fact.[22] Although its ramifications are complex, the point was made quite simply by Robert M. MacIver when he wrote, "Most other kinds of

---

[18] Robert K. Merton, "The Self-fulfilling Prophecy," *Antioch Review*, Summer, 1948; reprinted in *Social Theory and Social Structure*, rev. ed., The Free Press of Glencoe, Ill., Chicago, 1957, pp. 421–436. Robert M. MacIver, *The More Perfect Union*, The Macmillan Company, New York, 1948.

[19] "Dialectical Sociology: Toward a Resolution of the Current 'Crisis' in Western Sociology," *The British Journal of Sociology*, vol. XXIII, September, 1972, pp. 263–274.

[20] *Ibid.*, pp. 270–271.

[21] As Merton remarks, "Predictions of the return of Halley's comet do not influence its orbit." "The Self-fulfilling Prophecy," *op. cit.*, p. 423.

[22] See his *The Poverty of Historicism*, Routledge & Kegan Paul, Ltd., London, 1957.

philosophy do not affect the nature of the things they profess to explain, however foolish or however wise the philosophy may be, but this kind [political philosophy and sociology] makes and remakes the system that controls our lives."[23]

The problem, as can be seen, is more epistemological than sociological; that is, it concerns the nature of sociological knowledge rather than the nature of human society. It persists as a puzzle and a paradox. But it need not delay us in our search for the elements of the social order. In this book we pitch our inquiry on a level of abstraction high enough (though simple in the reading) to remove the contingencies of circumstance and to exhibit the form and structure of society itself in independence of particular societies. Some sociological propositions, in short, transcend the limitations of period and locus and win a certain autonomy in relation to the categories of time and space.

Two other methodological issues require a brief word in this introductory chapter. The first concerns the assertion, made in the preceding section, that sociology is both a rational and an empirical science. The sense in which this is true will now be examined. There are two broad avenues of approach to scientific knowledge. One, known as empiricism, is the approach that emphasizes experience and the facts that result from observation and experimentation. The other, known as rationalism, emphasizes reason and the theories that result from logical inference.

The empiricist collects facts; the rationalist coordinates and arranges them. To use an analogy, though it oversimplifies and somewhat distorts the distinction, the empiricist is a man who goes out and collects as many facts as he can, brings them back to his office, and throws them carelessly on his desk. The rationalist gathers no facts. He spends his time building pigeonholes in which facts of every possible kind may be filed, whether or not there are any actual facts to put into them. If the empiricist works alone the net result of his activity is a disorderly desk. If the rationalist works alone the net result is empty pigeonholes. When the two of them work together they know which facts to save and which ones to throw away; they have not only facts but also an orderly set of facts, with each one neatly filed in its proper place.

In the history of philosophy these two approaches or doctrines are radically opposed, and most philosophers in the Western tradition have defended either rationalism or empiricism. In Great Britain, for example, such philosophers as Bacon, Hobbes, Locke, Berkeley, Hume, and Mill supported the empirical point of view, whereas in France the followers of Descartes, the first modern philosopher, preferred to emphasize the uses of

---

[23] *The Web of Government*, The Macmillan Company, New York, 1947, p. 404.

reason. John Locke, in a quotation from Aristotle that may be regarded almost as the motto of empiricism, said *"Nihil in intellectu quod non prius fuerit in sensu"* (There is nothing in the intellect that is not first in the senses). To which Leibniz, the rationalist, responded, *"Nisi intellectus ipse"* (Except the intellect itself). Obviously, sociologists cannot be expected to solve a problem to which two thousand years of philosophical study and speculation have been able to provide no wholly satisfactory answer. In sociological inquiry, therefore, the two doctrines are put together and made to work together. Both theories and facts are required in the construction of knowledge. A theory unsubstantiated by hard, solid, and sometimes intractable facts is nothing more than an opinion or a speculation. Facts by themselves, in their isolated and discrete character, are meaningless, useless, and frequently trivial. One may paraphrase Immanuel Kant and say that theories without facts are empty and facts without theories are blind.

All of the modern sciences, therefore, no matter how much they may move between the empirical and the rational poles of method, avail themselves nevertheless of both empirical and rational resources. Sociology is no exception. It happens that American sociology, for example, has adhered perhaps a little more closely to the empirical pole than German sociology. It happens also that over periods of time sociology, like other sciences, shifts its emphasis in one direction or the other. The result of the empirical emphasis in American sociology has been vast conglomerations of facts, so many facts indeed as sometimes to be embarrassing. A major requirement of the development of sociology in the near future will be to transform these conglomerations into systems, this disorderly collection of facts into theories of society that will be in harmony with the facts. And that is why we say, without by any means solving the intricate and complex methodological problems involved, problems of continuing concern to both sociologists and philosophers, that sociology is both a rational and an empirical science.

The second methodological issue concerns the use of language, to which reference has also been made above. The student of the natural sciences comes away from his first few weeks of instruction with a sense of accomplishment. If his course is astronomy, for example, he learns that the constellation he is accustomed to seeing on clear nights in the northern sky, the one that he calls the Big Dipper, is Ursa Major. If he studies zoology he learns that the name of the summer annoyance known to him as a fruit fly is *Drosophila melanogaster.* In chemistry he learns that the salt he has been using all his life is sodium chloride.

Thus the student begins to acquire a new and technical vocabulary, a new set of names, scientific concepts, to apply to some of the phenomena that have previously presented themselves to his experience. This gives him a sense of accomplishment, and possibly also a sense of pride. He is becoming a scientist, he is learning a scientific vocabulary, he is beginning to see the world from the point of view of the scientist and to talk about it in professional terms. He has the impression that he is acquiring new knowledge when he learns to apply new names to old notions and to familiar things, and in a sense this is new knowledge of an important kind, even if it is not, as the student may be inclined to assume, new knowledge about the things he is talking about.

All sciences have these technical terminologies, their own sets of concepts, professional words in which to talk about the subjects or phenomena under investigation and in which to communicate knowledge about them. Such terminologies are indispensable, for they reduce the vagueness, the ambiguity, and the confusion that surround the use of ordinary speech. They prevent what Bacon called the Idols of the Market Place from introducing the errors, prejudices, and assumptions contained in language itself into the statement of scientific propositions. Words have color, they induce emotional responses, they have an aesthetic quality; and these characteristics, so desirable in literature, can impair the quest for objectivity in science. Technical terms, however arduous the process of learning them, thus have their important scientific uses, and the student is correct in feeling a sense of accomplishment after learning them.

In sociology, however, the situation is somewhat different—or at least it appears to the reader to be different. After two or three weeks of studying this book he will learn few if any words that are not already in his vocabulary. He already knows such words as "society," "culture," "community," "status," "role," "organization," "association," "group," and "institution," and reading them again in this place gives him no sense of accomplishment. It is important for him to realize, however, that they are not in fact the same words with which he is familiar in other contexts. They only look the same.

The sociologist, like other scientists, has a technical vocabulary. Instead of inventing new labels, however, taken from the Latin or Greek, he takes ordinary English words and gives them a technical meaning, ascribes a particular scientific significance to them. These words do not, therefore, necessarily mean what the student has been accustomed to think they mean. "Culture," for example, does not mean refinement in artistic or literary taste, or good manners, when it is used in sociology and anthropology. Thus, the reader does have to acquire a new vocabulary, a set of scientific concepts, even though, as words, they are old and familiar acquaintances.

It must be admitted that, at the present time, the technical vocabulary of sociology is not so settled or so firmly established as the technical vocabularies of some of the older sciences. Sociologists do not themselves always use the same words in the same technical senses. This situation will not present any problems to the reader, but we should be less than candid if we concealed it from him. Sociologists earnestly desire a well-ordered, systematic set of concepts, and have made much progress toward that end. But the goal is not yet achieved. It is possible, therefore, that some words in the following chapters will not be used in precisely the same sense as they are in other books of sociology. Where this may lead to confusion we shall inform the reader of other usages. Where such usages are only of incidental interest or where a knowledge of them would only impede the inquiry, we shall ignore them. In any event, we shall conform to the terminological practices of the majority of contemporary American sociologists.

We would conclude this section with another word of caution. Both "science" and "scientific method" can be construed in too narrow a sense. We have been calling sociology a science but we have been doing so in the broad meaning of the Italian *scienza* and the German *Wissenschaft*. In this sense science means any disciplined inquiry and the scientific method is any systematic effort to acquire knowledge when that effort is informed by the attitudes of mind we have described. We have said that it is a mistake to identify science with a particular kind of content. It is similarly a mistake to identify it with a particular kind of technique. Thus, the techniques of sociology—survey research, experimental designs (as in studies of small groups), and statistics (especially with the swift assistance of computers[24])—have become increasingly powerful and precise. They have become so powerful, in fact, that they present peculiar and sometimes paradoxical problems. Two temptations constantly confront the sociologist who has become an expert in the use of these techniques. The first of these, less serious, is that he will want to spend most of his time improving them, refining them, and making them into even more effective instruments of measurement and discovery—and indeed some sociologists succumb to this temptation. For them the remark of the German logician, Herman Lotze, is especially pertinent: "The constant whetting of an axe is apt to be a bit tedious if it isn't proposed to cut anything with it." The second is more insidious because it is often unrecognized. It concerns the fact that sociologists may be inclined to ask only those questions for which methods of research are available rather than finding methods to help them solve the

[24] A distinguished sociologist, Philip M. Hauser, has remarked that the computer is the only instrument ever devised by the mind of man that can make a quarter of a million errors in a thousandth of a second. And for some mysterious reason it still takes, even in this computerized age, four to six weeks to change the address of a magazine subscription.

more important of their problems. In other words, methods and problems are sometimes turned around in their significance. The method tends to determine the problem rather than the problem the method. The method thus becomes the independent variable, the problem the dependent one.

This situation has two consequences. The first of these is that large areas of potential research may remain uncultivated simply because no one has yet developed a method for dealing with them. The methods are missing, so to speak, and so the problems remain unsolved and even uninvestigated. One example of this, suggested by James S. Coleman, is trust.[25] The trust that two people have in one another is surely one of the most important components of their relationship; indeed, an entire structure of relationships in the larger society (including credit) is built upon trust. And yet there are few sociological studies of this phenomenon. The reason almost surely is that no one has devised a method for studying it.

The second consequence is related to the first. When too much attention is paid to science in the narrow sense, an inverse relationship tends to arise between the precision of the methods employed and the significance of the results. Thus, it is frequently the case that the more precise the methods, the less significant the knowledge derived from them. We sometimes learn to do very well things that are not worth doing and we sometimes expend resources of time and money learning things that are not worth knowing. James Thurber, asked to review a scientific treatise on penguins, complained that the book told him more about penguins than he wanted to know. And Tolstoy, in *War and Peace*, remarks that history is like a deaf man, muttering answers to questions that no one has asked him. (Do we need to know where Homer was born or where Socrates was buried?) The same can sometimes be said about sociology, especially when methods take precedence over ideas. Technical virtuosity, however useful, is no substitute for vision.

We can maintain, finally and with some pleasure, that sociology belongs not only to the sciences but also to the realm of humane letters. Indeed, the attributes we have assigned to the scientific method—objectivity, skepticism, humility, and the rest—will appear, upon reflection, to characterize any kind of responsible inquiry, whether in the sciences or in the humanities. Sociology, dealing as it does with human affairs and humane concerns, can help to bridge the gap between two kinds of inquiry and contribute to both kinds of knowledge. Methods and concepts are important and necessary, especially in the empirical discovery and logical construction of a body of knowledge. But they do not in themselves suffice.

[25] "The Method of Sociology," in Robert Bierstedt (ed.), *A Design for Sociology: Scope, Objectives, and Methods*, The American Academy of Political and Social Science, Philadelphia, 1969.

In the last analysis we are asked to remember that "it is not the lofty sails but the unseen wind that moves the ship." Similarly, "It is not the methods and the concepts that move our sociology along, but memory and desire— the memory that other men in other times have also asked questions about society and the desire that our answers, in our time, will be better than theirs."[26]

6. The Definition of Sociology

We have now looked at our subject from various points of view. But we have not offered, in a single sentence, a statement that defines sociology. Some authors prefer to omit a definition altogether on the ground that definitions are difficult to construct and easy to misunderstand or misconstrue. One might contend, with some cogency, that this entire chapter is an extended definition of sociology. Although there is considerable justification for this opinion, a short, but not too short, summary statement may nevertheless be useful. It is not enough to say that sociology is the study of society. This definition, though true, is laconic and even, to a degree, tautological. Without discoursing further on the difficulties involved, we shall adopt the following definition of sociology:

Sociology is an inquiry into the structure of society, an endeavor to achieve an orderly arrangement of the components of that structure, to delineate the relationships of these components to one another, and to discover, if possible, the general processes of social change.

7. The Uses of Sociology

We have said that sociology is concerned primarily with the acquisition of knowledge, not its utilization, and that sociology as such is a pure and not an applied science. Do these assertions imply that sociology is devoid of utility for the student who embarks upon its study for perhaps the first time and who, in the usual case, has no intention of becoming a sociologist? The answer is no. However "pure" a science it may be, sociology has intellectual consequences for anyone who studies it.

In the first place, like all of the liberal arts and sciences, sociology is a liberating discipline. It liberates the student from the provincialisms of color and class, of region and religion. It encourages him to consider society as a natural phenomenon, as natural as any other phenomenon in the universe. It helps him to take an objective view of his own society, to learn that it is

[26] Robert Bierstedt, "Sociology and Humane Learning," *American Sociological Review*, vol. 25, February, 1960, p. 9.

* this is a poor "definition"

one among many, to see the manner in which his own groups interact and combine with others to form the great society in which he lives, to understand that the social forces that built the civilization of ancient Egypt and those that built the civilization of contemporary America are, in essential characteristics, the same. Sociology thus gives a perspective to history and an insight into the life of man on earth. Man, as Aristotle noted long ago, is a social animal. Everything he is or does or thinks is related in some fashion to the fact that he lives with other people and is never wholly isolated from society.

In the second place, sociology can help the student to recognize and to appreciate the social factors in the environment that surrounds him—his relations with his fellows, the life of the community in which he lives, and the nature of the greater community in which he finds himself at this particular juncture of historical circumstances. Society, after all, is no local phenomenon. It is universal, and as permanent as the life of man itself.

For the student who decides to specialize in sociology, the more practical, as distinguished from the intellectual, consequences of this program of study are readily apparent. Sociology is a profession in which technical competence brings its own rewards. Sociologists, especially those trained in research procedures, are in increasing demand in business, government, industry, city planning, race relations, social-work supervision, advertising, communications, administration, and many other areas of community life. A few years ago all a sociologist could do with his sociology was to teach it. Although teaching, especially in colleges and universities, will always draw sociologists, sociology has now become "practical" enough to be practiced outside of academic halls. Careers apart from teaching are now possible in sociology, and expertly trained people are needed to work in many of its sectors and subdivisions. The various areas of applied sociology, in short, are coming more and more into prominence on local, state, national, and international levels.[27]

Finally, it may be mentioned that sociologists have become university deans, university presidents, heads of foundations, high officials of international organizations such as UNESCO and the Common Market, and even presidents of their countries. Thomas G. Masaryk, the first president of Czechoslovakia, was a sociologist, and so also is Rafael Caldera, elected president of Venezuela in 1968. Another sociologist, Amintore Fanfani, served as premier of Italy from 1958 to 1959 and from 1960 to 1962, and as president of the General Assembly of the United Nations in 1965.

---

[27] For a comprehensive treatment of this subject see Paul F. Lazarsfeld, William H. Sewell, and Harold L. Wilensky (Eds.), *The Uses of Sociology*, Basic Books, New York, 1967.

8. The Ultimate Goals of Sociology

Enough has now been said about the nature of our subject to provide a rough indication of the immediate goals and purposes of sociology. The immediate goal of sociology is to acquire knowledge about society. The immediate purpose of sociological reasoning and research is to describe in detail the structure of society, to exhibit the eternal recurrences and regularities in society, and to analyze the social components in all human activity.

Like all of the sciences, however, sociology is not content with descriptions, exhibitions, and analyses. It has a more remote and ultimate purpose. It seeks also the causes of things. The final questions to which sociology addresses itself are those that have to do with the nature of human experience on this earth and the succession of societies over the long centuries of human existence. The rise of man and the succession of his civilizations—is this a process that has rhyme and reason in it, or is it merely a cosmic accident in which no order and regularity can be discerned? "The glory that was Greece and the grandeur that was Rome"—are these purely chance phenomena, forever insusceptible to logical and causal explanation? What are the factors responsible for the disintegration of one social structure, like that of the medieval world, and the coming into being of another? Do human societies, like the individuals who comprise them, grow old after a while, and weary, and finally disappear from the face of the earth? Is there an ebb and flow in the affairs of men, a systole and diastole of human history? These too are problems of sociology. No one can answer such questions today, and men who speculate about them are called philosophers of history. But someday, if sociology, through its intimate analyses of the dynamics of society, can achieve some understanding of problems of this kind and contribute to their resolution, it will fulfill its initial promise and its ultimate destiny.

2

THE NATURAL CONDITIONS

OF HUMAN SOCIETY

BEFORE WE enter into our study of human societies themselves, it is desirable to consider first certain nonsocial or natural conditions that make societies possible and that have something to do with the similarities and differences to be discerned in them. Among these nonsocial factors are geographic, biological, and demographic factors.

Geographic factors assume an especial importance because human societies are always located at a certain place and the nature of this place exerts an influence upon the character of the society. There are no human societies, so far as we know, on any planet of the solar system except our own, because the natural conditions on other planets are not favorable to the existence of life. Similarly, there are no human societies 10 miles above the surface of the earth nor 10 miles below its surface. There are no human societies at the South Pole and none at the North Pole. The manner in which factors of this geographic kind set limits to social possibilities and sometimes determine social potentialities is the subject of Chapter 2.

In Chapter 3 we turn to a discussion of biological factors. Human societies are what they are, to some extent at least, because man is a certain kind of species and because his body has certain anatomical and physiological characteristics. Biological factors, too, set limits to the social possibilities of human societies and in certain ways help to determine the form and structure of these societies. Indeed, the view once prevailed that societies were similar to organisms and could be understood

therefore only in biological terms and
with the help of biological concepts.
Although no one today supports this view,
it is still necessary to consider the role of
the biological factors.

In this respect in addition we have to
reflect upon the influence of a special—
and sometimes especially troublesome—
kind of biological factor known as the
demographic factor, and this we do in
Chapter 4. The demographic factor has
to do primarily with people in their
quantitative aspects, that is, the number
of people who inhabit the planet and the
increase in this number in recent
centuries, the concentration of people in
various places and regions, the rates at
which people are born and procreate and
die, the movements of peoples within
their national boundaries and beyond,
and changing trends and tendencies in all
of these statistics. All of them, as can be
imagined, have something to do with the
societies that will later become our
principal interest.

We shall note particularly in this section
that influences of this kind do not operate
in one direction only, that if geographic,
biological, and demographic factors
influence to some extent the nature of
human societies, so also do social and
cultural factors in turn alter the face of
the earth, affect the structure and function
of the human body, and have some effect
upon the number and distribution of
people. Causation in sociology is never
simple, and it is seldom one-sided. In the
following chapters, then, we discuss the
influence of these natural conditions upon
human societies.

Chapter 2

THE GEOGRAPHIC FACTOR

HE EARTH itself has something to do with the societies that appear upon its surface. From earliest times, when men first turned their attention to the problems of sociology, they noticed that geographic factors exert an influence and that no serious attempt to understand society can be successful without an examination of this influence. They disagree, however, concerning the importance of geographic factors. One philosopher, for example, has asserted that "geography is a most enlightening science. In describing the habitat of man it largely explains his history."[1] Another philosopher[2] is reputed to have said, with considerable impatience, "Do not speak to me of geographical determinants. Where the Greeks once lived the Turks live now. That settles the question."

Since these are contradictory positions, both cannot be right and both cannot be wrong. Our task in this chapter is to attempt to judge these opposing claims for geography and to estimate as correctly as possible the influence of geographic factors upon human societies. We may anticipate our conclusion by suggesting that geographic factors, though seldom decisive, are seldom negligible either, and are therefore a necessary consideration in any study of society.

[1] George Santayana, *The Life of Reason*, Charles Scribner's Sons, New York, 1905–1906, vol. 3, p. 164.
[2] G. W. F. Hegel.

1. Geographic Interpretations

Gertrude Stein, that indefatigable writer of unintelligibilities ("Rose is a rose is a rose is a rose," and, "Pigeons in the grass alas"), once said, "In the United States there is more space where nobody is than where anybody is. This is what makes America what it is." No one knows whether Miss Stein was serious in this statement or not, and in any case such a question is one for the literary critic, not the sociologist. But there have been writers who have believed that geographic factors have to be assigned a paramount position in understanding the history of our own and other countries. Among these writers one of the most notable was Ellen Churchill Semple, a disciple of the great German geographer, Friedrich Ratzel. In 1903 she wrote a book in which she brilliantly interpreted and explained the history of the United States up to that time in terms of the influence of topography and soil and climate.[3] Miss Semple is a twentieth-century representative of a point of view that is as old as the history of human thought. It is not our intention here, nor is it necessary in a book on sociology, to trace the history of this idea back to ancient times.[4] But we shall take note of some of the extreme forms of the geographic interpretation in order to exhibit the nature of the problem with which we have to deal.

One of the earliest writers to dwell upon geographic factors was Hippocrates, the great physician of antiquity. He wrote a book called *On Airs, Waters, and Places*, in which he came to the conclusion that climate exercises a considerable influence upon the human temperament and that temperament, in turn, influences the kinds of government that men devise. He believed, for example, that Europeans, since they live in a climate of changing seasons, are vigorous, brave, and fierce, whereas Asiatics, who enjoy a more equable climate, are calm, mild, and gentle. Where he noted exceptions, as in the Far North of Europe or the Far South of Asia, these too he attributed to the climate. Where the climate is relatively unvaried, the people are uniform; where the climate changes under the influence of the seasons, the people are diversified. In the former situation they are placid and unhurried, in the latter alert and energetic.

Aristotle, generally considered the greatest philosopher of the Grecian age, adopted these arguments somewhat uncritically, characterizing the peoples of the North as high-spirited but so low in intelligence that they are unfit for political organization. Peoples of the South, on the other hand, are

---

[3] *American History and Its Geographic Conditions*, rev. ed., Houghton Mifflin Company, Boston, 1933. See also her *Influences of Geographic Environment*, Henry Holt and Company, Inc., New York, 1911.
[4] This has been done for us in a number of books. See for example Franklin Thomas, *The Environmental Basis of Society*, Appleton-Century-Crofts, Inc., New York, 1925.

intelligent and inventive, but so lacking in spirit that they are content to live as slaves. Since the Greeks are neither Northern nor Southern peoples and since their climate combines the best features of both regions, they have both spirit and intelligence and consequently are the best-governed people on earth and the best suited to rule the rest. Similarly, Vitruvius, an early Roman writer on architecture, decided that in extremely cold climates moisture is not drawn from the body and consequently that Northern peoples "are of vast height, and have fair complexions, straight red hair, grey eyes, and a great deal of blood, owing to the abundance of moisture and the coolness of the atmosphere."[5] Their large supply of blood makes them brave in time of war. Southern peoples, on the other hand, have an insufficient supply of blood because the sun sucks too much moisture out of their bodies. They are consequently "of lower stature, with a swarthy complexion, hair curling, black eyes, strong legs, and but little blood."[6] Pliny, another famous Roman, indulges in similar and even more extreme sentiments.[7]

Such arguments as these will doubtless appear fanciful to the modern reader. Yet they are repeated again and again in the early history of social thought. It is of incidental interest, perhaps, to note that each writer decides that his own narrow corner of earth, the place wherein he dwells, has the best climate and is therefore best suited to exercise dominion over all nations.

If later writers have refined these arguments somewhat and approached the subject with more knowledge and more sophistication, their general essence and import are the same. As one more example, from a period of history closer to our own, we may observe the following extreme statement of this position by a French philosopher, Victor Cousin, who lived in the nineteenth century:

> Yes, gentlemen, give me the map of a country, its configuration, its climate, its waters, its winds, and all its physical geography; give me its natural productions, its flora, its zoology, and I pledge myself to tell you, *a priori*, what the man of that country will be and what part that country will play in history, not by accident, but of necessity; not at one epoch, but in all epochs.[8]

These examples will doubtless suffice—although we need not stop with the nineteenth century. As we shall see, the late Yale geographer Ellsworth

---

[5] Vitruvius, *The Ten Books on Architecture*, book VI, chap. i, section 3. Quoted in *ibid.*, p. 35.
[6] *Ibid.*
[7] *Ibid.*, pp. 37–38.
[8] *Introduction a l'Histoire de la Philosophie.* Quoted by Lucien Febvre, *A Geographical Introduction to History*, Routledge & Kegan Paul, Ltd., London, 1925, p. 10.

Huntington wrote a number of books in which he espoused the thesis that civilization is a function of climate and defended it with ingenuity and enthusiasm. For the record, on the other hand, it should be said that few professional geographers today would subscribe to a simple environmental determinism.

In order to solve our own problem, let us take a closer look at it. Geographic factors in general, as Sorokin has defined them, include:

> . . . all cosmic conditions and phenomena which exist independent of man's activity, which are not created by man, and which change and vary through their own spontaneity, independent of man's existence and activity. In other words, if we take the total environment of a man or that of a social group, and subtract from it all environmental agencies directly or indirectly created or changed through man's existence and activity, we will have left approximately what is known as geographical environment.[9]

These factors thus include the motions of the earth, its position in the solar system, the motions of its single satellite, its proximity to the sun, the velocity of its revolution and rotation, the chemical composition of its crust, the nature of its enveloping atmosphere, the distribution of its land and water masses, the size and location of its continents and islands, the winds that play upon its surface, the clouds that float in its skies, its mountains and lakes, its prairies and rivers, its deserts and oceans, its animals and plants, the rain that falls upon it, the alternation of its seasons and the steady progression of day and night, the indentations of its coast lines and the altitudes of its hills, its variations in temperature and humidity, the age of its rocks and the slope of its terrains, the fertility of its soil and the mineral resources beneath its surface. All these and many more might be listed as geographic factors, factors that men themselves did not create and that they are almost completely powerless to change or control. But this is too long a list. Some of these factors are themselves functions of other factors, and it is therefore necessary to introduce some arrangement into them. We may therefore classify them into four major groups as follows: (1) the motions of the earth, (2) the distribution of land and water masses, (3) climate, and (4) natural resources. We shall examine the manner in which each of these major factors exerts an influence upon society.

First of all, however, it is appropriate to admit a proposition that is not susceptible to denial or contradiction: A proper conjunction of cosmic conditions is necessary for the existence of life upon this planet. So far as we know, no other planet in the solar system supports life, and without life,

---

[9] Pitirim A. Sorokin, *Contemporary Sociological Theories*, Harper & Brothers, New York, 1928, pp. 101–102.

of course, there can be no society.[10] An examination of the conditions necessary for life, however, is a problem for biology, not for sociology. Even where there is life there may be no human life and consequently no human societies. There are no societies on the tops of the highest mountains and none in the centers of the seas. Societies do not thrive on the ice sheets of the poles nor in the sands of the Sahara. The size of the earth itself and the acres of its arable land set limits to the number of people who dwell upon it. From these observations we may draw a preliminary conclusion that will help us to assay the role of the geographic factors in general. Geographic factors are limiting factors; they set limits to the variation of social phenomena; they determine the boundaries within which social events can occur. In this sense at least we may say that certain geographic conditions are necessary conditions in the existence of human societies.

2. The Motions of the Earth

Certain social consequences are inherent in the fact that the earth is a slightly pear-shaped spheroid that rotates upon its axis and revolves around the sun. The rotation of the earth determines that there shall be a steady alternation of night and day, day and night, and human activities adjust themselves to this alternation. The revolution of the earth determines that there shall be a steady progression of the seasons—spring, summer, autumn, winter, and then spring again—throughout a large portion of the globe. The social consequences of this rotation and revolution are many, some of which we shall mention here.

The fact that people work and play in the daytime and sleep at night is almost too obvious to require any attention at all. But rest and sleep are biological necessities, not geographic ones. Furthermore, some people work at night and sleep in the daytime. If every person in the world got up in the morning with the rising of the sun and went to bed in the evening with its setting, there would be a close and universal relationship between the earth's rotation and the social life of man. The degree to which this does not happen indicates that other than geographic factors are operating in the alternations of work and play and sleep and rest and in all the other activities in which men perforce indulge.

Similar observations may be made about the progression of the seasons. A North Dakota farm has one appearance in the wintertime and an entirely different one in the summer. The farmer's work changes as the sun moves through its solstices. Similarly, the pace of a great city like New

---

[10] It is also true, as we shall see, that without society there can be no *human* life.

York changes perceptibly in the months of midsummer, when the air close to the pavements shimmers in the heat of the sun and no breeze blows in the canyons between the skyscrapers. Many human activities alter their pace and character with the round of the seasons, and so we have the school year and the agricultural year and the retail-trade year and the industrial year and the fiscal year and the recreational year and so on through many examples.

But here again we have to note that the progression of the seasons is not only a geographic but also a social fact. The revolution of the earth does not determine that Independence Day should be in July, Memorial Day in May, and Labor Day in September. Nor does it require that the college year should extend from late September to early June. June may be a favorite month for weddings in our society, but is this because the vital juices stir in the springtime or because the end of the college year provides a convenient time for the ceremony? In the peasant societies of old Europe November was preferred as a "marriage month," because it was then that the harvest chores were over, and in ancient Greece the favored month was January.

If we move from such pleasant vital statistics as these to unpleasant ones, we can observe that there are more suicides in the merry month of May than in the melancholy month of November, but once again we are at a loss if we attempt to explain this phenomenon solely in terms of the seasons.[11] Also, in northern latitudes crimes against property are high in the winter and crimes against persons are high in the summer. Are winter and summer therefore to be taken as causes of these differential crime rates?

There is no question that there are cycles in many human activities and that these cycles sometimes follow the cycles of the seasons, but no man can say that it is this way and not otherwise because of the revolution of the earth around the sun. The countryman knows the seasons well and adjusts his life to them, but the clerk in the investment house does the same work day after day, in autumn and winter, in summer and spring.

Writers on these subjects have sought correlations between the seasons and the phenomena of social life. Ellsworth Huntington, for example, has asserted that the seasons of the year in which people are born is of far greater importance than is generally recognized. In some seasons, for example, the proportion of female births to male births rises, at certain seasons a higher proportion of the babies born are mentally defective or destined to suffer from tuberculosis, and at still other seasons an unusually

---

[11] The great French sociologist, Emile Durkheim, in his classic work on this subject thoroughly examined the role of geographic factors in the incidence of suicide and came to negative conclusions about their effects. See his *Suicide: A Study in Sociology*, The Free Press, New York, 1951. The original edition, *Le Suicide*, was published in Paris in 1897.

large number of babies are born who later on achieve eminence and fame.[12] Similarly, William F. Petersen has attempted to show that the season of the year in which an individual is conceived determines, for reasons of "meteorological turbulence," whether that individual will turn out to be a president of the United States, a genius at science or literature, a mental defective, a lunatic, or a criminal.[13]

On the basis of statistics compiled by writers like these, it is claimed that men of eminence, for example, are nearly all born during the early months of the year and few, if any, during the months of the late summer and fall. One may, of course, note that Franklin D. Roosevelt was born in January and that the birthdays of Abraham Lincoln and George Washington occur in February. To conclude from such statistical instances—or coincidences—as these, however, that there is an optimum or best season for the conception of eminent men and another season for the conception of the less eminent is to make statistical inferences do more work than they can properly perform.[14] To insist upon the validity of such inferences is to leave the realm of such positive sciences as geography and sociology and to wander perilously close to astrology.

No one doubts that there are daily cycles, annual cycles, weekly cycles, and monthly cycles in the social life of mankind and that some of these cycles have something to do with geography. Daily cycles occur because of the rotation of the earth upon its axis, annual cycles because of the revolution of the earth around the sun, and monthly cycles because of the revolution of the moon around the earth. But what accounts for the weekly cycles? Here we find no geographic or astronomic counterpart. The six days of labor and the seventh of rest is a Biblical injunction, not a geographic one.

Clocks and calendars, the metronomes of our life, are made by man, and neither daylight saving time nor standard time is inherent in the universe or required by its nature. One loses a day when circumnavigating the earth from east to west and gains a day when traveling in the opposite direction, but the international date line cannot be found in the Pacific Ocean. It exists only on the maps. The passage of time may be an ineluctable fact of nature, but man invented the time zones, choosing the

---

[12] Ellsworth Huntington, *Season of Birth*, John Wiley & Sons, Inc., New York, 1938.

[13] *The New York Times*, November 18, 1936, p. 24. See also William F. Petersen, *Man, Weather, Sun*, Charles C Thomas, Publisher, Springfield, Ill., 1947. This same author has even given us a geographic explanation of the Lincoln-Douglas debates. See his *Lincoln-Douglas: The Weather as Destiny*, Charles C Thomas, Publisher, Springfield, Ill., 1943.

[14] The simple expedient of examining an almanac discloses that more presidents of the United States were born during the last three months of the year than during the first three, by a score of 13 to 11. September has produced only one, however, and June none at all. October and November are tied for top place, with five each.

meridian at Greenwich as an arbitrary place at which to begin. And so we are led to the conclusion that, although the motions of the earth have much to do with the life of the human beings who inhabit it, most human activities must be explained by other factors.

3. Land and Water Masses

Switzerland has no navy worthy of the name, whereas England has been noted for its sea power throughout much of modern history. The explanation seems simple and geographic. Switzerland is a small and landlocked country, ringed about by the tall and stately Alps. England, on the other hand, is an island. What would be more "natural" than that an island people should look to the sea and fare forth over the broad expanse of oceans to create an empire based upon maritime power? Switzerland needs no navy because its defense lies in its mountain barriers. England does need one because its defense, on the contrary, rests in the waters that surround it.

The ease with which we can attribute this difference to the differential distribution of land and water masses should make us suspicious. It is true that Switzerland needs no navy, but other countries with only limited access to the sea—countries like Germany, for example—have built navies in modern times. And islands that support human societies, islands like Iceland and Bermuda and Ireland and the thousands of islands in Pacific Polynesia, have not ventured far into the field of naval construction. Furthermore, England herself, an island throughout all the centuries of recorded history, had no navy until the sixteenth century. Clearly other than geographic factors are at work, for an island society does not automatically produce a navy, nor even a maritime trade. Once again we see that without a proper conjunction of geographic factors a certain social phenomenon will not appear. But this phenomenon may not appear *with* this proper conjunction. The geographic factor is necessary but not sufficient to explain it.

It would, of course, be erroneous to assume that geographic factors, particularly those that have to do with the relative arrangements of land patterns and water patterns on the surface of the earth, are sociologically negligible. Maritime peoples tend to develop maritime occupations, to become fishermen and sailors, and prairie people cultivate the soil and become husbandmen and farmers. The commerce of the world tends to follow the arteries cut by geology because these are the geographic paths of least resistance. Mountains and rivers and lakes and oceans have been barriers to travel and trade and colonization and settlement. But man has learned to conquer them all. He now digs his holes through the tall mountains to make a turnpike and climbs over broad rivers on roadways of steel and cement.

Political boundaries frequently follow natural boundaries, but just as frequently do not. Cities grow where natural conditions are favorable, at the confluence of rivers or where rivers run into the seas, but great cities also rise from the plains. If the enthusiastic geographer says that the great city of Chicago developed "naturally" at the southern end of Lake Michigan because the lake was a barrier to eastern and western trade, he will have difficulty using his theory to account for the growth of Milwaukee, 90 miles to the north. He will have even greater difficulty explaining the rise of Indianapolis, the largest city in the United States not on a navigable body of water.

The City of New York enjoys one of the finest natural harbors in the world and owes much of its preeminence in international trade and commerce to this geographical advantage. But in colonial times New York was inferior as a port to both Boston and Philadelphia. If it later surpassed these cities its growth, in part, was due to another geographic factor, the accessibility of a vast and enormously rich hinterland up the Hudson River and over the water-level route to the West. But the same harbor, the same river, and the same hinterland were in the same places centuries before New York was a city or even a port.

To take still another example, the geographer might say that the Manhattan Island of today is a thicket of skyscrapers because of two geographic factors: (1) Manhattan has a solid rock foundation and can therefore support these skyscrapers, and (2) since Manhattan is entirely surrounded by water, the city in its growth had no direction to go but up. The sober geographer might remind his eager colleague, however, that the rock was just as solid and the rivers just as wide before Peter Minuit bought the island, for trinkets worth twenty-four dollars, from the Indians who lived in the woods north of what is now Wall Street. And where, he will ask, were the skyscrapers then? Geographic conditions are constant, or nearly so. It is the social and cultural factors that are the variables. And the most elementary logic teaches us that it is impossible to explain a variable by a constant. No one, neither geographer nor sociologist, will question the important role that the English Channel has played in the history of the European peoples and particularly, of course, of the Angles and Saxons and Jutes. The 18- to 22-mile water barrier between Folkestone and Boulogne, Dover and Calais, has released an island from the cares of a continent and has permitted the English to develop an insular civilization of a very high degree. The Channel has served as a defense in war and it enabled the island dwellers for a century and a half to hold the balance of power in Europe. Without it there would have been no Dunkirk in World War II, and the Nazi armies would have swallowed London as easily as Paris.

If, however, this famous stretch of water was a barrier to Hitler, and to Napoleon more than a century earlier, it was no barrier, but only an obstacle, to Julius Caesar, to William the Conqueror, and—in the other direction—to General Eisenhower. Since the invention of the airplane, of course, the Channel is hardly even an obstacle, and the insularity of the British nation, though it may or may not be a social fact, is no longer a geographic one. If there is a certain provincialism in the English mind, as evidenced perhaps by the reluctance of the Englishman to learn foreign languages,[15] it may be attributable to an imperial pride in a great civilization rather than to the fact that the English Channel separates the island from the Continent.

With respect to the influence of scenery upon the human temperament, there are as many theories as there are varieties of scenery. Of these we shall mention only one, an old theory recently advanced again, not by a geographer, but by an associate justice of the United States Supreme Court. Justice William O. Douglas, who likes to climb mountains, has the following to say about them:

> Mountains have a decent influence upon men. I have never met along the trails of the high mountains a mean man, a man who would cheat and steal. Certainly most men who are raised there are as wholesome as the mountains themselves. . . . When man pits himself against the mountain, he taps inner springs of his strength. He comes to know himself. . . . If man could only get to know the mountains better, and let them become a part of him, he would lose much of his aggression.[16]

The trouble with this theory is that one can argue the reverse with equal enthusiasm and sentiment. Mountains, one may say, restrict the free movement of a man, interrupt his vision, and frustrate his efforts to wrest a living from the soil. They isolate him from his fellows in the neighboring valleys and induce in him a sense of suspicion and distrust. It is the man on plain and prairie who can lift his eyes to the far horizon and gain a sense of distance and of space. The plainsman cultivates his land and acquires a sense of accomplishment. He listens to his corn grow during the hot summer days, and in the cool of the evening, as the crickets sing, he is at peace with himself and his fellow man.

[15] And, more humorously, by a headline which once appeared in a London newspaper: "Storm Raging over Channel; Continent Isolated."
[16] *Of Men and Mountains*, Harper & Row, Publishers, New York, 1950, p. 16.

Now, obviously, these points of view cannot both be right, because they are contraries. But they can both be wrong, because they are not contradictories. Any mature sociological judgment must, in the absence of additional evidence, regard them as equally fanciful—not devoid of merit, perhaps, as poetic propositions, but hardly adequate as scientific conclusions.

Unfortunately, the theory of the professional geographer on this matter is little better. The mountaineer, says Ellsworth Huntington, is resentful and quarrelsome, and much bolder than the plainsman. He envies the wealthier denizens of the lowlands and often tries to steal a share of their possessions. In some sections of the world raids from mountain tribes occur every year at the harvest, particularly in Persia and Afghanistan. In addition, feuds are more common in the mountains than in the lowlands, and these feuds may continue many generations after the original cause of the quarrel has been forgotten. The tendency to steal and to maraud Huntington attributes to the poor quality of the soil, which forces the mountaineer into poverty and desperation. The tendency to feud and quarrel he attributes to the natural isolation of the mountaineer's life and his lack of access to a court of justice. "Such things would not happen," says Professor Huntington, "if the isolation of the mountains had not forced people to look out for their own rights."[17]

The mistake here, as in both of the arguments above, lies in regarding isolation as a geographic rather than as a social concept. The reader will easily realize that one can be as effectively isolated from human companionship in the middle of a heavily populated city, say at Times Square in New York or Piccadilly Circus in London, as in the trackless wastes of the wilderness or on the rim of a high mountain. Geographic conditions may make social interaction difficult, but they seldom prevent it. Geographic conditions may make social interaction easy, but they do not assure it. In the years immediately following World War II it was extremely difficult for Russians and Americans to "fraternize" in the city of Berlin, but one would hardly attribute this difficulty to geography. Physical distance is one thing and social distance is another, and the relationship between mountains and moods requires much more research and investigation before theories like any of those mentioned here can subdue the skepticism of the sociologist.[18]

It is sometimes claimed, not unreasonably, that the nature of any terrain affects the fundamental mode of occupation in which the members

---

[17] Ellsworth Huntington, *Principles of Human Geography*, 5th ed., John Wiley & Sons, Inc., New York, 1940, pp. 223–224.

[18] It may be of incidental interest to note that one of the most active associations of collegiate mountain climbers in the United States is at the University of Iowa. There are no mountains within hundreds of miles of Iowa City.

of a society will indulge and that the mode of occupation, in turn, affects their art, literature, religion, and perhaps also their philosophic systems. Even the attributes of the deities whom people worship may have something to do with the geographic circumstances in which various religions arise. Thus, the members of a coastal society, for example the fisherfolk of Brittany, will pray to a god who has the power to quell the storms and pacify the sea from which they earn their living. An agricultural people, on the other hand, like the farmers of Illinois, may be expected to pray to a god who can guarantee a long growing season and freshen the soil with frequent and gentle rains. A prominent American historian has written that "an urban industrial society would certainly not write its twenty-third psalm in the images and metaphors of a pastoral people. Its first sentence would not end with the word 'shepherd'; but I cannot guess what word would be used instead."[19] Here, of course, it is a question whether the geography or the economy determined the metaphor, but in any event the psalm means as much today to the worshiper in a tiny Christian mission in the rice fields of Indochina as it does to the member of a metropolitan church in the city of Cincinnati.

We have to conclude, therefore, that, important as the arrangement of land and water masses may be, its influence is a negative, not a positive, one. It may determine what can be and what cannot be in society, but not what actually is. And so we find increasing support for an imminent conclusion that geography governs the possible, not the actual.

4. Climate

In the summertime, when the weather is warm, men and women in northern latitudes wear fewer clothes, spend much of their leisure time out of doors, go—in the United States—to baseball games and automobile races and county fairs and picnics, and, if they are in an economically privileged class, take vacations at the seashore or in the mountains. In the wintertime, when the weather is cold, they put on warmer clothing, stay indoors much of the time, go skiing or skating, travel less in their automobiles, and rely on shorter holiday periods to break the monotony of the season. Clearly climate has something to do with the nature of human activity. Of all the geographic factors we have mentioned, climate is possibly the most important, and we shall therefore devote this section to a discussion of the ways in which it exerts an influence upon society and upon human activities.

---

[19] Herbert Heaton, "The Economic Impact on History," in J. R. Strayer (ed.). *The Interpretation of History*, Princeton University Press, Princeton, N.J., 1943, pp. 105–106.

Graham Hutton, an Englishman who was stationed for some years at the British Consulate in Chicago, succumbed to a familiar compulsion of sojourners in a foreign land and wrote a book about the region of this country that he had come to know.[20] In this book he claimed to have noticed that Middle Westerners die before their time and exhibit the physical appearance of age and care long before their contemporaries in other parts of the country. He attributed this phenomenon to the extremes of temperature in the middle regions of the United States, to the fact that the inhabitants of these regions expend so much energy adjusting to the winter cold and the summer heat that they grow old before their time. This, of course, was a personal impression, and the author supplied no statistics to support his observations. If he had looked at the mortality statistics, he would have found exactly the reverse. Statistical tables of longevity rates for the various states indicate that the inhabitants of the Corn Belt area have a longer life expectancy than those of any other region of the country.

But statistics in themselves can neither support nor refute such a theory. The mortality rates in these states do not include the farmers who, having successfully tilled their rich black soil, retire to the more equable climes of Florida and California to "soak up the sun" in their declining years. Mortality rates are high and life expectancy low in the state of Arizona, for example, precisely because its climate is so salubrious that many people, especially those suffering from pulmonary afflictions, go there to live and ultimately to die. Thus, a state that has the most favorable climate for patients suffering from tuberculosis can also have the highest death rates attributable to this disease. Statistics of this kind must always be treated with the greatest caution. The high mobility of the American people makes it almost impossible to use them to support climatic conclusions.

Another example of the misuse of statistics is provided by Ellsworth Huntington, the geographer quoted earlier, who has asserted that the proportion of people of Middle Western origin whose names are listed in *Who's Who in America* is appreciably lower than that of indigenous inhabitants of the Eastern and Western seaboards, after correction for date of settlement and age of statehood. The statistics are doubtless correct. But we cannot use them to infer, as Huntington does, that the climate of the Middle West is therefore unfavorable to achievement. Only certain kinds of achievement are selected for inclusion in *Who's Who*. A full professor in a major university is almost automatically invited to list his name and record in this publication, but where are the master farmers of America? It is not necessary to refute Huntington's facts in order to reject his conclusions.

We are duly and properly impressed by the information that hell in the

[20] *Midwest at Noon*, University of Chicago Press, Chicago, 1946.

Eskimo religion is a cold place because the ultimate in unpleasantness to an inhabitant of the polar regions would "naturally" be a frigid temperature. Similarly, we can appreciate the fact that the Christian hell is a hot place, because, we "naturally" suppose, Christianity was originally a Mediterranean religion and was founded in a warm region of the earth. But Christianity has since spread all over the globe, and its hell was as hot in Cotton Mather's harsh Massachusetts winters as it was in the Eastern Mediterranean homelands of the prophets. Clearly other than climatic factors determine the temperature of hell.

That climate exercises an influence upon human energy and activity we should not be constrained to deny. Huntington introduces figures to show that physical strength, mental activity, and health are correlated with variations in temperature and humidity. He studied the productivity of workers in the textile factories of New England and the South and the daily mathematics grades of the cadets at the United States Military Academy at West Point.[21] Huntington notes further that there is an optimum temperature for mental work and another optimum for physical work. The optimum figure itself fails, however, when the climate is monotonous, for "changes of temperature, provided they are not too great, are more stimulating than uniformity" and "a fall in temperature, in certain latitudes, is more stimulating than a rise."[22]

One could continue with many more examples. Crime, suicide, morbidity, and mortality rates are all affected by climatic factors. There is no reason to suppose that phenomena of other kinds are not similarly affected. Anyone who has attempted to do his daily work in the middle of an enervating heat wave knows for himself that such factors are important. It is easy to be lazy when the temperature is abnormally high, and society itself supports our indolence. During the heat waves that frequently assail much of the United States in the summer, factory workers and clerical workers are often excused from their labors and permitted to go home. These facts no one would wish to deny. Climate exercises an effect, and it is not a negligible one.

But we must conclude, even in this respect, that whatever importance the climatic factor has, it is relatively minor in comparison with the social factors that influence the activity of men. Regional variations in climate are large in the United States. The weather in Maine and Minnesota is different from the weather in Florida and Southern California, and the climate of

[21] Ellsworth Huntington, *Civilization and Climate*, Yale University Press, New Haven, Conn., 1915, p. 79. In this latter case, however, he found it necessary to eliminate such social factors as football games, the junior prom, holidays, examinations, and reprimands in order for his correlations of achievement and climate to hold.
[22] *Ibid.*, p. 119.

Oregon is more attractive than the climate of Iowa. But the societies and civilizations in these states, in all essentials, are the same. The same subjects are taught in the schools and the same general occupations are pursued by the people. The main streets of the small towns and cities of Nevada and North Dakota are virtually indistinguishable from those of Arkansas and Minnesota. Where there are differences they are attributable, for the most part, to other than climatic factors. The Indian boys and girls who lived on the banks of the Mississippi centuries before the discovery of that river by De Soto lived one kind of life, and the American boys and girls who live there today live a completely different kind. But there is no evidence that the climate of the region has changed in any significant way during the course of the last one thousand years.

Ellsworth Huntington has emphasized more than any other writer the influence of climate upon civilization. He has drawn maps showing that regions of the earth which have an equable and temperate, but variable, climate are also distinguished by a high productivity in the arts we ordinarily associate with civilization. But even he has conceded that great nations have appeared in widely diverse climates, both in the hot plains of Mesopotamia and Yucatán and in the cool hill country of Norway and Switzerland. He has admitted in addition that Illinois and southern Mongolia, which differ enormously in civilization, lie in the same latitude and have the same average temperature.[23] The fact that we can find the same kinds of societies in widely different climates, and different kinds of societies in the same climate, encourages us to conclude that, though climate is one of the natural conditions that make human societies possible, it does not determine in any inevitable manner the infinite details of those societies.

5. Natural Resources

Ever since the explosion of the first atomic bomb, a new type of prospector has been scouring the earth. He is not the prospector of a century ago—a tramplike character wandering off by himself, his pick and pans packed on his mule, watching the swift water as it runs down the mountain streams of the West. This modern prospector is likely to be a man with a high degree of technical education, and he carries with him some scientific instruments, among the most important of which is a Geiger counter. He travels by airplane and possibly explores by helicopter. He is looking for uranium ore.

Uranium ore is not, of course, evenly distributed over the face of the earth, nor are the other mineral resources that mean so much to the life of

---

[23] *Ibid.*, pp. 2–3.

man. Some nations have more of it than others, and some have none of it at all. Now it is perfectly obvious that the nations with rich deposits may be more powerful, in a political and military sense, than those with none and that this geographic factor, which exists independently of any human activity, has much to do with diplomacy and international relations. And so with respect to each mineral resource—coal, iron, oil, copper, manganese, tin, and all the others. We have to say, therefore, that natural resources have a great deal to do with the wealth and comparative position of nations. And even further, natural resources have something to do with the general state and condition of society. It is difficult to imagine what contemporary civilization would be like if there were no such things on earth as coal and iron and oil. Without these mineral resources an industrial civilization would be inconceivable. In order to make something one must first have the ingredients. It would be ridiculous to minimize the social consequences of this important geographic factor and indeed there are separate areas of inquiry, notably industrial geology and economic geography, in which these problems are investigated in detail.

It must be apparent, however, that it is not the presence of natural resources, in or under the crust of the earth, that is important but rather the use that is made of them. Without use they would be quite devoid of sociological significance. The precious metals and common ores were part of the earth before the Industrial Revolution, but they exercised little influence upon earlier societies. The largest supply of uranium ore in the world is about as useful as a pile of sand to a society that lacks a science of physics. The coal fields of western Pennsylvania and southern Illinois existed for many centuries before Columbus discovered America, but they contributed nothing to the societies of the native Americans. If coal cannot automatically create a nation, neither, as the case of Sweden shows, can its absence retard its development. And here we see again that the role of the geographic factor is essentially an uncreative one. It may limit the directions that social development can take, but it does not determine them.

One cannot, in short, have a coal mine where there is no coal; and so coal is a necessary condition of coal mines. But there can be coal without coal mines; and so the former is not a sufficient condition of the latter. Coal on this continent was a constant for many centuries, but the societies that appeared here were variable. We may conclude again, therefore, that geographic factors, though necessary to explain human societies, are not sufficient. Something else is required to account for the fact of society and the differences that particular societies exhibit both in time and in space.

We cannot conclude this section without mentioning the greatest of all resources, the resources of the soil itself. Most of our food comes directly or indirectly from the soil. Without a proper combination of soil and sun and rain, the earth would yield none of its sustenance and societies could not subsist. The land has incalculable consequences for the men who dwell upon it and who cultivate it with hand and hoe and disk and plow. The land is the ultimate source of all wealth, and the difference between rich land and poor land has much to do with the prosperity and power of nations. If Greenland had the soil of Iowa, for example, and Iowa Greenland's glaciers, Iowa would not be the state where the tall corn grows and Greenland might—*might*—be one of the breadbaskets of the world. The social consequences of soil resources are immeasurable, and so obvious that they require no elaboration. But if exhausted soil supports no societies, neither does virgin soil, no matter how productive it may potentially be, and so once more we see that it is not the land itself but the use that men make of it that gives it its significance for sociology.

The exhaustion of the soil, however, and the depletion of other natural resources, in societies that have become accustomed to their use, can have momentous social consequences. For this reason conservation has become the concern of governments. But the soil no more exhausts itself than do metals mine themselves. These processes are social processes and so it is to sociology that we must look for their explanation.

We are frequently told that the deserts are on the march, and in truth no less than one-third of the surface of the earth is now arid land. We look at the vast regions of North Africa and the Middle East—Algeria, Tunisia, Tripolitania, Cyrenaica, Egypt, "the Biblical wildernesses of Sinai and the Negev, the lost lands of Babylon and the salt deserts of Persia"—and reflect that no less than fifteen civilizations flourished there and then "foundered in the dust of their own creation."[24] As we thus reflect we are reminded of Shelley's "Ozymandias":

> I met a traveler from an antique land
> Who said: Two vast and trunkless legs of stone
> Stand in the desert. Near them, on the sand,
> Half sunk, a shattered visage lies, whose frown,
> And wrinkled lip, and sneer of cold command,
> Tell that its sculptor well those passions read
> Which yet survive, stamped on these lifeless things,
> The hand that mocked them and the heart that fed;
> And on the pedestal these words appear:
> "My name is Ozymandias, king of kings:
> Look on my works, ye Mighty, and despair!"

[24] The expressions in quotation marks are taken from Ritchie Calder, "Need One-third of the World Be Desert?" *The New York Times Magazine*, July 9, 1950, p. 16. See, by the same author, *The Inheritors: The Story of Man and the World He Made*, William Heinemann, Ltd., London, 1961.

Nothing beside remains. Round the decay
Of that colossal wreck, boundless and bare
The lone and level sands stretch far away.

Shelley's sonnet suggests, perhaps, that no society can withstand the onslaught and invasion of the sand. But it would be a superficial analysis indeed that would attribute the victory of the desert to the action of climate and wind, and to the lowering of the water table underneath the Sahara. A careful analysis attributes this phenomenon not to the maleficence of natural factors but to the destruction of the North African forests by the succession of civilizations and to the practices of the men who founded and inherited them. The historic fertility of the Saharan lands has long since been confirmed—where, after all, did Hannibal get his elephants?—and similarly the existence of large fresh-water seas lying far beneath the surface. It is not climate, therefore, that destroyed the bounty of nature, but man himself. Scientists now working for United Nations agencies—the Food and Agricultural Organization and UNESCO—in the Saharan Research Center, have been growing oats, barley, vines, artichokes, onions, asparagus, carrots, potatoes, tomatoes, and mandarin oranges in the middle of what was only recently a desolate waste. If man destroys the soil he can also reclaim it. He can make a garden grow where plumes of sand now blow endlessly off the dunes.[25]

The natural resources of the earth, including its soil, are thus susceptible both to the uses and the misuses of men. By themselves they set limits to the societies that men may construct and the activities in which they may indulge. But they do not by themselves determine the kinds of societies, nor the kinds of activities, that these shall be. Geography supplies the natural conditions for the answers to some of our sociological problems, but it does not supply the sufficient conditions that wholly satisfactory answers require.

6. Geographic Factors and War

In the early months of World War II the German army conquered Poland, quickly overran the Low Countries, pushed the British off the Continent at Dunkirk, turned the flank of the Maginot Line, and marched triumphantly across the Place de la Concorde and up the Champs Elysées in the city of

[25] These fascinating facts, and many more, can be found in the article mentioned in the preceding footnote. A more recent article, in *The Times* of London, informs us that scientists working under the auspices of the Chinese Academy of Sciences are using artificial means to melt the glaciers of Kansu and Sinkiang in an effort to turn the deserts of Inner Mongolia into good farmland. *The Times*, Tuesday, March 14, 1961, p. 11.

Paris. The banner of the Swastika was riding high over one of the most civilized cities on earth and German military power was at its zenith. Why did not Hitler and his generals immediately turn this power against England? The answer is easy—the English Channel.

Had Hitler made an attempt to invade the British Isles at that time, he would almost certainly have succeeded. England, for the first time in many centuries, would have been subdued, and the history of World War II would have taken a different course. The task that confronted the United States after Pearl Harbor would have been of a different order of magnitude altogether if the hooked cross rather than the Union Jack had been flying over the Houses of Parliament in December of 1941. Who can doubt, whatever the ultimate outcome of the war, that the existence of the English Channel at that time saved the United Kingdom? What was a geographic barrier became, for Hitler, a psychological hazard as well and so he failed to grasp the greater victory that was so clearly within his reach.

The modern history of Western Europe, and of the world, would assuredly have been different had there been no such strait as the English Channel separating England and the Continent. One might say that there will always be an England because of it and that there might never have been an England without it. But this is idle speculation. Of the thousands of straits that separate land masses over the face of the earth, why is it that this one, and not innumerable others, assumes such a rich historical significance? For an answer to this question one must look not to geography but to history and politics and sociology.

No one can read the chronicles of war without attributing some importance to geographic factors, no matter how difficult their role may be to determine. Military strategy requires the assistance of geographic knowledge. No strategist may ignore the factors of wind and weather, the topography of the earth and the tides of the sea, or the elemental fact of distance itself. The mountain fastnesses of the Alps have permitted Switzerland to maintain her neutrality and her peace through all the European wars of the nineteenth and twentieth centuries. China has ultimately defeated all of her foreign conquerors by absorbing them in the vastness of the Chinese earth. And "General Winter" has been an incalculable aid in helping the Russians to repel all invaders of their soil.

So important indeed are geographic factors in the planning and prosecution of a war that a new science, known as geopolitics, has made its appearance during the last decades. This science was founded by Sir Halford Mackinder, a Member of Parliament and a professor at the University of London who, in 1904, read a paper to the British Geographical Society entitled "The Geographic Pivot of History." In this paper Professor Mackinder maintained that the great Russian-Siberian land mass was the "heartland" of the earth and that whoever controlled this almost illimitable territory—one-sixth of the habitable land surface of the globe—was in a good position to rule the rest of the world. He declared in addition that British sea power, at that time supreme, was only of peripheral importance in comparison with this heart and center of the land. This theory gains grandeur and cogency if one looks at the earth on a north polar projection, that is, from a point of vantage directly above the North Pole, and sees how much of it indeed, in contrast with the puny territories of the Western nations, Russia occupies.

Few persons paid attention to this thesis at the time it was proposed, nor even when Sir Halford developed and amplified it in his later books. One of those who did, however, was a German geographer named Karl Haushofer, an intimate of Hitler. Haushofer founded a school of geopolitics and gave the German dictator geographic justification for making war upon the Russians.

Suggestive as this theory is, it is also shortsighted if it implies that geographic position and size of land mass are alone sufficient to determine the locus of political power. Both of these conditions may be political advantages, but to rank them as political determinants is to accord them unjustified sociological importance. As a matter of fact, the entire school of geopolitics has been subjected to heavy criticism. Such criticism was inevitable in any case, as is apparent from even a superficial reading of history. Neither the dynasties of the Egyptian Ptolemies, nor the Roman Empire, nor the British Empire of the modern age, nor yet again the contemporary power of the United States can be explained by the theory of the Eurasian heartland. Power is a pure sociological concept, and geographic resources constitute only one of its several components.

Geographic factors assume importance also, of course, in the sphere of military tactics. In the late weeks of May, 1944, for example, the military might of the Allied Forces was poised on the island of Britain for an invasion of the Continent of Europe. To General Dwight D. Eisenhower, Supreme Commander of the Allied Forces, was given the authority to decide when the huge task force should move. When all else was in readiness, with his armies and navies restless with anticipation, he had to delay his decision once because of an improper conjunction of weather and tidal conditions off the coast of Normandy. Only when these conditions changed for the better a few days later was he able to issue his famous command, "Let 'er rip!" and set in motion the process that resulted in the destruction of the Hitlerian dream of empire.

But to attribute the success, or even the initiation, of this gigantic enterprise to the weather alone is like attributing a gunshot wound to the atmospheric conditions that influenced the trajectory of the bullet. Who can doubt that—whatever the weather, and whether or not it was auspicious—the fate of Hitler was sealed when the power of the Allies was first mounted against him and that this power would have prevailed in spite of time and tide?

Similarly, the Russian winter, as mentioned above, has always been an invaluable ally of the Russian, tsar and dictator alike, as several would-be conquerors have discovered to their dismay. But where is the historian who would say that this war or that war, or any war at all in the long and checkered course of human history, was decided by geography? To say so would be to contravene both historical fact and sociological principle. Geographic factors are surely not negligible in the history of warfare, but neither are they by themselves decisive.

Furthermore, it must not be forgotten that geographic factors that once were influential have since been reduced to insignificance by the inventive genius of man. In a concluding section of this chapter we refer to the reciprocal influences of social factors upon geographic conditions. At the moment we may intimate that nowhere perhaps is this counterinfluence more apparent than in the course and process of war. A million foot soldiers may fail to pass the barriers of the Andes or the Alps, but the lone aviator flies over them with ease and even with condescension. Clouds may envelop an airstrip, but instrument landings assure continuous service. Radar pierces the thickest fog, and neither weather nor distance is an obstacle to long-range navigation. Indeed, several of the important naval battles of World War II were fought with the opposing fleets out of sight of each other. For the future, unfortunately, these observations too are anachronisms. Neither distance nor climate, nor yet the weather, can prevent or even impede an attack by intercontinental ballistic missiles.

7. Geographic Factors and Civilization

The role of geographic factors in the origin, development, and disintegration of the great civilizations has fascinated sophisticated minds from the Greek Hippocrates of ancient times to the American Huntington and the English Toynbee of more recent date. Why is it that some societies rise to the level that we should be inclined to call "civilized"—a word that in its etymological and nonevaluative sense means simply "urbanized"[26]—whereas other societies remain in a state of primitivism, fail to master the achievements of reading and writing, and contribute nothing to literature and science and philosophy? Why is it that some societies—nonliterate

[26] For an elaboration of this theme see the author's "Indices of Civilization," *American Journal of Sociology*, Vol. LXXI, March, 1966, pp. 483–490.

societies—have a language but no alphabet, techniques but no science, legends but no literature, customs but no laws, religion but no theology, art but no aesthetics, and, finally, a *Weltanschauung*, or world view, but no philosophy? Can these differences, too, be attributed to the influence and operation of geographic factors?

Here the geographer can make a case that, on the surface at least, possesses a high order of plausibility. In the beginning of this chapter it was agreed that a certain favorable conjunction of geographic factors—one might with equal accuracy say cosmic factors—is necessary for life itself and that without life there can be no society. We now wish to inquire whether, given these conditions, geographic factors further operate in some cases to stimulate and in others to obstruct the rise of civilizations from a primitive "historylessness." We may speculate, for example, that where geographic conditions are too favorable the people have no incentive to invent the arts and instruments of civilization. The inhabitants of some of the islands in the southern and western seas need little exertion in order to survive. An abundant supply of food may even drop from the trees into their laps. There may be such a thing, in other words, as an environment that is too propitious, one that in its very luxuriance fails to stir its natives into the restless striving that results in the development of a civilization. When geographic conditions, on the other hand, are too unfavorable—when a harsh, barren, and forbidding environment requires the expenditure of too much human energy in order simply to survive, as in the case of the frozen lands of the Eskimo—here too no high civilization can be expected to develop. This theory, as has been said, appears to be a plausible one; it has, moreover, been elevated into a philosophy of history by the speculative sociologist Arnold J. Toynbee.

Toynbee believes that civilized societies arise as a result of a "response" to certain "challenges," among which the challenge of the environment is initially the most important. Thus, Toynbee finds that each of six early civilizations—the Egyptian, Sumerian, Chinese, Mayan, Andean, and Minoan—arose in response to an environmental challenge—the desiccation of the soil, jungle and river swamp, flood and extremes of temperature, the overabundance of the tropical forest, a bleak climate and a grudging earth, or—in the case of the Minoans—a hostile sea. They illustrate for Toynbee "the truth that, in the genesis of civilizations, the interplay between challenges and responses is the factor which counts above all others."[27]

Toynbee, no extremist, notes that in the genesis of certain other

[27] Arnold J. Toynbee, *A Study of History*, abridged by D. C. Somervell, Oxford University Press, Fair Lawn, N.J., 1946, pp. 68–79.

civilizations social rather than geographic factors presented the principal challenges, that in the incidence of some civilizations no direct physical challenge is apparent, and that even where physical challenges are present they may have been accompanied by human challenges now concealed forever in the unknown recesses of history. But he leaves the impression that "ease is inimical to civilization," that the adversities of an unfavorable environment are an historical advantage, and that only men who must master these adversities can create a civilized society.

The adversities of natural circumstance may nevertheless be too formidable to overcome. Between the extremes of ease and adversity there must be a golden mean, an optimum condition of environment, which induces neither to starvation nor to satiety. Where can such an optimum be found? Toynbee discovers that history supplies numerous examples. Of these we shall mention only two. The height of the Scandinavian civilization, he says, appeared not in Norway, Denmark, or Sweden, but in Iceland, the seat of the first parliament in the world and the scene and source of some of the grand sagas of Norse literature. When these same Scandinavian seafarers attempted to duplicate their feats 500 miles to the west on the island of Greenland, their efforts met with failure. There the environment was altogether too harsh, the challenge too severe.[28]

The colonization of the North American continent affords another illustration. The "winning of the West" in the United States was accomplished not by the inhabitants of Virginia and the Carolinas, where the environment was favorable, but by the Yankees, who had already conquered the stern coasts and stony soils of New England. "Evidently," concludes Toynbee, "the Mason and Dixon Line roughly corresponds with the southern limit of an area of optimum challenge."[29] But there is also a northern limit. This northern limit may be discovered in New England. When we speak of New England, says our eminent sociologist, we mean primarily Massachusetts, Rhode Island, and Connecticut, and not Maine, Vermont, and New Hampshire. Recognizing the contributions of Massachusetts to American civilization as beyond compare, Toynbee goes on to say:

> Maine, on the other hand, though actually a part of Massachusetts until her establishment as a separate state in 1820, has always been unimportant, and survives to-day as a kind of museum piece—a relic of seventeenth-century New England inhabited by woodmen and watermen and hunters. These children of a hard country now eke out their scanty livelihood by serving as

[28] *Ibid.*, p. 146.
[29] *Ibid.*

"guides" for pleasure-seekers who come from the North American cities to spend their holidays in this Arcadian state, just because Maine is still what she was when many of these cities had not yet begun to arise out of the wilderness. Maine to-day is at once one of the longest-settled regions of the American Union and one of the least urbanized and sophisticated.[30]

Environmental factors, at their optimum in Massachusetts, thus reach the point of diminishing returns in Maine. The theory is further "confirmed" by the fact that as we go still farther north we find the least "progressive" of the Canadian provinces in New Brunswick, Nova Scotia, and Newfoundland. Finally, we meet in Labrador, as previously in Greenland, the maximum challenge—geographic conditions so severe that a civilized society can neither arise nor survive in the icy wastes.

The down-Easters and the Dixielanders who read this book can doubtless supply their own answers to this theory without any help from the author. If Toynbee is saying in these passages that geographic factors set limits to the kinds of human societies that can appear upon this earth, he is saying no more than we have said throughout this chapter. If he is implying in addition, however, that a civilization is an inevitable function of an optimum conjunction of geographical circumstances and challenges, his conclusions are running ahead of the supportable data. A thoughtful student may be inclined, for example, to wonder why, if the severe climate of New England stimulated the colonists to build a great civilization, it did not similarly stimulate the indigenous North American Indians who inhabited the region long before the hardy and persecuted band of Pilgrims arrived on these shores in 1620. To this possible and indeed weighty objection Toynbee, in his fashion, supplies an answer:

> It is, of course, easy enough to cite examples of communities that have failed to respond to particular challenges. That proves nothing, for almost every challenge that has eventually evoked a victorious response turns out, on inquiry, to have baffled or broken one respondent after another before the moment when, at the hundredth or the thousandth summons, the victor has entered the lists at last. Such is the notorious "prodigality of nature," of which a host of examples spring to mind.[31]

The recourse here to a biological analogy—the prodigality of nature—may surely be regarded as somewhat less than satisfactory. It leaves unexplained how the successful instances differ from the unsuccessful ones when the geographic circumstances are the same. Versatile as some of these theories

---

[30] *Ibid.*, p. 147.
[31] *Ibid.*, p. 141.

are, therefore, and few will question the versatility of Toynbee's, they do not yet possess the cogency that would give them the stature of sociological knowledge. In most of them, as the reader has doubtless observed, a significant factor has been omitted—the influence of man himself and the stimulus he receives from association with his fellows.

Similar theories, of course, have been constructed to account for the disintegration of civilizations, but since they exhibit the same defects as those explaining the origins of human societies, it is not necessary to discuss them in detail. We shall, however, mention Huntington's theory of the decline and fall of the Roman Empire because it is one of the most prominent and intrinsically interesting of these theories. Huntington maintains that Rome prospered and achieved its grandeur in a climate that was more stimulating than that of any part of Italy today and that when the empire began to totter in the fourth and fifth centuries its decline was due primarily to a deficiency of rainfall. Since Huntington had no statistical records of a Roman meteorological bureau to study, he had to exercise considerable ingenuity in order to discover that the rainfall declined in these centuries. He accomplished this task by "dendrochronological" analysis— that is, by using tree rings as a measure of time; counting back, a year for a ring, until he arrived at the period of history in question; and finding, with great good luck for his theory, that the rings were closer together at that time, a fact which indicates a sparse supply of rain. There is, however, a serious obstacle in the way of accepting his theory. The rings he counted were on the cross sections of California Sequoia trees, which are among the few living things on earth that were alive in the days of the Roman Empire. If one cares to make the geographic leap from California to Italy and then the additional logical leap that transforms this interesting correlation into a causal factor, then one is at liberty to attribute the decay of this great civilization to the reluctance of the heavens to water the Roman earth. To sociologists, however, the theory seems more like astrology than ge- ography, and it has been so resoundingly criticized by P.A. Sorokin that no one since has had the temerity to resurrect it.[32]

A final example of the uses of geography to explain momentous trends in the course of human history is provided by a news story that once appeared in *The New York Times*. The story reported a lecture delivered by a geographer who maintained that the emergence of the Soviet Union to historical prominence in the twentieth century coincided with a general

[32] Pitirim A. Sorokin, *Contemporary Sociological Theories*, Harper & Row, Publishers, New York, 1928, pp. 186–192. Indeed, Sorokin's treatment of the geographical school of sociology (chap. III, pp. 99–193) merits continued attention. For Huntington's theory see his *World Power and Evolution*, Yale University Press, New Haven, Conn., 1919, and the previously cited *Civilization and Climate*.

warming of the earth's temperatures, a warming that began around 1850 and notably accelerated around 1920. Previously the winters had been too cold, and Russian energies too sluggish, but now with a more favorable climate these energies were released to the service of building an important and powerful nation.

This story, it should be observed, was not considered of sufficient significance to warrant a place on the front page, and the headline writer capped it with a pun—"Soviet Rises by Degree." It should also be observed that the geographer in question presented his theory as an "appearance" rather than as a conviction. The implication remains, however, that a rising temperature was not wholly unrelated to the growth of Russia as a great power in the twentieth century—otherwise there would have been no story. This theory, incidentally, has been propounded by others, although without quite so direct a reference to Russia. In its general form it is based upon the observation that the city of each of the great civilizations of the West, beginning with the Egyptian empire, has had its location in a more northerly latitude than its predecessor.[33] What can be said about this point of view?

In the first place, any summary rejection of it would be inappropriate. The theory may, after all, have a great deal to be said in its favor, as its proponents believe. We may note, however, that acceptance of it requires two assumptions rather than one. It requires us to believe, first, that the temperatures of the earth are indeed rising and, second, that this rise is causally related to historical events. There are several proponents of the first of these assumptions, geographers who have asserted, for example, that the mean annual temperature of New Haven, Connecticut, say, is now comparable to the former mean annual temperature of Baltimore, Maryland, that the glaciers are slowly retreating to the north, leaving warmer air behind them, and that we are in a period of "climatic amelioration." Other meteorologists, however, discern no such long-term trend, maintain that early statistics are too unreliable to support a satisfactory curve, and—with the usual caution of the weatherman—suggest that such warmer-than-normal seasons as have appeared in recent years may be strictly temporary phenomena. Still others maintain, in exact contrast to these views, that the temperature has dropped a half degree Fahrenheit in the last several decades on some 80 per cent of the earth's surface.[34] It is further contended, again in contradiction, that thermal pollution of rivers and lakes and

---

[33] See, for example, Vilhjalmur Stefansson, *The Northward Course of Empire*, Harcourt, Brace and Company, Inc., New York, 1920; and S. C. Gilfillan, "The Coldward Course of Progress," *Political Science Quarterly*, 1920, pp. 393–410.

[34] J. Murray Mitchell, U.S. Weather Bureau, at a meeting of the World Meteorological Organization in Rome, October 7, 1961.

oceans, occasioned by the hot wastes from nuclear power plants, will melt the glaciers of the north and that the released waters will in time inundate and destroy the coastal cities of the world. There is already some evidence that the rise in sea level, which for some three thousand years was about 4 inches per century, jumped to 3 inches in the eight years from 1964 to 1972. In other words, we have nothing but contrary opinions, and none of them wins the unanimous assent of the meteorologists. Predictions in meteorology seem to be as precarious as those in demography!

But even if the evidence for increasing warmth were to be accepted, it would by no means follow of necessity that a rise in temperature has caused the recent emergence from hibernation of the Russian Bear. To indulge in such an assertion is to ignore not only the history of Great Russia but also the entire history of the West. It is true that serfdom, as a social institution, did not disappear in Russia until after the opening of the twentieth century, long after it had disappeared in the countries of Western Europe, and that, in a sense, the Industrial Revolution is only now beginning to exercise its effects upon the population of one-sixth of the land mass of the earth. But it would be as easy to account for these facts by pointing to the several periods of social isolation from the West that characterized the course of Russian history during various regimes as to explain them by the climatic theory.

It is not altogether clear, furthermore, that Russia possessed no civilization of a high order before the recent and putative temperature rise. Although this civilization may have been confined to the upper classes—people who were in contact with Western Europe, who used French in their polite conversations, and who employed English governesses—it should not be forgotten that the nineteenth century was the great age of Russian literature and that Gogol, Pushkin, Tolstoy, and Dostoevski are all nineteenth-century names. Was the nineteenth century, too, a period of "climatic amelioration" for Russia? Can temperature alone account for the differences between the Russia of the imperial tsars and the Russia of the Communist dictators? And what about other countries that share the latitudes of Russia—Finland, Norway, Sweden, Denmark, Iceland, England, and Canada? Does their rise to historical eminence also coincide with the rise of a column of mercury in a tube? On these questions we remain in the realm of conjecture.

And so we conclude this section with the same observations we have made throughout. One cannot deny that a proper conjunction of geographic factors—soil and sun and wind and weather—are necessary for the very existence of human societies and that changing conjunctions of these factors may have something to do with the historical destinies of these societies. But to say that they are necessary is not to say that they are sufficient. To deny that they are negligible is not to assert that they are decisive. The problem of social causation is more complex than this. We must exercise unusual caution in regard to the influence of geographic factors upon the rise and fall of civilized societies, and upon the other social phenomena mentioned in this chapter, in order that we may neither ignore these factors completely nor assign them an insupportable significance.

8. The Reciprocal Influence of Social upon Geographic Factors

Before concluding this chapter we should like, in this short section, to emphasize that the influence of geographic factors upon societies is not a one-sided affair. It is a truism, of course, that throughout the entire course of his existence, man has steadily and systematically altered the face of nature. But it is a truism, nevertheless, that has a profound importance for sociology in general and for the substance of the present chapter in particular. Climate conditions culture, but culture also conditions climate.

Man cannot initially control the chemistry of the soil or the configuration of the land or the quantity of the waters or the duration of the seasons or the salinity of the sea or the lodes of precious metals or the succession of the tides or the rivers' currents or the heat of the noonday sun. To all of these and to many more he must adjust and in some measure adapt his life. But he changes many of these factors as he adjusts to them. He cultivates the soil, and thereby changes its composition. He can quite literally move mountains. If he cannot determine the temperature and humidity of the atmosphere, he can at least build houses to shelter himself from the elements and can, in addition, condition the air that immediately surrounds him, either warming it or cooling it to suit his needs and his fancy. He cannot control the weather, but he can attack the clouds with dry ice and silver iodide to make them yield their rainfall.[35] As mentioned above, he can reclaim a desert for agriculture. Civilized man with his cultural equipment can inhabit regions of the earth, at least for a time, in which primitive man without this equipment could not survive.[36]

Man cannot control the river's current, but he can dam the stream, capture its energy, and send that energy in turn to distant places on the thin

[35] This last became a new military technique during the Vietnam War and was used to muddy roads, weaken dikes, flood communications lines, provide a cloud and rain cover for infiltration, and even, with additional chemicals, produce an acidic rainfall capable of interfering with radar. There was some skepticism about the effectiveness of these measures, but "geophysical warfare," like "environmental engineering" in general, became an ominous prospect.

[36] A distinguished geographer, the late Isaiah H. Bowman, who was president of The Johns Hopkins University, once remarked that we possess all the techniques required to build a society at the South Pole and that the reason we do not do so is that it is too expensive. The same can now perhaps be said about the moon.

wires that hang from the hydroelectric towers. Tornado and flood and hurricane and drought can terrify him and sometimes shorten his life, but he builds defenses against them all and ultimately survives their depredations. He carves highways out of the slopes of mountains and airstrips out of the jungle; he bridges the rivers and tunnels underneath them; and he spans the continents with strings of steel on which diesels and electric locomotives run. Ultimately, of course, he must adjust to natural conditions beyond his control, but in adjusting he alters them—sometimes beyond recognition. The mark of man is upon the earth in all but the most inaccessible regions.

Sometimes, unfortunately, it is a harmful mark. There is increasing danger that man will destroy the natural environment that is essential to the continuance of life. Our rivers are polluted with pesticides, garbage, sewage, detergents, and chemical wastes. The waters at our shorelines are so full of pollutants that in some areas the fish and shellfish industries are approaching a state of disaster. Our air is poisoned by the fumes of millions of exhaust pipes, by the waste products of fossil fuels, and by biologically hazardous isotopes from uranium reactors. Hamlet was indeed prophetic when he said, "This most excellent canopy, the air, this brave o'erhanging firmament, appeareth nothing to me but a foul and pestilent congregation of vapors." Not even space itself is immune from the infestations of man. By February, 1972, 5,850 catalogued objects had been rocketed into orbits of one kind or another, and the space in the earth's vicinity was beginning to resemble a flying junkyard. The activities of man persistently upset the balance of nature. So thoughtless are some of these activities, so heedless of consequence, that scientists are sometimes inclined to wonder if there is intelligent life on earth!

The seventies are bringing to our attention with increasing force a solid and immutable geographic fact; that fact is the size of the earth itself. Our planet, in truth, is a small one, and the question is how much demographic and industrial growth it is able to sustain. Is it time for us to reject the appeal of development and settle instead for a stationary state of society, as John Stuart Mill recommended more than a century ago? Our ears are now assaulted by words like "ecology," "ecosystem," and "ecocide," and we are entreated to attend to our environment while it is still inhabitable. Prophets of catastrophe among us speak forebodingly of an exponential depletion of resources and tell us that to grow is to die. They say that we are on the slippery path that leads to an ecological Armageddon, and they predict with the help of computers that the day of doom, when man finally outgrows his earthly home, will arrive early in the twenty-first century.

The population aspects of this problem are treated in a succeeding chapter. That it is a serious problem few citizens would be constrained to deny. Indeed, it was the subject of an international Conference on the Human Environment convened in Stockholm in 1972 and attended by representatives from 109 countries. Many of them recognized that development means industrialization, that industrialization requires the production of energy, that the production of energy depletes resources and pollutes the "ecosphere" (meaning the land, the water, and the air, all three), and that a higher standard of living for some presents the threat of disaster for all. The representatives of the less developed countries regarded some of this reasoning as a form of neocolonialism and wondered why they should delay the industrial growth that can raise their standard of living and help to abolish poverty, disease, and illiteracy. For them a smokestack is still a sign of progress and even a source of scenic satisfaction. In any event, it is a complicated problem and one that offers not a choice between good and evil but rather a choice between two evils—either poverty or pollution —and the additional danger of having not one or the other but both.

Many variables, of course, are included in this pessimistic picture. There are those on the other side, however, who dismiss these portents of disaster and regard their bearers as victims of a new kind of fanaticism. From their point of view social mechanisms have been discovered in the past to stave off calamity, and there is no reason to suppose that they will not be discovered in the future. Necessity, as we have tediously been told, is the mother of invention.[37] Already governments like those of the United States, the United Kingdom, and the Soviet Union have spent billions of dollars to reduce pollution and have committed more billions for similar expenditures in succeeding years. Reports of the death of Lake Erie, for example, have been exaggerated, fish are once more being caught in the Thames at London, and the Soviet Government plans to build a 3-mile-long dam at the northern end of the Black Sea to reduce the salinity of the water and restore important fisheries. Classical economic laws will continue to bring exploitation and conservation into a benign equilibrium. Finally, technological innovation will continue to solve social problems, even those of impressive magnitude. Currently, plans are afoot to tap geothermal energy; that is, to convert into electricity the heat from molten rock 2 to 6 miles beneath the surface of the earth. Experiments in this direction are under way in Mexico, New Zealand, Iceland, Japan, Italy, and the United States, and it is a potential source of energy that would be entirely free of pollution.

[37] As someone has observed, if computers had existed in 1874 they would have predicted an exponential growth of horsedrawn carriages and trucks, thus creating a problem of manure pollution in city streets that no one would be able to solve.

The controversy between the doomsday school and its critics would seem to confirm very little except the wisdom of Thomas Hobbes' observation that to every argument an equally good one can be opposed. We need not weigh all of the arguments in order to recognize that by tampering with his environment man creates hazards for his societies. We should indeed take seriously the view of the distinguished economist, Robert L. Heilbroner, that the indefinite viability of the planet is a premise to be questioned seriously.

In any event the process of civilization may be looked upon as a constant accumulation of instruments that insulate men and their societies from the forces of nature. The geographic factors exert their most direct and immediate effect upon the most primitive societies. It is primitive man who meets a pristine nature. As men develop a culture, they exert an ever greater control over nature. The storm stays the hunter, but the mailman, as the saying goes, makes his appointed rounds in spite of snow and rain and gloom of night.[38] The dangers that beset the man of the twentieth century and the anxieties that afflict him are seldom, and then only in small part, attributable to the inclemency of the elements. They are frequently, and in a larger measure, attributable to the inclemency of man himself. A snowstorm may disrupt a city and clog its channels of communication, but a strike of stevedores, subway employees, or elevator operators can have the same effect. An earthquake can level several cities at once, but so can nuclear missiles on their errands of war. Few readers of this book have ever been seriously threatened by a wild animal; all live under the shadow of a radioactive cloud.

What we are trying to say here is that if societies are never wholly independent of the operation of geographic factors, neither are these factors insusceptible to social and cultural influences. Compare the virgin forest and the field of hybrid corn, the island of Manhattan in 1474 and in 1974, the uninhabited seacoast and Miami Beach, and do not forget the Outer Drive of the city of Chicago built on land itself reclaimed from the lake. Nature is vast and man is puny, but this, of all comparisons, is the least significant. Every item of culture that man devises or invents is a new sentence in his declaration of independence from nature, and although his independence can never be complete, it is incommensurably greater than that enjoyed by any other animal. It enables him to assert his own dominion over the earth that sustains him and gives him life.

---

[38] The inscription over the main entrance of the post office in New York City, as adapted from Herodotus, reads as follows: "Not snow, nor rain, nor heat, nor gloom of night stays these couriers from the swift completion of their appointed rounds."

9. Conclusion

In this chapter we have indicated a number of ways in which geographic factors exert an influence upon human societies and have indicated also how this influence is sharply limited by the nature of these societies themselves and by the social and cultural factors that are the products of human ingenuity. What these social and cultural factors are we shall explain in detail as this book proceeds, for they constitute its central thesis. But we have now finished one of our preliminary tasks, an exhibition of the relationship between the earth and the societies it supports. Geographic interpretations of society have the dignity of age and may be found, as we have shown, even in classical antiquity. Each generation of social thinkers produces its quota of such interpretations, and it is reasonable to suppose that they will continue to appear in the future. For the *fact* of the dependence of society upon a favorable conjunction of geographic factors is not in question. The problems arise when we attempt to measure the degree of that dependence.

The geographic factors themselves we have classified into four major groups: (1) the motions of the earth, (2) the distribution of land and water masses, (3) climate, and (4) natural resources. All of them are important; none may be ignored. Together they make possible the existence of society. But none of them singly, nor all of them taken together, can explain the infinite variations in human societies. For this explanation the most precise, the most detailed, and the most comprehensive geographical knowledge does not suffice.

In the concluding sections of the chapter we described, albeit in inadequate detail, some of the theories that attribute the strategy and tactics of war and the rise and fall of civilizations to the operation of geographic factors. As products of the ingenuity of the human mind they are not devoid of interest and even of fascination, but we cannot yet accept them as contributions to sociological knowledge. We nevertheless recommend that readers who have more than a superficial interest in sociology—which means an interest in human societies everywhere—give these theories additional attention. The venture will repay the effort.

Our own conclusions, which we have stated throughout, may be summarized as follows. The influences that geographic factors exert upon human societies are neither decisive nor negligible; they are limiting but not determining; they are necessary but seldom sufficient to answer the questions that present themselves for sociological analysis. Geographic factors set limits to possible variations in human societies; within those limits they determine neither what variations do in fact occur nor when and where they appear. Geographic factors account for what can be and for what cannot be in human societies, but they do not account for what is. Geographic factors are relatively constant and, as far as we know, have been relatively constant during all the years of recorded history. Social events and social phenomena, on the other hand, are almost infinitely variable. And it is logically inadmissible to explain a variable by a constant. Geographic factors may, on certain occasions—for example in case of earthquake or hurricane—disrupt the orderly course of societies and of social intercourse, and in these cases they serve as sufficient causes and not merely as necessary ones. But these are extraordinary occurrences, and it is always more difficult to explain the ordinary than the extraordinary.

To ignore the role of geographic factors altogether, therefore, is to commit a sociological error. But to give them more significance than they warrant in each particular situation is to commit an error equally serious. Geographic factors are indeed important, and no one would contrast the societies of Arab and Eskimo without recourse to them. Geography is an enlightening science, as our first philosopher said, but, as our second philosopher said, it cannot explain why, to modernize the example, where the Indians once lived the Americans live now. It cannot in itself explain the rise of the American or of any other civilization. As human societies grow in complexity and as culture accumulates, geographic factors steadily decrease in sociological significance. Geography, in short, governs the possible, not the actual. History is not a simple function of habitat, nor culture of climate; neither mistral nor monsoon determines morality, nor soil society.

Chapter 3

THE BIOLOGICAL FACTOR

NOTED AMERICAN anthropologist is reputed to have remarked that "your carcass is the clue to your character." An equally noted American psychologist steadily maintained, in flat contradiction, that the human child is infinitely plastic and that from any infant he could produce on demand a doctor, lawyer, merchant, or chief—given, of course, the proper environment and training. Here indeed we have a difference of opinion. Just as we began our preceding chapter with contradictory quotations from two philosophers, so here we have an argument between an anthropologist and a psychologist about the role to be assigned to biological factors in the development of adult men and women. The importance of biological factors has seldom been denied, but on the other hand it has always been a problem to estimate their influence in the never-quite-finished product that is a human being. In our study of sociology a similar problem confronts us. As suggested in our introductory chapter, sociology is not concerned with individuals as such, either with their behavior or their character. Concerns like these belong to the sciences of psychology and social psychology. But as sociologists we do need to inquire into the biological attributes of social processes, to seek the biological foundations of social phenomena, and to discover if possible the biological ingredients in human and historical events. We have already learned that human societies are what they are, to some extent at least, because of the operation and influence of geographic factors over which men have little or no control. Are they also what they are because of a comparable operation and influence of biological factors? An initial answer to our question, as in the former case, must be in the affirmative. Again we shall anticipate our conclusion, however, by suggesting that the biological factors, like the geographic discussed before, are limiting rather than determining factors in the formation and persistence of human societies, that they are necessary but not sufficient for the explanation of what happens in these societies, and that they govern the possible but not the actual.

Now it is perfectly and even absurdly apparent that, if the human animal were twice as tall on the average, or only half as tall, as he happens to be, many of the familiar objects that surround us would be similarly changed in size. If some groupings of mankind just happened to be twice as strong, in a muscular sense, as other groupings, the effect, similarly, could be fairly serious and might possibly provide, for example, a biological foundation for such social phenomena as a slave system or a caste system. Again, if ants had the brains of men and men the instincts of ants, one might predict, although not of course in precise detail, that the juxtaposition of these two groups of living things would be radically altered.

If men and women lived ten years on the average rather than the Biblical three score years and ten, if they produced children in litters of a dozen or more instead of in a viable maximum of five, if they could permanently subsist either above the surface of the earth or below the surface of the water, or if, finally, they had to compete for survival with other and equally intelligent creatures of different physiognomy and bodily form—all of these "if's," however fantastic or lugubrious, would alter the character of the societies in which human beings live. If thumbs were not opposable, or vision binocular, or reproduction sexual, the societies we know would not exist. For that matter, the situation envisaged by the comic poet Samuel Hoffenstein—

Breathes there a man with hide so tough
Who says two sexes aren't enough?[1]

[1] From *Treasury of Humorous Verse* by Samuel Hoffenstein. Published by Liveright Publishers, New York City. Copyright R 1955 David Hoffenstein. Copyright 1947 Liveright Publishing Corporation.

would introduce some radical and possibly interesting changes into the nature and character of society. For all of these absurd reasons, if for no others, it is important at least to inquire into the role and operation of the biological factors.

By biological factors we mean those having to do in general with the genetic constitution of the human organism. They concern the things we have and do because we are members of a particular species, because we share the planet with other species, and because we live in a somewhat delicate ecological balance with these others. Like the geographic factors, the biological elements are relatively autonomous, relatively independent of our wishes and desires. We are informed on ancient authority that no one, by taking thought, can add one cubit to his stature. Man is ineluctably a species of animal life, a species somewhat presumptuously called "sapiens," and the nature of this "wise" species has something to do with the societies men construct.

A race of morons could not possibly produce a society in which the science of mathematics would become an admired achievement—although it must immediately be said that a most gifted people might also fail to produce such a science in the absence of factors of a different kind, to be discussed in another chapter of this book.

To be more specific, some of the questions we wish to explore in this chapter concern the respects in which societies do or do not resemble a biological organism; the role of race and of racial differences in society; the biological basis of race; race mixture; the relationships between brain size and intelligence, anatomy and character, and epidemiology and history, or pestilence and society. In short, in this chapter we seek to discover the role that biological factors of various kinds play in the social life of man. In the present state of our knowledge our conclusion, of course, will lack precision. We cannot say, for example, that the ingredients of a given social situation are 20 per cent geographic, 30 per cent biological, and 50 per cent something else. To ask for such a quantitative answer is meaningless. Nor can we expect a comprehensive answer. We can treat only a few biological factors, selected from a larger number. But if our discussion is neither precise nor comprehensive, we want it at least to be suggestive, to indicate the importance to society of the fact that its members also belong to a biological species.[2]

1. Organisms and Organismic Analogies

The view that society itself is an organism, conforming to the laws that govern other organisms, will doubtless seem curious to the contemporary

[2] The sexual question is treated separately, in Chapter 14.

reader. This idea, however, can be found throughout our Western history, and it received an especial impetus in 1859, with the publication of Darwin's *Origin of Species.* For a considerable period thereafter it was a popular position in sociology, and the early sociological vocabulary, heavily influenced by developments in biology, was consequently filled with such terms as "organism," "heredity," "selection," "variation," "accommodation," "adaptation," "instincts," "struggle for existence," and "the survival of the fittest." As late as the third decade of this century a famous textbook in sociology could use words like "parasitism," "symbiosis," and "commensalism"[3]—all biological concepts.

The notion that occupies us here is not that society is like an organism, but that society—or, in earlier times, the state[4]—actually is an organism. This notion can be found in some of the Greek philosophers, the thinkers of the Orient, the Schoolmen of the Middle Ages, and so on down to our own time. As suggested above, it became rampant in the latter half of the nineteenth century and the beginning of the twentieth.

In the work of some writers of this persuasion we find assertions that society has the same characteristics as a biological organism. including multiplication, growth, differentiation, illness, death, regeneration, integration of parts, cohesion, purposivity, spirituality, structural perfectibility, and energy transformation. We find the view that the cell is the basic unit, that tissue is a complex of cells, the organ a complex of tissues, the person a complex of organs, and society a complex of persons—the progression making society the highest form of organism, with organism itself defined as "a united mass of living substance which is capable of preserving itself under certain exterior conditions." We find, too, the notion that phenomena like armies, police, clothing, roofs, safes, and fortresses are "protective social tissue" corresponding to the epidermal tissue of animals. We find the view that society, like other organisms, has organs to serve it and that the state is masculine, the church feminine. And we find the conclusion that, "since society is composed of living creatures, it can be but a living creature." It was ridiculously easy for writers of this school to discover social counterparts for the nervous system, the respiratory system, the digestive system, the reproductive system, and other parts of the human anatomy.

Finally, we find in the works of the great Herbert Spencer himself a chapter entitled "A Society Is an Organism," with such additional chapters as "The Sustaining System," "The Distributing System," and "The Regulating System." It was Spencer who attempted to transform a biologi-

---

[3] This term we use ourselves, in Chapter 17.
[4] The Greeks, for example, made no distinction between community and society on the one hand and the state on the other.

cal theory—the theory of evolution—into a theory of society. For Spencer the origin of societies was the same as the origin of species; both societies and species were subject to the laws of evolution, a process that he made perfectly "clear" in the following definition: "Evolution is an integration of matter and concomitant dissipation of motion; during which the matter passes from an indefinite, incoherent homogeneity to a definite, coherent heterogeneity; and during which the retained motion undergoes a parallel transformation." The best comment on this "definition" was made by a contemporary of Spencer who "translated" it as follows: "Evolution is a change from a no-howish untalkaboutable all-alikeness to a somehowish and in general talkaboutable not-all-alikeness by continuous sticktogether-ations and somethingelseifications." This comment speaks for itself—we need add only that the "organicists" themselves sooner or later submitted to criticisms of their doctrines and abandoned them for more moderate analogies.[5]

The Darwinian conceptions of evolution, natural selection, and the survival of the fittest came in this period to be applied not only to the development of societies but also to art, literature, music, philosophy, science, religion, and almost every other achievement of the mind of man. "Evolution," in fact, became the key word in all intellectual inquiry, and Darwin and Spencer were the key names of an era in the history of thought. Today few sociologists actually read Spencer, but his ideas are receiving renewed attention as, for example, in the late work of Talcott Parsons.[6]

Whatever one may now say about Spencer and his sociological theory, there is no doubt that the biological theories of the social structure have met a deserved demise. No one today considers society a biological organism or derives any but a momentary profit in so regarding it. Biological *analogies*, on the other hand, will doubtless persist; for it is often convenient to say that in certain respects society or some part of it is *like* an organism or some part of it, that some social processes *resemble* some biological or physiologi-cal processes, and that some social functions can be compared with or are analogous to some organic functions. Thus, for example, it does no harm to refer to the network of communications in the United States as the nerve system of American society. It does no harm, that is, if we always realize

---

[5] It is only fair to say that Spencer also discussed the ways in which societies differ from organisms. The more extreme views are to be found in the works of Lilienfeld, Schäffle, and Worms.
[6] See Parsons' *Societies: Evolutionary and Comparative Perspectives*, Prentice-Hall, Inc., Englewood Cliffs, N. J., 1966, and *The System of Modern Societies*, Prentice-Hall, Inc., Englewood Cliffs, N. J., 1971.

that such a comparison is merely an analogy, a manner of speaking, a literary device with no intrinsic or empirical significance.

There is one special type of biological analogy, as we shall have occasion to observe later, that will almost certainly continue to appear. The temptation to refer to the rise and fall of nations and of empires in terms of the life cycle of organisms will probably never be wholly resisted by philosophers of history. But the reader of these theories, like the sophisticated student of sociology, will recognize that he is dealing with analogies, not identities, and that where similarities of this sort arise they are superficial and external. However well they serve to illustrate, they can seldom explain.

2. Race

So much has been written about racial differences, and so much suffered because of them, that one begins a discussion of the subject with trepidation. In the histories of all societies some of the darkest chapters tell of torture and terror because the people who lived in them were visibly different, in some respect or other, from people who lived somewhere else, in some other society. And some of the fiercest pride has been taken, too, in characteristics, genetic in origin, with which people themselves have had nothing to do, which are not human achievements in any sense of the word but only biological accidents. All peoples, in fact, have dreamed of a racial "purity" when there is no such purity anywhere in the world, except possibly in the most primitive and most isolated of societies. It has taken us many thousands of years to learn that there is only one species of mankind on earth—Homo sapiens—and that we all belong to it.

The notion that "blood will tell," however, that superior societies are built by superior races, is both old and erroneous. One finds it in ancient religious writing, in classical literature and philosophy, in the sacred books of the East, and indeed in the expressions of all peoples. It is a belief retained by many people today, even in our own "enlightened" country and century, and particularly by those who for one reason or another have been denied the benefits of education. It is not necessary here to trace the history of an idea so persistent. Suffice it to say that this belief was given perhaps its clearest intellectual expression in the nineteenth century, in the writings of Count Arthur de Gobineau and Houston Stewart Chamberlain. The work of these two men in particular, one a Frenchman and the other an Englishman, found its way into the political philosophy of Nazi Germany and gave to Adolf Hitler the catastrophic delusion that an "Aryan" was somehow superior to a Jew.

Early in the nineteenth century the notion took hold—in Germany—

that the Germans were a superior people.[7] Friedrich Schlegel, a leader of
the romantic movement in that country, was one of the first to suggest that
it was the Teutons who, by regenerating a decaying Roman society, saved
both Christianity and civilization. Around 1840 F. A. Pott announced that
the superlative gifts of the German clans would henceforth control the
destinies of the European nations. Pott endowed these clans "with one of
those 'irresistible impulses' which constitute the metaphysics of history and
social theory, this particular one pushing them ever westward in a path of
conquest toward the setting sun."[8] Schlegel and Pott, however, were only
two representatives of a point of view that was to become an anvil chorus as
the century ran its course.

Count Arthur de Gobineau published his *Essai sur l'inégalité des races
humaines* in four volumes during the years 1853 to 1855. In the dedication to
this erudite and influential book he writes as follows:

> Passing from one induction to another, I was gradually penetrated by the
> conviction that the racial question overshadows all other problems in history,
> that it holds the key to them all, and that the inequality of the races from
> whose fusion a people is formed is enough to explain the whole course of its
> destiny.

And further:

> I convinced myself at last that everything great, noble, and fruitful in the
> works of man on this earth, in science, art, and civilization, derives from a
> single starting point; it belongs to one family alone, the different branches of
> which have reigned in all the civilized countries of the universe.[9]

From premises and conclusions like these our author also finally "convinces
himself" that the races are in fact unequal, that there are superior and
inferior races. The first carry the torch of civilization; the second are
condemned to helplessness and historylessness. The latter are unfortunately in the majority; they have been unable to produce anything of cultural

---

[7] In thus indicting the Germans, the student is urged to remember that a similar indictment
applies to all peoples, the most primitive as well as the most civilized. Indeed, in many
primitive languages the word for members of one's own society is also the word for human
beings. It happens merely that historical consequences were more serious in the German case.
[8] Frank H. Hankins, *The Racial Basis of Civilization*, Alfred A. Knopf, Inc., New York, 1926, p.
16. Hankins continues: "The magic of this impulse so infected the imagination that so sound
an anthropologist as E. B. Tylor a generation later equipped this moving tide of humanity with
a special Aryan cart for the transport of wives and infants." Our discussion follows that of
Hankins, whose outstanding book carries as its subtitle "A Critique of the Nordic Doctrine."
[9] These two passages are quoted by Hankins, *ibid.*, p. 34.

significance in spite of thousands of years of existence, and their "organic sterility" is such that no environment, no matter how favorable, can fertilize it. De Gobineau agrees that "the progress or stagnation of a people does not depend upon geographic conditions," but he raises to the rank of supreme importance another factor, the racial, to which sociologists have to respond with a similar skepticism.

By superior race, of course, de Gobineau meant the so-called "Nordic," "Aryan," or "white." This, in the age of the gods, was the one absolutely pure race, a race that an infusion of foreign blood has constantly contaminated and that has consequently suffered degeneration. Although "the white race originally possessed the monopoly of beauty, intelligence and strength, by its union with other varieties hybrids were created, which were beautiful without strength, strong without intelligence, or, if intelligent, either weak or ugly." And further, "peoples degenerate only in consequence of the various admixtures of blood which they undergo," a degeneration which "corresponds exactly to the quantity and quality of the new blood."[10]

Race mixture was thus anathema to de Gobineau. Indeed, he felt that miscegenation had proceeded to such an alarming degree by the middle of the nineteenth century that no one could view the future with anything but apprehension. Human beings would grow progressively more alike, no race would be better than any other, and mediocrity would triumph. Finally, "human herds, no longer nations, weighted down by a mournful somnolence, will henceforth be benumbed in their nullity, like buffaloes ruminating in the stagnant meres of the Pontine marshes."[11]

The theories of Houston Stewart Chamberlain are similar to those of de Gobineau in every respect except that they make less pretense at being scientific. Chamberlain's book, which appeared some forty-odd years after de Gobineau's (1899 to be exact), was translated into English with the title *Foundations of the Nineteenth Century*. The author himself was born in England, of aristocratic parents, but he carried on a lifelong love affair with Germany, where he became a friend and follower of Richard Wagner, the great composer, and married Wagner's daughter. The admiration was mutual. Chamberlain's writings made the best-seller lists in Germany and Kaiser Wilhelm encouraged their distribution by financial appropriations.

Indeed, as Hankins suggests, it was the work of Chamberlain that helped to create in the German people an illusion of a special mission on earth, a mission touched by divinity, which gave them not only the right

[10] *Ibid.*, pp. 35–36.
[11] Quoted by Pitirim A. Sorokin, *Contemporary Sociological Theories*, Harper & Row, Publishers, New York, 1928, p. 229.

but also the duty to march against inferior peoples. In his book it is the Teuton who creates civilization. Civilization in fact is synonymous with Teuton society. The superman is not merely an idealized hero invented by the philosopher Nietzsche.[12] He exists. He is the man with Teuton blood.

De Gobineau and Chamberlain are representatives of a point of view that, as we have noted, has an ancient and dishonorable history. The notion that civilization is synonymous with blood, or in any way a function of biology, is one that no evidence has been found to support. When one considers the number of people who have devoted their lives to seeking such evidence, he must be impressed by the fact that they have consistently been unsuccessful, that none of the evidence they have produced has remained immune from refutation or has failed, in fact, to collapse at the slightest touch of scientific criticism.

Count Arthur de Gobineau is one of the more respectable advocates of a theory that, in the hands of others, has often been merely an excuse for arrogance. These others it is unnecessary either to recount or to contemplate. There is not the slightest reason to suppose that racial factors as such have anything to do with the rise and fall of nations or that, in the absence of other differences, there will be substantial dissimilarities in the structures of the societies created and maintained by different racial groupings of mankind.

3. The Biological Basis of Race

If we can accord no credence whatever to the views of the racial writers as just expressed, we have to exercise some caution in the opposite direction lest we deny that racial differences do exist, that the members of the human race can be classified into various subgroups in terms of known and sometimes visible physical differences. Many sociologists appalled by the political uses to which these differences have been put, have denied that races exist or that discernible differences have a biological basis. They have been tempted to tell us on the contrary that the notion of race is a myth or a superstition. This error may be on the side of the angels, but it is an error nevertheless. Race may be an unfortunate concept, but it is hardly a mythical one. Let us inquire into this matter a little further.

There is a complex organic compound called phenylthiocarbamide— PTC for short. Improbable as it may seem, some people in the world can taste this substance and some cannot. It has been discovered that the ability to taste it is inherited, that tasting ability is attributable to a dominant gene,

[12] Nietzsche, a contemporary of Chamberlain and, like him, a friend of Wagner, did sing the praises of the superman. But he was also an opponent of anti-Semitism and so little German in feeling that he perversely tried to trace his own ancestry to Poland.

nontasting to a recessive gene, and that about 70 per cent of Europeans and Americans are "tasters" and the remaining 30 per cent "nontasters." Even within the former group, however, there is much variability; that is, some of the 70 per cent say that the stuff tastes only mildly bitter, others swear that it is quite bitter, and still others react so strongly that they become nauseated.

It has also been discovered that the percentages of tasters and nontasters differ in various parts of the world, that the incidence of tasting, for example, is relatively high among American Indians and Chinese and relatively low among the Eskimos. As just mentioned, these are genetic differences; they have to do with the genes, with biological inheritance. Nevertheless, we do not classify all human beings into two races on the basis of this biological difference—tasters and nontasters. Why don't we?

Several decades ago it was discovered that sometimes there is a blood incompatibility between mothers and their own babies and that this is due to the presence or absence of an "Rh" factor, so called because knowledge about it was gained first through experiments with Rhesus monkeys. This Rh substance is also produced through the operation of a dominant gene and is present in the blood of 85 per cent of white persons and absent in the blood of the remaining 15 per cent. When an Rh-negative mother carries an Rh-positive baby (in which the father's gene, being dominant, prevails), a serious type of anemia or jaundice, called *erythroblastosis foetalis*, can develop and this, in turn, can be fatal to the baby.[13]

As in the case of tasting, percentage figures on the presence of the Rh factor differ in various parts of the world. If the ratio is 85 per cent positive to 15 per cent negative among white persons, it is 92 per cent positive to 8 per cent negative among American Negroes, and almost 100 per cent positive among Chinese, Japanese, and American Indians. Again let us note the fact that this is a genetic or hereditary characteristic; it is a result of the genes that people carry. Nevertheless we do not classify all human beings into two races on the basis of this biological difference—Rh positives and Rh negatives. Why don't we?

The readers of this book already know that there are four different blood types, A, B, AB, and O, which are important to distinguish for the purpose of transfusions. These differences in blood groups are also genetic, the genes for types A and B, which are of almost equal strength, being dominant over the genes for type O. It is also known that there is a different incidence of these types in various parts of the world. A high percentage of American Indians, for example, have blood type O, but the Blackfoot and Blood tribes in Montana constitute an important exception in that they

---

[13] Blood transfusions at birth have now reduced the mortality rate almost to zero.

predominate in type A. Asiatic peoples have a high proportion of group B, but this group is also characteristic of Abyssinians and of the Pygmies in the Congo. Peoples living in widely separated parts of the world—Eskimos, Portuguese, and Australian aborigines—resemble one another quite closely in blood-type distribution. Once again, these blood types are a genetic or hereditary factor; they result from the genes that people carry. Nevertheless we do not classify all human beings into four different races, called A, B, AB, and O, based upon this biological index. Why don't we?

Everybody knows, finally, that some people have dark skins and some have light skins. Except for the influence of ultraviolet rays upon those addicted to sun bathing (or "sun baking," as the Australians call it), skin color too is a genetic trait and one that a given individual is unable to change or modify in any permanent way. Skin color is determined by various pigments, all of which are present in all human beings. The differences are due to different combinations of these pigments and these differences are hereditary. Some descendants of African tribes have relatively light skins, some East Indians have fairly dark skins, and Americans exhibit skin coloration ranging from the very light to the very dark. Nevertheless, we classify human beings into at least two different races, black and white, on the basis of differences in skin color. Why do we?

People can obviously be classified into various groups in terms of the four variables we have now mentioned—the ability to taste phenylthio-carbamide, the presence or absence of the Rh factor in the blood, the blood type in general, and skin color. There are many other genetic variables that might also have been cited, but these four should be sufficient for our purposes here. The point we wish to make is that each of the four variables described is independent of the other three. People who are quite similar with respect to one of them may be quite different with respect to the others. The classification of people into groups on the basis of these genetic factors, therefore is quite arbitrary. The differences exist, to be sure, and they are genetic, but on biological grounds it is clearly arbitrary to select one rather than another as a basis for classification. One has to admit, of course, that skin color is visible and a known variable whereas the other three are scientific discoveries. But even if we arbitrarily select criteria for classification and arrange the population of the earth into groups in terms of them, it is often difficult, if not impossible, to place particular individuals into these groups. It is even more difficult to maintain that there is a racial type or average member of such a group. As a distinguished biologist, Paul Amos Moody, has written:

No *individual* ever is "average"; each individual differs from every other in some respects ("identical" twins most closely approach an exception to this statement). We find the same situation when we attempt to classify *individuals* as belonging to one race or another. John Doe, for example, has dark brown skin and kinky hair; he belongs to blood group A, is Rh-positive, round-headed, and a "taster." Richard Roe has dark brown skin and wavy hair; he belongs to blood group B, is Rh-negative, long-headed, and a "non-taster." Despite all the differences between them people generally would classify them both as Negroes on the basis of their one point of similarity: dark brown skin. A third individual, George Goe, has little skin pigment, has wavy hair, belongs to blood group B, is Rh-negative, long-headed, and a "non-taster." Despite the many similarities between George and Richard people generally would probably not classify them as belonging to the same race, their decision being based on the single point that George has little skin pigment while Richard has much.[14]

Professor Moody continues:

> Of course our imaginary example is oversimplified; many more characteristics than these are involved in classifying people. But the other characteristics are of the same kind as those mentioned, and when we classify *individuals* as belonging to this race or that we are being just as arbitrary in placing emphasis upon some characteristics and ignoring others as we were in classifying our three hypothetical individuals above.[15]

Why, as Professor Moody asks, does our greatest lack of perspective concern skin color? For this there can be no sound—or even unsound—biological reason. In terms of the perpetuation of the species, for example, one can construct a most cogent argument for developing "race" prejudices against those whose blood has a different Rh factor from our own, and this is an argument that would have a genetic foundation. We might similarly develop a biological argument for prejudice against those with different blood types because their incompatibility would interfere with the facility of transfusions at a time, let us say, of atomic disaster. The reason we choose skin color rather than blood type as a basis for classification and consequent prejudice is apparently that differences in skin color are visible and differences in blood type are not. The reason is thus seen to be sociological in character and not only biological.[16] The same conclusion would apply to any other characteristic or trait, visible or invisible, that we might happen to choose.

[14] Paul Amos Moody, *Introduction to Evolution*, Harper & Row, Publishers, New York, 1953, p. 232.
[15] *Ibid.*
[16] It is also geographical, of course, in that people with certain visible physical characteristics trace their origin, by and large, to different parts of the world.

There is another kind of argument often presented by those who seek biological evidence for the alleged superiority of whites over blacks. It is contended that in the evolutionary design of nature whites have evolved farther than blacks from their common simian ancestry, that whites are thus biologically "ahead" in the line of biological development and that blacks have lagged behind.

To support this view its protagonists point to three differences in particular. They say that blacks on the average have darker skin, longer arms in relation to total bodily height, and a greater degree of prognathism (that is, a more obtrusive or protruding jaw). All three of these assertions, incidentally, happen to be true. The inference then is readily drawn that in all three respects blacks are "closer" to the order of primates than whites are and the desired conclusion is triumphantly proclaimed. It is an argument, however, that also works in reverse. It happens to be true, too, that whites on the average have relatively thin lips, that they have straight rather than curly hair, and that they have much more bodily hair than blacks. In these three characteristics it is clear that whites are "closer" to the order of primates than blacks.

As a matter of fact, it is interesting to note—and the foregoing example is an excellent illustration—that the most remarkable ingenuity has been expended in efforts to prove that one group of mankind is somehow superior to another. As previously mentioned, however, none of these efforts, ingenious and strenuous as they have been, has produced any findings able to survive contradiction. Of all the arguments that have been advanced by all kinds of investigators, "scientific" and otherwise, not one remains as acceptable evidence for such superiority.

One argument, which even convinced a number of men of science for a while, may merit an additional word, although both the circumstances and the conclusions now seem archaic. When psychologists and other scientists began to study the results of the Army Alpha intelligence tests administered to inductees in World War I, the facts seemed steadily to point in the same direction. There could be no doubt whatever that white soldiers on the average scored higher than black soldiers. Was this the final, long-sought scientific proof that whites are more intelligent than blacks? Many were inclined to answer in the affirmative, and this answer found its way into some of the textbooks of the time.

More extended study, however, disclosed other interesting results. Urban dwellers on the average scored higher than rural dwellers, and Northerners on the average scored higher than Southerners. Where is the racial factor here? When the figures were taken in different combinations, still other facts emerged. It was discovered, for example, that Northern urban blacks scored higher on the average than Southern rural whites.

Thus the factor of race was overwhelmed by the factors of education and opportunity, and one more bit of "evidence" for racial superiority followed its predecessors into the discard.

The issue was opened to renewed debate, however, in 1969 as the result of a long article published by Arthur R. Jensen of the University of California at Berkeley.[17] Jensen maintained that the role of cultural factors in intelligence had consistently been overemphasized and, by contrast, the role of biological factors underemphasized; that genetic factors, when separated out by versatile statistical procedures, account for a large part of the difference in intelligence quotients in different populations; that the important environmental influences are prenatal ones; and that, although extreme environmental deprivation may prevent the child's realization of his potential, the most favorable environmental circumstances cannot raise a child's intelligence above its genetic limits. These, in Jensen's view, are the reasons both for the failure of "compensatory education" in the United States as applied to minority and economically disadvantaged groups and also for the persistence of such racial differences in intelligence as have been discerned.

Jensen's critics contend, on the contrary, that he has drawn illogical conclusions from inadequate evidence, that his statistical procedures are faulty, that his claim for the high heritability of intelligence remains wholly unsubstantiated, and that his point of view, taken in its entirety, is a "counsel of despair." We need not respond to the technicalities of the controversy to conclude that, although there are doubtless genetic factors in whatever we choose to mean by intelligence (as there are, for example, in the determination of height), they are conditioned and sometimes severely affected by environmental influences. The social inequities between black and white in the United States are so great that, as the president of the National Academy of Sciences has said, it is impossible to do reasonable research on the question of racial differences in intelligence and, if such differences are found, on the further question whether they are attributable to genetic or environmental factors.

4. Mankind—One Species

Red squirrels and gray squirrels in the forests of this country do not interbreed with each other. They thus constitute two different species of the same genus. Since an interchange of genes does not occur between them, they are said by biologists to be in a situation of reproductive isolation, a situation in which species do not interbreed even when they have the

---

[17] *Harvard Educational Review*, vol. 39, no. 1, winter, 1969, pp. 1–123.

(geographic) opportunity to do so. Reproductive isolation can result from a number of factors. In the first place, copulation between males and females may be impossible because of gross lack of fit between the genital organs. This is frequently the case in the animal and insect kingdoms and is sometimes called mechanical isolation. In the second place, interbreeding may be impossible because the breeding seasons of two species may not coincide. This is frequently true with respect to different kinds of insects and flowers.

In other cases copulation is possible and does occur between members of different species but does not—for one or more of several reasons—result in an effective exchange of genes. Such reasons include (1) failure of the sperm to fertilize the ovum; (2) inviability of the resulting hybrids, that is, inability to live; or (3) sterility of the resulting hybrids even in the instances when they reach sexual maturity (mules are perhaps the best-known example in this category).

The point about reproductive isolation is that it occurs only in subhuman orders of species. It is unknown to mankind. Every kind of normal man on earth can mate fruitfully with every kind of normal woman, producing offspring who are viable and who, at sexual maturity, will have a similar facility. Various peoples, of course, are geographically isolated from others, and this separation, over long periods of time, has resulted in the differences that we can today observe between South African Bushmen, let us say, and Polar Eskimos, between the American Indians of the Southwest and the Arabs of North Africa. Such differences come about through natural selection and through the perpetuation of certain mutations that appear to be favorable, or at least not unfavorable, in certain geographic regions. But there is not, and so far as we know has never been, reproductive isolation among humankind. The organs fit, and sex knows no season.[18] In other words, all men now on earth belong to one and the same species.

The races of mankind are thus seen to be subspecies rather than species, the distinguishing characteristics of the former being (1) absence of reproductive isolation and (2) a smaller degree of genetic differentiation. "The differences between races," as Moody says in his discussion of the subject, "are more likely to take the form of variations in *frequencies* of occurrence of certain genes than they are to manifest themselves in the form of possession of certain genes by one race, with absence of those genes in another."[19] His conclusion on the matter merits attention:

---

[18] One is reminded of La Rochefoucauld, who said, "Man is the only animal that drinks when he is not thirsty, eats when he is not hungry, and makes love at all seasons." To which it must unhappily be added, "and kills when he is not angry."

[19] Moody, *op. cit.*, p. 229.

Modern races are descendants of ancient races, but probably no one modern race is the descendant of any one ancient race alone. Our inability to draw any clear-cut lines between races gives added confidence that such is the case. The genes have been continually "reshuffled" as time, in geologic copiousness, has gone by.[20]

If races, as subspecies, do exist, what are they? Most authorities now classify them into four groups that exhibit geographical and minor genetic differences. These are Mongolians, Caucasians, Negroes, and Australoids. These were never "pure" races, however, and in any event their differences are probably doomed to ultimate extinction. The world has become so small that race intermixture is increasing rather than decreasing, pockets of relative geographic isolation are disappearing, and it is doubtful if genetic mutations, if and when they occur, can be limited to any one of these groupings.

The current inhabitants of the United States of America, including presumably the majority of the readers of this book, are the most hopelessly mixed up of all peoples. Unless they are direct descendants of American Indians, a small statistical chance, their ancestors came in recent times from every continent. Most, of course, came from Europe, and Europe was previously the most mixed-up place on the globe. The Irish, for example, are a mixture of Picts, Scandinavians, Asturians, Spaniards, Celts, Campignians, Angles, Normans, and Norsemen. The English are a mixture of Celts, Danes, Romans, Normans, Belgae, Beaker Folk, Angles, Saxons, and Jutes; the Germans of Celts, Vikings, Romans, Franks, Slavs, Huns, and Saxons; and the Italians of Etruscans, Sabines, Latins, Goths, Gauls, Normans, Phoenicians, Greeks, Germans, Swabians, Franks, and Saxons.[21] The origins of most national groups are similarly diverse. After coming to the United States, moreover, families often became even more mixed up, so that many present-day Americans, the end products of these events, are mixtures of mixtures. But now, in any event, all can claim the same nationality. It must be remembered, however, that there is no American race. There is only one human species to which all men, for better or worse, belong. This is a biological fact, but not yet, unfortunately, a social fact.

We may summarize these observations on race as follows. Biological differences do exist between peoples, and these differences enable us to classify them into several distinctive groupings. The classifications themselves will differ, however, depending upon the criterion that is chosen. If

[20] *Ibid.,* p. 234.
[21] Amram Scheinfeld, *The New You and Heredity,* J. B. Lippincott Company, Philadelphia, 1950, pp. 496–497.

we happen to choose skin color we get one set of groups; head shape gives us another, stature still another, and so on. Peoples who have inhabited the same general regions of the earth over long periods of time and who have been geographically isolated from other peoples show differences of skin color attributable to the operation of such factors as light and heat. But there is no reproductive isolation among human beings.

We may call these different groups races if we wish—we have to call them something, and to deny the differences is to commit an error at least as serious as to exaggerate them—but differences of this biological kind have nothing to do in any sense with the superiority or inferiority of one group with respect to another. Skin color has no more to do with historical achievement than has stature, and stature has no more influence in this regard than does the curious ability of some and not others to taste phenylthiocarbamide. Homo sapiens is one genus and one species.[22]

It would be pleasant if we could conclude our discussion of race with these biological observations. Unfortunately, as W. I. Thomas once said, "If people define situations as real they are real in their consequences." If people believe that one race is superior to another, their belief has consequences. The consequences are social, however, rather than biological, and we shall explore them in a later chapter of this book. The *fact* that there are minor biological differences between the races of mankind has nothing to do with the societies these races construct. The *belief* that these differences are important, however, can have a great deal to do with the character of their societies. It is this second question that will later detain our attention.

5. Brain Size and Intelligence

One biological factor would seem to have a great deal to do with human actions and events and would normally elicit, therefore, the sociologist's attention. We refer to brain size or cranial capacity. Evolutionary increase in brain size, at a constant or inconstant rate, might be expected to explain, at least in part, the evolution of human societies. As Charles Darwin put it in *The Descent of Man* (1871), "No one, I presume, doubts that the large proportion which the size of man's brain bears to his body, compared to the same proportion in the gorilla or orang, is closely connected with his higher mental powers."[23] "On the other hand," as Darwin also warned, "no one

[22] For an enlightening treatment of the entire subject of race by a physical anthropologist, see William Howells, *Mankind in the Making*, Martin Secker & Warburg, Ltd., London, 1960, chaps. 18–22.
[23] Modern Library Edition, New York, p. 436.

supposes that the intellect of any two animals or of any two men can be accurately gauged by the cubic contents of their skulls."[24]

The construction of cranial indices, in fact, is an exercise that has its quirks. If cranial capacity is a criterion of intelligence then La Chapelle Man, with 1620 cc, should have been somewhat superior to Gottfried Wilhelm Leibnitz, one of the great philosophers and mathematicians of modern times, whose capacity was only 1422 cc. If brain weight is a criterion then whales and elephants would have a decided advantage over men. When we put the picture into another perspective, however, we discover that it is not brain weight by itself, but the proportion of brain weight to total bodily weight that should be taken into account. On this reckoning the proportion for the whale is 1 to 8,500 whereas that of man is 1 to 50.[25] The absolute size would therefore seem to have a great deal less importance than the proportionate size. But the quirks remain. In contemporary slang we characterize our stupid friends as "bird brains," and yet the proportion of brain weight to body weight in birds—1 to 35—is higher than in men. In the capuchin monkey the proportion is 1 to 17.5 and in the newborn human infant it is 1 to 6. For that matter, the brains of adult males are significantly larger than the brains of adult females, but female brains on the other hand are somewhat larger in proportion to total bodily weight. Brain size in short, both absolute and relative, seems to have some relationship with intelligence, but its precise nature has so far defied exact scientific statement.

In any event, the fossil evidence seems to indicate that there has been no substantial change in the size of the human brain in the last 200,000 years. The Neanderthal man had a brain almost as large as ours.[x] He would be an asset to a contemporary football team and, like other athletic assets, he could probably get through college without too much difficulty. The problem seems to be not how to grow bigger brains but how to make better use of the ones we have. As a matter of fact, except for minor details (most of them dental), there is little evidence that any part of the human body is now involved in an evolutionary process. It is true that American college students of the present generation are taller and heavier than their parents, and that coeds have bigger feet,[26] but it is doubtful whether these changes represent a genuine evolutionary development in the biological sense. Most students of the subject prefer to attribute them to improved nutrition, living conditions, and medical care and to the consequent diminution in the

x) larger!

[24] *Ibid.*
[25] Authorities give different figures ranging from 1:44 to 1:50.
[26] Freshmen at Vassar and Smith, for example, are two inches taller and ten pounds heavier than they were in 1900.

incidence of childhood diseases.[27] It is possible, in fact indeed even probable, that not evolution but rather the reverse has set to work on our human species. Consider, for example, the following observations of Julian Huxley:

> In the human phase, the biological mechanisms of evolution—physical heredity and natural selection—are now subsidiary to the psycho-social ones. Though undoubtedly man's genetic nature changed a great deal during the long protohuman stage, there is no evidence that it has been in any important way improved since the time of the Aurignacian cave men. What has been improved since then are the tools of action and thought and the ways of accumulating and utilizing experience: and these improvements have had truly prodigious results in a very brief period of time. Indeed, during this period it is probable that man's genetic nature has degenerated and is still doing so. In general, the more elaborate social life is, the more it tends to shield individuals from the action of natural selection; and when this occurs, as we have already seen, harmful mutations accumulate instead of being weeded out. As a result of this process, there can be no reasonable doubt that the human species today is burdened with many more deleterious mutant genes than can possibly exist in any species of wild creature.[28]

We have indulged in these few remarks on biological evolution because we want to emphasize the absence of correlation between the changes that have taken place on the biological level and those that occur on the historical level. It is logically impossible, as we have noted before, to explain a variable by a constant. Social phenomena can seldom be explained by reference back to biological foundations. The biological differences between people can seldom, if ever, explain their social differences. Biological factors supply the necessary conditions for human social life but, like the geographic factors, they fail to explain its manifold variations or subtle complications. For this explanation we need recourse to other factors.

6. Physical Type and Social Career

If neither race nor brain size has anything directly to do with social phenomena—that is, if these biological causes do not directly produce social

---

[27] Dr. Harry L. Shapiro, Curator of Physical Anthropology at the American Museum of Natural History, is an exception. He points out that people are growing taller in other parts of the world too, in places like Japan and Hawaii and Western Europe, and that increased stature has appeared as well in such "backward" parts of the United States as the Ozark mountain hills and the "Tobacco Road" country of the South.

[28] Julian Huxley, *Evolution in Action*, Harper & Row, Publishers, New York, 1953, pp. 172–173.

results—can we find some other physical characteristic that does? We have to concede, of course, that a certain collocation of biological factors is required for the appearance of a particular social effect. For example, it is unlikely that a tone-deaf person will ever become a virtuoso on the violin, that a very frail person will establish a world's record in the shot-put, or that a very stupid one will make world-shattering contributions to mathematical physics. There is no certainty, on the other hand, that talent will express itself in the absence of social opportunities to do so. And it is clear that persons with absolute pitch, huge muscles, and high intelligence do not automatically become violinists, shot-putters, and mathematicians if they happen to be born in societies in which there are no such activities as violin playing, shot-putting, and mathematical inference. Again we are encouraged to conclude, in accordance with our useful formula, that biological factors supply the necessary but not the sufficient conditions for the appearance of social phenomena of this sort. Biological factors, like the geographic, govern the possible, not the actual, in human societies.

The quest for biological correlates of social phenomena, however, has never ceased. Psychologists, for example, are always interested in possible relationships between physical type and temperament. In classical antiquity it was believed that the body was filled with, or composed of, four liquids or "humours"—blood, phlegm, black bile, and yellow bile—and that temperament depended upon an excess of one or another of them. An excess of blood, for example, made a sanguine person (cheerful, hopeful, warm, ardent, confident), an excess of phlegm a phlegmatic one (lethargic, dull, sluggish, apathetic), an excess of black bile a melancholic one (depressed, sad, pensive), and an excess of yellow bile a choleric one (angry, irascible, irritable). This theory prevailed from the time of Hippocrates (460?–377? b.c.) to the time of Shakespeare and beyond.[29] Remember Shakespeare's Caesar attaching suspicion to those who are too lean?

> Let me have men about me that are fat,
> Sleek-headed men and such as sleep o'nights.
> Yond Cassius has a lean and hungry look,
> He thinks too much; such men are dangerous.[30]

Efforts to find linkages between physical characteristics and personality, however, have almost completely collapsed. The relationship is at best a

---

[29] The theory of Hippocrates, incidentally, is related to the metaphysical views of the earlier Pythagorean philosophers, who held that all things were compounded of four primary and fundamental qualities—the hot, the cold, the wet, and the dry—and that these themselves, in combination, characterized the four elements—earth, air, fire, and water.

[30] *Julius Caesar*, I, ii.

tenuous one. Physique and temperament may be related, but so far no one has been able to exhibit a sufficient number of relevant facts or an acceptable theory. The notion that a jutting jaw or a low forehead predisposes a man to crime wins no more credence than that red hair predisposes a girl to outbursts of temper. Are fat men addicted to jollity, pale men to poetry, long-fingered men to surgery, and weak-eyed men to reading books? In legend and in literature the answer, perhaps, is in the affirmative. In sociology the negative view prevails.

7. Animals, Insects, and Microbes

A fascinating tale can be spun about the influence of animals, insects, and microbes upon human beings and their societies. The planet, after all, does not belong solely to us, the species that studies it and writes about it. It belongs also to herrings and hyenas, to lice and lions, to cows and corn borers, to giraffes and gypsy moths. We are only one species among many and we exist in a kind of delicate ecological balance with these others. We prey upon some of them and they, of course, return the compliment. Nature exhibits an endless cycle of eating and being eaten, and from this process our own kind is not exempt. As a great bacteriologist has somewhat unpleasantly put it:

> There is probably as little conscious cruelty in the lion that devours a missionary as there is in the kind-hearted old gentleman who dines upon a chicken pie, or in the staphylococcus that is raising a boil on the old gentleman's neck. Broadly speaking, the lion is parasitic on the missionary, as the old gentleman is on the chicken pie, and the staphylococcus on the old gentleman.[31]

The delicate juxtaposition of ecological factors can be further illustrated by another example—the relationship that Darwin and Huxley discerned between the number of old maids in a region's population and the abundance of its clover crop. Old maids, it seems, have a propensity to keep cats. As the cats increase, the field mice decrease, because more of them are eaten by more cats. If the number of field mice decreases, the number of bumblebees increases, because the mice feed on bumblebee larvae. As bumblebees increase, so also does the clover, because the clover flower is pollinated primarily by bumblebees. In short, as the number of old maids increases, so also does the yield of clover.

But this is only half the story. An increase in the clover yield contributes to the prosperity of farmers, induces them to marry, and thus

[31] Hans Zinsser, *Rats, Lice and History*, Little, Brown, and Company, Boston, 1935, p. 8.

reduces the number of old maids. This reduces the cats, increases the mice, reduces the bumblebees, and reduces the clover crop. In short, an increase in the clover crop ultimately causes its decrease. And similarly, an increase in the number of old maids ultimately brings about their decrease, which again results in increase, and so on in a cycle revolving forever.[32]

Stories like these illustrate the important point that there is an ecological balance between man and the animal and insect kingdoms, and that any alteration in one will in some way or other affect the other. There is also, as we shall see in the following chapter, an ecological relationship between the human species and its food supply.[33]

Dr. Hans Zinsser, the bacteriologist quoted above, has written a fascinating history of typhus fever, in which he indulges in the following remarks:

> Our chief purpose in writing the biography of one of these diseases is to impress the fact that we are dealing with a phase of man's history on earth which has received too little attention from poets, artists, and historians. Swords and lances, arrows, machine guns, and even high explosives have had far less power over the fates of the nations than the typhus louse, the plague flea, and the yellow-fever mosquito. Civilizations have retreated from the plasmodium of malaria, and armies have crumbled into rabbles under the onslaught of cholera spirilla, or of dysentery and typhoid bacilli. Huge areas have been devastated by the trypanosome that travels on the wings of the tsetse fly, and generations have been harassed by the syphilis of a courtier. War and conquest and that herd existence which is an accompaniment of what we call civilization have merely set the stage for these more powerful agents of human tragedy.[34]

[32] The situation is not always so amusing. Consider the following quotation: "Because of a lack of understanding of ecological principles the efforts of well-intentioned conservationists and agriculturalists are frequently badly misdirected. A story is told of certain sheep ranchers who became convinced that coyotes were robbing them of their young sheep. As a result the community rose up and by every possible means slaughtered all the coyotes that could be located for miles around. Following the destruction of the coyotes, the rabbits, field mice, and other small rodents of the region increased tremendously and made serious inroads upon the grass of the pastures. When this development was realized, the sheep men executed an about-face, abruptly stopped killing the coyotes, and instituted an elaborate program for the poisoning of the rodents. The coyotes filtered in from surrounding areas and multiplied, and finding their natural rodent food now scarce they were forced to turn to the young sheep as their only available source of food." George L. Clarke, *Elements of Ecology*, John Wiley & Sons, Inc., New York, 1954, p. 19. See also Lorus J. Milne and Margery Milne, *The Balance of Nature*, Alfred A. Knopf, Inc., New York, 1960.
[33] These relationships in general enabled Charles Darwin to consummate one of the sublime feats of the human mind. His study of the giant orchid of Madagascar convinced him that there must also exist an insect, hitherto unknown and unobserved, to pollinate it. This insect would have to have in particular a proboscis fitted to the dimensions of the orchid. Shortly afterwards such an insect was discovered—the huge hawk moth of Madagascar.
[34] Zinsser, *op. cit.*, p. 9–10.

And again:

> Soldiers have rarely won wars. They more often mop up after the barrage of
> epidemics. And typhus, with its brothers and sisters,—plague, cholera,
> typhoid, dysentery,—has decided more campaigns than Caesar, Hannibal,
> Napoleon, and all the inspector generals of history. The epidemics get the
> blame for defeat, the generals the credit for victory. It ought to be the other
> way round.[35]

The title of Dr. Zinsser's book, *Rats, Lice and History*, clearly indicates his
belief that rats and lice have a great deal to do with history and, accordingly,
with society. Certainly the story of human epidemics, from the earliest
times to the present, would shed some light upon human events. A study of
the bubonic plague alone, the Black Death that ravaged Europe toward the
end of the fourteenth century and killed, according to some estimates, as
many as twenty million Europeans, would suggest that bacteriological
phenomena may not be ignored as an influence in society. Further evidence
in support of this position is the fact that the Ona Indians of South America
were decimated by the measles in 1925.[36] And an examination of the
history of syphilis would doubtless supply additional confirmation and
contribute much to sociological inquiry.[37]

The distribution of various species of animals and fish can also exert
an influence in society, particularly upon the occupations of men and the
economies of nations. Let us consider an example offered by a writer named
Richard Lewinsohn. He explains that the fish trade in the late medieval
period was operated on an international basis by the Hanseatic League, an
organization of North European cities, numbering at times more than
seventy, that promulgated and protected the reciprocal relations of individual traders. The main catch was herring, which the League supplied to
Europe. Lewinsohn maintains that "the rise of Amsterdam was made
possible by the herring industry," and goes on to write:

> Meanwhile the Hanseatic League had been enjoying a virtual monopoly in the
> Baltic Sea. In about 1500, however, the herring stayed away, disappeared
> completely. To this day no one knows whether it was marine currents, the
> depredations of larger fish, or a plague that brought about this catastrophe. In

---

[35] *Ibid.*, p. 153.
[36] Carleton S. Coon, *The Story of Man*, Alfred A. Knopf, Inc., New York, 1954, p. 183.
[37] Zinsser makes the doubtless immoral suggestion that a complete victory over syphilis might
be damaging to the further course of civilization: "It has often been claimed that since so many
brilliant men have had syphilis, much of the world's greatest achievement was evidently
formulated in brains stimulated by the cerebral irritation of an early general paresis." *Op. cit.*,
p. 62n.

any event it was a terrible blow to the Hanse. Many historians believe that this biological event, rather than later political conflicts, started the downfall of that great commercial organization.[38]

Only historians who have given detailed and diligent study to this period of history can decide the question, of course, and they exhibit no unanimity. Nevertheless, the possibility that herring had something to do with one of the earliest and most successful efforts at international economic cooperation, and its subsequent decline, is not altogether to be discounted. On the other hand, it is equally fair to remark that herring was in especially great demand in the late medieval period in Western and Northern Europe as a Lenten staple and that, if some religion other than Catholicism—one, for example, without any dietary provisions—had been prevalent at the time, the League might have had a totally different history. Medieval Catholicism, of course, is not a biological factor. Once again, therefore, we see that biological factors, even when their influence is acknowledged, are not sufficient in themselves to explain social or historical phenomena.

In the preceding pages we have discussed a number of efforts to relate social conditions and effects to biological components and causes. If none of these efforts has been wholly successful, neither can they be wholly ignored. The problem of the biological factors exhibits the complexity of sociological analysis and inquiry. If the explanation of a single phenomenon, like the Hanseatic League, presents difficulties of the magnitude indicated here, one can only stand in awe before those presented by a consideration of history and society in the large. Sociology is not yet ready to provide this larger explanation.

8. Summary

In this chapter we have attended all too briefly to the role of biological factors in the construction or causation of social phenomena. We began with the simple and irrefutable observation that society is what it is, to some extent at least, because the human organism is what it is. It is an organism endowed with abilities and disabilities, faculties and faults, unusual capacities and indubitable limitations. It belongs to a species that shares a planet with others, and with these others it must come to terms, preserving the balance of nature. No thorough-going sociology can neglect certain basic biological facts, like bisexual reproduction for example, nor deny their influence in society.

---

[38] Richard Lewinsohn, *Animals, Men and Myths*, Harper & Row, Publishers, New York, 1954, p. 140.

Society, however, is not itself an organism, and accordingly we devoted an early section of the chapter to an examination of the curious view that it is, a view that permeates the history of social and political philosophy and that had an especial vogue at the turn of the century. We attended next to the writers on race, to those who have indulged in ingenious and sometimes desperate efforts to associate civilization with one color of skin rather than with another. These attempts, like the biological analogies, are today devoid of scientific significance, as they have always been devoid of scientific cogency. That there are small biological differences between various groupings of mankind cannot be denied, but it is impossible to maintain that these differences have anything to do with the differences in their societies. Nor do we find close correlations between physical type and social careers, in spite of astonishingly diligent and even brilliant attempts to discover them. We noticed, however, that there is an ecological balance between men and other species—animals and insects and microbes—and suggested that alterations in this balance may have serious social consequences.

We may say in conclusion that throughout the entire recorded course of history Homo sapiens has been the same species, of about the same stature and size and weight and intelligence and longevity. The succession of human events, always different and constantly changing, that have characterized this history can hardly be attributed to changes in the anatomy and physiology of the human organism because, as we emphasized in the preceding chapter, it is not logically possible to explain a variable by a constant. We arrive therefore at the conclusion that biological factors, necessary as they are as a foundation for human life and accordingly for human societies, are nevertheless not sufficient for the explanation of these societies. For this explanation other than biological factors have to be sought. What these factors are we shall begin to explore in another part of this book.

All of us, finally, confront the rather chilling thought that now, in the twentieth century of the Christian era, the species may be standing on the threshold of extinction. Just as the dinosaurs in an earlier era became maladapted to their environment and perished as a result, so Homo sapiens may suffer similar consequences because of a brain that grew too big. Although the brain continues, of course, to serve the survival of the individual, it may no longer serve the survival of the race. It may be indeed that the organ whose capacities distinguish man from all other animals will prove in the gathering twilight to be dysfunctional in the evolutionary sense. It may be that man's very genius at discovering the secret of the atom will result in the destruction of the discoverer. A cosmic spectator may someday note with cosmic amusement that men did not really last very long in comparison with the dinosaurs and that it was the height of pretension for the former to refer to the latter as "unsuccessful animals." It may be that man, that amazing species, both "reprobate ape and apprentice angel," was far too clever for his own good. Maybe, as our atomic scientists suggest, it is even now only twenty minutes to midnight.

Chapter 4

THE DEMOGRAPHIC FACTOR

N THE PRECEDING two chapters we learned first that the location of a human society on the earth's surface has something to do with the kind of society it will be, and second that the nature of the human species similarly exercises a never-to-be-neglected effect. We learned in short that two kinds of natural conditions —the geographic and the biological—determine to some extent, as necessary but not sufficient factors, the kinds of societies in which we live. We called these conditions "natural" because they are relatively, but not wholly, impervious to human interference and design.

In this chapter we concern ourselves with still another kind of condition that exerts an influence upon our societies. This is also a natural condition, in a sense, although, as we shall see, it is much more susceptible to human decision than the first two conditions are. We can do little to change the composition of the earth's crust and little to change the shape of our own physique but there are things we can do to alter in one way or another the operation of the factor we are about to discuss. We call this third factor the demographic factor, and it has to do with people themselves (*demos*, people) in their most purely quantitative characteristics. Demographic phenomena are almost wholly statistical and these statistics in fact are among the most interesting in the world because they are statistics about ourselves. The very first demographic question— first in time, one supposes, and clearly first in importance—is how many people are there, living now, on this planet. How many were there last year, a hundred years ago, a thousand? How many will there be next year, ten years from now, a hundred?[1]

Questions like these, however prominent, are still rather primitive so far as demography is concerned. The number of people living at any given time, as a pure number, may be a much less important fact to know than whether the population is increasing or decreasing, and at what rate. If it is changing in either direction the change may be a short-term or a long-term phenomenon, and again it is necessary to know the difference. Furthermore, the increase, if such it is, may be due either to an increase in the birth rate or to a decrease in the death rate, and the first of these produces a society different in some respects from the second. Ordinarily, of course, both of these rates are undergoing changes in relative independence of each other at the same time. Again, the population is not evenly distributed; in some parts of the world people are so crowded that locomotion is difficult and, as Petersen has observed, goods that once were free have now become commodities—"water in the semiarid West, air in smog-ridden Los Angeles, space in any city to park a car."[2] In other parts people have to travel considerable distances to find a town or a village, or a gasoline pump. Still others are wholly uninhabited. Almost half the world's population lives on 5 per cent of its land area, and 57 per cent of its land area contains less than 5 per cent the population. Furthermore, people are not stationary objects. They have always moved restlessly across the surface of the earth, decreasing the population in one place and increasing it in another. And finally, the composition of the population may differ from one place to another. In some societies there may be more males than females, in others the reverse; in some the old may predominate over the young, and in others the contrary; some populations may exhibit an ethnic homogeneity and others may in this respect be quite diverse. All these and many more are demographic questions and all of them attract the attention of demographers. But they are obviously important to other sociologists as well.

The subject of demography, as one of the subdivisions of sociology, is not without its hazards, both intellectual and political. One would think on first reflection that of all the subjects in the curriculum and of all the sciences in the university, the subject of population would be the most objective, the least susceptible to the distortions of prejudice, and the most reliable, therefore, in its conclusions. People, after all, can be counted. Their births and deaths, their increase and decrease, and their changing ratios can all be captured by cardinal measurement. Basic quantities are

[1] Note that our curiosity does not ordinarily extend as far into the future as it does into the past. That is why history is more important than prophecy.

[2] William Petersen, *Population*, The Macmillan Company, New York, 1961, p. 38.

involved, and cardinal numbers, not ordinal comparisons of variable criteria, and the questions and their answers should be wholly free from bias. And yet, unfortunately, almost exactly the contrary is the case. The findings bend this way or that, depending upon whether the demographers are optimistic or pessimistic in temperament, Catholic or Protestant in religion, Russian or American in nationality, propagandistic or scientific in approach, and tender-minded or tough-minded in general intellectual orientation. In the field of population, as in most of the sectors of sociology, it is almost impossible to avoid having a point of view, and this point of view will almost certainly influence the way in which one reads and interprets the numbers.

1. The Story of Demography

The systematic study of demography, like sociology itself, is relatively recent, but the problem of people, like most social questions, has occupied the inquisitive minds of all ages. The earliest writers had something to say about population, its increase and decrease, and the attendant social consequences. Operating for the most part on the basis of facts that were little more than their own observations, they nevertheless considered the problem and made recommendations about it—recommendations that were related to public policy. Their views on public policy, in reciprocal fashion, influenced the demographic theories they developed.

The story of demography has as one of its origins the writings of the ancient Chinese sages, among whom the name of Confucius always occupies a prominent place. They presented the notion that too many people in a given area or nation, for example, will reduce the economic productivity per worker, influence adversely the general level of living, and have strife and conflict as its consequences. They had the notion also of an ideal relationship between land and people, any deviation from which would result in dislocation of the economy, and they entertained as a corollary an early conception of an optimum population. They believed in the necessity, or at least the desirability, of moving people from overpopulated to underpopulated areas and concluded that this was one of the functions of government. They discussed in some detail the factors that operate to check population growth—such as insufficient food, premature marriage (because it was thought to increase infant mortality), war, and, surprisingly, the high cost of weddings which in turn, of course, reduced the marriage rate.

The Greek philosophers too had something to say about population. Both Plato and Aristotle, for example, were concerned with the best government of the city-state and they both recognized that the number and quality of the people who inhabited the city had something to do with the matter. They wrestled especially with the question of size. The society had to be large enough to be economically self-sufficient and large enough, too, to be able to defend itself, but not so large, on the other hand, as to make government difficult. Some Aristotelian mean, in short, was required and both philosophers addressed themselves to the determination of the number of people that an ideal state should have. Plato specified the exact number of 5,040 citizens, which would indicate a total population of around 60,000 (since citizens comprised only a minority of the total), and did so for the curious reason that the number 5,040 has fifty-nine divisors and for the less curious reason that this number "will furnish numbers for war and peace, and for all contract and dealings, including taxes and divisions of the land."[3]

Aristotle discussed Plato's views and suggested that great care had to be taken concerning the number of citizens and that "the limit should be fixed by calculating the chances of mortality in the children, and of sterility in married persons." The neglect of this subject, he went on to say, "which in existing states is so common, is a never-failing cause of poverty among the citizens; and poverty is the parent of revolution and crime."[4] In another passage, discussing the laws and constitution of Sparta, Aristotle mentioned how the legislators encouraged the citizens at the time of the Theban invasion to have large families. They did this by exempting from military service the fathers of three sons and exempting from all the "burdens of the state" fathers of four. "Yet it is obvious," Aristotle said, "that, if there were many children, the land being distributed as it is, many of them must necessarily fall into poverty."[5] Although Aristotle was not as precise as Plato about the number of citizens, he was clearly interested in the relationships that obtain in a society between population and property, and interested in both of these as relevant to the stability of the state.

In making his own recommendations for the proper ordering of a state Aristotle wrote as follows:

> First among the materials required by the statesman is population: he will consider what should be the number and character of the citizens, and then what should be the size and character of the country. Most persons think that a state in order to be happy ought to be large; but even if they are right, they have no idea what is a large and what a small state. . . . And even if we reckon greatness by numbers, we ought not to include everybody, for there must always be in cities a multitude of slaves and sojourners and foreigners; but we

---

[3] *The Laws*, Book V, 737–738.
[4] *Politics*, II, chap. 6, 1265b.
[5] *Ibid.*, 1270b.

should include those only who are members of the state, and who form an essential part of it. The number of the latter is a proof of the greatness of a city; but a city which produces numerous artisans and comparatively few soldiers cannot be great, for a great city is not to be confounded with a populous one. Moreover, experience shows that a very populous city can rarely, if ever, be well governed; since all cities which have a reputation for good government have a limit of population.[6]

He concluded this section by remarking, "Clearly then the best limit of the population of a state is the largest number which suffices for the purposes of life, and can be taken in at a single view."[7] In succeeding sections he considered not only the quantity but also the quality of the citizens, that is, their character, and with this concern he passed from demography as such over into sociology proper, the whole being, for Aristotle, a part of politics.

Both Plato and Aristotle referred in various parts of their writings to methods of population control directed toward either increase or decrease as the situation seemed to require. In the former category, for example, we find the encouragement of immigration as well as rebuke for young men who fail to marry and reward for those who do; in the latter, legal restriction of those "in whom generation is affluent," colonization and emigration, child-exposure and other kinds of infanticide, abortion, and homosexuality, the last of which Aristotle mentioned as a practice of the Cretans. Other Greek writers who concerned themselves with these problems include Xenophon, who had something to say about the population policies of the Lacedaemonians and the Persians; Herodotus, who referred on a number of occasions to population growth and to migration; and Thucydides, who mentioned migration as a means of relieving population pressure.[8]

In antiquity, as in our own times, the attitudes that legislators and others might take toward population problems depended first of all upon the size and kind of unit in which the questions arose. Thus the Greeks, with their system of numerous and relatively small city-states, had a fairly local attitude whereas the Romans, like the Chinese, thought more in terms of the empire it was their task to administer. In the Greek situation, accordingly, emigration and immigration were of more significance than

---

[6] *Ibid.*, 1326b.

[7] *Ibid.*

[8] The appropriate references are for Plato, *Laws*, V, 739–741; IV, 707–709; V, 736; VI, 754; for Aristotle, *Politics*, VII, 16; II, 10, 11; VI, 5. For extensive treatment, including bibliographical notes, see *The Determinants and Consequences of Population Trends* (Population Studies, no. 17), United Nations, New York, 1953, p. 22. This superior study, to which the present chapter is heavily indebted, will be referred to subsequently as *Determinants and Consequences*.

they were in the Roman or the Chinese situation, where the territory of the respective empires was so vast that migration became meaningless as a solution to a population problem. Furthermore, in these latter situations increasing numbers of people, and therefore of potential soldiers, and again therefore of military power, was a goal to be promoted. The Romans and the Chinese in consequence advocated population policies that encouraged growth and expansion rather than restriction and retreat. In these examples one finds an obvious sociological principle; namely, that as the size of the political unit increases from tribe, city-state, nation, and empire, so also does the utility of migration as a means of population control diminish. In other words, there is an inverse relationship between the size of the political unit and the efficacy of migration as an instrument of population control.

In accordance with this principle it is not surprising either that the Romans should have taken less interest in population as such and that, when the subject did arise, they were concerned to encourage population growth for the greater glory of the empire. Thus we find the few Roman writers who touched upon it devising ways of stimulating the increase of people, and to this end they disapproved of celibacy, defended the importance of reproduction, and recommended rewards for the birth of children. Cicero opposed the plan of Plato for a communal ownership of wives and advocated monogamy instead because he thought the latter institution more productive of offspring. Cicero also mentioned various checks to population growth, including flood, epidemic disease, famine, war, revolution, and the depredations of wild animals.[9] Pliny has a notation or two on immigration in his *Historia naturalis*, but otherwise the Roman references are rather sparse.

Medieval thinkers in the West also had little to say about population, and what they did say was couched of course in a moral and religious context rather than a political or scientific one. In accordance with the tenets of Christianity they were opposed, as one might expect, to such measures of population control as abortion, infanticide, child-exposure, divorce, polygamy, second marriage, and even, for some persons, first marriage.[10] On the other hand, and again as would be expected, they approved of virginity, continence, celibacy, and, for those who married at all, monogamy. Most of them favored an increase in population, supporting perhaps the Biblical command to "be fruitful and multiply," although some, on the other hand, advocated clerical celibacy on the ground that it would reduce the rate of population growth. In general, however, they were sensitive to the catastrophes—famine, war, disease—with which mankind

[9] *De re publica*, IV, 5; *De officiis*, II, 5.
[10] See Chapter 14, Women and Men.

is afflicted, and saw no reason therefore to think in terms of population control of any kind. These attitudes prevailed during the following centuries and it is not until the end of the eighteenth century that we find important warnings against continued and uncontrolled increase. Indeed, the new world of the Western Hemisphere, empty except for a few aborigines, added an almost limitless territory to be filled with people and removed for a long time any threat of overpopulation that Europeans might have felt.[11]

In the intervening centuries only two writers stand out as figures in the history of demography, one of them Ibn Khaldun (1332–1406) of the fourteenth century and the other Giovanni Botero (1543–1617) of the sixteenth and early seventeenth. Ibn Khaldun, the greatest sociologist of the Moslem world, developed a cyclical theory of population change and related it to a more general cycle in the life of societies.[12] Botero anticipated Malthus in suggesting that no matter what the size of the population, man continues to reproduce at about the same rate and that this situation, in the long run, can have serious consequences wherever there are limits to the capacity to find subsistence. The limitations that the requirements of subsistence place upon what would otherwise be an unlimited process is the notion that engages our attention in Botero's work.[13]

The mercantilists of the seventeenth and eighteenth centuries, interested in what has been called analytical rather than merely descriptive demography,[14] continued to advocate—as a kind of favorable balance of people, payments, and power—a large and growing population, one that would have military as well as economic and political advantages. It is in this period that we find the beginning of a more systematic and analytic demography, especially in the work of John Graunt (1620–1674), Sir William Petty (1623–1687), and, almost a century later, Johann Peter Süssmilch (1707–1767). Graunt, often called the father of modern vital statistics, announced four basic demographic principles: (1) that vital phenomena exhibit statistical regularities, (2) that urban death rates exceed rural death rates, (3) that the death rate is higher for the young and for the old than for those in the middle ages of life, and (4) that male births exceed female births in number although the proportion of the sexes is nevertheless approximately equal. Graunt has the honor in addition of having constructed the first life table of the population of London.[15]

Petty in his turn was dominated, as he said, by considerations of

---

[11] In England, for example, putative overpopulation was used as an argument in favor of a colonial policy.

[12] *Determinants and Consequences,* p. 24, note 19. See also Muhsin Mahdi, *Ibn Khaldun's Philosophy of History,* George Allen & Unwin, Ltd., London, 1957, especially pp. 216–221.

[13] His *Delle cause della grandezza delle città* was published in 1558. See the brief treatment in the *Encyclopedia of the Social Sciences.*

[14] That is, interested in theories rather than merely in censuses.

[15] *Natural and Political Observations Made upon the Bills of Mortality,* 1662.

"Number, Weight and Measure." He made many contributions to the economic theory of his time and noted some of the effects of a continuous increase in population—effects that included "wars and great slaughter."[16] Süssmilch, one of the distinguished figures in the history of statistics, wrote a comprehensive work in which he ascertained the variations in mortality rates with respect to different variables (age, sex, residence, and so on), emphasized the regularity and order that demographic phenomena exhibit, estimated the world population of his day to be one billion, and offered the hypothesis that this number would double periodically but at a rate that would vary inversely with the increasing size of the total.[17] These are only some of the many observations that Süssmilch made on a wide range of statistical and demographic problems. The work of all three of these men will indicate the status of demographic theory up to the end of the eighteenth century, when there was published in England a book so important to all of the social sciences that its author merits a section by himself.[18]

2. The Great Demographer

Thomas Robert Malthus, an English clergyman who lived from 1766 to 1834, published in 1798 one of the most influential and important books in the entire history of sociology. It was in this book that Charles Darwin found one of the keys that opened the door to the principle of natural selection and, in broader terms, the theory of evolution, which was in turn the most remarkable scientific discovery of the nineteenth century. It was in this book also that David Ricardo found the idea that emerged in his own theory as the iron law of wages. The book that Malthus wrote was entitled, in its first edition, *An Essay on the Principle of Population as it Affects the Future Improvement of Society, with Remarks on the Speculations of Mr. Godwin, M. Condorcet, and Other Writers.*

This title, a long one in accordance with the custom of the day, accurately suggests the origin of the book. Malthus had been carrying on an argument with his father about the merits of views advanced by Condorcet and Godwin, two philosophical optimists who believed in the infinite

---

[16] See C. H. Hull, *The Economic Writings of Sir William Petty*, 2 vols., Cambridge, England, 1899; especially vol. II, pp. 537–548.

[17] His *magnum opus*, published in 1775, was entitled *Die Göttliche Ordnung*, signifying that there is a divine order in the rates at which births and deaths occur.

[18] It is worth mentioning that Benjamin Franklin also wrote a book on demography, his *Observation concerning the Increase of Mankind and the Peopling of Countries*, in 1751. He suggested that there is no limit to the prolific nature of either plants or animals except the crowding that interferes with acquiring the means of subsistence. It is perfectly possible to suppose that one nation alone, say the English, could in the absence of other inhabitants populate the entire earth.

perfectibility of the human race. Condorcet wrote a history of human progress (*Esquisse d'un tableau des progrés de l'esprit humain*, 1795) and looked forward to a time when all inequalities, animosities, and miscellaneous troubles would have vanished from human societies, when all would speak the same language, all survive disease, and when men, finally, would be so rational that they would refrain from "filling the earth with useless and unhappy beings." William Godwin expressed sentiments of a similarly roseate hue in his *Enquiry concerning Political Justice* (1793).[19] Malthus was less optimistic. He sensed danger in the continued increase of population and decided to investigate the matter in some detail. The result was a book that went through seven editions by 1872 and many more since, has been translated into most of the world's languages, and poses a problem that can neither be minimized nor ignored. The problem has not yet in fact received a satisfactory solution.

Malthus believed, in brief simplicity, that the programs of the reformers of his day in their efforts to relieve "the unspeakable ills of society" were doomed to failure. Their plans were palliatives, not remedies. In order to get to the heart of the matter of poverty and human misery it was necessary to consider the population itself and especially the rate at which it increased. If allowed to increase without checks of any sort the population, Malthus said, would double every twenty-five years and thus increase in geometric ratio in accordance with the series 1, 2, 4, 8, 16, 32, 64, 128, 256, and so on. Food supply, on the other hand, even in circumstances "most favorable to human industry," could not possibly increase in more than arithmetic ratio, in accordance with the series 1, 2, 3, 4, 5, 6, 7, 8, 9, and so on. Malthus concluded, therefore, that "in two centuries the population would be to the means of subsistence as 256 to 9; in three centuries as 4,096 to 13, and in two thousand years the difference would be incalculable."

It was the formula, not the fact, that gave so percussive an impact to the theory. Others before Malthus had noticed the necessary relationship between the productive powers of the earth and the reproductive capacities of the race, and indeed Coleridge criticized Malthus for indulging in a painful elaboration of the obvious and declared that the sense and nonsense in the *Essay* were also related as an arithmetic to a geometric series. The mathematical ratio as introduced by Malthus, however, seemed far more exact and compelling than any verbal statement could be. For what he had done was to call attention to the properties of a geometric series, which are awesome indeed. We may take a moment to examine them.

---

[19] For example: "There will be no war, no crimes, no administration of justice, as it is called, and no government. Besides this, there will be neither disease, anguish, melancholy, nor resentment. Every man will seek, with ineffable ardour, the good of all."

Consider the brain-teaser about the amoeba and the milk bottle. An amoeba, let us say, reproduces itself every two minutes; that is, it produces two new amoebae which, in two more minutes, produce four new ones, and so on. Let us assume that one amoeba placed in a quart milk bottle and reproducing at this rate will fill the bottle in thirty minutes. How long, then, will it take to fill the bottle if we start with two amoebae instead of one? The unwary will answer fifteen minutes, because fifteen is half of thirty. As with all brain-teasers, however, the unwary response is the wrong response. The right answer is twenty-eight minutes. If we put two amoebae into the bottle rather than one we are in exactly the same situation at the beginning that we were in after the first two minutes in the original case, and thus we cut two minutes off the time required to fill the bottle.

The beginning of the process, however, is not nearly so important as the end. That is, two minutes before the half hour, if we start with one amoeba again, the bottle is only half full and two minutes later, at the half hour, it is full. To fill a second bottle will require not another half hour but only another two minutes. In other words, in another two minutes another bottle will be needed in addition to the first one in order to contain the multiplying amoebae, which, incidentally, are multiplying throughout at the same rate. If the rate itself increases to more than one fission every two minutes the process is compounded into an even more rapid increase, and this is what the neo-Malthusians fear with respect to the growth of the world's population.

Population does not increase, however, without checks, and Malthus recognized that these were of two kinds, positive and preventive. Positive checks were those that might affect any species and that shorten the natural life span, such as epidemics, diseases, wars, plagues, famines, and the effects of unwholesome occupations, hard labor, and climatic exposure. Preventive checks, on the other hand, which only man can employ, would include celibacy, late marriage, and sexual abstinence or, as Malthus put it, "moral restraint"—which, he acknowledged, "does not at present prevail much among the male parts of society."[20] Since Malthus recognized that

[20] It is not true, incidentally, as one finds curiously repeated even in some recent introductions to the *Essay*, that Malthus himself had eleven daughters nor, as Marx reported, that he was wholly celibate. He had in fact three children, two daughters and a son. The emphasis upon moral restraint occurs not in the first but in the second edition of the *Essay*, in which dour pessimism gives way to a cautious optimism and in which population and prosperity are found to be compatible after all. The differences between the two versions was noted by Walter Bagehot with the dry comment that "In its first form the *Essay on Population* was conclusive as an argument, only it was based on untrue facts; in its second form it was based on true facts, but it was inconclusive as an argument." See the excellent discussion by Gertrude Himmelfarb in the Introduction to the Modern Library edition of the *Essay*, Random House, Inc., New York, 1960, where the Bagehot quotation appears. For the lively responses to Malthus in the English literature of the nineteenth century see Harold A. Boner, *Hungry Generations*, King's Crown Press, New York, 1955.

the need for sexual experience was quite importunate, second only to the need for food, the outlook for the future did not appear to him to be bright.

Now things have not worked out the way Malthus thought they would a century and a half ago. Neither the increase in population nor the increase in the food supply conforms exactly to the Malthusian predictions. Other factors, which he could not have known, have come to influence both of these processes and to produce results that differ from those that he predicted. Indeed, in some periods and places, as for example in the United States in some parts of its history, food production increased faster than the population. There is nevertheless—and this must always be the first mark to the credit of Malthus—some limiting relationship between population and food supply. Malthus may not have understood all of the details of demography, but it is his dramatic essay that captured the attention of social science. As Kingsley Davis has written, "Despite the outpouring of books, pamphlets, and articles on population theory, it is hard to cite a single scientific advance since Malthus' day that this literature has contributed to the subject."[21] His is indeed one of the great names in the history of sociology.

With the theory of Malthus we enter a new era and the writings on population become so numerous that it is no longer profitable or possible to pursue them. The story of demography from the beginning of the nineteenth century onward is the story of a continuing controversy between the Malthusians and the anti-Malthusians—a controversy that is not yet stilled. Before concluding this historical section, however, we must make brief reference to the views of Marx and the Marxian theoreticians on this subject. Most of them, including Marx himself, were inclined either to deny that there was a population problem, or to attribute it to deficiencies in the organization of society, or to insist that it was characteristic only of capitalistic societies (which require an excess labor force), or to say merely that it was a problem that could occur only in certain stages of economic development. Marx conceded that Malthus was sensitive to the reality of class conflict but denounced him nevertheless as a "shameless sycophant of the ruling classes." Marx was skeptical about the establishment of universally valid laws of population growth and insisted, in conformity with his general sociological theory, that different modes of production brought about different kinds of population phenomena. Surplus population was a problem only in capitalistic societies where, in fact, it was an intentional consequence of capitalistic enterprise. Post-Marxian writers have continued

[21] "The Sociology of Demographic Behavior," in Robert K. Merton, Leonard Broom, and Leonard S. Cottrell, Jr. (eds.), *Sociology Today*, Basic Books, Inc., Publishers, New York, 1959, p. 313.

to doubt that an excess population is any more than a temporary imbalance due to archaic systems of economic organization and to insist that the problem, if such it is, will disappear with the coming of the socialist state.[22]

3. A Note on the Census

If we try to trace the population of the world from earliest times it is obvious that for many thousands and perhaps hundreds of thousands of years we have to rely upon inferences and estimates. Primitive and prehistoric societies maintained no census bureaus. For that matter the men who lived in the earliest of times did not know how to count, and it is impossible to say therefore how many people lived in their societies, or how heavily populated they were in relation to the land area they occupied, or what diseases they died of, or how many died in proportion to the number born, or how many moved from one place to another. These, and many similar facts, can never be known with any accuracy or precision. The ingenuity of the demographers, however, has resulted in some careful reconstructions and the guesses that we have, about early historical societies at least, are good guesses indeed.

The word "census" itself comes from the Latin *censere*, to value, or tax, and in ancient Rome one of the duties of the censor was to take a register of the number and property of the citizens for the purpose of imposing taxes. For this reason censuses have frequently been unpopular and have often been denounced as instruments of tyranny. One of the factors accounting for the inaccuracy of the early censuses was the desire of the citizens to conceal their wealth in order to keep their taxes as low as possible. A second factor was that the total population of a state or nation was considered to have a military importance and was therefore "classified information"—that is, confidential or secret. A third factor, entering much later than the other two and relating to the growth of democracy in the modern sense, is the notion that there are certain facts into which it is inappropriate for government to inquire. Thus, to inquire into a citizen's religion, for example, though clearly productive of data useful to sociology, may be regarded as unwise, not because the citizens lack candor but because they believe the question—if answers are compulsory—exceeds the proper role of government in a free society. (Like a woman's age, it may be important to know but impolite to ask.) Finally, census data, though

[22] E. K. Fedorov, Secretary General of the U.S.S.R. Academy of Sciences, said in 1962 that it will be many millennia before population becomes a problem, that the resources of mankind should not be discounted, and that we have only begun to mine our riches. See his article in the *Saturday Review*, February 11, 1962, pp. 17–20. For the Marxian literature in general see *Determinants and Consequences*, pp. 32–36.

quantitative, have no inherent reliability. A king can require a subject to answer a question but no earthly majesty can make him tell the truth. And then, of course, there are the many societies in the world where census data were until quite recent times nonexistent and to which therefore the canons of accuracy have no meaning.

Most of the early efforts at census taking were directed only at certain classes of the population. Thus, censuses taken in ancient Rome were limited, for one reason or another, to a count of citizens alone, or males alone, or adults alone, or households alone. The Chinese and the Incas had census enumerations but their results are not easy to interpret.[23] Contemporary estimates of early populations are quite ingenious and sophisticated, but it is useful to remember nevertheless that they are still estimates and inferences based upon such things as archaeological evidence; numerical allusions in literature; figures in manuscripts; records of grain imports, tax levies, and soldiers; and similar data. It is interesting to note in this connection that even contemporary inaccuracies have to be discovered, when possible, by internal and analytic means and with the help of techniques that are sometimes quite complicated, because there is no external standard other than the census itself in terms of which its accuracy can be determined.

The taking of periodic, as opposed to occasional, censuses is a fairly recent development in Western history. There was an attempt to count the entire population of the city of Nuremberg in 1449 and this is perhaps the earliest effort at completeness. The count was ordered by the city fathers because a siege was threatened and both the available food supply and the number of inhabitants were facts it was of imperative necessity to know. The results, incidentally, were a closely guarded military secret and remained so for 200 years. Censuses of other municipalities and of the Swiss cantons were taken during the fifteenth and sixteenth centuries, but the counting of total populations of large countries seemed for some time to be beyond the pale of possibility.

There is some question as to which of three countries—Canada, Sweden, or the United States—was the first to institute census-taking on a regular basis, and it is surely not necessary to settle the question. Attempts were begun in all three of these countries a little after the middle of the eighteenth century. The Constitution of the United States (1787) requires that an "enumeration shall be made within three years after the first meeting of the Congress of the United States and within every subsequent term of ten years" (Article I, Section 2), and the reason for this provision,

---

[23] On the former see A. J. Jaffe, "A Review of the Censuses and Demographic Statistics of China," *Population Studies* (U.K.), vol. 1, no. 3, December, 1947, pp. 308–337.

of course, was not scientific but rather political in the best sense of the word. That is, since membership in the House of Representatives, as was decided in one of the great Constitutional compromises, was to be determined by population rather than apportioned equally by states, it was necessary to know what the population was and to make arrangements for periodic recount. That the census itself does not always assure prompt and equitable reapportionment, however, is something that the Supreme Court has been compelled to recognize. In any event, the first American census was taken in 1790 and, as a democratic innovation, its results were immediately made public.

The European countries began soon thereafter to take censuses of their own—France in 1800, England in 1801, Belgium in 1846 (a census administered by the statistician Quetelet), Italy in 1861, Germany in 1871, and Russia in 1897. By the end of the nineteenth century almost all Europeans were being regularly counted and by 1930 the practice of census taking had been extended to more than two-thirds of the population of the world. The *Demographic Yearbook* of the United Nations contains census statistics for over two hundred countries and territories and an examination of this important publication will disclose that almost all of the world's peoples are now being counted with a remarkable degree of accuracy.

4. The World's Population

So far as we know, men have been living on this planet for at least a hundred thousand years and possibly as long as a million years. During all these eons of past time the population was sparse. The few people there were, were thinly spread in the areas of the earth that would support them, and their settlements were small, containing seldom more than a dozen or two families. The rate of increase with each passing generation was also small—so small as to be almost insignificant. Two dozen people living a hundred thousand years ago and increasing continuously at the rate of only twenty per one hundred thousand per year would have been enough to produce the present population of the world. This, as we have seen, is the effect of a geometric series which, like compound interest, magnifies even small annual increments into total increases that very quickly overwhelm the principal itself. If we take 600,000 B.C. as a reasonable date at which human life began on earth, we discover that from that time to the present a total of some 77 billion people have enjoyed a longer or shorter sojourn here. Only about 12 billion of these people, however, lived before 6,000 B.C., and so 99 per cent of this estimated time span of human existence produced only 6 per cent, leaving 94 per cent of the people to be produced in the remaining 1 per cent of the time. A similarly impressive fact is that of all the people who have ever lived on earth in this fantastic span of time, roughly 4 per cent are alive today.

In the early centuries the number of people in any given area on the earth's surface was rather directly determined by the amount of food that area could supply. Geographic and especially climatic factors, as we have seen, set narrow limits to human choice and the early representatives of our species were dependent upon gathering rather than upon producing their food. They gathered whatever they could find that would sustain them—roots, berries, fish, shellfish, and small animals. They did not work directly to increase the food supply either by breeding animals or by growing grain. As a result they were often hungry, and the threat of starvation was never far removed. Fortunately, man has versatile ingestive and digestive equipment and can adapt himself to a wide variety of foods. As an English anthropologist has written, "He has the incisors of a rodent, the molars of a plant eater, and the canines of a carnivore; . . . an added length of gut for the digestion of green food, gastric juice for the conversion of starch to sugar, pepsin for the metabolism of proteins, and pancreatic fluid for the emulsification of fats."[24]

The transition from food gathering to food producing is a technological change of rather considerable moment, but it did not apparently result in an immediate growth of population. One of the results of the new agricultural surplus was an increase in the leisure time that some or all of the members of the community were able to enjoy. It is the leisure, and after a time of unknown duration the growth of a leisure class, that made possible for the first time the appearance of an entirely new social phenomenon—the city. As Petersen says, and we shall remark again in another chapter, "A sizable number of persons who do not have to grow their own food is the sine qua non of urban existence."[25] By our own criteria the primeval city was a very small place. Ur and Erech had no more than 25,000 inhabitants each and the largest of the ancient cities, Thebes, had fewer than a quarter of a million.[26]

Skipping numerous centuries and turning from urban to imperial units, we learn that at the time of the death of Augustus (A.D. 14) the estimated population of the Roman Empire was around 54 million, or possibly a little more, with 23 million of them in Europe and 6 million in Italy proper. For Egypt at the end of Ptolemaic times we have a figure somewhere between 8$\frac{1}{2}$ and 10 million. Estimates for China in the early centuries of the Christian era range from 50 to 70 million—although it is

[24] Audrey Richards, *Hunger and Work in a Savage Tribe: A Functional Study of Nutrition among the Southern Bantu*, The Free Press of Glencoe, New York, 1948, pp. 7–8. Quoted in Petersen, *op. cit.*, p. 317, note 7.

[25] Petersen, *op. cit.*, p. 321.

[26] *Ibid.* The question of cities meets us again, in Chapter 16.

difficult to know with any precision the area that is included. Demographers accept for ancient India a figure of between 100 and 140 million. The population of the world during the lifetime of Christ was probably around 300 million.

With the advent of early modern times the population had risen to some 500 to 550 million, but the trend of growth was neither continuous nor large nor universal throughout the globe. The general pattern from the medieval period to roughly the seventeenth century has been summarized as follows:

1. Wide fluctuations, with relatively small net increase, and in some cases net decrease, in ancient centres of dense population: China, India, Mesopotamia, the Near East and Egypt;
2. Similar but less violent fluctuations with an emergent trend toward population increase, in southern and western Europe—with marked decreases at different times in Greece, Spain, and the Danubian region;
3. Pronounced increase in the "frontier regions" of central and eastern Europe. Little information is available concerning the growth of population in the frontier regions of other continents during this period.[27]

Population statistics are still uncertain in the seventeenth and eighteenth centuries. Demographers assume a slow increase after the middle of the seventeenth century, but no one knows how the rate of increase, if any, compares with that of any of several earlier centuries. As we have seen, the practice of census taking was still rudimentary at this time, and figures for the world itself during this and the following two centuries continue to fall into the category of educated estimates rather than of settled facts. The best of these estimates are those of W. F. Willcox and A. M. Carr-Saunders, as follows:

Population of the World

1650–1900*	Willcox	Carr-Saunders
1650	470,000,000	545,000,000
1750	694,000,000	728,000,000
1800	919,000,000	906,000,000
1850	1,091,000,000	1,171,000,000
1900	1,571,000,000	1,608,000,000

* The appropriate references are W. F. Willcox, *Studies in American Demography*, Ithaca, New York, 1940; and A. M. Carr-Saunders, *World Population; Past Growth and Present Trends*, Oxford, 1936. Both sets of figures are taken from *Determinants and Consequences*, p. 11.

[27] *Determinants and Consequences*, p. 10

Both sets of estimates are included here in order to afford some notion of the degree of difference between two distinguished demographers for the period in question. Actually, as a single glance suffices to show, the difference is not very large and we can therefore accept either set—or a compromise figure between them—with a good bit of confidence.

We come now to the most recent period in the population story, the period from 1920 to the present. It shows a startling picture. Let us first examine the bare statistics as they are given to us by United Nations estimates.

Population of the World

1920–1967*	
1920	1,834,000,000
1930	2,008,000,000
1940	2,216,000,000
1950	2,406,000,000
1960	2,901,834,000
1970	3,632,000,000

* *Determinants and Consequences*, p. 11. The 1960 and 1970 figures, however, are from the *Demographic Yearbook*, United Nations, New York, 1961 and 1971 respectively.

If we look at a graphic representation of population growth during the entire time we have been discussing, something a little over 100,000 years, we shall see the following picture:

World Population Growth

The view from here—if "here" means the twentieth century—is from a rather considerable height. A curve that rose almost imperceptibly for 100,000 years changed direction, 300 years ago and is now rising very rapidly indeed. It is a dramatic change and one that has many implications.

Thomas Robert Malthus is here again, as he was almost two centuries ago, insisting that we pay attention.

5. The Far-from-lonely Crowd

As in Malthusian times, we are assailed on all sides by voices in a great debate. Are there too many people in the world today? Should the human proclivity to reproduction be somehow reduced? What does "too many" mean? Is it not possible that the marvelous resources of science will be able, through new discoveries if necessary, to stay the threat of starvation that overpopulation would otherwise bring in its train? Does the concept of overpopulation itself make any sense? Suppose science learns, as Godwin, in answer to Malthus, said it would, how to feed the world's population from a single flower pot? What happens, on the other hand, in the absence of such a panacea, when aid to underdeveloped countries merely reduces the death rate without affecting the birth rate and produces a net effect of more poverty and suffering than before the aid began? What can be done, what need be done—if anything—to curb, curtail, or control man's apparently reckless urge to multiply? Or is the whole thing a pseudoproblem, emphasized only by those who have little faith in the divine order of Johann Peter Süssmilch, in the power of divine decisions to cure the temporary disproportions that sometimes occur? Or is it a genuine problem but one that will disappear, as the Marxists say, with the coming of the Communist state?

The answers to these questions are now the subjects of public controversy. Not only biologists, sociologists, and demographers proper, but statisticians, politicians, theologians, and philosophers have begun to express their opinions. To some of them, the neo-Malthusians, the problem has become the most serious—with the exception of thermonuclear weapons—that mankind has ever had to face. The problem is so ubiquitous in fact that no literate person has been able to avoid some involvement with it. The answers given depend not so much upon the facts themselves, which are hardly in dispute, but upon such anterior philosophical, sociological, or religious positions as provide the context in which the facts are viewed. Let us look at the situation in the worst possible light.

The facts themselves we have already described, in both statistical and graphic form. Their meaning, however, can only be grasped by looking at them again and by stating them this time with the stark insistence and penetration of the English language.

Consider first the figures of 1, 2, and 3 billions of people. A billion of anything is a number that cannot be grasped or comprehended by any human faculty. Imagination, ordinarily more powerful and more wayward, is in this curious instance less versatile than reason. One knows rationally but not imaginatively the difference between a billion and a million. To the imagination they are both large numbers. Only reason, aided by arithmetic, can distinguish between them.

It is not our task, however, to philosophize about large numbers but rather to deal with the story that the numbers tell. Look at the graph again and consider that it took all of the years from the origin of the species—at the very least 100,000 years—to the year 1830 to produce a world population of 1 billion people. This process was not, we know, a steady one. There were advances and retreats, periods of rapid growth and periods too of decimation caused by disease, defeat, and natural catastrophe. With whatever fits and starts, surges and lags, the number of 1 billion was reached around the eighteen hundred and thirtieth year of the Christian era, a mere second ago in the history of recorded time. How long did it take then to bring the figure up to 2 billion? Only 100 years—the period from 1830 to 1930. And how long for 3 billion? Only thirty-one additional years—the brief period from 1930 to 1961. And now, at the present rate of increase, it will take only fifteen more years to add a fourth billion, and only ten years after that to add a fifth. There is every likelihood indeed that, unchecked in the meantime, the world's population will rise to 6 billion by the end of the present century.

If we look at these figures in a slightly different way we shall recognize that all of the years of human history, both recorded and unrecorded, to the year 1900 were required to produce a population of $1\frac{1}{2}$ billion. The twentieth century alone, a minute span of only 100 years, will have produced at its end another $4\frac{1}{2}$ billion. One century, a brief moment by the clock that measures eons and ages, will have produced three times as many people as a thousand centuries produced before.

Consider now some miscellaneous items, unrelated to one another but all related to population. India at the moment of writing this page is adding 8 million people to its total every year. China adds 12 million per year, or 1 million per month. The population of Mexico will double—from 50 million to 100 million—in the next twenty years. The earth itself added every year of the decade of the sixties from 46 million people to 65 million at the end, the former figure equivalent to a country the size of France. Every four years, again using the lower figure, it added enough people to populate another country the size of the United States. For that matter, Asia alone now adds more people to its population every year than emigrated to the United States from Europe during the whole of the nineteenth century. Two-thirds of the people in the world go to bed hungry every night, and every morning there are approximately 180,000 more infants clamoring for breakfast. So great are the disparities among continents that one-third of the world's population consumes two-thirds of its food supply and, sadly, vice versa. And in the time it takes the average family in the United States to have dinner, 417 people starve to death. Every week more than enough people are born to add to the world another Baltimore, Houston, Cleveland, St. Louis, Milwaukee, or Washington, D.C., every two weeks another Philadelphia, every month another Chicago, and every two months another New York.

If statistics are more understandable, or more palatable, in smaller doses, consider that about 7,500 babies are now born every hour on the clock—which means 125 per minute, day and night. And this number of 125 is itself increasing with the passage of every calendar day; that is, people are increasing in number every day and the rate at which they are increasing is also increasing. There is in truth a population "explosion," although the word itself is perhaps more dramatic than scientific. All it means—and that, perhaps, is enough—is that there are many more people on earth at the present time than ever before and they are adding to their numbers more rapidly. The earth in short is now a thickly populated planet and the crowds that appear upon it can no longer be lonely. As the gifted American writer John Updike rather trenchantly put it in one of his stories, "The race is no longer a tiny clan of simian aristocrats lording it over an ocean of grass; mankind is a plague racing like fire across the exhausted continents." [28]

6. The Population of the United States

The population of any particular country has no more intrinsic interest for sociology than the population of any other. Sociology, on the contrary, is concerned with those phenomena and processes that repeat themselves in era after era in human history and from place to place around the globe. It is this relatively abstract view which, as we have seen, distinguishes sociology from such disciplines as history and ethnography. Sociology of all sciences should escape the provincialisms and the parochialisms that would result from the examination of all social problems from the inside of a particular society—which, after all, is only one society among many. Nevertheless, for our present purpose the population of the United States is a useful example of a trend toward expansion and it can be utilized therefore as a piece of inductive evidence for one of the most important of the influences that are currently affecting the contemporary world. For it is clearly the case that the population of the United States, like that of many other countries, is rapidly increasing.

Those of us who live in the United States, incidentally, are easily

[28] "Lifeguard," *The New Yorker*, June 17, 1961, p. 30.

persuaded that the difficult problems of humankind always happen somewhere else; that our own country is notably immune from the social processes that affect other less developed and less happily endowed countries; and that we are in all respects a favored nation under the sun. It is true, of course, that we are favored in many respects. But it is not true that our natural advantages enable us to escape all of the problems that beset other societies. Of these the problem of population is one to which we have no privileged solution—although it may not appear to be a problem because we also have an embarrassing plethora of foodstuffs. We represent in fact just one more example of what is an exceedingly rapid population growth when compared with other societies at other periods of history.

Some of the present consequences of this growth are shown in other chapters, especially when we consider the city and the suburb. Here we want to note only two of the more salient features of the demographic character of the United States. The first of these is that only three countries in the world have a larger population—China with an estimated 760 million, India with an estimated 550 million, and the Soviet Union with around 243 million, all in 1966. The United States, with 205 million, is thus the fourth most populous country in the world today. If we look at population densities rather than at the numbers themselves, there is some shifting of rank among these four. India goes to the top of the list as the most densely populated, with 317.2 persons per square mile; China is next with 172.7, the United States third with 50.5, and the Soviet Union fourth with 24.1. Thus, the United States is twice as "crowded" as the Soviet Union, China over seven times, and India twelve and a half. It is also interesting to note, incidentally, that more than half of the population of the world lives in one or another of these four countries.

A second salient feature of the population of the United States is that in its growth from roughly 4 million people in 1790 to the 63 million of 1890 the figures duplicated with a curious precision the geometric increase that Malthus predicted for all populations everywhere in the absence of positive and preventive checks. Thus, during this hundred-year period the population doubled every twenty-five years and the curves of actual population growth and of a Malthusian projection almost exactly coincide. The actual growth was even slightly higher than the Malthusian rate because of the effects of immigration, which did not decline until some time after 1920. From 1890 to the present, however, the population did not increase as fast as the Malthusian formula would have predicted. The declining rate of increase is due in part to the decline in the birth rate from the beginning of the period to almost the end of it. It is due also to the virtual end of the immigration process, which filled the American space at so prodigious a rate during most of the years of American history, and especially during the years from roughly 1885 to 1920. Immigration was reduced sharply during, and as a result of, two world wars, and it is of some interest to observe that during three years of the great Depression, from 1932 to 1935, 183,000 more people left the United States than came here to live. In the 1960s immigration averaged under 400,000 a year.

In any event, the most palpable of present facts about the United States is that its population too is increasing to a size that some people, not all of whom are looking for a place to park, regard as something more than comfortable. On the other hand, the rate of growth began to decelerate in 1955, a deceleration that continued during the sixties and became dramatic in the early seventies. Indeed, it appeared that the country, for the first time in its history, might reach zero population growth, a consequence devoutly to be wished by a group calling themselves Zero Population Growth, Incorporated. Their happiness could, of course, be premature. Even with a birthrate of 2.11, which is the magic figure required to reach "ZPG," the population would continue to increase for seventy more years because of the increasing number of females approaching the childbearing ages.[29] Only one thing is certain, and that thing is that the National Park Service is strained to its utmost capacity.

7. What of the Future?

In his altogether excellent book on population, the American sociologist William Petersen distinguishes between population projections and popula-

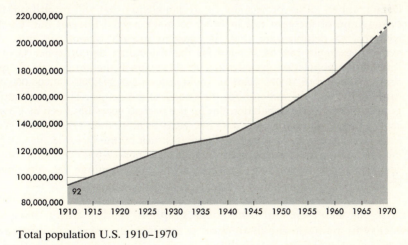

Total population U.S. 1910–1970

[29] The decimal part of the 2.11 is required to compensate for those females—largely on account of infant mortality—who do not live long enough to reproduce or who otherwise fail to do so. The number of women in the age range 15–44 was 42 million in 1970; in 1990 the number will be 60 million.

tion forecasts. The former, the projections, are constructed solely of demographic materials, that is, trends that can be predicted from the size and profile of a population alone, including known birth, death, and migration rates. The latter, the forecasts, introduce in addition some of the more intangible and precariously known social and economic variables, in so far as these can be estimated at a given time. Forecasts, in consequence, can be most hazardous. How can the demographer be expected to know, for example, that a depression will occur ten years hence, that a major war will wipe out large numbers of people, that an effective and inexpensive contraceptive pill will be invented, that a religious taboo on conception control will be reexamined, that a reduction in the birth rate will become a major policy of a large nation, that a cure for cancer will be found, and so on through many possibilities? As Petersen says in this connection, even the sociologists who are specialists in economic, technological, social, and cultural developments are "not only generally unable to predict their future development but also often unable to summarize their past trend accurately."[30]

Nevertheless, changes will occur, whether they are predictable or not. In fact, changes *must* occur. It is an interesting intellectual exercise to consider a population projection, to inquire into what can happen as a result of the operation of demographic factors alone. We appeal to Petersen again for an example:

> Demographers often project the future population that will result from the current rate of increase not in order to make a valid forecast but, on the contrary, to demonstrate that the present growth *cannot* continue. An extreme example can be cited from the Australian demographer George Knibbs: If a population grew from a single couple at the annual rate of 1 per cent, at the end of 10,000 years it would require 248,293,000,000,000,000,000 earths to furnish the material for the bodies of the people. The actual rate of growth of the world population during the past 30 years has been at 1.2 per cent per year, and during the past five years at more than 1.5 per cent. With such a calculation as Knibbs made, one is struck by the fact that the current increase of the human species is a highly temporary phenomenon, which could not have begun very long ago and cannot continue for very much longer.[31]

Of course, as Petersen and other demographers readily admit, it is not always easy to maintain the distinction in practice between projections and forecasts. In what follows we shall indulge in neither of these but rather in

[30] William Petersen, *op. cit.*, p. 299.
[31] *Ibid.*

what may candidly be called sheer speculation. We want to consider some of the things that could happen, that are not altogether beyond the realm of possibility.

The first of these possibilities is that there is some kind of automatic check built into the population process, some natural means of preserving an ecological balance between any species and its food supply, something that happens as a wholly natural phenomenon and without intervention of human plan or design. It is possible, for example, that reproduction rates are themselves a function of population density, that they decline when the density becomes too great and increase again when it becomes so low that it threatens the continued existence of the species. Nature would thus ensure, through biological processes as yet unknown, the continuance of the species and at the same time protect it against its own excess.

It may be said at once that no such theory enjoys the benefit of acceptable evidence. Such evidence as there is comes chiefly from observations on the lower animals and not even this has won a unanimously favorable reception. It has been reported, for example, that glandular secretions are somehow involved in this process; that the tension of overcrowding results in the enlargement of adrenal and pituitary glands, which in turn increases susceptibility to disease and reduces fertility, milk production, and resistance to infection. This phenomenon has been observed among red-back voles in the sub-Arctic regions of Finland, where overcrowding even in the presence of an adequate food supply is said to have had these results; in animals in the Philadelphia zoo; and in other studies of small animals. On the other hand, no enlargement of the glands of male lemmings has been observed even at the peak of their abundance. No one doubts, of course, that there are irregular cycles which affect the self-destructive migrations of these animals, but the explanation is still a mystery to biological science. A four-year study of woodchucks on a 20,000-acre plot in Pennsylvania shows that the population tends to be stabilized at approximately one woodchuck per acre and that this balance is quickly restored when it is experimentally altered—even when the number is reduced by half. The suggestion is offered again that this is due to some kind of hormone response.[32]

These theories, as mentioned above, are matters of much controversy among biologists and there is no way of knowing whether, even if true, they would describe a phenomenon that similarly applies to the human species. We merely want to suggest the possibility that increasing population density itself might be a detriment to increasing population—even

---

[32] A brief survey of these theories is contained in *The New York Times*, January 14, 1962, sec. 1, p. 65.

without the increased mortality that a drastically reduced food supply would bring about—and thus operate like an automatic check. On the other hand, as opponents of the theory have been quick to point out, those parts of the world that have the highest birth rates at the present time are also those that are the most crowded. It is doubtful in fact if any purely biological theory of density control can sustain itself in application to human societies. Too many other factors are at work and the theory itself, however attractive on purely speculative grounds, offers no present satisfaction.

The second possibility is that present trends will be reversed for other reasons and that what today looks like a population explosion will tomorrow make us wonder whether the anxiety was justified. We have seen that, although the total world population and its present rate of growth are striking in magnitude, the increase as a whole was subject to many surges and retreats throughout the course of its curve. Long-term trends are in fact unpredictable, and if the demographers have been wrong before, it is easy—even if not altogether safe—to suppose that they can be wrong again. It is asking too much of social science to predict that present trends will continue. Estimates that are wrong in one direction can also be wrong in the other. No conscientious demographer would attempt to conceal the difficulties involved in prediction. As the superior United Nations study expresses it:

> It has been amply demonstrated that population trends, although they are more stable than many other attributes of human societies, are subject to considerable changes within periods of a few decades or even a few years. Prediction of future population with confidence would be possible only if (1) universal laws of population had been established, and (2) the relevant future social and economic circumstances influencing population change could be known in advance.[33]

It is quite possible that a rapidly increasing world population will react against itself, not for the biological reasons mentioned above, but because statesmen everywhere will become increasingly conscious of the problem. Petersen remarks, in one of his many felicitous statements, "It is a useful rule of thumb in social analysis that any trend, once it goes beyond a certain point, tends to build up a resistance that eventually leads to a reversal."[34] With respect to population it has happened again and again in the history of

---

[33] *Determinants and Consequences,* p. 151.
[34] Petersen, *op. cit.,* p. 302.

the race and there is no reason to suppose that it will not happen again. If people become sufficiently worried, or sufficiently crowded, or increasingly unable to feed themselves and their children, then they are likely to take some kind of action to reduce their numbers in the future. When their efforts are assisted by their government, encouraged by public opinion, and condoned by their religion, then they are in a position to affect a trend.

There are of course, in the world today, some powerful taboos against any kind of birth control or contraception and they appear even in otherwise contradictory ideologies. Even the strongest of taboos, however, are subject to change. In Holland and Germany as late as 1890 it was considered blasphemous to add artificial fertilizers to the soil in order to increase the yield. It was a taboo that no longer prevails. A notable reduction in the birth rate was accomplished in Ireland by postponing the age of marriage,[35] and more recently in Japan by governmental dissemination of contraceptive information. In the latter country, only recently threatened by a population problem, the birth rate in 1962 reached the lowest point in its entire history. Something similar, or with similar effect, could happen in other parts of the world, not excluding China, India, and Latin America. All one can know with certainty is that the planet cannot long sustain the birth rate that its people now have and that, if the race survives, a change will by mathematical necessity have to occur.

A final possibility is a paradoxical one. There is indeed a solution to the population problem. The trouble with it is that it is too effective a solution—it would finish mankind as well. The dreaded engines of nuclear warfare are more potent by an infinite factor than any known to history and there is no question that they can reverse the demographic trends that have been in operation since the beginning of the sixteenth century. It is possible indeed that they can decimate the race for centuries to come and make room on all the continents for new numbers of human beings—beings genetically different, perhaps, from ourselves in ways unpleasant to contemplate. Thus a new species would inhabit the earth, begin again to reproduce itself, and, in some sidereal time, have a population problem of its own.

---

[35] In the eighteenth century Irish girls married as early as sixteen years of age and the population doubled in the sixty years from 1781 to 1841. The resulting condition, combined with the great potato famine of the forties, encouraged emigration in very large numbers. It also reestablished an old tradition which required a man to receive his inheritance before he could marry and fortified a taboo on sexual intercourse for more than one generation of married partners living in the same household. As a result the age of marriage became higher and higher and the population was reduced again to its eighteenth-century level by 1951. In that year, 45.6 per cent of the females and 67.4 per cent of the males in the age group 25 to 34 were unmarried.

8. Summary

In this chapter, which is by no means an introduction to demography,[36] we have tried to invite attention to some of the basic facts of human existence—the number of people who have lived on earth, who live here now, and who may be expected to live here in the future. The size of the world's population at any particular time is not yet a social fact—though it has social consequences—and for this reason we have preferred to include the demographic factor among the natural conditions of human society. If further justification be needed we can say that for most of the centuries of human habitation upon the planet, the increase or decrease of population was a purely natural phenomenon, unplanned by human genius and undirected by human design. The human species grew in numbers in the manner that we have described, but the long-term growth depended upon natural propensities and the temporary retardations upon natural hazards. Indeed, for many of these centuries men cannot have been aware of the population trends to which their own reproduction contributed and in this sense we can say that population processes are a part of those larger biological processes that affect any species.

In any event, we had an opportunity to trace the history of the human concern for the increase and decrease of population and to mention reputed results on military strength, on economic productivity, and on the general welfare. We saw that the ancient Chinese and the ancient Greeks alike took cognizance of the factors that affect population trends and we observed the recommendations they made for the demographic character of the well-ordered state. The question of conscious population control, which elicits so much interest and anxiety today, attracted the attention of these old philosophers as well. The story continued through the Roman, medieval, and early modern period in Western history and we came at last to the great demographer, Thomas Robert Malthus, and the theory that won him first rank in his discipline and a permanent place in intellectual history.

Our next undertaking, with an aside on the census itself, was to tell the story of the world's population from the beginning to the present time. We had occasion to emphasize the sharp change of direction that began some three hundred years ago and to ask what this might portend for our descendants and the societies in which they are destined to live. We saw that the crowd is no longer lonely and that there are more of us now than ever before—and even more tomorrow. Some of the consequences of this rapid growth we encounter in later discussions of the sex and age ratios of a population and also in the chapter on city and suburb.

[36] An excellent introduction to the subject can be found in Theodore Caplow, *Elementary Sociology*, Prentice-Hall, Inc., Englewood Cliffs, N. J., 1971, pp. 196–263.

Neither Malthus at the end of the eighteenth century nor we in ours can predict with any accuracy or success the future food resources of the earth, any more than we can measure the resources of the human mind. The energy of the sun and the sustenance of the sea may help us to increase beyond current imagination the number of people who can live on the earth's surface. Atomic energy can work pleasant miracles as well as unpleasant ones, and the chemical industry is still in its infancy. A cautious view of the demographic situation will take into account not only the human propensity for procreation but also the human talent for invention.

We may conclude, at least, with the safe observation that without people there would be no societies and that the number of people, whether many or few, has something to do with the prospects and potentialities of these societies. An increasing population presents one kind of problem, a decreasing one another. There can be too many people, and too few, for certain social purposes. But population, though clearly a biological factor, is just as clearly not an autonomous one. It depends upon the relationship of birth rates to death rates, and this relationship in turn is now susceptible to human influence and arrangement. Human ingenuity and belief—for example, medical technology on the one hand and religious ideology on the other—transform a biological propensity into a social process. And medicine and religion, like the agriculture and engineering that increase the food supply, are human achievements, not biological necessities.

WE HAVE NOW completed our discussion of the natural conditions of human society. We have indicated, by principle and example, that geographic, biological, and demographic factors all operate in the formation of human societies and help to determine the characteristics of these societies. In each case, however, we have observed that the influence of these factors, with certain exceptions, is negative rather than positive. We have seen that they set limits to the variations in societies but do not, within these limits, determine the details of social structure and of social development. It is important to know what these limits are, and we have therefore discussed them at some length. But we are now ready to turn more directly to the central themes of sociology and to treat, in even greater detail, the factor that above all exerts a positive and determining influence in society. This factor is culture.

"Culture" is one of the most important concepts in contemporary social science. It is used in psychology, social psychology, political science, and economics. It is the central concept in anthropology and a basic concept in sociology. We therefore devote this section, comprising

CULTURE AND SOCIALIZATION

three chapters, to this concept
and this phenomenon. In the first
of these chapters we discuss the meaning
of culture, and in the second the
content of culture. The subject of the
third is the acquisition of culture, the
process commonly known as socialization.

Chapter 5

THE MEANING OF CULTURE

HE AVERAGE American boy learns that the square
of the hypotenuse of a right-angled triangle
is equal to the sum of the squares of the other
two sides. He also learns that bodies attract each
other with a force directly proportional to
their mass and inversely proportional
to the square of the distance between
them. He knows that the speed
of light is roughly 186,000 miles per
second and that the evening star,
which shines so brightly in the
western sky in the springtime, is not
a star at all but the planet
Venus. If he were an Eskimo or a Fiji Islander,
he would know none of these things. On the
other hand, he does not ordinarily learn how to
catch a seal nor how to make a kayak nor
how to make a bull-roarer nor how to tend a
yam plot. If he were an Eskimo
he could do the first two of these
things, and if he were a Fiji Islander
he could do the second two. How
are we to explain these differences?
It is fairly obvious, on the basis
of the preceding chapters, if
not indeed of common sense, that
no examination of temperature
or topography or any other geographic
factor can provide a satisfactory
explanation, except for the fact that seals
and yams do not grow in the same
places. It is perhaps less obvious, but
no less true, that no examination of the
human organism or of the human
brain would enable us to predict that
these differences would appear.
We have to seek our explanation,

therefore, in a factor of another kind, the factor of culture. What then is culture?

1. The Definition of Culture

The word "culture" is in every English-speaking student's vocabulary before he begins to study sociology. Nearly everyone knows the difference between a "cultured" person and an "uncultured" one. Culture in this sense has something to do with personal refinement. Possession of it indicates that one knows how to conduct himself in all of the social situations to which he is likely to be exposed and in which he participates. It implies the pursuit of perfection. It means, as Matthew Arnold once said, a knowledge of the best that has been thought and said in the world, an ability to see life steadily and see it whole. A man or woman of culture is expected to prefer Bach to rock; he knows the difference between the philosopher Plato and the planet Pluto; his palate presumably prefers filet mignon to corned beef and cabbage, and French champagne to corn liquor; and he would rather read Shakespeare in blank verse than a tabloid in what could be mistaken for prose. The man of culture has a good manner, and good manners. He has something we are likely to call good taste. Above all, he is expected to follow the Kantian injunction and treat all other people as ends in themselves and not as means only.

It is not easy to say precisely what culture is in this sense. One of the best definitions, perhaps, is that of A. Lawrence Lowell, a former president of Harvard University, who identified culture with "enjoyment of the things the world has agreed are beautiful; interest in the knowledge that mankind has found valuable; comprehension of the principles that the race has accepted as true."[1] One may be inclined to hope that a bachelor of arts degree symbolizes possession of culture, but unfortunately this is not always the case.

In any event, however, this is not the sense in which we use the word "culture" in sociology. The sociological meaning of the word is quite different and, accordingly, we have here an illustration of the fact mentioned in the introductory chapter that the sociologist takes words out of the language of everyday conversation, gives them a technical meaning, and thus makes concepts out of them. In sociology "culture" does not mean personal refinement.

Historians give the word "culture" still another meaning, though one that is somewhat related to the popular concept of the term. They use it to refer to the so-called "higher" achievements of group life or of a period of

[1] "Culture," *At War with Academic Traditions in America*, Harvard University Press, Cambridge, Mass., 1934, p. 117.

history—specifically art, music, literature, philosophy, religion, and science. Thus, a cultural history of modern Europe would be an account of historical achievements in these fields and the adjective "cultural" would differentiate this kind of history from political history, economic history, industrial history, military history, or a history of manners and customs.[2] As common and indeed as universal as this usage is among historians, however, this again is not the way the word "culture" is used by contemporary sociologists. We need yet another meaning of the word. In sociology and anthropology "culture" means neither the refinement of a person nor the refinements of society.

In these sciences, and indeed in the other social sciences as well, culture has come to mean not the so-called "higher" achievements of group life—art, religion, philosophy, science, and the rest—but *all* the achievements of group life. It includes not only sonnets and symphonies and statues but also trinkets and tomahawks and tractors. A jet plane and a tank and a helicopter are as much a part of culture in the sociological sense as are the plays of Eugene O'Neill, the poems of Robert Frost, and the novels of Ernest Hemingway. A violin is a part of culture and so is a screwdriver; and so, too, are candlelight at dinner and a lunch box at noon, prayer and profanity, a cent and a cigarette, an art museum and a sewage-disposal system.

Many sociologists and anthropologists have attempted to construct adequate and comprehensive definitions of culture in this sense, and there are consequently hundreds of these definitions in the literature. One of the earliest, and most quoted, was formulated by E. B. Tylor, an English anthropologist, in a book published in 1871: "Culture is that complex whole which includes knowledge, belief, art, morals, law, custom, and any other capabilities and habits acquired by man as a member of society."[3] Another definition, formulated by two anthropologists who gave considerable thought to this problem, is as follows: "By 'culture' we mean those historically created selective processes which channel men's reactions both to internal and to external stimuli."[4] For our purposes, however, in order to avoid as many terminological difficulties as possible and in order to retain

[2] See for example Preserved Smith, *A History of Modern Culture*, 2 vols., Henry Holt and Company, New York, 1930, 1934. This outstanding work does, however, include manners and morals within its scope.
[3] E. B. Tylor, *Primitive Culture*, John Murray, London, 1872, vol. 1, p. 1.
[4] Clyde Kluckhohn and William H. Kelly, "The Concept of Culture," in Ralph Linton (ed.), *The Science of Man in the World Crisis*, Columbia University Press, New York, 1944, p. 84. For a comprehensive, though highly technical, discussion see A. L. Kroeber and Clyde Kluckhohn, *Culture: A Critical Review of Concepts and Definitions*, Papers of the Peabody Museum of American Archaeology and Ethnology, vol. 47, no. 1, Harvard University Press, Cambridge, Mass., 1952. Available in paperback.

the virtues both of simplicity and of comprehensiveness, we shall define the word as follows: *Culture is the complex whole that consists of all the ways we think and do and everything we have as members of society.* The implications of this definition, together with certain qualifications, will become clear as we proceed with the discussion.

2. Synonymous Expressions

Learned Ways of Behavior

Before considering the content of culture, a task reserved for the following chapter, we want to help clarify the nature of this phenomenon by considering various expressions that are sometimes used as synonyms of culture. The first of these is the phrase "learned ways of behavior." When identified in this way, culture is not behavior as such but the grooves or channels in which human behavior proceeds. Unlearned behavior, such as the knee-jerk reflex, the eye-blinking reflex, and so on are purely physiological and not cultural. Shaking hands and shaving, on the other hand, are cultural. The emphasis upon learning is important. Homo sapiens, as we are pleased to call ourselves, is poorly supplied with instincts. In marked contrast to other species of animals, and especially to various species of insects like ants and bees, man has to learn to do most of the things he does.[5] There is no instinct or other biological endowment that teaches us to tie a shoelace, boil a potato, fry an egg, eat with a fork, drink from a glass, comb our hair, brush our teeth, pull a zipper, make change, read a newspaper, push a lawnmower, drive a nail, strike a match, write a check, ring a doorbell, turn a faucet, drive a car, and do many other things that we do every day without thinking. All of these simple things, and thousands like them—to say nothing of more complicated activities like finding the roots of a quadratic equation, writing a sonnet, or running for office—have to be learned. They are all a part of culture. Whether or not we learn them depends, if we are normal individuals, not upon any biological inheritance or genetic constitution, but upon being members of a society in which these activities are regularly performed. We learn to do all of the things mentioned not because we have a normal complement of physiological capacities—this is a necessary but not a sufficient reason—but because we are born into a society whose culture contains them. The Ona Indians, who live at the southern tip of South America, can do none of these things, and

---

[5] "There is no human being, if he be even a few weeks old, who reacts completely freshly to any stimulus situation. Very few human responses indeed can be explained entirely through even the most complete knowledge of the individual biological equipment." Kluckhohn and Kelly, ibid., p. 85.

yet there is no evidence that they are biologically inferior to the natives of Ohio, who can do all of them.

Culture, in other words, is transmitted not through the germ plasm but only through learning, and learning requires social interaction. The genes may have a lot to do with genius, but the chromosomes have nothing to do with culture. Several sociologists have asked us to look at a group of squirming and squalling newborn babies. They come in various sizes and shapes and colors. But no physical examination of them, no matter how minute, can tell us which of them will become a Protestant and which Catholic, which will learn English and which some other language, which will someday salute one flag and which another. If, however, we know the culture to which the infants will be exposed, we can answer all of these questions with ridiculous ease. Culture, in short, is learned.

The fact that culture depends upon social interaction can be illustrated by noting that individuals who are deprived of society at an early age, who are deprived, that is, of the companionship of other people, do not acquire a culture. A case of this kind has been observed and described by Kingsley Davis. This is the case of Anna, an illegitimate child found in the attic of a Pennsylvania farmhouse. The child was given no attention, no training in anything, no exercise, and just enough food to keep her alive. When discovered, she could not walk or talk or even sit upright, and she was believed to be both deaf and blind. As Professor Davis commented, her condition showed "how little her purely biological resources, when acting alone, could contribute to making her a complete person." By the time Anna died, at the age of ten, she had learned how to follow directions, play with beads, identify colors, build with blocks, play with dolls, keep her clothing clean, wash her hands, and brush her teeth. Thus, although she never caught up with others of her age group, she did make notable progress in spite of her overwhelming and ultimately fatal handicap.[6]

There have been reports of people who have been isolated from society at more advanced ages. In New York City, for example, a misguided mother imprisoned her draft-age son in a sealed room, sending him food by means of a dumbwaiter, and kept him there in a successful effort to keep him out of the Army. At the end of his incarceration, however, he was of no use to the Army or to any other organized group. He had lost most of the attributes we normally associate with human beings.

This case, and others like it, indicates that no one can acquire culture without association with human beings and, once acquired, it can gradually

---

[6] Kingsley Davis, Human Society, The Macmillan Company, New York, 1949, pp. 204-205. Professor Davis earlier reported on this case in two articles in the *American Journal of Sociology*.

be lost through deprivation of this association. Extraordinary as it may seem, human beings need other human beings in order to become human and in order to remain human. We are not born human but become human by acquiring the culture of our society. The man without a culture, in this sociological sense, is a feral man, a "wild" man, more like an animal than a human being. The human child, whom someone has wittily and also sensibly defined as an alimentary canal with a lot of noise at one end and utter irresponsibility at the other, literally has to be domesticated, and this process of domestication is the process of acquiring a culture. Whether or not a child can learn depends upon his biological equipment. What he learns depends upon his culture.

The Social Heritage

If culture has to be learned, even though the learning is unconscious imitation, so also it has to be taught, even though the teaching is unconscious instruction. If a generation fails, for one reason or another, to transmit a part of its culture to the succeeding generation, that aspect of the culture will simply disappear and may have to be reinvented or rediscovered at a later date. Thus, there are various things that people living at an earlier period of history knew how to do but that people living centuries after them can no longer do. No one today, for example, knows the secret of Egyptian embalming and no one today can duplicate the art of violin making that reached a peak of unique perfection in the work of Stradivarius in the eighteenth century. No one today knows the formula for making the stained glass used to ornament medieval cathedrals. Contemporary technicians of course know how to stain glass, but some part of the medieval formula has been lost through a failure of transmission. No one knows how many other secrets of industry and art have similarly been lost. We have learned to do many things that were quite unknown to our predecessors in other periods of history, but we have forgotten some things, too, that were commonplace to them.

Culture may thus be conceived of as a kind of stream flowing down through the centuries from one generation to another. When we think of it in this way it becomes synonymous with the social heritage, and some sociologists use this term rather than culture. Each generation contributes something to this stream, but in each generation, too, something is left behind, some "sediment" drops to the bottom and is lost to society. For the most part what is lost is no longer required; it disappeared because it became obsolete. No one today—except possibly someone working on a Hollywood production—wants to build a trireme, the ship with three banks of oars that the men of classical antiquity used to navigate the seas. No one today carries in his pocket a nutmeg grater, an item almost as common in eighteenth-century England as a cigarette lighter is in twentieth-century America. This implement, which came in various shapes, was used by the gentleman of that period to grate nutmeg in taverns where spices were not supplied with the liquors.[7] Our museums, in fact, are full of relics of all kinds from earlier civilizations that are no longer an essential part of our contemporary culture but that are yet important to our archaeologists and antiquarians and historians and indeed to all of us because they help us to understand the past.

Although metaphors are dangerous, especially when taken literally, we may say that culture, or the social heritage, is the memory of the human race. Few of us today, perhaps, would have the wit to invent a wheel or the genius to devise an alphabet. Few of us can even make a match or a safety pin or a lead pencil. Fortunately, we do not have to do these things. All of them were already a part of our culture when we were born. It is instructive to think about what society would be like without this accumulation of culture, what our lives would be without it. *Human* beings as we know them would not, in fact, exist, and Homo sapiens would simply be another species of animal. It is culture, par excellence, that distinguishes us from the other animals, and although animals of some species, notably the anthropoid apes, have a not inconsiderable learning ability, the fact that they have no language prevents them from communicating what they learn to the next generation. Language, of course, is the most important of all the vehicles for the transmission of culture. Without language culture cannot accumulate. And language itself, as we shall see, is a most important part of culture.

Culture, in the sociological sense, is also something that is shared, not something that one person alone can possess. An isolated inventor may succeed in making a gadget in his laboratory that does all sorts of unusual and wonderful things, but if no one ever uses it except himself, it does not become a part of culture. The Patent Office has patented thousands of inventions that have never caught hold in society and that are never used. These inventions do not then become a part of the culture of our society. Similarly, if the new ideas that people constantly have never find public expression and if the new ways of doing things that they constantly devise are not adopted by other people, they might as well never have been thought of or devised. For culture is shared. It is always something adopted, used, believed, practiced, or possessed by more than one person. It depends upon group life for its existence.

As we suggested in the chapter on geography, man—like all of his

---

[7] A collection of silver nutmeg graters may be seen in the Smithsonian Institution in Washington, D.C.

cousins in the animal world—must ultimately adjust to his physical environment; he can develop and vary only within limits set by that environment. In marked contrast to the other animals, however, man does not adjust directly to this environment. Culture always intervenes and, in most cases, aids the process of adjustment. Just as our houses shelter us from the storm, so also does our culture insulate us from natural dangers and assist us to survive.

Few of us, indeed, could survive without culture, although the earliest men must have been able to do so. For us, in fact, nature does not exist "in the raw," and we do not need to respond to it without the help given us by our social heritage. A modern civilized man going naked into the wilderness, without knife or ax or match, might possibly survive and might even thrive, but if he was also without a single scrap of knowledge, his survival would be problematic. And the knowledge that would enable him to survive in such a circumstance would have its source in his culture. Robinson Crusoe is not, of course, a fictional example of a feral man, for he took his culture with him when he was stranded on his ocean isle. Because he had absorbed a culture he did not have to start from scratch. Nature, on the other hand, sometimes reminds us that culture is not enough for survival, as in times of earthquake, flood, volcanic eruption, tornado, hurricane, and blizzard, and also in periods of excessive heat or cold. But without culture we should have difficulty surviving in even the best of weather.

We may ask what would happen if this social heritage suddenly disappeared; if, for example, a nuclear war should lay waste the civilized earth and destroy the accumulation of culture. An English sociologist, writing before the advent of nuclear weapons, speculates about the effect of a similar eventuality as follows:

> If the earth were struck by one of Mr. Wells' comets, and if, in consequence, every human being now alive were to lose all the knowledge and habits which he had acquired from preceding generations (though retaining unchanged all his own powers of invention, memory, and habituation) nine tenths of the inhabitants of London or New York would be dead in a month, and 99 per cent of the remaining tenth would be dead in six months. They would have no language to express their thoughts, and no thoughts but vague reverie. They could not read notices, or drive motors or horses. They would wander about, led by the inarticulate cries of a few naturally dominant individuals, drowning themselves as thirst came on, in hundreds at the riverside landing places, looting those shops where the smell of decaying food attracted them and perhaps at the end stumbling on the expedient of cannibalism.[8]

---

[8] Graham Wallas, *Our Social Heritage*, Yale University Press, New Haven, Conn., 1921, p. 16.

It requires, as one can see, a strong imagination to conceive the nature of the world in the absence of culture.

The Superorganic

Because culture, from one point of view, has a certain degree of independence from inorganic and organic factors, it is sometimes called "the superorganic." This synonym implies that there are three orders of phenomena—the inorganic, the organic, and the superorganic—and that the first of these is investigated by the physical sciences, the second by the biological or "life" sciences, and the third by the social sciences and the humanities. The choice of the word "superorganic," introduced into the literature by Herbert Spencer and emphasized again by A. L. Kroeber,[9] is unfortunate if it implies, as it may, that "culture" is somehow superior to "nature" or that what is cultural is not natural. We have already suggested that a modern city is as natural as is an anthill, and the point is worth reiterating here.

But the word "superorganic" is useful when it implies that what may be the same phenomenon from a physical or biological point of view may be quite a different phenomenon from the cultural point of view. Thus, a piece of cloth of the same color, composition, and texture may be used as a headdress in one society, a diaper in another, and a flag in still another. Similarly, paper of the same grade and quality may appear as a diploma, as a commission in the armed services, or as a bill of indictment in a court of law.

To use another example, a tree means different things to the botanist who studies it, the gardener who tends it, the old woman who uses it for shade in the late summer afternoon, the farmer who picks its fruit, the motorist who collides with it, and the young lovers who carve their initials in its trunk. The same physical objects and physical characteristics, in other words, may constitute a variety of quite different cultural objects and cultural characteristics. On the other hand, the same cultural meaning may be objectified in a variety of different physical ways. The American flag has the same significance for Americans whether they see it printed on paper, flying as cloth from a pole, or stamped in metal. And the Lord's Prayer is the Lord's Prayer whether sung by a choir, read by a minister, recited in unison with others, or repeated silently to oneself.

The same considerations apply, of course, to the relationship between organic facts and their cultural significance. How men are garbed

---

[9] A. L. Kroeber, "The Superorganic," *American Anthropologist*, vol. 19, 1917, pp. 163–215. This important paper is reprinted in A. L. Kroeber, *The Nature of Culture*, University of Chicago Press, Chicago, 1952, pp. 22–51.

—whether as priests, soldiers, miners, plumbers, professors, prisoners, judges, or professional baseball players—has a great deal to do with how they are viewed in their society, but, so far as biological type is concerned, an admiral may be quite indistinguishable from a bishop or a swindler. Thus the adage that clothes make the man—or woman—is a statement full of sociological meaning. On the other hand, admirals, bishops, and swindlers come in a variety of constitutional types. To use another example, the sexual act, physiologically the same, may in one situation be seduction, in another adultery, in another prostitution, in another rape, and in still another the lawful intercourse of married partners.

The word "superorganic," therefore—if one will refrain from attaching metaphysical connotations to it—fixes our attention upon the social meaning of physical objects and physiological acts and emphasizes the fact that this social meaning may be relatively independent of physical and biological properties and characteristics. In this sense "the superorganic" becomes a useful synonym for "culture."

Design for Living

We have now indicated that culture sometimes refers to learned behavior, sometimes—as in the phrase "stream of culture"—to the social heritage, and sometimes to the superorganic. Each one of these expressions exhibits and emphasizes a particular characteristic of culture. There remain several simpler and perhaps less precise synonyms.

Sometimes culture means simply the "way of life" of a people or their "design for living." Kluckhohn and Kelly define it in this sense as follows: "A culture is a historically derived system of explicit and implicit designs for living, which tends to be shared by all or specially designated members of a group."[10] This concept of culture is particularly useful in distinguishing one society or group from another. Here the reference is not to culture in general but to particular cultures. Thus, the culture of the Mexicans is different from that of the French, the culture of the Hopi Indians of the Southwest is different from that of the Kwakiutl Indians of the Northwest, and the culture of the contemporary Russian student is different from that of the contemporary American reader of this book. There is an American way of life, a way of life that is important to Americans. It is our design for living. Similarly, other peoples have ways of life that are important to them and that they cherish.

The way of life, or design for living, includes many things, and this conception is far from being as simple as it seems. Cultures in this sense are capable of almost infinite variety—within biological and geographic limits,

[10] Kluckhohn and Kelly, *op. cit.*, p. 98.

of course—and such cultures as appear on earth do not necessarily coincide with the political boundaries of national states or with the epochs and eras of historical time. But it is permissible to speak of the American way of life as American culture, the Japanese way of life as Japanese culture, and so on. All peoples have their designs for living and this, in a most general sense, is what we can also mean by their culture.

We now have a list of expressions that sociologists and anthropologists frequently use as synonyms for culture: (1) learned behavior, (2) the social heritage, (3) the superorganic, and (4) design for living. Each one of these expressions emphasizes a slightly different aspect of a complex phenomenon. The first one suggests that culture is learned and taught and shared and cannot be possessed by an individual in isolation from society. The second suggests that culture is transmitted from one generation to the next, that it constitutes an "inheritance" from the past in the social sense and that in each generation something is added and something is lost. The third one suggests that culture varies in relative independence of physical constituents and biological components and has an independent meaning. And the fourth suggests that culture varies also from one society or group to another, in different places at the same time and in the same place at different times. But these synonymous expressions do not as yet indicate with sufficient clarity the nature of culture, its forms and content, and so we shall need to pursue this subject further in the following chapter. At this point, however, it seems desirable to impress the reader with the great importance of culture in human life and in human society.

3. The Importance of Culture

It is almost impossible to exaggerate the importance of culture in human life. Neither a single individual, a particular social group, nor an entire society can be understood without a reference to culture. It is culture that, in the wide focus of the world, distinguishes individual from individual, group from group, and society from society. It is culture that distinguishes us as a species from the other animals, including the higher orders of animals most like ourselves. It is culture that makes us human. What each individual contributes to his culture is small indeed; what he takes from it is beyond all possibility of measurement.

We remarked in the introductory chapter that in some respects we are like all other people, in some respects like some other people, and in certain other respects like no one except ourselves. The first of these respects is the proper concern of biology and physiology, the last of individual psychology. It is the second, the respect in which we are like, or unlike, some other people, that is of special interest to sociology. In this section, therefore, we want to discuss the ways in which culture determines what we do, and to examine some of the various ways in which it influences our activities.

It may seem obvious at first that seeing is a purely physiological act, that what we see depends upon what is in front of us when we open our eyes. Actually, what we see depends upon our culture. Strange as it may seem, we have to learn to see, and what we learn to see depends to a large degree upon the society in which we grow up. A blind man who suddenly recovers his sight will not be able to tell which of two objects in front of him is a cube and which is a pyramid, even though he has already learned to make these distinctions through the sense of touch. The boy "couched by Chesselden"—the subject of a famous case discussed in the *Philosophical Transactions of the Royal Society of London*, in which a Dr. Chesselden removed the cataracts from a boy's eyes—would not at first believe that the small picture in front of him was a picture of his father, on the ground that so large a man could not be put in so small a space.[11] Indeed, the spectacles some of us wear to correct our vision actually "correct" the world that presents itself to our eyes. And spectacles, of course, are an item of culture unknown to some societies.

Even more dramatic, perhaps, is the fact that although peoples all over the world—the astronauts excepted—see the same moon, they see different things in it. Americans see a man in the moon, and sometimes another man looking over the first man's shoulder. The natives of Samoa see in the moon a woman who is weaving the stuff that clouds are made of. Native American Indians of the Northwest see such things in the moon as a duck, an eagle with outstretched wings, and a horned toad, who has hopped there in order to escape a wolf. To the Indians of the East the moon contains a little gray rabbit, with long ears and outstretched paws. Natives of the South Pacific see in the moon a grove of trees; they hope to dwell there when they die and to feast forever on the trees' golden fruit. The French see in the moon the evil countenance of Judas Iscariot, and the Australians a huge, searching cat's eye. The mothers of Puritan New England told their children that the figure in the moon was a goblin with large ears, a wart on his nose, and scissors in his hand—the scissors to be used to snip off the noses of those who were impolite to their parents. And—loveliest of all perhaps—Irish legend tells us that the young girl who drinks white wine and rosewater and who then looks at the moon through a silken handkerchief will see there the face of her future bridegroom.[12]

---

[11] The first man to prove that we have to learn to see was a philosopher, George Berkeley (1685–1753), who published his *Essay towards a New Theory of Vision* in 1709.
[12] The author is indebted for these facts to Mary Gene Evans, "What's in a Moon?" *The New York Times Magazine*, October 12, 1947, p. 34.

If what we see depends upon our culture so also, and much more obviously, does what we wear—and indeed whether we wear anything at all. Nudity is immoral in some societies and quite moral in others. Variations in costume are in fact immense and can almost always be used to distinguish societies from one another, as well as to distinguish different groups and strata within the same society. Egyptian, Greek, Roman, ancient Briton, fifteenth-century Spaniard, eighteenth-century Frenchman, and twentieth-century Russian all have different and distinctive clothing. What we wear and how we wear it depends upon our culture. And thus clothing too is a part of culture.

Some peoples live in round houses set in circular patterns. We live in rectangular houses set in rectangular patterns. The polar Eskimo builds his house of snow, the Navaho of mud, the Hopi of sandstone, and the contemporary American of a variety of materials including wood, brick, concrete, and stone. Even within the same society we can see an astounding range of variation from the sharecropper's hovel in the cotton fields to the Towers of the Waldorf-Astoria in New York City. The story of architecture through the ages could show us in detail, if we had time to tarry, how the structures men build to shelter them as they eat and sleep reflect their different cultures.

Equally striking are the food preferences of different peoples. Some subsist on fish; others on berries and roots. Some drink milk; others abhor the thought of it. Europeans, in fact, are frequently astonished to learn that American men drink this white fluid product of the cow even after they have grown up. The French look upon water as a liquid good only for washing. Snakes, scorpions, feathers, worms, monkeys, frogs, lizards, lice, wasps, bees, beetles, snails and even clay and rotten wood and canned peaches can be found among the foodstuffs of various peoples. No Eskimo has more pride than the one who can offer his guest a mixture of caribou eyes, auk slime, ptarmigan dung, and fermented brain of bear, the whole thoroughly prechewed by the host to make it soft and palatable. In this department of culture there is no doubt whatever that one society's meat is another society's poison. What is digestible, of course, is ultimately a function of physiology, but it is more immediately a function of culture.

Furthermore, distinctive types of food are associated with certain contemporary societies. Borscht (beet soup), sauerkraut, spaghetti, onion soup, mutton, and apple pie almost automatically suggest Russia, Germany, Italy, France, England, and the United States respectively. An American may object on moral grounds to the drinking of wine, but he will usually not hesitate to give his children Coca-Cola. The Frenchman, on the other hand, who will serve diluted wine to the smallest of his children, may regard Coca-Cola as a noxious liquid to which he objects on moral grounds.

As a matter of fact, a bill was once introduced in the French National Assembly intended to bar the sale of Coca-Cola in France both on the grounds of health and of morality.[13]

Thus, the houses we live in, the clothes we wear, the food we eat, and the beverages we imbibe can be explained not by biological needs for shelter, warmth, food, and drink, but only by culture. And here we have a new illustration of the important point discussed in earlier chapters. *That* we eat and drink is something to be explained by physiology, but *what* we eat and drink, on the contrary, can be explained only by culture. The necessary factor is the biological one; the sufficient factor is culture. Of course, biology and geography and even physics set limits to the range of cultural variation. Men cannot build their houses from the top down, nor build them of materials that are unavailable to them. No people may eat indigestible or poisonous foods and continue to survive, and the length of time a man can fast is clearly limited. But the tremendous, the almost illimitable and infinitesimal, variations on the range of possibilities are to be explained and understood only in terms of culture. Culture is therefore the key that opens the door to an analysis of human societies and human beings. Let us consider some additional examples.

One might be tempted to think that the shedding of tears, like other expressions of emotion, is a physiological process to be accounted for in terms of the functioning of the tear glands when excited by the appropriate stimulus. There is no evidence that these glands are constructed differently or function differently in different groupings of people, although minor variations attributable to age and sex have been noted. But no physiological examination of these glands, no matter how microscopic or minute, will explain why they operate on certain occasions in some societies and not on similar occasions in other societies.

American men do not, for example, shed tears in public, except on the occasion of bereavement—or, possibly, on the occasion of losing an important basketball game. Weakness in this respect is culturally tabooed, and boys in our society are taught as early as possible to restrain their tears in circumstances of sorrow and anger as well as pain. American men, however, are permitted grimaces, if not tears, in certain situations, say in the dentist's chair. In certain American Indian tribes, on the other hand, the young braves were subjected to an ecstasy of torture and passed the test only when they endured it without a flicker of facial expression. It cannot be

---

[13] French newspapers supporting passage of the bill objected to the "coca-colonization" of France and warned against a new illness called "coca-colique." *Le Monde*, a moderate newspaper, denounced the "dangers that Coca-Cola represents for the health and civilization of France" and maintained that "the moral landscape of France is at stake." The bill, incidentally, failed of ultimate passage.

maintained that there are constitutional differences in the ability of men of different societies to withstand pain. The answer again is cultural. When we reflect, in fact, that an adult American male is permitted to laugh in public but not to cry, that the adult Iroquois male is permitted to do neither in public, and that the adult Italian male is permitted to do both, we can easily see that other than physiological factors are at work.

It is frequently maintained, to choose another example, that some peoples are more aggressive, more warlike, more pugnacious than others. As evidence for this proposition we are asked to compare the Icelanders, the Swiss, and the Swedes with the Spartans, the Prussians, and the Blackfoot Indians. But this evidence lends no weight to the hypothesis that the difference is temperamental or that it is grounded in psychology and physiology. If such factors were physiological they could be presumed to be constant throughout history. But aggression, pugnacity, and militarism are sporadic in their appearance. Wars occur in most societies but not in all, and even in the societies in which they do occur they are not constant phenomena. Such variables as these, therefore, must be explained by another variable, culture, and not by the constant that is the organic constitution of the human species. Similarly, men may seek profits and power and pelf, but neither capitalism nor dictatorship nor crime can be directly related to their biological nature. Every attempted explanation of social phenomena in purely biological terms leads sooner or later to a stop sign at the end of a blind alley.

Furthermore, men become saints in some societies for actions that would land them in jail in others. Or they are crucified in some periods of history for "offenses" for which they are apotheosized in others. They gain sanctity in some societies by living alone in the wilderness, fasting and praying for many years, but in other societies similar actions would merely be considered queer. St. Simeon Stylites, a medieval hermit, became a saint because he lived for more than thirty-five years on top of a pole. In our society flagpole sitting once appeared as a commercial advertising stunt and won notoriety, but no sanctification, for its practitioners.

The contemporary American student may think it is perfectly natural to be reading these lines from left to right and is likely to imagine that any other way of reading would be wrong. He has forgotten, however, that once upon a time, most likely in the first grade of his primary school, he had to be taught to read in this direction and that it is not something he did automatically or naturally. A little reflection, furthermore, will convince him that the explanation is cultural. Hebrew and Persian, for example, are read from right to left and Chinese and Japanese from top to bottom, and these directions too seem natural to the people who read and write these languages.

If what we do is so greatly conditioned by our culture—eating and drinking, laughing and crying, reading and writing, loving and hating, playing and working, and all the other activities in which we indulge—so also is what we think. Once again we have a subject on which many books could be written, and have been written. Of the many illustrations of this point, therefore, we shall have to confine ourselves to only a few.

As a first consideration, what we think about may already be determined in large part by the particular language that is so essential a component of our culture. We cannot think at all without words, and words are bits of culture.[14] It may be that an entire attitude toward the universe— what the Germans call a *Weltanschauung*, or world view—is already contained in the language that we learn because we are born at a particular period of history and in a particular society. How, for example, could we ponder such philosophical problems as quantity, quality, relation, substance, and causality if these words did not belong to our language and if the ideas corresponding to them did not belong to our culture? Indeed, a German philologist, Fritz Mauthner, once remarked that if Aristotle had spoken Dakotan, an American Indian language, the whole history of Western philosophy would have been different. The perennial problems of philosophy, as a French philologist, Louis Rougier, once suggested, may not be perennial problems at all, in the sense that they have less to do with the universe itself than with the grammatical structure of the Indo-European languages. And Bertrand Russell, the English philosopher, once suggested that the principal reason why we classify things into subjects and objects is that the sentences of the language we happen to speak contain subjects and predicates.

This, however, introduces some difficult sociological problems, problems relevant to the sociology of knowledge. For our present purpose we need only reflect upon the following remarks made by Aldous Huxley in one of his novels:

Our "souls" are so little "us" that we cannot even form the remotest conception how "we" should react to the universe, if we were ignorant of language in general, or even of our own particular language. The nature of our "souls" and of the world they inhabit would be entirely different from what it is, if we had never learnt to talk, or if we had learnt to talk Eskimo instead of

---

[14] It is one of the paradoxes of knowledge, incidentally, that thinking without words is impossible and thinking with them is often imprecise. This, however, is a problem for the philosophers, especially those who concern themselves with logic and semantics. See our discussion of Bacon's Idols of the Market Place in Chapter 1.

English. Madness consists, among other things, in imagining that our "soul" exists apart from the language our nurses happen to have taught us.[15]

How a language itself gets to be what it is and to contain the words it does is again a function of culture. The Eskimos, for example, have many words for "snow," whereas we have only one, which is qualified in use by adjectives. For them drifting snow, falling snow, light snow, heavy snow, wet snow, and melting snow all have different names. Similarly, the Arabs have different names for kneeling camels, standing camels, old camels, young camels, and pregnant camels, whereas we use adjectives rather than nouns to announce the differences.

As a final example from the field of language we may refer to the fact that Shakespeare, an Englishman, has a strong appeal to the Germans but scarcely any appeal to the French. The only possible explanation is a cultural one—one that concerns the "genius" of a language. Consider only the first line of one of the great soliloquies of Hamlet:

To be or not to be, that is the question.

In German this line gains, if possible, even greater grandeur and power:

Sein oder nicht sein, dass ist hier die Frage.

But in French the depth and significance disappear, and the line becomes faintly ridiculous:

Être ou ne pas être, telle est la question.

Something has disappeared that was there in the English and German. The words remain—it is a literal translation—but the profound philosophic beauty of the line has vanished into a linguistic limbo from which it is difficult to recapture its full and profound meaning.[16]

All societies seem to have ideas that are peculiar to their culture and that cannot be precisely translated into the language of another society. For

[15] *After Many a Summer Dies the Swan*, Harper & Row, Publishers, Incorporated, New York, 1939, pp. 309–310. In fact, as Max Müller has reminded us, "Every man, even the freest thinker, is a slave to the language in which he has been brought up." *The Science of Thought*, New York, 1887, vol. I, p. 273.

[16] The reverence of the Germans for Shakespeare is so great, incidentally, especially in the translation of A. W. von Schlegel, that they have ceased to think of him as English. Thus, a German attending a performance of the New York Shakespeare Festival was heard to remark to her companion that it wasn't at all bad, but not, of course, as good as the Schlegel original!

this reason translations from one language to another are difficult at best. One has to sacrifice either the flavor of the original or its meaning. As a famous French translator has said, *"Les traductions sont comme les femmes. Quand elles sont belles, elles ne sont pas fidèles; et quand elles sont fidèles, elles ne sont pas belles."* (Translations are like women. When they are beautiful they are not faithful, and when they are faithful they are not beautiful.)

Some words, in addition, cannot be translated at all into another language, except by circumlocution, because there is no word in the second language that corresponds to them. The German word *Weltanschauung*, for example, to which we referred earlier, cannot be exactly rendered into English. We translated it literally as "world view," but to the German the word implies much more—an entire philosophy of life. The full meaning cannot be conveyed by any English expression. The French word *rapport* likewise cannot be translated into English, and consequently we use it in its French form in English speech. We say, for example, that the first task of the social worker is to establish rapport with her client, and by this we mean something more than sympathy because sympathy subtly implies condescension, an implication that is absent in the French original. Many words in the German philosophic vocabulary are Latin rather than Germanic in origin because the late medieval translators of the works of St. Thomas Aquinas could find no German equivalents for the Latin concepts and therefore had to "Germanize" the Latin originals.

English also has words and expressions that are untranslatable. "Fair play," for example, usually appears as *fair-play* in French and German discourse. For that matter, the American "OK" defies translation into any language in the world, including English. A headline on the sports page of an American tabloid—CUBS COOL BUCS—would baffle a European with the most accurate and precise knowledge of academic English, and the famous headline which once appeared in *Variety*, the newspaper of the American entertainment world—STIX NIX HIX PIX—can be understood by only a minority of Americans themselves.[17]

If what we think and what we say are functions of our culture, so also of course is what we learn. We can obviously learn only what is in our culture and, in complex societies, only a small part of that. The Eskimo adolescent learns how to conceal a bent sliver of bone in frozen meat as a means of catching a polar bear. The Orokaiva boy learns how to make fly and fish traps. The Mundugumor youth learns that in order to achieve adult status in his society he will have to kill a human being—or did learn this,

---

[17] Perhaps we should provide a translation. The headline means that motion pictures of rural life do not sell well in rural areas.

rather, before the practice was stopped by the colonial authority. American boys and girls learn natural history and political history, algebra and geometry, English literature and, possibly, sociology. They also learn at various ages how to roller skate, ride a bicycle, and drive a car. And they learn baseball. No one who has had no contact with American culture could possibly explain the meaning of an unassisted triple play.

Whether we learn, and how much we can learn, is of course a function of intelligence. But what we learn is a function of culture. Not everybody in our society can become a famous mathematician or musician, in spite of the fact that mathematics and music are a part of our culture. A certain native talent is required for accomplishment in these fields. On the other hand, we have no way of knowing how many unsung geniuses exist in other parts of the world whose native talent for mathematics or music can find no expression because these achievements are no part of their culture. Nothing we know about intelligence permits us to draw the conclusion that an Eskimo or an Orokaiva adolescent could not, in another cultural setting, learn the elements of the differential and integral calculus as well as an American college student. The differences here are cultural, not biological. A striking story in this respect comes to us from Paraguay. In the interior of that country there lives a primitive tribe known as the Guayaki, a tribe with a Stone Age culture, subsisting on honey and wild beasts. These people once abandoned a two-year-old girl in moving from one encampment to another. The girl was discovered by a professor at Lima University, Peru, who was exploring in the region. He took her back to Lima, where he and his wife raised her as part of their family. By the time she was seventeen she had become a brilliant student of biology, and her teachers and associates were predicting an outstanding career for her in that field of intellectual endeavor.[18] It is instructive to contrast this case with that of the Pennsylvania child mentioned earlier in this chapter.

Not only our knowledge and our education but also our goals and our aspirations are set for us by the culture of our society. What we are and what we want to become can therefore be understood only with reference to culture. No Zūni Indian wants to be a successful bond salesman, no Eskimo wants to win the Nobel prize for literature, no Hottentot wants to become an atomic physicist, no Andaman Islander wants to run the four-minute mile, no Zulu wants to become a professor of philosophy, and no Bantu wants to become a burlesque comedian. Similarly, no American wants to become a witch doctor. The occupational choices of nonliterate peoples, of course, are quite restricted, if indeed they have any choices at all. The

---

[18] This story is reported by Claude Lévi-Strauss, who, incidentally, is one of the world's most distinguished anthropologists.

situation is different with respect to literate peoples because they have cultural alternatives. But in all cases the goals and aspirations coincide with the possibilities contained in the culture.

One of the pleasures of anthropology is that it discovers and exhibits facts and contrasts from exotic cultures, and the reader who wishes to pursue this kind of information has a fascinating literature in store for him. For our purposes we have said enough to indicate that the pattern of life that people follow in various societies depends, always within appropriate geographical and biological limitations, upon the culture of those societies. We have surely said enough to satisfy even the most skeptical reader that culture is the key concept in all attempts to explain and to understand the social life of man.

4. Culture and Biology

If we look at the world's societies from past to present, from primitive to civilized, and from East to West, we shall be impressed with the almost illimitable variations that they display. They are all made up of human beings who live in groups with one another, but their ways of doing things, their patterns of living—their cultures, in short—exhibit thousands of differences in detail and in design. As biological specimens all people are pretty much alike. They all have two eyes, two ears, four limbs, a nose, and a mouth; and further anatomical observation discloses only the most superficial and indeed inconsequential differences. It is in the realm of culture, not biology, that the differences become significant and consequential. There are therefore certain relationships between culture and the organism that we now wish to examine.

Sometimes cultural and biological factors operate in harmony; sometimes they work against each other. It is obvious that the imperious needs of the body may force us to violate the standards of our culture and to commit antisocial acts. A man who is starving is not one who is overly impressed with the sanctity of the laws concerning property nor with the beneficence of the economic system under which he lives. A society under siege, where physical mobility is limited, or one experiencing the crisis of famine, does not exhibit the cultural patterns that are normal or usual in that society. Biological disabilities of one kind or another—for example, impairment of the brain—may result in social irresponsibility. All of these facts are obvious and require no elaboration.

What may not be so obvious is that cultural factors exert influences upon biological factors, and may ultimately alter their character. A striking and even terrifying illustration is the effect of atomic radiation upon animal and human reproduction. Furthermore, what is considered normal and abnormal may be a matter of cultural definition. Epilepsy, even when abnormal in the sense that it is of infrequent occurrence, has sometimes been considered a sacred disease in societies other than our own, and the man or woman who is "fortunate" enough to be afflicted with it may be surrounded by special privileges. Symptoms associated with paranoia[19] in our society may confer prestige upon people who possess them in certain primitive societies. Indeed, some anthropologists have maintained that paranoid behavior is "normal" behavior in some societies.[20]

It is important for us to recognize, however, that cultural patterns may have deleterious effects upon the physiology and anatomy of the human organism and that practices that are culturally approved, and even required, may at the same time be biologically harmful. It is customary and instructive to refer to primitive societies for illustrations of this point. Thus, stretching the lips, filing the teeth, scarification of the flesh, piercing of tongues and ears, induced obesity, and artificial pigmentation of the skin have all been used as means of bodily ornamentation in various nonliterate societies. Indeed, the art of tattooing continues to be practiced in literate societies.

Initiation rites of one sort or another found in many societies, not excepting some called civilized, involve flogging, burning, mutilating, the tearing of flesh, the forced ingestion of strange foods and drugs, or body-racking ordeals of hunger and thirst. People have starved in the midst of plenty because the food physically available to them was, for one reason or another, culturally tabooed. The cannibal chieftain cannot readily understand why people in some societies would rather go hungry than eat their neighbors, and he thinks it the height of foolishness to abstain from adding enemies to the menu. Diet, as we have seen, is a cultural and not a physiological phenomenon. And a little brown man in India, whose name was Gandhi, fasted on several occasions to what seemed the limit of organic endurance in order to embarrass a government.

The effects of certain cultural practices on anatomy may be further indicated by a wide range of illustrations drawn from the various occupations of our own society. The blacksmith possesses, on poetic authority, a mighty arm; cauliflower ears are the marks of boxers; enlarged hearts are associated with athletes in general and especially with those who are

---

[19] The name for the mental disease in which the victim suffers from delusions of persecution.

[20] Considerable caution has to be exercised in this regard, however. "In general the psychopathologies that get rewarded among primitives are only the mild or transient ones. A markedly deteriorative psychosis, even a persistent and pointless delusion, such as a man's acting out the belief that he was a tree, would be rated and deplored by them much as by us. It is the lighter aberrations from objective reality that can win social approval." A. L. Kroeber, "Psychosis or Social Sanction." *The Nature of Culture, op. cit.,* p. 318.

successful at track and field events. Baseball pitchers suffer a number of ailments that are regularly encountered in no other activity. Among these ailments, according to a physician who made a specialty of them, are bursitis, synovitis (inflammation of the synovial membrane), calcified deposits in the tendons, myositis (inflammation of the muscles), osteoarthritis, unusual fractures and dislocations, and a severe pain somewhat inelegantly known as "pitcher's elbow." The incidence of bursitis, an inflammation of the small sac between the joints of arm and shoulder, is also high among stenographers. And college professors, as a class, possibly because they read so many lines of type and so much of their students' poor handwriting, almost universally develop impairments of vision. Indeed, spectacles are practically a badge of the teaching profession. Miners suffer from silicosis and house painters from lead poisoning. All of these cases, and many more we could mention, illustrate how the various occupations of our culture influence, and sometimes damage, the structure and functions of the human organism.

Certain other aspects of the culture may also have a deleterious effect on health. For example, the high incidence of ulcers in our society, which occur much more often in males than in females, is often explained by reference to the competitiveness of our contemporary culture. On the more trivial side, it may be conjectured that tight collars and neckties and belts interfere with circulation. No law school graduate however, would present himself to the personnel director of a Wall Street law firm without a collar and tie, even though the interview situation itself is sufficient to raise the blood pressure and to activate the sweat glands.

Of similar interest in this regard is the harm that American women do to their bodies in order to conform to cultural standards of feminine beauty. Diets and so-called "success schools" represent a direct interference of cultural factors with physiological functioning. High heels are inimical to healthy feet and directly affect the anatomy of the arch, and yet fashion requires them on many occasions.

More interesting still, perhaps, is the fact that standards of feminine beauty are themselves cultural standards and not physical ones. They are susceptible to a quite incredible variation from one society to another and to radical changes within the same society in the course of time. In certain parts of Africa, for example, the most desirable females are the fattest ones. When the girls reach the marriageable age their mothers take them away from the tribal encampment, stuff them with rich and heavy foods, and rub them with butter, which they use as a cosmetic rather than as a food. If the young lady gains so much weight that she can hardly walk, the regimen is considered a success and she has no trouble finding suitors when she returns to the tribe. Indeed, the story is told of a talented and internationally famous American actress who, at a ceremonial dinner in London, captivated all of the guests with her personal charm and grace and wit. She managed also to chat amiably with the guest at her left, an African chief, who, at the conclusion of the dinner, said to her in his impeccable Oxford accent, "I could easily fall in love with you if only you were black and fat."

Once again, however, it is not necessary to go to London, or to Africa, in order to illustrate a point. In our own American society in as short a period as fifty years changes have occurred in standards of feminine beauty that one could describe, with some understatement, as interesting. The "pin-up girl" who adorned so many bulkheads and barracks walls of the Vietnam War bears little resemblance to her older sister of the Korean War. The sex is the same, but the surface has undergone alteration.

The human body itself is no mere physiological phenomenon but, much more importantly, a cultural phenomenon. It means different things to different peoples in different times and places. The diseases with which it is afflicted, the demands that are made upon it, and the trials and travails that affect its mortal life—all these can be understood only by taking culture into account. Physiology is not enough. Whether the body is to be considered the noble and splendid temple of physical beauty or the outward and somewhat bothersome shell for an immortal soul, or a combination of both, depends entirely upon culture. The human body is a physiological fact, but it is a cultural value.

In short, except for the few totally unconditioned reflexes—for example, the knee jerk or the blinking of the eyes—it is difficult to find physiological functions that are purely physiological in character. A knee jerk is physiological but a kickoff in football is cultural; a blink is physiological but a wink is cultural. With only a few exceptions, and those relatively unimportant ones, all of these functions appear in situations that are clearly set and regulated by culture. The more basic the function, the more stringent becomes the cultural regulation, and the satisfaction of such biological needs as food, sex, and elimination is accomplished only in terms of norms that are cultural in both origin and essence. Satisfaction and denial alike, in all the important cases, require not biological but cultural explanations.

This is obviously a theme that can be expanded to many pages. We have chosen only enough examples to show that, although biological factors indubitably have a great deal to do with culture, it is no less true that cultural factors, in turn, exert a remarkable influence upon biological and, especially, physiological functions. Biologically man may be only an inexpensive compound of chemicals, destined to disintegrate and utterly disappear, but culturally neither poet nor philosopher nor singer of songs, nor yet indeed sociologist, can do him justice.

5. Cultural Diffusion

We have remarked that differences in culture distinguish one society from another. We shall later have occasion to emphasize that these differences also distinguish one group from another within the same society. But culture does not come in sealed containers. So long as people move restlessly over the face of the earth, they will carry bits of culture from one place to another. Travelers and traders, soldiers and settlers, missionaries and migrant workers—all these and more have been instrumental in effecting a process known as cultural diffusion. By means of this process culture comes to be widely distributed, and what is invented or discovered in one society is spread to other societies all over the world. The modern arts of communication and transportation, the ease with which peoples meet, and the points at which societies are in contact have all facilitated cultural diffusion to such an extent that some things can now be found in almost every society, except perhaps the most isolated and most primitive.

Thus, there is the story of the African explorer who, penetrating with his party into the darkest parts of that once unknown continent, found a tribe of people never before seen by a white man, and among them a naked child sitting on a Standard Oil can. The author of this book, traveling some years ago in central Czechoslovakia, found few villages in that region without Ford tractors, Singer sewing machines, and Eastman Kodaks. As is well known, Coca-Cola can now be purchased in almost every part of the world. Similarly, Swiss watches and French wines and English tweeds and Russian caviar and Spanish sherry and Swedish automobiles can be found in almost all parts of the United States.

If material items are thus diffused, so also are ideas. The Christian religion, for example, has spread from its origin in the Eastern Mediterranean to almost every country. Scientific knowledge, in the absence of political restrictions, moves easily and rapidly from one society to another. Astronomical data have been exchanged between scientists whose nations were formally at war. Important books are translated into many languages. For that matter, our numbers and letters come originally from the Arabs and the Phoenicians respectively. Every ship that travels from one port to another is a vehicle of cultural diffusion, not merely with respect to the goods it carries in its hold, but also with respect to the customs of its crew.

It would be possible to fill many pages with examples of cultural diffusion, but at the moment we are interested in one particular lesson that this process teaches us. This lesson is that none of the complex societies to be found on earth today created more than a very few of the total number of cultural elements to be found in it. All of them have "borrowed" elements from other societies. Indeed, Ralph Linton estimated that in no case does the number of indigenous or native elements exceed 10 per cent of the total culture. Professor Linton's description of the elements of our own American culture that have come from other societies is so justly famous that it has been quoted in many books. We want to quote it again:

> Our solid American citizen awakens in a bed built on a pattern which originated in the Near East but which was modified in Northern Europe before it was transmitted to America. He throws back the covers made from cotton, domesticated in India, or linen, domesticated in the Near East, or wool from sheep, also domesticated in the Near East, or silk, the use of which was discovered in China. All of these materials have been spun and woven by processes invented in the Near East. He slips into his moccasins, invented by the Indians of the Eastern woodlands, and goes to the bathroom, whose fixtures are a mixture of European and American inventions, both of recent date. He takes off his pajamas, a garment invented in India, and washes with soap invented by the ancient Gauls. He then shaves, a masochistic rite which seems to have been derived from either Sumer or ancient Egypt.
>
> Returning to the bedroom, he removes his clothes from a chair of southern European type and proceeds to dress. He puts on garments whose form originally derived from the skin clothing of the nomads of the Asiatic steppes, puts on shoes made from skins tanned by a process invented in ancient Egypt, and cut to a pattern derived from the classical civilizations of the Mediterranean, and ties around his neck a strip of bright-colored cloth which is a vestigial survival of the shoulder shawls worn by the seventeenth-century Croatians. Before going out for breakfast he glances through the window, made of glass invented in Egypt, and if it is raining, puts on overshoes made of rubber discovered by the Central American Indians and takes an umbrella, invented in southeastern Asia. Upon his head he puts a hat made of felt, a material invented in the Asiatic steppes.
>
> On his way to breakfast he stops to buy a paper, paying for it with coins, an ancient Lydian invention. At the restaurant a whole new series of borrowed elements confronts him. His plate is made of a form of pottery invented in China. His knife is of steel, an alloy first made in southern India, his fork, a medieval Italian invention, and his spoon a derivative of a Roman original. He begins breakfast with an orange, from the eastern Mediterranean, a cantaloupe from Persia, or perhaps a piece of African watermelon. With this he has coffee, an Abyssinian plant, with cream and sugar. Both the domestication of cows and the idea of milking them originated in the Near East, while sugar was first made in India. After his fruit and first coffee he goes on to waffles, cakes made by a Scandinavian technique from wheat domesticated in Asia Minor. Over these he pours maple syrup, invented by the Indians of the Eastern woodlands. As a side dish he may have the eggs of a species of bird domesticated in Indo-China, or thin strips of the flesh of an animal domesticated in Eastern Asia, which have been salted and smoked by a process developed in northern Europe.

When our friend has finished eating, he settles back to smoke, an American Indian habit, consuming a plant domesticated in Brazil in either a pipe, derived from the Indians of Virginia, or a cigarette, derived from Mexico. If he is hardy enough he may even attempt a cigar, transmitted to us from the Antilles by way of Spain. While smoking he reads the news of the day, imprinted in characters invented in Germany. As he absorbs the accounts of foreign troubles he will, if he is a good conservative citizen, thank a Hebrew deity in an Indo-European language that he is 100 per cent American.[21]

6. Summary

In this chapter we have attempted to explain the meaning of "culture," a concept that has been called the most important analytical tool in contemporary social science. In anthropology and sociology this word does not mean what it does in ordinary conversation nor even what it is likely to mean to historians. It refers, rather, to the entire complex of what man has and does and thinks as a member of society. It includes all the ways of living and doing and thinking that have been passed down from one generation to another and that have become an accepted part of a society. It is culture that distinguishes man from the lower animals, especially from those, like the anthropoid apes, with whom he otherwise has so much in common. It is culture that distinguishes the human child from the feral child and that indeed makes him human. Culture consists of everything we have learned to think and do and use as members of society, as people who are in constant social interaction with other people.

The concept of culture has a number of synonyms that are used in the literature to emphasize some of its important characteristics and to focus attention upon them. Among these synonyms, we discussed (1) learned behavior, (2) the social heritage, (3) the superorganic, and (4) design for living. Each of these synonymous expressions, as we have said, emphasizes a different aspect of a complex phenomenon and focuses attention upon different characteristics, all of which, however, are essential to an understanding of the basic concept.

Next, we discoursed at length upon the importance of culture in human life and indicated how it determines what we see, what we think, what we learn, how we talk and read, the houses we live in, the food we eat, the liquids we drink, and so on through a myriad of examples. We then considered somewhat briefly the reciprocal influences between biological

---

[21] Ralph Linton, *The Study of Man,* Appleton-Century-Crofts, Inc., New York, 1936, pp. 326–327. See the entire chapter entitled "Diffusion," pp. 324–346. Note that even the "100 per cent American" is Arabic, Latin, and Italian in origin.

and cultural factors and again gained an opportunity to stress the importance of culture.

Finally, we pointed out that the culture of each society is only in small part a product of its own invention and discovery and that by far the largest part, except in the case of the most isolated society, has been introduced from other societies and from other times. Culture, in short, is diffused from one society to another, and this process of cultural diffusion is a constant social process whenever societies are in contact and whenever and wherever peoples meet.

We thus have seen that whether we take a single individual in the course of his day or a single individual in the course of his life, everything he thinks and does and has and uses and *is*—apart, of course, from personal peculiarities and idiosyncrasies—is a function of his culture. Similarly, whether we take a society in a single day of its existence or follow it through its entire history, we cannot understand it without understanding its culture. In the broad spaces of the world and in the long stretches of historical time, it is culture that makes some people like and unlike other people in all the significant senses in which they are similar and different. And it is culture that makes societies like and unlike other societies.

If we were to end our discussion of culture at this point, however, we should be guilty of an oversimplification. Culture, after all, is a large and complex phenomenon, and cultural contrasts are easy to make. One of the real services of anthropology has been to illuminate these contrasts and to exhibit the tremendous range of cultural variation in human societies. As sociologists, however, we are not so much interested in the differences that societies exhibit as in the structural similarities that make all societies in a sense alike. We need, therefore, to inquire whether culture has certain structural characteristics wherever it appears. In order to answer this question, we must refine the concept still further and examine the form and content of culture in greater detail. These tasks occupy us in the following chapter.

Chapter 6

THE CONTENT OF CULTURE

HE PRECEDING chapter has emphasized the fact that people in different societies all over the world have different cultures. They think different thoughts, do different things, and use different implements and utensils. For this reason their lives run different courses and the cycles of day and year and season wear different aspects. The natives of Polynesia and the citizens of Paris accumulate different kinds of knowledge and cultivate different arts. The Eskimo and the Ethiopian nourish themselves with different foodstuffs and indulge in different ceremonies. The Spartan of the ancient Greek city-state and the Spaniard of the sixteenth century worshiped different gods and found different modes of enjoyment and relaxation and recreation. The Egyptian helot, the Roman hoplite, the Greek philosopher, the medieval monk, the Renaissance politician, the Elizabethan poet, and the Russian aristocrat of the nineteenth century all led different lives, entertained different ideas, and pursued different goals. No anatomical inquiry, however intimate and detailed, can explain these differences. The explanation is to be sought rather in the realm of culture.

This, at least, is the lesson of the preceding chapter, and it is a point worth repeating again and again. But culture is a complex and comprehensive phenomenon. In order to use the concept as a tool of sociological analysis it is necessary not only to define it and to insist upon its importance but also to break it down, as it were, and to consider its various components. In this chapter, therefore, we want to examine the structure of culture and inquire into its content.

One of the principal goals of sociology is to discover the sources of the fundamental order that society exhibits, the order that makes it possible for human beings to interact with one another and to live together in the same house, the same town, the same country, and the same world. If we are to do this we need, for one thing, to know a great deal more about culture than we were able to discuss in the preceding chapter.

It is apparent that, underlying all of the cultural diversities and disparities to be found in societies throughout the world and throughout the course of history, there are certain cultural similarities. People may worship different gods in different ways, but they all have a religion.[1] They may follow different occupations, but they all earn a living. Their vocal cords may vibrate in different rhythms, but they all speak a language. They may have different ideas about the universe and about man's place in it, but they all have some kind of answer to the question of human life and destiny. Their rituals and ceremonies may be so diverse as to defy exhaustive description, but they all, nevertheless, do have rituals and ceremonies. The material culture of a primitive society may be quite simple and, by our standards, poor in quality, that of a civilized society quite complex and rich in quantity, but all societies without exception have a material culture. If we have chosen, in the preceding chapter, to emphasize the differences in culture, we want in this one to demonstrate that culture everywhere can be broken down into the same categories and that everywhere it has the same components.

1. The Content of Culture

Many sociologists have classified the content of culture into two large components, material culture and nonmaterial culture. One sociologist, in fact, has used this distinction as the basis for a theory of cultural change.[2] The concept of material culture is clear enough. But the concept of nonmaterial culture is not quite so clear, except in the sense that it is a residual category, including everything that is not material. "Everything that is not material," however, may include items of several fundamentally different kinds, and this tendency to obscure significant distinctions is a

---

[1] Even in a country that is officially nonreligious there is a prophet (Karl Marx), a "holy" book (*Das Kapital*), a redeemer (Lenin), a hymn ("The Internationale"), a church (the Communist party), a heaven (the classless society), and an Apostles' Creed (*The Communist Manifesto*).
[2] The reference is to William F. Ogburn, whose theory is discussed in Chapter 20.

logical weakness of residual categories. We shall therefore adopt a threefold classification of the content of culture.

Our classification stems directly from the definition of culture as the complex whole that consists of all the ways we think and do and everything we have as members of society. Thinking and doing and having are three of the most fundamental categories in the grammar of any language. They give us the three components of culture—ideas, norms, and things. The last of these is the material culture mentioned above. Ideas and norms are both nonmaterial culture, but we distinguish them because they perform different functions in society and operate in different ways. We thus have the major categories or headings under which we can later locate the detailed items that make up this large phenomenon. The basic table on which we shall build now looks like this:

Culture

(Thinking)	*(Doing)*	*(Having)*
Ideas	Norms	Materiel

We shall discuss these three components of culture in some detail and fill in the table as we go along.

2. Ideas

If it is impossible, as we shall see, to count the material possessions of a people in a given society, it is inconceivable that anyone could take an inventory of their ideas. No questionnaire, no matter how extensive, could disclose them all. Many of them may be subliminal, in the sense that the people themselves may be only dimly aware of them or not aware at all. In literate societies ideas are recorded and written down and stored in books and libraries. Ideas thus make up the literature of the society in the broadest possible sense of that word. In nonliterate societies they constitute the lore and the legends of the tribe. The sociologist is not interested in the truth or falsity of the notions that prevail in various societies but only in the fact that some notions do prevail and help to determine the unique character of the lives that people live in these societies. It matters not whether these ideas are compounded into myths or into scientific truths about the universe, although we shall later make a distinction between ideas on the one hand and ideologies on the other. Men and societies are sustained by false notions and true notions alike, and what may seem true in one society may seem false in another, and the other way around.

The Greeks believed in many gods, gods of both sexes, who loved and laughed like human beings as they disported themselves on Mount Olympus. The Pilgrims who settled the first English colony in Massachusetts believed in one god, a male deity, who frowned upon pleasurable pursuits and who particularly did not like to see his people wasting their time or their substance. The Eskimos believe in several gods, but the most important one is a beautiful female deity named Sedna who lives with her father at the bottom of the sea and who, when she is pleased with her people, sees to it that they get enough to eat. The Russians, officially at least, believe in no god. All of these are but major variations in the religious ideas to be found in the world's societies. The minor variations, especially if we look at both literate and nonliterate societies, are infinite.

We find a similarly vast and heterogeneous collection of political ideas. Some peoples believe that their chiefs or kings are divinely ordained to rule them and to lead them into paths of power and glory. Some believe that the strongest should rule, or the wealthiest, or the wiliest, or the most excellent, or the most wise. Still others will support any small group that manages to gain control. And others believe in government through representation by the majority of the governed. Some, finally, adhere to an hereditary principle and attach significance to a royal family. These again are only major variations among many minor ones.

The people of some societies have certain ideas that are totally lacking in others. In our own society, for example, we believe that parallel lines in Euclidean space never meet, that bodies in a vacuum fall with the same velocity in independence of their mass, that pure water at sea level freezes at 32 degrees Fahrenheit, that the differential of x^2 is $2x$, and that—fateful equation—$e = mc^2$. The Watusi of Africa, the Maori of New Zealand, the Ona Indians of South America, the Hopi Indians of North America, the Polynesians of the South Seas, and the Laplanders of the northern regions have none of these ideas. The people of some societies do not know that there is any connection between sexual intercourse and the birth of a child, and some believe, on the contrary, that repeated intercourse is necessary to make the child grow in the womb. Some peoples believe that the birth of twins is clear evidence of adultery on the part of the mother. In different societies, also, people believe in the supernatural talents of medicine men or in the reality of voices from the spirit world or in the exorcism of witches by bell, book, and candle.

The ideas that people have and that are accepted in their societies (for otherwise they do not become a part of their culture) are inexhaustible in number. In the examples we have just used we have drawn only from the fields of religion, political philosophy, and science. It is impossible even to imagine, let alone to record, all of the ideas that have appeared in all the various societies from the beginning of historical time to the present and that still appear in contemporary societies. But it is easy to see that each society has its own collection and that the ideas of one differentiate it from all the others. What people think, in short, is an important component of their culture. Whether or not it is the most important component, in that it determines the character of the other two and through them the nature and historical destiny of a society, is a sociological issue that we discuss in the last chapter of this book.

We have already remarked that some of the ideas entertained by the members of a society are true and that others are false. Sociologically speaking, it is important to recognize that both kinds of ideas, the false as well as the true, influence human conduct and illuminate the contours of a society. Thus, the false notion, mentioned above, that the birth of twins is evidence of adultery may result in the corporal punishment of the mother. The false notion that the world is flat prevented the Portuguese navigators of the period preceding the voyages of Columbus from sailing very far out of sight of the coast line, lest their ships fall over the edge and into the abyss. The notion that the world is coming to an end in a specified number of days periodically induces the members of certain religious sects to sell all of their possessions and to climb to the highest hill in order to prepare for their transfer to another and presumably happier world. A proper Bostonian lady began at the advanced age of ninety-eight to study Hebrew in order, as she explained, to be able to greet her Creator in his native tongue. The notion that war is inevitable helps to hasten its coming. The false notion, entertained by many Americans, that the Negro is somehow inferior results in the patterns of prejudice and of segregation that are found in our country.

Examples of this sort could easily be multiplied. To generalize, however, we may say that there are three classes of ideas—those which are true, those which are false, and those whose truth or falsity has not been determined—and that all three kinds exert an effect when they are entertained by numbers of people and become an integral part of their culture.

From another point of view we may classify ideas into such categories as scientific propositions, legends, myths, superstitions, proverbs, and aphorisms. The number of scientific ideas in a culture, even a complex, "civilized," and "scientific" culture, is always less than the total number of ideas in that culture. Many phenomena mystify the human mind, and when men do not have scientific explanations they will construct others that, no less than the former, influence their conduct. Thus, there are home remedies for afflictions of one kind or another; auspicious dates, not including Friday the thirteenth, for launching great enterprises or for planting crops; weather predictions—"Rain before seven, clear before eleven," for example—that belong to folklore rather than to meteorology;[3] and so on.

The legend of George Washington and the cherry tree, invented out of whole cloth by Parson Weems, an early biographer of our first President, has been used to inculcate the virtues of truth telling in generations of American school children.[4] "Early to bed and early to rise makes a man healthy, wealthy, and wise," and all the other maxims of Benjamin Franklin are further examples of ideas that have exerted, and that continue to exert, an incalculable influence upon our society. Indeed, ideas, or ways of thinking—whether found in science, religion, literature, art, or in the folklore of the tribe—are an important component of culture. Like the cribs in which we are placed at birth, they are ready for us when we enter our society, and we accept a very large number of them, as we do the cribs, without criticism and without conscious deliberation.

At this point we can find in one column of our table of culture:

Culture

Ideas	Norms	Materiel
Scientific truths		
Religious beliefs		
Myths		
Legends		
Literature		
Superstitions		
Aphorisms		
Proverbs		
Folklore		

The task of classifying ideas is a complex one, and no one, perhaps, has succeeded in constructing a list that will be satisfactory for all purposes. We shall not contend that the list above is satisfactory. It may be maintained, for example, that some literature is devoid of ideas, that in the prose of Gertrude Stein and the poetry of E. E. Cummings, for example, the sound of the words and their arrangement are sometimes more important than

---

[3] Meteorologists have discovered, interestingly enough, that some of the weather lore present in our society has a basis in fact and can be supported by scientific evidence. This situation is not strange if we reflect that much of this lore grows out of human experience, which is only more refined and more rigorously systematized in science.

[4] The author is indebted to J. E. Hulett, Jr., for the observation that this legend tells us more about the culture of colonial society, and especially about father-son relations in that society, than it does about the truth-telling proclivities of the young George Washington.

ideas, which are the central concern in other writing. This objection we should be disposed to concede. It is possible, of course, for some writing to be altogether innocent of ideas. But for the most part this is not the case. The literature of a society ordinarily does express ideas, and these ideas become a part of the intellectual heritage of the people who live in the society. One may raise other objections to the classification, however. It may be contended on the one hand that the listing is not exhaustive of all types of ideas and on the other that the separate items are not mutually exclusive. But it will nevertheless serve to indicate the sort of things that we should include in the first of our major components of culture.

3. Norms

The concept of norms, one of the most important concepts in contemporary sociology, serves as a label for the second large component of culture. When we use this concept we refer not to ways of thinking but to ways of doing. Most of the things we do as members of society and most of the things we refrain from doing are cultural in character. When we talk about what people do in society we are interested, as sociologists, not in their behavior as such, but rather in the type of behavior that is considered socially acceptable or unacceptable. We are interested, in short, in conduct.

Behavior, as we have noted, may be mere impulse or response; conduct, on the other hand, implies the presence of norms, which are cultural. Our conduct conforms to certain standards, standards that are considered appropriate in the society in which we live. These standards and rules and expectations are what we call norms and, as we shall see, they are of several kinds. Conduct runs along in grooves; it is channelized in specific ways in each society, and it is these grooves, or channels, that constitute the norms. Without norms social life would be impossible and there would be no order in society. Without norms we should never know whether to shake hands with a new acquaintance, rub noses with him, kiss him, or give him an affectionate push. Society itself is a kind of order, which is made possible by the presence of norms, and norms are the essence of social organization. A good portion of this book is devoted to an examination of the implications of these statements, and another chapter is devoted in its entirety to the subject of norms. At the moment, therefore, we want only to illustrate the nature of a norm and to indicate its meaning.

Let us forget about sociology for a moment and imagine that we are at Yankee Stadium in New York on a warm summer afternoon late in the season. On the diamond, in front of us, the Leopards and the Camels (for this is a fictitious scene) have played a tight and almost scoreless game of baseball for eight and a half innings. In the fourth inning, however, the

Leopards managed to push a run across the plate on a scratch hit, a stolen base, a sacrifice bunt, and a long fly to the outfield. The score at the moment is as follows:

Leopards	000 100 000
Camels	000 000 00

The two teams are fighting for second place in the league and this game is an important one since, for reasons of schedule, the loser may not be able to overtake the Beavers, who are in first place. In the bottom half of the ninth the Camels come to bat for their last chance. It is the inning of sudden death, and we are all sitting on the edge of our seats.

The first batter, Bill Hanselman, is retired on a pop-up foul to the third baseman. One out. The second batter, Leo Lasswell, gets a clean single through the box and out into center field. One out and Leo on first. The next batter, a pinch hitter named Fritz Markle, after running the count to two balls and two strikes, raps the ball sharply on the ground into deep short. The Leopard shortstop, the best in the league, gathers it in and tosses to the second baseman for the force play. The throw to first, however, is not in time, and Fritz is safe on the initial sack.

At this point we notice, to our amazement, that Leo Lasswell is standing on third, having run across the diamond through the pitcher's box from first. The base umpire, Gabby Lewis, strides over to third in all his official majesty and thumbs Leo out of the game. Leo, who is never at a loss for words, refuses to leave, and the dialogue, inaudible to the spectators, goes something like this:

"Ya big bum," screams Leo. "Nobody tagged me. Nobody even threw the ball to third."

"What," bellows Gabby, "has that got to do with it? Get out of here!"

"Calm down, Gabby," answers Leo. "Even a blind man like you can see that if I had gone to second I would have been out a mile. That's why I had to go to third. From here mebbe I can score, and we need the run. Look at the scoreboard!"

"But . . . but . . . ." sputters the umpire, flabbergasted by the argument; "you have to touch second on your way to third and you were nowhere near second base."

"You're so right," replies Leo, more reasonably now. "But I did touch the pitcher's slab on the way over, to make up for missing second. If you'd have been awake you would have seen me hit the rubber."

"But you can't do that, you jughead!" explodes Gabby, "it's against the rules."

"Rules, schmules," mutters Leo. "Rules are nothing but conventions. Rules are made for baseball players, not baseball players for rules. We gotta give up the rules. Otherwise we might lose the game."

At this moment three men attired in white, whose approach Leo has not observed, come up to him and, with a kind of professional gentleness, induce him to leave the game and go along with them.

We have of course, omitted all of the profanity in the above exchange and included all of the tired clichés of the sports writers. It is time, in fact, to dismiss the sad spectacle. It is perfectly apparent to everyone that baseball would be impossible without rules. If umpires capriciously decided that some balls could be caught on the first bounce and others on the fly, if pitchers demanded five balls instead of four and two strikes instead of three, if players batted in any order and ran the bases in any direction, if managers put sometimes nine and sometimes fifteen men on the field, and so on, there would be no such game as baseball. In such circumstances there would be no order on the diamond, but only confusion, pandemonium, and chaos. The rules of baseball are its norms.

What may not be so apparent is that what happens in the stands is similarly guided by rules. The spectators pay a stipulated price for their tickets, enter at certain gates, and depart by certain others. In very small groups of people it will be noticed that the women go through these gates ahead of the men and that the men, not the women, buy the tickets. Tickets, in turn, are sold by ticket sellers and not by policemen or peanut vendors. Some people, not necessarily the strongest, sit in boxes, and others, not necessarily the weakest, occupy the bleachers. The hawkers who sell popcorn and peanuts, candy and chewing gum, will accept products of the United States Mint for their wares but not Austrian schillings or Polish zlotys. Nor do they sell beer at one price to the poor and another to the rich. The spectators do not attempt to sit in the dugouts, nor do they try to take a turn at bat. They are permitted, however, to offer advice, and this they do with enthusiasm.

And so with all the situations in society. Society is not a game, but it too has its rules. Not all of the rules of society are enforced by umpires or other officials, however, and some are almost self-enforcing in a sense, as we shall see. Furthermore, the rules of society are of several different kinds, and many of them operate in a fashion somewhat different from the rules of baseball. But everywhere, in all societies, there are rules, and it is these rules that are the norms of these societies. The category of norms, as the second large component of culture, includes rules, expectations, and standardized procedures—in short, ways of behaving in almost all of the situations that we confront and in which we participate.

Let us consider another norm, one that is a procedure rather than a rule. Suppose, for example, that we wish to communicate with someone who is in the vicinity but outside the range of our voice and vision. There are several ways in which we may do this. We may go out and try to find this person and communicate with him orally. We may light a fire and send some smoke signals. We may beat a drum according to a prearranged code known to both of us. We may hire an errand boy and give him the message to deliver. In our society, however, it is unlikely that we shall adopt any of these alternatives. It is more probable that we shall either telephone or write a letter. Using the telephone and writing letters are thus norms of communication in our society. We adopt them almost without thinking because they are standardized procedures.

There are other norms associated with these simple actions. When we write a letter, for example, we ordinarily place the date and place of origin at the top of the paper. We begin with a salutation that includes the word "dear." This word is not a term of endearment, and it implies no particular intimacy or affection. Indeed, we use it in addressing people we do not know at all, as well as in addressing people we may actively dislike. The salutation is nevertheless a norm to which we all conform. Similarly, we end the letter with something called a "complimentary close"—"Yours very truly" or "Sincerely yours," for example—and we sign our names even if the rest of the letter is typewritten. In other words, there are certain accepted ways of writing a letter, and these ways are norms. The norms differ for personal letters and business letters, but the writer in each case conforms to them. Deviation from them attracts attention and is somehow jarring or unsettling to the recipient, as when we receive a typewritten letter to which our correspondent has forgotten to append his signature.

Similarly, if one wants to take a book out of a library, there are certain accepted and standardized ways of doing it. These ways, or norms, may be slightly different for different libraries, but in general they are pretty much the same for all of the libraries in our society. One might simply take the book off the shelves, hide it, and walk off with it, but to do so would clearly violate a norm. One is expected to walk and talk quietly in a library, to have the book checked out by signing for it in some way, not to deface or mutilate it, to bring it back on or before the date it is due, and to pay a fine for a tardy return. One is not expected to make love to the librarian, to ask her for a summary of the news of the day, to request her to read the book and give a précis of its contents, to inquire if she attended church last Sunday, or to ask her if she is satisfied with her salary. A given individual in this situation may, of course, do only some of the things expected of him and may, in addition, do some of the things not expected, but the conventional procedures are norms nevertheless. They are outlines of expectations in this situation.

The same observations may be made about all of the social situations in which we find ourselves. Thus, not only writing a letter and using a library, but setting a table, making a speech, attending a class, playing in an orchestra, watching a football game, buying groceries, depositing money in a bank, parking a car, riding an airliner, purchasing tickets—all of these activities and a myriad others involve norms. The norms that affect direct social interaction with other people are perhaps especially apparent, but almost every situation we confront contains them, whether other people are immediately present or not. They may thus be thought of as general guides to conduct.

We said "almost" in the preceding paragraph because there are certain exceptions, situations that are not "covered" or controlled by norms. These are situations that are trivial, novel, or rare. As an example of the first, society makes no effort to guide or control the order in which we put on our shoes, whether the right one first or the left. The matter is utterly trivial. Society is similarly indifferent in our choice of "Good morning" as a greeting even though it is fifteen minutes after noon. No one accuses us of falsehood. As an example of the novel, we know what Alexander Graham Bell said to his assistant ("Watson, come here; I want you.") in the first telephone conversation in history, but there was no norm to which he could conform. There was no precedent, and thus no norm. There are no norms, in short, for wholly unprecedented situations. Finally, as an example of the rare, what does one say when writing a letter to a close friend whose brother has just been indicted on a homicide charge? One hopes that this situation is so rare that no norm need come into being and that each situation of its kind can be handled in its own context by the individuals who are unfortunately involved. With these few exceptions, however, which do not affect the stability and order of society itself, norms are ubiquitous and universal.

By and large, whatever we do, whenever and wherever we do it, falls into certain patterns that are set for us by our society. There are norms for meeting people and norms for taking leave of them, norms for writing and norms for speaking, norms for eating and drinking, norms for playing and working, norms for dating and dancing, norms in classrooms and in cafeterias, norms in hospitals and hotels, and so on for every conceivable activity in almost every conceivable situation. Wearing clothes, sleeping at night, eating three meals a day, cheering the home team, drinking from a glass, marrying one wife at a time, paying bills on the first of the month, speaking a language, writing from left to right, taking examinations at the end of a semester—all these and countless thousands more are norms.

It is apparent too that the norms of one society are different from the norms of another. When we greet a person in our society we are likely to shake hands, but not to rub noses. American males do not kiss each other—the notion is abhorrent to us—but a French general bestowing a medal upon a soldier will kiss him on both cheeks. Some peoples, as we have seen, eat snakes and scorpions and snails; others eat sausages and sauerkraut. Some peoples use water for drinking, others only for washing. Beef and milk, as we have also seen, are considerable items in the diet of some peoples; others regard the cow as sacred and look upon the consumption of any of its products as reprehensible from a religious point of view. Some peoples converse in English, others in Swahili. The rules of grammar, similarly, are norms. It is not good English to carelessly split infinitives, and prepositions are poor words to end sentences with.

In a later section of this chapter we shall consider the question of whether there are any absolute or universal norms. Here we want only to emphasize that the norms, like the other major components of culture, tend to vary from one society to another and in all societies through the periods of their historical existence. As suggested above, norms are of central concern to sociology not only because they regularize human conduct but also because they contribute order and stability to human societies. A norm, in short, is a standardized mode of procedure, a way of doing something that is acceptable to our society. It thus belongs to the second column in our table of culture.

4. Materiel

We have now discussed ways of thinking and ways of doing and are ready to introduce the third major component of culture—what we have as members of society. This component consists of things; it is the material culture or, as we shall call it, *materiel*. Materiel, of course, is the most tangible, the most obvious, and the most easily understood of the components of culture. This category includes all of the material items that the members of a society have and use. It would be an enormous, if not an impossible, task to list all the materiel of even a very small and simple society, and this difficulty increases in dimension as we move to the large and complex societies with which we are best acquainted. No one could possibly take a complete inventory of all the material things to be found in the culture of the United States in the twentieth century. No matter how extensive, no such list would ever be complete. The task of classifying these items—from safety pins to lunar modules and from thumbtacks to sky-scrapers—would itself stagger the imagination. Neither the Sears Roebuck catalogue by itself nor all the catalogues together would exhaust the material possessions of the American people, the things they have and use. It would be difficult enough to count and classify the material objects in a single house. Materiel has a way of accumulating, like old and treasured objects in an attic, so that each generation in a complex society has more of it than its predecessor. The automobile, the radio, the airplane, the motion-picture projector, the television set, and the lunar module, for example, were all unknown to men who lived only a hundred years ago.

When an archeologist digs up an ancient city or subterranean village, it is the remnants of the material culture that he finds. The norms of the people who once lived there and the ideas they entertained cannot be disclosed by ax and spade. But the fact that these norms and these ideas can be inferred, to some extent at least, from the material remains and that the archeologist can reconstruct the life of these societies indicates that there is a close connection between materiel and the other parts of culture. "The world is so full of a number of things" that, whether or not we should all be as happy as kings, they exert an ineluctable influence on our lives.

Quantitatively speaking, some societies have a richer collection of materiel than do others. We may be inclined to call the former more "advanced," the latter more "primitive." But such a judgment should not imply that one society is therefore superior to another. Gadgets and gimmicks do not necessarily contribute to happiness, however much they may facilitate the accomplishment of certain tasks. Furthermore, the tasks themselves may not be worth doing. If, however, we cannot evaluate societies in terms of their material culture, we can at least compare them and differentiate them on this basis. We should not expect, for example, to find a spark plug in the Watusi society, a baseball bat in Bali, a monastery in Iceland, a prayer stick in Salt Lake City, a bull-roarer in Dubuque, a swimming pool among the Eskimos, an astronomical observatory on Sakhalin Island, and so on. Each society, in other words, has its own collection of material culture traits, and this collection, in spite of the cultural diffusion discussed in the preceding chapter, helps to differentiate it from all the rest.

Some sociologists do not like to include materiel under the concept of culture on the ground that culture consists only of ideas or that it has a meaning only after it has been "internalized," so to speak, and becomes a customary part of the conduct of the members of a society. We ourselves, in discussing the superorganic, which is one of the synonyms of culture, pointed out that the same material objects may have different meanings to the members of different societies. Beads and mirrors, for example, may be mediums of exchange in some societies and ornaments in others. The cost of armaments has induced someone to remark that the difference between primitive and civilized peoples is that the former use shells for money and the latter money for shells. These facts, of course, we have no disposition to deny.

But it is necessary to notice that the material culture of a society precedes the birth of a given individual in that society and to that material culture he must adjust his life. Our own children today learn to roller-skate, to ride wagons and scooters and tricycles and bicycles, and later to drive automobiles, because these vehicles are presented to them by their society and are a part of their culture. The size of the house in which we live and the arrangement of its rooms affect our patterns of daily living. Similarly, the arrangement of buildings and streets in our cities and the location of railroads, highways, and subways have a great deal to do with our physical movements. Highways and bridges and buildings—to say nothing of knives and forks and spoons—are laid out for us when we appear upon the scene, and such material arrangements as these influence our behavior and determine our conduct in both general and specific situations. No motorist wishing to drive from New Jersey directly to Manhattan is going to cross the Hudson River except by way of the George Washington Bridge, the Lincoln Tunnel, or the Holland Tunnel, and one who tries another route is either going to drown or find himself in Bellevue Hospital under close observation. Materiel, like other aspects of culture, is inexorable in its way and, in some senses at least, is more rigid and unyielding than ideas and norms. The question of "internalizing" this culture is in many cases academic because frequently there is no alternative.

If we fail to pursue this subject further, the reason is not that it is unimportant but that illustrations are ridiculously easy to accumulate. A society that has clocks and watches in its material culture will exhibit a different tempo from one in which these instruments are absent. Changes in societies produced by the introduction of automobiles, airplanes, radios, and television sets are almost beyond reckoning, and their ramifications can seldom be predicted in detail. We may conclude this section with the observation that in primitive societies the physical environment consists largely of the geographic features discussed in our second chapter but that in complex societies such as our own, and especially in our cities, the physical environment consists in addition, and in a large and more important part, of the material culture.

Our table of culture, as constructed up to this point, looks like this:

Culture

Ideas	Norms	Materiel
Scientific truths		Machines
Religious beliefs		Tools
Myths		Utensils
Legends		Buildings
Literature		Roads
Superstitions		Bridges
Aphorisms		Artifacts
Proverbs		Objets d'art
Folklore		Clothing
		Vehicles
		Furniture
		Foodstuffs
		Medicines

The items under both ideas and materiel could obviously be extended. So far we have no similar listing under norms. Norms, however, are so important that we devote a succeeding chapter to them in its entirety.

5. Ideologies

We have now discussed, in a preliminary fashion, the three major components of culture—ideas, norms, and materiel. Some kinds of culture may not fit clearly into only one of these compartments but may belong rather to two or even three of them. A work of art, for example, may partake of the nature of all three. Thus, it has a material component, the pigment and canvas in the case of a painting, an idea that informs it, and aesthetic norms to which it conforms. Similarly, in the case of music, a solo by a virtuoso on the violin would not adequately be described by referring to the wood of which the instrument is made nor could his performance be regarded merely as running the rosined tail of a dead horse over the entrails of a dead cat. The music also means something. It reflects the ideas of composer, interpreter, and audience alike, even though, unless it is program music, these ideas may be difficult to articulate. Finally, the playing of the selection also conforms to certain norms. A violin solo is appropriate in certain circumstances and inappropriate in others, and an awareness of aesthetic norms enables us to judge that there are differences between the renditions of the same selection by a great artist on the one hand and a beginner on the other. A work of art, in short, exhibits all three of the components of culture.

So also we find phenomena that relate two of these components to each other and that stand, in a sense, between them. We shall refer to combinations of ideas and norms as *ideologies*, which would appear in our table as follows:

Culture

Ideas		Norms	Materiel
	Ideologies		

When we are presented with an idea, we are likely to ask whether it is true or false, and we have already had occasion to observe that true and false ideas alike exert an influence in our societies. When we are presented with a norm, a way of doing things, on the other hand, we are likely to inquire whether it is "right" or "wrong," or "good" or "bad," or "efficient" or "inefficient." In some cases, however, we raise these questions about ideas too. We want to know not only whether certain ideas are true or false but also whether they are good or bad, and frequently this second question is more important than the first. Ideas that are evaluated in this way are what we call ideologies.[5] More precisely, an ideology is an idea supported by a norm. We are encouraged to believe it, not because it is true, but because such belief is regarded as right and proper in our society. Let us examine this matter a little more closely.

Some of our ideas, and particularly those we should include in the category of scientific knowledge, are morally neutral. Thus, the Pythagorean theorem is true in terms of the axioms and postulates of Euclid. We do not ask whether it is a "good" theorem in addition; indeed the question is meaningless. No one, except perhaps our geometry teachers, exerts any pressure upon us to believe it, nor do we gain moral stature when we declare that it is true. The situation is the same with respect to the ideas contained in the whole of mathematics, those contained in the textbooks of the various sciences, and those to be found in almanacs, telephone directories, catalogues, statistical tabulations, and historical records. These ideas may be true or false, but not good or bad, proper or improper; they are not ideologies, and we gain no moral approbation by accepting or rejecting them.

There are other ideas, however, that we are expected to believe not

---

[5] Some writers might prefer to call these "values." This, however, involves one of the most difficult of all problems of philosophy; in fact, an entire subdivision of philosophy—named axiology, or value theory—is devoted to it. It seems desirable, therefore, to avoid the word.

because they are true—indeed the question of truth may be impossible to determine—but because they are considered right or good or proper in our society. These are the ideologies, the ideas that we have a social obligation to believe, the ideas that we are required to believe if we wish to remain in good standing in our social groups. All societies exert pressure upon their members to adhere to some beliefs and to reject others. Propositions asserting, for example, that there is only one God, that the human soul is immortal, that monogamy is the preferable form of marriage, that atheism is wrong, that extramarital sex experience is immoral, that free enterprise is good, that infant industries ought to be protected by tariffs—all these, and hundreds like them, are ideologies. All who share the contemporary culture of the United States are expected to hold these beliefs, and the man who publicly challenges any one of them will be given short shrift by most of his associates and by the members of his larger social circle. An almost sacred quality adheres to these ideologies, and any deviation in principle is regarded as "un-American."

The Declaration of Independence, known to every American and celebrated on the Fourth of July, states as a self-evident truth that all men are created equal. This proposition is an ideology, not a scientific truth. Indeed, we know on scientific grounds that it is false. Men are not equal Some are tall and some short, some fat and some thin, some black and some white, some intelligent and some stupid, some rich and some poor, and so on through an entire catalogue of differences. But such considerations are obviously irrelevant to the proposition. The proposition means that all men are equal in the sight of God and should be equal in the sight of their government. In this sense the proposition is ideological rather than scientific. One expresses his "Americanism" by supporting this ideology, and belief in it is a patriotic obligation. We are proud to acknowledge this proposition and we regard the Declaration that contains it as one of the ringing documents of human history.

It is apparent that all societies, even the most primitive, have ideologies and that these ideologies are an intimate and important part of their culture. Each society regards its central ideologies as sacred and tolerates no skepticism with respect to them. Indeed, it is a significant sociological fact that the pressure to believe them is frequently stronger than the pressure to conform to the norms of conduct to which they are related. Thus, in our society it is easier to commit adultery than it is to advocate it.

In the late thirties, for example, the English philosopher Bertrand Russell was appointed to the faculty of The City College of New York in order to offer instruction in mathematical logic. The appointment aroused violent and ultimately successful opposition on the ground that Lord Russell, in one of his early books, had recommended that the taboo on adultery be reconsidered and suggested that its relaxation might contribute to the stability of marriage. It is important to recognize that the philosopher himself was not accused of committing adultery, nor did his opponents make it altogether clear what relation his views on morals might have to his teaching of mathematical logic. The fact that he had once questioned an ideology was sufficient. Funds for his salary were dropped from the college budget and the incident was closed.

In all religions, similarly, sinners may sometimes be "saved," but unbelievers never. The sinner may live a life spotted with infamy, but appropriate penance may absolve him from its consequences. The heretic, on the other hand, may lead a pure and virtuous life, perhaps almost saintly in character, but his conduct will not necessarily save him from damnation. Thus, it is pardonable to violate the norms if only one accepts the ideology. It is unpardonable, on the other hand, to reject the ideology no matter how closely one conforms to the norms. Skepticism, in short, is more serious than sin. This sociological phenomenon, evident in every time and society, is a paradox. We mention it because it indicates the very great importance of ideologies in the social life of man.

6. Technologies

Between norms and materiel we find another phenomenon, which we shall label *technologies*. Technologies are sometimes referred to as technical norms or, more simply, as techniques. Thus, it is not enough to have the materiel, to own the tool, to possess the utensil. One must also, in the convenient American phrase, have the know-how. One may have all of the parts of an automobile, boxed and correctly labeled, and not know how to put them together. One may have the automobile and not know how to drive it. Similarly, there are norms for using tools. It is considered inappropriate, and indeed it is usually inefficient, to use a chisel as a screwdriver or a screwdriver as a chisel. To do so violates a technical norm. We are therefore admonished always to use the right tool for the job. The new bride, to take another example, may have all of the ingredients for baking a cake, but unless she puts them together in accordance with the norms specified in the recipe, the result may be less than satisfactory.

Technologies, of course, differ from society to society, and societies may accordingly be compared with respect to their levels of technological achievement. During a critical labor shortage in the oil fields of Borneo some years ago, British and Malayan operators received permission from the Sarawak government to recruit about seven hundred primitive Dayaks for the job. These Dayaks, once the famed head-hunters of Borneo, enjoyed picking off their enemies with arrow, dart, and blowpipe and taking their heads as souvenirs. It is doubtful whether the average American would know how to use these weapons, at least for this purpose. The Dayaks, on the other hand, did not become very effective laborers in the oil fields. One reason was that they would rather have been back in the hills, hunting, fishing, and tending rice. A more important reason, however, was their total lack of the relevant technological skill. They had to be shown, for example, that a wheelbarrow can be moved much more easily if it is lifted by the handles.

A discussion of the technological component of culture could obviously extend to many pages. Some sociologists regard technology as the most important constituent of culture and make it a prime factor in their explanations of social change. This is an issue that we meet again in the last chapter of this book. Here we need only emphasize that technologies, like ideologies, are an integral part of the culture of a society.

Culture

Ideas	*Norms*	*Materiel*
	Technologies	

7. Subsidiary Culture Concepts

The words "culture" and "cultural" appear in numerous combinations with other words, all of which it is important for the student of sociology to know. The combinations are labels for various kinds of social phenomena that he needs to understand in order to appreciate the nature of society. Since these subsidiary concepts occur again and again in the literature of the social sciences, it is necessary for us to define them.

Culture Trait and Culture Item

When we talk about a very small bit of culture, we use the terms "trait" or "item." A spark plug, for example, is an item of material culture, the notion that the world is round an item of ideational culture, and the practice of shaking hands with acquaintances an item of culture classified as a norm. We should be inclined to use the word item when referring to materiel, either item or trait when referring to an idea, and, probably, the word trait when referring to a norm. There is nothing precise about this usage, nor is it standardized in the literature, except that the term culture item or culture trait does refer to a small bit of culture in any one of the three components.

Culture Complex

Small bits of culture seldom, if ever, exist in isolation from others, except perhaps on a dump heap. Item combines with item and trait to form culture complexes. Thus an automobile engine, made up of a number of parts not all invented at the same time—or, for that matter, even an entire automobile—may be referred to as a culture complex. So also may the combined notions that the earth is round and that it revolves around the sun. And handshaking may be considered only one practice in a culture complex of meeting and greeting practices that include polite forms of address and so on. Again, the usage is not precise in detail, but when we refer to a combination of culture items or culture traits we are likely to use the concept "culture complex."

Culture Pattern and Culture Configuration

Combinations of culture traits and culture items—culture complexes—themselves combine with other combinations and give us culture patterns or culture configurations. Thus, gasoline engines and automobiles combine with other mechanical complexes to make a "machine age" or a mechanically minded or technological society. And an industrial society displays a pattern different from one whose culture contains no machines. Similarly, theories of the nature of the earth and of the solar system combine to comprise a scientific discipline of astronomy, a philosophic discipline of cosmology, and a superstitious discipline of astrology. Astronomy, cosmology, and astrology thus constitute culture patterns or culture configurations.

Finally, to continue our third example, all kinds of polite practices combine to make up the distinctive culture patterns of etiquette or the configurations of hospitality that characterize various societies. Sometimes "pattern" is the larger term and sometimes "configuration," but they both refer, despite imprecise usage, to the major constellations of culture that appear in all societies and that distinguish one society from another. These words, in fact, frequently designate combinations, not only of ideas or norms or materiel, but of all three together. All of these terms—trait or item, complex, and pattern or configuration—represent a continuum from simple entities to complicated unities, and no one can presume to graduate this continuum precisely or to draw any clear boundary lines between the various categories.

8. Acculturation

The process of acquiring the culture of a different society from one's own is called *acculturation*. When in Rome we are advised to do as the Romans do. If any of these acquired patterns lasts and becomes a part of our regular behavior, we have been acculturated, to that extent, to a Roman culture pattern. An American student who learns in England to take tea in the afternoon or in France to drink wine with his meals is becoming acculturated to the English or French culture, as the case may be. The results of acculturation can be seen also in the American who, having spent his two or three years abroad as a Rhodes scholar, brings an Oxford accent back to his native Oklahoma.

Acculturation occurs on a large scale when one society is invaded by another. The conquerors attempt to impose their way of life upon the conquered and, however successful this imposition, the conquerors in turn begin to adopt some of the practices of the conquered. This process is inevitable when peoples meet. Societies jealous of their culture try to prevent acculturation by forbidding "fraternization" or by erecting other obstacles to social intercourse, but such attempts are rarely successful. Transcultural social intercourse always results in at least some acculturation. Sometimes, of course, the traits of one culture do not harmonize well with those of another and their transmission is resisted. Thus, the American Indians eagerly adopted the firearms and the "firewater" of the English colonists but were somewhat reluctant to embrace the colonists' religion and their attitude toward work.

Acculturation can be seen on a grand scale in the millions of European immigrants who settled the continental United States and became assimilated to an American culture. In three generations the family of the Polish immigrant is indistinguishable, except perhaps by name, from that of the immigrant from Greece. Their grandsons salute the same flag, sing the same songs, attend the same university, and possibly play on the same football team. We popularly refer to this process as the "melting pot"; in sociological terms it is "acculturation." It is also called "assimilation" when the emphasis is upon a social rather than upon a cultural process. In any event, Americans can understand this phenomenon better, perhaps, than those of other nationalities because all of them have a history of acculturation in their own families.[6]

This process is not always a smooth and easy one and some peoples are acculturated more readily than others, but it never fails to happen when people of one culture have social relations for any extended period of time with people of another. The Englishman may continue to dress for dinner even in the steaming jungles of Malaya, but he is not wholly immune to Malayan customs. The Greek in New York City may continue to read Greek newspapers in Greek, but he will find in them some of the American comic strips, also in Greek. Acculturation can easily be observed in cities that are "crossroads of the world," cities like Singapore, Manila, Hongkong, Tokyo, Cairo, Istanbul, New York, Caracas, Rio, Montevideo, San Francisco, Geneva, Paris, and London.

[6] On this subject see Milton M. Gordon, *Assimilation in American Life*, Oxford University Press, New York, 1964.

Acculturation, like education, is a constant process in society. Education is the process by which we acquire the culture of our own society. Acculturation is the process by which we acquire the culture of a contemporary society other than our own. Acculturation is the result of the contact of cultures. When we speak of cultural diffusion, which was discussed in the preceding chapter, we focus our attention upon the movement of traits and complexes themselves. When we speak of acculturation, essentially the same process, we think rather of the adoption of traits and complexes by people who are in contact with other societies and other cultures.

9. Cultural Lag

Cultural lag, a concept introduced by William F. Ogburn, refers to a situation in which one part or phase of culture lags behind another and causes imbalance or disharmony in the society. Since we indulge in a more detailed discussion of this phenomenon in a later chapter, we may confine ourselves here to a few examples that will make its meaning clear.

There is traffic congestion in all of our cities at the present time because the rate of highway construction and the progress of urban traffic engineering have not kept pace with the rapidly increasing number of automobiles that use these highways. Off-street parking facilities are notoriously inadequate, and this situation has presented almost insurmountable problems to municipal governments. The revival of mass transit, to remove the glut of automobiles, is again a delayed development. Here we can see a cultural lag between the rate of accumulation of material culture and societal adjustment to it. As another example, medical science is now able to transplant organs from one human body to another, but there are at the moment of writing no legal or ethical codes to deal with the serious problems that can arise.

The law in general, as we see in a later chapter, is quite frequently a laggard, and in many instances does not change quickly enough to meet social requirements. Political arrangements generally lag behind technological, demographic, and other kinds of changes. In many respects the world itself, because of rapid advances in the arts of communication and transportation, is a single economic unit, but it is very far from being a single political unit. Educational arrangements also frequently lag behind technological innovations. Radio, television, and the movies are familiar to us all as entertainment devices, but their educational potentialities are far from being exploited to the full. Sometimes an idea or an invention may appear decades or even centuries before it is utilized by society. Finally, we may observe that it takes some time to get new words into the dictionary and some time also to get them out after they become obsolete. Thus we see that cultural lag is a simple concept, but one that is heavily weighted with sociological significance. We shall encounter it again in this book.

10. Cultural Survival

Sometimes culture traits, items, or complexes survive in a society long after their original function has disappeared and sometimes even after the initial reason for their establishment has been forgotten. The sleeves of men's jackets still have three or four buttons at or near the cuff, but these buttons serve no function whatever, except possibly a decorative one. According to one theory Frederick the Great of Prussia introduced these buttons on uniforms in order to discourage his soldiers from indulging in the somewhat unaesthetic—to say nothing of unhygienic—practice of wiping their noses on their sleeves. The military salute, once evidence that one had no hostile intent toward a stranger or other chance acquaintance—since it is impossible to salute and shoot at the same time with the same hand—is now used as a symbol of military discipline and rank. Military drill, once important as a means of moving a body of foot soldiers from one place to another in the shortest possible time, is merely a cultural survival in an age of rockets and jets and atoms. It may still have a function in inculcating discipline and in making habitual an immediate and unthinking obedience to orders, but this was not its original purpose.

Etiquette still prescribes that a gentleman walking with a lady stay on the side of the walk that is nearer the street. This custom had a point in a day when runaway horses were a possibility, to say nothing of the time when garbage was dumped from second-story windows into the street. These reasons no longer apply, but the custom persists. As a final example, there is the story of the wall outside of a village in Ireland. The villagers ceremoniously stop and bow before this wall when entering or leaving the village. If asked why they do this, they will be unable to offer a reason, except to say that they have always done so, and their fathers before them. We may be sure that once there was a reason but that, whatever it was, it has long since been forgotten.

11. Culture Conflict

The term *culture conflict* is an ellipsis; that is, it is people—groups or societies—who are in conflict with one another, not cultures. Their contention, however, usually has a cultural base, and it is therefore convenient sometimes to use the concept of culture conflict. Religious wars, which have filled so many sorry pages in the history of the Western nations, are good examples. The cow is a sacred animal in the Hindu culture but not in the Moslem culture. Hindu and Moslem live side by side in India, and their different attitudes on this one subject alone are perennial occasions of conflict. Similarly, Protestant and Catholic live side by side in the United States, and their differences on abortion, contraception, and education are also productive sources of conflict. Numerous other examples will readily suggest themselves.

12. Ideal Culture and Real Culture

The ideal culture of a society is the culture its members think they have; the real culture is the culture they actually have. In all societies there is a discrepancy between the ideal culture pattern and the real culture pattern. If an American citizen were asked to tell a visitor from a foreign land something about how Americans think and live, his description would probably be somewhat less than realistic. He might say, for example, that the United States is a democracy, that all men are created equal, and that all have the same legal rights and social privileges. He might neglect to mention, however, that some Americans, whose skin color happens to be of a darker hue, do not enjoy these rights and privileges equally with other citizens. He might say that Americans believe in and practice monogamy, but the divorce and remarriage rate might lead the visitor to suspect that Americans actually practice something that could better be described as serial polygamy. The citizen again would not hesitate to declare that American culture is a religious culture, but he would refrain from saying in addition—possibly because he is unaware of the fact—that only about half the population are members of any organized church and that fewer than half regularly attend church services of any kind.

Anthropologists similarly have difficulty sometimes in discovering the real culture pattern of the primitive peoples whom they study and investigate. An informant may tell the anthropologist, for example, that sexual dalliance with the daughter of the tribal chieftain is an offense punishable by death. But further investigation may reveal that, although this information is invariably given—and given in good faith—the real situation is somewhat different. Actually, and tacitly, such dalliance may not have been punished by death for many generations, and it may, on the contrary, confer tremendous prestige upon any tribal male who can get away with it. Verbal descriptions, however universal, may cloak or even contradict a culture pattern that is equally universal.

The distinction between ideal and real culture is expressed by some anthropologists in terms of *overt culture* and *covert culture*, or *explicit culture* and *implicit culture*. Indeed, these latter terms may be preferable since the former are laden with philosophical connotations that are quite irrelevant to the question at issue. The terminology, in other words, is not currently settled or consistent, but there is no difficulty about the distinction itself. One sociologist, for example, has emphasized the important fact that things are not always as they seem in society and that culture traits and culture patterns, and indeed other social and cultural phenomena, have both manifest and latent functions that may be quite disparate, or at least different from each other.[7] Thus, to use one of his illustrations, the manifest function of a political party is to recruit votes for the party's candidates, but one of its latent functions in a large city is to distribute charity and legal aid to the precinct poor. The manifest function is thus political; the latent function is charitable. The latent function in this case may possibly be performed more effectively by the party than by the social-work organization whose manifest function it is to do it. The student of sociology, therefore, has to be alert for differences, whatever their label, between the ideal and the real, the overt and the covert, the manifest and the latent.

13. Cultural Relativity

In a novel by Hans Ruesch we are taken to the land of the polar Eskimo and introduced there to a family of four: Ernenek, the father; Asiak, the mother; and two children—Papik, a boy, and Ivaloo, a girl.[8] One spring, when the sun begins to stay up all night and it is time for traveling to the south, the family visits the trading post of a white man, where they hope to trade some foxskins for a gun—not because Ernenek needs a gun but because he enjoys the loud noise it makes when someone pulls the trigger. They learn there for the first time that the white man's customs are different from theirs and that while they remain at the trading post they are not permitted to do some of the things that are quite "natural" (that is, cultural) to them, such as, for example, taking off their clothes in the unbearable heat inside the trader's one-room cabin. After the first day's adventures Asiak is moved to remark to Ernenek that something seems to be wrong with the white man:

> Why doesn't he know that a small igloo is quicker to build and easier to keep warm than so huge a house? He must walk to what he needs, instead of just reaching out for it, and sometimes he doesn't find what he is looking for despite the glaring light. He may have a lot of guns but somebody doubts if

[7] Robert K. Merton, *Social Theory and Social Structure*, Revised and Enlarged Edition, The Free Press of Glencoe, New York, 1957, chap. I.
[8] Hans Ruesch, *Top of the World*, Harper & Row, Publishers, New York, 1950, Pocket Book edition published April, 1951. Quotations are taken from the latter edition.

they are any good for killing game, or why would he eat those ill-smelling things out of iron boxes? And why does he drink fire-water that burns your throat? And why doesn't he allow taking off one's clothes when it is too warm? And why does he never smile? And why doesn't he laugh [have sexual intercourse] with the women of the Men, and objects even to other people laughing?[9]

In short, there are many things about the white man that Ernenek and his family do not understand. Most of all, they cannot understand why the white man refuses the utmost in hospitality that the Eskimo is able to offer; namely, the use of his wife as a sleeping companion. In the story Ernenek kills a white man because of the grave insult that refusal implies. When Ernenek and his wife recount the episode to another white man, the dialogue goes as follows:

"You said the fellow you killed provoked you?"
"So it was."
"He insulted Asiak?"
"Terribly."
"Presumably he was killed as you tried to defend her from his advances?"
Ernenek and Asiak looked at each other and burst out laughing. "It wasn't so at all," Asiak said at last.
"Here's how it was," said Ernenek. "He kept snubbing all our offers although he was our guest. He scorned even the oldest meat we had."
"You see, Ernenek, many of us white men are not fond of old meat."
"But the worms were fresh!" said Asiak.
"It happens, Asiak, that we are used to foods of a quite different kind."
"So we noticed," Ernenek went on, "and that's why, hoping to offer him at last a thing he might relish, somebody proposed him Asiak to laugh with."
"Let a woman explain," Asiak broke in. "A woman washed her hair to make it smooth, rubbed tallow into it, greased her face with blubber and scraped herself clean with the knife, to be polite."
"Yes," cried Ernenek, rising. "She had purposely groomed herself! And what did the white man do? He turned his back to her! That was too much! Should a man let his wife be so insulted? So somebody grabbed the scoundrel by his miserable little shoulders and beat him a few times against the wall—not in order to kill him, just wanting to crack his head a little. It was unfortunate it cracked a lot."
"Ernenek has done the same to other men," Asiak put in helpfully, "but it was always the wall that went to pieces first."
The white man winced. "Our judges would show no understanding for such an explanation. Offering your wife to other men!"

---

[9] *Ibid.*, p. 58.

"Why not? The men like it and Asiak says it's good for her. It makes her eyes sparkle and her cheeks glow."

"Don't you people borrow other men's wives?" Asiak inquired.

"Never mind that! It isn't fitting, that's all."

"Refusing isn't fitting for a man!" Ernenek said indignantly. "Anybody would much rather lend out his wife than something else. Lend out your sled and you'll get it back cracked, lend out your saw and some teeth will be missing, lend out your dogs and they'll come home crawling, tired—but no matter how often you lend out your wife she'll always stay like new." [10]

Here we have a situation in which the norms of one society, the American, contradict the norms of another, the Eskimo. The same action that in one society constitutes the sin of adultery constitutes, in the other, a gesture of hospitality. What is right in one society is wrong in the other, and the other way around. As we look at societies throughout the world, and throughout the course of historical time, we find many examples of this kind. It is difficult to find absolute standards in human societies. Standards are relative to the culture in which they appear. This is the principle of cultural relativity. In its simplest terms it means that actions that are moral in some societies are immoral in others, that propositions considered true in some are false in others, and that conduct that is approved and even required in some is disapproved and even forbidden in others. This principle, which anthropological investigation of nonliterate societies all over the world has helped to support, has been known to social thinkers since the earliest times and was given a complete and lucid expression by Boethius (*c.* 475–525), author of *The Consolation of Philosophy*, in the following words: "The customs and laws of diverse nations do so much differ the one from the other, that the same thing which some commend as laudable, others condemn as deserving punishment."[11]

The principle of cultural relativity raises questions of great complexity. One of these questions concerns the possibility of universal norms, that is, norms that prevail in every society, ancient and modern, primitive and civilized, Eastern and Western. Are there any actions that are commended alike in all societies or condemned alike in all? Are there, in short, any absolute norms? On this question the sociological evidence is inconclusive and may even, in the opinion of some writers on ethics, be irrelevant. Anthropologists and sociologists themselves are not in complete agreement on this issue.

One might assume, for example, that the premeditated murder of another human being is forbidden by the norms of all societies and of all

[10] *Ibid.*, pp. 87–88.
[11] *De Consolatione Philosophiae*, Loeb Classical Library, vol. II, p. 215.

human groups. But the norm does not, in so-called civilized societies, apply to the soldiers of a country with which one's own country is at war. Indeed, the soldiers who kill the largest number of enemies are decorated for valor. In many primitive societies the norm does not apply to the stranger, and wanderers risk their lives entering the outskirts of tribal villages not their own. If the murder of enemies and strangers is permitted under specified circumstances, one might perhaps assume that the premeditated murder of a friend is not, that such an action is always prohibited. But here again there are exceptions. Some societies support even the killing of a friend under certain conditions—for example, if the "friend" is found *in flagrante delicto* with one's wife. And, whether or not wives are to be considered "friends," they too may justifiably be done away with in some societies for actions that may or may not be considered offenses in other societies. Even in a civilized society, with a long tradition of law, it is difficult to get a jury to convict a man who murders the seducer of his wife. Thus, there is no universal taboo against homicide, and circumstances that proscribe it in certain societies may prescribe it in others.

Perhaps the closest we can come to a universal taboo is the taboo against incest, that is, sexual relations between close blood relations—brother and sister, mother and son, or father and daughter. And yet, incest is known to occur in all societies, not excluding our own. The reasons for this taboo, so nearly universal, have fascinated psychologist and anthropologist alike, but no thoroughly satisfactory explanation has been discovered. Furthermore, the taboo is officially relaxed in certain cases. Brother-sister marriages have been required in some families, for example, in the ancient Egyptian royal house and the ancient Hawaiian royal house, to preserve the purity of the royal bloodline.

One might speculate further that cruelty to young children would be universally tabooed. But infanticide, especially female infanticide, has been practiced in a number of nonliterate societies. In literate societies, on the other hand, to take only one illustration, children were forced to work long hours in factories and mines under incredible conditions in Western European societies during the period known as the Industrial Revolution.[12] For that matter, child abuse is a serious social and medical problem in such an apparently civilized nation as the United States.

Earlier anthropologists and sociologists were fascinated by cultural relativity and took delight in exhibiting instances of it, such as the one we

---

[12]This practice once produced the following bitter poem:
The golf links lie so near the mill
That almost every day
The laboring children can look out
And see the men at play.

have used (also with delight) from the Eskimo. It is a useful lesson to learn. But if we look at the situation a little more closely and with a little more sophistication, we can perhaps find a universal norm after all. It is called the norm of reciprocity, and it is at least conceivable that it appears in all societies. The Eskimo husband is being hospitable to his guest. Is it not the case that all hosts in all societies are expected to be hospitable to their guests? And are not guests expected, on some future occasion, to reverse the roles and invite their erstwhile hosts to become their guests? The form of the hospitality may vary over a wide range, but the norm remains and one becomes increasingly uncomfortable when he is unable to conform to it. Thus the English laborer, impoverished by retirement, has to give up his evenings at the local pub: "I don't want anybody to stand me a drink, because I can't pay my round. When I'm asked, I always find some reason for refusing, because I know I can't do anything in return." Thus also the discomfort of the upper-middle-class wife who, through circumstances she is temporarily unable to control, finds it impossible to repay the social obligations she has accumulated. The very notion of an accumulation of obligations implies the existence of a norm of reciprocity, and it is possible that it obtains in all human societies.[13]

It is also possible, as Theodore Caplow has sagaciously observed, that all peoples, everywhere, react in much the same way to social snubs, dirty jokes, and political speeches, and this too would suggest the presence of universal norms.[14] Finally, it is probable that in every society men and women are offended by hypocrisy.[15] It is good, in short, to know about cultural relativity, but it is also good to know that throughout the world the human beings who inhabit it share in general the same hopes and aspirations, suffer the same disappointments and defeats, and construct for themselves the same kinds of norms.

It is important in any event to distinguish between a cultural absolute and a cultural universal. It is conceivable that some norms could become universal without at the same time becoming absolute; that is, it could happen that at some time in the future all peoples in every society in the

---

[13] See Alvin W. Gouldner, "The Norm of Reciprocity," *American Sociological Review*, vol. 25, April, 1960, pp. 161–178.
[14] *Elementary Sociology*, Prentice-Hall, Inc., Englewood Cliffs, N. J., 1971, p. 112.
[15] At the 1948 session of the General Assembly of the United Nations, which adopted the Universal Declaration of Human Rights, the delegate from Saudi Arabia (among seven others) abstained from voting on the ground that no one could have the right to change his religion at will. The delegate from Pakistan considered this position to be a misinterpretation of the Koran: "I think we are permitted to believe or disbelieve. He who will believe, shall believe; he who cannot believe, shall not believe. The only unforgiveable sin is to be a hypocrite." Quoted in Joseph P. Lash, *Eleanor: The Years Alone*, W. W. Norton & Company, Inc., New York, 1972, p. 79. Eleanor Roosevelt was chairman of the commission that drafted the Declaration.

world would adopt the same general type of clothing that is now worn by the Western European and American peoples. We should not infer that because, in this hypothetical instance, a practice had become universal it had also become an absolute, that there would then be only one right kind of clothing to wear. On the other hand, the ethical philosopher might say that there are indeed absolute values or norms even though they are not universal, that underlying all of the diversities and differences to be found in the range of culture there is an abstract principle of right and wrong, of good and evil—and the religious philosopher would certainly say so. But here at least this important question may remain an open one, for the problem is one of ethics rather than of sociology.[16]

14. Ethnocentrism

Ethnocentrism is a corollary of the principle of cultural relativity. It means the ethnic-centered tendency to evaluate other cultures in terms of our own. It means that the ways of thinking and the ways of doing that we observe in other societies are measured and judged in terms of the ideas and norms prevailing in the society with which we are most familiar. Archimedes, the ancient Greek physicist, once remarked that if he had a place to stand, and a lever long enough, he could move the world. We too lack a place to stand, a place from which we can with complete objectivity investigate the ideas, ideologies, and norms of all societies. Since we lack this place to stand we tend, quite normally it appears, to stand in our own society as it were and to judge all others in terms of it.

Thus, as we have seen from the illustration used above, we easily conclude that Eskimo hospitality is immoral, as indeed it would be in our society. The Eskimos' practice of putting their aged parents out on the ice to die similarly seems abhorrent to us, and we should place it in the category of homicide or, more specifically, geronticide. From the Eskimo point of view, however, the man or woman who becomes too old to keep up with the tribe, to travel the vast distances that must be covered in the course of a year in the search for enough food to keep alive, jeopardizes the continued existence of the community; and the existence of the community is considered more important than the survival of the individual.

On the other hand, certain practices of ours, such as catching seal and using only the skin and discarding the rest, seem to the Eskimo wasteful to the point of immorality. Similarly, although the Eskimo can understand how one man can kill another man in anger, he is totally unable to

---

[16] For a thoughtful treatment of this subject see Abraham Edel, *Ethical Judgment*, The Free Press of Glencoe, New York, 1955.

comprehend the phenomenon of organized war and, indeed, when informed that white men indulge in this practice, he is somewhat incredulous and tends to regard it as ridiculous. Poor benighted Eskimo!

Ethnocentrism in fact is one of the Baconian Idols of the Cave, to which we referred in our first chapter. No one, not even a sociologist, can avoid it altogether, but the sociologist has a professional responsibility to be aware of it and accordingly to judge foreign ideologies and foreign norms in terms of the functions they perform in the societies in which they appear rather than in terms of the standards that he takes from his own society.

Ethnocentrism is the name of the tendency to believe that only other people are foreigners, never ourselves. The Englishman, for example, who tries to purchase an article in a department store in Argentina is asked by the clerk, in an endeavor to be helpful, whether he is a foreigner. "No," he replies, with some surprise, "I'm British." Similarly, Winston Churchill once wondered why it was so difficult for people to learn the English spelling of those "foreign places" in which they lived. This tendency, however, is difficult to avoid. Sometimes the language we speak forces us into an unwilling ethnocentrism. Throughout this book, for example, we refer to residents of the United States as Americans. This practice is ultimately inexcusable because Venezuelans, Brazilians, Uruguayans, Panamanians, Mexicans, and Canadians, for example, are also Americans, and we do not include them when we use this adjective. Unfortunately, however, the English language supplies us with no word that corresponds to the United States as "English" does to England, "German" to Germany, "French" to France, "Mexican" to Mexico, and so on. There is no respectable alternative, in fact, and, like everybody else, we are more or less forced to adopt a usage of which we disapprove and which is both arrogant and impolite.

There is one possible solution to this kind of ethnocentric impasse. We might judge societies, if we are inclined to judge them at all, in terms of the degree to which they conform to their own norms rather than the degree to which they conform to ours. In other words we would evaluate them according to the discrepancy that could be discerned between their real culture on the one hand and their ideal culture on the other. By this test, of course, we might find our own society "inferior" to many others, and especially inferior to societies that we call primitive. On the other hand, the notion that we ought to practice what we preach may be an ideology taken from our own culture and one that is quite irrelevant in others.

In short, the ethnocentric predicament in sociology is as difficult to avoid or to resolve as is the egocentric predicament in philosophy. In any case, it comes to be a problem for an advanced sociological theory and especially for the sociology of knowledge. The reader of this book will want to guard against the tendency to judge other cultures in terms of his own and to assume that some exotic custom is unseemly or immoral in another society simply because those adjectives could be properly applied to it in our society.

15. Temporocentrism

Temporocentrism is the temporal equivalent of ethnocentrism. The author has defined it as "the unexamined and largely unconscious acceptance of one's own century, one's own era, one's own lifetime, as the center of sociological significance, as the focus to which all other periods of historical time are related, and as the criterion by which they are judged."[17] All of us are inclined to believe, or rather to assume without question, that the present is more important than the past and that the whole of historical time is significant only for what it means to us. We thus tend to judge earlier societies in terms of criteria that are relevant to our own rather than to theirs and to weigh their virtues and defects in terms of standards drawn from our own contemporary century.

This temporocentric tendency induces us to place what must, in the long course of history, seem to be an exaggerated emphasis upon our own period. We assume, for example, that the crisis of our age is somehow more "critical" than the crises of other ages. We tend to ascribe a unique importance to the problems of our own era and to regard them as more complex than the problems that faced the man of imperial Rome, for example, or the man of the Renaissance. We are afflicted with a sense of urgency, a feeling that these tasks need to be undertaken, these problems solved, this action accomplished before it is too late. The stark warning, "it is later than you think," seems to mean more to us, in our temporocentrism, than it could possibly have meant to men of any other period of history. We believe that what we do, here and now in our own century, will have an overwhelming impact upon the centuries of future time. This belief could conceivably be warranted; but on the other hand what we do here and now may later be viewed as only a minor ripple on the stream of history, bubbles that arise somewhere and disappear before the next bend of the river. Finally, it is impressed upon us, in sermon, commencement address, and daily newspaper, that we are living in an age of transition. So Adam might have remarked to Eve on the occasion of their departure from the Garden of Eden.

Temporocentrism, in short, results from a lack of historical perspec-

---

[17] Robert Bierstedt, "The Limitations of Anthropological Methods in Sociology," *American Journal of Sociology*, vol. 54, no. 1, July, 1948, pp. 27–28.

tive. It afflicts in large measure the untutored man who has had no opportunity to study history. But it afflicts also the social scientist who, in his concern for the problems of the present, seems often to have little respect for history. Much of contemporary sociological research, for example, especially in the United States, is concentrated upon the "specious present" and neglects an extended temporal orientation. In some contemporary anthropological literature this tendency is perhaps even more apparent. An anthropologist, indeed, has defined history as "principally the inaccurate narration of events which ought not to have happened, precipitated by persons who ought to be forgotten, and written by arid pedants who deserve to be condemned to the perpetual torment of reading their own works."[18] The author of this definition conceded that it was "willful hyperbole," but in any event it is a view that sociologists cannot share. If an indifference to history is productive of temporocentrism, hostility to history is even more productive of it.

Sociology needs the deepening sense of time that only the study of history can supply. Travel is generally conceded to be broadening. But it is not often noticed that we can travel in time as well as in space and that such travel is inexpensive indeed. We need no steamship tickets, no passports, and no visas in order to spend a day with Socrates in Athens or an evening with Shakespeare at the Globe theater in London.

The German poet Goethe once remarked, "Wer fremde Sprache nicht kennt, weiss nichts von seiner eigenen" (He who knows no foreign language knows nothing of his own). The same applies to societies. If we know only one society—our own—we know none. Only by avoiding the errors of both temporocentrism and ethnocentrism can we hope to escape our own time-bound, space-limited, and culture-constricted experience and begin to understand the nature of human societies in all times and places.

16. Counterculture

In most periods of Western history, perhaps in all, men and women have been dissatisfied in greater or lesser degree with the societies in which they found themselves. Their dissatisfaction has been expressed in one or a number of forms, but in all of them there is an effort to visualize and sometimes to practice a kind of communal life in which the miseries and pains, the trials and travails of their own surroundings would somehow be erased and they would discover a new world or create a new society in which all ideals are realized, all hopes fulfilled, and all ambitions achieved. Whether viewed as a protest against the old society or the brave construc-

---

[18] Earnest Albert Hooton, *Twilight of Man*, G. P. Putnam's Sons, New York, 1939, p. 194.

tion of a new one, the result is a *counterculture*, a culture which stands in a contrary or even contradictory juxtaposition to the societies of their ancestors and contemporaries. To some of them, civilization itself hampers the growth of the human spirit and finally stifles it; it is necessary therefore to cast the old aside and to start all over again with a new set of social arrangements.

Many of these new arrangements are the visions of philosophers, men whose constructions remain in the imagination and are never converted into practice. These are the writers of utopias (*utopia*; literally, "no place") and they can be found as early as the ninth century B.C. Lycurgus, for example, who was guardian of a king of Sparta in that early period, drew up an ideal constitution and set of laws for that city which, he hoped, would drive out of society such evils as insolence, envy, avarice, and luxury. Other writers on utopian themes include, from a much larger roster, the names of Plato (*The Republic*); Aristophanes (*The Ecclesiazusae*; actually a burlesque of Plato); Zeno, the Stoic philosopher, who conceived (in a book also entitled *The Republic*) of a society without marriage, religion, laws, money, or property; and Iambulus, who dreamed of a voyage to the Islands of the Sun. In later centuries an entire series of utopias appeared, including such famous ones as Sir Thomas More's *Utopia* (1516), Tommaso Campanella's *City of the Sun* (1623), Francis Bacon's *The New Atlantis* (1627), James Harrington's *The Commonwealth of Oceana* (1656), Fénelon's *Telemachus* (1699), and, three examples from a much later period, Edward Bellamy's *Looking Backward* (1888; which sold over 1 million copies and was translated into many languages); Gabriel Tarde's *Fragment d'Histoire Future* (1904); and H.G. Wells' *A Modern Utopia* (1905). The list is much longer.

Tarde, a brilliant sociologist, whose book was translated into English as *Underground Man*, made allowance, in accordance with Herbert Spencer's principle of "separation," for a city of painters, a city of sculptors, a city of musicians, of poets, of chemists, of psychologists—indeed, a city of specialists of every kind—except philosophers (including sociologists): "For we were obliged after several attempts to give up the idea of founding or maintaining a city of philosophers, notably owing to the incessant trouble caused by the tribe of sociologists who are the most unsociable of mankind."

Others throughout history have actually founded and tried to live in utopian or otherwise experimental societies. In the United States such communities as Brook Farm, Oneida, New Harmony, the Amana Colonies, the Amish, the Hutterites, and, in Canada, the Doukhobors, come to mind. For most of these there is an effort, usually supported by strong religious sentiment and belief, to save a culture from the ravages of unwanted change, and in these cases the surrounding culture appears to them, of course, to be the counterculture.

To describe only one example, in 1830 two disciples of the French sociologist Saint-Simon attempted to put into practice his religious principles as outlined in a book entitled *Nouveau Christianisme* (*New Christianity*, 1825), founded a College of Apostles, together with disciples and missionaries, and formed a community first in Paris and then in the suburbs dedicated to the principle that "each man will be placed according to his capacity, and rewarded according to his work."[19] The members wore a distinctive costume consisting of a blue tunic, a white vest, a red neckband, white trousers, and red beret. The vest, incidentally, buttoned only in back to stress the fraternal dependence of the apostles upon one another. The community was dedicated also to the principle of the total emancipation of women, and one of its "apostles" even traveled to Constantinople in search of the female Messiah. The movement succumbed to the police after only two years, however, on suspicion of sexual communism and revolutionary activity.

The term "counterculture" in the United States in the 1970s is likely to mean neither classical utopian thought nor any of the older communal ventures but rather an effort to escape a detested society on the part of the young, who experiment with still newer forms of communal living, who try to avoid the scorned conventions of ordinary life, and who seek a new existence and a new identity. In the sixties and seventies their communes could be found all over the country, from the tenements on St. Marks Place in New York City to the redwood forests of northern California. They lived in groups of a dozen or so up to two or three hundred, the latter sometimes augmented by as many as a hundred transients, using as shelters old farmhouses, old barns and shacks, and stray pieces of lumber put together with an often enviable ingenuity. Many left their old names behind and called themselves Bingo Jim, Giraffe, Peter the Wolf, Dan Coyote, Adrian Avenger, Jamestown, Little Sister, and Alicia Bay Laurel, the last of whom wrote several books, including one entitled *Living on the Earth*, which achieved a measure of fame. They dedicated themselves to ballads and guitars, often to drugs, and tried to free themselves from the constraints of a "straight" society. Violence finally defeated the members of "Galahad's Pad" in the East Village, and what will happen to the others is impossible to know.[20]

---

[19] This principle was later expressed by Karl Marx in *The German Ideology*, as "from each according to his abilities, to each according to his needs," and became one of the slogans of the Communist International.

[20] Their story is told with great sensitivity by the sociologist Lewis Yablonsky in his book *The Hippie Trip*, Pegasus, New York, 1968.

17. Summary

This entire chapter, in a sense, is itself a summary treatment of the subject of culture. In the preceding chapter we defined this concept and attempted to indicate the very great importance of culture in the social life of mankind. In this chapter we have looked into the components of culture, components that are directly related to our definition. We have said that it is useful to conceive of culture in terms of three large compartments—ideas, norms, and materiel—and two combined compartments—ideologies and technologies. Although it is impossible to list with any precision the kinds of ideas and the kinds of materiel to be found in culture, we indicated nevertheless the sort of subheadings that might be used. We have not yet, however, subjected the norms to a similar treatment.

In the second half of the chapter we considered a number of subsidiary cultural concepts—traits, items, complexes, patterns, and configurations—and indicated how these terms are employed. Such additional phenomena as acculturation, cultural lag, cultural survival, culture conflict, and ideal and real culture next detained our attention. We pointed to the principle of cultural relativity and suggested that both ethnocentrism and temporocentrism can easily preclude objectivity in sociological reasoning and research. And, finally, we introduced a few brief notes on the phenomenon of the counterculture.

All of these topics deserve, of course, a more extended treatment. They embrace, in fact, a large part of the literature of anthropology and sociology. We hope we have said enough, however, to give the reader some appreciation of the meaning and content of culture.

Chapter 7

THE ACQUISITION OF CULTURE

N THE PRECEDING chapters we emphasized the importance of culture in everything we think, and do, and have, and indeed used these verbs in the derivation of our definition of culture. We suggested that it is culture that determines what we eat and drink, what we wear, what work we do, what God we worship, what knowledge we rely upon, what poetry we recite, and so on through the entire catalogue of our activities. We now want to take a slightly different view of the matter, to observe it from a different vantage. We want to look at the individual and see how he acquires the culture to which he is exposed, to learn if possible the mechanisms that operate in this process in all societies, and to watch the development of personality in the interaction of the person and his culture. We want to look, in short, at what has come to be called the socialization process, the process by which original nature is transformed into human nature, the process in terms of which every human individual becomes an acceptable member of his society. In exploring this subject we shall have occasion to deal with the nature of the interaction between self and society, with the self as subject and as object, with the old question of heredity and environment, with the agencies of socialization, with personality itself, and with the self as an actor and role player in the drama that it is the destiny of all of us to endure and enjoy.

1. The Encounter: Self and Society

Strictly speaking, the initial encounter is not between self and society at all because at the first stage, as we shall see, the self does not yet exist. Here, however, we want to suggest something else; namely, that the infant at birth, the organism that is to become human in its exposure to culture, is not simply a lump of clay that receives impressions and is shaped, as on a potter's wheel, by external influence and instrument. The organism is not wholly passive, wholly inert, wholly malleable, and no one who has ever seen an infant in action would believe it to be so. There is response, of course, but there is impulse too. The organism not only responds to the stimulus but also seeks it out. The baby roots around for the nipple to which it will then respond by sucking movements of the lips—movements indeed that precede the discovery. We are not saying that the stimulus is altogether absent, but only that it may be internal—like, for example, the peristalsis of the walls of the stomach, which stimulates the search for food—and not a part of the culture as such. The organism is an engine, in short, with its own motive forces, and this in effect, as Aristotle noticed long ago, is what distinguishes an animate from an inanimate object; this is what it means to be alive. The organism not only receives the culture; it also, so to speak, goes to meet it.

The nature and number of these motive forces have puzzled philosophers for centuries and they are still largely unresolved problems in psychology and social psychology. In the early years of the present century an instinct theory prevailed. The first two books published in the field of social psychology, one by the sociologist E. A. Ross and the other by the psychologist William McDougall—both in the year 1908—subscribed to this theory and indeed gave it great impetus in the social and psychological sciences. The existence of instincts somewhere in the organism made the explanation of human behavior an exceedingly simple process. Why do men and women mate? Because of the sexual instinct. Why do they have children? Because of the philoprogenitive instinct. Why do they earn money? Because they have an acquisitive instinct. And why do they save it? Because they have a hoarding instinct.

All this was very simple and very easy—until someone, notably the sociologist L. L. Bernard, noticed that it was too simple and too easy. For it became clear after a while, as the number of instincts multiplied, that the instinct theory could explain everything and therefore could explain nothing. For, as we shall have occasion to remark again in this book, a theory that explains too much is as useless as one that explains too little. The questions and answers above seem reasonable enough. But similar answers to additional questions begin to sound a little strained. Why do people play games? Because they have a competitive instinct. Why do they play baseball? Because they have a baseball-playing instinct? And why do they study sociology? Because they have a sociology-studying instinct?

It became obvious, in short, that the instinct theory was rather like a large warehouse in which every conceivable kind of instinct was stored. Whenever it became necessary to explain any snippet of behavior one had only to enter the warehouse and find the appropriate instinct—and thus one had the explanation. The number of different kinds of behavior was almost limitless, but then so was the number of instincts in the warehouse. It became fairly obvious in fact that until and unless one found a physiological correlate or a biological base the instinct was nothing but an artifact—a label, as it were—that might serve as a descriptive tag but was wholly devoid of explanatory power.

One solution to this problem, when the instinct theory was discarded, was to find instead a small number of "prepotent reflexes," "unlearned drives," or, more currently, "wants." A textbook in social psychology, for example, lists in its treatment of motivation an affiliation want, an acquisitive want, a prestige want, a power want, an altruistic want, and a curiosity want.[1] Once again, however, whether we use reflexes, drives, or wants—or interests, propensities, or urges—we have merely a series of synonyms for instincts. What we have thrown out of the front door reappears at the back in a different dress, and the problem remains unsolved.

Whatever the answer to the difficult problem of motivation may be, it is clear that the organism has motions of its own and meets its environment in various ways. It also has various unlearned reflexes—the Babinski, the knee-jerk, and the blinking reflex—which serve as indicators of physiological normality but have little sociological importance. We have said before in this book that, compared with other animals and insects, the human infant is poorly supplied with instincts, but there are things nevertheless that it does not have to learn, such as anger at constraint, fear of falling, the need to eat, and, later on, the urge to sexual expression. The life of man in society is thus a confrontation of organism and culture, each of which contributes something to the behavior that results. The point is that man encounters his culture and in a sense has a tussle with it. He does not merely receive it.

[1] Like all such lists, this one has its problems. No one wants curiosity, for example, as one wants prestige. Curiosity is simply a synonym for wanting to know. If there is any want involved it is a wanting to know or, in the authors' jargon, a knowledge want. Incidentally, the philosopher James K. Feibleman has long maintained that the desire or drive to know must be ranked with such other basic drives as hunger and sex. How else can we explain the ubiquity of curiosity, the eagerness to learn a secret or listen to gossip, the desire to be what the sociologist David Riesman has called an "inside-dopester," to be "in the know"?

2. Heredity and Environment

If organism and culture each contributes something to the human being the individual will become, then we would seem to have the problem of heredity and environment, or heredity *versus* environment, to be perhaps a bit more accurate. For a long time a controversy raged in psychology and the social sciences as to which of these two distinguishable things, heredity or environment, is more important, which makes the major and which the minor contribution. Later on the controversy became quiescent, and it seemed as if the question had been resolved firmly in favor of the environmentalists. Still later the question again became moot, especially with regard to racial differences in intelligence, as we saw in an earlier chapter, and with regard to sex differences in intelligence, temperament, and achievement, as we see in a later chapter. It is possible that the question is unfortunately phrased. It may be as meaningless as asking which contributes more to the motion of an automobile, the engine or the gasoline.

There are more serious difficulties. One cannot be sure, when the problem is sufficiently refined, that the two things, organism and environment, are in truth as distinguishable as they may superficially seem to be. An American writer of a generation or more ago, A. F. Bentley, a gentleman farmer who distinguished himself in three fields (political science, social psychology, and philosophy), once published a paper with the facetious title, "The Human Skin: Philosophy's Last Line of Defense," in which his question, like ours today, is far from facetious. At what point does a custom that is cultural, and therefore external to the organism, become a habit that is physiological, and therefore internal to it? Where now is the dividing line, the point of transition? When does the custom of brushing our teeth or of using a knife and fork become a habit and therefore a "natural" activity of the organism? When does the pleasant custom of smoking become a habit that is hard to break and when does the sad practice of drug taking become an addiction that is impossible to cure?

And when, seen from the other side, does what is internal to the organism become an item of culture? At what point do the orator's words or the singer's notes cease to belong to orator and singer, as it were, and become objective phenomena in an external world? When do the words that flow from the tip of a writer's pencil onto a piece of paper cease to be a part of him and become instead a part of a larger universe so external that others can read them and then internalize them again? Where is the dividing line between words that begin as ideas and end as ink? We have here, one would suppose, another riddle. It is a riddle we do not propose to solve, but merely to state in order to indicate that things are not as simple as they seem and that what is distinguishable when seen from one point of view may be blurred and confused when seen from another.

The sociologist Sorokin has suggested one of the best analogies perhaps of the relationship between the individual and culture, or the individual's heredity and the culture's environment. It is something like the relationship between the phonograph and the record. What the phonograph will play depends upon the record that is placed upon its turntable. It is the record that determines whether the music will be popular or classical and whether the language that issues from it is Italian or French—and so on through all the varieties of records. But how well the music will be played, the quality of the tone, depends upon the phonograph. The same record will sound quite different when played upon a phonograph that is a child's inexpensive and squeaky toy and upon one that is a massive and costly instrument designed for stereophonic reproduction. And so also for individuals. Whether they speak French or Italian, salute this flag or that, worship one God or many, depends, as we have seen, upon their culture. But the quality of their performance, its timbre and tonality so to speak, depends upon their hereditary talents and capabilities. Some will be better at music or atomic physics, or pole vaulting or ice skating, than others, but they can be neither good nor bad at them in societies where these activities are not pursued.

We need not argue, therefore, about which is more important, heredity or environment, because both are important in ways that defy a quantitative comparison. As we have indicated before, a Mongolian idiot has no chance of becoming a mathematician, but neither has the most gifted individual in a society in which there is no mathematical science. The geneticist will continue to study the mechanisms of heredity—whether in Indian corn, fruit flies, race horses, or human beings—and will particularly try to find connections between genes and certain attributes, chromosomes and certain characteristics. The sociologist will continue to take both heredity and environment into account. It is clear in any case that without the organism the culture would be only an archaeological relic, as dead as the ruins of Pompeii or the rose-red city of Petra, half as old as time. Without the culture, on the other hand, the organism would remain an organism, a feral, not a human, being. Both are obviously necessary to create a human person with the attributes and faculties, the conduct and characteristics, we associate with our socialized species.

3. The Self as Subject

Everyone who is alive, in any society, has a consciousness of self. The self is what he means, in the English language for example, by the word "I" when he is not thinking of himself. The stipulation of not thinking is important because as soon as one thinks of himself, or of his use of the "I," or even of "I" in quotation marks, the self becomes object rather than subject and the essence of the "I" disappears. The nature of the self, as seen by the self, subjectively and from the inside, is one of the great mysteries to which neither science nor philosophy has anything but partial and inadequate answers. As soon as we say "the nature of the self," as in the preceding sentence, we have already made an object of it, and the self as subject has vanished into a limbo where there is no language and where words are useless. The self as subject is a self that transcends the possibility of explanation. It is as difficult to identify this self as it is to find it and to give it a location.

Let us consider the problem of location for a moment—and let the author who I am talk to the reader who you are in the first person. Let us ignore the usual formality, in short, in order to get closer, if we can, to the self as subject. Of all the pronouns it is the I that is most baffling and complex. I know perfectly well what you are—for one thing I can see you and listen to you talk (I can imagine you reading this book)—and I know what he is and she is and they are (we both do) for similar reasons. I even know what we are, because "we" surely means the two of us or the three of us or all of us, as distinguished from the rest, the others, the ones that the "we" excludes. But what am I? When I say that I do not know what I am, I do not even know whether there are three different "I"'s in that expression, two different "I"'s, or only one. One reason for my difficulty is that any effort to think about it—i.e., my I—already turns it into an "it," an object, and that is precisely what, at the moment, I do not want my I to be.

But let us proceed to the problem of location. If I do not know what I am, can I not at least say where I am? This too is difficult. I think that I am somewhere behind my eyes—at least I have the impression that I look through them when I see—but now that I have put the words down on paper the notion seems a bit ridiculous. I know the eyes are mine (the left one, for example, has been near-sighted for years), but now I am confused again about what the "mine" might refer to. Modern surgical techniques could transfer them to someone else. But nothing could transfer the I that now owns them to someone else and if it could be done the I would probably no longer be me but rather someone else.

I am surely dependent upon my body because I did not exist before my body did, and it is a genuine (and religious) question whether I shall continue to exist when my body dies. And so, you see, I have something to do with my body. But if I look for me somewhere inside this body there is no particular place that I can find myself. In fact, this whole body is mine to do with what I want. I can feed it, fill it and empty it as the Greek philosopher got tired of doing, lay it down for a nap (in which case I disappear for a while), run it up or down the stairs, take it swimming, or make it—one hand of it that is—move a pencil across a sheet of paper. All of these things *I* can do to *it* and therefore I cannot be identical with it but rather something else. I am never far away from my body, it is true, except perhaps in revery, and what I should do without it I really do not know. I have the impression that it is always somewhere around, where I am, and I should no doubt be quite uncomfortable without it. But that seems only fair, for sometimes it is quite uncomfortable with me, as when I give it too much to eat or drink, or make it work too long without rest.

My body has changed a great deal since I—or it—was born, but I think somehow that in spite of these changes I am still the same I, not a different one, and that I shall continue to be the same I until I die. But what accounts for this sameness, this continuing identity through all these changes—graying hair, for example, and increasing weight—I do not know. This problem is the problem of identity, with which the philosophers often struggle. In the eighteenth century some "coffee-house intellectuals," —Pope, Arbuthnot, Gay, and others—wanting to make fun of the philosophers, wrote anonymously a book called *The Memoirs of Martinus Scriblerus*. In this book they told the tale of a sock. This sock, after it is worn a while, gets a hole in it. You darn this hole and wear it some more and soon there is another hole. And so on. There will come a time, after continuous darning, when not a single one of the original threads remains. The question of Martinus Scriblerus then becomes—Is it the same sock?

The same question, of course, can be asked about me and my body. I do not exist without my body and yet every single cell of this body reproduces itself, it is estimated, every seven years. This means that no part of my body seven years ago is part of my body today, and I am puzzled therefore about what has happened to me in the meantime. Am I the same I or a different one?

I think it is time to stop this speculation about me. You have the problem too, or at least I think you do. Who are you anyway? I don't mean what is your name, what is your street address, what is the color of your hair, or whether you are tall or short or fat or thin. I mean, who are you? Do you also have an I that baffles you when you try to explain your being to your self? Have you ever been tempted to think that you might have had another body than the one you have, say a body of a different color or a different age? Isn't it curious, when you stop to think about it, that you are you today and that there has never been another you in any period of history? How strange that you should be you, and I I, and that there is no confusion of identities between us. Suppose the arrangements of life and consciousness and existence were such that when we became dissatisfied with our body we could thrust ourselves into another and then continue both to be ourselves and to have ourselves permanently, through all of future time? Would we then be able to know more about this ineffable self that refers to itself as I?

Lawrence Durrell, in the first of the novels in his Alexandria quartet, has one of his characters—Pursewarden, a writer—ask still another question about the self. He wonders whether it is continuous or whether it exists only in successive moments of self-consciousness. But this is only an echo of David Hume, the Scottish skeptic, who long before said that when he sought this mysterious thing he never found a self as such but only a succession of sensations.

Observations like these, tantalizing as they may be, have of course no end to them. All of them are speculative, some seem surrealistic, and others may come close to nonsense. What I am from my point of view and what you are from yours are questions not open to inquiry. The subjective self is mine, or yours, and that is all we can say. As soon as we start to talk about it, it changes into an objective self, and it has then disappeared as subject. It becomes the object of our concern, as it does in the section that follows.[2]

4. The Self as Object

We now leave the subjective self to the solipsists and turn to the only self that can be an object of inquiry—the objective self. Where does this self arise? Are we born with it or is it something we have to learn to recognize and to know? Is it something the individual brings with him as he confronts society or is it something that he receives from society as a gift of the confrontation? How, as the English philosopher W. J. H. Sprott engagingly puts it, do little Shirley and little Raymond begin to absorb their culture? How, more importantly for present purposes, do they acquire their Shirley-hood and Raymond-hood?[3] This at least is a question to which social psychology and sociology have some answers.

One of the earliest of sustained attacks on this problem was made by Charles Horton Cooley, a sociologist who dedicated his entire career to the advancement of two primary propositions—one, that the mind is social, and two, that society is mental. The second of these propositions is quite out of fashion and no one subscribes to it in Cooley's terms, but the first is

---

[2] One may wonder in addition whether the difference between the subject and the object is a fact in the universe, hard and obdurate, or whether it is something that occurs only because of the exigencies of language. Is it only the nature of language and not the nature of the universe that requires us to differentiate between subject and object? Is this because the sentences we speak have subjects and predicates? Or do our sentences have subjects and predicates as an accurate reflection of the nature of the universe—a universe that actually contains subjects and objects? These questions belong to the philosophy of language and to the sociology of knowledge, but they can occur, of course, to any thoughtful mind.

[3] W. J. H. Sprott, *Social Psychology*, Methuen & Co., Ltd., London, 1956, p. 126.

of overriding importance and has won the general assent of all of his successors, even when they have demurred on its details. A characteristic passage appears at the very beginning of his book, *Social Organization*, where he insists that "self and society are twin-born, we know one as immediately as we know the other, and the notion of a separate and independent ego is an illusion."[4] Indeed, Cooley objects to the famous formulation of Descartes—*Cogito ergo sum* (I think, therefore I am)—on two grounds. Before mentioning them let us examine the Cartesian situation.

René Descartes (1596–1650), the inventor of analytic geometry and the founder of modern philosophy, was also a gentleman soldier of some repute. In the year 1619, while on his way to join the army of the Emperor Maximilian, then in winter quarters, he found himself in a little village near Ulm, in a sheltered hut with its comfortable fire. He fell to musing about the potentialities of human reason and indeed began to wonder if he could prove his own existence by reason alone, without recourse to observation and experience. He began by trying to doubt the existence of everything in order to discover what, if anything, would remain when the doubting had been pushed to its ultimate limit and had exhausted all of its possibilities. He doubted first the existence of the external world. The external world could be an illusion, for it seems to be dependent upon sensations that could be erroneous or misleading. The water that is warm to cold feet, for example, is cold to warm hands, as Plato had noticed long before. Next Descartes doubted the existence of God, a doubt that was similarly fortified by philosophical precedent. Finally, he doubted that he himself existed, and this too he convinced himself that he was able to do. There was one thing, however, that he could not doubt—and that was that he was doubting. To doubt is to think; to think is to be; therefore—triumphantly—I am. *Je pense, donc je suis*: I think, therefore I am.

One of the flaws in this argument is in the restoration of the "I." The end product of the doubting was only doubting and it was a dubious leap from an unspoken premise that permitted Descartes to assume that doubting required a doubter and that it was he (whose existence he had doubted) who was doing the doubting. How did he know, moreover, having doubted everything else, that a predicate or a participle required a subject and that that subject was himself? Once the first step was taken, however, Descartes found it comparatively easy to restore the other things that he had doubted—God, in an argument reminiscent of St. Anselm in the eleventh century, and the external world as a corollary of the existence

---

[4] Charles Horton Cooley, *Social Organization*, The Free Press of Glencoe, New York, 1956, p. 5. The book was originally published in 1909.

of God. As the American philosopher Morris Raphael Cohen once pointed out, no one who uses the method of Cartesian doubt is ever satisfied until he has recovered everything he has doubted.

Whatever the logical flaws in this procedure, Cooley objected to it: "In the first place it seems to imply that 'I'-consciousness is a part of all consciousness, when, in fact, it belongs only to a rather advanced stage of development. In the second it is one-sided or 'individualistic' in asserting the personal or "I' aspect to the exclusion of the social or 'we' aspect, which is equally original with it."[5] In Cooley's view self-consciousness can arise only in society and indeed it is inseparable from social consciousness. Self-consciousness does not in fact appear in children until they are about two years of age and then only in conjunction with the consciousness of others as well. The self, in short, is social.

In the earlier of Cooley's two major works, *Human Nature and the Social Order* (1902), he contributed a number of useful and indeed striking insights, together with his famous "looking-glass" conception of the self. The first of the insights that attract our attention is that "I" is, after all, a word, that a word is a part of a language, and a language is a social product.[6] Without society there would be no communication, without communication no language, and without language no "I." "To think of it as apart from society is a palpable absurdity."[7] A second insight, less relevant to his central thesis but interesting nevertheless, is Cooley's observation that we sometimes transfer the "I" to an inanimate object with which we are closely associated and which is ours. Examples would be a golf ball or an automobile, as in "I am in the rough to the left of the green," and "I am in Parking Area C." The first of these examples is Cooley's and he quotes with approval the somewhat similar observations made by William James in his *Principles of Psychology* (1890): "A man's self is the sum total of all he can call his, not only his body and his psychic powers, but his clothes and his house, his wife and children, his ancestors and friends, his reputation and works, his lands and horses and yacht and bank-account. All these things give him the same emotions."[8]

More important, however, is the looking-glass conception mentioned above. The way we imagine ourselves to appear to another person is an essential element in our conception of ourselves. Thus, I am not what I think I am and I am not what you think I am. I am what I think you think I am. The proof of this view seemed clear to Cooley from the consideration that "We are ashamed to seem evasive in the presence of a straightforward

---

[5] *Ibid.,* p. 6.
[6] *Human Nature and the Social Order,* The Free Press of Glencoe, New York, 1956, p. 180.
[7] *Ibid.,* p. 181.
[8] *Ibid.,* note to p. 170.

man, cowardly in the presence of a brave one, gross in the presence of a refined one, and so on.''[9] That we exhibit a different self in different social groups is fairly clear and it is only a small step therefore to the inference that we *are* a different self in different groups; to the additional inference that we depend upon the presence of others for our conception of our selves; and to the conclusion again, now strengthened by this additional evidence, that the self is social and that self-consciousness would not exist in the absence of society. These, at least, are Cooley's important contributions to the problem.

The role of others in self-perception was the fruitful starting point for the theory of the self propounded by George Herbert Mead (1863–1931), the philosopher and psychologist who taught and wrote for many years at the University of Chicago. Mead agreed wholeheartedly with Cooley that it is absurd to look at the self, or the mind, from the viewpoint of an individual organism. Although it may have its focus in the organism, it is without question a social product and a social phenomenon.[10] What are the specific mechanisms, then, in terms of which this social self comes into consciousness? One suggestion comes from the realization that almost all behavior is behavior in interaction with others and therefore involves adjustments and adaptations to them. This is the way it is when dogs are fighting, cats are playing, and humans are conversing. Everything that one of the participants does is a response to what the other one does, for this is the nature of interaction. So far we have consciousness by each of the other but not necessarily as yet any self-consciousness. The more we interact with others, however—and interaction increases in the process of living itself—the more we learn to anticipate the responses of others and to learn, for example, the future significance of present gestures. We watch for signs of pleasure or displeasure in the other person and learn to interpret them correctly. These signs ordinarily take the form of gestures and facial expressions, and after a while these gestures and expressions indicate to us what we are expected to do in a given situation.

In this way, in reverse so to speak, our own gestures become meaningful to us. That is, we learn the meaning of our own gestures when we respond to them ourselves, implicitly, as the other does explicitly. The gesture, in short, evokes in ourselves the response we intend to elicit from the other—we take the attitude of the other. Thus we are always replying to ourselves, silently, when we are talking to others. This tendency is apparent in teaching, for example. We have to restrain ourselves from blurting out the answers to the questions we have asked of those we are

---

[9] *Ibid.*, p. 184.
[10] *Mind, Self, and Society*, The University of Chicago Press, Chicago, 1934, p. 133.

trying to teach. One result of this process, in the course of our normal interactions, is that we begin to carry on an internal conversation, a conversation with ourselves, not in the manner of the village idiot, who talks aloud to himself and answers questions no one has asked him, but rather as one who is responsive in anticipation to one's own words and gestures. It is in this process, according to Mead, that we find the genesis of the self and the origin of self-consciousness. For, as Sprott remarks in discussing this point, unless we make the very large assumption of a primal selfhood it is difficult to see how a self-consciousness could otherwise arise except in the process that presents ourselves to ourselves as something somehow different from others.[11]

The next step is to notice that, although we take the attitude of the other in order to discover the self, the others with whom we interact are different others and we therefore respond to them differently. We take the attitudes of a number of others, just as we engage in a number of different interactions. We do not, however, become a different self with respect to each different other—although we do, of course, respond to different persons differently—and Mead now has the difficult problem of explaining the continuity of the self—its consistency, so to speak—throughout these changing interactions with different others. He solves the problem with the quite original suggestion that we consolidate all of these different others into a "generalized other" and this generalized other in turn is identical with the social group or the community to which we belong. The responses that finally result in selfhood are not the discontinuous responses to different others but rather the continuous responses we make to a generalized other. The situation is exactly like that found in every one of us when we say, or more likely think, "What will people think if I do this, or that?" The "people" in this expression are not any particular persons but rather a generalized person, a generalized other, that is coextensive with the community of our associates. In this way the social explanation of the self is complete.

There is at least one other notion in Mead that merits a moment of attention and reflection, and that is his distinction between the "I" and the "me." The "I" is what we have called above the subjective self, and the "me" is the objective self. The I is both subjective and spontaneous, the me results from a recognition of the self as the bundle of attitudes and responses that is derived from the generalized other. The I initiates action but it becomes, in cognition and memory, the me. We do not, as we have seen in our earlier discussion, ever know the I because as soon as we know it—i.e., cognize it or recognize it—it has already become an object, and thus

---

[11] Sprott, *op. cit.*, p. 129.

the me. It is the I that is unique; the me is the product of the generalized other. The I is spontaneous, therefore, and the me conventional. The me cooperates with the community because the community is its source and origin as the generalized other.

The separation of the self into an I and a me can serve as a transition to the Freudian view of the matter, to which we now briefly turn. If Mead used these two components, Freud used three—the id, the ego, and the superego or, as they appeared in the original German, the *Es*, the *Ich*, and the *Über-Ich*.[12] The id represents our appetites, those inborn drives that prompt us to act. It seeks pleasure and avoids pain—and gives added resonance to the famous sentence of Jeremy Bentham (1748–1832) that "Nature has placed mankind under the governance of two sovereign masters, Pain and Pleasure." The id furnishes the impulse, the impulse to do what we want because it is what we want to do, without regard to friends or society, conscience or morality.

We are not, however, permitted to do what we want. We are not allowed to steal the steak in our neighbor's freezer, to initiate conversation with the prettiest of passing females, or to hit the person who infuriates us with his willful stupidity. We are required to adjust our desires to the reality of a world in which they may not be fulfilled. It is the second mechanism of the mind, the ego, that helps us to do this. It mediates between the impulses of the id and the moral exigencies of the world in which we live. It is the ego that weighs the claims of the id against the demands of society, making now some space for impulse and now some reins for restraint, and thus contributing to the long-term adjustment of the individual. The ego is thus the manager of the self.

The moral restraint that society imposes also has its agent in the self—and this is the superego. The superego tells us what is right and what is wrong; it is the "Sunday school" of the mind, the conscience of the individual. It tells us what we ought and—more frequently perhaps—ought not to do. It imposes upon us the moral imperatives of society. It inhibits the freedom of impulse. The id and the superego, then, stand in opposition, the one to the other. If all of our impulses cannot be gratified, however, neither can they all be restrained without serious harm to the individual. It is the task of the ego then to serve as the umpire in this permanent contest.

The contest, incidentally, is an internal one and is not identical with the process, to be described in the following chapter of this book, in which

---

[12] Philip Rieff suggests that the Latin words, now used invariably in English discussions, as contrasted with Spanish and French for example, have contributed to the complexities of the Freudian "rhetoric" and obscure what a simple translation—the It, the I, and the Super-I— would otherwise make clear. See his study *Freud: The Mind of the Moralist*, Anchor Books, Doubleday & Company, Inc., Garden City, N.Y., 1961, note to p. 64.

the sanctions applied by our companions induce us to conform to the norms. This, on the contrary, is the self in conflict with itself. As Philip Rieff so clearly expresses it:

> No small part of Freud's impact upon the contemporary moral imagination derives from his idea of the self in conflict. He conceives of the self not as an abstract entity, uniting experience and cognition, but as the subject of a struggle between two objective forces—unregenerate instincts and overbearing culture. Between these two forces there may be compromise but no resolution. Since the individual can neither extirpate his instincts nor wholly reject the demands of society, his character expresses the way in which he organizes and appeases the conflict between the two.[13]

The id meets the superego head-on, as it were. They are always on a collision course. It is in this contrary juxtaposition that the awareness of self arises and it is this conflict that gives us our conception of it. It is in the repression of impulse that we become conscious of the fact that there is something else in the universe than our selves, and it is this consciousness that gives us also the sense of self.

There are thus certain similarities in the theories of Cooley, Mead, and Freud. All three, however different their intellectual orientations, arrive at a theory of the self that requires society. For none of the three is self-consciousness possible without the presence and, in one case, the repressions, of society. Thus in three writers we have a view of the self that is explicitly sociological. The individual has a self only because he first acquires a society.

It may be that the reader of this book will be reluctant to accept any such sociological theory of the self. The trouble is that the demonstrable facts we have on this subject are insufficient to support a general theory and the theories therefore still have in them some flavor of speculation. It may be that in spite of Cooley, Mead, and Freud, there is a primal self-consciousness after all, a subjective self that has an initial and permanent independence of all external influences whether these originate in the inhibitions of a society or in the obduracies of the physical universe. We have no disposition to argue the case, either here or elsewhere, because, as Nietzsche said, "One's own self is well hidden from one's own self." However this may be, we should doubtless all agree that, whether or not we have a primal self-consciousness, we need a language to make it articulate—even to make ourselves aware that we have it—and language is both product and vehicle of culture. We cannot know the meaning of "I" and

---

[13] *Ibid.*, p. 29.

"me" and "mine" until there are such words in the language as "I" and "me" and "mine," and we learn these meanings only in intercourse and association with our fellows—with you and yours, and them and theirs. The subjective self, the elusive self, may not require any cultural assistance for its existence, but the objective self cannot dispense with such assistance. To this extent at least, the self is social.

5. Personality and Culture

On the first page of this book we made the now rather common observation that in certain respects we are like all other people, in certain other respects like some other people, and in still others like no one except ourselves. We have said that the second of these propositions is particularly appropriate to sociology and we shall see later that people do fall into similar groupings depending upon their possession of characteristics they have in common. A logical inference from this proposition would be that all those who are exposed to the same culture are alike, and it would be difficult to explain therefore how each human personality could be unique. The truth is that not everyone is exposed to exactly the same culture, not even those who are children in the same family. We need therefore to explore this complicated situation in a little more detail in order to see how culture is related to personality.

Let us notice first of all that culture is not a monolithic entity, a hardened mold into which each individual is poured at birth, a cookie cutter designed to produce innumerable individuals all exhibiting exactly the same traits and attributes. Culture is not a uniform pattern that impresses itself alike upon all who are exposed to it, nor is it a uniform that all must wear. Consider, for example, the regional differences in culture that occur within a single society. There is a difference between a Middle Westerner and an Easterner in the United States, a Highlander and a Lowlander in Scotland, a Prussian and a Bavarian in Germany, a Venetian and a Sicilian in Italy, and so on, in addition to other differences that they might exhibit. There are different traditions born of different regions, and these tend to create different personalities and different temperaments. The Middle Westerner is more open, friendlier, "breezier," it may be, the New Englander more reserved and, some would say, more dignified in his contacts, especially initial ones, with other people. These differences are fairly obvious and there is no need to expatiate upon them except to say that any culture that is shared by a large number of people reasonably distributed in space is a mosaic of subcultures—subcultures created by region and religion, class and occupation, education and political belief. Not all of the children in the same society confront the same culture because of the many subcultures that every complex society contains.

In the second place, the culture may present alternative lines of action that are equally acceptable and yet one of them may affect the personality in one way and the second in another. In our own culture, for example, babies may be breast-fed or bottle-fed and both procedures are in conformity with the norms. There are those who would contend that breast feeding is preferable to bottle feeding on the ground that the greater intimacy with the mother contributes to a greater emotional security. Whether or not this is the case, few would doubt that there could be a differential effect upon personality. Similarly, infant feeding may be periodic or permissive, on either a definite or a "demand" schedule, and again both alternatives are permitted by the culture and may exert slightly different influences upon the personality. The point is that there are cultural alternatives as well as cultural specifications and not all cultural patterns are cultural imperatives.

Newly arrived members of a society do not confront the same culture for still another reason. Culture does not transmit itself. It is transmitted only by individuals and these individuals have absorbed different bits and pieces of the culture to which they in their turn were initially exposed. No two sets of parents, even of the same race, religion, and region, will transmit to their offspring the same cultural items and traits. One of the problems of marital adjustment (a continuous process) in fact stems from the circumstance that the two individuals involved, even when they have the same ethnic antecedents, the same religion, the same social class background, and a comparable education, will bring to each other different cultural emphases and conform to slightly different norms. One of the couple will squeeze the tube of toothpaste from the bottom (as it should be squeezed!) and the other at the top. After the children come, the culture that one pair of parents transmits will be different in perceivable particulars from the culture that is being transmitted to the new generation next door in the same housing development. Each family, in a sense, has its own subculture.

If the cultures exhibit these slight discrepancies, so also does the social situation in which the infant finds himself and which also has an effect upon the development of personality. The social group that the only child belongs to in his family is clearly not the same social group in which two children are members—or three or five or eight. A child who has brothers only is in a different social and cultural situation from one who has only sisters, and his own sex is an additional variable in the situation. Birth order is still another factor that can affect the personality and it is obvious again that first and last children have both advantages and disadvantages that do not accrue to the middle children. Closely related to this is another variable, the age of the parents, and once more it is easy to see that a child of young parents has a better chance to learn to water-ski, for example, than the child of older parents. Even with roughly the same culture, in short, the social situation in a single family is different for each of its younger members, and consequently the personalities that develop can be different too.

Variety is endless in human life, and various also are the influences to which the developing personality is exposed. Several more factors that encourage idiosyncrasy still require a remark or two. We have not yet said that if the culture is not uniform, neither is it static. In the complex societies that we know best it is changing all the time and, so far as we can determine without fixed points for comparison, at a rapid rate as well. Even if the ages of parents could be held constant, children born into the same family a decade apart would encounter a different culture—and in some respects a dramatically different one. Culture is a dynamic, changing thing, and presents with every passing period new facets and a new frontier.

We have to notice too that the original material that comes to the culture to be shaped and formed and conditioned and directed is also highly variable. No two biological organisms, no two newly born babies, are exactly alike in every talent, attribute, and trait—although the case of identical twins comes close to being an exception. There are biological differences too, genetic in character, that make every human infant different from every other and able, in consequence, to respond in different ways to the same or similar cultural stimuli. We should not overstress the biological basis of personality, but we must not understress it either. As we have said before, to the adult human being both heredity and environment have their share to contribute.

We may mention finally that the culture itself can place a greater emphasis upon individuality than upon conformity. Culture can offer alternatives as well as specifications and its norms, as we shall see, are areas of permissiveness as well as guides for conduct. Initiative, inventiveness, originality, adaptability to new situations can all be values that are ranked highly in a particular culture, just as their contraries can be ranked highly in others. Wherever we find an emphasis upon individuality we have a cultural factor operating to diminish what would otherwise be a cultural uniformity.

We have offered a number of reasons why culture does not sculpture personalities into a common mold: (1) cultures themselves lack uniformity in their spatial distribution; (2) cultures are transmitted atomistically, as it were, by persons who possess different collections of items and traits; (3) the social situations in which personalities are acquired produce additional cultural varieties; (4) cultures may change rapidly even in brief periods of time; (5) the individual's organic constitution accounts for its share of variation; and (6) the culture may encourage individuality and even, in some respects, idiosyncrasy. For all of these reasons there may appear in a given culture a wide range of variation in personality type, and indeed this tends to be the case.

There are those who maintain nevertheless that the relationship between culture and personality is quite close and that culture encourages the development of certain types of personality and discourages certain others. They argue that cultures are congenial to the development of certain kinds of personalities because of the ideas and ideologies they contain. In some the virtues of humility, modesty, and withdrawal, for example, may win rewards in personal esteem and in others the contrary traits of boastfulness, self-acclaim, and aggressiveness. Some may stress order and efficiency and neatness whereas in others these attributes would receive only a secondary emphasis, if indeed they are considered important at all. Still others may give a high priority to ambition, material success, and "getting ahead." Different goals, aspirations, hopes, and fears may all receive a different stress and in this way a particular culture may encourage the development of a particular kind of personality. Those who support this view offer as evidence the case of our own culture, for example, where there is a sharp differentiation of sex roles and where boys, therefore, are taught to be masculine—that is, to develop those personality traits associated with maleness—and girls on the other hand are taught to be feminine. That these differences are all culturally determined, however, is a theory that we treat with some skepticism in another chapter of this book.

Other evidence comes from the study of cultures quite different from our own and appears in the literature of anthropology. The most famous of these studies perhaps are Ruth Benedict's *Patterns of Culture* and Margaret Mead's *Sex and Temperament in Three Primitive Societies*, both of which were published in 1935. In these books we are told that the Zuñi Indians are calm, the Kwakiutl competitive, the Dobuans suspicious, the Arapesh amiable, the Mundugumor treacherous—and these differences in temperament are attributed to the culture. Similarly, writers like Abram Kardiner and Ralph Linton have utilized the concept of a "basic personality structure" that is supposedly congenial with the total range of institutions to be found in a given culture.[14]

The cogency of these claims for the cultural determination of personality would seem to depend very largely upon one's definition of personality. Writers in this field have different conceptions of it and among the various definitions we find such expressions as an integration of habit systems, a totality of physiological and psychological reaction systems, a cultural mold, the events whose locus defines the individual in relation to surrounding individuals, the individual's social stimulus value, a structural whole, definable in terms of its own distinctive structural attributes, a

[14] See Abram Kardiner *et al.*, *The Psychological Frontiers of Society*, Columbia University Press, New York, 1945; and Ralph Linton, *The Cultural Background of Personality*, Appleton-Century-Crofts, Inc., New York, 1945.

structural organism-environment field, a primordial stuff, a pattern of accidentally imposed conditionings, an achieved inner structure, and the dynamic organization of those psychophysical systems that determine the individual's unique adjustment to his environment. Some of these expressions are paraphrases, others quotations culled from a number of psychologists. Some of them, as can be seen, stress the organic and some the environmental, some the individual and some the social, some the personal and some the cultural—and indeed these adjectives may be regarded in this context as three sets of synonyms.

Now it is fairly clear that if we define personality as "a cultural mold," then we can easily accept the view that personality is determined by culture. It is true by definition. If, on the other hand, we regard personality as some kind of "primordial stuff," then we must reject this view. It is false by definition. Our own conclusion would go to neither of these extremes. We would tend to subscribe to an intermediate position and say that neither psychology, with its emphasis upon individual differences, nor sociology, with its emphasis upon cultural similarities, can by itself give an adequate account of personality. It would seem to be a superior strategy to regard personality as a biosocial phenomenon, the study of which belongs properly to a social psychology or—what is the same thing, though a more awkward expression—a psychological sociology.

We should like, however, to stress two facts about the confrontation of the individual and his culture—one, that it is a two-way process, not like the pouring of an infinitely plastic substance into an unyielding container, and two, that the process is a continuous one, not something that begins in infancy and ends at adulthood. One might say with respect to the first of these observations that the word "process" is too mild, that actually there is a struggle going on that frequently results, for the individual, in frustration and anxiety. "One lives," as Ernest van den Haag has poetically expressed it, "in the tension between society and solitude,"[15] and this is the tension too that gives pertinence to the Freudian theory of the self. Sometimes the cultural impress does not "take," sometimes it stimulates the individual to "counterattack," sometimes, even when cultural patterns are apparently accepted, tensions may flare up later and result either in personality disorders or in an effort to change the offending part of the culture.

Furthermore, individuals react in different ways to these cultural pressures and impressions. As Gardner Murphy suggests, "One child is easily molded with regard to food but fights constantly against socialization

---

[15] In Ernest van den Haag, *Passion and Social Constraint*, Stein and Day, New York, 1963, p. 126.

of his aggressive impulses; the reverse may be true of another child."[16] Complete uniformity and a total absence of innovation would be the stagnant result of a process in which every individual bore the unchanging imprint of a monolithic culture. It is easy, in short, to exaggerate the effect of culture upon personality—an exaggeration that was fashionable in the culture and personality theories of several decades ago. Personality is not a passive creation of culture—as the differing temperaments of siblings should have shown us. Yet one cannot wholly ignore the influence of culture either. However useful the concept of "basic personality structure" may be, there is a difference between the typical Englishman, the typical German, the typical Turk, and the typical Brazilian. The trouble is that few of these Englishmen, Germans, Turks, and Brazilians are typical.

6. The Agents of Socialization

Personalities do not come ready-made. The process that transforms the primitive organism—the puking, mewling, bawling, caterwauling infant— into a reasonably respectable human being is a long process and one that is apt to be arduous for all concerned. As sociologists we are inclined to see the culture on the one side and the individual on the other and wonder what effect each has upon the other. To look at the problem in this way, however, is in part erroneous and in part artificial, because on the one side—the individual—we have a concrete entity, and on the other—the culture—we have an abstraction. How an entity interacts with an abstraction is not a meaningful question. We can give it meaning, however, by eradicating the abstraction, as it were, and by emphasizing something we have previously recognized, namely, that culture is always transmitted by people in interaction. It is transmitted through the communication they have with one another, and communication thus comes to be the essence of the process of culture transmission. It is the basic—though not the only[17]—instrument of socialization, and a versatile instrument it is too, since it operates between those who do not know one another as well as between those who do. Let us consider this instrument in a little more detail so that we may disclose the specific kinds of communication through which the child acquires his culture.

It must be fairly apparent that the process of culture transmission begins for every one of us in the family, and that the parental—and

---

[16] Gardner Murphy, *Personality*, Harper & Row, Publishers, Incorporated, New York, 1947, p. 905.
[17] There are other mechanisms too, for example imitation, which was treated so brilliantly by the French sociologist Gabriel Tarde (1843–1904).

especially the maternal—influence upon the infant is the most important of all. Given the basic abilities that are genetically present and transmitted through the germ plasm, this most intimate of all human relationships, that between mother and child, must be accorded the largest significance in the socialization process and in the shaping of these abilities and capacities in ways that the culture helps to determine. The father, of course, is important too, but his role is defined in somewhat different ways in different cultures and in some, as is seen in a later chapter on the family, the father is less important than the mother's brother. Nevertheless, it is the father in most societies who transmits to his sons the knowledge and the skill in particular activities that males in these societies are expected to acquire. In any event, these are the communications—with mother and father—through which the child receives an introduction to his culture, an introduction which, in advanced societies, is somewhat prolonged in time. He receives additional communications from his older siblings, who have gone through the same process—with certain differences due to birth order, as we have already recognized, and to the number and sex of the siblings.

The role of siblings in the socialization process leads us by an easy transition to the role of peer groups. Peer groups, as the word implies, means those groups made up of the contemporaries of the child, his associates in school and in Sunday school, in playground and in street. He learns from these children, as indeed they learn from him, facts and facets of the culture that they have previously learned, at different times, from their parents. The members of peer groups have other sources of information about the culture—their peers in still other peer groups—and thus the acquisition of culture goes on, with much of the socialization process a function of precisely these kinds of groups.

As time goes on, of course, the peer group surpasses the parental and family group in importance, and by the time the children are in high school, in our culture, they have begun openly and candidly to reject the parental influence in favor of the obvious superiority of the information and guidance they receive from their contemporaries. This seems to be an inevitable occurrence in rapidly changing societies—it might be called the displacement of the parents by the peers—and no one doubts that it occurs in ours. The teen ages are the ages par excellence of parent-child misunderstanding. Mark Twain gave his own inimitable recognition of this fact when he said, "When I was sixteen my old man was so stupid I could hardly stand to have him around; but when I got to be twenty-one I was surprised to see how much he had learned in the meantime."

Certainly it is true that the peer culture takes precedence over the parental culture in the adolescent years and the advice of one's contemporaries, whether overtly or covertly communicated, sets the standard in almost every aspect of conduct. We should not assume, therefore, that the socialization process is completed by the time the teen ages are reached. On the contrary, this is the time when the pressures for conformity are perhaps at their height, when deviance in the ordinary affairs of life is punished most severely by one's associates, when conformity is required with a daily and almost hourly insistence. The American high school might be described, in fact, as a hotbed of conformity. No one who suffers it is competent to write about it and those who write about it can no longer remember it with precision. An exception is Phyllis McGinley, who wrote an exquisite description of it in a poem entitled "A Certain Age," a part of which we quote:

> All of a sudden, bicycles are toys
> Not locomotion. Bicycles are for boys
> And seventh-graders, screaming when they talk.
> A girl would rather
> Take vows, go hungry, put on last year's frock,
> Or dance with her own father
> Than pedal down the block.
>
> This side of childhood lies a narrow land,
> Its laws unwritten, altering out of hand,
>
> But, more than Sparta's, savagely severe.
> Common or gentry,
> The same taboos prevail. One learns, by ear,
> The customs of the country
> Or pays her forfeit here.[18]

Parents and peers, however, are not the only agencies of the socialization process. There are teachers too and thus the school comes to play its own important role. It is hardly necessary to discuss that role, so obvious is it in every society that has an institution of education. It is in the school that the culture is formally transmitted and acquired, in which the lore and the learning, the science and the art, of one generation is passed on to the next. It is not only the formal knowledge of the culture that is transmitted there but most of its premises as well—its ethical sentiments, its political attitudes, its customs and taboos. The children in the earlier school may uncritically absorb the culture to which their teachers give expression; they

---

[18] Reprinted in *Times Three, Selected Verse from Three Decades*, The Viking Press, Inc., New York, 1960, p. 45. By permission. By the time these words appear in print, of course, bicycles may have become popular in the American high school, as their use has increased in the rest of society. The sociological point Miss McGinley makes in her lines, however, remains unchallenged. In high school the cost of nonconformity is high.

may in the high school respond with increasing skepticism. But wherever they are, and at whatever age, the communications they receive from their teachers help to socialize them and to make them finally mature members of their societies.

There is another source of socialization, one that appears of course only in literate societies, and that is the printed word. The civilization that most of us share is constructed of words. Words rush at us in torrent and cascade; they leap into our vision, as in billboard and newspaper, magazine and textbook, and assault our ears, as in radio and television. "The media of mass communication," as our commentators, sociological and otherwise, like to call them, importune us with their messages and these messages too contain in capsule form the premises of our culture, its attitudes and ideologies. The words are always written by some one and these people too—authors and editors and advertisers—join the teachers, the peers, and the parents in the socialization process. In individual cases, of course, some of these influences are more important than others, and in any case there are inconsistencies and even contradictions among them. The responses can also differ. Some of us respect tradition; others fear the opinions of their peers; and still others prefer to listen to the "thousand tongues" of conscience. In the words of David Riesman, the first of these groups is tradition-directed, the second other-directed, and the third inner-directed. In Riesman's theory these three groups have different orders of preponderance under different historical conditions, but all three modes of socialization result in conformity of a kind and all three thus contribute to the transmission of a culture by some and its acquisition by others.[19]

7. Summary

In this chapter we have tried to take some of the mystery out of the process by which culture is transmitted from one generation to another in human societies. Our emphasis hitherto in this book has been upon the culture and the society; here we have turned to the individual and have suggested that what is culture transmission from the point of view of the society as a whole is socialization from the point of view of the individual. In earlier chapters we asserted that we are not born human, but become human in our association with others who already possess a culture. In this chapter we have endeavored to show how this association is the underlying mechanism by which culture is acquired.

[19] For Riesman's theory see his famous book *The Lonely Crowd*, Yale University Press, New Haven, Conn., 1950. Also, abridged, in Anchor Books, Doubleday & Company, Inc., Garden City, N.Y., 1953. The book was written in collaboration with Nathan Glazer and Reuel Denney.

It is necessary to recognize, however, that culture is not a simple, monolithic entity that is transmitted en masse and all of a piece to every new human individual who is exposed to it. Culture is a complex and variable thing—flexible, loose, not always integrated, sometimes rigid, sometimes permissive, sometimes inconsistent in its parts, and in truth amorphous. In other words, the systematic character of culture, which we have taken pains to elaborate in the preceding chapters, is not always apparent to the father who is scolding his child, the schoolmates who indicate their disapproval of something he is doing, and the teacher who finds the mistakes in his arithmetic. Socialization, in short, involves a partial, not a total, culture because human beings are involved and human beings have their whims, their idiosyncrasies, and their infinite variety.

In discussing the socialization process in general we had occasion to refer to a number of issues and problems that are related to it. First of all we suggested that the organism that confronts society and that is receptive to its culture is not, after all, an inert and passive organism. It is lively, intent, active. It goes to meet the culture; it seeks the stimuli to which it will respond; it is, in short, alive. The forces that motivate it have never been altogether clear, either in physiological or sociological terms, and the problem of motivation, therefore, remains unsolved. We thought it appropriate nevertheless to indicate some of the difficulties associated with it and to describe what happened with respect to one of these theories, the instinct theory that enjoyed so long a reign in the history of psychology.

Although we have previously considered the biological factor in society we thought it appropriate in this chapter also to look once again at the ancient issue of heredity and environment, primarily because it is an issue that occupies so much of the time and attention of social scientists and psychologists. A number of problems remain, of course, but they no longer engage the passions of partisans who would claim that heredity is more important than environment, or the other way around. As sociologists we can best use Sorokin's model of the phonograph which performs according to its quality a wide variety of musical selections depending upon the record that is placed upon its turntable. In the socialization process we may say therefore that the attributes of the organism are necessary conditions and the culture a sufficient condition to explain the personality that develops.

The following sections of the chapter dealt with the self—both the subjective self and the objective self. The first of these two subjects is a matter of almost pure speculation, as the section shows, because it is a subject that abounds in paradoxes. After playing with these paradoxes for a few pages we turned to the objective self, which is rather more amenable to investigation. In this section we explored the theories developed by Charles Horton Cooley, George Herbert Mead, and Sigmund Freud, and found in all three eminent cases that the self is social, that it requires society for its full explanation, and that our consciousness of it—our self-consciousness—arises in our interaction with others.

In the next section we examined with some skepticism the view, fairly popular in recent decades, that culture is the sole determinant of personality. This position, plausible on the surface, nevertheless presents many difficulties. These difficulties seriously affect the concept of a basic personality structure and they appear especially because of variations in both the cultural and the social situations that face the individual in his developmental career. A culture would have to be much less variable than it is, and social situations would have to be much more constant, in order to construct this basic structure. Some attributes of personality are indeed traceable to culture. National differences and religious differences, to mention only two, encourage the development of different personality traits. But again, individual differences and variations in social situations make it difficult if not impossible for consistent personality types to emerge—to say nothing of different initial constitutions. The story of personality is one of the most complex of the problems that belong to social psychology. We do our sociology no service when we make personality entirely a function of culture. Personality in truth, as we said, is a biosocial phenomenon and one that can be understood neither by psychology nor sociology in independence of the other.

We concluded, briefly, with an emphasis upon four of the most important of the agents of socialization—parents, peers, teachers, and the mass media—suggesting how each contributes its share to the never-ending process that begins with the human infant, only barely qualified for admission to the human race, and ends with his acceptance as a member of society. In between the initial material and the end result there is the socialization process, the process by which all of us acquire the culture that we shall, in turn, transmit to the next generation as it arrives upon our scene with its own pressing need to be socialized.

4

SOCIAL ORGANIZATION

IN THIS SECTION we arrive at the vital center of sociology. It is important to realize, however, that when we turn from culture to social organization we are not changing the subject. Social organization is a part of culture, just as art, science, philosophy, and kitchenware are parts of culture. Ideas and materiel engage the interest of all the social sciences, and of the humanities too, but the norms are of particular interest to sociology because they constitute the basis, the very foundation, of the social structure. In the first chapter of this section, therefore, we treat the norms in detail and indicate how they contribute this essential service to society. But norms alone are not enough. They are only one of the elements of social organization. Furthermore, norms are not "free-floating" phenomena. They are attached to something, and the "something" to which they are attached is statuses, the subject of the second chapter in this section. We shall see that

society is a network of statuses and
that norms and statuses together constitute
its structure.

The subject of statuses leads directly
to a discussion of groups because, as will
become apparent in the third of these
chapters, every person in society has as
many statuses as there are groups of
which he is a member. Groups are
indeed central to sociology, and we shall
accordingly give them an extensive
treatment.

Two closely related phenomena—
associations and institutions—receive
attention in a chapter of their own, and
the section concludes with separate
chapters on two rather complex but
significant subjects, authority and power.
We thus have seven elements that constitute
the structure of society—norms, statuses,
groups, associations, institutions,
authority, and power.

The section as a whole should provide
the reader with a firm sense of the social
order and a knowledge of the factors that
contribute structure and stability to
human societies wherever they may
appear.

Chapter 8

NORMS

OCIAL RELATIONS assume a
remarkable and, it sometimes
seems, an almost miraculous order
and stability. Every day we interact
with dozens of people, some of whom
we know and some of whom we do
not know. How is this possible? How
does it happen that social relations
between people of all kinds and
varieties, of all ages and both
sexes, run along even as
smoothly as they do? The answer
is to be found in the norms that
prevail in every society and that
constitute an important component
of its structure. In Chapter 6, on
the content of culture, we pointed out
that culture is comprised of three
phenomena—ideas, norms, and
materiel. We suggested there that
there are several kinds of ideas and
also several kinds of materiel. We
began to construct a table of culture
to illustrate not only the major
categories but also some of the
subdivisions. The column under
norms, however, is still vacant.
We now turn, therefore, to a more
detailed discussion of norms, a
subject of fundamental significance
to sociology.

No science can include all three
of the components of culture within its
purview, for they obviously
comprehend the whole of human
activity and of human achievement.
It is the business of philosophy, for

example, to study ideas as it is of physics and chemistry to study the material universe. Culture is too complex—too big—to be thoroughly examined by anything but a universal science, and no such science exists. Philosophy itself once performed that function, and in ancient Greece all knowledge was a part of her eminent domain. But the days of the system builders are past, and no one human mind can now embrace the whole of human knowledge. Nor can any one science or discipline embrace it.

The concept of culture, as we have seen, is one of enormous importance for an understanding of human society and for an insight into why people do the things they do. But sociology is not and cannot be concerned with culture in its entirety. The science of anthropology can to some extent lay claim to such a concern, but only in so far as it is an inquiry directed to nonliterate peoples. When the society is small and relatively simple it may be possible for an investigator to encompass it all—its climate, cookery, economy, language, government (if any), religion, myths and legends, child-raising practices, sexual practices, burial customs, techniques, taboos, and even the personalities of its people. But such a task would be impossible for a society of any significant size or degree of complexity. In this case various specialists, such as geographers, economists, linguists, political scientists, theologians, literary critics, historians, engineers, psychologists, and philosophers all attend to their own particular areas of investigation, and only in the work of all of them put together can we begin to have an idea of what the total culture is like.

The sociologist has a specialty here too. His concern is with the ways in which people live together, interact with one another, and adopt and follow certain usages that characterize their society and distinguish it from others. These ways are also a part of the culture and have been developed through a long process of cultural construction. In no society do individuals live alone for extended periods of time. In all societies people learn to get along with other people and in fact to have more or less constant social relations with other people. And there are established ways for doing this, just as there are established ways for growing yams or for building canoes or for chopping down trees or for speaking a language. These established ways are called norms.

1. The Nature of a Norm

In the preceding chapter we introduced the subject of norms with a reference to a mythical baseball game. It became obvious immediately that baseball, like other games, would be impossible without rules. These rules are norms, and one may say that they constitute the structure of every game, from baseball to bridge. We then looked up into the grandstand and noticed that the spectators were conforming to rules too. These rules also are norms, the norms appropriate to viewing a baseball game. There are penalties for violating these norms, just as there are for violating the norms on the diamond. A man, for example, who insists upon the right to occupy a box seat when he has only a bleacher ticket will be firmly escorted to the bleachers or, if he continues his insistence, out of the ball park. The official in this case is called a policeman rather than an umpire, but, as we shall see, police action is by no means the only way or even the most important way of encouraging conformity to norms.

What is true of baseball in this respect is equally true of all the situations of society. Whatever order and regularity they exhibit is attributable to the presence of norms to which the participants, in various degrees, conform. A norm, then, is a rule or a standard that governs our conduct in the social situations in which we participate. It is a societal expectation. It is a standard to which we are expected to conform whether we actually do so or not. It is a cultural specification that guides our conduct in society. It is a way of doing things, the way that is set for us by our society. It is also, as we shall see, an essential instrument of social control.

In producing this book the author and publisher have conformed to a large number of norms. To mention only a few, the book is divided into chapters, the chapters are numbered and named, the table of contents is at the beginning, the indexes are at the end, the footnotes are at the bottom of the page, and the pages are numbered consecutively in Arabic numerals. If we had tampered with these norms in the slightest particular, for example if we had put the indexes at the beginning or the table of contents at the end,[1] or if we had put the footnotes at the top of the page instead of at the bottom, the result would jar the reader and make him wonder whether we knew what we were doing. He might not express his discomfiture in exactly these words—he might not express it at all—but he would know that we had violated a norm.

Similarly, the author has tried to use "correct" English. English is correct when it conforms to the norms of grammatical usage. we begin our sentences with a capital letter and end them with a period? This last sentence looks as if something were drastically wrong with it. The words mean what they say, but in writing them the author has violated the norms of punctuation. The result is disturbing. It is wrong. Thus the norms surround us all of the time, but we are so accustomed to them that we seldom notice them except when we violate them—or begin to read sociology.

It should be remarked that a norm is not a statistical average. It is not

---

[1] In many French books the table of contents is at the end and there is no index.

a mean, a median, or a mode. It refers not to the average behavior of a number of persons in a specific social situation, but instead to the expected behavior, the behavior that is considered appropriate in that situation. It is statistical only in the sense that a significant number of people in a group regard it as a standard procedure. It is a norm in our society, for example, to say "Please" when requesting a favor and "Thank you" when a favor is received, but no statistical count of the actual frequency of occurrence of these polite expressions is available. Nor would such a count be relevant. The norm is considered the standard procedure, whether or not anyone conforms to it, follows it, or observes it in a specific situation.

Similarly, the norm requiring premarital chastity in our society is almost certainly in process of change. But as long as conformity to it is expected by the majority, or is given frequent expression, no statistical account of deviation from it—were such a count possible—would change it. It is the expectation rather than the behavior that is relevant. Norms, in other words, to use a familiar Shakespearean expression, are sometimes more honored in the breach than in the observance, but their character as norms may remain unimpaired. In these cases we can discern a discrepancy between the ideal culture and the real culture of a given society or social group.

2. Norms and the Individual

We are frequently admonished by our elders and our teachers to think about what we are doing. The late philosopher Alfred North Whitehead once remarked that this advice is nonsense if it is meant to apply to the ordinary affairs of life. As a matter of fact, he continued, the more things we can do *without* thinking the better off we are.[2] If we had to reflect and deliberate and think about what we are going to do when we enter a store, classroom, cafeteria, or ticket line and meet a clerk, teacher, cashier, or ticket seller, we should be able to accomplish only a very small number of our objectives in the course of a day. The principal function of the norms for the individual is thus to reduce the necessity for decision in the innumerable

---

[2] The case of the centipede is illustrative:
  "The centipede was happy quite
      Until a toad in fun
  Said, 'Pray, which leg goes after which?'
  That worked her mind to such a pitch,
  She lay distracted in a ditch,
      Considering how to run."

—Credited to Mrs. Edward Craster, 1871

social situations that he confronts and in which he participates. Without them we should be faced from moment to moment with an almost intolerable burden of decision. Let us take the case of a hypothetical undergraduate and see how the norms of our society make it possible for him to get through the day without spending all of it in merely thinking about what to do and how to do it. When he wakes up in the morning he does not have to decide whether or not to wear shoes, whether to shave with a razor or with a pocket-knife, whether to greet his housemates in English or in some other language, whether to put the subject before the predicate in his sentences, whether to stir his coffee with a spoon or a fork, whether to say "Hello" or "So long" upon leaving his breakfast companions, whether to drop a quarter, a dime, or a token into the turnstile of the subway or the till of the bus or, if he is driving, whether to pass an approaching car on the right or the left, whether to smoke in the classroom or not, when to talk and when not to talk in class, whether to play baseball or cricket in the afternoon, and so on through more examples than could be put in even a much longer sentence than this one.

Now most of these examples and alternatives doubtless seem ridiculous and even silly. But the reason they seem so is precisely because there *are* norms in these situations. Without norms all of these decisions would have to be made. One can only imagine the confusion that would result in the absence of norms. Some people would be going through the cafeteria line in one direction and some in the other, and only a few would get fed. Indeed, it can readily be seen that without norms social relations would be haphazard, chaotic, and possibly even dangerous. It is the norms, therefore, that give order, stability, and predictability to social life and that, in consequence, are exceedingly important elements of the social structure. A situation of complete normlessness, or anomy, as Durkheim called it, would be intolerable, and no normless or anomic society could long endure. As anarchy is the contradiction of government, so anomy is the contradiction of society. Where there are no norms, there is also no society. We have thus discovered in the norms one source and locus of the order that society exhibits and have answered one of the basic questions set by sociological inquiry.

3. Varieties of Norms

Just as there are numerous kinds of ideas and numerous kinds of materiel, so also there are many kinds of norms. We are now ready to distinguish them and to complete our table of culture. We shall first merely list various phenomena that belong to this column:

Culture

Ideas	Norms	Materiel
	Laws	
	Statutes	
	Rules	
	Regulations	
	Customs	
	Folkways	
	Mores	
	Taboos	
	Fashion	
	Rites	
	Rituals	
	Ceremonies	
	Conventions	
	Etiquette	

Obviously such a list is unsatisfactory for systematic purposes because some of these words are almost synonymous and in any case there is much overlap. Unfortunately, there is no standard classification of the norms in the sociology texts and each sociologist has presented a somewhat different list. But we should be able to avoid verbal quibbles and semantic complications if we say merely that all of the norms may be subsumed under three major concepts—folkways, mores, and laws—which we shall discuss in turn.

Before we do this, however, we want to make two preliminary observations. The first of these is that the norms are both prescriptive and proscriptive; that is, the norms both prescribe, or require, certain actions and proscribe, or prohibit, certain other actions. We are required to wear clothes in our society and forbidden to go naked in the street. We are required to pass examinations in college courses at most universities and forbidden to obtain help from other people in doing so. We are required to register at specified times and we are not permitted to graduate without paying the prescribed fees. We are required to drive our automobiles on the right side of the road in the United States and are forbidden to run through a red light. Frequently the prescriptions and proscriptions come in pairs; that is, we are required to do something and forbidden not to do it, or forbidden to commit an act and required to omit it. Proscriptive norms, when they are not legal prohibitions, are known as taboos.

The second observation is that some of the norms pervade an entire society and others, less pervasive, prevail only in certain groups. We shall call the former *communal norms* and the latter *associational norms*. An example of a communal norm would be the custom of shaking hands upon meeting a new acquaintance, a custom that appears throughout our society, in all groups and classes. The custom of wearing an Oriental costume at conventions, on the other hand, applies only to the members of the Ancient Arabic Order, Nobles of the Mystic Shrine. The custom of eating three meals a day appears throughout the American society, but the requirement of passing a legal examination applies only to those who desire to be admitted to the bar.

These two ways of classifying norms—as prescriptive or proscriptive and as communal or associational—represent categories that cut across the others we are about to discuss. They should be kept in mind, therefore, as we proceed.

4. Folkways

Folkways is a term introduced by the late William Graham Sumner, professor at Yale and one of the earliest of American sociologists, in a famous book of that name published first in 1907. The word means literally the ways of the folk, the ways people have devised for satisfying their needs, for interacting with one another, and for conducting their lives. Each society, of course, has different folkways, just as each has different ideas and different material things—and thus a different culture. The word "folkways" was meant to emphasize these differences, and Sumner's book is filled with comparisons and contrasts drawn from societies all over the world and especially from nonliterate societies. Nonliterate societies are useful for this purpose because the contrasts appear in bolder relief and readily illustrate the fact that what is "right" in some societies may be "wrong" in others. A more familiar word for the practices of the folk, of people in their separate societies, is "customs" and we shall use "folkways" and "customs" synonymously, with perhaps a slight preference for "folkways" because it has come to be accepted as one of the concepts of sociology.

Folkways, in short, are norms to which we conform because it is customary to do so in our society. Conformity to the folkways is neither required by law nor enforced by any special agency of society. There is no law that requires us to wear shoes, to eat breakfast in the morning, to sleep in a bed, to sign our letters, to attend baseball games, to eat hot dogs and peanuts, to drink water from a glass and tea and coffee from a cup, to speak English or to use Arabic numerals in our calculations. And yet we do all of these things, and thousands like them, without thinking. It is a matter of custom, a matter of usage. They are our folkways. People who live in other parts of the world may do none of these things because their folkways are different.

Just as we found it impossible to catalogue all of the material culture traits of a society, so also we cannot construct a comprehensive list of its folkways. They are far too numerous and such a list would be endless. No encyclopedia could contain all of the customs observed by all of the peoples of history, nor even by all of the peoples living on earth today.[3] We can, however, note that folkways are a universal characteristic of human societies and that no society does or could exist without them. They thus constitute an important part of the social structure and contribute to the order and stability of social relations. In this respect, of course, they have the same function as the other kinds of norms still to be discussed.

5. The Mores

The mores differ from the folkways in the sense that moral conduct differs from merely customary conduct. Our society requires us to conform to the mores, without, however, having established a special agency to enforce conformity. The word *mores* is the Latin word for customs, but we use it rather as synonymous with morals; it is, of course, the Latin source of the word "morals."[4] Sumner also introduced this word into the sociological vocabulary and said that the mores are those practices that are believed to conduce to societal welfare. Folkways, on the contrary, do not have the connotation of welfare.

It is hard to see how the custom of tipping, for example, conduces to societal welfare. It could be abolished without any serious threat to the continuation and preservation of society. Indeed, in some sections of the United States the custom is considered to be "un-American"—since it implies a class difference between the giver and the recipient of the tip. Quite different is the situation with respect, let us say, to sexual behavior. Deviations in this sphere are regarded as threats to the family and, consequently, to the society. The man who supports a wife and a mistress is—in our society, but not necessarily in others—regarded as immoral. However different the cultural patterns surrounding sexual activities in various societies, persons who violate these patterns—the mores—are

---

[3] There are, however, valuable collections. See, for example, *The Golden Bough*, by Sir James G. Fraser, in twelve volumes. A one-volume edition, abridged by the author, was published by The Macmillan Company, New York, in 1922. See also William Graham Sumner, Albert G. Keller, and Maurice R. Davie, *The Science of Society*, 4 vols., Yale University Press, New Haven, Conn., 1927, and the Human Relations Area Files at Yale.

[4] *Mores* is plural; the singular, *mos*, is not used in sociology.

viewed as a danger to the society and are dealt with in a manner shortly to be explored.

It would be a mistake, however, albeit a common one, to limit morals to the sexual sphere. The cadet who violates the honor code at the United States Military Academy by cheating on an examination is regarded as immoral by his associates. A general has remarked that this code becomes so much a part of every graduate of the Academy that, like the virtue of his mother and sister, it is not an appropriate subject for discussion. The man or woman who pushes to the head of the line and buys a ticket out of turn is similarly violating one of the mores. The author who uses the expressions of other writers in his work without giving due credit to them is also violating the mores. So, too, is a person who is cruel to children or to animals.

In one town great public indignation was aroused against a man who built a high and unsightly "spite fence" around his property in protest against a veteran's prefabricated house on the adjoining lot. His action, well within the law since he had built the fence on his own ground, was nevertheless regarded as immoral by the neighbors and by the townspeople in general. A group of them tore it down one night, and he did not replace it. The action of a wealthy woman who wills her fortune to her cats rather than to her nephews and nieces would similarly be regarded as immoral. One may recognize the legal right to do this and at the same time regard it as immoral.

6. Laws

The norms that we call laws are perhaps the most familiar. Nevertheless, although all societies have folkways and mores, not all of them have laws. Laws appear only in societies with a political organization, that is a government. Laws are expressly enacted by legislatures or decreed as acts of legitimate authority by political officials, and some societies are so small or so simple that they lack these formal functions. Laws, in addition, are always written down and recorded in some fashion; obviously, therefore, they cannot appear in nonliterate societies. Some writers, it is true, expand the meaning of law to cover all the customs or rules whose observance is somehow required and enforced by recognized authority, in nonliterate as well as literate societies, and in this sense there is such a thing as primitive law. For sociological purposes, however, it seems better to limit the term to formally enacted and recorded norms, especially because it then becomes possible to sharpen the important distinction between laws on the one hand and folkways and mores on the other.

Folkways and mores, to use one of Sumner's expressions, are *crescive*; that is, like Topsy, they just grow. A simple example can be found in the college classroom. Seats are normally unassigned and students sit where they like. After the first few meetings of the class, however, the students tend to occupy the same seats every day and may even develop a proprietary attitude toward them. Thus a seating pattern emerges that was wholly unplanned. Similarly, no one ever consciously planned the position of the verb in the English sentence.

Laws, on the other hand, are *enacted*, and consequently appear only in civilized societies. They are enacted by legislatures, interpreted and applied by the courts, and enforced by police. They are familiar to all of us and require no detailed examination here. Familiarity, however, should not blind us to the fact that the concept of law itself, its exact nature and operation, is a problem full of sociological and philosophical complexities to which the disciplines of jurisprudence and the sociology of law both address themselves. Here we should like to introduce only the incidental observation that the common expression "the unwritten law" refers in fact, not to the laws at all, but to the mores. The unwritten law is usually invoked in opposition to some written law, and such instances illustrate the fact that laws and mores are not always in harmony and are sometimes in actual conflict. Whatever else may be said about laws, it is clear at least that they are enforced directly, not by the opinion of the community operating informally, but by the authority of the state operating formally as the political agent and instrument of society.

7. Sanctions

Sanctions are the supporters of the norms, the punishments applied to those who do not conform and the rewards given to those who do. Negatively, they may be anything from a raised eyebrow to the electric chair; positively, anything from a smile to an honorary degree. The negative sanction for violating one of the folkways is to be considered odd, or queer, or boorish, or impolite. The negative sanction for violating one of the mores is to be considered immoral.

There are more or less subtle ways in which disapproval may be expressed. One of the less subtle is ridicule, a powerful social sanction because no one likes to be considered ridiculous by those whose opinions he values. One likes to stand in well with others, especially with those who constitute his intimate groups, and such a sanction, therefore, usually has an immediate and direct effect when promptly applied to those who do not conform to the folkways. Ridicule, or what has been called "the satiric sanction," is, in short, so effective that in some primitive groups it is the only negative sanction needed and the sanction that, above all others, is used to induce children to learn, and to abide by, the customs of the society. But this satiric sanction is applied in all social groups. We conform both to the folkways and to the mores because we dislike being different, because we do not like the disapproval of our friends, because, in fact, we need their approval in order to live with ourselves.

To be told that something or other "just isn't done," is in most cases a more powerful sanction than any "official" penalty could be. Similarly, when we do as others do we are rewarded with their approval, and approval is therefore a positive sanction that encourages us to conform. The ultimate negative sanction for both the mores and the folkways is ostracism, a studied refusal to communicate with the violator, the banishment of the offender from the groups to which he wants to belong, sending him to Coventry. No one likes to be exiled from groups he considers his own, from his circle of intimates and friends, and ostracism is thus one of the cruelest punishments known to man.

Finally, there are the negative sanctions applied to violators of the laws. These are clear and familiar and stated in the laws themselves. They of course include fine, imprisonment, deportation, and, for some offenses, death. Although the sanctions may differ in degree and sometimes in character for the different norms, they all tend to separate the errant individual from his group and to cast upon him the spell of loneliness.

Sanctions are similarly used to support conformity to the ideologies of the groups of which one is a member. As mentioned in an earlier chapter, the sanctions that support the ideologies are often stronger than those supporting the mores, and what might be called "misbelief" frequently has more serious consequences than misbehavior. An American millionaire who contributed heavily to leftist causes once remarked that he could get drunk every night and still be held in highest esteem, but because of his political beliefs he was considered a traitor to his class. We have here an illustration of a sound sociological principle. Immorality, in short, attaches to ideas as well as to conduct, and it is the approved ideologies whose sanctity is most jealously guarded by the group.

Citizens who conform—and most of us do—are usually unaware of the strength of the pressures that operate to induce this conformity. Only when one is himself the victim of ostracism is it possible fully to appreciate the seriousness of this sanction. The records of history provide countless examples of individuals who were exiled from their groups for not conforming to the ideologies that these groups held sacred. The case of Spinoza is most instructive in this respect and it can illustrate the point better than many pages of description.

Baruch de Espinoza or, as we have come to know him, Benedict

Spinoza (1632–1677), one of the greatest philosophers of modern times, belonged to a family of Spanish Jews who, several generations earlier, had found sanctuary in Holland after Ferdinand and Isabella had banished them from Spain in the year that Columbus discovered America. The Jews prospered in Holland, which was one of the most liberal and enlightened of European countries. Spinoza, however, as a young philosopher, had come to question certain views concerning God, the angels, and the soul that were integral ideological components of both the Jewish and the Christian religions. The fathers of the synagogue, not wishing to incur the displeasure of their Christian neighbors, who had been hospitable to them, offered the young man a sum of money if he would keep silent about these views and maintain at least an external conformity with the ideologies. Spinoza refused, and on July 27, 1656, he was excommunicated, as the historian says, "with all the sombre formalities of Hebrew ritual":

> During the reading of the curse, the wailing and protracted note of a great horn was heard to fall in from time to time; the lights, seen brightly burning at the beginning of the ceremony, were extinguished one by one as it proceeded, till at the end the last went out—typical of the extinction of the spiritual life of the excommunicated man—and the congregation was left in total darkness.

There is dread and grandeur in the writ of excommunication:

> The heads of the Ecclesiastical Council hereby make known, that, already well assured of the evil opinions and doings of Baruch de Espinoza, they have endeavored in sundry ways and by various promises to turn him from his evil courses. But as they have been unable to bring him to any better way of thinking; on the contrary, as they are every day better certified of the horrible heresies entertained and avowed by him, and of the insolence with which these heresies are promulgated and spread abroad, and many persons worthy of credit having borne witness to these in the presence of the said Espinoza, he has been held fully convicted of the same. Review having therefore been made of the whole matter before the chiefs of the Ecclesiastical Council, it has been resolved, the Councillors assenting thereto, to anathematize the said Spinoza, and to cut him off from the people of Israel, and from the present hour to place him in Anathema with the following malediction:
>
> With the judgment of the angels and the sentence of the saints, we anathematize, execrate, curse and cast out Baruch de Espinoza, the whole of the sacred community assenting, in presence of the sacred books with the six-hundred-and-thirteen precepts written therein, pronouncing against him the malediction wherewith Elisha cursed the children, and all the maledictions written in the Book of the Law. Let him be accursed by day, and accursed by night; let him be accursed in his lying down, and accursed in his rising up, accursed in going out and accursed in coming in. May the Lord nevermore

pardon or acknowledge him, may the wrath and displeasure of the Lord burn henceforth against this man, load him with all the curses written in the Book of the Law, and blot out his name from under the sky; may the Lord sever him forever from all the tribes of Israel, weight him with all the maledictions of the firmament contained in the Book of the Law; and may all ye who are obedient to the Lord your God be saved this day.

Hereby then are all admonished that none hold converse with him by word of mouth, none hold communication with him by writing; that no one do him any service, no one abide under the same roof with him, no one approach within four cubits length of him, and no one read any document dictated by him, or written by his hand.[5]

8. Associational Norms

The state, which embraces and supports the legal norms, that is, the laws, is only one of the associations of society. All organized groups have their rules and regulations, their formal statutes that set out the obligations and responsibilities of the members to one another and to the association itself. These norms we call associational norms.

The policeman who represents the state, or a subdivision thereof, has no interest, for example, in the time of night that a college girl returns to her dormitory after an evening engagement. The dean of women, on the other hand, depending on the parietal rules, may have a highly developed curiosity about matters of this kind. A college or university, in other words, has its own formal rules and regulations, which are separate from the laws of the state and which may or may not coincide with them. These are the norms of the association. And so also do all of the associations of society have their own norms.

These norms pertain, of course, only to the members of the association. Frequently they are more stringent and more comprehensive in their regulation of behavior than are the laws of the state. Thus, the monk in his monastery, the member of the Olympic swimming team, and the teacher in the public school enjoys more privileges perhaps but also suffers more restrictions than do those who, let us say, are merely citizens. Each of these associations imposes its own set of norms upon the individuals who belong to it.

It is interesting to observe in this connection that a subsidiary association of the state, the United States Navy, is much more rigid and specific in its regulation of the daily conduct of its members than is the state

---

[5] The writ and the quotation immediately preceding are taken from R. Willis, *Benedict de Spinoza*, London, 1870, pp. 34–35, as quoted by Will Durant, *The Story of Philosophy*, Simon and Schuster, Inc., New York, 1926, pp. 168–169.

itself. Furthermore, in the society at large only a few offenses against the criminal law—murder, kidnapping, treason, and rape in some jurisdictions—are punishable by death. The military code of the Navy, however, visits this penalty upon many more offenses than these. The sanction of death, for example, may be applied, upon conviction by a general court-martial and in accordance with the Articles for the Government of the Navy, to anyone in the presence of an enemy "who treacherously yields or pusillanimously cries for quarter."[6] Cowardice in the community is an offense against the mores; in the Navy it is in addition a violation of a statute, or associational norm.

In some cases, in a complex society, the rules and regulations of an association may conflict with the laws of the state, as for example in the case of a criminal gang, a gambling syndicate, or even a college fraternity that requires a pledge to steal a highway sign in order to qualify for initiation. The relationship between the laws of the state and the statutes of other associations within the community is a complex subject and many of the problems of government arise precisely in this relationship.

The sanction for violation of associational norms is quite clear. Continued violation brings dismissal from the association and consequent withdrawal of the rights and privileges of membership. The dean of women has the authority to suspend the undergraduate woman who keeps later hours than the university statutes permit. The American Bar Association will similarly suspend from membership a lawyer guilty of violation of its norms, and the American Medical Association will expel a physician who indulges in unethical conduct, as specified in its official codes.

The principal difference between the laws, which are the norms of the state, and the norms of other associations is that the former apply to everyone in the country—since everyone, including those who are not yet citizens, comes under the jurisdiction of the state—whereas the associational norms apply only to members of the association. One assumes the obligation to conform to the latter only by formally joining the association, and frequently a formal pronouncement of allegiance is a condition of membership. The laws are simply broader in their application. Only by relinquishing one's residence and going to a foreign country can one avoid them, but then he falls immediately under the jurisdiction of another set of laws. When one withdraws from the university, on the contrary, he ceases to be bound by its regulations.

Actually, as we shall have occasion to see, the state is an association like the others, only larger, more pervasive, and more comprehensive. It is

---

[6] This fine literary expression, dating back to Revolutionary times, was altered in 1951 to the weak phrase "is guilty of cowardly conduct."

an association to which all of the inhabitants of a society in some sense belong. But it is nevertheless one association, one organized group, among many. Laws, too, are thus associational norms. They have a special name—"laws"—only because the state is a special kind, and an especially important kind, of association in modern complex societies.

In summary, then, when we speak of laws, we mean the norms of the state; when we speak of other formal rules and regulations, we mean the norms of other associations in society. In both cases the norms have become institutionalized, that is, regularized and enacted. The differences between them are only differences of degree: (1) laws are more pervasive than other associational norms in that they are universally and, in theory, evenly applicable throughout the society; and (2) sanctions are applied in a different manner by the state than by other associations. The state is the only association of society that may legitimately apply the sanction of force to guarantee conformity to its norms.[7] No other association is permitted to incarcerate or kill those who violate its rules.

9. Relationships between the Norms

There are some exceedingly interesting relationships between folkways, mores, and laws. In the first place, although each of these norms is supported by slightly different sanctions, we should not therefore assume that the mores are necessarily more coercive than the folkways, or that the laws are necessarily more coercive than either the folkways or the mores. The negative sanctions may, in some cases, be more severe as we proceed in this order from folkways to laws, but the greater severity does not necessarily induce greater conformity. Furthermore, a small fine is not necessarily more severe or onerous than, say, ridicule. The man who violates the laws by indulging in criminal enterprises and who violates the mores by keeping a mistress as well as a wife may nevertheless, to avoid ridicule, dress without ostentation in the best of conservative taste and conform to all the norms of fashion and etiquette.

In the fifty states of the Union there is such a multiplicity of laws that all of us have on some occasion or other violated one of them. If it is a crime to violate a law we are all criminals, and certainly the incidence of juvenile delinquency in our society is 100 per cent. Is there anyone who drives an automobile, for example, who has not at some time or other exceeded the speed limit in a particular zone? We violate many laws with impunity, and largely because everyone else does, too. Many laws are obsolete and remain on the books long after the need for them has disappeared and long

---

[7] The family, within limits, is an exception to this observation.

after observance, by general consent, has been discontinued. Such laws are among the cultural survivals mentioned in an earlier chapter.[8]

Although we can violate certain laws without fear of punishment, we would all think twice before violating one of the folkways or mores; for sanctions are swiftly applied to such violations, and these sanctions have the support of the community. None of the readers of this book would fail to keep an appointment voluntarily made, none would eat peas with a knife, and none would demand a gift of money from his banker on the ground that the banker is well supplied with the stuff and has more than he needs. No law forbids any of these practices. In other words, we may not conclude that the laws are necessarily more effective instruments of social control than are the folkways and mores. In certain instances, such as those requiring the payment of taxes, they may be more effective, but in many other instances they may be less effective.

Societies so primitive that they lack the institution of government obviously have no laws. But all societies, without exception, have folkways and mores. No society could exist without them and, as we have seen, without them the orderly social intercourse of human beings would be impossible. The laws that appear in complex societies are to some extent a crystallization of the mores of these societies. They support the mores with an additional sanction—enforcement by the state and its police power. The mores gain formal recognition in the laws. But the mores exist before the laws are enacted and may change while the laws remain in force. The law, in other words, is frequently a laggard. In most cases, in fact, it is the law that fails to keep pace with the mores, retards the processes of social change, and represents the conservative influences in society. This is not invariably true, however. Sometimes laws are enacted before their provisions have the support of the community, and in these cases, as we shall see, it is difficult if not impossible to enforce them.

Folkways are usually considered to be more changeable—and more rapidly changeable—than the laws. Folkways associated with fad and fashion, for example, may change from year to year and even from month to month. Most folkways, moreover, never receive formal recognition in the laws and hence are not subject to this additional stabilizing influence.

---

[8] Obsolete laws make amusing reading. Until 1950, for example, when the old colonial statute was finally repealed, any citizen of the state of Rhode Island found within the boundaries of the Commonwealth of Massachusetts was legally liable to execution by hanging. Many of these laws are simply absurd. It is against the law in Natchez, Mississippi, for example, for elephants to drink beer, in the state of Tennessee to take the fish of another person off the hook, in Walden, New York, to give a drink of water to another person without a permit, and in Wichita, Kansas, for a father to use a gun in order to frighten away his daughter's suitors. For these and other examples see D. Hyman, *It's Still the Law*, David McKay Company, Inc., New York, 1961.

The laws indeed are so numerous, so comprehensive, and so important in complex societies that many specialists are specifically and professionally concerned with them—lawyers, judges, legislators—and jurisprudence is a special branch of knowledge. The law is so important that it is sometimes believed to have a divine source and origin and somehow to transcend the mundane affairs of men. This sentiment seems implicit, for example, in the inscription on Langdell Hall at the Harvard Law School—*"Non sub Homine, sed sub Deo et Lege."* (Not under Man, but under God and Law.) Sociological analysis indicates, however, that this sentiment proceeds from erroneous assumptions. The laws, like the other norms, arise in the course of time from the use and wont of society.

If the laws represent in many cases a crystallization, or formal recognition, of prescriptions and proscriptions already contained in the mores, it is also true, because of cultural lag, that conflict between the mores and the laws is not only a possible but a frequent occurrence in contemporary societies. Obsolete laws illustrate this point. Sometimes the conflict between these two kinds of norms assumes a dramatic significance. A newly elected city attorney in Wilmington, Delaware, sworn to uphold the laws, once decided to take his oath of office seriously. Wilmington at this time had a series of "blue laws" on its books that forbade work of any character on Sunday. The city attorney enforced these laws and brought consternation to the citizens. No one could buy or sell the Sunday newspaper, no one could ride a bus, milk deliveries could not be made, medicine could not be prescribed or sold, and the life of the city was threatened with a complete stoppage. The lesson was obvious, and it was quickly learned.

The disparity between the mores and the laws is not always so dramatic as the above illustration suggests. Nevertheless, as societies become more complex such disparities are inevitable. And in these cases, indeed in all cases of conflict, it is the mores, not the laws, that prevail. If the conflict is such that something has to "give," it is the laws rather than the mores that succumb. The historical evidence in support of this proposition is overwhelming. Indeed, many centuries ago the Roman historian Tacitus expressed it in a famous question—*Quid leges sine moribus?* (What are laws without mores?)

The superiority of the mores in this respect has induced someone to enunciate the following principle: *When the mores are adequate, laws are unnecessary; and when the mores are inadequate, laws are useless.* This "principle" is obviously untrue, since it would make laws either unnecessary or useless and require us to conclude that they might as well be abolished. A principle that is untrue can nevertheless be instructive. Let us examine it.

It says in the first place that when the mores are adequate, laws are unnecessary. This is precisely the situation in which small, nonliterate societies find themselves. They all have mores without laws. Such a society can dispense with laws, but it cannot, of course, dispense with mores. The folkways and mores of complex societies also supply an illustration. Thus, no law forces us to begin our letters with "Dear" and none forces us to end them with a complimentary close. Similarly, with respect to the mores, no law compels us to refrain from cheating at cards, to give credit where credit is due, and to go to the end of the line when purchasing tickets. Our associates, not the police, take care of matters like this, and it is they who require conformity.

But we cannot infer from these examples that laws in general are unnecessary. They may be supererogatory in small societies where everyone knows everyone else and where social relations are on a personal basis. They are essential, however, in large societies where social relations, as we shall see in some detail in the following chapter, are functions of status rather than personality and where there are many overlapping social groups.

In our own society, as we have said, there are some who would not pay taxes if not required to do so by law—law, incidentally, that is fully supported by the mores. But the mores cannot by themselves ensure obedience because their sanctions cannot operate effectively in this case. If one were subject to no legal penalty for nonpayment of taxes, he could violate the mores in this respect with impunity. His associates would not discover his offense and could not therefore express their disapproval. Some offenses, in fact, can be secret and can thus evade the publicity that would bring the moral pressures into play.

Furthermore, a complex society is comprised of many social groups and these groups have different mores and different folkways. A complex society, in short, has no homogeneous culture. When the norms of these diverse groups conflict, as they frequently do, some more pervasive authority, one representing the entire society, is needed to adjudicate between them. And this is the function of the laws. The first half of the principle is therefore false.

The second half, however, is true. When the mores are inadequate, laws are useless. We have already suggested that when the mores of the majority are strongly opposed to the laws, it is the laws that have to give way. The history of prohibition legislation in the United States will remain a perennial example of this fact. Taken together with the sumptuary laws of other societies in other periods of history, this legislation supplies sufficient evidence in support of the principle. Sumptuary laws are those determining what people may eat or drink or wear, and they have seldom, in any society, accomplished their purpose. There appear to be certain areas of life that are immune to legislation and that the laws cannot successfully invade. Control in these areas is reserved for the mores and folkways.

There is the story, for example, of the Russian czar who, wishing to discourage the wearing of mustaches by his subjects on the gound that hirsute adornments of this character should be reserved for the higher nobility, placed a fairly high tax on this practice. To his surprise the result was more mustaches than before. Under the new decree the mustache became not only a decoration for the upper lip but also a sign that the wearer was wealthy enough to afford the tax.

As another example we may refer to the laws against brevity in bathing suits that New York City, in common with many other cities attempted to enforce on the public beaches in the early years of this century. The spectacle of policemen patrolling Coney Island with ruler and tape, measuring the distance from the hem of the garment to the kneecap, seems a little ridiculous to us today. No legal rule and no policeman's ruler could stay the course of "progress" from the knee to the hip, just as no law could save the disappearance of the top from the man's two-piece bathing suit. Here again we have a situation that is governed by the mores and not by the laws.[9] There are, of course, exceptions to these observations. The Geneva of John Calvin, the Edinburgh of John Knox, and the New England of Cotton and Increase Mather all held tight control over matters that are otherwise left to custom. In these three cases, however, we have theocracies in which the laws of the state are supported by the rules and sanctions of religion. They sustain themselves for a period of time, but then they too succumb.[10]

If the mores do not support the laws, the laws might as well never have been passed; for no political authority on earth, including that represented by all the resources of a totalitarian state, can for an indefinite period enforce a law that directly contradicts the mores—or even the

---

[9] For examples of sumptuary legislation in ancient societies see Emile Durkheim, *The Division of Labor in Society*, George Simpson trans., The Free Press of Glencoe, New York, 1960, p. 159.

[10] Another example of sumptuary legislation is an act passed by the British Parliament in 1770: That all women, of whatever age, rank, profession, or degree, whether virgins, maids, or widows, that shall, from and after such Act, impose upon, seduce, or betray into matrimony any of His Majesty's male subjects by the scents, paints, cosmetic washes, artificial teeth, false hair, Spanish wool, iron stays, hoops, high-heeled shoes, etc., shall incur the penalty of the law now enforced against witchcraft and like misdemeanours, and that the marriage, upon conviction, shall stand null and void.

folkways of a majority.[11] The achievement of law may be the apex of civilization; it is, in fact, one of the things we mean by civilization. But sociology teaches us still to remember, with Dr. Samuel Johnson:

> How small of all that human hearts endure,
> That part which laws or kings can cause or cure!

Should the laws then be used to enforce morality? This is a question that has stimulated vigorous debate. One view is that the laws should control one area of human life and the mores another and that these areas are separate and independent. Crime would thus be the concern of the laws and indecency (or sin—a word that in an irreligious age almost requires quotation marks) the concern of the mores. In this view the laws, for example, should have nothing to do with any kind of sexual behavior between freely consenting adults when conducted in private. The laws should not be used to enforce morality primarily because they cannot be; they are powerless to perform this function and it is the better part of wisdom to acknowledge this fact. It is important both for the sake of intellectual and social order to maintain a distinction between what is illegal and what is immoral. The law, in short, is not a branch of morality and should not be its support. One trouble with this view, of course, is that it is not always easy to distinguish between acts that harm other individuals and acts that offend them, to separate crime and sin. To which of the two categories, for example, does bigamy belong? And to which abortion? The complex questions contained here became the subject of a sparkling and profound debate in the 1960s between Lord Patrick Devlin, one of England's most eminent jurists, and H. L. A. Hart, the distinguished professor of jurisprudence at Oxford University.[12] The debate will doubtless continue.

We may now summarize this discussion of the relations between the folkways, the mores and the laws: These three kinds of norms are supported by various sanctions, ranging from ridicule and obloquy through ostracism and excommunication, to fine, imprisonment, and, in some cases, death. The sanction that supports an associational norm may be simply loss of membership, although usually some obloquy accompanies formal suspension from an organized group. The laws, though more

---

[11] In February, 1953, the Legislature of the sovereign state of Georgia enacted a law banning the use of "and/or" and requiring the use of a new word "andor." There is no evidence that this usage has been adopted. Needless to say, as our principle teaches us, Julius Caesar himself could not introduce a new word into a language and make it stick.

[12] Patrick Devlin, *The Enforcement of Morals*, Oxford University Press, 1965, and H. L. A. Hart, *Punishment and Responsibility: Essays in the Philosophy of Law*, Oxford University Press, 1969. See also the latter's *The Concept of Law*, Oxford, 1961.

formal, are not necessarily more coercive in their effects than are the folkways and mores; some folkways indeed are more coercive than some laws, especially when the latter are obsolete. And finally, when the mores are inadequate, laws are useless. If we mentioned earlier a question by Tacitus, we may conclude this section with the equally apposite remark by Aristotle that "a law derives all its strength from custom."[13]

10. Why We Conform to the Norms

We have seen that society, as represented by our associates, exerts a steady pressure upon us to conform to the norms and that in the case of some norms—the laws—these pressures are institutionalized and applied by special agencies. It is easy to see that we do not enjoy the disapproval and displeasure of our fellows, that we can hardly sustain the pain of ostracism from our own groups (unless perhaps, like Spinoza, we are philosophers), and that we thoroughly dislike the loss of mobility occasioned by imprisonment. It is easy to see in addition that we do enjoy the approval and approbation of our fellows and that in most cases this is a large reward indeed and one that we endeavor to earn by our conformity. But hope of reward and fear of punishment are not the only reasons we conform to the norms of our society, however pleasant or unpleasant these sanctions may be. There are other bases for conformity, and it is these that we wish to explore in this section, without discriminating now between folkways, mores, and laws.

Indoctrination

The first reason we conform to the norms is that we have been indoctrinated to do so. From our earliest childhood we are taught to observe the norms of our society. Like other aspects of culture they are ready for us when we arrive upon the human scene and we accept them, as we accept the ideas and the materiel, without conscious thought or reflection. We are taught, for example, to take our meals at certain times of the day, to use certain kinds of utensils at the table, to address our elders with respect, to omit certain vulgarities from our speech, to write and read from left to right, not to strike a child smaller than ourselves, and so on through an infinity of illustrations.

The "socialization" of the child, in effect, is the process of learning the norms of his own society. After a while, these norms seem to him the right and proper way of doing things, and sometimes, indeed, the *only* way. In

---

[13] *Politics.* 1269*a*. There is an echo in Durkheim: "Law expresses customs, and if it acts against them, it is with a force that it has borrowed from them." *Op. cit.*, p. 146.

many cases, therefore, we conform to the norms because we know no alternatives—for the same reason, in short, that we use English instead of Hindustani. This is the process of indoctrination, a process that is constant and continuous from the beginning of our lives.

Habituation

The second reason we conform to the norms is that we become habituated to them. As we have seen in an earlier section, what is customary in many cases becomes habitual. We are indoctrinated in the use of knife, fork, and spoon, and after a while their use is a matter of habit. It is not easy, for example, for a child to learn the "correct" way of using a knife and fork, and the English way of using these implements is different from the American. What is "correct," of course, as we have seen, is defined by the folkways of the society. But, once the prescribed method is learned, it is similarly not easy to use a knife and a fork in an "incorrect" way. Repetition has thus made a habit, and a folkway comes to be rooted, in a sense, in the organism. When one has become habituated to a practice, he observes it automatically, without reflection or effort. From this time on, it is more difficult to violate the folkway, as it were, than to conform to it. And so we see that habituation reinforces the norms and guarantees the regularity of conformity.

Utility

A third reason why we conform to the norms of our society is that frequently we can appreciate their utility. As reflective individuals we can see that norms are useful, that they enable us to interact with others in a way conducive to the best interests of all, that they contribute to the ease of social intercourse. It is apparent to us, for example, that the fair way of distributing tickets to a play for which only a limited number of seats are available is to sell them first to those who come first to purchase them. We see the rationality in the expression "first come, first served." We recognize that an orderly line or queue is a superior device, socially speaking, to a disorderly rush, in which, someone, perhaps ourselves, might be trampled. This norm does not always work, of course, as our cartoonists have often made clear in depicting the shoppers at a bargain counter in a department store. But in general we do not permit the largest and the strongest of our associates always to go to the head of the line because we recognize that he can force his way there. Such a situation would lead to chaos and to the victory of force over order.

We recognize further that the flow of traffic at busy intersections is smoother and less dangerous when lights are installed. Thus, we stop at a red light and go on a green one, not only because we are indoctrinated and habituated to the practice, but because we recognize that this kind of regulation is useful to everyone, ourselves included. The fear of sanctions, that is, the fear of receiving a ticket from an unseen policeman, is perhaps the least important of the reasons why we obey the changes of the traffic lights. It is reasonable to obey the traffic laws, in short, because, as the slogan has it, "the life you save may be your own." In other words, in many social situations we recognize the rational efficacy of the norms to which we conform. We may even recognize their efficacy when we do not, in fact, conform to them; that is, we may on occasion run a stop sign when we are in a hurry and so invite the possibility of an accident, but we do not therefore advocate the abolition of stop signs. We can see that they are useful.

Group Identification

A fourth reason why we conform to the norms is that conformity is a means of group identification. We may conform to the norms of our own social groups, for example, rather than to those of groups to which we do not belong, not because we regard our own as superior (which they may not be in fact) and not because we are particularly indoctrinated or habituated to them, but because in conforming to them we express our identification with these groups. The Eskimo shoe may in any rational evaluation be superior to our own—that is, it may produce fewer fallen arches—but we do not for this reason wear Eskimo rather than American shoes. The folkways, in short, are not always rational. But we conform to them nevertheless because they are our own, because they identify us with our own society and our own social groups.

A factory laborer may carry his lunch to work even though it is easier, in his particular domestic situation, to eat in a restaurant. But to do the easier thing might also result in a separation or dissociation from his fellow workers, all of whom bring their lunches from home. In such cases, although the apprehension of a sanction, group disapproval, may be operating, there is also a positive incentive to conformity as a means of exhibiting identification with one's own groups.

The American sociologist, Robert K. Merton, with his customary perspicacity, has detected another phenomenon here. That is the phenomenon he has called the reference group. In some situations we conform not to the norms of the groups to which we actually belong but rather to those of the groups to which we would like to belong, those with which we would like to be identified.[14] Thus, the medical student, the law student, and the graduate student begins to observe and to conform to the norms of

---

[14] As Merton himself says, "People take the standards of significant others as a basis for self-appraisal and evaluation." See his essay "On Sociological Theories of the Middle Range," *On Theoretical Sociology*, The Free Press, New York, 1967, p. 40.

doctors, lawyers and professors before he has been admitted to membership in these groups. Similarly, the upwardly mobile individual may, prematurely from one point of view, try to conform to the norms of etiquette and speech of a higher social class than his own because he seeks identification with this class. There is, in short, a difference between actual group and reference group. But always group identification is important.

11. Bohemians and Babbitts

It must be apparent that there are varying degrees of conformity to the norms of societies and of groups. Some people conform closely to them; others not so closely. Thus, we have "conformists" and "nonconformists" in all societies. There are "deviates" even in primitive groups where the norms, and indeed the total culture, have a universal application throughout a small community. We may refer to those who are relatively nonconformist as Bohemians and to those at the opposite end of the scale, who are relatively conformist, as Babbitts.

The word "Bohemian" does not, in this instance, refer to a resident of Bohemia, a section of Czechoslovakia. It means instead one who sets himself off from the rest of the society and who regards himself as immune from the sanctions that society imposes upon its other members.

The word "Babbitt," on the other hand, comes from the famous novel of that name by Sinclair Lewis. The principal character in the novel is George F. Babbitt, a "realtor" in the fictional city of Zenith, located somewhere in the Middle West. Mr. Babbitt may grumble and he may even try to rebel, but in the end he always conforms. In one of his most rebellious moods he deliberately dries his hands on the guest towel in his own bathroom. Now it is perfectly clear that no one in his right mind uses guest towels in his own bathroom. (Guests don't even use guest towels!) But Babbitt gains great satisfaction from his violation of a norm. He tries in other ways to express his individuality—by making comments, for example, that can be construed as friendly to labor and that are therefore censured by his business-class associates. The processes by which his groups bring him back into line are brilliantly portrayed by the novelist throughout, and now, although the book is too old to interest the contemporary student, it remains true that in it Sinclair Lewis made a number of valid sociological observations, as he did indeed in his other novels.

Anyone who deviates too much, of course, challenges the order of his society and will suffer the sanctions that we have already discussed. But it should also be observed that we do not ordinarily approve of people in our society who are sticklers for the rules, who seem to consider the norms absolute standards to be observed no matter what the situation or what extenuating circumstances it may contain. In other words, those who conform too closely to the *ideal* culture, as opposed to the *real* culture, may also be subject to ridicule. Caspar Milquetoast is the caricature of such a conformist. Mr. Milquetoast will obey the law no matter how much personal inconvenience his obedience may entail and no matter how much ridicule he may sustain. He will obey a law even when it is admittedly obsolete.

The letter of the law, as we know, frequently violates its spirit, and the same may be said about norms. A certain amount of prevarication or the uttering of light falsehoods is a necessity in polite social intercourse. The hostess tells the departing guests that they must come again soon even if she knows, and they know, that a return visit is not desired. Many invitations to "come and see us sometime" are extended only to conform to a conversational norm, to the norms of etiquette, and are meant by no one to be taken literally.

In the ideal culture, therefore, and in the ideal society, everyone conforms to the norms and to the same degree. In the real culture there are many degrees of conformity. These two kinds of culture produce two sets of norms, one in the ideal pattern, which everyone professes, and another in the real pattern, to which people in fact conform. There are Bohemians and Babbitts in all societies and in all social groups. The norms, in short, do not bear equally upon all the members of a society. People are not automata; they have their likes and their dislikes, their idiosyncrasies of behavior and belief. There would be no variety in a society in which all were Babbitts. There would be no order in one in which all were Bohemians.

As a matter of fact, even Bohemians conform to the norms of their own Bohemian groups, no matter how much these norms may differ from the norms of the surrounding society. However much the "hippies" and "yippies" of the late sixties and seventies deviated in dress and hair style from the general societal norms, they were rigid conformists in their own groups. They were keeping time to a different tune, as Cooley once expressed it, but they were nevertheless keeping time.

12. Differential Norms in a Multigroup Society

As the above example indicates, one does not conform to all of the norms in a complex society but only to those of his own groups. This consideration introduces a complicating factor into any treatment of the norms. For each society of any size is made up of many diverse groups with different and sometimes even contradictory norms. Of the thousands of examples that might be used to illustrate this point, we shall choose only a few.

A member of the Catholic Church may not eat meat on Good Friday, except in certain specifically approved circumstances, without violating a norm. This norm exerts no effect whatever upon the Good Friday menus of Protestants. A Catholic similarly violates a norm if he uses a contraceptive device or patronizes a birth-control clinic. A Protestant, however, may do both of these things. Differences of this kind obviously cause complications in a society and constitute barriers to understanding. Here, however, we are interested simply in the fact that the same norms do not operate in all groups. What is "wrong" in some groups is "right" in others, even within the same society, and thus we come to recognize again the relativity of the norms. In order to conform to a norm of his peer group a college student may have to violate a norm imposed by his family group. In order to conform to a norm of his religion a man may have to violate a law. And so on through endless examples.

Each group in society, to a certain extent at least, has its own norms, to which its members are expected and required to conform. There is no social group without its norms, no matter what these norms may be. Even temporary and transient groups have their norms. In his Pulitzer-prize-winning novel, *The Grapes of Wrath*, John Steinbeck tells us about the "Okies" who migrated from Oklahoma to California when the dust storms blew their land away. These migrants developed certain norms to which they all conformed as they journeyed along Highway 66 on their way to the "promised land," where jobs and food were thought to be plentiful. When they camped along the highway at night, those who had food recognized a moral obligation to share their meager supplies with others in the group who were even less fortunate. There was never enough to go around, but it was shared nevertheless. There was no similar obligation, however, to share gasoline, which was also a precious commodity, and no one expected the gift of even half a gallon.

Mention of John Steinbeck invokes another illustration or two, this time from his novel *Cannery Row*. The men who lived and worked in Cannery Row and who worked occasionally along the fishing wharves would not patronize the house of prostitution located on the row. The girls who worked there were their friends, and a commercial relationship with one of them was tabooed. The mores of the group required that they patronize a house in another neighborhood altogether. Similarly, the girls wore street dresses rather than evening dresses to the party the inhabitants of the row gave to "Doc," the marine biologist who was their friend. Evening clothes were their working clothes, and one does not wear working clothes to a party, even in Cannery Row. These fictional illustrations have their real-life counterparts. The norms of some groups do not harmonize with the norms of other groups. Sometimes they are in flat contradiction.

Differences such as these are characteristic of complex societies and they have a number of important implications which it may be appropriate to mention. In the first place, the diversity of norms belonging to different social groups sharply sets off a complex society from a primitive society. Primitive societies in general do not have more than one set of religious beliefs and practices; they do not have several political parties or political points of view clamoring for recognition; their members conform or do not conform, as the individual case may be, to only one code of morality; they lack a series of diverse standards for judging the artistic achievements of their members; and so on throughout the list of various norms. They thus present a more or less unified picture to the observer, and their culture exhibits a high degree of integration. Although individuals may deviate, as they do in all societies, their deviation is from a single set of norms.

The situation is quite different with respect to complex societies. Such societies, including our own, are comprised of an almost infinite variety of different groups, all of which, as we have seen, have different norms to which the members are expected to conform. What is deviance in one group may be conformity in another. A Babbitt may rebel against the norms of the "Babbitt warren"—as some cynic has called American middle-class Middle Western culture—without becoming a Bohemian. A Bohemian, on the other hand, may conform quite closely to the norms of Bohemia in all the ways in which these norms contradict the norms of the larger society, and even take pride in his conformity. The man who rebels against *all* of the norms of his society is not usually a Bohemian but rather a hermit, one who separates himself both physically and socially from his community. In complex societies like ours there are Catholics and Protestants and Jews, Republicans and Democrats, white-collar workers and "no collar" workers, modernists and traditionalists in the arts, materialists and idealists in philosophy, and so on through an imposingly large number of examples. A multigroup society such as ours, therefore, does not exhibit the degree of cultural integration that is characteristic of primitive societies. Our differential norms and ideologies give us a many-faceted culture.

As a second consequence, societies that have many different sets of norms create special problems for the individuals who live in these societies. The same individuals belong at the same time to different groups and are expected to conform to different norms. When these norms contradict one another, or when they conflict, the individual is forced into making a choice between them, a problem that seldom presents itself to the primitive in his simple society. What does the conscientious objector do, for example, when he receives his order to report for induction into the armed forces? Conformity to one norm is tantamount to violation of another. What does the college student do when his friends encourage him to indulge in certain practices that he knows would incur the disapproval of his parents? In a rapidly changing society the norms of an older generation seldom coincide in all respects with the norms of the younger. We thus have conflict situations arising as a result of social change.

Some sociologists believe that such conflict situations are largely responsible for the high incidence of mental disease in our society. It is not that there are too many norms to which the individual is expected to conform, but too many contradictory norms. Business norms differ from religious norms, family norms from undergraduate norms, political norms from ethical norms, and so on. It is difficult to be a good pacifist and a good citizen at the same time. It is difficult to be a good citizen of the world, that is, a good internationalist, and a good patriot at the same time. It is not even easy, in all circumstances, to be a good parent and a good neighbor at the same time. In other words, the second consequence of the multiplicity and variety of norms in a complex society is that individuals are presented with problems that would not otherwise occur and, accordingly, spend much of their lives trying to adjust to conflicting obligations.

There is a third consequence of the multiplicity and variety of norms in a complex society. Differences in norms are barriers to understanding. We have emphasized throughout this chapter that without norms the social interaction of people would be difficult, dangerous, and in some cases impossible. Indeed, a normless situation is a situation of anomy and anomy represents chaos, just as society represents order. But it must also be apparent that different and contrary norms are barriers to easy and regular social intercourse. Anyone, to take an exceedingly simple situation, who has ever tried to communicate with another person in an alien tongue has some appreciation of the difficulties involved. But differences in language are only one kind among all the differences that separate people from one another. The Catholic family that both pays taxes and supports the parochial school finds it difficult to understand why some of his tax money cannot be used for Catholic education. The Protestant family, on the other hand, feels just as strongly that public money should not be used to subsidize private schools. And so there is a barrier to the social intercourse of Catholic and Protestant. It is an inevitable phenomenon in multigroup societies.

13. Miscellaneous Norms

Although folkways, mores, and laws are the principal kinds of norms that we find in society, there are several other kinds to which we want now to devote a brief discussion. Among these norms are fashion, rite, ceremony, ritual, and etiquette. All of these might be included under the concept of folkways, except that for the most part they are not the ways of an entire "folk" but only of selected groups within a society. They nevertheless function as folkways in limited groups and are supported by similar sanctions.

Fashion

We have noticed that people like to be like their associates and friends. They also like to be different. One of the reasons they conform to the norms is that in doing so they identify themselves with their groups. But they also want to express their individuality. Fashion is a device beautifully suited to reconcile these opposing tendencies, the desire to conform on the one hand and the desire to be different on the other. Fashion may be defined as a permitted range of variation around a norm. Fashion operates in many spheres, but it is most familiar, perhaps, in the sphere of dress. The folkways prescribe that we wear clothing of a special kind in our society; thus, in general, trousers and shirts for men and dresses, or blouses and skirts, for women. But these requirements are very general indeed, and many variations are possible within the basic pattern. These variations—in style, color, design, and so on—permit the expression of individuality. The norm is thus not a thin line but an area of permissiveness. If one dresses too conservatively or too radically, of course, eyebrows will be raised, and this is the group sanction of disapproval coming into play. We are frequently reluctant to purchase an item of apparel or, once it is purchased, to wear it for fear it will make us too conspicuous. In the absence of norms no such reluctance would occur. But within the area defined by a norm, variations are both possible and desirable.

It is the function of fashion, in short, to permit and to regulate variety, and to alleviate what would otherwise be a dull and deadening uniformity. The desire to express one's individuality in modes of dress seems to operate in all social groups, even in those groups where uniform dress is required, as for example in military organizations. Thus high-ranking Army officers in World War II frequently adopted distinctive outward signs of their individuality. One general, for example, wore a battle jacket rather than the traditional blouse; another was identified with sunglasses, a corncob pipe, and a sweat-stained cap; a third took an especial delight in his highly polished helmet and pearl-handled revolvers; another usually attached a hand grenade to his blouse; and still another was seldom photographed without his beret. Similarly, groups within the Army adopt distinctive shoulder patches and other decorations to set themselves off from others; monks and nuns of the various Catholic orders wear distinctive habits; and nurses who receive their training at different hospitals symbolize their respective affiliations by special caps. Thus fashion is a device that enables us to be both like and unlike other people, to conform to the norms and at the same time to express our individuality, to be different without breaching the customs of our contemporaries.

The great French sociologist, Gabriel Tarde, who emphasized in his writings the importance of imitation, made an interesting distinction between custom and fashion. In conforming to custom, he said, we imitate our ancestors, in conforming to fashion we imitate our contemporaries. Edward Sapir observed that "fashion is custom in the guise of departure from custom."[15] However fashion is defined, its function is clear. It is also clear that the sanctions that support conformity to fashion in dress are powerful indeed. No woman would go to a dance in a dated dress. The success of fashion designers and, indeed, of the entire clothing industry may be attributed, in large part, to the reluctance of men and women to be out of style. It is in this sphere, the sphere of fashion, that the operation of folkways and their supporting sanctions becomes, perhaps, most apparent. Similar sanctions support all the folkways of society and operate in a similar way.

The vagaries of fashion in dress, of course, constitute much too large a subject for us to pursue in any detail. It would be a mistake, however, to limit fashion to matters of dress. Fashion extends its sway over many areas of conduct and belief. If people wear fashionable clothes they also indulge in fashionable amusements, eat fashionable foods, read fashionable books, and die of fashionable diseases. There are fashions in art and in literature, in science and religion. The works of Herman Melville, for example, are in fashion for a period and are then superseded, say, by the works of Henry James, and each of these periods produces its own quota of biographies and critical studies. Not even the learned professions are immune from the influences of fashion. Certain subjects of inquiry, certain modes of interpretation and analysis, certain kinds of problems attract attention for a while and come into style, only to recede in favor of something else. There are even fashions in mathematics. When such changes are relatively rapid or superficial or trivial or unexpected or irresponsible or bizarre, they are called fads rather than fashions. In any case, fads and fashions alike are constant phenomena of social life. People follow them and conform to their requirements, and thus these vogues too operate as norms.

[15] "Fashion," *Encyclopaedia of the Social Sciences*, The Macmillan Company, New York, 1931. In this perceptive article the following passage also merits reflection: "Most normal individuals consciously or unconsciously have the itch to break away in some measure from a too literal loyalty to accepted custom. They are not fundamentally in revolt from custom but they wish somehow to legitimize their personal deviation without laying themselves open to the charge of insensitiveness to good taste or good manners. Fashion is the discreet solution of the subtle conflict."

Rites, Rituals, and Ceremonies

Rites, rituals, and ceremonies lend dignity and a kind of special significance to various events of social life. By investing certain happenings with particular importance, they help on the one hand to sustain the orderly process of society and on the other to break the tedium of monotony. They mark some occasions with solemnity and introduce gaiety and rejoicing to others. Above all, they serve to identify the individual with his groups, his community, and his nation, thus supporting and intensifying his loyalties.

The function of ceremony is quite clear and needs no extended or elaborate discussion. We tend to ceremonialize the exploits of our fellows and to ceremonialize, too, the major crises and transitions of life. The birth of a baby, confirmation, graduation, the inauguration of a president, the opening of a new store or a new branch office, the return of a military hero to his homeland, a promotion, the publication of a book, a new record in athletics, admission to membership in any one of thousands of different organizations, the signing of a law or treaty, an anniversary, a victory, a landing on the moon—all these events, some trivial and some sublime, are given special marks of attention.

In all societies such significant occasions as births, deaths, and marriages are accompanied by some kind of ceremony, which serves as an announcement to society at large that an important event has taken place. The ceremony confers public recognition upon it. When the event is one of transition from one state to another—from the unbaptized to the baptized, from the single to the married, from childhood to adulthood, or from the living to the dead—the accompanying ceremony is called a *rite de passage*, or a rite of passage. There is no intrinsic reason, perhaps, why a student who has earned the required credits, paid his bills, and passed his final examinations should not receive his college degree by mail. It is felt, nevertheless, that the transition from undergraduate to graduate status is important enough to merit public recognition and public reward. The ceremony of commencement provides this recognition. Commencement, therefore, is a rite of passage. Different societies, of course, ceremonialize different events. In some societies a girl's first menstruation is made the occasion of a joyous ceremony; in others, such as our own, public mention of menstruation is tabooed, that is, prohibited by the mores.

Ceremony, as can be seen, performs an important function in the life of a society and in the life of the individual as well. It regularizes or standardizes situations which people confront and in which they would otherwise have no appropriate guides for action. The cigars that the new father presses upon his associates at the office help him over a "crisis"—in which he feels foolish enough, but proud at the same time. The cigars ease the tension, as do the highly unoriginal remarks that are made on such occasions. The ceremony, simple as it is, cloaks a genuine sentiment and allows it expression at the same time. The solemnity of a funeral serves a similar function. Death presents a crisis to those who survive. What would these survivors do on so serious and so painful an occasion if their society did not provide for them an appropriate mode of action, a recognized sequence of duties to be publicly performed? Once again we can see how a norm solves a problem, helps us to meet a crisis, and relieves us of what would otherwise be a heavy burden of decision.

Rites and rituals serve similar purposes. A rite is a ceremony, and the two words are frequently used synonymously. Sometimes, however, the word "rite" carries an additional connotation. It sometimes conveys a sense of secrecy, of a ceremony known only to the initiated, of practices secured from the prying eyes of the curious. Thus, an initiation ceremony in any fraternal association or lodge, guarded as it is from the uninitiated, is usually referred to as a rite. Rites then are not usually open to an entire community but are rather ceremonies reserved for the members of particular groups and hidden from public view. All secret societies have their rites and so also do groups that have relatively high qualifications for membership. An oral examination for the degree of doctor of philosophy, for example, serves not only as a test of the candidate's qualifications—this is its manifest purpose—but also as a kind of rite, symbolizing, when successful, the student's right to join a somewhat limited and select circle.

Ritual, too, is a kind of ceremony, but this word carries the additional connotation of repetition; that is, a ritual is a ceremony that is periodically and repeatedly performed. Such religious practices as the Catholic Mass are rituals, for they are regularly performed. The various holidays—formerly "holy days"—observed throughout the calendar year provide additional examples of ritual. New Year's Day, Memorial Day, the Fourth of July, Labor Day, Thanksgiving, and finally Christmas follow each other in regular succession in the American calendar, and holiday celebrations are therefore rituals. The various groups that make up the American, or any other, society also have their rituals—if only their regular weekly or monthly meeting. Ritual, in short, introduces temporal regularity and a precision of detail into many of the events that characterize our social life. The role of ritual in inducing a sense of group identification and, in addition, of group loyalty is also readily apparent.

Etiquette

Etiquette shares with ritual the property of precision. It is a code of precise procedures that governs the social interaction of people. Like other norms it contains the notion of propriety. It is proper, that is, to give or send a gift to those whose week-end hospitality one has enjoyed, to place a guest of honor, if female, at the right of the host at a formal dinner, if male at the right of the hostess, to send a gift to the bride to whose wedding one has been invited, to wear formal attire on certain occasions, to respond promptly to an engraved invitation, especially one containing the symbols "RSVP" (*Répondez, s'il vous plaît*), and so on through thousands of examples.

The etiquette governing a wedding ceremony is precise and rigorous in its specifications, as is also the etiquette prescribed for the assumption of command of a battleship or the formal reception on board of an admiral. The details of these ceremonies are outlined in advance and the obligation to conform to them is inherent in the situations to which they apply. Arbiters of etiquette appear in society, and it is they who decide that it is proper to complete the cut for the dealer in a game of bridge and improper for a young man to give an item of wearing apparel to a young woman before he is formally engaged to her.

Sociologically speaking, etiquette as a system of norms has three purposes. In the first place, like other norms, it prescribes standard procedures to be followed on specific occasions. Secondly, it indicates membership in a certain social class. In the third place, it serves to maintain social distance where intimacy or familiarity is not desired.

We may say another word about the last of these functions. If one postpones for too long a transition from formal to informal modes of address, that is, if one continues to address his acquaintances by titles of rank or by the formal salutation of "Mr." or "Mrs." or "Ms." accompanied by last names, the delay indicates to the other person that closer relations are not desired. Sometimes we want to avoid a more personal relationship with some of our acquaintances. In order to accomplish this with propriety we continue to treat them with a strict politeness and a rigid etiquette. As E. T. Hiller observed: "Unwanted approaches are repelled by confronting the other with decorous conduct, thereby supplying a reminder that he or she is to remain at a social distance beyond the bounds of exclusive relations."[16] In this respect, therefore, etiquette serves as a standardized means of discouraging intimacy in social relations.

14. Summary

In this chapter we have discussed in detail the component of culture that is of central concern to sociology. We have seen that it is the norms which give structure, stability, and order to society, that without them social

[16] E. T. Hiller, *Social Relations and Structures*, Harper & Row, Publishers, Incorporated, New York, 1947, p. 106.

interaction would be dangerous, difficult, and chaotic, and the individual would be faced with an almost intolerable burden of decision. We have defined a norm as a pattern or expectation, a cultural specification, a rule or standard that governs our conduct in the social situations in which we participate. Sometimes, of course, as we have observed, situations arise in society that are trivial, novel, or rare, situations for which there is no precedent and consequently no norm, but in the vast majority of situations the norm is there, as a part of our culture, to guide our conduct.

We then went on to show that human societies exhibit norms of several different kinds. We noted first that norms are both prescriptive and proscriptive, that they require certain kinds of conduct on the one hand and prohibit certain kinds on the other. We noticed also that norms are communal when they pervade an entire community or society and associational when they function within a particular organized group in society. Although there is no standardized classification of norms in the sociological literature, it is convenient to arrange them in three classes—folkways, mores, and laws. Folkways and mores for the most part are communal norms; laws are the associational norms that appear in the political organization of society. Associations other than the state have their rules and regulations too, and these requirements are also classified as associational norms.

We next suggested that the norms of any society are supported by sanctions, the positive sanctions of reward and the negative sanctions of punishment. Among the negative sanctions we listed ridicule, ostracism, fine, imprisonment, and death. Although laws are enforced by special agencies of society, we emphasized nevertheless that the laws are not necessarily more coercive in their operation than the folkways and mores. There are, in fact, certain areas of conduct and especially of belief that are immune from legislation and that are governed by other than legal norms. We exhibited in this connection the sociological force of the question asked by Tacitus—*Quid leges sine moribus?*—and announced the principle that when the mores are inadequate, laws are useless. In another section we remarked that the sanctions of reward and punishment, of approval and disapproval, do not completely explain why people conform to the norms of their societies and suggested such additional reasons as (1) indoctrination, (2) habituation, (3) utility, and (4) group identification.[17]

---

[17] From the point of view of social psychology it could be argued that indoctrination and habituation are the same process and involve the same learning mechanisms, that this process is called indoctrination when considered from the teaching side and habituation when considered from the learning side. Like problems of motivation and learning in general, however, this question is not one that the sociologist needs to solve. On the sociological level, at least, the distinction is significant and useful.

Attention was next invited to the fact that there are degrees of conformity to the norms in all societies and in all social groups. In all of them, even the most primitive, there are Bohemians and Babbitts, those who are in relative rebellion and those who are in relative conformity. Extreme conformity to a specific set of norms, regardless of circumstances, incites the sanction of disapproval, as does extreme nonconformity. Even Bohemians, however, conform closely to the norms of their own groups. Indeed, there is no social group without its norms no matter how "antisocial" it is considered by the members of the larger society that surrounds it.

In the concluding sections of the chapter we observed that different groups in a large complex society have different and sometimes conflicting norms and that this situation (1) sharply differentiates simple and complex societies, (2) creates problems and difficulties for their members, and (3) introduces barriers to understanding. Finally, we offered a brief treatment of some miscellaneous norms, including fashion, ceremony, rite, ritual, and etiquette.

We may repeat in conclusion, and with an added emphasis, that the first task of sociology is to discover the locus of the fundamental order that society exhibits. We have discovered this locus in the norms. No society and no social group can exist without them. As we have seen, it is the norms that make possible the orderly social intercourse of people in societies and thus serve the individual as guides to conduct. It is the norms, along with their sanctions, that serve as instruments of social control and thus support the orderly processes of society. And it is the norms, from the point of view of sociology itself, that constitute one of the basic components of the social structure. It is the norms, in short, that contribute order and stability to human societies wherever they may appear on earth and it is the norms that make possible the safe and orderly intercourse of men and women as they meet and act and talk with others of their kind.

s WE HAVE repeatedly observed, it is the business of sociology to examine and to analyze the nature of the fundamental order that society exhibits. A part of this task we have now accomplished. We have noticed that the order and regularity of social interaction are attributable to the existence of norms, which guide and canalize the relations that people have with one another. It is the norms that give predictability to these relations and interactions, form them into patterns, and thus give a structure to society.

We now wish to discuss another phenomenon, intimately related to the norms, which also contributes to the order we find in society. This is the phenomenon of status. We shall see that the norms are not "free-floating" in society but that, on the contrary, they are "fastened down" somewhere, and that they are attached, in fact, to statuses. We shall see in addition that society is a network of statuses. A consideration of status will also help us lay a foundation for our subsequent treatment of groups, associations, and authority. The concept of status, in short, is one of the most useful of the analytical tools at the disposal of contemporary sociology.

We encounter, however, a small conceptual difficulty at the outset. Some sociologists think of status in terms of rank order either in society at large (upper class versus lower class) or in an organized group (president versus vice-president), a rank that always carries a connotation of higher or lower and often, if not usually, of greater or lesser influence and prestige. Others think of status as more nearly equivalent to position or condition, without any necessary connotation of rank. Thus, in the second sense, class status, which does have a connotation of rank, is only one kind of status. Other kinds are marital status, age status, sex status, kinship status, membership status, and so on—statuses that have nothing to do with rank. First cousin and second cousin, for example, are different associational statuses, but there is no sense in which one of them is "higher" than the other. We have adopted the second of these conceptions because it seems to conform more closely to the norms of English usage. Marital status, for example, whether single, married, divorced, widowed, or remarried, is sought on almost every kind of questionnaire an individual is called upon to complete. Furthermore, there is no other convenient word that can be used for both ranked and unranked statuses (the "position" of vice-president sounds all right, but not the "position" of cousin or customer) or that so accurately conveys the meaning of the phenomenon. In what follows, therefore, although we shall mention stratified statuses, status has no necessary implication of rank or of rank order but indicates instead a more general phenomenon.

1. The Importance of Status

This entire chapter bears witness to the importance of status, and the reader cannot be expected to appreciate this importance until he has finished it. Nevertheless, the following story can illustrate that the total meaning of certain social phenomena depends upon the status of the individual involved. It concerns the doctor who, upon completing his examination of a young woman, said, "Mrs. Jones, I have very good news for you."

"My name," the young woman replied, "is Miss Jones, not Mrs. Jones."

"In that case," said the doctor, "I'm afraid I have very bad news for you."

This is not a very good story but it does illustrate the importance of status. The same physiological condition that in one status would be good news is bad news in another.

Comparable situations appear constantly, if less dramatically, in the lives of all of us. A significantly large number of the social interactions between people in a complex society such as ours are status interactions and not personal interactions. A student, for example, has social relations with barbers, bank tellers, bus drivers, ticket takers, registrars, and deans. It is of vital importance to recognize that he can, and probably does, have social relations with all of these people without knowing their names or indeed anything else about them—except their status. Nor, in turn, do they need to know his name or anything about him—except his status. It is conceivable, and even probable, that when a student first comes to the university he is acquainted with none of the university staff, either administrative or academic. Nevertheless, even without this personal knowledge or acquaintance, he manages to register for his courses, rent a room, pay his fees, buy his books, and attend the classes of instructors he has never seen before.

Registration itself, with its attendant red tape and filling out of forms, is a miracle of social organization, a process made possible only by norms and statuses. Hundreds and even thousands of freshmen interact with dozens of university officials, and none of them knows more than a few of the others personally. In this situation not even the names of the individuals concerned have any initial importance; the operation is conducted solely in terms of statuses and the norms attached to them. We invite the reader to reflect for a moment upon this phenomenon. Is it not a genuine miracle that all of these people, with so little personal acquaintance, can carry off in so orderly a fashion so complicated a process as registration for a new university term? It is indeed a miracle, the miracle of social organization. It is a miracle made possible, and even quite simple, by norms and statuses.

Society is full of these miracles of social organization. Consider a cafeteria. The customer's status entitles him to certain services; it does not give him the right to walk behind the steam table and scoop out his own mashed potatoes. The people who work there, from the cooks to the cashiers, perform their functions in accordance with the statuses they occupy. The customer receives his check and pays his money, not just to anyone, but to the cashier, who has a status obligation to receive it as the customer has a status obligation to pay it. The cashier may be female, young, and pretty, but nothing in her status, nor in the customer's, requires her to give him her telephone number along with the change. Again we may emphasize that an individual receives service solely in accordance with his status as customer. He may be completely unknown to the entire personnel of the cafeteria and they in turn may all be strangers to him. If all the customers had to have an introduction to the manager and all of his employees before they could patronize the establishment, it is difficult to see how the aims of cafeteria and customer could be met.

Consider a football game. Eleven men take the field for the opening kickoff against eleven other men, who may be total strangers to them. Formal introductions are not in order. They are quite unnecessary. The players begin to interact, to block and to tackle, in terms of the status relationships set up by the structure of the game. Personal feelings, whether of friendship or of animosity, have little to do with the situation, although they may of course affect it in more or less subtle ways.

The same observation can, of course, be made in regard to other sports. The fact that the Yankee center fielder, Joe DiMaggio, played for a large part of his career against his own brother, the Red Sox center fielder Dominic DiMaggio, did not affect the quality of the competition between these two teams. On the other hand one of the greatest double-play combinations known to baseball—Tinker to Evers to Chance—presented an entirely different picture. The year these players set the major-league record, Tinker and Evers were so hostile to each other that they did not exchange a word off the field during the entire season. Here we have a phenomenon frequently ignored in explanations of human behavior that lean too heavily upon psychological factors. Although personalities are important in interindividual interaction, they pale into relative insignificance in comparison with status in many of the relations that characterize modern society.

It is not necessary, in short, for the shortstop and the second baseman to be good friends, or even to be acquainted, in order for them to perform effectively and well at their positions. What they do is determined by the positions themselves—the statuses—and the norms attached to them. One can thus predict, without knowing anything about the players, that in an ordinary game the first baseman will make the largest number of put-outs and the pitcher the largest number of throws and that, if it is a major-league game, the first baseman will be left-handed and the third baseman right-handed. The norms, which involve rights, duties, privileges, obligations, perquisites, and prerogatives, are attached to statuses and not to individuals. This is a vital sociological principle and one that we shall have occasion to emphasize again and again.

We want to exaggerate this point a little for purposes of emphasis. Our friends the psychologists like to think of social relations in terms of the character and temperament of individuals, their likes and dislikes, intimacies and animosities, and so on, laying stress upon their personalities. This, of course, is both appropriate and necessary in so far as primary-group relations are involved, that is, when people interact with members of their intimate and friendship groups and evaluate each other intrinsically and personally. In the case of secondary-group relations, however, which are so numerous in complex societies, the situation is different. Here the relations are determined by the statuses of the individuals involved. These statuses, in turn, have nothing directly to do with the character and temperament of the individuals themselves but are components, instead, of the structure of society.

Every day those of us who live in all but the smallest hamlets interact with dozens of people with whom we are personally unacquainted, and these interactions are conducted with a decent order and efficiency. We may ride daily on bus or subway without knowing anything about the personality, the domestic situation, or the marital preferences of the driver or guard. The subway motorman we seldom see. We buy magazines and newspapers from clerks who are total strangers. And at work—if we are, say, bank tellers, salesmen, reporters, telephone operators, or executives—we deal efficiently with many other strangers. If we are shipping clerks, for example, we prepare shipments for customers whose names we do not recognize to be sent by truck and train by handlers we do not know.

We carry on correspondence, itself a highly important form of social interaction in a complex society, with persons whose signatures we do not recognize. If we are in the Navy we may be sent to the ends of the earth on orders signed by the Chief of Naval Personnel, and it matters not whether this Chief be Admiral X, Admiral Y, Admiral Z—or Christopher Columbus. We pay taxes to a director of internal revenue and yet only an insignificant percentage of Americans, not including the author of this book, are able to name the director in the district to which their checks are mailed. Some of us pay dues to national associations whose treasurers might be anybody so far as we are concerned. And some of us get married by ministers we have never seen before and never expect to see again. How is all this possible? It is possible only because of what we have deliberately called the "miracle" of social organization. It is possible only because people occupy statuses in terms of which these interactions can proceed.

All of this is really very simple and very obvious. Nevertheless, like many simple and obvious things, it usually escapes attention. If anyone imagines, however, that it is unimportant, let him reflect upon situations in which statuses are mistaken or unknown. Most of us have doubtless been in a store of some kind and have asked a question of a "clerk" who turned out to be not a clerk but another customer. In this situation some embarrassment ensues. It happens so often indeed that there is a norm to "cover" it, a norm that calls for an apology on the part of the person who mistakes the status. The familiar response "I'm a stranger here myself" similarly indicates an incorrectly estimated status. A new student at the University of North Carolina once asked a passer-by to help him up the steps with a trunk, only to discover, some time later, that his willing assistant was the president of the university.

Finally, when one meets a new person conversational gambits are directed first toward the determination of statuses. The sex status of the individual is apparent and the age status is almost as apparent, but such questions as "Where are you from?" and "What do you do?" are designed to discover the regional status and the occupational status, and only after such information is elicited does one know what norms to apply as the conversation continues. Furthermore, if we are single males of a certain age and the new acquaintance is a girl of a certain age, we may be most interested to see whether she is wearing a ring on the third finger of her left hand. Other conditions being favorable, the presence or absence of a symbol of marital status will determine whether or not we ask her for a date. These examples, and thousands more that could easily be supplied, will indicate the very great importance of status in a complex society.

2. Status and Role

The concepts of status and role have a growing significance in the social sciences. We want now to define them and to distinguish between them.

A *status* is simply a position in society or in a group. Every society and every group have many such positions and every individual occupies many such positions—as many, in fact, as there are groups to which he belongs. His status will differ with the type of group; that is, he will have one kind of a status in an organized group, for example, and another kind in an unorganized group. The problem of groups will be the subject of our next chapter, and we shall not elaborate upon it here. In any case, the status is the position afforded by group affiliation, group membership, or group organization. It is "set" in the structure of the group or of the society before a given individual comes along to occupy it. It is an item of culture.

A *role* is the dynamic or the behavioral aspect of status. Statuses are occupied, but roles are played. A role is the manner in which a given individual fulfills the obligations of a status and enjoys its privileges and prerogatives. A role is what an individual *does* in the status he occupies. It is obvious that different individuals do different things in the same statuses, and it is the concept of role that enables us to take account of these differences.

This use of the concepts "status" and "role" has more than the grammatical advantage mentioned at the beginning of the chapter. It conforms to the usage adopted by other sociologists as well. Talcott Parsons, for example, writing of the participation of actors in a social relationship, says that this participation has two aspects:

> On the one hand there is the positional aspect—that of where the actor in question is "located" in the social system relative to other actors. This is what we will call his *status*, which is his place in the relationship system considered

as a structure, that is a patterned system of *parts*. On the other hand there is the processual aspect, that of what the actor does in his relations with others seen in the context of its functional significance in the social system. It is this which we shall call his *role*.[1]

A few illustrations will help to clarify the distinction. The Presidency of the United States is a status. Attached to this status are many norms. The person who occupies the position of President, whoever he may be, has certain duties, responsibilities, and obligations and, in turn, enjoys certain privileges, perquisites, and prerogatives. These duties and so on are attached to the office, that is, to the status, and not to the individual. Nevertheless, different incumbents of this high office perform its functions in different fashions. The role played by Thomas Jefferson was different from the role played by Andrew Jackson, and the role played by Herbert Hoover was different from the role played by Franklin Delano Roosevelt. The status is roughly the same, but the roles exhibit numerous variations. We say "roughly the same" because the status also changes in the course of time. New norms are added to it and old ones removed. Thus, some Presidents exercise emergency or war powers and other do not. Some have grants of authority with respect to international trade and tariffs that Congress denies to others. The authority of the office expands at some periods and contracts at others.

The status of president of a university presents a similar picture. It is a status obligation to sign the diplomas of the graduating seniors and to confer honorary degrees and, by authority of the faculty, degrees in course. These duties the president cannot escape—although the first of them can be done by automation. In any event, two different incumbents will approach these tasks in different ways. The presidency of Harvard University is a status. The role played in that status by James Bryant Conant, however, was different from the role played later by Nathan M. Pusey.

But we do not need such exalted illustrations. The position of first baseman on a baseball team is a status. Anyone who occupies this status has to do certain things and to expect certain kinds of plays. He is obligated not only to field his position but also to receive the ball from the other infielders after they have fielded theirs. The box score of an average game will show that the first baseman has made the largest number of put-outs and that he has most frequently served as the end man in double plays. One can, in fact, say a great deal about this position and the duties and

[1] *The Social System*, The Free Press, Glencoe, Ill., 1951, p. 25. See also Robert K. Merton, *Social Theory and Social Structure*, revised and enlarged edition, The Free Press, Glencoe, Ill., 1957, pp. 368–370.

responsibilities that accompany it without having any particular first baseman in mind. All of these duties and responsibilities are attached to the status itself and not to any particular individual.

With respect to role, on the contrary, the situation is altogether different. The status of first baseman is the same no matter who occupies it, but the identity of the individual has everything to do with the role of first baseman. The status is the position itself. What one does with it is a matter of role playing. The fact that one can describe the various positions on a baseball team and indeed the nature of the game itself without mentioning the name of a single individual who has ever played these positions is an indication of the importance of status.

We may pause a moment to point out that the different interests of sociology and social psychology appear clearly in this distinction between status and role. Status is a sociological concept and a sociological phenomenon. Role, on the other hand, is a concept and a phenomenon of social psychology. Individual idiosyncrasies in personality and ability and behavior account for the fact that different individuals play different roles in the same status. Both of these phenomena, however, status as well as role, are dynamic and constantly changing. The role, obviously, changes with each incumbent in a status. The status changes as the norms attached to it are altered. Over the course of time new obligations and new responsibilities may be added to a status, or old ones removed. Sometimes vigorous role playing may expand the functions of a status, and sometimes these functions change because of exigencies in the system of which the status is a part. When an association increases in size, for example, its officers may acquire new duties, or new statuses may be established.[2] When we say, therefore, that role is the dynamic aspect of status, we do not imply that statuses are static. Both statuses and roles are dynamic elements in the life of a society. The former, however, are cultural, the latter behavioral.

Whenever we have a distinction between two things, it is useful for the sake of clarity to ask whether one of them can appear without the other. At least one writer, for example, has asserted that there is no status without a role and no role without a status. This assertion, however, is incorrect. Although statuses and roles are usually correlative phenomena, it is possible to have one without the other. A status without a role is simply an unfilled position in an association. When a President of the United States dies in office, his status is assumed immediately by the vice-president,

---

[2] In recent decades many universities have added a new status in their administrative ranks, the office of provost. The provost is responsible for the management of the entire university under the immediate direction of the president. He is a kind of assistant president but not an assistant to the president, which is a relatively minor position and one usually outside "the chain of command."

whose status, in turn, becomes vacant. The status of vice-president remains an official part of the government and is filled at the next election. But in the interim there is a status without a role. Similarly, when the president of a university resigns it may take some time to find a suitable successor. Meanwhile the status of president remains a part of the university organization, even though it is temporarily unfilled. The duties of the presidency during this period may be parceled out among several assistants, but none of them enjoys the privileges of the status.

On the other hand, it is possible to play a role without occupying a status. Most women, for example, play the role of nurse when a member of their family is ill. Nurse is a status in a hospital, but in the home it may be a role. Finally, all of us know people who are great practical jokers, the "life-of-the-party" type. There is something in their personality that casts them in the role of clowns. They do not, however, occupy the status of clown. Clown is a status only in the circus. Similarly, one may play the role of a teacher without occupying the status of a teacher.

To state this point in formal sociological language, we may say that a status is an *institutionalized* role.[3] It is a role that has become regularized, standardized, and formalized in the society at large or in any of the specific associations of society. Historically speaking, the role always comes first, but at any given moment in a complex society a status precedes the incumbency of a given individual. Thus, although, as we have said, status and role are correlative and closely related phenomena, it is possible to have one without the other. The structure of society, however, is comprised of statuses, not roles. It is statuses, together with norms, that give order, predictability, and even possibility to social relations.

3. Ascribed and Achieved Statuses

Some statuses are ascribed to individuals; others are achieved by them. Ascribed statuses derive from membership in involuntary groups, achieved statuses from membership in voluntary groups. Age status and sex status, for example, are both obviously ascribed, not achieved. These statuses depend upon biological conditions and there is little we can do about them, beyond disguising our age by a few conceits and subterfuges. Kinship statuses also are ascribed. We do not choose our relatives, neither our sisters nor our cousins nor our aunts. The writer knows of a young couple whose little boy protested strenuously when informed that he was soon going to be a brother. "I don't want to be a brother," this four-year-old insisted, "I just want to be me." Brother, of course, is a kinship status and,

---

[3] The concept of institution is discussed in a later chapter.

as in the case of other kinship statuses, is thrust upon the individual without his having any choice in the matter. Marital and parental statuses, on the other hand, are achieved. One does not have to become a husband or a wife or a parent.

One similarly has no choice about his place of birth, and consequently his regional and national statuses are ascribed rather than achieved. These statuses may later be changed, but there is no initial choice. Nor does one choose, except in rare cases of "passing," his racial status. This too is ascribed. One's status as a member of a particular religious group, for example. Protestant, Catholic, or Jew, is also initially ascribed. We simply begin our lives with the religious status of our parents. A different religious status, however, may later be achieved. Initial class status is likewise ascribed; that is, at birth we take on the class position of our parents and we have no choice as to which "side of the tracks" happens to claim us in our childhood. A different class status, like a different religious status, may later be achieved. In other words, some of our statuses are initially ascribed and later achieved.

Marital status and parental status, as we have said, are achieved. So also is educational status. The status of college graduate, however easy it may be to acquire, is achieved. It is not simply ascribed. Occupational status is similarly achieved. One does not become a mechanic, contractor, professor, or banker by ascription. Political-party status is another example of an achieved status in our society; that is, one achieves the status of Republican or Democrat. As a matter of fact, most associations (that is, organized groups) are voluntary, and the statuses derived from membership in these associations are consequently achieved statuses.

E. T. Hiller introduced an additional refinement in his treatment of statuses, namely, the concept of assumed status. Thus, for him, ascribed statuses are those assigned on the basis of involuntary attributes, such as age, race, and sex; assumed statuses are options that a person may or may not exercise, such as marital status or occupational status; and achieved statuses are those that one must win with superior skill or knowledge, usually in competition with others. It is apparent that this threefold classification has considerable merit in that it preserves the ordinary connotation of the verb "to achieve," but somehow it has attracted the attention of few other sociologists.[4]

In any event, it may be suggested that statuses which are achieved in some societies are ascribed in others. In medieval society, for example, religious status, class status, and usually occupational status were ascribed.

---

[4] E. T. Hiller, *Social Relations and Structures*, Harper & Brothers, New York and London, 1947, pp. 335–337.

They could not be achieved, nor could the original ascription be changed. In a totalitarian society of the sort we have seen in the twentieth century, political status is ascribed and any attempt to achieve it is dangerous. The occupational status of Queen Elizabeth of England is ascribed, as a simple function of kinship. In some societies the occupational statuses of all of the members are functions of age and sex and kin, and in these societies the sons are expected to follow in the footsteps of the fathers. In societies with rigid class structures and little social mobility, class status is ascribed and cannot be achieved. In a caste society, such as that of India, caste status was also a function of kinship status and remained for the individual a permanent ascription. In highly fluid societies, on the other hand, where the class structure is relatively open and where social mobility is possible, class statuses may be achieved. In other words, societies differ in the proportions of ascribed and achieved statuses that their structures contain. We should be inclined to say that one mark of a free society, in the political sense, is the large number of achieved statuses that its organization makes possible. In a free society the number of voluntary associations, and consequently of achieved statuses, is at a maximum.

4. The Individual and His Statuses

It must be apparent that each individual in a complex society such as ours occupies many different statuses during the course of a single day and an extremely large number of different statuses during the course of his life. An average college sophomore, for example, may be a student to his teachers and to the townspeople, an undergraduate to the registrar, a customer to his barber, a depositor to his banker, a passenger to the bus driver, a pedestrian to the motorist, a son to his parents, a brother to his sister, a clerk to the manager of the department store where he works on Saturdays, a second-string quarterback to his football coach, a chairman to the members of one of his committees, a trumpet player to the conductor of the band, an American to all foreigners, a male to all the girls, a patient to his doctor, a parishioner to his minister, and so on. In short, during the course of a single day he is student, sophomore, undergraduate, customer, depositor, passenger, pedestrian, son, brother, clerk, quarterback, chairman, trumpet player, patient, parishioner, American, and male. But even these do not exhaust his statuses. These are only some of the statuses he occupies at the present time. If we try to add to them the statuses that he has occupied, or will occupy, during the course of his life, our task would be endless. No such enumeration could exhaust the list, and this diversity, of course, is one of the distinguishing marks of a highly complex society. The smaller and simpler the society, the fewer the statuses that an individual can occupy.

We are born into a society that already contains customers and clerks, teachers and students, and all the rest. We do not as a rule create the statuses we shall occupy; they are already a part of the structure of our society. The student who sees and understands this point has in his possession a basic and genuine sociological insight. Here is a phenomenon that, like others we have mentioned, contributes order and stability to human societies. One may, of course, beat new paths and branch out into new directions, playing roles never played before and possibly, after winning social acceptance for these roles, creating new statuses. Specific statuses, like other elements of culture, come into being at certain periods in the life of a society and, also like other elements of culture, become at other periods obsolete and disappear from the social structure. Statuses too, as we have observed, are dynamic and are caught in the flow of circumstance that afflicts all things social. But the individual, for the most part, finds the statuses that he may occupy already established in the society in which he is born.

As we remarked earlier, in the chapter on culture, no twentieth-century American boy wants to become a witch doctor because there is no such status in his society. No Zulu youth wants to become a bond salesman because in his society, similarly, such a status is lacking. The influence that statuses thus exercise upon the careers of individuals in particular societies is quite important. Only by taking these statuses into account can we fully understand the behavior, the activities, and indeed the entire lives of people in diverse societies.

Some statuses, of course, are more important than others in determining the individual's position in society, and different societies have different criteria of importance. For this reason the sociologist E. T. Hiller introduced the useful concept of "key status." In our American society it is occupation that is the key status, the status which tends to assume a greater importance than the others and to take precedence over them. Mr. Smith may be a deacon in his church and a minor functionary in his lodge; he may be a native of the state of Wyoming and he may vote the Republican ticket. What interests us most about Mr. Smith, however, especially when we meet him for the first time, is what he does for a living. Is he an undertaker, a lawyer, or a banker? The answer to this question will not only determine for us his occupational status but give us a clue in addition to several other statuses, for example, his social-class status. Thus, we can say that in our society it is the individual's occupational status that tells us most about him. "What do you do?" is a key question, the one that fixes most securely the position in "social space" that an individual occupies.

In other societies kinship statuses or religious statuses or even political statuses may be more important and thus become the key status. In primitive societies age, sex, and kin are of overriding significance. In India the caste status was once of primary importance. In contemporary Russia it is the political status that holds supremacy. Finally, in the society of ancient China the intellectual status of a man took precedence, and it was the wise and learned follower of "the First Holy One," Confucius, who received the veneration of his fellows.

5. Some Status Relations

Many of the statuses in society are linked in a somewhat constant relationship with others. In our society, for example, there is a large number of paired statuses that go together, as it were, and have their own norms. Let us look at some of these pairs:

Parent—Child	Priest—Confessant
Husband—Wife	Nurse—Patient
Doctor—Patient	Social worker—Client
Lawyer—Client	Tax collector—Citizen
Teacher—Student	Hostess—Guest
Brother—Sister	Meter reader—Householder
Minister—Parishioner	Teller—Depositor
Owner—Manager	Conductor—Musician
Attorney—Witness	Officer—Enlisted man
Sales manager—Secretary	City editor—Reporter
Coach—Player	Policeman—Motorist
Landlord—Tenant	Buyer—Salesman
Artist—Model	Captain—Crew
Bus driver—Passenger	Personnel manager—Job applicant
Customer—Clerk	President—Cabinet member
Foreman—Worker	Employer—Employee

This list could obviously extend for many pages if we were to attempt to indicate all of the paired statuses in our society. These, however, are enough to serve as evidence of the significance of the sociological phenomenon with which we are concerned. They illustrate the fact that a very large number of the relations we have with other people in a complex society are status relations rather than personal relations—although they may of course be both—and that the norms that appear in such a society are not just norms in general but norms that are attached to specific statuses. The norms in fact are quite different in these different status relations.

For example, every month a man enters our houses without knocking and proceeds directly to the basement. Now it is not customary to enter other people's houses without knocking; in fact, in the Anglo-Saxon countries at least, the inviolability of the home is protected by tradition and by law. Nevertheless, here is a man who walks in without asking permission. The explanation, however, is quite simple. He is the meter reader. He wants to read the gas meter so that his company can calculate how much we owe for services. No guest, on the other hand, no matter how well known, feels free to enter a house without knocking. We do not even walk abruptly into the houses of our closest friends. Thus, what is permitted in one status, that of meter reader, is prohibited in another, that of guest, even though the personal relations between guests and hosts are much closer than those between meter readers and householders. We do not, in fact, need to know anything at all about the meter reader except his occupational status. We do not ordinarily know his name, marital status, degree of education, income, politics, or religion. All of this information is irrelevant. We have here a pure status relation.[5]

Consider another example. One of the strongest taboos in our culture is placed upon questions of money and income. No student would think of asking his professor what the latter's income is and how much of it he manages to save. This taboo is so strong that the best of friends do not ordinarily exchange this information with each other. The norm, however, does not apply to all statuses. An official whose name we do not know, the director of internal revenue, asks us this question every year, and we are required to answer it truthfully by April 15. In the status relationship involving tax collector and citizen, in other words, the taboo is relaxed, and there is an exception to a norm that is otherwise almost universal. The banker from whom we solicit a loan has a similar right and even an obligation to ask the income question. Information we should hesitate to give to even close friends, therefore, is given freely in accordance with the norms of other statuses.

As a final example of this point consider the fact that there is a strong taboo upon nudity in our culture. This taboo, nevertheless, does not apply in several of the status relationships listed above and is no part of the norms attached to them. It is relaxed completely in the patient status of the doctor-patient relationship and also in the model status of the artist-model relationship. A male doctor, in other words, can *in that status* request a young woman to remove her clothing when she occupies the status of patient, and the artist can make a similar request of his model. In the statuses of husband and wife, and of small children, the taboo is similarly

---

[5] Skeptical readers of this book have expressed doubt about the meter reader's entering without knocking. As a custom, of course, it may be disappearing as more and more meters are located outside the house. The custom has nevertheless been observed both in a small city in Iowa and in a small suburb of New York.

absent, but these are special cases because of the intimate personal relations involved and do not illustrate the point so well.

These examples show rather conclusively that the norms are attached to statuses and that different norms are attached to different statuses. As we have had occasion to say before, this variety is the mark of a highly complex society, one in which statuses are highly differentiated. Illustrations of this point can be multiplied indefinitely. Penitents tell priests whose identity they may not know the most intimate secrets of their lives, patients mention to their psychiatrists facts they would conceal from all other persons, communications between lawyers and their clients are privileged, husbands and wives cannot be required on the witness stand to testify against each other, an army officer may with complete impersonality send a number of soldiers to certain death, an employee may lose his job because of the decision of a remote official with whom he is wholly unacquainted, and a judge may sentence a convicted criminal to years of imprisonment. None of these norms has anything to do with the personal traits, the character, or the personality of the individuals involved. In such status relationships we have, par excellence, a sociological situation and a sociological phenomenon.

6. Status Conflicts and Reversals

What happens now when an individual occupies two statuses whose norms are contradictory, when in conforming to the norms of one of his statuses he has to violate the norms of another? This is a fairly familiar situation in a complex society and it always creates a problem. A Quaker who receives an induction notice from his draft board cannot at the same time conform to the norms of his religious status and to the norms of his citizenship status. They are in conflict. Here the individual himself will have to choose, although in this particular case the law provides an alternative solution. In many other cases, however, the situation is not so simple.

A California high-school teacher was once dismissed from her position for criticizing the members of the school board. The grounds for dismissal were that no teacher has a right to indulge in such criticism. Citizens, however, do have that right, and the teacher is also a citizen and a taxpayer. This argument, however, did not save this particular teacher her job. A privilege attached to one status that the individual occupies is not necessarily attached to another of his statuses and may even be denied him in the latter.

Citizens are similarly free to write to their Congressmen and are frequently encouraged to do so. Naval officers, however, do not have this privilege. A communication to a Congressman from an officer on a matter of pending legislation is a direct contravention of naval regulations and is considered, in addition, a violation of the "chain of command." As a matter of fact, a naval officer may not communicate officially with any other member of the Navy or with the Secretary of the Navy except through this complicated chain of command. His letter has to pass through his commanding officer, the Commandant of the Naval District, and the Chief of Naval Personnel before reaching the Secretary, and all of these intervening officers must read the communication and forward it with either their approval or disapproval. With respect to the law, communications in some statuses are "privileged" and in others are not. A priest may not be required to testify against a penitent or a lawyer against his client. A newspaper reporter, however, can apparently be required in some states to divulge a private source of information, and this problem is now a subject for litigation in the courts. It is possible that the norm will be changed and a new privilege added to the status of reporter. A parent may chastise a child and, in some jurisdictions, a teacher or principal may chastise a pupil, but a parent may not chastise a principal. One who tried it in a Middle Western state was convicted of assault. A university professor may, as a citizen, vote for, support, and speak in behalf of any candidate for political office. Since his university affiliation is known, however, he may jeopardize his appointment if his candidate is an unpopular one. Citizens in general, in short, have many privileges that are withdrawn from them when they occupy certain other statuses in the society.

The point of these illustrations is simply that different norms are attached to different statuses. The same action that is permitted in one status may be prohibited in another. The same action may even be prescribed as an obligation in one status and proscribed as a crime in another. No one but a medical doctor, for example, may administer a drug to a patient, and he may legally be charged with negligence if he fails to administer it under the appropriate circumstances. It is illegal for anyone who is not a member of the bar to accept payment for legal advice, and it is currently a question, therefore, whether accountants may advise corporations on matters of taxation. Justices of the Supreme Court of the United States, on the other hand, although most of them are members of the bar, may not practice law or even informally give legal advice to their friends. Military personnel are required on certain occasions to wear a uniform, but a civilian can be arrested for wearing one and indicted on a charge of impersonation. Except on the stage and at costume parties, men may not publicly masquerade as women, and vice versa.

Sometimes we find interesting reversals in status privileges and obligations. The President of the United States is at the very top of an organizational hierarchy. Nevertheless, he takes orders from the officers of the Secret Service who are legally charged with guarding the security of his person. An admiral exercises military command over all officers in the Navy who are subordinate to him, including the lieutenant commanders who serve as doctors in the Medical Corps. When he assumes the status of patient under the care of one of these doctors, however, it is the lieutenant commander who gives orders to the admiral. Authority is thus determined entirely by status, and the same individuals may stand in reverse relationships to each other when they occupy different statuses.

In the Navy, also, a junior officer is required by the rules of etiquette to open a door for a senior officer and give the latter precedence in going through it. Suppose, however, that the junior officer is a female ensign and the senior officer a male lieutenant. The community norm requires the young man to open the door for the young woman. Which norm and which status is controlling? The Navy, jealously protecting its system, once issued a formal ruling on this matter and directed all personnel to conform to its norm and not to the community norm. The ruling failed to reckon with a long tradition of chivalry, however, a tradition that continues to support the community in this situation, and it was the community norm that prevailed.

When Elizabeth, then Princess of England, and the Duke of Edinburgh visited Hamilton, Ontario, a number of years ago, they attended church in the statuses of husband and wife rather than in the statuses of heiress presumptive and royal consort; that is, Elizabeth entered the front pew before her husband and he sat on the aisle. The controlling norm in a social situation is thus determined by the statuses that the participating individuals occupy, and it is different for the same individuals in different statuses.

These examples are relatively trivial. There are situations, however, that have more serious consequences. One of them concerns military justice. The attorneys assigned to defend military personnel at courts-martial are themselves military officers and are subordinate to the officers who bring the charges. If they defend their clients as vigorously as they possibly can, which as lawyers it is their professional obligation to do, they may quite easily incur the displeasure of their superiors and thus jeopardize their own careers. The only answer to this problem would seem to be the engagement of civilian attorneys who owe no obligation to anyone except their clients. Otherwise the military can exert pressure, by the nature of status itself, upon its own lawyers, destroy the adversary character of the proceeding which is fundamental to Anglo-Saxon law, and deny to the defendant his full measure of due process.

It must be apparent that individuals become accustomed to the norms of their key statuses and that it is not always easy to adjust to the norms of a new status. Confusion is the normal consequence of such status transitions.

It is difficult, therefore, for a young man who is accustomed to the status of civilian to conform to the norms required of the status of soldier. And this, of course, is the reason why the Army and the Navy have to spend some time indoctrinating new personnel into the norms—the rules, traditions, etiquette, and so on—of a military organization. Some individuals never make a complete adjustment to what is, in effect, a new society and a different culture.

It is not often realized, however, that a similarly difficult adjustment is required of individuals who move from military status to civilian status. Men who have attended the service academies, the military "trade schools" and who have spent a large part of their adult lives as Army or Navy officers face a severe problem when they first attempt to conform to the norms of civilian status. There is the story, not confirmed, of an admiral who became president of a university. When he walked out on the platform, at his first appearance before the student body, the students rose as a voluntary token of respect to their new president. He, however, bellowed "Seats!" to them in the peremptory tone of a military command—an egregiously rude thing for a civilian official to do and yet something that would have been quite appropriate had the situation contained naval statuses. An assistant professor of economics called on this same president to discuss a matter of departmental policy. After some minutes of conversation the president said to the professor, "You may go." This dismissal would have been appropriate had the statuses been admiral and, say, lieutenant commander, because the senior officer in the Navy grants permission to the junior to leave his presence. In the university statuses of president and assistant professor, however, the remark was quite out of order. Here we find social relations between two individuals clearly suffering because of status confusions.

A general who became president of a university experienced embarrassments similar to those of the admiral. At the conclusion of a vote by the university council, a faculty governing body over which he presided, he would sometimes say, with abrupt finality, "Mimeograph the order and distribute it to all concerned." A secretary would have to remind him as gently as possible that the vote did not constitute an "order" to anybody and that mimeographed distribution from the president's office would be wholly inappropriate. Subordinates in a military organization, incidentally, do not "remind" their superiors of anything; they "invite their attention" to it.

We use these examples of status conflict—and of course many more could be added—because it is in these situations that one can see, by contrast, the importance of statuses and the norms attached to them. Without statuses and their accompanying norms social interaction between people who do not know one another could not be carried on and a complex society would consequently be impossible. When statuses are misinterpreted, social interaction breaks down. When they are unclear, social interaction becomes difficult. Fortunately, most statuses are clearly articulated and recognized; one knows the norms attached to them because he has absorbed the culture of which they are a part. Early in life the child learns the difference between parent and neighbor, cousin and classmate, teacher and janitor, minister and policeman, guest and magazine salesman. In many cases recognition is facilitated by signs and symbols.

7. Symbols of Status

Some statuses are highly "visible," especially those based upon the biological categories of age, sex, and ethnic-group affiliation—the last, however, only if skin color is involved. But many statuses that do not depend on biological differences are also easily recognizable. Nationality statuses, for example, are frequently, but not always, distinguishable by differences in dress and usually by language or accent. Often regional or territorial statuses can also be identified by accent or idiom. Fraternal orders and lodges have emblems of a particular kind that serve to fix the status of membership and to allow recognition by others. Identification by this means of membership status in, say, a Masonic lodge frequently makes it possible to cash a check in a community where one is otherwise not known. A title on an office door or below the signature in a letter serves as a specific symbol of both status and rank, and the status of wife, as we have mentioned before, is symbolized in our society by the wedding ring and in other societies by a distinguishing costume, headdress, or other ornament.

Occupational statuses especially are frequently symbolized by various kinds of costume. These vary all the way from a complete uniform to a distinctive kind of cap or hat and on to a badge of one sort or another pinned to the lapel. Policemen, priests, and soldiers, for example, are easily distinguishable by differences in dress. Construction workers wear hard hats, and these words in turn became labels for the occupation. In hospitals the white uniforms of the doctors and nurses prevent them from being mistaken for patients or visitors. Outside the hospital the doctor's little black bag serves as much as a symbol of status as it does as a container of instruments and pills. (His automobile usually carries the caduceus, traditional symbol of medicine, and sometimes a special license plate beginning with the abbreviation "MD.") Briefcases are status symbols for diplomats, professors, and attorneys. Rank within an occupation, moreover, may also be designated by differences in dress. Officers and enlisted men in the armed services, for example, are distinguished from each other by distinctive uniforms, and, in addition, the Army officer wears a symbol of rank on his shoulders, the Navy officer on his sleeves.

In the many cases where no distinctive uniform or other kind of dress or ornamentation indicates occupational status, other signs appear. Frequently these signs of status are special kinds of material culture traits. The male secretary of a corporation executive may be indistinguishable in dress from his "boss," but his desk will be smaller and its appointments less luxurious. He may or may not have a private office, but if he does it will be smaller than that which the executive occupies. A stranger walking into any business or corporation office seldom has any uncertainty about the positions that the various employees occupy in the hierarchy. Material culture items as status symbols may be found in every office in the society, whether the office itself be in a factory, a department store, a publishing house, a hospital, or a university. The physical position of work is also a status symbol; that is, clerks in stores are found behind counters, customers in front of them. In this way we can recognize waiters, hotel clerks, bartenders, barbers, and taxicab drivers anywhere in the world.

In general, all of these status symbols are perfectly clear in our complex society and confusions arising from misinterpretation are relatively rare. Material culture items, in short, serve as status symbols in all societies, and a rich collection of material culture makes possible a high degree of precision in status identification.

8. Status Succession

Statuses, as we have seen, are highly differentiated in complex societies. They also tend to be arranged in such a manner that individuals occupy them in regular sequences. Thus, obviously, one is a child before one is an adult, a wife before a widow, and so on. Statuses in organized groups exhibit similar sequences. One is a freshman before he is a sophomore, an undergraduate before he is a graduate student. Faculty ranks also have their progression—instructor, assistant professor, associate professor, and professor. Among university administrators a given individual is frequently a dean before he is a president, although a dean has been defined as a person who knows too much to be a president and not enough to be a professor. Military ranks present a similar situation, and it is rare indeed that an individual passes from his initial rank to his highest rank without occupying, in turn, all of the intervening ranks. Exceptions, however, are possible in most of these situations.

In business organizations too one finds regular progressions, so that an individual usually knows, at the time of his employment, the steps or ranks between his initial status and the one he hopes ultimately to achieve.

Here, however, the situation may be somewhat more fluid than in a military organization; it is not uncommon to skip ranks, to move for example from general sales manager or general counsel to president over the heads of seventeen vice-presidents. The statuses themselves, however, are clearly stratified with respect to one another and the larger the association the greater the degree of stratification. We shall meet the question of stratified statuses again when we come to consider the general question of social stratification. Here we want to suggest only that in a complex society statuses are not only differentiated, that is, set off one from the other, but also stratified, that is, arranged in various ranks, and that stratified statuses exhibit a kind of stepladder pattern of which individuals are cognizant as they set foot on the first step.

It has been suggested, in so far as individuals are concerned, that the total course of life represents a certain regular progression in terms of status. First of all one accumulates at birth a number of statuses by ascription. The period from childhood to late middle age is one of steady status accumulation, a steady rise in the number of statuses achieved. Old age represents a period of status relinquishment. One does not, of course, relinquish ascribed statuses, but achieved statuses tend in the later years steadily to diminish.

Many of these statuses become "inactive," and others, especially occupational statuses, are surrendered altogether. The president of the corporation retires and is given the somewhat honorary and less functional status of chairman of the board. The conductor who has traveled so many millions of miles in the service of his railroad is required to retire and to begin living on his pension. The retirement is ceremonialized by higher officials of the railroad who ride with him on his last trip and who present to him a watch or other token, the whole business comprising a kind of *rite de passage*, to which we referred in the preceding chapter. The distinguished professor retires and is given, with or without ceremony, the title of professor emeritus.

In one sense a new status of this sort is still achieved, but it is largely honorific and inactive. It may be an important achieved status, but the role accompanying it has a diminished significance. In other words, an individual both occupies the status of professor and plays the role of professor when he teaches his classes and conducts his seminars, but when he later achieves the status of professor emeritus, he finds no corresponding role to play in his new position. Here again, therefore, we have an example of a status without a role.

It is obvious that this period of status relinquishment is also a period of severe adjustments for the individual. It is a problem that, in our own society, is of increasing concern because of the changing age composition of the population. The time that the individual must retire, however, is determined by cultural and not alone by biological factors; that is, a baseball player relinquishes his key status, at the outside, in his late thirties, a professor in his late sixties. Joseph Paul DiMaggio, one of the great center fielders of an earlier era was an "old man" at the age of thirty-six and Joe Louis, the heavy-weight champion of the same era, was "old" even "younger." A professional philosopher, on the other hand, may be "young" and "promising" at the biological age of forty-five. Status relinquishment in any case presents its problems, and status transitions are regular phenomena in the lives of individuals in all societies.

9. Associational and Communal Statuses

Although we occupy many statuses simultaneously, we play roles in them only intermittently. The meter reader, for example, is a meter reader only, so to speak, when he is reading meters, that is, when he is on the job. Before eight in the morning and after five in the evening, on weekends and on holidays, he does not play the role attached to his occupational status. Similarly, one plays the role of vice-president or cashier of a bank, for the most part, only when actually at work in the bank or when engaged in banking business. This is the case with respect to many of the occupational statuses in society. They are significant only when we are playing the accompanying roles. These are what have been called, by the sociologist Max Weber for example, *associational statuses*; that is, they have relevance only within an association or organized group.

Certain other statuses, on the contrary, carry over as it were into the community and have relevance to both associational and extra-associational situations, even when we are not playing the roles demanded by them. We call these latter *communal statuses* in contrast to the former, which are associational statuses. Thus, a priest is always a priest in all of his social relations and not merely when he is celebrating the Mass or hearing a confession. All of his other statuses, even such kinship statuses as son, brother, and cousin, diminish in significance, and it is as priest that other individuals respond to him in all kinds of social situations. This status, in short, carries over into the community and operates not only when he is within the association, in this case the Church, but also when he is outside it. He wears his "uniform" on most occasions and not merely when he is playing the specific role or performing the specific obligations of his status. He is a priest both inside the association and outside it, associationally and extra-associationally. Society thus contains both associational statuses and communal statuses.

This distinction requires an additional refinement. The status of Navy officer, for example, is derived from membership in an association, the Navy, and carries over extra-associationally into the community and into social relations with those outside the service. The officer, however, also has status within the Navy. On his own ship or shore station he will have an official position, a billet, which is his status in the organization. He may be a commanding officer, and such a billet is possible whether he is an ensign or a captain.[6] As a commanding officer he will be addressed as "Captain," whatever his rank, by those whom he commands. On every large ship in the Navy there is a "first lieutenant." This is the officer, whatever his rank, who is charged with the responsibility for the "house-keeping" of the ship. Another billet of a similar kind is fire-control officer. Naval officer is thus a communal status; commanding officer, first lieutenant, or fire-control officer is an associational status, one limited to the particular group in which the officer performs his naval duties. Billets in the Navy are thus associational statuses; naval ranks are communal statuses.

This same situation prevails in other groups. The bank official's communal status is banker; his associational status within the bank may be vice-president in charge of corporation loans or vice-president in charge of taxation and finance or vice-president in charge of public relations, and so on. Similarly, the communal status of university professors is professor or "educator." Within the university, however, there are certain associational statuses, such as chairman of the department of philosophy or secretary of the educational-policies committee or member of the governing board for intercollegiate athletics. These associational statuses provide additional illustrations of the point that individuals in a complex society occupy many statuses at the same time, even though they do not play all of the corresponding roles simultaneously.

10. Multiple Statuses in a Single Group

The members of a single small group in society may represent a large number of statuses, and the relations between these members may be conducted sometimes in terms of some of these statuses and sometimes in terms of others. Let us see how this can happen, for example, in a small group of factory workers. Let us suppose we have eight men working together in the same department of a large factory—Russo, Mulvaney, Murphy, Watson, Swenson, Rubin, Schmidt, and Dobrowski. These men

---

[6] An ensign may be a commanding officer, say on a PT boat or at a small shore station. A captain, on the other hand, may not be a commanding officer, say when he is assigned to the staff of the Chief of Naval Operations. In short, with respect to their billets an ensign may be a "captain," and a captain may not.

work together under a foreman, whose name is Keller, and who, like other foremen in the factory, belongs to an administrative hierarchy made up, in ascending order of authority, of supervisors, superintendents, managers, a general manager, a president, and the chairman of the board. At the moment, however, we are interested not so much in the hierarchy as we are in Russo, Mulvaney, Murphy, Watson, Swenson, Rubin, Schmidt, and Dobrowski. Let us inquire into their statuses.

First of all they are all adult males, they are all workmen on the same level in the same factory, and they are all members of the same union. These are strong bonds of association, particularly because the occupational status is a key status in their society. But they do not share all of their statuses. Although they are all good Americans and have good American names, they represent different national origins. These have now only a minor importance, but there are nevertheless certain nationalistic traditions to which they differentially subscribe and certain bits of nationalistic culture which are not common to the entire group. Russo's family originally came from Italy, Mulvaney's and Murphy's from Ireland, Watson's and Rubin's from England, Swenson's from Sweden, Schmidt's from Germany, and Dobrowski's from Poland. Certain festivals, certain ceremonies, and certain songs thus have special meanings for these men. Mulvaney and Murphy, for example, in their status as Irishmen, are always out parading on St. Patrick's Day. With respect to religious status, Mulvaney, Murphy, Russo, and Dobrowski have a strong tie in common, for these four are all Roman Catholics, even though they are not all members of the same church and do not, in consequence, necessarily see one another on Sunday. Rubin is Jewish, Swenson and Schmidt are Lutheran, and Watson is a Presbyterian. In general they respect one another's religious beliefs, but their different religious statuses introduce certain hesitations, certain taboos, into their general conversation, and give the four Catholic workmen a stronger consciousness of kind than they would have if the entire group were Catholic.

Dobrowski and Watson are neighbors and thus travel to work in the same car pool. Their children play together and are constantly in and out of each other's houses. Watson and Swenson are the only Republicans in the group and, since there are no taboos on political conversations, heated but friendly arguments are numerous during the months preceding a presidential election. In so far as baseball is concerned they tend to follow the fortunes of major-league teams in cities of their own region. In this fact, unimportant as it may seem, we can detect the relevance of regional statuses. Rubin, Schmidt, and Murphy, furthermore, live in the same general area and are patrons of the same tavern, where they like to stop for a couple of beers after work in the afternoon. Swenson is a recent widower, and the sexual conversation of the group, ordinarily uninhibited, is at the moment somewhat muted in deference to Swenson's bereavement. Russo is unmarried, and this status makes him the butt of many of his comrades' jokes and ribald remarks. Rubin and Dobrowski are members of the company's bowling team, and this status gives them a certain standing in the factory as a whole.

None of these men, in their status as workmen, may directly approach the general manager of the company. Orders from the general manager are received through the intermediate officials, and suggestions and complaints move in the opposite direction through the chain of command. Russo, however, is the union steward, and in this capacity—that is to say, this status—he negotiates officially with the general manager on matters of union-company business. In one of his statuses, in other words, he is required to communicate by way of the chain of command and in the other he may communicate directly. He may even, in his union status, issue an ultimatum to the general manager and may be required to do this by a directive from the national office of his union. In his status as workman, of course, such an ultimatum would be unthinkable. In other words, patterns of communication conform to the norms of the statuses involved.

Keller, the foreman, is ineligible for membership in the union and on matters of this kind he is somewhat set apart, and both he and his men are conscious of his authority. Keller and Schmidt, however, are both members of the same Lutheran church and their ancestors once lived in the same German village. Their "unofficial" social relations are consequently somewhat closer than their different factory statuses would suggest. Rubin, Swenson, and Russo are all war veterans and see each other at meetings of the American Legion Post, of which they are members. If the different religious status of these three tend to set them apart, their common status as veterans and as members of the legion serves to bring them together.

It is obvious that one could go on for some time discussing the statuses of these men, the eight workers and the foreman. No such discussion could exhaust the implications of their statuses. We have tried only to indicate that both in readily apparent and also in subtle ways their common and different statuses exert influences upon and help to determine the social relations that they have with one another. And so it would be with any group of people we might find—in an office, on a village street, in an apartment house, on board a ship, in a classroom, at a meeting, in a grocery store, in a court of law, or anywhere in society. All of them interact with one another in terms of the norms of the various and several statuses that they occupy, and this is the factor that confers order and predictability upon their relations.

If multiple statuses appear in a single group, it is also true that many people in different groups have similar and even identical statuses. Every criminal trial in a court of law, for example, exhibits the same formal pattern. In two trials the personnel may be quite different—different judges, different attorneys, different bailiffs, different defendants, different witnesses, different jurors, different newspapermen covering the trial, and different spectators. Without specifying any of these individuals, without naming them or identifying them, without knowing anything about them except their statuses, we immediately know a great deal about what they will do, how they will interact with one another, what kinds of authority will be exercised, and where they will sit in the courtroom.

The situation, in short, has a structure, a structure comprised of norms and statuses. When we know these norms and statuses we know in general the procedure that will be followed. We do not need to know the individuals involved nor—and this is most important—do they need to know one another. If the trial takes place in a large city the people in the courtroom may never have seen one another before, and when the trial is over they may go their separate ways without ever seeing one another again. This is surely one of the "miracles" of social organization. Society itself, in contrast to anomy, is a network of statuses.

11. Status Relations and Personal Relations

If we were to maintain that social relations between people proceed *only* in terms of statuses, we should be guilty of a gross exaggeration, not to say a clear contradiction of fact. Norms and statuses make it possible for people who do not know one another to interact, and thus make possible also the very existence of a complex society. But people do get to know one another. They evaluate one another—to use E. T. Hiller's terms—"intrinsically" and "personally" as well as "extrinsically" and "categorically."[7] People do occupy statuses, but they also play roles in these statuses, and some of them play them in one manner and others in another. People respond emotionally and temperamentally to other people and not only formally and officially. People grow fond of some people and grow hostile or remain indifferent to other people. And here we see that social relations have not only a sociological character, in terms of the structure of society, but also a psychological character, in terms of the structure of personality. This latter inquiry is properly the subject of social psychology, but we should be remiss if we neglected to mention it.

As a matter of fact we have here a phenomenon that cannot be

[7] E. T. Hiller, *Social Relations and Structures*, Harper & Row, Publishers, New York, 1947, chaps. 13, 14, 38.

ignored if we are interested, as all sociologists must be, in acquiring a complete understanding of social relations. Parent-child relations, for example, are not only status relations, but relations involving total personalities. Parents have obligations and responsibilities toward their children, and in turn enjoy certain privileges of authority over their immature decisions and pride in their growth and development. They also normally love their children. The relationship is one of complex emotional commitments. In this situation the purely status character of the relationship recedes into the background, even though it is never wholly without significance and even though it is ultimately defined in the law. And so also for many other relations in society, relations between spouses, friends, acquaintances, neighbors, relatives, and so on. In these relations character and temperament and personality take precedence over status.

Here, however, we are interested in another phenomenon. We want to indicate that what are initially status relations may come, through repetition, to be personal relations. Initial interactions between customers and clerks, for example, are status relations, and in this sense, as we have emphasized throughout, they are independent of the personal characteristics of the individuals involved. It is in the status relation that "the customer is always right." Nevertheless, customers come to know personally the clerks with whom they have frequent transactions. Clerks and customers begin, after a while, to evaluate one another personally and intrinsically rather than merely categorically and extrinsically. Customers have favorite clerks and clerks have favorite customers.

The housewife does not at first know the butcher in the supermarket where she purchases her meat. After a while, however, if she becomes a regular customer, she begins to greet the butcher by name and he returns the compliment. They inquire after each other's health, and a little later the housewife, now known as Mrs. Jones, asks the butcher, now known as Mr. Smith, whether he enjoyed his vacation. She wonders too whether Susie, the butcher's four-year-old, has recovered from her attack of measles, and he wonders whether Harry, the housewife's eighteen-year-old, is going to be drafted before he finishes college. Mr. Smith and Mrs. Jones now appreciate each other as persons, and Mr. Smith begins to anticipate Mrs. Jones's needs and to save for her some of his choicer cuts of meat. Mrs. Jones, in turn, always buys her meat from Mr. Smith and not from the other butchers in the department.

A moment's reflection will result in the conclusion that this sort of thing happens in a great many of our social relationships. Certain bus drivers, for example, are more cheerful than others, and we are glad to ride with them. Certain business associates appeal to us more than others. Students like some teachers, not necessarily the most competent, better than others, and teachers too have more positive responses to some students, not necessarily the most brilliant, than to others. Corporation executives choose their assistants not only in terms of their status qualifications but also because of their personal qualities—and sometimes because of the personal qualities of their wives.

In taking cognizance of this phenomenon, however, we do not want to overemphasize it. The status relationship as such continues to be important, and individuals continue to conform to the norms that their statuses involve. The butcher does not have lower prices for Mrs. Jones than he does for his other customers. After three straight singles in the eighth inning of a tight game, a manager does not hesitate to replace his pitcher no matter how much he likes him as a person. In selecting the concertmaster of the orchestra, the conductor chooses not his best friend but the best violinist. When the director of internal revenue begins to do favors for his friends, he is indicted for misfeasance and removed from office. Social relations in a complex society are combinations of personal and status factors.

These observations will also be pertinent in the following chapter, where we show that personal factors are not wholly absent from even the most highly and rigidly organized groups and that in all of these groups or associations an informal organization arises to take its place beside the formal organization. The distinction between the formal and the informal organization of associations is one that has engaged the systematic attention of sociologists. Whether we concern ourselves with a factory, a business office, a baseball team, a church, a newspaper, a university, or an army; whatever the association, we find these two kinds of organization, one built upon status relationships and the other upon personal relationships. The analysis of status that we have just completed will serve as a foundation for our subsequent treatment of this subject.

12. Summary

We began this chapter with some intimations of the importance of status and suggested that the total meaning of many social situations depends upon the statuses involved. The appearance in public together of a husband and wife occasions no comment; the appearance in public together of a husband and somebody else's wife, on the contrary, can easily elicit disapproval. Marital status is indeed a significant status, but it is only one of thousands of different kinds of status that a complex society exhibits. Taking them all together we can explain the nature of social organization and of social relations. Without them such regular phenomena as a Saturday afternoon football game, the World Series, an election, a meeting, a concert, a university term, a congressional session, a trial at law, and an infinite number of other events would be impossible. We have gone so far as to assert that the organization of society is, in fact, a phenomenon no less miraculous than the regular procession of the planets around the sun and that without some such concept as status it would remain a mystery.

We emphasized in addition that a very large number of the social relations between individuals in a complex society are status relations and that it is status which enables us to interact in an orderly, harmonious way with hundreds and even thousands of people who are outside the range of our personal acquaintances—the ticket seller, the usher, the registrar, the barber, the taxi driver, the subway guard, the bank teller, the representative in Congress, the chairman of the local draft board, the clerk in the department store, the cashier in the restaurant, the bartender, the Chief of Naval Personnel, and the director of internal revenue. We emphasized, even to the point of exaggeration, that social relations of this kind are conducted in accordance with the norms attached to these statuses and in independence, at least initially, of the character, temperament, and personality of the people involved. Relations of this kind have an enormous importance in a complex society, and the structure of complex societies can be understood only in terms of them.

We next introduced a distinction between status and role. Status is a structural phenomenon and role is a behavioral phenomenon; status is a concept in sociology, role a concept in social psychology; status depends upon social structure, role upon the personalities and capabilities of individuals. Although status and role are usually found together, it is possible to imagine situations involving status without role and role without status. People occupy statuses; they play roles. The norms, however, are attached to the statuses. Since the norms are constantly changing in a changing society, statuses too—as well as roles—are dynamic phenomena. Statuses and roles may, however, change in relative independence of each other. New statuses arise in society and old ones disappear. In occupational statuses especially, competent and capable incumbents may expand the range of obligations and privileges whereas incompetent and incapable incumbents may exert an opposite influence. Some statuses, for example that of Kentucky colonel, are honorary statuses and have no roles associated with them.

We noted that statuses may be either ascribed or achieved and then turned our attention to the fact that every individual in a complex society simultaneously occupies a large number of different statuses, even though he does not, of course, simultaneously play the correlative roles. If we take into account not only the statuses that an individual occupies at a period of time, say during his sophomore year at college, but throughout his life, then this number is exceedingly large. In all societies, however, key statuses appear, statuses by which an individual is principally identified.

The nature of this key status varies from society to society and varies also from one period of history to another.

Another section of the chapter was devoted to illustrations of status relationships. We noticed in this respect that many statuses—landlord-tenant, teacher-student, doctor-patient, and so on—are paired statuses and that the norms attached to some of these are quite different from the norms attached to others. Since people occupy different statuses at the same time, the possibility of contrary and even contradictory norms arises and accordingly we gave some attention to status conflicts. Conflicts of this sort introduce vexing problems into the lives of individuals in a complex society and are almost wholly unknown to members of simple societies. Similarly, individuals become accustomed to the norms surrounding their statuses and frequently find it difficult to adjust to new statuses—as in the case of a civilian becoming a soldier or a soldier a civilian again.

Statuses, when not biologically "visible," are usually indicated in various ways, and we consequently discussed such symbols of status as costume, badge, title, and items of material culture. The statuses that constitute an important part of the culture of complex societies, in addition, are highly differentiated and stratified and, although we postponed the discussion of stratification as such until a later chapter, we observed that statuses are arranged in regular patterns with respect to one another. There are, in short status progressions and successions and, from the point of view of the individual, periods of status accumulation and periods of status relinquishment. Finally, for purposes of illustration, we discussed an imaginary group of factory workers and indicated some of the statuses that they occupy and the ways in which these statuses both help and hinder their social intercourse. At the end of the chapter we introduced one additional distinction, that between status relations and personal relations, and indicated how personal factors enter into many status relations and frequently change their character.

The reader who has followed the discussion up to this point will now have some sense of the structure of society. He will be able to appreciate the sociological fact that norms and statuses together constitute this structure. He will see that norms are attached to statuses and not to persons and that social relations in a society of any size or complexity are possible only because of the presence and prearrangement in that society of a systematic network of statuses. He will see society in short as a network of statuses and will understand the contribution that status makes to the fundamental order of society.

The locus of statuses is in groups, and each individual in society, accordingly, has as many statuses as there are groups of which he is a member. We need next, therefore, to inquire into the nature of the groups that appear in human societies. This is the task of the following chapter.

Chapter 10

GROUPS

HEMISTS and physicists have arranged
all substances that appear on earth
into a small number of classes,
called elements, and of these all other
things are compounded. Biologists,
similarly, have arranged plants and animals and
insects into a small number of classes, called species,
and of these all living things are varieties.
Sociologists, however, have not yet achieved a
satisfactory classification of social groups. The task
is difficult. The student can appreciate
one of the difficulties by pausing
to reflect upon the enormous number
of groups that a complex society
contains. Indeed, there are probably
more groups in any sizable society than
there are individuals in that society.
The gross number of groups in a society,
however, is hardly an important problem
—at least when presented in this
form. Obviously the number
depends entirely upon how
we define a group. If we say that
all those born at 5 A.M. on a
Tuesday, for example, constitute
a social group, then the number
of such groups is immense,
since there is an immense number
of moments in a week when
people have been born. If we can
say that any collection of
people, large or small, on any
street, street corner, path, or village
green in the world constitutes
a social group, no matter
how momentary or transient the
gathering may be, then again the

number of groups is immense. If we say that such examples are nonsense because some groups are important and others are unimportant, then we have the complicated problem of deciding what we mean by "important" and "unimportant." Clearly there are issues of great complexity involved here, and it is the responsibility of the sociologist to make an effort to resolve them. In this chapter, therefore, we confront the problem of groups and their classification.

1. "No Man Is an Island"

No man normally lives alone. The greatest philosopher of antiquity and possibly of all time—Aristotle—remarked in a statement which has been quoted again and again that man is a social animal (*zoon politikon*). Aristotle also remarked that only a beast or a god is fit to live alone.[1] With the exception of hermits, shepherds, lighthouse keepers, prisoners in solitary confinement, and possibly a few others, no human being lives alone for any extended period of time. So necessary in fact is association with our fellow human beings that survival is problematic without it, personality deterioration accompanies its absence, and total ostracism from one's groups is probably the cruelest punishment—short of death itself— that men are ever called upon to endure.

Since the large majority of us do not live alone, we consequently live in groups—all kinds of groups. Inevitably most of us are, or have been, members of a family. We have friends, or at least acquaintances. We live in a certain place, and accordingly our street, our neighborhood, our city, our state, and our country represent kinds of groups. We are male or female, old or young, and so we belong to at least two groups based upon biological characteristics. We have an occupation or profession or at least some kind of pursuit, activity, or hobby, and consequently we are frequently associated with those who have similar pursuits, and have something in common with them whether we associate with them or not. Probably everyone who reads this book has, at one time or another, served on a committee, and a committee, too, is a kind of group. Everybody who happens to have read a certain book, including this one, constitutes a group. A classroom is a kind of group and so is a corporation. A university is a kind of group and so are all college students, but they are not groups of the same kind. All those who profess the same religion, who salute the same flag, who have the same ethnic origin, who are in the same income-tax brackets, who subscribe to the same newspaper, and so on through an infinity of examples are in some sense or other members of the same groups.

---

[1] Or, added the irreverent Nietzsche in the nineteenth century, a combination of both—that is, a philosopher.

All criminals constitute a group and so also do all forgers, all teachers and all professors, all artists and all poets, and in each of these cases it can be seen that the first group completely includes the second. There are also groups whose members are not individuals but only other groups, such as for example the Association of American Railroads and the American Council of Learned Societies. Strange as it may seem, there are groups that have no members at all, such as female Irish astronauts. And finally there are even imaginary groups, including the inhabitants of Mars and of the lost continent of Atlantis.

The problem of classifying all of these groups, actual and potential, real and imaginary, is one of considerable difficulty. We shall not survey the numerous efforts to solve it in the literature of sociology but shall instead present a classification of our own. Before doing so, however, we should like to say that, although there are various simple ways of classifying groups, some of these methods are either useless, illogical, or both. Thus, one alternative is simply to list all possible groups and arrange them in alphabetical order in accordance with their names. Unfortunately, an alphabetical order is not a logical order and the result of this alternative is merely a directory, with no sociological significance. Such a directory may be useful if we are interested in street addresses or telephone numbers, but such information is more practical than sociological. Furthermore, some kinds of groups, for example crowds and cliques, have no names, and consequently such a listing would perforce omit such groups entirely. Some groups, furthermore, do not have any regional or territorial locus, that is, there is no place at which they can be located, and these too would be missing from such a list. There is no locus, for example, for the group comprised of all those who write poetry. In this case we could list all kinds of poetry "societies," but poets who do not belong to these societies could not be included. No directory or list, in other words whether arranged in alphabetical order or in some other way, can provide the kind of classification we want. Whatever its practical utility for certain purposes, it would have neither logical nor sociological importance.

Another simple, and eminently logical, means of classifying groups is to take a total population, say the population of the United States, and ask how many possible combinations and permutations are mathematically possible for the given number of people. There are well-known algebraic formulas for carrying out these computations, and the answer, though astronomically large, is easy to arrive at. An American sociologist once recommended a modification of this method for classifying groups.[2] Here,

---

[2] George A. Lundberg, "Some Problems of Group Classification and Measurement," *American Sociological Review*, vol. 5, June, 1940, pp. 351–360. See also his *Foundations of Sociology*, The Macmillan Company, New York, 1939, pp. 339–374.

however, the problem of group classification becomes a mathematical problem rather than a sociological problem, and the resulting categories, though logical, are not very useful. Nor do they have much significance. A large number of "empty pigeonholes," no matter how orderly their arrangement, does not contribute to our knowledge of groups.

The circumstances of group classification, in short, are somewhat perverse. The more practical our classification happens to be, the less logical it becomes; and the more logical, the less practical. In other words, as in so many other situations, we cannot have everything at once. For the sociological analysis of groups we have to surrender something both of logical rigor and of practical utility. Similarly, the classification can be neither too abstract nor too concrete without losing sociological significance.[3]

In this connection it should be recognized that classifications do not, as such, exist in the nature of any phenomena. Categories are imposed upon phenomena for various purposes, and different classifications of the same phenomena may therefore be equally correct or incorrect, although not all equally logical or equally useful. In other words, we may classify a great many things in a great many different ways, and the classification we ultimately choose will be the one most relevant to our particular purpose. This again is a simple point. The population of the United States, for example, may be classified by sex into two categories, male and female. The same population may be classified by age into two categories, those under thirty and those over thirty, or indeed into a large number of age categories. This is what is meant by saying that our categories sometimes cut across one another.[4] Similarly, the books on our shelves can be classified by height, weight, color, content, number of pages, date of publication, or authors' names. In this case we could have seven different classifications of the same books, all equally correct but not all equally useful. The same observation applies to the problem of group classification in sociology. The same groups can be classified in a variety of different ways depending upon the characteristics in which we happen to be interested at a particular time.

Let us quit this level of logical discourse, however, and take another look at an imaginary undergraduate and some of the groups to which he belongs. In the first place, he belongs to an age group. This is a matter of biological determination primarily but also, as we have seen, of cultural

---

[3] It is obvious that if we operate on a high enough level of abstraction, we can integrate anything (everything in the universe belongs to the category of being), and if we operate on a low enough one, we can differentiate anything (there are no two identical things in the universe). That is why, in the nature of inquiry, it is necessary to deal with classes of things and that is why taxonomy is important.

[4] The U. S. Bureau of the Census once, with unconscious humor, published a table carrying the following legend: "American population broken down by age and sex."

determination. Biological age as such is an important determinant of membership in many groups, of eligibility for some and of ineligibility for others, and is itself constitutive of group membership. In all probability our student would not be attending college if he were eight or eighty instead of the eighteen he is. His age, while helping to attach him to some groups separates him from others, especially those comprised of people much younger or much older. As his age changes he will relinquish his membership in some groups and apply for admission to others.

It is also apparent, since we have been using the masculine pronoun, that our student belongs to that half of the human race which is male rather than female. This has a great deal to do with his conduct, for reasons that are both biological and cultural, and determines in addition many of his group memberships and affiliations. Age and sex groups are not, of course, organized groups, such as those that require him to pay dues and attend meetings, but they are of incalculable importance in fixing many of his statuses in society.

The student has a family at home and this group, of course, has been exceedingly important to him. Its importance, however, will begin to wane in the next few years, now that he is away at school, and someday he may start another family of his own. As a resident of his home town and as a temporary resident of his university town, he is a member of two different communities and in each of these he calls a particular neighborhood his own. His father's income, his father's occupation, and the location of his father's house have something to do with the social class to which he belongs and a social class too is a kind of a social group. His county, state, region, and country delineate his locality or territorial groups.

He has had many friends and acquaintances during his life, "peer groups" as they are sometimes called, including boyhood gangs and cliques, and these, constantly changing as they are, also constitute social groups. He has been a member of a basketball team and of an orchestra, has served on a respectable number of committees both in school and at the university, has been in many audiences and numerous crowds, and—since he has had a number of short-time jobs—has belonged to many occupational groups. The various associations that he has formally joined—his church, his university, the YMCA, and so on—are still other groups of which he is a member. In fact, if we should try to list or to imagine all of the groups to which he has belonged at some time or other, our list would soon become large, unmanageable, and chaotic. If we should try to include all of his temporary and transient groups in addition, our list would be virtually inexhaustible; and if we should strive for an absolutely complete enumeration, our attempt would certainly be doomed to failure. It is the necessity of introducing some order into this chaos that makes systematic classification of groups essential in sociology.

2. A Classification of Groups

We are members of some groups through the circumstance of statistical arrangement. We are members of other groups because we are conscious of having something in common, some shared attribute or characteristic, with other people. We are members of still other groups because we enter into social relationships with other people. And, finally, we are members of groups because we join them and have our names inscribed on the membership rolls. These observations provide clues to distinctions between four different kinds of groups that we shall call, respectively, (1) the statistical, (2) the societal, (3) the social, and (4) the associational. These are not perhaps the best possible names, or labels, for these different kinds of groups, but in the absence of better ones they will have to do. Let us examine them in order and explain them in some detail. We should note first of all, however, that they arrange themselves on a kind of logical continuum depending upon the presence of certain important sociological properties, (1) consciousness of kind, (2) social interaction, and (3) social organization—properties that result in groups of fundamentally different characteristics.

Statistical Groups

Statistical groups are "formed," not by the members themselves, but by sociologists and statisticians. The members of such groups are not usually conscious of belonging to them and indeed "belonging" is too strong a word, inasmuch as "membership" in such groups carries with it neither obligations nor privileges. Many sociologists do not include these groups at all when discussing this subject on the very reasonable ground that, since no social interaction is involved, no social relations exist and social relations constitute the specific business of sociology. Now it is perfectly true that one can construct a large number of statistical groups that have no sociological significance whatever. Some absurd examples would be the people who were born on a Tuesday, those who at one time or another have tried to bring forth a musical note from a tuba, those who have seen the Mississippi River, and all authors whose books are exactly 376 pages long. Such ridiculous examples could be multiplied indefinitely. (Indeed, one imagines that they *are* multiplied indefinitely by those who compile baseball statistics.) As sociologists, however, we may want to talk about the group of people who have been elected to the Hall of Fame, or about the group of men who served in the British Cabinet during the reign of Queen Victoria, or about the group of people who were victims of the San Francisco earthquake of 1906. There is obviously no interaction in these groups, but if our classification is to be complete we want to make a place for them. In addition, many purely statistical groups have more than a merely statistical significance. Statistical groupings of some kinds have much to do with the entire character of a society. Thus, a society in which 10 per cent of the population is illiterate would be a different kind of society from one in which 90 per cent is illiterate. A society in which the majority of people are over thirty-five years of age would be different from one in which the majority are under that age. The proportion of the population that is right-handed rather than left-handed certainly exercises an influence upon the material culture and probably also upon the norms of a society.

	Consciousness of Kind	Social Interaction	Social Organization
A. Statistical	No	No	No

The number of people who, in a given year, are afflicted by a particular disease, say diphtheria, has much to do with the allocation of funds for medical research. The fact of having had such a disease, however, may not in itself stimulate or encourage social interaction among those afflicted, and people who, for example, have no more in common than a vaccination scar are not likely to enter into social relations with one another At the same time, one should not demean the importance of statistical groups of this kind. The number of public-school teachers who are unmarried, a fact that does not necessarily induce the members of this group to interact with one another, is nevertheless a fact that exercises an effect upon public-school education and that causes concern to many who are interested in the educational system of our country. Once again we may say that many purely statistical groupings, especially when they are majorities, have much to do with the total character and profile of a society. They constitute demographic rather than social arrangements, in the strict sense, but they cannot be ignored in any thoroughgoing sociological examination or inquiry.

Societal Groups

Our second category we shall call societal groups, though we have to apologize for the awkward adjective. Societal groups differ from statistical groups in one very important characteristic—consciousness of kind. The concept "consciousness of kind" was introduced into sociology by Franklin Henry Giddings, who taught sociology and the history of civilization for many years at Columbia University. Giddings was anxious to explain a phenomenon that every observation disclosed, namely, that wherever we look we find people in association with one another—that is, living in groups. This cannot be explained by instinct, nor can it be presumed that human beings live together because they intellectually recognize the utility of doing so. We can say merely that people do have a consciousness of kind, that they recognize others like themselves and want to associate with them.

The basic "why" of the matter is still unsettled today. It is fruitless to ask when men began living together in groups, for indeed it is impossible to imagine their ever doing otherwise. Certainly it is unreasonable to suppose, as several political philosophers of the "social-contract" school have done, that once upon a time all men lived alone, and suddenly, on one eventful day, decided to band together with others for mutual protection, not only against the elements and against other species, but also against predators of their own kind. Nor does it help to posit an instinct for gregariousness, that is, an instinct for living together. The "explanation" in this case is no explanation at all, but merely a label—"gregarious instinct"—used as a fig leaf to cover the nudity of our ignorance.

	Consciousness of Kind	*Social Interaction*	*Social Organization*
A. Statistical	No	No	No
B. Societal	Yes	No	No

As sociologists, we are satisfied to say that, whatever the basic cause or fundamental motive, people do live together, not simply with others of their species, but with groups of their own special and particular kind. Consciousness of kind is a strong stimulus to social relations. We are aware that some people are like us in certain significant respects, and we go in groups with those in whom we recognize a common trait. Consciousness of difference, on the other hand, as we shall have many occasions to see in the following chapters, is frequently a barrier to social intercourse—excepting, of course, consciousness of difference in sex.

Societal groups differ from statistical groups, therefore, in this important respect. Societal groups are composed of people who have a consciousness of kind, who are aware of the similarity or identity of the traits or characteristics that they all possess. In these groups there are usually external and visible signs of similarity by which the members recognize one another, including such signs, for example, as age, sex, skin color, style of clothing, language, accent, response to particular patriotic symbols, and so on. Examples of societal groups are females, the aged, Negroes, Southerners, Bostonians, circus people, plumbers, golfers, and the blind. Societal groups—including, as they do, all ethnic groups, all regional groups, all national or state groups, and all occupational groups— are distinctive and important in any society. We do not imply, however, that plumbers necessarily associate with one another simply because they are plumbers, nor that parliamentarians necessarily associate with one another simply because they are parliamentarians, but only that consciousness of such similarities is a powerful stimulus to social intercourse and to the formation of organized groups. In mixed groupings and in heterogeneous collections of people it will be those who recognize similarities of this kind who begin to gravitate together and to associate with one another.

We do not, unfortunately, know which of various ties—religious, national, ethnic, occupational, social class, or political—is the stronger. A French political philosopher once said that "two parliamentarians, one of whom is a revolutionary, have more in common than two revolutionaries, one of whom is a parliamentarian." We might wish that this assertion were true, but we do not know that it is. Karl Marx believed that the workers of the world, because they all suffered oppression, would be or could be united and that the tie of oppression would top all others in importance and effect. His belief, however, failed to take into account sufficiently the tie of nationalism, which continues to be intense as we approach the last quarter of the twentieth century. Affluent members of affluent trade unions in capitalistic countries such as the United States are far from revolutionary in their political opinions, and most of them keep their patriotic sentiments at a higher pitch than do many other groups in the country.

One can even speculate that upper-class solidarity is stronger than working-class solidarity because the rich, being more mobile, are more international in their acquaintanceships and consequently in their sentiments. The rich of all nations congregate with others of their kind at such "watering places" as Acapulco, Palm Beach, Deauville, St. Moritz, and Monaco. In *Grand Illusion*, one of the great achievements of cinematic art, dramatic emphasis is given to the fact that the French officer incarcerated in the German military prison and the commandant of the prison, both members of the nobility in their respective countries, have much more in common than the former has with his untitled French co-prisoners and the latter with his German subordinates.

Social Groups

We use the word "social" here in its narrowest sense, that is, to imply social contact and communication, social interaction and social intercourse. Once again the label is awkward and even ambiguous, but there seems to be no better one. In any event social groups are those in which people actually associate with one another and have social relations with one another. They can be of many kinds—friendship or acquaintance groups, classroom groups, cliques, crowds, audiences, congregations, kinship groups, passengers on the same ship, neighborhood groups, play groups, and numerous others. In these groups there is not only consciousness of kind or of some like interest but also social interaction—extending from polite conversation, or simply mutual awareness, at one pole to the most intimate relationships at the other.

	Consciousness of Kind	Social Interaction	Social Organization
A. Statistical	No	No	No
B. Societal	Yes	No	No
C. Social	Yes	Yes	No

To some groups we belong because of statistical accidents; to others because we have some trait or characteristic in common with other people; and to still others, our fourth category, because we formally join them and become members in an official sense. We are not merely members of social groups, however—"membership" is too formal and official an expression. These are the groups in which we live, groups composed of people whom, for the most part, we know personally and either like or dislike. In other words, we have something much more here than mere consciousness of kind, important as that is. We have social interaction.

Associational Groups

We come finally to a most important kind of group in modern complex societies, the associational group. An associational group, or, more simply, an association, is an organized group. It satisfies the criteria of the other kinds of groups and has in addition a formal structure, that is, an organization.

It is almost impossible to exaggerate the importance of associations in the society in which we live. We all belong to many of them. Our college or university is an association, the community chest is an association, and so is the Red Cross; a committee is an association, a football team is an association, and so is an orchestra; Rotary and Kiwanis are associations and so also are the League of Women Voters and the American Association of University Women; the United States Steel Corporation is an association and so is the United States Government; the Army and the Navy are associations and so are the International Ladies' Garment Workers Union, the Society for the Prevention of Cruelty to Animals, the National Association for the Advancement of Colored People, the Missouri Synod of the Lutheran Church, the American Association for the Advancement of Science, the United Nations, the Union of Soviet Socialist Republics, the Society for the Preservation and Encouragement of Barbershop Quartet

Singing, and the Society for the Prevention of Calling Pullman Porters George.[5]

	Consciousness of Kind	Social Interaction	Social Organization
A. Statistical	No	No	No
B. Societal	Yes	No	No
C. Social	Yes	Yes	No
D. Associational	Yes	Yes	Yes

Associations, in short, are groups of people who, conscious of common or similar interest, band or join together in some organized way in order to pursue those interests. Associations may be formed for any conceivable purpose, from mining a metal to undermining an empire. They may even be formed for the purpose of ensuring privacy and for discouraging social relations of a more intimate sort. The typical London club can serve as an example of this last, as illustrated by the story of the young member who accidentally bumped into an old member on the stairs and who immediately offered his embarrassed apologies. "Don't bother to apologize," replied the old member. "Indeed, I am most grateful to you. I have been a member of this club for thirty years, and you're the first person who has ever spoken to me." Another story of a similar sort, and doubtless similarly apocryphal, concerns the old member who summoned an attendant and said, "Please remove the admiral from the divan. He's been dead for three days. And besides, he's sitting on a copy of *Punch*."

The point of the preceding stories is simply that associations may be formed, and some now exist, that have as their function the most ridiculous activities the human mind can devise. In the following chapter, specifically devoted to this subject, we emphasize the tremendous proliferation and multiplication of associations in modern complex societies and examine in some detail the nature of organization, the phenomenon that distinguishes associations from other kinds of groups. At the moment we are interested merely in this preliminary classification and in the simple table of arrangement that indicates how these various kinds of groups—the statistical, the societal, the social, and the associational—are related to one another.

To indicate how these groups can grow out of one another, let us consider an example. Redheaded people do not ordinarily associate with one another simply because they are redheaded. All people who have red hair,

[5] To curious associations we may add the one formed by a minister in Indiana, an association for the prevention and discouragement of the formation of associations, whose password was "No."

nevertheless, do constitute a statistical group, and it is important for clothing manufacturers, dress designers, hairdressers, and various others to know roughly how many redheaded people there are. It is a fact that has statistical, but not yet much sociological, significance.

Suppose, however, that the government, through some capricious legislation, should impose a tax upon redheaded people. They would then become a societal group, a group rather conscious of their kind. They would be united not only in their possession of red hair, a factor not really sufficient to encourage social relations, but also in their opposition to the tax. They would then begin to greet each other as fellow-sufferers of discrimination, to talk, to argue, and to harangue the government—thus constituting a number of social groups, in our special sense of the word. If they would then formally organize and establish a Redheaded League in order to resist the legislation, the league would be the fourth kind of group, an association.

It should be remarked that this classification of groups into four categories represents a logical rather than a temporal continuum. Statistical groups do not necessarily, through some inevitable social process, become societal groups, nor do societal groups necessarily become social groups, nor social groups associations. It is conceivable that a statistical group could almost immediately become an associational group, and also that the reverse could happen when the association is dissolved. In other words, we are not talking here about some social process. Nor are the criteria of differentiation necessarily additive or cumulative. It is possible to conceive of associational groups whose members have few if any social relations with the other members. Into this category would fit the stockholders of a corporation, the policy holders of a mutual insurance company, subscribers to a consumers union, sponsors of a political movement, and, for that matter, the entire membership, as such, of a political party. We are suggesting, in short, an orderly arrangement of groups, which includes all of them on the one hand and permits distinctions between important kinds on the other. We should not be disposed to claim, however, that this classification is superior to others, nor that it is the best for every possible sociological purpose.

As previously mentioned, it has not always been easy for sociologists to decide what a group is or how the term should be used. Do the people who scurry for shelter from the rain and find themselves huddled together in the same doorway constitute a group? Are the people who happen to be reading the same newspaper editorial or watching the same television program a group, even though they are not linked in any other way and are, in fact, widely scattered in space? What about the people who just happen, at a given moment, to be somewhere in the vicinity of State and Madison

Streets in Chicago, or in Times Square in New York, or strolling along the King's Road on a Saturday afternoon in London? Or the people who happen to be in the same subway car or on the same transcontinental airline? Or, finally, those who, though belonging to an association, never attend any of its meetings and know none of the other members?

If social interaction is the sole criterion of a group, if "some degree of reciprocity" or "some measure of mutual awareness" is required, as several sociologists have maintained, then some important phenomena, including some of the groups mentioned in the preceeding paragraph, are omitted from sociological inquiry. The classification offered here enables us to include these groups and to emphasize in addition the importance of groups composed of people who do have social relations with one another.

Sometimes, of course, the lines between these various groups are not easy to draw with precision. We should say, for example, that the people who just happen to be in the same place at the same time constitute, in our terminology, a societal but not a social group. But they can very easily become a social group. Subway passengers in New York, for example, are notoriously indifferent to one another. But only the slightest of stimuli is needed to transform this societal group into a social group. The writer was in a fairly crowded car one evening in the spring when a very young, very tipsy Scandinavian sailor happened to stroll in from the adjoining car. He began to sing aloud in his native language, a gay, pleasant song, and the passengers, aroused from their reveries and their newspapers, responded warmly to his effort and began to exchange smiles with one another. With unexpected and indeed unusual solicitude for subway passengers, several of the men in the car asked the sailor where he wanted to go and made sure that he did not ride past his destination. After he left, the remaining passengers, augmented now by others who were strangers to the episode, returned to their reveries and their newspapers. The spell was broken. What for a few transitory moments had been a social group became once again a societal group, people with no more in common than their accidental togetherness at the same time and place, enough to give them a consciousness of kind but not enough, without this extra stimulus, to induce them to enter into social relations with one another.

The reader may pardon another example from the writer's experience. The English are among the most reserved people in the world and do not ordinarily like to initiate or to participate in conversations with strangers. Nevertheless, the writer happened at one time to find himself in a compartment on the train from Folkestone to London with four or five English people who apparently did not know one another. There was no conversation. The writer, with English money in his pocket for the first time, and baffled by the complexities of pounds, shillings, and pence, innocently requested an explanation from the man sitting next to him.

Immediately all of the inhabitants of the compartment, recognizing the writer as a foreigner, began to explain to him the intricacies of the coinage system and to respond to one another's remarks. From that moment conversation was continuous; the English went on to describe the delights of the countryside and the tourist attractions not to be missed, and it was altogether a pleasant ride to London. From this example, and many like it, we can draw a sociological inference of some importance, and this we do in a section to follow.

3. The Form and Content of Groups

Though keeping in mind the basic classification of groups presented in the preceding section, we now alter our viewpoint and consider a distinction between the sociological form of a group on the one hand and the sociological content on the other. It should be apparent that form and content are two distinct characteristics. We can ask, for example, whether a given group is large or small. This is a purely formal question. Or we can ask what is the purpose or function or principal activity of the group. This is a more substantive question, the answer to which is a matter of sociological content. In answer to the first question we may discover that it is a small group. In answer to the second that it is a recreational group, a basketball team. In terms of this distinction between sociological form and sociological content we can approach the subject of groups in a way that enables us to enumerate some of their most important properties.[6]

Let us reverse the order and consider the sociological content first. This is the characteristic in terms of which the layman would ordinarily be inclined to classify groups. He would want to know whether a given group is a basketball team or a football team, a department store or a drugstore, an automobile workers union or an electrical workers union, a fraternal organization or a charitable organization, a law firm or a soap factory, and so on. This, of course, is a sound procedure and such distinctions are important. Many sociologists themselves maintain that the function or purpose of a group is its most significant characteristic and the one which best distinguishes one group from another. Certainly it is a characteristic or property that may not be ignored. We need to recognize, however, that function or purpose or content, important as it is, is only one of the many properties of groups and that this property alone does not exhaust the possibilities of sociological analysis.

It is true, of course, that people form groups because they want to get something done, something that they cannot accomplish by themselves.

[6] This discussion is heavily influenced by the sociology of Georg Simmel.

No single person can play a game of tennis, operate a transatlantic steamship, administer a university, or manage a department store. Activities like these require cooperative effort. They imply the existence of groups. As we have noted, groups may exist, or may be formed, for almost any purpose or function. If we are to classify them all in terms of content, therefore, we shall have to restrict ourselves to a few large and comprehensive categories. From this point of view, then, we should have the following kinds of groups, all of which have some importance in modern complex societies: kin, family, ethnic, territorial, age, sex, political, governmental, language, religious, residential, class, occupational, recreational, propinquity, business, nationality, scientific, charity, insurance, educational, honorary, learned, and so on. The "and so on" is included because, though we have named many of the important types of group, no such list could ever be complete. Those mentioned, however, are major groups, and the adjectives describing them indicate what we mean when we talk about the content of groups. It is this characteristic that is likely to be the first thing we should want to know about any group.

As suggested above, however, such knowledge by no means exhausts the possibilities of sociological analysis. Groups also have formal properties, and only with the help of these can we introduce some important principles of group theory into contemporary sociology. In the case of each of these formal properties we find a set of dual categories, which we proceed to discuss in turn. We want, in short, to treat not the content of groups but their form.

Primary Groups and Secondary Groups

The concept of the primary group was introduced into American sociology by Charles Horton Cooley, whom we have met before in this book. By primary groups Cooley meant the intimate, personal, "face-to-face" groups in which we find our companions and comrades, the members of our family, and our daily associates. These are the people with whom we enjoy the more intimate kinds of social relations, not those whom we know merely by acquaintance or by reputation, but those with whom we have a close and constant social relationship.[7] The expression "face-to-face" should be interpreted figuratively, not literally. It is possible to have face-to-face relations with people who are not members of our primary groups and, conversely, we may not have face-to-face relations with those who are members of our primary groups. Bank tellers, bus drivers, and barbers, for example, are not necessarily people with whom we have primary-group relations, even though we see them face to face. On the other hand, all of us correspond, especially as we grow older, with close

[7] For Cooley's treatment see his *Social Organization*, Charles Scribner's Sons, New York, 1909.

friends whom we may not have seen for many years. It is the degree of intimacy, or social distance, rather than physical distance that determines the primary group.

In some languages, for example French and German, different forms of address symbolize the distinction between primary- and secondary-group relations. Thus "vous" and "Sie," meaning "you" in French and German respectively, are polite forms of address and are used when conversing with those whom one does not know well. When "tu" and "du," also meaning "you," are used instead, a marked change has come over the relationship. It has now become personal and primary. In English the use of first names in place of Mr. or Mrs. or some other title symbolizes a similar change, although not always with precision or with absolute certainty. In short, the primary group is a personal group, the secondary group an impersonal one; we have personal relations with members of the first and status relations with members of the second.

It may be observed that primary groups are not constant throughout the lifetime of an individual. The intimate relations we have as children with our brothers and sisters, for example, may not continue through the years of maturity. Distance and dissimilar interests may finally create barriers to social intercourse, especially in a society in which kinship relations receive so little emphasis. Friends of a decade ago, with whom we were once inseparable, may have followed a course of life quite different from ours and greet us now, if at all, only once a year on a Christmas card. The circle of our intimates, in short the membership of our primary groups, is constantly changing, a change as ineluctable as the passage of time itself. But wherever we are, at whatever age, we are members of some primary group—unless, of course, we have become hermits or solitary wanderers over the face of the earth.

It may also be observed that the primary group is always a small group. It may take several columns in *Who's Who* to list all the organized secondary groups of an unusually prominent person, but the untraveled man or woman who dwells in some remote hamlet may have as large a primary group as a president of the United States. Indeed, because the prestige so formally attached to the latter position constitutes a barrier to intimacy, a president may be the loneliest man in the world. The primary group, in short, offers intimate, personal relations; it is the group in which we satisfy our wish—indeed our need—for response.[8]

[8] One can hardly write a book on sociology or social psychology without mentioning the famous "four wishes" introduced into the literature by W. I. Thomas and Florian Znaniecki in their monumental work *The Polish Peasant in Europe and America*, Richard Badger, Boston, 1918. They are (1) the wish for response, (2) the wish for recognition, (3) the wish for security, and (4) the wish for new experience. It will be noticed that it is the primary group in which we satisfy our wish for response, the secondary group in which we satisfy our wish for recognition.

The concepts of E. T. Hiller which we discussed in the preceding chapter are also relevant in this connection. The relations we have with members of our primary groups are "personal" and "intrinsic"; those we have in our secondary groups are "categoric" and "extrinsic." In the primary group, in other words, we evaluate people intrinsically in terms of their personal characteristics, whereas in the secondary group we evaluate them extrinsically in terms of the social categories, or statuses, they occupy.

If John Jones, for example, is a member of an orchestra to which we also belong, we want to know what kind of musician he is, how well he performs on his instrument. This is an extrinsic evaluation. If John Jones, on the other hand, is a member of our primary group, we want to know what kind of person he is, whether or not, in an apt slang expression, he is a "good guy." This is an intrinsic evaluation. It should be pointed out that we do not always "like" the members of our primary groups. Relations of enmity can also be intimate and, as has often been suggested, we have to know a person fairly well in order to dislike him.

In one form or another this distinction between the primary and the secondary groups, between primary-group relations and secondary-group relations, appears somewhere in the writings of most sociologists. All of them make a similar classification, even though the labels they use may be different. Thus, if in Cooley we have primary and secondary,[9] in Tönnies we have "Gemeinschaft" and "Gesellschaft," in Durkheim "mechanical solidarity" and "organic solidarity," in Sorokin "familistic" relations and "contractual" relations. The "pattern-variables" of Talcott Parsons are an elaboration of this basic distinction. Indeed, it has been used—by Spencer, Durkheim, Tönnies, MacIver, and others—to describe two different kinds of social relationships.

We are constrained to suggest, finally, that the growth of secondary relations in complex societies neither diminishes the need for the primary group nor reduces its membership. No matter how large the groups of which we are members, no matter how highly organized they may happen to be, we shall always come to know some of the members more personally than others. Some will become friends. Some, in short, will become members of our primary groups. The need for intimacy and for primary-group response is constant. It is here that we have the sense of "togetherness" and of belonging. It is here that we are evaluated for what we are and not merely for what we can do.

Sometimes we change our primary group abruptly, as when we leave home for the first time in order to attend college or to take a job. What is

[9] Cooley himself did not use the term "secondary," as has been pointed out by Richard Dewey. See his article, "Charles Horton Cooley: Pioneer in Psychosociology," in Harry Elmer Barnes (ed.), *An Introduction to the History of Sociology*, The University of Chicago Press, Chicago, 1948.

commonly known as homesickness, an almost universal complaint at some time or other, is really nostalgia for a primary group from which we have removed ourselves. It is this factor that makes adjustment to a new situation difficult, whether a new job, a new school, a new regiment in the Army, or a new neighborhood in a new city. It has been observed indeed that soldiers with strong primary-group ties with their associates are less susceptible to battlefield psychoses than those who lack this intimate sense of belonging. Such soldiers, too, can better withstand the shock of domestic infidelity than those who have no one to whom they can intimately turn. And it has been proved again and again—first by the great French sociologist Emile Durkheim—that the incidence of suicide is highest in those whose primary-group ties are weakest.

Thus, in one of the classic studies in the history of sociology, Durkheim discovered that suicide rates in Western Europe were higher for Protestants than for Catholics. This puzzled him at first because the prohibition against taking one's own life appears in both Protestantism and Catholicism. He attributed the difference to the fact that Catholics, among whom religious exercises are more constant and regular, have a greater solidarity among themselves, a larger sense of belonging to a religious community. They have one church, whereas the Protestants have many denominations. Among freethinkers the rates are still higher. The Jews, who occupy a middle position, would seem to resemble the Protestants more than the Catholics, but they also have a more intensified sense of community because of the discrimination to which they have been subjected. The variable of marital status, to which Durkheim also attended, shows the same picture. The incidence of suicide is in ascending degree among the married with children, the married without children, the widowed, the divorced, and the unmarried (except that it is lower among the widowed with children than the newly wed without). Here again it seems to be the primary group bond that explains the differences. This is the phenomenon he called egoistic suicide.

There is another form of suicide which Durkheim called altruistic suicide, whose etiology is exactly the reverse. Too close an attachment to one's group, if suicide is one of the group's norms, can also explain the act. The Japanese samurai who disembowels himself in the rite of hara-kiri, the kamikaze bomber pilot who flies to certain death in order to be sure of hitting his target, the Indian widow who immolates herself on her deceased husband's funeral pyre, the ancient Scandinavian warrior in whose group death in bed was unthinkable, and the Prussian officer who, upon conviction by a court-martial, is given his pistol and knows exactly what to do with it—all are committing altruistic suicide. In these cases the primary group attachment is so tight that it overcomes the wish for survival.

Still a third form of suicide Durkheim called anomic. When any group of people is in a state of anomy, that is, when the norms break down almost entirely, then too the incidence of suicide rises. Such a state, for example, might result from famine, pestilence, invasion, or siege, and here again the primary groups may lose their hold.

The primary group, in short, has all kinds of consequences for our social life. It is always, in terms of our classification, a social group, and not a societal group or an associational group. It molds our opinions, guides our affections, influences our actions, and in large measure determines our loyalties. By "differential association," a concept introduced by a renowned criminologist, the late Edwin H. Sutherland, it encourages us to follow one occupation rather than another and determines in large measure whether we become poets or criminals, plumbers or philosophers. The importance of the primary group can hardly be exaggerated. This is not the group in which we merely work or study or play. This is the group in which we live, and have our being.

Secondary groups, by contrast, are all those that are not primary. They constitute a residual category that has no significance in and by itself. Nevertheless, as we have seen, a very large number of our social relationships in a complex society are relationships of this secondary-group kind; and if our secondary groups are frequently amorphous or unformed, the relations they represent are still of tremendous importance.

In-groups and Out-groups

In-groups and out-groups are of no specific size and may indeed be highly variable. An in-group may be as small as a family or as large as the world. And the out-group, then, is simply everybody who is not in the family or not in the world, as the case may be. An in-group is simply the "we-group," an out-group the "they-group." The in-group includes ourselves and anybody we happen to mean when we use the pronoun "we." The out-group, by subtraction, includes everybody else or, as we may somewhat paradoxically say, everybody who is excluded when we use the word "we."

When we say "we" we may mean only the members of our family, in which case only they constitute the in-group and everybody else is the out-group. We may, however, mean those who are in our sociology class, and in this case the class is the in-group and all those who are not in the class the out-group. An in-group may be everyone who lives in our town, or everyone who goes to our university, or anyone who lives in our state, or all of us who live east (or west) of the Mississippi River, or all Americans, and so on.

In her play *The Member of the Wedding* Carson McCullers caught the flavor of the in-group in the following dialogue between Frankie, a girl of twelve, and John Henry, her seven-year-old cousin:

Frankie: Shush, just now I realized something. The trouble with me is that for a long time I have been just an "I" person. All other people can say "we." When Berenice says "we" she means her lodge and church and colored people. Soldiers can say "we" and mean the army. All people belong to a "we" except me.

John Henry: What are we going to do?

Frankie: Not to belong to a "we" makes you too lonesome. Until this afternoon I didn't have a "we," but now after seeing Janice and Jarvis I suddenly realize something.

John Henry: What?

Frankie: I know that the bride and my brother are the "we" of me. So I'm going with them, and joining with the wedding.[10]

In-groups and out-groups, in short, are not actual groups except in so far as people create them in their use of the pronouns "we" and "they." The distinction is nevertheless an important formal distinction because it enables us to construct two significant sociological principles, which we shall now proceed to examine.

(1) The first of these principles is that in-group members tend to stereotype those who are in the out-group. This proposition means, to use Hiller's concepts again, that we tend to evaluate personally and intrinsically those who are in our in-groups, and categorically and extrinsically those in the out-groups. In simpler language, we tend to react to in-group members as individuals, to those in the out-group as members of a class or category. We tend to notice the differences between those who are in our in-groups and to notice only the similarities of those in the out-group. To Americans of occidental origin all Chinese tend to look alike and seem quite indistinguishable from one another, and we may be sure that the same is true in reverse. Similarly, Americans tend to feel that the English have no sense of humor, that all Frenchmen are winebibbers, and that all Germans are fond of sauerkraut. All of these propositions are false. As a matter of fact, some Frenchmen are both teetotalers and prohibitionists and some Germans cannot abide the sight of sauerkraut. Nevertheless, these are the stereotypes that have arisen.

To the American soldier and civilian alike during World War II, the Japanese enemy was a shifty and treacherous individual, universally equipped with horn-rimmed glasses. To the Japanese the American was a hypocritical and hairy devil—hypocritical because the Americans the Japanese knew best, missionaries and salesmen, seemed to have different systems of ethics, and hairy because members of the white race have more

[10] Copyright 1949, 1951, by Carson McCullers and reprinted by permission of the publisher, New Directions.

bodily and facial hair than do other peoples. Such ethnic and nationalistic stereotypes, common in all parts of the world, result from the sociological principle just announced.

Unfavorable generalizations, of course, are not restricted to other nationalities. In the United States whites have stereotypes of blacks, and vice versa. To the white in a time of racial tension, the black is a sullen and dangerous character who carries a knife that he is eager to use. He does not stop to think of the many editors, diplomats, actors, athletes, novelists, playwrights, and professors whose talents are a credit to the human race. To the black, on the other hand, the white is a treacherous oppressor who enjoys grinding the black down to a permanently inferior position in society. He, in his turn, does not stop to think of the multitude of whites—even in Rhodesia, South Africa, and the United States—who are truly unprejudiced and who devote their lives to the cause of justice and humanity for all men. Somehow it is always the least respectable traits to be found anywhere that tend to form the stereotype.

There are political, occupational, and religious stereotypes too, to which cartoonists especially have made significant contributions. Owners and managers, for example, are fat, cigar-smoking, diamond-studded capitalists in the left-wing newspapers, whereas the workers are brawny, upright sons of toil. Switch to a right-wing paper and the capitalists become the widows, orphans, and aged who have invested their life savings in a corporation devoted to public service, and the workers turn into agitators and racketeers. The father is bald and square, the son hirsute and hip. The farmer thinks the city dweller has ice water flowing in his veins and the city dweller is sure the farmer has hayseed in his hair. All bankers are dignified and distant, all baseball players are superstitious, all plumbers forget their tools, and all professors are absent-minded. The Jew is always Shylock or Fagin, never Einstein or Jesus.

Every in-group, in short, constructs out-group stereotypes. Social distance encourages categorization and discourages individual differentiation. The awkward words in the preceding sentence mean simply that all of us, the sociologically naive and the sociologically sophisticated alike, tend thoughtlessly to react to people who are in our in-groups as individuals and to people in our out-groups as members of a class. Knowledge of the principle, however, helps to reduce its unfortunate effects and to destroy the barriers that obstruct the easy intercourse of all peoples.

(2) The second principle that follows from the in-group—out-group distinction is that any threat, imaginary or real, from an out-group tends to intensify the cohesion and the solidarity of the in-group. This is a principle that can be illustrated on all levels and in groups of any size. Consider, for example, a family. In the normal family, brother sometimes quarrels with

brother and sister with sister. Let anyone outside the family make a slighting remark about a brother or sister, however, and the whole family bands together to repel both the remark and its author. As Mencius, the Chinese sage, said many centuries ago (so old are some of our principles), "Brothers who may quarrel within the walls of their home, will bind themselves together to drive away any intruder." Similarly, it is seldom wise to interfere in a quarrel between husband and wife. The danger is great that both of them will turn upon the peacemaker and remind him that it is a private fight.

Dictators are adept at utilizing this principle, and many a tottering regime throughout history has been saved by the pretense that the state is menaced by a hostile force and is a potential victim of aggression. This hostile force—this out-group—may geographically be an external or an internal one. It was external in the case of the Italo-Ethiopian War (1935–1936). Mussolini solidified his followers and silenced his opposition by pretending—successfully—that the Ethiopians were a threat to the power and the glory of the Italian empire. Hitler, on the other hand, used an internal out-group for the same purpose. It was the Jews, it will be painfully remembered, who threatened the purity of the "Aryan Race" (whatever that is[11]) and the cultural traditions of the greater Germany.

Similar observations may be made about certain social and historical phenomena in the United States. Criticism that is tolerated and even utilized when it stems from the in-group is resented and repelled when its source is in the out-group. Thus, Southern writers may candidly examine the conditions prevailing in the land below the Mason and Dixon line, but if a Northern writer examines these conditions with a comparable candor, his views will be resented as "Yankee interference" and will usually have the opposite of their intended effect. Indeed, voters in Southern states have returned to office politicians whose policies they did not particularly approve simply because these policies were severely censured in Northern, and especially New York, newspapers.

On the national level the familiar American expression "Politics stops at the water's edge" again exemplifies this in-group—out-group principle. It results in the so-called bipartisan foreign policy, which means that, although Republicans and Democrats may criticize each other freely on domestic issues, they band together as Americans and present a united front on any issue that seriously affects the relations of the United States with other countries. The Vietnam war, which seems to contradict the principle, actually confirms it. It divided the American people, instead of unifying them, because first a minority and then a majority were honestly not

[11] See Chapter 3.

convinced that a small, weak, and unindustrialized country in Southeast Asia could be a threat to the security of the United States. Finally, allies who work together to defeat a common enemy frequently fall apart at the conclusion of a war and begin to quarrel among themselves. The pages of history are full of examples.

But one need not stop at the national level. In terms of this principle the student of sociology is able to imagine an effective resolution of the tension that has marked Russian-American relations for several decades. The conflict would cease immediately in the event of a threatened invasion of this planet from outer space. An invasion from Mars, for example, would find the Russians and the Americans forgetting their differences and, as Earthmen, joining together to repel the invaders—unless, of course, the Martians turned out to be Marxians. Any threat from the cosmos itself, for example an imminent collision between the earth and another body, would have a similar effect.[12]

The out-group need not always be hostile. The presence even of a friendly representative of an out-group can exert a positive influence upon solidarity and cohesion. Thus, the English people in the railway compartment mentioned earlier had more in common—namely, their "Englishness"—with an American in their midst than they would otherwise have had. The presence of a foreigner emphasized their consciousness of kind and stimulated their social interaction. One more facet of this interesting principle appears with the recognition that an acquaintanceship marked by relative indifference when two people are in their own home town can suddenly ripen into friendship when the two meet each other thousands of miles away in a foreign country.

In his description of a botanist, H. G. Wells, in an old novel, caught with considerable literary impact the distinction between the in-group and the out-group.

> [The botanist] has a strong feeling for systematic botanists as against plant physiologists, whom he regards as lewd and evil scoundrels in this relation; but he has a strong feeling for all botanists and indeed all biologists, as against physicists, and those who profess the exact sciences, all of whom he regards as dull, mechanical, ugly-minded scoundrels in this relation; but he has a strong feeling for all who profess what he calls Science, as against psychologists, sociologists, philosophers, and literary men, whom he regards as wild, foolish, immoral scoundrels in this relation; but he has a strong feeling for all educated men as against the working man, whom he regards as a cheating, lying, loafing, drunken, thievish, dirty scoundrel in this relation; but so soon

---

[12] For other examples and for a discussion of the principle in general see Lewis Coser, *The Functions of Social Conflict*, The Free Press of Glencoe, New York, 1956; especially pp. 87–95.

as the working man is comprehended together with these others, as *English-men*, he holds them superior to all sorts of Europeans, whom he regards. . .[13]

This amusing bit, of course, is highly exaggerated, but there is no doubt that it makes the point.

The in-group, in short, is our group; the out-group is everybody else. We may remind the reader, in concluding our discussion of this point, that these groups have no specific or stable size. In one context the in-group may mean only the inhabitants of our house, in another the inhabitants of our planet. And we may state again the sociological principles that emerge from the distinction: (1) in-groups tend to stereotype out-groups, and (2) any threat, imaginary or real, from an out-group tends to intensify the cohesion and solidarity of an in-group.

Large Groups and Small Groups

Some of the other formal properties of groups are more familiar and require a less extended discussion. Some of them, in fact, are almost self-explanatory. Among these is the circumstance that some groups are large and others small. The size of a group, however, is one of its most important characteristics and one that has consequences of considerable sociological significance. Things happen to a group—any group—as it grows. Increase in size and decrease in size alike can alter initial arrangements and introduce changes into structure and function.

For the accomplishment of some purposes small groups are more efficient than large ones, and for other purposes the reverse is true. For certain purposes there is an optimum, or best, size, but what this size is, is not always easy to determine. Other things being equal, a large army is superior to a small one, a large country is more powerful than a small one, and a large corporation has more control over a market than a small one. But most committees become ineffective when they have more than a small number of members; one would hardly want many more than twelve teams in each of the major leagues; and nine and eleven members seem about right for baseball and football teams respectively. Fifty students and ten professors could hardly comprise a university, but when universities grow too large they lose something too. Contacts between students and their instructors, for example, become attenuated, formal, and infrequent. In the very largest universities students lose their identity and begin to see themselves as so many punched cards, on campus only to be processed.

Although it is not possible to pursue this subject in detail, certain consequences of size may be briefly indicated. First of all, as the size of a

[13] H. G. Wells, *A Modern Utopia*, Chapman & Hall, Ltd., London, 1905, p. 322.

group increases, so also does the division of labor. In very small groups all of the members may perform the same functions and indulge in the same activities. In large ones their functions are differentiated and their activities become specialized. In a small high school, for example, the same individual may teach English, history, and mathematics; direct the senior-class play; and serve as assistant coach of the basketball team. In a large high school these different activities require the services of as many individuals, and the English course is broken down into composition and literature, history into European and American, and mathematics into algebra and geometry. Similar observations apply to any group whatever, and one of the principal sociological differences between large societies and small societies is the complex division of labor that characterizes the former.[14] Indeed, prominent sociological theories, notably those of Herbert Spencer and Emile Durkheim, have been built upon the solid foundation of this fact. Durkheim, as mentioned before, saw societies as characterized by either mechanical or organic solidarity. In the former, solidarity is supplied by a "collective consciousness"; in the latter, by the division of labor.

Second, as associational groups increase in size, their structure of necessity becomes more rigid. There is need for more organization, for additional norms, and for more "red tape." In small groups many functions can be performed in an informal fashion; in large ones the specifications become more detailed. *The New York Times* is much more highly organized than is a small country weekly such as the Martha's Vineyard (Mass.) *Gazette.*

Finally, as a corollary of these two consequences, social relations in large groups are more formal and less personal (that is, less primary) than they are in small groups. An increase in size brings with it an increase in the number of secondary or status relations but no corresponding increase in the number of primary or personal relations; indeed, the latter may actually decrease. Thus, there are more secondary relations on an aircraft carrier than on a destroyer and in a large city than in a small village.

Majority Groups and Minority Groups

Related to the gross factor of size, but not identical with it, is the characteristic that determines whether the group is a majority or minority.

[14] This is an item of ancient knowledge. Xenephon (*circa* 362 B.C.) wrote as follows: "In small cities, the man that makes beds may make doors, ploughs, and tables, and perhaps houses; he is glad if even so he can find customers enough to provide a living, and it is plainly impossible that a man practising many crafts can be good at them all. But in great cities, because there is a large demand for each article, a single craft is enough for a living, or sometimes, indeed, no more than a single branch of a craft; we find one man making men's boots only; and another, women's only; and another, cobbling or cutting out merely, for a livelihood; one man lives by cutting out garments, another by fitting together the pieces." *Cyropaedia*, Book VIII, p. 2.

Majorities and minorities, of course, are always components of other groups and the terms have no meaning in themselves. It is obvious that majorities may be very small (two out of a group of three friends) and minorities very large (those who supported the defeated candidate in a presidential election), although not in the same context. But even in the same group a majority may be large or small. Thus, in a group of 100, both 51 and 99 would constitute a majority. This distinction, therefore, is not identical with the distinction of size.

The majority or minority property of groups has consequences of both a social and a political character. Ethnic-group tension or conflict, for example, is least when the majority group is very large and the minority very small, and greatest when the minority begins to approach the majority in size. Indeed, although the political consequences of majorities and minorities have been recognized for some time, the sociological ramifications have not yet received sufficient study. The political principle of majority rule has an importance beyond compare for the democratic state, and some groups—political parties—have as their primary function the recruitment of a majority.[15]

Long-lived Groups and Short-lived Groups

The duration of a group, its span of existence, is also one of the more important of its properties. Some groups have only a brief and momentary existence; others last for centuries. A committee formed for the sole purpose of collecting a fund or arranging a dinner disbands as soon as it has fulfilled its function. The crowd that gathers to watch a fire, to witness the aftermath of an accident, or to see a ship come into port melts away when the excitement subsides. Other groups, such as the veterans of a particular war or the members of the class of '34 at "dear old Siwash," are destined to last only as long as their members live. Still other groups have an existence independent of the lives of particular individuals for they have a flow of people in and out of membership. Universities and long-established business firms fit into this category. And finally, some groups manage to attain a great age. Among these may be mentioned the Parliament of Iceland, the Masonic Lodge, and the Church of Rome.

Voluntary Groups and Involuntary Groups

Some groups we join. Of others we are members, willy-nilly, without choice. Our age group and sex group and ethnic group, based as they are upon biological properties, are involuntary groups. Our language group,

---

[15] For a more extensive discussion of this subject see Robert Bierstedt, "The Sociology of Majorities," *American Sociological Review*, vol. 13, December, 1948, pp. 700–710.

similarly, is involuntary, since as children we learn the language of our parents or guardians. Our social-class group and our religious group, our regional group and our nationality group are all initially involuntary, although all of these, in our society, can be changed and thus, to some extent at least, can become voluntary groups. Our occupational group, our recreational group, our educational group, and indeed all of our interest groups are voluntary. No one is required by law to read a certain newspaper, to watch a given television program, to sell soap instead of suspenders, to become a grocer or a butcher. All such groups are voluntary. This distinction corresponds exactly with that made in the preceding chapter between achieved and ascribed statuses. It is in voluntary groups that status is achieved, in involuntary groups that status is ascribed. The reader will also recall that groups which are voluntary in some societies may be involuntary in others.

Open Groups and Closed Groups

All groups, of course, are closed to those who do not possess qualifications corresponding to the criteria by which the groups were formed. With certain exceptions, a young man may not be a student at Barnard or Bryn Mawr, nor can a young woman enroll at Williams or Amherst.[16] Nevertheless, some groups are relatively open and some are relatively closed. Thus, almost anyone of voting age can easily become a member of a political party, anyone can become a contributor to the community chest, anyone with the price of admission may attend a concert or a football game, and anyone can join a street crowd.

Many groups, both organized and unorganized, however, are relatively closed. A clique, by definition, is exclusive and selective, and thus closed in the sociological sense, as is also any friendship group. Families are closed groups by biology and by law. Professions, trades, and skilled occupations are also relatively closed. One has to be a member of the bar before he can become a member of the American Bar Association and one has to have a Ph.D. or equivalent qualification in order to become a member of most university faculties. No nonresident and no illiterate may vote in the City of New York. The Princeton Club of New York is closed to all except Princetonians, and the International Electrical Workers' Union is closed to all except electrical workers.

Horizontal Groups and Vertical Groups

We have not so far in this book mentioned the subject of social class and the class structure of societies, for this important and all but universal phe-

---

[16] The strong trend toward coeducation, as these lines are written, may ruin the particular examples. As we shall see in a later chapter, however, many groups are sex-exclusive.

nomenon is the concern of a chapter in the following section. Here we want to suggest only that some groups include members from all social classes and others receive their membership only from certain strata in society. The former we call vertical groups, the latter horizontal. A religious association, in theory at least, is usually of the former kind, as is a veterans' association. The Union League Club, on the contrary, is clearly horizontal, and so is the societal group composed of municipal recipients of public relief. Occupational groups tend to be horizontal because occupations themselves are stratified in complex societies. Ethnic groups, on the other hand, are vertical since they are, of course, made up of individuals in various social classes.

Independent Groups and Dependent Groups

Here we have an extremely simple distinction. Some groups exist, as it were, in their own right and others only as subgroups of larger groups; the former are independent, the latter dependent. The women's auxiliary of a lodge or other association is a dependent group. So also is a branch office of a corporation, the local office of a government agency, local chapters of national associations, and so on. A committee is almost always a dependent group. A private college or university is an independent association whereas a state university or city college, since it is a branch or bureau of a state or city government, is a dependent association.

In a society such as ours the number of dependent groups reaches astronomical proportions, and additional complexities are introduced by the fact that many dependent groups have coordinate affiliations with dependent groups in other associations. Purchasing agents, for example, constitute a dependent group within a university, but purchasing agents from various universities join together in an association of university purchasing agents to comprise an independent association. The distinction, as we have said, is simple, but the situations it helps to characterize may be quite complex.

Organized Groups and Unorganized Groups

We come, finally, to one of the most important of all the formal properties of groups. Some groups—among them the statistical, the societal, and the social—just are, or happen to be. Others, the associational, come to be through a formally articulated process known as organization. What, then, does organization mean? Here, it should be noted, we are speaking not of the organization of society itself—this, in a sense, is the subject of the entire book—but rather of the organization of associations, that is, of groups within a society. This is an important phenomenon, one whose significance for the modern complex societies in which we are primarily interested can hardly be overestimated.

In such societies a very large number of the social relations and social interactions between people are conducted in organized groups. It is the factor of organization that enables people who may be personally unacquainted with one another to interact, in a myriad of ways, in pursuit of a common goal. It is the factor of organization that, as we shall see, creates authority and determines that some in society shall command and others obey, some decide and others acquiesce in the decision. It is the factor of organization that confers permanence upon certain groups and the absence of it that makes other groups temporary and transient phenomena. It is the factor of organization, in short, that makes possible the very existence of the large, complex, technological society to which we all belong. And it is organization rather than tradition that, above all, distinguishes these modern societies from those small tribal societies to be found in the isles of the western seas and in the forests of the several continents.

Organization, in fact, is a subject that requires our most detailed and analytic attention and is therefore discussed at length in the following chapter. At the moment we want merely to emphasize its importance and to indicate that, of all the formal properties of groups, it may well have the highest degree of sociological significance.

We have now completed our listing of the formal properties of groups.[17] It will be noticed that the form categories cut across the content categories; that is, any of the content groups may have any combination of the formal properties. For example, a business corporation may be large or small, open or closed, of long or short duration, horizontal or vertical, and so on through the list, and so also may a recreational group, an ethnic group, a religious group, or any other kind of content group. It is for this reason that we have made the distinction between the sociological content and the sociological form of groups. And the principle, of course, works in the other direction too. An in-group may be a territorial group, an occupational group, a language group, and so on. By "we," that is, we may mean New Yorkers, students, or those who speak English. And so we now have two different ways of looking at groups, one in terms of their content, purpose, or function, and the other in terms of their form, properties, and characteristics. By putting these two ways together we can analyze any kind of a group and have a basis for comparing it with others.

4. Summary

This chapter in its entirety has been devoted to a discussion of groups, a problem at the very center of sociological inquiry. We began by suggesting

---

[17] The list, incidentally, is not exhaustive. One could introduce additional formal properties, but the ones included are the most important.

that all human beings, without exception, at some time or another and indeed at most times, live in groups. None is solitary and, in the more poetic language of John Donne, "no man is an island." The maze and multiplicity of groups are indeed among the most pervasive of all social phenomena, universally characteristic of every complex society and modern civilization. In fact, as intimated at the beginning, in such societies as these there are probably more groups than there are individuals.

We then asked how we might classify these groups and introduce an order among them for sociological purposes. This, for various reasons, is one of the most difficult problems in contemporary sociology. Many sociologists have attempted a solution, but a standardized classification has not yet been achieved. Furthermore, the more logical such classifications are, the less useful they tend to be; and the more useful, the less logical. In view of this situation we presented a relatively simple one, which we now summarily repeat:

	Consciousness of Kind	Social Interaction	Social Organization
A. Statistical	No	No	No
B. Societal	Yes	No	No
C. Social	Yes	Yes	No
D. Associational	Yes	Yes	Yes

We explained these four kinds of groups in some detail and indicated that, however inadequate the labels, the distinctions are important. All modern societies contain these four different kinds of groups.

Our next task was to discuss groups from two other points of view, one in terms of their sociological content and the other in terms of their sociological form. The content of a group, in this sense, is its function or purpose or description, whether territorial, religious, linguistic, athletic, academic, and so on. The form, on the contrary, depends upon its possession or lack of possession of certain sociological properties. These properties we treated in pairs, as follows: (1) primary groups and secondary groups, (2) in-groups and out-groups, (3) large groups and small groups, (4) majority groups and minority groups, (5) long-lived groups and short-lived groups, (6) voluntary groups and involuntary groups, (7) open groups and closed groups, (8) horizontal groups and vertical groups, (9) independent groups and dependent groups, and (10) organized groups and unorganized groups. Any detailed, thorough, and comprehensive examination of groups would take these categories into consideration, and such consideration, in turn, would illuminate the fundamental character of the groups that appear in modern societies.

Chapter 11

ASSOCIATIONS AND INSTITUTIONS

N CONTINUING our analysis of the structure
of society we have to consider in some
detail two more important phenomena—
associations and institutions. We have
seen how it is possible for people
to get around in society and to interact with
scores of other people with whom they are
personally unacquainted. We have seen how
it is possible for a student, for example,
to come to a university, rent a room,
register for courses, attend classes,
accumulate credits, patronize restaurants,
use the library, and even cash checks
without initially knowing the names
of the people who are involved in these
relations with him. We have seen that we
all occupy recognized statuses in society and
that these statuses, together with the norms
attached to them, contribute order,
regularity, and predictability to our daily
life and to the lives of our associates. We
have also observed that we are identified
with many groups—statistical, societal, social
and associational—and that we have as many
statuses as we have group identifications.
We have not yet discussed, however,
the kinds of groups in which we are
formally enrolled as members,
the groups in which we may hold
offices, the groups to which we pay dues.
We have not, in short, discussed the
"organizations" to which we belong.
Since sociologists have to use the word
"organization" so frequently,
especially in any attempt to explain the
structure of society, they do not call
these groups "organizations," but rather

"associations." An association, as indicated in the preceding chapter, is simply an organized group, and the two concepts "association" and "organized group" are precisely synonymous. We have observed that the fundamental characteristic of associations is that, unlike statistical, societal, and social groups, they have the attribute of organization.

We now have to explain exactly what this organization means and how a university, for example, differs from an ethnic group, an age group, a friendship group, and a circle of acquaintances. A university, of course, is an organized group, an association, and so are a corporation, an orchestra, and a football team. To say that these groups are associations because they are organized is not enough. Since such groups play so important a role in any complex society, we need to examine this characteristic in detail. What, specifically and precisely, is an association?

1. The Importance of Organization

Organization appears in a society simply because many of the things we do could not be done without it and many other things we do can be done much better because of it. Let us reflect for a moment on this fact. No game involving more than one player would be possible if it were not for organization, and we should, of course, be unable to play baseball or football or bridge, for example, by ourselves. There would be no such things as an orchestra or a university or a store or a court of law or a government without organization. Organization makes possible the complex activities in which the members of a complex society participate. Even if we as individuals had completely absorbed a culture, we should still be unable to accomplish many things without organized interaction with our fellows.

One could write a book by himself, and writing is certainly a solitary kind of activity, but one does not ordinarily write a book and also publish it by himself; that is, the man who writes the manuscript does not finance its publication, manufacture the paper on which it is printed or the cloth that goes into the binding, set it in type, run it through the press, transport the finished product to the bookstore, and sell it. All of these are separate activities, and the finished book is thus a product of many people working together in an organized fashion. The shoes we wear on our feet, the food we put into our mouths, the material culture items we use in our work, the newspapers we read, the automobiles we drive—all these and millions more are products of joint, organized activity. Without organization few of these items would be produced and without organization few of our accomplishments would be possible.

Every one of us is acquainted with the scratching and screeching sounds made by musicians who are tuning their instruments before a concert. A few minutes later, however, the conductor ascends the podium, quiet reigns for a moment, and then, with the downbeat of the baton, the orchestra launches into one of the masterworks of Beethoven and we have music. What is it that transforms noise into music, a cacophony into a symphony? The answer is organization. What is it that transforms individual musicians into an orchestra? The answer again is organization. Without organization there would be no such thing as an orchestra.

If we shift our gaze to the stadium during the "great autumnal madness," we can similarly see that without organization a football game would not be possible. Eleven men do not necessarily make a team. A team is an organized group, and it is vastly superior to eleven unorganized men in its ability to move a football down the field and across the goal line. Eleven men, even though each weighed over 300 pounds, would have no chance at all against a team. It is not, in short, individual size, personal strength, or brute force that makes a football team, but coordinated, organized activity. A team can defeat an unorganized group of eleven men under any circumstances. Indeed, eleven men could not play football together without some organization. With organization they constitute a team, an association.

For this same reason a very small body of organized police or of marines can control a very large crowd. A small number of men, constituting themselves as a government, can rule a nation. A small number of men constituting themselves as a board of directors can manage a vast corporation and assign and coordinate the duties of thousands and sometimes tens of thousands of employees. A small board of regents or of trustees can operate the enterprise of a university. All this is possible because of organization.

2. The Continuum of Organization

A crowd is unorganized; a corporation is organized. In these two instances the contrast is clear and easy to observe even before we know precisely what organization is. It would indeed be pleasant, sociologically speaking, if one could simply say that groups are organized or not organized, for then we should be able to arrange them in two distinct classes without confusion. Unfortunately, however, the situation is not so clear-cut. A crowd is unorganized and a corporation is organized, but what shall we say about a family, for example, or a gang, or a group of women who meet every second Thursday afternoon in order to play bridge? In these cases, and many like them, the situation is not so clear. We have to suggest, therefore, that organization and "unorganization" are not two clearly distinct categories but rather phenomena that shade off into each other. Organization, in other words, is a continuum with wholly unorganized groups at one end and highly organized groups or associations at the other.

Groups may range themselves at any point on this continuum, and many can be found at or near the middle. These we should say are partly organized. There are degrees of organization, in short, and organization is a continuous rather than a discrete variable. The most highly organized groups are those that can sustain a total turnover in their membership. Some of these, as we have seen, last for long periods of time, sometimes for centuries. These associations, though not independent of their personnel—for if there were no members there would also be no association—are nevertheless independent of any particular personnel. Less highly organized groups are more dependent upon particular personnel, and unorganized groups, of course, are wholly dependent upon the particular people who comprise them and have no structure that can maintain them through changes in personnel. We shall refer to this phenomenon again, but here we want to state the principle: The dependence of a group upon particular personnel varies inversely with the degree of its organization.

3. The Criteria of Organization

We are now ready to discuss the criteria of organization, the specific factors that distinguish an organized group from an unorganized group and give distinctive character to an association as contrasted with all other groups. These factors are as follows: (1) a specific function or purpose, (2) associational norms, (3) associational statuses, (4) authority, (5) tests of membership, (6) property, and (7) a name and other identifying symbols. We shall examine each of these factors in turn.

A Specific Function

Every association is formed for the pursuit of a particular interest or activity. As we have emphasized repeatedly, there are practically no limits on what that activity may be and not even the most potent imagination can exhaust the possibilities. There are associations for the advancement of beekeeping and for keeping alive the memory of men who would otherwise be unknown; there are associations for the preservation of peace and associations for preventing insult to the flag; there are associations for the promotion of margarine consumption and associations for the importation of exotic plants. Indeed, almost any conceivable purpose can be served by an association—good, bad, indifferent, or ever ridiculous.[1]

Associations need not be limited to one function or interest, however. Sometimes they embrace a number of functions. Sometimes these functions may all be major ones, although this is relatively rare. For the most part there is a principal function or activity and then a number of auxiliary or subsidiary functions. The principal function of a church, for example, is religion, but it may also become involved in the pursuit of charitable, ethical, athletic, recreational, educational, missionary, "sociable," and even political activities. The YMCA, as another example, is an association whose functions are religious, recreational, and educational at the same time. A university whose function is education will also have a football team—and sometimes it is difficult to determine which is the principal function and which the auxiliary. The auxiliary function of baseball, which is business, is alleged by some to be killing its principal function, which is sport. Even the smallest associations may have several purposes. The Thursday Afternoon Sewing Society obviously is interested both in sewing and in gossiping.

Robert K. Merton, who knows that things are not always as they seem in society, has introduced another distinction that has relevance here—a distinction between manifest and latent functions. It is clear, for example, that a candy store in a large city may be a front for the numbers racket; a motel, a brothel; and a much larger business may be a cloak for a criminal enterprise. Merton has in mind, however, something at once more subtle and more legitimate. The manifest function of a political party is to state the issues of an election and to get out the votes for its candidates. At the precinct level, however, many latent functions can be discerned. Here the party finds jobs for its "regulars," quashes traffic tickets, watches the relief rolls, settles quarrels, cuts red tape, and in general serves as a "helping" agency for all who are loyal to it. Reciprocation, of course, is expected. Similarly, the local tavern and drugstore may be better purveyors of advice to neighbors in need than the municipal welfare office. The voice of the bartender, like his ear, is blissfully free of bureaucratic tendencies, and he requires no carbon copies of anything.

We thus see in society, and especially in our own society, an

---

[1] Among associations that have come to the attention of the author are the American Ladder Institute, the Facing Tile Institute, the Instant Potato Products Association, the National Association of Bank-Women, the National Pecan Shellers and Processors Association, the Pie Filling Institute, the Sterile Disposable Device Committee, the International Association of Auditorium Managers, the National Broom Council, the Steel Tank Institute, and the Seed Pea Institute. The interesting thing about these associations is that they all have the same address and telephone number in the city of Chicago. Their affairs are administered and managed by another association which, with forty-four clients, claims to be the largest association in the world that handles the affairs of other associations.

imposingly large number of associations that carry on the interests of their members—interests that may be religious, educational, political, financial, recreational, charitable, patriotic, military, athletic, sociable, or indeed of any conceivable kind. It may be observed that none of these interests, except possibly the religious, can be pursued alone. Neither hermits nor Robinson Crusoes have any need to be charitable, patriotic, or political. In other words, interests of this kind are possible in the first instance only because people can and do act in concert with their fellows. Interests of this kind have their incidence and origin in society and can be developed and pursued only in society. And even those activities that individuals might be able to perform alone can be performed more efficiently in association with others. Here we see the basic reason why associations arise in societies.

The first characteristic of associations, therefore, is their function, the principal and subsidiary interests that their members pursue. It is this characteristic that distinguishes one association from another—an army from a political party, a university from a church, a library from a department store, a community-chest committee from a steel corporation, and so on through all the associations of society. This interest, or combination of interests, is the property to which we have previously referred as the content of the group. The content becomes an interest or function in the association.

Associational Norms

The second characteristic of an association is that it has its own norms. Certain conduct is appropriate in a university classroom, a factory, an office, a department store, a hospital, a government bureau, a military unit, and so on. Students and teachers, foremen and workmen, vice-presidents and secretaries, managers and clerks, doctors and nurses, bureau directors and assistants, officers and enlisted men, respectively, observe norms in their interaction that have their origin in the association itself and that would lead to inappropriate behavior if followed in other associations and in other circumstances. Certain procedures come to be established in association, and these procedures—or norms—distinguish one association from another and also distinguish the association from the more or less amorphous community in which it appears.

People interacting in a particular association, say a factory or an office or a classroom, follow communal norms too; that is, the norms of politeness, for example, are not specific to an association but operate everywhere in a society. Not all of the norms observed within an association, therefore, are associational norms as such. Nevertheless, some norms are unique to the association. Certain forms of conduct and certain procedures prevail only within an association. Thus, the requirement that every candidate for the degree of doctor of philosophy present, and successfully defend, a dissertation that makes an original contribution to knowledge is a norm that can be found only in the university. Similarly, the whole paraphernalia of grades, transcripts, credits, examinations, commencement ceremonies, and so on, are indicative of college and university norms, and none of these would be found in exactly the same form in a factory, office, store, or regiment. These others, however, have their own associational norms—work orders, billing procedures, sales slips, strategic plans, and many others, all appropriate to the specific association of which they are a part.

Whatever these norms may be, therefore, every association has them, and they are specific to the association itself. The norms of similar associations, that is, associations which, although separate, have the same functions and purposes and interests, tend also to be similar. This observation, however, introduces us to another kind of phenomenon, the institution, which we discuss later on in this chapter.

Associational Statuses

If associations have specific norms, they also have specific statuses to which the norms are attached. We have already distinguished between communal and associational status, and it is this latter kind of status, of course, that attracts our attention here. Right fielder is a status only on a baseball team, which is an association. It can be found nowhere else in society and it is not a communal status.[2] The status of vice-president in charge of production or of public relations is similarly an associational status, a status specific to an association and not one which, like husband or father, for example, has general significance in the community. It is this special set of statuses, in short, that constitutes the organization of an association and that determines the social relations which the members of the association have with one another.

It should be quite obvious that one could make an exceedingly long list of associational statuses, that is, of the various positions which help constitute the structure of organized groups and which are meaningful only within those groups. The communal status of a university student, for example, is simply student, in an undifferentiated fashion. Within the university, however, a given student is a freshman, sophomore, junior, senior, or graduate student, and these are associational statuses. Within the association, also, a student is a sociology major, a physics major, an "engineer," or some other sort of specialist. As an association increases in

[2] The communal status corresponding to this is more general—professional baseball player, for example, or athlete.

size and complexity, the number of associational statuses also grows until—in a very large association, such as a university or a corporation—this number is very great indeed. Within the association these statuses and their norms take precedence over the extra-associational statuses that particular members may have with relation to one another.

Two men may be the best of friends and even inseparable companions. In some associations to which they both belong, however, it is altogether possible that Mr. A's status will be subordinate to Mr. B's and in others that Mr. B's status will be subordinate to Mr. A's. In the orchestra of which they are both members, for example, Mr. A may be the conductor, Mr. B the first clarinet; on a community-chest committee Mr. B may be the chairman and Mr. A a member. This illustration, and many more that might be used, indicates the importance of associational statuses and indicates also that such statuses are peculiar to associations and do not necessarily extend to extra-associational relations.

We have now seen that the structure of an association consists, in part, of specialized norms and specialized statuses. This specialization is indicative of a most important sociological phenomenon—the division of labor. The division of labor is so important indeed that it explains in large measure both the difference between unorganized and organized groups and the difference between simple and complex societies. The division of labor is characteristic of all organization, and in a sense organization is synonymous with the division of labor. It is a phenomenon that has far-reaching consequences for the behavior of men in groups and for collective activity. It makes possible the accomplishment of certain purposes that otherwise could not be attained.

It is inconceivable, for example, that one could have a baseball team made up solely of pitchers, a football team made up solely of quarterbacks, a city government only of policemen, a bank only of tellers, a university only of deans, a restaurant only of cooks, a department store only of clerks, and so on. Organized action in these associations is possible only because there is a division of labor, because some people do some things and other people do other things. In attempting to make a touchdown, a football team, as suggested previously, is superior to eleven unorganized men who are trying to do the same thing. The statuses in the organized group fit together and complement one another. In football the division of labor has progressed to a degree that has engaged the attention of the public and the professional fascination of the sportswriters. The platoon system means that there are actually two teams, an offensive team and a defensive team. But the division of labor does not stop there. Professional teams have a man who does nothing but kick the points after touchdowns and another who does nothing but punt. These players are put in only to perform their specialties and then are immediately withdrawn. We confront in addition such newer statuses as wide receivers, right cornerbackers, middle linebackers, strong safeties, free safeties, and tight ends. There may be a question whether football is a "game" under these circumstances, but there is little doubt that the division of labor contributes to the efficiency of the organization.

The football team, however, with all of its contemporary division of labor, is only a small and relatively simple example of the intensive degree of specialization that characterizes the associations of modern society. Consider, for example, a modern hospital clinic. We have seen in our society within recent decades an increasing specialization in the practice of medicine. The days when every doctor was a general practitioner, or "GP" as he is called in the parlance of the profession, have disappeared and in their place we have a situation in which almost every doctor is a specialist. In a clinic in an average-sized city one may find these various specialists working together, each one complementing the knowledge and skill of the others. Thus, there are obstetricians, gynecologists, pediatricians, surgeons, anaesthetists, dermatologists, ophthalmologists, otolaryngologists, heart specialists, bone specialists, hematologists, roentgenologists, urologists, neurologists, psychiatrists, specialists in internal medicine, and so on. One may possibly regret that the personal touch of the family physician is no longer apparent in this situation, but few will deny that this division of labor contributes to the expertness of medical care.

Even this kind of division of labor, however, is relatively simple compared with that to be observed in such giant associations as, for example, international corporations and conglomerates. The organizational complexity of the largest of these is almost beyond comprehension. If an outsider cannot know it in detail, neither can most of the members, who are acquainted, for the most part, only with the organization of their own departments and divisions. It is clear that the various, coordinated, and complex activities of associations of this size can be carried on only with the help of a minute division of labor.

If additional illustrations are required the reader need only reflect upon the vast number of people, most of them doing different things, who make it possible for a householder in Maine to fill his furnace tank with oil from Texas, and the similarly vast number of people who enable a mother in Denver, Colorado, to telephone her traveling daughter in Istanbul. It is specialized norms and specialized statuses that make possible the division of labor—indeed are synonymous with it—and it is the division of labor, in turn, that makes possible the intricate activities of a modern association.

Authority

We frequently relate the concept of authority to the phenomenon of government. Actually, however, authority appears in all associations and not merely in those whose function is government. In one sense it might be said that every association, no matter how small, has its own government and that every association in society, in a very real sense, is a political phenomenon. Certainly every association has its own structure of authority. Organization, in fact, creates authority. Where there is no organization there is no authority, and where there is no authority there is no organization. Authority is thus one of the most important of the criteria of organization.

It is so important that we dispense with a discussion of it here and treat it in detail, and by itself, in the following chapter.

Tests of Membership

It is easy to join some associations and difficult to join others. All associations, however, require certain qualifications, however minimal, of those who seek membership in them. One may imagine, for example, and imagine correctly, that it is not very difficult to get into the army of any nation. During periods of military exigency, when manpower needs are urgent, it is said that medical examiners stop testing eyes and merely count them. Nevertheless, there are tests of membership—even in an army. Persons otherwise qualified by age may not be able to meet the physical and mental standards set for admission. Thus even an involuntary association has its tests of membership.

All associations without exception, in fact, are relatively closed. All of them have tests of membership. These tests may be quite simple and easy to meet, or they may be quite complex and difficult to meet, but in all cases there are tests of some kind or other. It is easy to get into the armed services and it is easy to join the Republican party; it is difficult, on the other hand, to become a member of the American Bar Association or the Daughters of the American Revolution. But no association is completely open. We can now see how a group can be involuntary and closed at the same time. An association like the Army, for example, has tests of membership, but all who meet these tests are required to join under a policy of universal conscription.

In this respect associations clearly differ from statistical and societal groups. Membership in an association is almost always an achieved status, seldom merely an ascribed status.[3] Everyone who joins an association must, at the very least, agree to conform to the norms that characterize it—that is, its statutes, rules, and regulations—and failure to do so results in loss of membership, the sanction employed to induce conformity. Agreement is itself a test of membership, and this requirement alone prevents any association from qualifying as an open group. Many associations have

[3] There are exceptions, but they are exceedingly rare. An hereditary monarchy is one.

special initiation ceremonies in addition, rites intended to impress upon those who join them the fact that membership is a privileged status and to indicate also that the tests of membership have been satisfied. One is even "sworn in" to the Army, and the swearing in, an act that has both symbolic and legal significance, is the ceremony that serves this function.

Property

All associations, except possibly the simplest and smallest have property of their own. The dues that are collected, for example, belong neither to the treasurer nor to any other member, but to the association itself, and such sums are expended in the name of and in behalf of the association. As sums are expended, property of one kind or another accumulates. Such property may be anything from the penant that belongs to a "den" of cub scouts to the assets of the Bank of America. It may include all kinds of material culture items, for each association has its own materiel just as it has its own norms. We should expect to find chalk and blackboards, for example, in a college, counters and cash registers in a department store, bats and balls in a baseball team, and so on.

Material culture items by themselves, of course, are not property. Property implies not only the items but also norms of ownership, of the right to use, and thus involves both materiel and norms. What is property in one society may not be property in another because the norms are different. We include this observation only as an incidental remark and cannot pursue here an analysis of the nature of property. We do want to insist, however, that property is a sociological phenomenon and not merely an economic one. And certainly it is never a mere physical phenomenon.

When we consider the fact that each association in society has its own special set of norms and its own distinctive materiel, it seems possible to say that, in one sense at lease, each association has its own culture and that each association represents to some degree at least a subculture of a total culture. Each association is also a unique society, a society within a larger society, as, for example, the Eastern Sociological Society.

A Name and Other Identifying Symbols

We may conclude our discussion of the formal properties of associations by indicating that every one of them has a name—whether it is the Government of Venezuela, Local 376 of the Plasterers Union, the Society for the Preservation of Manx Cats, or the Egyptian Army—and usually other identifying symbols as well. Frequently the more highly organized associations indicate the name in the first sentence of their constitution, charter of organization, or other formal instrument that sets out their norms and specifies their statuses. But it is not only the larger associations that are identified by name. Every committee, even though it is a dependent association, also has a name, usually one that indicates its purpose—for example, a committee to investigate space requirements for members holding official positions or a committee to make policy recommendations, and so on through all of the multifarious committees that spring up constantly in organized groups.

In addition to the name, of course, there may be other symbols of identification—mottoes, slogans, songs, colors (as in school colors), "yells," ribbons, seals, crests, coats of arms, trade-marks, and so on. These are sometimes called "symbolic culture traits" and they, like names, serve to identify associations and to distinguish them from others. Secret societies have their secret languages, their grips and codes and passwords, and these serve a similar function. The growth of advertising has resulted in a tremendous increase of symbols of this kind for manufacturing and commercial companies and all such firms have in addition a distinctive letterhead.

We have now examined the major properties of associations and have indicated how these properties distinguish organized groups from the unorganized groups in society. These properties in summary are (1) a specific function, (2) associational norms, (3) associational statuses, (4) authority, (5) property, (6) tests of membership, and (7) a name and other identifying symbols. It will be apparent that some of these are corollaries of others; that is, the division of labor is a function of the differentiation of statuses, authority is a function of the stratification of statuses, and property is a combined function of associational norms and materiel. We have nevertheless chosen to discuss them separately for reasons of clarity.

It will be observed that all of these properties have to do with internal associational structure, the nature of organization itself. In a later chapter we consider the relations that different associations have with one another—inter-associational relations—and indicate in some detail how the growth of large-scale associations influences the character of a complex society.

4. Formal and Informal Organization

At the end of our chapter on statuses we suggested that Mr. Smith and Mrs. Jones, who interact initially in the status relations of butcher and customer, come after a while to know each other and that their relationship, while still a status relationship, becomes also a personal relationship. We said that this sort of thing is indeed a usual occurrence in society and that, whenever two or more people interact frequently or regularly in a status relationship, personal elements begin after a while subtly to influence and possibly to change the nature of the relationship. We now want to suggest that this same phenomenon occurs in associations.

The relations between the various members of an association, which may at one time be almost purely status relations gradually become personal realtions as well; and thus there arises, alongside the formal organization of the association, another kind of organization, which may be called the informal organization. In every association in society, therefore, we find two different kinds of organization, the formal organization on the one hand and the informal organization on the other. The former is comprised of status relations, the latter of personal relations. The social interactions of the members of an association seldom conform precisely with the norms attached to the statuses that constitute its formal structure. Personal factors always intervene. It is the recognition of this point that makes possible the distinction we are about to discuss.

Let us consider for a moment a newly constructed and newly commissioned ship in the Navy. When this ship—let us assume it is a destroyer—is commissioned, it has to be fitted out with a crew or, in Navy terminology, a ship's company.[4] A number of individuals, who may never before have seen or even heard of one another, are assigned to occupy certain statuses in an organization whose pattern is repeated throughout the Navy. Thus, one of these individuals will be assigned to the status of commanding officer, another to the status of executive officer, another to the status of engineering officer, and so on through the entire table of organization. As these individuals report for duty they interact with one another without confusion in terms of the statuses to which they have formally been assigned. *In no other way* would it be possible to move the ship from the yards and to navigate it upon the seas. This process, as we have frequently emphasized, is a miracle, the miracle of social organization.

But our analysis should not stop at this point. On the shakedown cruise the members of the ship's company begin to get acquainted with one another. The officers and men begin to take the measure of their captain and he, in turn, begins to take their measure. The shakedown cruise, in short, tests not only the mechanical workings of the ship but also the competence and the character of the individuals who comprise the ship's company. Certain of these individuals will begin to exhibit leadership traits in relative independence of their official positions or associational statuses. Certain others, in spite of statuses that require the exercise of authority, will

---

[4] The Navy, incidentally, is so insistent upon its terminology—as an identifying symbol of its associational stature—that even the complement of shore stations is referred to as a ship's company, and college dormitories taken over by the Navy lose their floors, walls, ceilings, staircases, and toilets and acquire instead decks, bulkheads, overheads, ladders, and heads.

perhaps appear reluctant to play a leadership role. The crew will very quickly size up the captain. Is he a stickler for the rules, a martinet, or is he a "right guy," a "human being"? Is he going to run the ship—and let there be no mistake about it—or is he going to withdraw behind the privileges of his rank and surrender command in all but name to his executive officer? Which of the officers on board, in independence of their statuses, will win the admiration and the confidence of the enlisted men? Which individual will contribute most to morale, to the *esprit de corps* of the group, and give the men pride in their company and in their ship?

It is apparent that all of these questions could be answered in terms of the norms and statuses that comprise the organization of the ship's company. The commanding officer may indeed be the leader in fact as well as name, and he may be the sort of person who inspires his company, a man they will follow without question, and one whose decisions, in their estimation, will usually be right. It is unlikely, however, that this will always be the case. Sometimes the man assigned to the status of commanding officer may forfeit the respect of his subordinates and sometimes he may be indifferent to it.

In any event, as the members of the ship's company begin to know one another personally and to evaluate one another's strengths and weaknesses, merits and deficiencies, certain men will begin to stand out from the others, their advice will frequently be requested, and others will defer to them. Some will be avoided and others will be sought out for companionship and friendship. In other words, there will arise in these situations something that may be called an informal organization of the ship's company, an organization that may or may not coincide with the formal organization as set out by the Articles for the Government of the Navy. The members of the ship's company occupy statuses—but they also play roles. And their role playing alters the character of the formal organization in ways that are not predictable.

We may now leave the Navy with the observation that what happens in a ship's company also happens inevitably in any association in society and that in all of them we find an informal organization existing simultaneously with the formal organization. We may now proceed to discuss this distinction in the language of sociological analysis. The formal organization of an association consists of the formally recognized and established statuses of the members in accordance with the rank of the offices and other positions they occupy, together with the rules and regulations that set out the obligations, duties, privileges, and responsibilities of these positions. The statuses of non-office-holding members, their duties and privileges, are also of course a part of the formal organization—formal because formally recognized and concurred in as a condition of membership. Social relations between the members are conducted formally in terms of these statuses, in conformity with explicit norms, and in accordance with "extrinsic" and "categoric" evaluations of persons. In the formal organization statuses have differential prestige in independence of the persons who occupy them.

Since this independence is difficult, if not impossible, to maintain in the dynamics of associational life, however, an informal organization arises alongside the formal. The informal organization consists of roles rather than statuses, of the patterns of dominance and submission, affection, hostility, or indifference that form among the members in accordance with their intrinsic and personal evaluations of one another. These role patterns may or may not coincide with or conform to the status hierarchy of the formal organization. In the informal organization social relations occur on the basis of the esteem that the members have for one another in independence of their statuses. In short, in formal organization social relations proceed in terms of the prestige of statuses and in accordance with explicit associational norms; in informal organization they proceed in terms of the esteem for persons and in accordance with implicit societal (that is, extra-associational) norms. Prestige attaches to statuses; esteem to persons.[5] The former is a component of formal organization, the latter of informal organization.

Now it is apparent that in some associations there may be a close coincidence between the formal and the informal organization and that this coincidence may be relatively permanent. In such cases the statuses that carry the greatest prestige are occupied by the persons who are held in the highest esteem. On the other hand, an association may exhibit a wide discrepancy between its formal and informal organization. In these cases the prestige continues to attach to the status but esteem is withheld from the person occupying the status, who thereupon becomes a figurehead. An officer in this situation has the formal authority of his position but not the informal influence sustained by esteem. It is also apparent that an association functions best when the informal organization supports the formal organization and that when the discrepancy between these two types of organization becomes too great the continued existence of the association is endangered.[6]

We may now summarize these observations in convenient form by listing the attributes of formal organization in one column and those of informal organization in another:

[5] This important distinction between prestige and esteem was introduced into the literature by Kingsley David. See his *Human Society*, The Macmillan Company, New York, 1949, pp. 93–94.
[6] The preceding three paragraphs have been taken, with modifications, from an article entitled "The Sociology of Majorities," by Robert Bierstedt, *American Sociological Review*, vol. 13, no. 6, December, 1948, pp. 707–708.

Formal organization	*Informal organization*
Associational norms	Communal norms
Statuses	Roles
Prestige	Esteem
Authority	Leadership
Superordination	Dominance
Subordination	Submission
Extrinsic evaluation of persons	Intrinsic evaluation of persons
Status .relations	Personal relations

One may make an even broader distinction between the phenomena which appear in the left column and those which appear in the right by saying that the former are essentially sociological in character and can be explained only by sociological analysis, whereas all of the latter (except communal norms), involving as they do the personality and temperament of individuals, belong more appropriately to social psychology. Interpersonal relations, in short, cannot be understood without the aid of social psychology and interstatus relations, on the other, cannot be understood without the aid of sociology.

The importance of this distinction frequently escapes the attention of those who are interested in problems of motivation. The nature of formal organization—that is, of social structure in the broad sense—has a great deal to do with matters ordinarily consigned to psychology. We may introduce two examples. Victory in the World Series goes to the team that wins four out of seven games. Since the financial returns to the players are so great the players would be strongly motivated to stretch out the series to the full seven games, evening up the score as it were until the last game, which would then be the only real contest. This could conceivably be done without conscious planning and without conscious deliberation. In other words, there would be no question of "throwing games," as in the case of the old "Black Sox" scandal, but of something so subtle that it could hardly be detected.

What prevents this possibility? The answer is to be found in the norms—the rules—that govern the World Series. No matter how many games are required to reach a decision, the players share in the receipts of only the first four games. Thus, it is to their advantage to finish the series as quickly as possible. If more than four games are required, the players are literally working for nothing at a time when, having worked all season, they are all anxious to go hunting. In this situation the norms clearly influence the motivation.

As a second example, consider a situation that once occurred in a

Naval training unit. The officer candidates attached to the unit were required to participate in setting-up exercises before breakfast under the command of a chief petty officer. It was easy to get an exemption from these exercises, on the ground of a slight cold or other indisposition, by going to sick bay and getting a slip from one of the pharmacist's mates, all of whom were extremely cooperative. As a result the number of exemptions grew steadily until one day about half of the personnel had sick excuses signed and authenticated by the medical department.

The executive officer of the unit now had a mild problem of malingering to solve. He could easily have reduced the number of exemptions by ordering the medical officer to authenticate each case personally or by ordering him to reprimand the pharmacist's mates and to supervise their work more closely. He discovered, however, a much more effective way of accomplishing the desired result. He changed a norm. He issued an order depriving all personnel of town liberty in the evening if they had a calisthenic exemption in the morning, on the ground that men too ill for setting-up exercises were too ill to have a night on the town, a privilege ordinarily granted to all personnel. Needless to say, the number of sick excuses dropped as if by magic to the normal two or three. The problem was solved without raising the unpleasant issue of malingering and without interfering with the judgment of the medical department. As both of these illustrations show, organizational structure has a very great deal to do with behavior.

We can now make two general observations about the relationship between formal and informal organization. The first of these is that the best conceivable formal organization will not suffice to make a successful association unless it receives support in the informal organization; that is, the most orderly and efficient structure does not automatically produce a successful associational administration if the members have no good will toward one another, if there are personal hostilities, if, in short, the members do not like one another and cannot get along together. The exercise of authority in such situations brings nothing but resentment, and resentment, in turn, makes the orderly intercourse of people difficult if not impossible. In the extreme case authority itself disappears and nothing remains but force.

The second observation concerns the reverse situation. The best good will in the world will be insufficient for the successful pursuit of an associational activity if the formal organization is deficient. For this reason it is undesirable, for example, to have divided responsibility at the top, to have two persons vested with coordinate authority to make final decisions on matters affecting the association. Two good friends placed in such a situation will very quickly become enemies because conflict between them, in their status relations, is inevitable. This phenomenon can be illustrated again and again in the history of particular associations. The most efficient and satisfactory association, in short, is one in which the formal organization is supported by the informal organization. When the discrepancy between the two becomes too great, the association, as we have said, is in danger of dissolution.

One final observation proceeds from this distinction between formal and informal organization. Society itself exhibits these two forms of organization. For it is apparent that when we speak of the state we are speaking of the formal organization of society; when we speak of the community, on the other hand, we are speaking of the informal organization of society. The laws are associational norms that belong to the formal organization; the folkways and mores are communal norms that belong to the informal organization. Government officials, both appointed and elected, occupy statuses in the formal organization; politicians and patronage dispensers play roles in the informal organization.

This situation, however, is greatly complicated by the fact that people organize to pursue political interests. Thus the informal organization of the government presents a picture of highly organized special-interest groups that, like political parties, are associations in their own right.[7] We return to this subject in a later chapter. Here we want merely to emphasize that the state represents the formal organization of society and the community its informal organization.

In this section we have briefly discussed the important distinction between the formal and the informal organization of associations. The growth of associations, and of associational relations, is one of the most characteristic features of a complex society. Not all social relations are associational relations, however, and not all associational relations are status relations. Frequent and regular social intercourse among the members of an association induces them to evaluate one another personally and intrinsically, and thus personal relations enter into and sometimes support, sometimes confuse, the status relations. As a result we find in every association, no matter how rigidly structured, an informal organization that arises to coexist with the formal organization.

The formal organization is comprised of statuses, and prestige is attached to these statuses in independence of the persons who occupy them. The informal organization, on the other hand, is comprised of roles,

---

[7] A President's cabinet, incidentally, is part of the formal structure of government; his "kitchen cabinet" part of the informal structure.

and esteem is awarded to persons in independence of the statuses they occupy.[8] Authority is found only in formal organization; leadership, on the contrary, appears in the informal organization and also, or course, in the unorganized community. A policeman, for example, represents authority, not leadership.

Associational norms and associational statuses determine the social actions of the members of associations, and these actions in turn affect the structure of the association. It is the structure that sustains an association throughout changes in personnel; it is the members themselves, and especially a majority of members, who sustain it throughout changes in structure. The relationships between the formal organization of an association and its informal organization are always subtle, always complicated, and always interesting. And it is in this area, particularly with respect to the political organization of society, that sociology and political science meet on common ground.

5. Institutions

The concept of institutions is one of the most important in the entire field of sociology. Unfortunately, however, it is a concept that has been burdened by ambiguity and that has received inconsistent articulation and definition in the sociological literature. Some writers, for example, will call any large-scale organized group an institution and reserve the word "association" for the smaller organized groups in society. The distinction between institutions and associations then becomes a simple distinction of size.

Simplicity, however, does not always induce clarity, and no one knows how large a group must become, in these terms, in order to merit the name of institution. As a matter of fact, it would not be wise to encourage this usage. For purposes of a systematic sociology there is a much more important—not to say much less equivocal—distinction to be made between institutions and associations, even though it unfortunately deviates from ordinary speech in which prisons, hospitals and universities, for example, are called institutions.

An association, as we have said, is any organized group, whether large or small. Because of its organization, it has some structure and some continuity. It has, in addition, an identity and a name. An institution, on the other hand, is not a group at all, organized or unorganized. An institution is an organized procedure. An institution is a formal, recognized,

---

[8] This is the Jeeves–Bertie Wooster syndrome. No reader of P. G. Wodehouse would fail to hold Jeeves, the "gentleman's gentleman," in the highest esteem; and none on the contrary would grant his employer, poor Bertie, any esteem at all.

established, and stabilized way of pursuing some activity in society. In succinct terms, then, an association is an organized group, an institution is an organized procedure. An institution, in addition, is a norm just as folkways, mores, and laws are norms, but it differs from these other norms in a manner that we presently explain.

If we have stated the distinction, we now need to illustrate it in order that it may become clear. Let us therefore forget the noun "institution" for a while and consider instead the verb "to institutionalize." Human beings perform thousands of activities during the course of their lives. Some of these activites are institutionalized and some are not. Thus, almost all of the males in our society at one time or another have played a game of baseball. On college campuses and on sandlots "pickup" games are common and indeed can be found almost any day during the season. The same game is played in an October "classic" called the World Series. The difference between the pickup game and the World Series game is that baseball in the former situation is uninstitutionalized and in the latter institutionalized.

Similarly, two boys trying in fun to knock each other down and two prize fighters in Madison Square Garden trying to do the same thing are engaged in essentially the same activity. The first, however, is uninstitutionalized, the second institutionalized. In other words, the same activity that in one situation is uninstitutionalized in another is institutionalized, that is, formally pursued in accordance with a special and somewhat rigorous set of norms.

Consider another example. Every person in our society at some time or another plays the role of a teacher, that is, teaches someone else how to do something. The small third-grader teaches his smaller sister how to draw the number 2. A mother teaches the child how to put on his overshoes. A girl teaches a friend how to play bridge. A father teaches his son how to drive a car. Boys teach each other tricks. But although everyone at some time or other engages in the activities of teaching and learning, not everyone occupies the status of teacher of the status of student. The status, as we said earlier in this book, is an institutionalized role. Teaching and learning are activities to be found in all societies, but they become so important in some societies that they are institutionalized; in these societies, therefore, we have an institution of education. The same activity occurs both in the classroom and in thousands of places outside the classroom. In the classroom, however, it is formalized, regularized, and established—in short, institutionalized.

The dissemination of news is similarly something that occurs in all societies. People "pass the word" from one to another on matters of mutual interest. In complex societies, however, this activity—the dissemination of news—is institutionalized and we have, in consequence, the institution of journalism. In most societies, also, people worship or otherwise acknowledge the unseen powers who control their destiny. Worship comes to be performed in regular, recognizable, and even ritualistic ways, however, and so in all societies we find the institution of religion. In all societies, too, people are confronted with the necessity of earning their living, and this acitvity has become universally institutionalized. In all societies, therefore, we have economic institutions and, in complex societies, an institution of business. Finally, in all societies people have ways of caring for the ill and in complex societies these ways become the institutions of nursing and medicine.

An institution in short—returning to the noun—is a definite, formal, and regular way of doing something. It is an established procedure. In any society certain actions are repeated again and again, and it is this repetition that confers a pattern upon the action and that makes of it a recognized procedure. The procedure in turn, when established, becomes the institution. Society is always at work transforming event into precedent, and precedent into institution. It should be observed, however, that even when an activity is institutionalized in a society, it continues to be carried on also in uninstitutionalized ways. Thus, news is still disseminated by word of mouth even though we have the institution of journalism, and teaching and learning continue to take place in informal ways even though we have the institution of education.

It should also be observed that different societies institutionalize different activities. These differences can be discerned most easily in the simpler societies. For example, although most societies have priests, some have neither medicine men nor political chieftains, and some have one but not the other. In other words, the care and cure of the ill can be institutionalized in some societies, political leadership in others, and intercession with the gods in still others. In very simple societies institutions are relatively undifferentiated; that is, in some of them medicine men, political chiefs, and priests may be indistinguishable, so that instead of three different institutions—medicine, government, and religion—we may have them all combined in one. As societies grow in size and complexity, institutions become progressively more differentiated, an accompaniment of the division of labor, until in societies like our own this differentiation is detailed and minute.

We may next inquire in what respect an institution, which we have defined as an established procedure, differs from the other norms, particularly from the folkways and mores. The answer is quite simple and introduces us to another characteristic of institutions. The folkways and mores are sustained and sanctioned by unorganized groups within a society and by entire communities. Institutions, on the other hand, always require specific associations to sustain them. Wherever we find an institution, therefore, we find also at least one association—and usually many more—whose function it is to pursue the institutionalized activity.

The custom of shaking hands, for example, is a folkway that is supported by the unorganized community. The salute, on the other hand, is an institutionalized greeting supported by such associations as armies and navies. Teaching and learning, as we have said, are customary activities in all societies. The institution of education, however, cannot appear without such associations as schools and colleges. Institutions and associations are thus concomitant and correlative phenomena. Folkways and mores are uninstitutionalized norms and require no associations to support them. Laws, on the other hand, are institutionalized norms that appear only in the political organization of society and that require an association called a government for their enactment and enforcement. Government, incidentally, is an institution; *a* government is an association.

In any society in which we find the institution of journalism, therefore, we also find newspapers, and these newspapers are edited and published by associations. Journalism is the institution; *The New York Times, The St. Louis Post-Dispatch, The Baltimore Sun*, and so on are associations. Without such associations there would be no such institution as journalism. Similarly, education is the institution; the University of Hawaii, Harvard University, Indiana University, Smith College, Bennington College, Thomas Jefferson High School, and so on are associations.

Institutions, in short, are impossible without associations, and most associations operate in institutionalized ways; that is, they pursue their principal and auxiliary functions in ways that have become established in the society and that are roughly the same in all associations. The formal process of education is so much the same in all of these associations that it would be difficult to distinguish a classroom situation in one of them from a classroom situation in another.

As previously indicated, popular usage is confused on the distinction between these two phenomena, associations and institutions. Two simple tests can dispel the confusion. The first of these is that an association has a location; it makes sense to ask where it is. An institution, on the contrary, does not have a location, and the question makes no sense. Thus, a university can be located in space; education cannot.[9] The second test is

---

[9] This is true even if an association has many dependent associations that are widely diffused in geographical area. In these cases there is always a central headquarters or home office. Phi Beta Kappa, for example, has chapters in many universities and colleges and its members are spread throughout the globe. Nevertheless, it has a central office, and the chapters themselves have their own definite locations.

that it is possible to belong to an association. Thus, one can become a member of a committee, a club, or a corporation; one cannot become a member of journalism, education, or religion. One can join a church and one is a member of a family. A church and a family are thus associations. Religion and marriage, on the contrary, are institutions. This distinction and these tests can best be illustrated, perhaps, by studying the following list, in which associations and institutions are contrasted.

Associations	Institutions
A corporation	Business
A railroad	Transportation
An army	War
A college	Education
A newspaper company	Journalism
A church	Religion
A television network	Television
A baseball team	Baseball
A family	The family
A government	Government
A hospital	Medicine
A night club	Entertainment
A theatrical company	The drama

It is obvious that one can belong to or join any of the phenomena listed in the left-hand column and to none of those in the right-hand column.

Several sets of terms in the above list may benefit by elaboration. A family is called an association; the family, on the other hand, is an institution. A family means a particular family—the Adams family, the Kennedy family, the Jukes family, or the family of the reader of this book. This family, or any family, is an association. It was formed originally by two people "associating" with one another in the institution of marriage, and it will last only as long as its individual members live. A family—any family—is thus an association. *The* family, on the other hand, is an institution. No one belongs to *the* family, but only to *a* family. *The* family is society's way of regularizing the functions of procreation, the care and training of the young, and the inheritance of property. In short, *a* family, a particular, is an association; *the* family, a universal, is an institution.

The family, incidentally, is a universal institution in society. There is no society anywhere on earth that does not have the institution of the family; in all of them in all periods of history procreation has been institutionalized. In all societies, of course, including our own, procreation can occur in uninstitutionalized ways, but this carries with it the stigma of illegitimacy.

As another illustration let us reiterate that *a* government is an association, government an institution. The Government of the United States, or of France, for example, is a very highly organized group comprised of both elected and appointed officials and other personnel. These are members of the American, or of the French, Government. Government, on the other hand, as a regular and recognized way of governing—that is, of making political decisions, enacting and enforcing laws, and maintaining formal order in a society—is of course an institution. This institution, unlike the family, does not appear in all societies; there are some societies so primitive that one cannot discern in them a separate institution of government. These societies have no political organization as such, and no one in them is recognized as a member of a ruling association. All complex societies, on the other hand, have an institution of government, and there is a corresponding association—*a* government—that supports the institution and that carries on the institutionalized activity of ruling or governing.

In a complex society, of course, we find many different institutions. These institutions give a characteristic profile to an entire society and make possible the comparative analysis of different societies. We may observe throughout history, for example, that there are religious societies, military societies, family societies, political societies, business societies, and so on, depending upon the prominence or dominance of one or another of these kinds of institutions. The medieval society was predominantly a religious society, and the Roman Catholic Church was its most important association. Ancient Sparta and modern Prussia, on the contrary, were predominantly military societies, and here military status was accorded the highest rank. In the old Chinese society the family was the dominant institution, and in totalitarian states it is the political institution that takes precedence over others. Our own society in the twentieth century is often called an industrial society, since industry is frequently believed to be its most important institution. It is through institutions, in short, that one can approach the general problem of cultural integration.

In concluding this chapter on associations and institutions we should like to make the final observation that several associations may serve the same institution and that a single association may have a number of institutionalized activities. We have already noticed that a number of colleges and universities serve the institution of education, a number of newspapers serve the institution of journalism, a number of corporations serve the institution of business, and so on. This, of course, is obvious. But it is also apparent that a single association may have a number of functions, both principal and auxiliary, and thus serve different institutions.

A university in contemporary American society, for example, is dedicated primarily to the institution of education. It also has something to do, however, with the institution of intercollegiate athletics. And this institution in turn involves it in the institution of business. The status of a university treasurer may frequently be indistinguishable from that of a corporation executive. In addition, large universities, both public and private, may own and administer properties, hold patents, lend and borrow money, serve the government in military research, rent and sell real estate, operate an investment business, and so on through many other economic activities. A large modern university, in sum, represents many more institutions than education.

The same phenomenon may be observed in the case of other associations. A large publishing company, for example the McGraw-Hill Book Company, which published this book, is ostensibly a corporation devoted to the institution of business. But this company also serves the institution of education through its publication of textbooks in all fields of learning. More than that, however, the company encourages and stimulates research in the sciences and scholarly disciplines and once contributed a sizable sum to Yale University for the purpose of collecting and editing the Boswell papers. *The New York Times*, an association devoted to the institution of journalism, also contributes to learning by providing a subsidy, in the amount of $1 million, for editing and publishing the papers of Thomas Jefferson. The *Times*, through its "Hundred Neediest Cases" at Christmastime, supports in addition the institution of charity. And finally, the United States Government, an association whose manifest function is to serve the institution of government, serves in addition more institutions than can reasonably be listed.

We have here, in the growth of institutional functions served by single associations, one of the most important sociological phenomena of a complex society. We may also notice, in concluding this discussion, that as associations grow in size, whether these associations are universities, corporations, newspapers, churches, or governments, they tend to increase their institutional activities. The number of institutions represented by a single association is a direct function of its size, and this statement, of course, is a sociological principle.

6. Summary

In this chapter we have provided an introductory treatment of associations and institutions, that is, of organized groups of people and organized ways of doing things. Our first task, accordingly, was to emphasize the importance of organization. Without organization there would be no universities, colleges, and schools; no steel corporations, automobile factories, and oil refineries; no newspapers, banks, and governments. All of these are possible because people have learned to associate with one another in an organized way. If it were not for organization we would still be leading the village and tribal lives of our most primitive ancestors.

Organization, of course, is not a constant in society. There are some groups that have a bare minimum of organization and in fact are hardly organized at all. There are other groups that have an extremely high and rigid degree of organization. In other words, the associations of society may be placed on a continuum with the least organized groups at one end and the most organized groups at the other. We noticed in this connection that as groups become more highly organized they win a greater independence of particular personnel, and that the most highly organized groups of all can sustain a total turnover in their membership without a significant change in their structure. It is these highly organized groups that often endure for many years and sometimes even for centuries.

We then proceeded to ask exactly what organization was. In answering this question we found seven characteristics, or criteria, that distinguish an organized group from an unorganized group: (1) a specific function or purpose, (2) associational norms, (3) associational statuses, (4) authority, (5) property, (6) tests of membership, and (7) a name and other identifying symbols. In treating these topics we had occasion to dwell upon the very great importance of the division of labor that proceeds from the presence of associational norms and statuses and also to indicate how the division of labor helps to differentiate a simple society from a complex society.

The next section of the chapter was devoted to the distinction between the formal and the informal organization of associations. We summarized this point by stating that whereas in the formal organization social relations between members proceed in accordance with the statuses they occupy and the explicit norms of the association, in the informal organization these relations proceed in accordance with the roles the members play and the implicit norms of the community at large. In the formal organization the members evaluate one another extrinsically and categorically in terms of the authority attached to their statuses, in the informal organization they evaluate one another intrinsically and personally in terms of affection, hostility, or indifference. The operation of any association thus reflects a subtle combination of its formal and informal organizations.

In some associations, as we observed, the informal organization closely supports and sustains the formal organization, leadership traits are exhibited by those who occupy the statuses to which authority is attached, and the discrepancy between the two forms of organization is very small. In some associations, on the other hand, this discrepancy may be quite large, leadership may be exercised primarily by those not in authority, those in authority may be merely figureheads, and the formal organization may receive little support in the informal.[10] It is obvious that, when the discrepancy between the formal and informal organizations becomes too large, the association is in danger of dissolution.

Finally, we noticed that the most favorable formal organization will be of no avail if, in the informal organization, there is no will to make it work. On the other hand, the best will in the world, in the informal organization, will contribute nothing to the operating efficiency of the association if the formal organization is deficient. In this connection we introduced two illustrations to indicate how structure can influence behavior in general and motivation in particular.

The concluding section of the chapter was devoted to an analysis of institutions. If associations are groups of people organized for the purpose of doing things, institutions are the organized ways of doing them. We accordingly defined an institution as a regularized, formalized, recognized, and established way of doing something, a mode of procedure. People belong to associations; they do not belong to institutions. Associations have a locus; institutions do not. Among examples of this distinction we noted that a university is an association, education an institution; that a corporation is an association, business an institution. We noticed in addition that more activities are institutionalized in complex than in simple societies. The structure of an association itself, with its specific norms and statuses, represents an institutionalized mode of social interaction. Even in complex societies, where many activities are institutionalized, these same activities continue to be carried on in uninstitutionalized ways. We observed that a large number of associations may represent the same institution and that a single association may represent several different institutions. Associations and institutions, like all things social, are susceptible to change in the course of time, but in both there are elements of permanence. An association can frequently sustain a change in institutional function, and an institution can survive the disappearance of particular associations. Associations and institutions are thus closely related but nevertheless distinct phenomena.

Finally, we may reiterate and give special emphasis to the observation on a preceding page that society is always at work transforming event into precedent and precedent into institution.

We are now ready to direct our attention to the nature of authority, which, as we have said, is a universal characteristic and prime criterion of organized groups.

---

[10] It is interesting to note that in most large-scale associations there are honorific statuses to which personnel may be "promoted" after they have ceased effectively to play their roles. Thus, as we have seen, a president of a corporation may be promoted to the chairmanship of the board, a promotion that necessitates a relinquishment of duties and responsibilities. Status relinquishment also, of course, comes as a function of age, as indicated in a preceding chapter.

Chapter 12

AUTHORITY

N THE VAST complexity that is a human
society the exercise of authority is a
constant and pervasive phenomenon.
Society indeed is impossible without
order—in a larger sense, as we have
maintained throughout this book, society
is synonymous with order—and it is
authority that serves as the foundation for
much of the order that society exhibits.
Every day thousands of persons interact
with thousands of others in relationships
that involve superordination and
subordination, the issuance of commands
and obedience to them, the
announcement of decisions by some
and the acceptance of these decisions by
others. Here, as we intimated in the
preceding chapter, we have a phenomenon
of rather considerable sociological significance
and one to which we now turn our attention.*
What is it, in short, that confers upon some
men the right to command, upon others the
obligation to obey? Why should anyone
exercise this right, anyone owe this duty?
How does authority contribute to
the order that most of the members of a
society desire, those who obey as
well as those who exact obedience?
And how does it operate in the
structure of an association? These are
some of the questions we shall try to answer.

---

*This chapter is a revision of an article entitled "The
Problem of Authority," which first appeared in *Freedom
and Control in Modern Society*, edited by Morroe Berger, Theodore
Abel, and Charles H. Page, D. Van Nostrand Company,
Inc., New York, 1954, pp. 67–81.

If we seek examples of the exercise of authority we shall find them in every organized sector of society. It is authority that enables the jailor to hand to Socrates the cup of hemlock with the rueful but reasonable expectation that he will drink it; authority that enables the elders of the synagogue to execrate, curse, and cast out Spinoza with "all the maledictions written in the Book of the Law;" authority that permits a President of the United States to remove an imperious general from his commands. On less exalted levels it is authority that enables a vice-president to dictate to his secretary, a sales manager to assign territories to his salesmen, a personnel manager to employ and discharge workers, an umpire to banish a player from a baseball game, a policeman to arrest a citizen, and so on through innumerable examples. It is easily apparent that authority is by no means a purely political phenomenon in the narrow sense of the word. For it is not only in the political organization of society, but in all of its organization, that authority appears. Every association in society, no matter how small or how temporary it may be, has its own structure of authority.

1. Authority and Competence

Before discussing the nature of authority proper it will be convenient if we first distinguish it from two other phenomena with which it is sometimes confused. The first of these is competence. Thus, we commonly speak of a given person an "an authority" on a given subject. There are "authorities" on baseball, football, bridge, etiquette, music, the merchant guilds of medieval London, Balzac, celestial navigation, and indeed on everything else. In this sense authority is related to influence but not to power, and in this sense it has nothing to do with legitimacy and nothing with obligation. It is recognition of competence that encourages us to accept the opinions of those who have achieved prominence in their special fields of endeavor. There is nothing compulsory about this acceptance, and if we accept opinions of this kind it is a tribute to eminence rather than an obeisance to authority. We voluntarily respect the competence of others, but authority requires our submission. When the situation involves competence, furthermore, one may choose one "authority" rather than another. Competence, in other words, exerts influence; authority exacts obedience.

It is interesting to note in this connection that our language tricks us into error. When we speak of an order or a command having been issued by "competent authority," we do not, curiously enough, mean competence at all. We mean not that the authority is competent, but that it is legitimate. In a subordinate position, for example, we will obey the command of a superior whose authority we acknowledge even when it seems unreasonable to us to do so, and disobey a command that seems reasonable if we question the authority of the alleged superior to issue it. Superior knowledge, superior skill, and superior competence need not be involved in the exercise of "competent authority." As Talcott Parsons has pointed out, the treasurer of a corporation may have the authority to sign checks disbursing the corporation's funds, but this does not imply that the treasurer is a better check signer than any one of hundreds of others.[1] Nor does the exercise of authority carry any necessary connotation of personal superiority. The manager of a baseball team is not a better pitcher than the player he removes nor, in turn, is the player inferior to the umpire who banishes him from the game. A professor may be a more competent scholar than the dean who declines to renew his appointment, a lawyer more learned in the law than the judge who cites him for contempt, a worker a more competent carpenter than the forman who assigns his duties. As Robert M. MacIver has written, "The man who commands may be no wiser, no abler, may be in no sense better than the average of his fellows; sometimes, by any intrinsic standard, he is inferior to them. Here is the magic of government."[2] Here indeed is the magic of all social organization.

2. Authority and Leadership

The second phenomenon with which authority is sometimes confused is the phenomemon of leadership. Unfortunately, it is Max Weber, one of the greatest and most influential of all sociologists, who is largely responsible for this confusion. Weber distinguished three kinds of authority which he called the traditional, the rational-legal, and the charismatic.[3] By traditional authority he meant, for example, the political decisions made by the elders of a small tribe or by its head man before the process of government is fully institutionalized. This would be a group that, in our terminology, ranks relatively low on the continuum of organization. But it is nevertheless genuine authority inasmuch as the group confers upon the status of elder, head, or chief the right to make these decisions. Rational-legal authority, on the other hand, appears in groups that rank relatively high on the continuum of organization—modern governments, for example, the myriad of associations that appear in contemporary industrial societies, and in bureaucratic structures.

Charismatic authority, however, is not authority at all, but leadership. By charisma Weber meant, in its literal etymological sense, a gift of grace

[1] Page 58, note 4 in Max Weber, *The Theory of Social and Economic Organization*, Talcott Parsons, editor, Oxford University Press, New York, 1947.
[2] *The Web of Government*, The Macmillan Company, New York, 1947, p. 13.
[3] For Weber's treatment see *The Theory of Social and Economic Organization*, Talcott Parsons, ed., The Free Press, Macmillan, New York, 1947, pp. 328–363.

which, imputed to a leader by his followers, gives a divine sanction, stimulus, and even justification to his actions. A charismatic leader is believed to be different from other men; he rises above them because he is touched with divinity; there is something of the celestial afflatus about him, and an almost tangible magnetism. He operates beyond the boundaries of legitimacy. He needs no extant organization in society because he creates his own, a new and sometimes revolutionary one. And he may be "good" or "evil." Thus, Jesus was a charismatic leader; the Pope is not. Gandhi was a charismatic leader, Nehru was not. Martin Luther King, Jr., yes; Ralph David Abernathy, no; Lenin and Hitler, yes; their successors, no. Of course we are dealing with a continuum here too. Franklin D. Roosevelt and Charles de Gaulle, for example, may or may not be regarded as charismatic leaders. There would be arguments on both sides. Finally, it is interesting to note that persons whose achievements are so impressive that they set them apart from the multitude are sometimes suspected of charisma,[4] and indeed it is of significance for the sociologist of religion that the attribution of charisma seems to be the initial stage in apotheosis.

But leadership—even charismatic leadership—is not authority. As in the case of competence, no one is required to follow a leader and no one involuntarily satisfies a leader's desire or grants a leader's wish. The fiat of the leader lacks legitimacy. One may follow or not, and no sanction, except possibly the informal sanction of being regarded as odd by other followers, is applied to those who abstain. The situation with respect to authority is quite different. A leader can only request, an authority can require. The person subjected to an order by "competent authority" has no alternative but to obey.[5] The examination must be taken at the appointed time, taxes must be paid, the draft induction notice must be observed.[6] Obedience to an authoritative command is not a matter of a subordinate's arbitrary decision.

---

[4] The biographer of John Maynard Keynes, for example, permits himself to speculate as follows: "In making a final appraisement of Keynes' influence, some may seek to attribute it to a gift or special power that lies outside the range of normal human qualities; they may seek for some mysterious aptitude, some nameless gift, bestowed on him from the unseen world." R. F. Harrod, *The Life of John Maynard Keynes*, Harcourt, Brace & Company, New York, 1951, p. 646. The author immediately rejects his own suggestion; but if sophisticated scholars can allude, however lightly, to such a possibility, it is easy to see how the multitude, in any society, might concede charisma to those whose extraordinary achievements win them extraordinary devotion.

[5] Unless, as we shall subsequently see, the situation is rearranged in such a manner that the subordinate is able to withdraw from it.

[6] An amusing story comes from England concerning the Londoner who, upon receiving his draft induction notice, replied, "See Luke 14:20." ("I have married a wife and therefore I cannot come.") To which the War Office answered, "Your attention is drawn to Luke 7:8." ("For I also am a man set under authority, having under me soldiers, and I say unto one, Go, and he goeth; and to another, Come, and he cometh.")

Leadership depends upon the personal qualities of the leader in the situations in which he leads. In the case of authority, however, the relationship ceases to be personal and, if the legitimacy of the authority is recognized, the subordinate must obey the command even when he is unacquainted with the person who issues it. In a leadership relation the person is basic; in an authority relation personal identity is irrelevant.

We may summarize these observations by noting that an authority relationship is one of superordination and subordination; the leadership relationship, on the contrary, is one of dominance and submission. These are independent variables. Superordinates may or may not be dominant individuals in a psychological sense; subordinates may or may not be submissive. Leadership qualities, of course, are frequently involved in a man's rising to a position of authority in an association, but this is another process. Frequency is not necessity, as can be seen in numerous illustrations, from the monarch to the sheriff, where no test of leadership, or of competence, is imposed. The exercise of authority need not involve a personal relationship of any kind. As suggested immediately above, those who exercise authority, especially in the large-scale associations of complex societies, are frequently unaware of the individual identities of the persons over whom authority is exercised, and, conversely, the latter may be unaware of the personal identity of the former. In a military establishment, for example, thousands of men are sent to the far corners of the earth by an official whom they have never seen and whose name they may even fail to recognize. This official, in turn, is unacquainted with the men thus subjected to his command, and he may not see or even sign the paper that dispatches them to their destinations. It would be inappropriate to contend that there is any leadership as such in this situation. Leadership, in short, like competence, is a species of influence; authority is a function of power.

3. Authority and Organization

Once we have distinguished authority from competence and from leadership we are prepared to indulge in statements of a more positive character. Our first observation is perhaps the obvious one that authority is always a property of social organization. Where there is no organization there is no authority. Authority appears only in the organized groups—the associations —of society, never in unorganized groups or in the unorganized community. An absence of organization implies an absence of authority. There is authority only within an association, never in the interstices between associations. The exercise of authority, furthermore, never extends beyond the limits of the association in which it is institutionalized and which gives it support and sanction. The manager of a camera store, for example, may require his clerks to sign in and out when they arrive and leave, but such an order can have no effect upon his customers. The collector of internal revenue may not examine a candidate for the degree of doctor of philosophy, a policeman may not overrule an umpire on a close play at second base, the Chief Justice of the United States may not tell the board of directors of American Civil Liberties Union how to decide an issue of policy, and so on through all the situations of society.[7] We have thus discovered the locus of authority. If we are asked where in society authority appears we shall reply that it occurs in associations—always in them—and never anywhere else.

A certain flavor of dogmatism appears in the preceding sentence and we should try to dispel it with some elaboration. The notion that authority never appears except in associations is one for which we have perhaps provided sufficient illustration. But the notion that authority always appears in associations may arouse the skeptical impulse of the reader. On this point we have already referred to Max Weber's concept of traditional authority and have agreed that even groups that are minimally organized in any rational or legal sense of the word nevertheless exhibit and express this important phenomenon. It could not be otherwise. Some person, or some smaller group within the society, must decide whether to abandon the settlement or to maintain it for another night in its current place, whether to attack the enemy that threatens or to strengthen the defenses at home. Whatever the decision, the authority of the person or council that makes it must receive the recognition and acknowledgment of the group. In the absence of such recognition nothing would happen. The only alternative is consensus, and this is difficult if not impossible to achieve as the group increases in size. Even in the successful case some authoritative voice must determine—and announce—that consensus exists. Fortunately or unfortunately, human beings almost always agree to disagree and thus require the invention of some social technique to arbitrate and ultimately to resolve their differences. This is something that does not yet work on the international level—there is no genuine law on this level—and it breaks down on the domestic level in the cases of riot and revolution.

But we return to authority. We want to suggest, and indeed insist, that authority exists in the smallest and most temporary of associations. Consider a committee. Even a committee of three, all of them longtime

---

[7] An instance of error in this respect concerns an American general. On a tour of inspection at an army post he became annoyed at a telephone lineman who paid no attention to his passing and who continued to work at the top of the pole. The lineman refused in addition to obey the general's peremptory command to come down from the pole and stand at attention. At this point the general, near apoplexy as the story goes, demanded to know the man's name and company. The name is unimportant; the company was the Bell Telephone Company.

friends, will have a chairman. One of the three has the authority to take the initiative, to arrange a date for a meeting in which they will transact their business, whatever it is, and to communicate the committee's decision or recommendation to the larger group of which it is an appendage. Committees, incidentally, almost always have an odd number of members in order that a majority view may be discerned. This is one aspect of the significance of majorities in groups and societies, a significance that has been too little recognized.[8] But the point is clear. We have said that authority appears only in associations, and in all of them, and we have regarded it therefore as one of the necessary criteria of organization. We now reiterate also that it always appears in associations. Every organized group in society—small or large, temporary or permanent—has its own structure of authority.

4. Authority and Status

We may now suggest in addition that authority is always attached to statuses and never—Max Weber to the contrary notwithstanding—to individuals. Furthermore, the exercise of authority is a function of norms that are themselves attached to statuses. An individual exercises the authority of a status only so long as he occupies that status and ceases to exercise it when he resigns, or when he is removed, or when his term of office expires. An officer in the army—in fact, an officer in any association whatever—issues commands, allocates responsibilities, and expects achievement not in his own name but rather in virtue of the authority vested in his status. An ex-president of a university does not confer degrees upon the graduating class, an ex-chairman of the board does not determine the policies of the finance committee of the corporation (although he may influence them), and an ex-President of the United States neither signs nor vetoes bills passed by Congress.[9] The exercise of authority is wholly and indeed exclusively a function of associational status.

If authority is created in the organization of an association it is necessary, accordingly, to examine the process in which an unorganized group is transformed into an organized one. In this process several things happen. In the first place, informal procedures and patterns of interaction come to be standardized as norms. In the second place, roles come to be standardized as statuses. It is the institutionalization of procedures into norms and roles into statuses that results in the formal organization of the

---

[8] On this subject an old paper of the author's may be helpful. See "The Sociology of Majorities," *American Sociological Review*, Vol. XIII, December, 1948, pp. 700–710.

[9] During the final months of his term of office, although his authority remains intact, a president's influence begins to disappear. This is the familiar "lame duck" phenomenon. It vividly illustrates the distinction between influence and authority.

association. They are its organization. More particularly, the role of leader, which one or several members of the groups have been playing, comes to be institutionalized in one or several statuses to which authority is now attached in accordance with the norms. These roles become statuses in order that the stability of the association may be assured and its continuity guaranteed.

It is apparent that no association of any size or degree of complexity can maintain a constant membership. The inexorable process of life itself determines that the personnel of the association will change over the course of time. Some associations cannot survive the individual departures of the people who constitute them because they have no method of recruitment.[10] Any association whose members wish it to survive and to gain an independence of particular personnel must institutionalize its roles into statuses and must create authority where initially there was only leadership. The leader who has been instrumental in organizing the association may subsequently be indisposed or withdraw from the circle of his followers. Unless his role has been institutionalized such a contingency would jeopardize the association's existence. After it has been institutionalized the leader may even be deposed from his position of authority, and a successor named, without damage to the group. A structure is thus necessary if associations are to survive the flow of individuals in and out of membership. The supreme test of the organization of an association, as we have previously mentioned, is satisfied when it can sustain a total turnover in personnel.

The formal organization of an association, in short, is constituted of norms and statuses. The norms are attached to the statuses and not to the persons who occupy them. The norms involve rights, duties, privileges, obligations, prerogatives, and responsibilities as they are attached to particular statuses in the structure of the association. The right to exercise authority, that is, the right to make decisions and enforce them is now attached to certain statuses, and this right receives the support of all those who belong to the association and who conform to its norms. The exercise of authority, however, is not only a right. It is also a duty. The occupation of certain statuses carries the obligation to make decisions in the name of the association and the obligation to enforce them.

We have said that authority is never exercised except in a status

---

[10] This is Simmel's "broken-plate" pattern. A group of friendly individuals, with an important tie in common, may decide to meet twice a year in tribute to their companionship. At the first meeting a plate is broken and each member takes away with him one of the broken pieces. At his death the piece is restored to the group. When the last piece is returned, of course, the group ceases to exist. This is the pattern of verterans' associations and alumni groups to which we have referred in a previous chapter.

relationship. When a person who lacks the appropriate status tries to influence or control the action of another, we can be sure that it is leadership, not authority, that is being exercised. Sometimes, of course, there is a penumbra of uncertainty with respect to the authority vested in a status, and the right to make a decision, as in jurisdictional disputes, may be more seriously contested than the policy the decision involves. "Who's in charge here?"—as the slang expression would have it—is indeed a necessary question. One of the marks of a good executive is his ability to construct and to maintain a table of organization in which the lines of authority are straight and clear, and well known to all personnel.

It is clear that authority is wholly a function of the formal organization of an association. It makes no appearance in the informal organization. It would nevertheless be improvident to ignore the fact that personal factors do enter into status relationships and that the latter are seldom "pure" except in cases where the two individuals involved are unaware of each other's identity. We have seen that persons evaluate each other intrinsically in terms of their personalities and not only extrinsically in terms of their conformity to the norms that their statuses impose upon them. We have also seen that the informal organization of an association sometimes takes precedence over its formal organization. Subordinates in these situations frequently exhibit capacities as leaders and play leadership roles; superordinates, on the other hand, may withdraw informally from the responsibilities of their statuses and exercise only a nominal authority. Nor can we ignore the familiar phenomenon by which the possession of a status involving authority exerts an influence upon personality. Otherwise submissive individuals "dress'd in a little brief authority," sometimes assume an authoritarian air, and otherwise dominant individuals, stripped of the perquisites of status, sometimes exhibit a new humility. The almost universal and indeed welcome intrusion of psychological factors, however, does not alter the fact that authority itself is exercised in a status relationship and not in a personal relationship and that it is a function of the formal, not the informal, organization of an association.

5. The Rationale of Authority

What, then, sustains the authority exercised by some people over others? Why should a subordinate obey a superordinate especially when he disapproves of the command? Why, in fact, does subordination not imply agreement, insubordination dissent? Why does an inferior obey a superior whom he may clearly dislike, whom he may never have met, or to whom in other relations he may be utterly indifferent? A preliminary answer to these questions has already been suggested: Both the superior and the inferior recognize that they are operating in a status relationship and that personal sentiments have no relevance to the exercise of authority in the situation. Indeed, a person is expected and even required to exercise the same kind of authority over friends and intimates that he does over enemies and strangers. In the ideal case the exercise of authority is wholly objective, impartial, impersonal, and disinterested. The judge who has violated a traffic regulation is expected to fine himself. Indeed, in the ideal case —and the writer is indebted to Talcott Parsons for this suggestion—authority is as impersonal as a traffic light.

These observations, however, do not quite answer the more general questions. The reasons people submit to authority, in the larger focus, are the reasons that encourage them to obey the law, to practice the customs of their society, and to conform to the norms of the particular associations to which they belong. We have in an earlier chapter discussed the reasons why people conform to norms and this discussion needs no recital or repetition here. But the reasons why men in general conform to the norms do not explain why particular men accept particular authority—especially in situations where the person who exercises authority introduces new norms, when he exercises, in effect, a legislative function. What supports the authority in these instances?

The answer to this question is that authority in these, as in all other cases, is supported, sanctioned, and sustained by the association itself. The person who exercises it is recognized as an agent of the group. He represents the group. He acts not in his own but in the group's name. Insubordination now is a threat not to a personal relationship but to the continued existence of the group. It is an assault upon the group, a denial of the validity of its norms, and, even more significantly, an attack by an individual upon a majority. Since authority is attached to a status, in a system of statuses supported by the majority of the members, and since this system of statuses is synonymous with the organization of an association, it is apparent that any disinclination to accept the status arrangement and the exercise of authority involved in it implies a disinclination to accept the group itself. It is the majority of the members of an association who support its structure and who sustain the authority exercised in particular statuses in accordance with particular norms. If we seek the rationale of authority, therefore, we find it in the very factors that induce men to form associations in the first place, to join together in organized groups, and to perpetuate these associations. It is the desire for stability and continuity which guarantees that the exercise of authority will be maintained in the statuses of the association, not only as an underwriting of particular decisions, but as a bulwark behind the association itself. An individual who rejects this authority is jeopardizing the continued existence of the association. The ultimate answer, therefore, to the question of what sustains the authority exercised in an association of any kind is that this authority is sustained by a majority of the association's own members.

6. Authority: Coercion or Consent?

We have finally to inquire whether authority is a phenomenon exercised by coercion or by consent. Does the person who accepts a command from superior authority do so, in short, because he has to or because he wants to? A possible answer to this question stems from a distinction between voluntary associations on the one hand and involuntary associations on the other. In a voluntary association membership is a matter of consent, and people voluntarily give their allegiance to it. They conform to the norms of the association for the same reason that they conform to the rules of the games they play; that is, they conform because the desire to play exceeds the desire to win. Similarly, they accept the authority of others in voluntary associations because the desire to belong exceeds the desire to make independent decisions on matters of associational concern. The candidate for the degree of doctor of philosophy accepts the authority of his examiners to ask him questions, the football player accepts the authority of the coach to determine strategy and tactics, and the employee accepts the authority of his employer to assign his duties. In voluntary associations, too, a member may escape the yoke of authority by the simple expedient of resigning. In voluntary associations, in short, authority rests upon consent, and it might be appropriate in these circumstances to define authority as institutionalized leadership.

In involuntary associations, however, the situation is different. A soldier may not defy the order of a superior officer, a citizen may not ignore the demands of the tax collector, and a prisoner clearly may not refuse to accept the authority of his guards. In certain associations, in other words, voluntary withdrawal is impossible, and these are what we should be inclined to call involuntary associations. In associations like these it would be unrealistic to deny that coercion is present in the exercise of authority. It is in these situations that authority becomes a power phenomenon, and it is in these that we can define authority as institutionalized power. In voluntary associations, then, we could say that authority is institutionalized leadership, in involuntary associations that it is institutionalized power. In the former authority rests upon consent; in the latter, upon coercion.

This solution, however, is not quite satisfactory. In the first place it is not always easy to distinguish between voluntary and involuntary associations. There are associations, in addition, which one may voluntarily join but from which one may not voluntarily withdraw. And there are associations that are voluntary for some but involuntary for others. In the second place, and probably more important, authority that may or may not be accepted hardly qualifies as authority in accordance with the ordinary connotation of the term. There is something mandatory, not merely arbitrary, about authority and no analysis can quite rationalize this mandatory element away and retain the full significance of the phenomenon. Furthermore, even in voluntary associations a member who declines to submit to constituted authority is ordinarily required, in an exercise of authority, to resign. If he refuses to resign there must be still another exercise of authority to compel his withdrawal from the association and to repel the threat to the group as a whole that his insubordination entails. In view of these considerations it would seem that our problem requires a different answer.

In order to retain the central connotation of the concept we are examining it seems desirable to assert that authority is always a power phenomenon and to define authority as institutionalized power. It is power that confers authority upon a command. But it is sanctioned power, institutionalized power. The power resides in the majority of the members, the majority that supports and sustains the association and its norms. It is the majority that, in accordance with whatever rules and regulations it adopts, can create a status, confer authority upon it, and keep it there. The formation of an association, its stability and its continuity, involves the formal delegation of the power that resides in the majority to one or a number of the group's members as agents of the whole. This is what we mean by the institutionalization of power as authority.

It is true, of course, that an individual's membership in an association may be a matter of consent and he may similarly be free to withdraw. But so long as he remains a member, the authority exercised by his superordinates is mandatory and not a matter of voluntary determination. The consent in these cases applies to membership in the association and not to the acceptance of the commands of constituted authority. Membership may be voluntary, but acceptance of authority is mandatory. It is one of the conditions of membership. Stated alternatively, an individual may be free to belong or not to belong to a particular association, but as a member he is not free to reject the authority exercised by other individuals in accordance with the norms of the association. Considerations like these encourage us to conclude that when consent is involved, as it is in voluntary associations, it applies to the fact of membership and not to the acceptance of authority.

7. Conclusion

In this chapter we have tried to stress the importance of authority, not only as one of the criteria of organization but as one of its essential components.

We first distinguished authority from competence and from leadership, then indicated that the locus of authority is always in associations and not elsewhere in society, and suggested, with perhaps an unnecessary emphasis, that authority is always attached to statuses and not to persons. We then considered the process of organization, in which authority is created, offered an inferior and, in our opinion, a superior answer to the question whether authority is a matter of coercion or consent, and finally defined it as institutionalized power. We should maintain in conclusion that it is impossible to understand the phenomenon of authority without recourse to the concept of power, and accordingly it is the problem of power that attracts our attention in the following chapter.

Chapter 13

POWER

SOCIOLOGICAL INQUIRY provides few problems as perplexing as the problem of power. It is as perplexing in its way as the problem of electricity in physics. As a matter of fact, social power is like electrical power. We see the effects and manifestations of both but not the phenomenon itself. Social power is transformed into order, force, and authority; electrical power into light, heat, and motion. The misapplication of both, to be macabre for a moment, can result in death. But the essence of these phenomena is elusive. Not even the dictionary can give us a satisfactory definition of electricity and indeed can only call it "a fundamental entity of nature." We can similarly—and truthfully—say that power is "a fundamental entity of society," but with an awareness that we are not saying very much, if indeed we are saying anything at all. Our relative ignorance of the nature of power is itself a curious phenomenon. The word has been in our vocabularies for as long as we can remember and we frequently use it. But we find ourselves unable to define it. We here confront the dilemma of St. Augustine who confessed that he knew perfectly well what time was—until someone asked him. (*Si non rogas, intelligo.*) In this chapter, however, we shall dare to ask what social power is and we shall try to offer an answer. In the process we shall also hope to communicate the notion that power is a matter of central sociological importance.*

1. Power and Society

The power structure of society is not an insignificant problem. In any realistic sense it is both a sociological (i.e., a scientific) and a moral (i.e., a social) problem. It has traditionally been a problem in political philosophy. Like so many other problems of a political character, however, it has roots that lie deeper than the *polis* and reach into the community itself. Its primitive basis and ultimate locus are to be sought in society, and not only in government, because in government it is already institutionalized. It is apparent, furthermore, that not all power is political power and that political power—like economic, financial, industrial, and military power—is only one of several and various kinds of social power. Wall Street, for example, can compete with the government of the United States in exercising power over foreign trade and in affecting the exchange rate of foreign currencies.

Society, in fact, is shot through with power relations—the power a father exercises over his child, a master over his slave, a teacher over his pupils, the victor over the vanquished, the blackmailer over his victim, the warden over his prisoners, the judge over the convicted defendant, an employer over his employee, a general over his lieutenants, a captain over his crew, a creditor over a debtor, and so on through an impressively large number of social relationships. The reader of the preceding chapter will recognize that some of these are examples of authority. But all of them are examples of power because authority is a species of power. It is worth an incidental note that not all these examples of power enjoy the support of the state. To some of them the state is indifferent, to others it is opposed.

Power, in short, is a universal phenomenon in human societies. It is present in almost all social interaction. It appears even in courtship.[1] It appears almost everywhere, in fact, except in the ideal family, in friendship, and in those social relations in the narrower sense that the sociologist Georg Simmel called relations of "polite acquaintance," the kind of interaction, for example, that appears at cocktail parties and at wedding receptions. Most other social relations contain elements of power. What, then, is this phenomenon? In trying to answer the question we shall adopt

---

* This chapter is a revision of an article entitled "An Analysis of Social Power," *American Sociological Review.* Vol. XV. December, 1950, pp. 730–738.
[1] On this subject, and on power in general, see Peter M. Blau, *Exchange and Power in Social Life*, John Wiley & Sons, New York, 1964, pp. 76-85.

the procedure of the preceding chapter and first distinguish it from other phenomena with which it has often been associated and often confused.

2. Power and Prestige

Social power has variously been identified with prestige, influence, eminence, competence, dominance, rights, strength, force, and authority, and it was the distinguished Lord Chancellor of England, Francis Bacon, who identified it with knowledge. Since the intension of a term varies, if at all, inversely with its extension—i.e., the more things a term can be applied to the less precise its meaning—it is necessary to distinguish power from most of these other phenomena. Let us begin by separating power from prestige.

A close association between power and prestige was made by the American sociologist E. A. Ross in his classic work on social control. "The immediate cause of the location of power," he said, "is prestige." And further, "The class that has the most prestige will have the most power."[2] Now prestige may certainly be construed as something that is sometimes related to power, in the sense that powerful groups tend to be prestigious and prestigious groups powerful. Prestige clearly separates man from man and group from group and it has, as one of its consequences, one kind of stratification that appears in human societies. But we can always escape confusion if we can find, no matter how close the relationship, one phenomenon in the absence of the other. We can do this with respect to power and prestige and consequently the two phenomena are not identical. They are in fact independent variables. Prestige is frequently unaccompanied by power, as in the case of scholars elected to membership in the American Academy of Arts and Sciences, and power may similarly be unassociated with prestige, as in the case of a group of gangsters preying upon the small independent stores in the Bronx in New York City. Physicists, in our world, have great prestige, but not much power. Policemen, on the other hand, have significant power but—except perhaps in London—little prestige. The Phi Beta Kappa Society has high prestige in American academic circles, but no power. Prestige, in short, does not suffice to create power, and the two phenomena, both sociologically important, are not identical and may or may not appear together.

Similar observations may be made about the relationship of knowledge, eminence, skill, and competence to power. All four of these may

[2] *Social Control,* The Macmillan Company, New York, 1916, p. 78. Dennis Wrong is most enlightening on the relationship between power and social control. See his "Some Problems in Defining Social Power, "*The American Journal of Sociology,* vol. 73, no. 6, May, 1968, pp. 673–681.

contribute to prestige, but they may be quite unaccompanied by power. When power does accompany them the association is incidental rather than necessary. Thus the most erudite archaeologist, the most famous sculptor, the most talented pianist, and the most competent automobile mechanic in the world might all four be devoid of power. Knowledge, eminence, skill, and competence, although they may accompany it, have nothing intrinsically to do with power.

3. Power and Influence

When we turn to the relationship between power and influence we find a more intimate connection, but once again it is necessary to make a distinction. It is necessary because influence is persuasive whereas power is coercive. We submit voluntarily to influence but power requires our submission. The mistress of a king may influence the destiny of a nation, but only because her paramour permits himself to be swayed by her designs. In any ultimate reckoning her influence may be more important than his power, but it is inefficacious unless it is transformed into power. The power a teacher exercises over his pupils stems not from his superior knowledge (this is competence rather than power) and not from his opinions (this is influence rather than power), but from his ability to apply the sanction of failure to the student who does not fulfill his requirements and meet his standards. The competence may be unappreciated, and the influence may be ineffective, but the power may not be gainsaid.[3]

Furthermore, power and influence can occur in isolation from each other and so they also are independent variables. We should say, for example, that Karl Marx exerted an incalculable influence upon the twentieth century, but this poverty-stricken exile who spent so many of his hours in the British Museum was hardly a man of power. Even the assertion that he was a man of influence is an ellipsis. It is the ideas that were—and continue to be—influential. The Soviet dictator Stalin, on the other hand, was a man of power, and power may dispense with influence. Influence may convert a friend, but power coerces friend and foe alike. Influence attaches to an idea, a doctrine, or a creed, and has its locus in the ideological sphere. Power attaches to a person, a group, or an association, and has its locus in the sociological sphere. Plato, Aristotle, St. Thomas, Shakespeare, Galileo, Newton, and Kant were men of influence, but none of them exercised any noticeable power. One need only compare Aristotle, for example, with his famous pupil, Alexander the Great. Napoleon Bonaparte

[3] In this case, however, as shown in the preceding chapter, the power is transformed into authority.

and Abraham Lincoln were men of both power and influence. Genghis Khan and Adolf Hitler were men of power. Archimedes was a man of influence, but the soldier who slew him at the gates of Syracuse had more power.

When we speak, therefore, of the power of an idea or when we are tempted to say that ideas are weapons or when we assert, with the above-mentioned Napoleon, that the pen is mightier than the sword, we are using figurative language, speaking truly as it were, but metaphorically and with synecdoche.[4] Ideas are influential, they can change the course of history, but for the sake of logical and sociological clarity it is preferable to deny to them the attribute of power. Influence in this sense, of course, presents quite a serious and as complex a problem as power, but it is not the problem we are now discussing.[5]

4. Power and Dominance

It is relatively easy to distinguish power from dominance. Power is a sociological, dominance a psychological phenomenon. The locus of power is in both persons and groups, and in almost all of the important cases it is in the latter. The locus of dominance, on the contrary, is only in individuals. Power is a function and resource of the organization and opposition of associations, of the arrangement and juxtaposition of groups, including classes, and of the structure of society itself. Dominance, on the other hand, is a function of personality or of temperament. It is a personal trait. A timid robber, who flaunts his gun, has more power than his unarmed victim, however dominant or aggressive the latter may be in his normal social relationships. Furthermore, and one of the most interesting facets of this distinction, dominant individuals play roles in powerless

[4] We frequently speak of the power of the press. The President of the United States, for example, to say nothing of the Cabinet, the Congress, and even the Court, listens intently to the voice of *The New York Times,* and *The Times* of London is not known as "The Thunderer" for nothing. But neither newspaper can elect a single candidate to political office, and neither editor nor columnist, however influential, can issue an order that will initiate a governmental policy or force a change in one. To revert to our earlier analogy, power is lightning, not thunder.

[5] For sophisticated treatments of influence, see William A. Gamson, *Power and Discontent,* The Dorsey Press, Homewood, Illinois, 1968; Talcott Parsons, "On the Concept of Influence," *Public Opinion Quarterly,* Vol. 27, Spring, 1963, pp. 37–62; James S. Coleman, "Comment on 'On the Concept of Influence,'" *Ibid.,* pp. 63–82; and Parsons' rejoinder to Coleman, *Ibid.,* pp. 87–92. For an unusually clear and correct use of the concepts of influence, leadership, power, and authority in the study of a United States congressman, in this case the Chairman of the Ways and Means Committee of the House of Representatives, see John F. Manley, "Wilbur D. Mills: A Study in Congressional Influence," *The American Political Science Review,* vol. LXIII, no. 2, June, 1969, pp. 442–464.

groups and submissive individuals play roles in powerful ones. Some groups indeed acquire an impressive power in society, especially political power, because there are so many submissive individuals who are persuaded to join them and who meekly agree to the norms and ideologies that membership imposes. A clear example of this is the growth of the National Socialist Party in Germany in the 1930s. We can easily see, therefore, that dominance is a problem in social psychology, power a problem in sociology.

This distinction, among others, illustrates once more the impropriety of associating sociology too closely with psychology, or even social psychology. Individual and group phenomena are fundamentally different in character. The subjective factors that motivate an individual to participate in social action, the ends he seeks and the means he employs to achieve them, have little to do with the objective social consequences of the action. A man may join the army, for example, for any number of reasons—to achieve financial independence, to earn early retirement, to conform with the law, to escape a delicate domestic situation, to withdraw from an embarrassing emotional commitment, to see the world, to escape the pressure of mortgage payments, to fight for a cause in which he believes, to wear a uniform, to do what his friends are doing, or to do what he believes is right. None of these motivations will affect very much the power of the army that he joins. Similarly, people do not have children because they wish to increase the birthrate, to raise the classification of the municipal post office, or to contribute to the military strength of the state. The births, however, may have all three of these consequences, and many more besides. And finally, to return to our subject, a dominant personality does not confer power upon the man who possesses it. Power, in short, is one thing, dominance quite another.

5. Power and Rights

It is a little more difficult to distinguish power from rights because the latter term is itself ambiguous. It appears indeed in two senses that are exactly contradictory—as those privileges and only those that are secured by the state and as those that the state may not invade even to secure.

A complex example of the latter concerns the work of the Federal Communications Commission in the United States. The commission is committed by law to observe and enforce a so-called "fairness doctrine." This means, in view of the limited number of television channels available, and in view also of the fact that the airwaves belong to the people and not to private corporations, that all points of view and the entire spectrum of opinion on any subject should receive full and equal treatment. This requirement has caused serious difficulty and embarrassment in giving equal time to the very small political parties which could not otherwise gain access to television except at prohibitive expense and which, in any case, have no chance of winning an election.

But there is a more serious problem involved. Some television stations in smaller communities, properly qualified, and owned or subsidized by particular religious denominations, devote almost all of their time to the propagation of their own particular faith. The fairness doctrine would seem to require that other religious denominations have an opportunity to answer and to advocate their own doctrines. But who, if the local supply of channels is exhausted, is empowered to decide? Who will determine the allocation of time? The First Amendment to the Constitution of the United States constructs a famous wall of separation between church and state and it can be argued therefore that no official agency of the government, including the Federal Communications Commission, can make a decision on religious grounds, even in the interest of fairness. We may encounter here a prohibition of the kind that has often been sustained by the Supreme Court of the United States. This example is introduced only to illustrate the complexity of the problem and to show that there are certain rights—in this instance the right of access to the air—which, as we have said, it can be argued that the government may not invade even to secure.

We do not, fortunately, need to pursue the ramifications of this particular problem. Nor do we need to pursue the distinctions between various kinds of rights, including "natural rights" and natural law (like fairness for example) which are elaborated in the history of jurisprudence, in the sociology of law, and in theology, to recognize that a right always requires some support in the social structure. No individual can successfully claim a right that is unrecognized in the law and nonexistent in the mores.[6] Rights in general, like privileges, duties, obligations, responsibilities, perquisites, and prerogatives, are attached to statuses both in society itself and in the separate associations of society. One may have a right without the power to exercise it—for example, the right to vote in certain communities in the American South—but in most cases power of some kind supports whatever rights are claimed. Rights are more closely associated with privileges and with authority than they are with power. A right, like a privilege, is one of the perquisites of power and not power itself. There is, of course, a further distinction between rights and privileges. Military leave, for example, is a privilege and not a right; it may be requested but it may

---

[6] Odd and extravagant claims, of course, are sometimes made. A woman once claimed the right of using the house of the president of a Middle Western university, and indeed on one occasion lodged herself in the living room, on the grounds that the university and all of its buildings belonged to the taxpayers of the state and that the president's house was therefore a public facility.

not be demanded. Similarly, promotion in any association, except some-times for reasons of seniority, is a privilege and not a right.

6. Power, Force, and Authority

We have now distinguished power from prestige, from influence, from dominance, and from rights, and the three concepts of strength, force, and authority remain. Physical strength detains our analysis only for a moment because it has almost no sociological significance. Hard muscles can conquer flabby ones and a big man can usually defeat a small one (unless the latter knows karate) in physical combat, but two men—the Herculean feats of television detectives notwithstanding—can almost always subdue a single man when all other resources of the three are equal. As Thomas Hobbes noted long ago, "One man is not much stronger than another." It is ludicrous to suppose that anyone exercises authority over another because of his size. Size and strength are both negligible factors in civilized societies. Physical strength, however, is a form of power, and its use is force, as we shall now proceed to see in a larger perspective.

It is the concepts of force and authority that give us a solution to our problem. Power is not force and power is not authority, but it is intimately related to both. We want, therefore, to propose three definitions and then examine their implications: (1) power is latent force; (2) force is manifest power, and (3), as indicated in the preceding chapter, authority is institu-tionalized power. The first two of these propositions may be considered together. They look like circular definitions and, as a matter of fact, they are. If an independent meaning can be found for one of these concepts, however, the other may be defined in terms of it and the circularity will disappear.[7]

We may therefore suggest an independent definition of the concept of force. Force in sociology is remarkably similar to force in physics and here we have an interesting linkage between nature and society. In both cases force means the production of an effect, an alteration in movement or action that overcomes resistance. It is an interference with a body at rest or

---

[7] As a matter of purely technical interest, it may be observed that all definitions are ultimately circular. Every system of inference contains undefined or "primitive" terms in its initial propositions because, if it were necessary to define every term before using it, it would be impossible ever to talk or write or reason. There would be no word with which to begin. An undefined term in one system, however, may be defined in another. Although we may still perhaps have a logical deficiency here, it is not necessarily a practical deficiency if the circle, so to speak, is not too small. When we find an independent meaning for one of the terms in a couplet of circular definitions we are, in effect, enlarging the circle. The problem involved here has engaged some of the best minds in the history of logic, including Whitehead and Russell, who discuss it in the Introduction to *Principia Mathematica*.

in motion that changes its state or direction; an interference with a person that changes what he is doing or intends to do. In the sociological sense, where it is synonymous with coercion, it compels a change in the course of action of an individual or a group against the wishes of the individual or the group. It means the application of sanctions when they are not willingly received. It means, further, the reduction or limitation or closure or even total elimination of alternatives to the social action of one person or group by another person or group. "Your money or your life" is a threat that, when acted upon, becomes a situation of naked force, the reduction of alternatives to two.[8] The blackmailer who exacts his tribute from his victim as the price of silence is again limiting alternatives—pay or be exposed. The bouncer who throws an obstreperous patron out of a bar or nightclub is depriving him of the alternative of staying for another round of drinks. The execution of a sentence to hang represents the total elimination of alternatives. One army progressively limits the social action of its enemy until only two alternatives remain for the unsuccessful contender—to surrender or die.[9]

Now all of these are situations of manifest power. Power itself is the predisposition or prior capacity that makes the use of force possible. Only groups that have power can threaten to use force and the threat itself is power. Power is the ability to employ force, not its actual employment, the ability to apply sanctions, not their actual application. Power is the ability to introduce force into a social situation; it is stance, not action; it is a presentation of the probability of force. Unlike force, incidentally, power is always successful; when it is not successful it was not, or ceases to be, power. The bankrupt corporation and the vanquished army are both powerless. Power symbolizes the force that *may* be applied in any social situation and supports the authority that *is* applied. Power is thus neither force nor authority but it makes both force and authority possible. Without

---

[8] The holdup man expresses his disjunction dramatically but incorrectly. What he really means is "Your money, or your life and your money."

[9] There is a further distinction to be made between force and violence. We should be inclined to say, although a continuum and not a dichotomy is involved, that violence is uncontrolled force, undisciplined force. A mob engaged in shooting, looting, and arson, as in the riots that occur in cities, is an expression of violence. The police that restrain, subdue, and finally control it are an expression of force. Unfortunately, as in the student demonstrations that have occurred in universities in the world's major cities, the police too have often become undisciplined—"lost their cool" as the slang phrase so aptly puts it—and have themselves indulged in violence. War, although fought by disciplined force on both sides, is always violent at the points where the opposing armies clash. Political assassination is always an act of violence and so, more generally, is the act of murder. In these cases it is the destruction of life, rather than the absence of discipline, that becomes the governing criterion. Violence is force used not to maintain or to restore order, but to destroy. It thus has a moral connotation whereas the concepts of power, force, and authority are morally neutral.

power there would be no force and without power there would be no authority.

7. Power and Formal Organization

The implications of the preceding propositions will become clearer if we turn our attention to the locus of power. We discover it both in the organized sectors of society and in the unorganized; that is, it rests, latent, both in associations and in the unorganized community. Furthermore, in associations themselves, its presence is discernible both in the formal and in the informal organization. The first of these presents a fairly simple problem. It is in the formal organization of associations, as we saw in the last chapter, that social power is institutionalized and transformed into authority. If social interaction proceeded wholly in accordance with the norms of the formal organization, and if the norms were always clear, then power would be dissolved without residue into authority. This would happen, however, only in a "perfect" or "ideal" association, and such associations do not exist in the actual world. In the real world uncertainties arise, situations are unanticipated, penumbral areas appear in which the norms are unclear or inadequate. Strong leaders expand the authority attached to their statuses; weak leaders diminish it. Questions occur about the distribution of authority, both horizontal and vertical. The table of organization becomes unstuck; it is something that looks good on paper, but only there. Miss Brewster, at the age of fifty-six, is being difficult. She is the secretary of the graduate department of economics, but she has survived the incumbencies of five different department chairmen, she knows all the rules, and she is beginning to decide which of the graduate students will make it through to their Ph.D. degrees and which will not. She does this not by examining them in economics, which she has neither the competence nor the authority to do, but by a selective application of the rules. Something is happening here that disturbs the structure of authority. A good "petty officer," as seen in this example, can often make or break his superior, even in a military association.

Sometimes authority clearly vested in an associational status may not be exercised because it conflicts with a moral norm to which the larger and surrounding community subscribes. A naval officer who surrenders his ship, in opposition to ancient tradition and stringent law, may escape a court martial because his superiors recognize that—because he made his difficult decision in the interest of saving human lives—the sentiment of the nation supports him. Sometimes an official may remove a subordinate from office without formal cause and without formal authority because such action, now involving power, also finds support in public opinion. Public opinion may require the resignation of an associate justice of the Supreme Court, a requirement that the Chief Justice himself has no authority to impose. Sometimes, on the contrary, a superior may have the authority to discharge a subordinate, but not the power, because retention of the subordinate is demanded by the community. One example was the inability of both the general manager and the owner of the New York Yankees to "fire" Babe Ruth, or even to trade him, when he was at the height of his fame, although there were numerous occasions on which they wanted very much to do so. The Yankee fans would have been outraged. On another level, the British monarch still has the authority to dissolve Parliament. It would shake the United Kingdom, however, if it were done without a specific request by the Prime Minister.

These situations abound and they are often quite complex. In a university it may not be clear whether a dean has the authority to decline to reappoint a professor when this action has been recommended by the chairman of the department with the concurrence of the department's members; or, more subtly, whether, if he uses his authority to deny a salary increase to the professor in question in order to encourage him to resign, he will be accused of maladministration if he exercises it. It may similarly be unclear whether a Bishop of the Episcopal Church has the authority to remove a rector from his parish when the latter has the support of a large majority of his parishioners. In other words, opposing power often makes it a matter of unwise policy for an official to exercise the authority that is specifically vested in his status. In recent years we have seen student power bring about student representation on policy-making committees, sometimes even on boards of trustees, and black power add to the curricula of many universities programs in Afro-American studies. In all of these cases we see power leaking into the joints of associational structure and affecting the formal organization.

8. Power and Informal Organization

Interaction in an association, as we have previously illustrated, does not proceed in precise or in complete conformity to the norms of formal organization. Power spills over the vessels of status, which only imperfectly contain it as authority. We arrive, therefore, at a brief consideration of informal organization, in which the prestige of statuses gives way to the esteem for persons and in which the social interaction of the members proceeds not only in terms of the explicit norms of the association but also in terms of implicit extra-associational norms whose locus is in the community and which may or may not conflict, at strategic points, with the associational norms. The examples we have already offered help us to anticipate what we have to say about the incidence and presence of power in informal organization.

No association is wholly formal in its social organization. Social organization, as we have seen, makes possible the orderly social intercourse of people who do not know one another and indeed can make personal acquaintance supererogatory. But in the continuity of associational life the members do become acquainted with one another and interact not only extrinsically and categorically, in terms of the statuses they occupy, but also intrinsically and personally in terms of the roles they play and the personalities they exhibit. Subgroups arise and begin to exert subtle pressures upon the organization, upon the norms that may be breached in the observance thereof, and upon the authority which, however firmly institutionalized, is yet subject to change. These subgroups may, as cliques and factions, remain within the association or, as sects and splinter groups, break away from it and form new and often competing associations. In any event, no formal organization remains wholly formal under the exigencies of time and circumstance. Power is seldom completely institutionalized as authority, seldom exhausted in organization. If power sustains the structure, opposing power threatens it, and every voluntary association is always at the mercy of a majority of its own members. It would be difficult to overemphasize the importance of this fact. In all associations, even involuntary associations, the power of people acting in concert is so great that the prohibition against "combinations" appears in the statutes of military associations and the right of collective petition is denied to military personnel.

Power appears, then, in associations in two forms, institutionalized as authority in the formal organization and uninstitutionalized as power itself in the informal organization. But this does not exhaust the incidence of power in the associations of society. It must be evident that power is required to inaugurate the association in the first place, to guarantee its continuance, and to enforce its norms. Here, in fact, we come close to the essence and etiology of social power. Half a dozen people, or a dozen, forming an association would not seem to represent much power. In agreement about the desirability of forming the association, for example, they represent only consensus. But in the association that they form they do indeed represent power, a power that enables them to initiate the association in any case in which there is resistance or even inertia. And, once formed, power supports it against opposing power, both internal and external, that would challenge or threaten its continued existence.

Power, in short, supports the fundamental order of society and the social organization within it. Power stands behind every association and sustains its structure. Without power there is no organization and without power there is no order. The intrusion of the time dimension and the exigencies of circumstance require continual readjustments of the structure of every association and it is power that sustains it through these transitions. Authority itself cannot exist without the immediate support of power and the ultimate sanction of force.

9. Power and Conflict

As important as power may be in associations, it is even more important where it reigns, uninstitutionalized, in the interstices between associations and has its locus in society itself. Here we find the issues and conflicts of our time—labor versus management, Protestant versus Catholic, militant black versus reactionary white, radical student versus conservative administration, business versus government, Republican versus Democrat, Tory versus Labor, Israeli versus Arab, the Soviet Union versus the United States, hawks versus doves in both countries, and indeed one side versus the other in all the wars and revolutions in history. If it is power that supports the social order it is power also that rends it asunder.

It is not the task of the present chapter to examine any of these conflicts but rather to confine the focus to the nature of power itself. And here we have two logical possibilities—power in the confrontations of like groups and power in the confrontations of unlike groups. Examples of the former are commercial companies competing for the same market, factions competing for control of a national student association, religious associations competing for adherents, newspapers competing for readers, magazines for advertisers, construction companies for contracts, political parties for votes, and so on through a large number of instances. Examples of the latter are conflicts between labor and management, between church and state, between the legislative and executive branches of government, between different subdivisions of the same bureaucracy, between the "Young Turks" and "the Establishment" in almost every large-scale association, and so on through an equally large number of instances. Power thus appears both in competition and in conflict and has no incidence in groups that neither compete nor conflict; i.e., in groups that do not share a common social matrix and have no social relations with one another, as for example, the American Council of Learned Societies and Rotary International. Power thus arises only in social opposition of some kind.

It is no accident that the noun "power" is related to the adjective "potential." It may seem redundant to say so, but power is always potential; that is, when it is used it becomes something else, in nature force, and in society either force or authority. It is, as we have said, latent force, potential force. It is the lion ready to spring, the leopard ready to pounce. It is the engine of a rocketship, still attached to its gantry, during the countdown that precedes blast-off. And so in society, on every level from the insignificant to the serious. Aces and kings in the hand represent power in the game of bridge. When played they represent authority according to the rules of the game, the authority to take tricks, and no one disputes the authority of the ace of trumps. Money and credit represent financial power; when spent or used they are transformed into property which, in turn, may become one of the sources of even more power.[10] Military power is the most awesome of all because its function, when necessary, is to be transformed into force. But it is power before it becomes force and indeed if it never does. This is the power that is attached to intercontinental ballistic missiles at rest in their silos or in submarines at sea. One desperately hopes that they will always remain at rest, but no one doubts that they represent power. It is a power that affects the destinies of nations. Indeed, the nations that have it are called "powers," and those that have the most of it are called "superpowers."

If power is one of the imperatives of society it may also be partly a pretense and succeed only because it is inaccurately estimated, or unchallenged. The encouragement of inaccurate estimates by the enemy, of course, is a familiar stratagem in war. But it occurs in many power relations. The threat of a strike may succeed when the strike will not. Blackmail may have consequences more dire than the exposure of the secret. The threat of a minority to secede from an association may affect it more than an actual secession. The threat of a boycott may achieve the result desired when the boycott itself would fail. In poker parlance—and indeed it is the same phenomenon—a "bluff" is powerful, but the power vanishes when the bluff is called.

10. The Sources of Power

We are at last in a position to locate the sources of power, which are three: (1) numbers of people, and especially majorities, (2) organization, and (3) resources.

It is difficult to overestimate the power that resides in numbers. As suggested before, other things being equal, two men can almost always force one man to do what they want, and ten men can do it even more easily. The power of a majority is so great that in many social situations there is a consensus about the right to express it as authority. This can be

---

[10] For an ingenious, but highly complex, working out of the analogy between money and power, see Talcott Parsons, "On the Concept of Political Power," *Proceedings of the American Philosophical Society*, Vol. 107, No. 3, June, 1963, pp. 232–262.

seen on many levels, from the trivial to the sublime. Thus, a group of three friends will ordinarily go to the movie that two of them want to see. On a larger stage, the party that wins the majority of votes is conceded the right to form a government. In a very profound sense, as Simmel once observed, this right is conceded because it can be taken. Majorities own so much power that they can be overcome only be dividing them into factions and "Divide and rule" (*Divide et impera*), therefore, is one of the oldest of imperial devices. Majorities are threatened, of course, when they are small, when the minority is increasing in size, and thus augmenting its power. For this reason it is the better part of wisdom to follow the admonition of Thomas Jefferson that slender majorities should not initiate large innovations. The tides of sentiment and opinion move too fast. But majorities are powerful, and the larger they are, both relatively and absolutely, the more powerful.

Given the same social organization, in short, and the same resources, the larger number can always control the smaller and secure its compliance. If the majorities have frequently and for long historical periods suffered oppression and exploitation, it is because they have not been organized or have lacked resources. Finally, the power of a majority appears in all associations, except in the rare cases in history when charisma blinds all followers and bends them to the leader's will. It is the power of a majority, even in the most formally and tightly organized associations, that either threatens or sustains the stability of the associational structure.[11]

Important as numbers are, however, as the primary source of social power, they seldom operate alone. As suggested above, majorities may suffer oppression for long historical periods; they may, in short, be powerless or possess only the residual power of inertia. We arrive therefore at the second source of social power—social organization. A well-organized and disciplined body of marines or police can control a much larger number of unorganized individuals, as in a riot or insurrection. An organized minority can control an unorganized majority. But even here majorities possess so much power that there are limits beyond which this kind of control cannot be exercised. These limits appear with the recognition that the majority can organize and thus reverse the control. There is such a thing, after all, as a successful revolution. An organized majority—we are tempted to say—is the most powerful social force on earth.

Of two groups, however, equal or nearly equal in numbers and comparable in organization, the one with access to the greater resources will have the superior power. Political power, as Chairman Mao has

---

[11] For an elaboration of this theme see the author's paper "The Sociology of Majorities,' *American Sociological Review*, Vol. 13, Decemeber, 1948, pp. 700–710.

observed, flows from the barrel of a gun. Similarly, Stalin once asked how many divisions the Pope was able to mobilize. And so resources constitute the third source of social power. Resources are of many kinds—money, credit, property, knowledge, skill, competence, cunning, acumen, deceit (as in the poker bluff), armament, and of course all of the things usually included under the term "natural resources,"—especially, at this moment of history, iron and uranium ore. They are all a part of the arsenal of power. Here, in fact, we are able to reintroduce the many phenomena we have previously distinguished from power. They are sources, not synonyms, of power. There are also supernatural resources in the case of organized religions which, as agencies of a celestial government, apply supernatural sanctions, as instruments of control. It is apparent that, in any power conflict, they can tip the balance when the other sources of power are equal and comparable. Important as they are, however, as sources of power, they are not themselves power. Unless utilized by people who are in organized association with one another they are devoid of sociological significance.

Finally, it may be of more than incidental interest to note that there is one kind of social situation in which the power of opposing groups is completely balanced. The numbers on each side are equal, their social organization is identical, and their resources are as nearly the same as possible. This situation reveals itself in games and contests in which power components are cancelled out and the victory goes to the superior skill. Whether the game be baseball or bridge there is insistence, inherent in the structure of the game itself, upon an equalization and thus cancellation of power, and this is the universal characteristic of sport and the basis of the conception of "fair play."[12] It would be foolish, of course, to assert that resources are always equal. One professional baseball team has financial resources that may not be available to another, and one bridge partnership may have better cards than its opponent. But such inequalities excite disapproval because they deny the nature of sport.[13] In the former case recruitment of talent—the player draft—proceeds in inverse order of the previous year's standings of the clubs, and tournament bridge is duplicate bridge so that all partnerships will play the same hands. When resources cannot be equalized, a game loses some of its savor, and sentiment supports the "underdog." We have here a most familiar, but nevertheless peculiar, situation—one in which power is so balanced as to be irrelevant. Sport may

[12] The game of poker is an exception. Here, unless there are betting limits, resources are not equalized among the contestants. And even with limits the player who can afford to lose the most has an advantage that represents power.

[13] About which, incidentally, a substantial sociological study has yet to be written. That none has appeared is surprising in view of the very great importance of sport in human life. Indeed, Honduras and El Salvador once went to war over the result of a soccer match.

be a moral equivalent for war, as William James wanted to believe, but it cannot unfortunately be a sociological equivalent. The situations are quite similar in many respects, but they are different in a crucial one. The difference between a conflict and a contest is that the former is a power phenomenon, and the latter is not.

11. Conclusion

In this chapter we have addressed our discussion to one of the most perplexing of sociological problems—the problem of power. We have taken a vague and ambiguous concept, a concept we all know but find difficult to define, and have attempted to sharpen the edges of its meaning. Among the propositions offered the following may serve as a summary: (1) power is a social phenomenon par excellence, the analysis of which is a particular responsibility of sociology; (2) it is useful and necessary to distinguish power from other phenomena such as prestige, influence, dominance, rights, force, and authority; (3) power is latent force, force is manifest power, and authority is institutionalized power; (4) power has its incidence in social opposition of some kind and, unlike authority, appears both in associations and in the interstices between them; (5) power is always potential and has its issue, in society, in either force or authority; (6) the sources of power can be found in a combination of numbers (especially majorities), social organization, and resources; and finally, *passim*, (7) power is a fundamental support of the social order on the one hand and a constant threat to that order on the other. Some of these propositions will doubtless encounter qualification and even dissent. We hope, however, that they will stimulate the sociological reflection of the reader.

We have now concluded our general survey of the subject of social organization. We have discovered certain constants in society, certain universal components of social structure—norms, statuses, groups, associations, institutions, authority, and power. These constitute the structure of all complex societies, the stability of which is sustained by supporting power and challenged by opposing power. No matter how great the cultural differences between a city on the Ganges and one on the Thames, one on the Tiber and one on the Hudson, the structure of the societies of which these cities are a part is the same. In all societies without exception, we find norms, statuses, groups, associations, institutions, authority, and power. Society itself has a structure, and these seven elements are the components of that structure.

In this section we have tried to present a sense of social structure, an appreciation of the nature of social organization, and an insight into the fundamental order that society exhibits. This is the first and most important task of a systematic sociological theory.

5

EVERYWHERE we look in society
we find people belonging
together with others in
groups. Some of these groups,
as we have seen, appear
through the accidents of
circumstance, because people
happen to be in the same place at the
same time or, separated in space,
because they share a similar or a
common interest. In the preceding
section we discussed the nature of
these groups, suggested a way of
classifying them, and
emphasized their position
with respect to the structure
of society. In this section
we want to leave this
relatively abstract level and
to turn our attention
instead to some of the
concrete groups that can be
found in a society.

A society is composed not of
an amorphous mass of individuals,
"windowless monads" in a swarm
of bodies. Nor does it exist as a
single entity, a monolith rigidly
molded and solidly integrated. It is made
up, rather, of knots and nodes,

SOCIAL DIFFERENTIATION

of clusters constantly changing—
in short, of *groups* of people in
ever-fluctuating relationships with
other people, some of whom are like and
some unlike themselves. It is in
reference to this diversity within society
that we use the phrase "social
differentiation." It is our task, therefore, in the
chapters that follow, to consider some of
the more important of these differentiations
in a complex society—men and women, the
family, city and suburb, class and
caste, color and creed, and finally,
associations and institutions. We shall see that
the profile of a society is exhibited in the
juxtaposition of its different groups.

ALE AND FEMALE created he them. The male, Adam, he created first, and then, as the story goes, he studied his product, noticed certain imperfections in it, and murmured to himself, "I think I can do better." Whereupon he created Eve. Whether Eve was "better" or not is a question on which both Adam and Eve doubtless had an opinion, and their descendants have been arguing it ever since. At least there is general agreement that Adam was created first and Eve second. Thus woman, made of a spare part, is God's second sex or possibly, as the philosopher Nietzsche once put it, God's second mistake. In any event we have two sexes—not one, not three—and this is one of the brute facts of the universe.

It is also, of course, one of the brute facts of society. The existence of two sexes, a biological differentiation, results in what is also one of the most important kinds of social differentiation, differentiation into two kinds of societal groups, men and women. In no society do the same norms apply with equal force to these two groups. In all societies there are different norms and different statuses for the two sexes. No society treats its men and its women exactly alike. In no society do they indulge in identical activities, share identical aspirations, or pursue identical goals in identical ways. In all societies they think differently, dress differently, and do different kinds of work.

One could argue, therefore, with perhaps only a slight exaggeration, that all societies have two cultures, a male culture and a female culture, and that these two cultures are quite different. More precisely perhaps, one might say that each society has at least three cultures—one male, one female, and one shared by the two sexes. In any event, it is certain that the biological fact of sexual differentiation has manifold social consequences, some of which we want to explore in this chapter.

1. The Dominant Sex

Certain movements of thought that appeared earlier in this century, including behaviorism, have tended to underemphasize differences in sex and to attribute them in any event to the influence of cultural, rather than biological factors. It has been contended, for example, that the dominance of the male is by no means a universal characteristic of human societies, that where it exists it is culturally induced, and that it is not based upon a biological advantage. It is argued in addition that male dominance, which is to be found in the societies with which most of us are familiar, is replaced by female dominance in certain other societies. It is even argued that in these latter societies it is women who initiate sexual behavior, who are the aggressors in courtship, and who make the marital decisions. In these societies, in contrast with others, prostitution is a male and not a female institution. Finally, it has been maintained that differences in the size and shape and strength of men and women are determined entirely by cultural conditioning and will disappear when equality of rights is achieved.

A writer who has adopted at least part of this theory is the well-known anthropologist Margaret Mead. In her studies in the South Seas, studies that have made her justly famous, she discovered within a single 100-mile area three tribes which seemed to her to illustrate the thesis that patterns of sexual behavior are not fixed in the physiological properties of the organism but are resultants rather of cultural factors. Of these three tribes she writes as follows:

> In one, both men and women act as we expect women to act—in a mild parental responsive way; in the second, both act as we expect men to act—in a

fierce initiating fashion; and in the third, the men act according to our stereotype for women—are catty, wear curls, and go shopping, while the women are energetic, managerial, unadorned partners.[1]

Miss Mead refers to the book from which this quotation is taken as her most misunderstood work. It nevertheless suggests that human nature is almost infinitely plastic and that the plasticity it exhibits extends even to the similarities and differences between the sexes. Sexual characteristics themselves, in this view, are highly variable and are molded by culture into a wide range of different forms. To writers of this school it is culture and not biology that will ultimately explain the distinctive thoughts and actions, the disparate passions and possessions of men and women as they live their separate lives in the same societies. Indeed, as Miss Mead says, her three tribes provided "a wealth of material on how completely a culture may impose, on one sex or both sexes, a pattern which is appropriate to only a segment of the human race."[2]

Other evidence, however, casts doubt upon the cogency of this conclusion. It may be that the social sciences themselves, with their emphasis upon the importance of culture, have exaggerated in some respects the manner in which sexual differences in society are matters of social achievement rather than of biological determination. In the early chapters of this present book, as the reader will recall, both geographic and biological factors were seen to be necessary but not usually sufficient for the explanation of social phenomena. Except for rare events and extraordinary circumstances, we concluded, we would be advised to seek our sociological understanding on the cultural level.

Without subduing the accents contained in those chapters, we want nevertheless to explore the possibility that biological factors may have more to do with the norms and statuses pertaining to sex than many writers have been willing to acknowledge. This is another way of saying that sexual differentiation in society may be more of a biological, and less of a cultural, phenomenon than has been supposed.

Our sex, perhaps, is the most important single thing about us. It has been suggested that if any of us were dropped by parachute into some hitherto forbidden country, to fall into the midst of an unknown tribe, the very first observation to be made about us would concern our sex. Our unwitting hosts, whatever their other reactions—whether friendly, hostile, or, less likely, indifferent—would see us first not as white or black, tall or

---

[1] "Preface," *Sex and Temperament in Three Primitive Societies*, Mentor Books, New American Library of World Literature, Inc., New York, 1950. Published originally by William Morrow and Company, Inc., New York, 1935. See also her *Male and Female*, William Morrow and Company, Inc., New York, 1949.
[2] "Preface," *Sex and Temperament.*

short, old or young, but as male or female. And we, in turn, would immediately distinguish our hosts from our hostesses. In such a situation, in short, the reactions on both sides would vary in a most significant way depending upon the perception of sex. And so it is for every situation we confront. If we are male, our society bends our conduct in one way; if we are female, in another.[3] In thousands of hospitals newborn male babies are wrapped in blue blankets and newborn females in pink blankets. Thus the culture begins immediately at birth to differentiate between the sexes. On the other hand, as a sociologist has wryly remarked, among the newborn of the same color no other kind of differentiation is possible. In any event, we want to ask what kinds of sexual differentiation are due to nature and what kinds to culture. We may begin with the sometimes surprising proposition that in several important respects it is men rather than women who are the weaker sex.

2. The Weaker Sex

Growth and Development

In the first paragraph of this chapter we observed that, in Biblical terms at least, there was general agreement that the male was created first and the female second. A New York psychiatrist, however, has reversed the creation story with respect to embryology. She argues that all human embryos are initially female and that without a suffusion of androgens, or male sex hormones, during the first five or six weeks, no males would develop.[4] Although the androgens are indeed required, they come from the fetal testes, and the inference that females are therefore prior to males, or even that humans are psychosexually neutral at birth, is a dubious one. Genetically, males and females are not sexually undifferentiated. Sex is determined at the moment of conception by the distribution of X and Y chromosomes; that is, the fertilized egg that is to become female has two X chromosomes and the one that is to become male has an X and a Y chromosome, the Y much smaller than the X.[5]

In any event, tossing the pink and blue blankets aside, maturation is both a biological and a cultural process; in fact, it is possible to think of it as

[3] For a comprehensive discussion of this subject, see Harriet Holter, *Sex Roles and Social Structure*, Universitetsforlaget, Oslo, 1970.
[4] Mary Jane Sherfey, *The Nature and Evolution of Female Sexuality*, Random House, New York, 1972.
[5] See David A. Hamburg and Donald T. Lunde, "Sex Hormones in the Development of Sex Differences in Human Behavior," in Eleanor E. Maccoby (ed.), *The Developemnt of Sex Differences*, Stanford University Press, Stanford, Calif., 1966, pp. 1–24.

two processes, which may or may not be well coordinated and which, in some respects at least, may be independent of each other. Thus, the age at which a boy becomes a man, and a girl a woman, may vary from one society to another in independence of similar rates of physiological change. Whether either sex is old enough to vote at the age of eighteen is a question that cannot be answered by a textbook of physiology. Whether young people are old enough to marry at that age is a question to which physiology and sociology might give contradictory answers. We have previously remarked that a prize fighter may be old at thirty and a philosopher young at forty-five. Age, then, is a matter of cultural—and not merely chronological—definition. But certain biological limitations may not be transcended and some of these have social consequences. Among them is the fact that the process of physiological maturation proceeds at a different pace in males and females.

Although the evidence is not altogether conclusive, several studies have indicated that the gestation period for boy babies averages from five to nine days longer than for girl babies. At birth the latter are already better developed than the former. Their bones are stronger, their reflexes better coordinated, their skulls literally in better shape. All babies are born with a soft spot on top of the head where the bones are not yet joined and through which one can feel the pulsations of the heart. This spot, called the *fontanelle*, facilitates the difficult passage of the head in parturition, and it usually closes altogether shortly after birth. The point is, however, that it usually closes earlier in girls and somewhat later in boys. The bones and muscles of little girls in general develop their strength earlier. Thus, little girls learn earlier than boys how to button and unbutton their clothing and how to turn doorknobs and faucets. Female superiority in wrist movement, fine finger movement, and manual dexterity continues throughout childhood. In addition, girls cut their teeth earlier, on the average, than boys and begin also to talk a little earlier.

The differences in rate of growth increase throughout childhood, and at puberty, when the primary and secondary sex characteristics assume their adult form and function, the discrepancies in maturation amount to an average of two years; that is, puberty occurs in girls at an average age of twelve, in boys at an average age of fourteen. In later adolescence, although the evidence is less clear here, the differences seem to continue, so that girls are physically mature by about the age of eighteen, two to three years ahead of their male contemporaries. The same disparity exists between the respective ages at which girls and boys are considered intellectually and emotionally mature. In this differential process we may have the clue to the cultural fact that in our society at least men tend to marry women younger than themselves. Indeed, the average age of bridegrooms tends to be two or three years older than that of brides, and the exceptional cases in which the bride is older tend to cause anxiety and comment in the society.

Thus, the definition of maturity is almost certainly a cultural definition, but maturation is with comparable certainty a biological process. Of the two the latter would seem to be virtually unchangeable, the former more variable.

If this is indeed the case it introduces certain problems into society. We may, for example, raise the question whether coeducation, which is now almost universal in contemporary American culture, is in fact superior to separate education for the sexes. The question may have an especial point in view of the fact that a young man and a young woman of the same age in the same classroom may be quite far apart with respect to all of the physiological and most of the emotional indices of maturity. This question we shall not attempt to answer here. We suggest only that an answer to it will be the more comprehensive as it takes into consideration both the biological and the cultural variables involved, and the more satisfactory as it conforms to whatever facts are the more unchanging and intransigent.[6]

Morbidity and Mortality

If doubt remains that men are the weaker sex, let us attend to the statistics of disease and death. Here it is a fact, however one explains it, that at every age of life more males than females contract diseases and die. This is a difference between the sexes that becomes apparent even before birth and that continues to advanced ages. The statistics show that death, though it may be no respecter of persons, is clearly a respecter of sexes, and that the female is more clearly favored at every age of life—except, of course, the very latest when, because all women too are mortal, the differential disappears.

We shall not take the space here to trace the morbidity statistics for every disease; we note only that, with the exception of certain gynecological difficulties and certain other afflictions like St. Vitus's dance and whooping cough, disease attacks more males than females. The mortality statistics are even more striking, as shown by changing sex ratios throughout life. In the first place the ratio of male births to female births is about 105.5 to 100, giving males a decided numerical advantage at the beginning. No one knows, of course, how many males are conceived in proportion to

---

[6] Lionel Tiger raises the same question. See his *Men in Groups*, Random House, New York, 1969, pp. 200–204. So also did Amram Scheinfeld more than a generation ago, in *Women and Men*, Harcourt, Brace & World, Inc., New York, 1944.

females but the probability is that the ratio may be as high as 120 or 130 to 100. The evidence consists of the higher prenatal mortality rate among males. In other words, more male embryos fail to survive the gestation period and more male embryos are aborted. Since there is no known embryological reason why the prenatal environment should be more dangerous for males than for females, the discrepancy can be explained only by the greater weakness of the male.

If the sex ratio at birth, as just mentioned, is 105.5 males to 100 females, at the end of the first year of life it has dropped further to 104.5 to 100. Consider what this means. It means that a great many more male babies die than female babies and that the first year of life is especially hazardous for the male. Male neonates (that is, newborn infants) are more susceptible to a greater variety of diseases than are female neonates, and their greater mortality rate is reflected in the statistics. Even more curious, perhaps, is the fact that not only the disease but also the accident rate is higher for male babies than for females. Since it is difficult to argue that parents take greater care of female babies than of males, or take greater precautions for their safety, the conclusion again appears inescapable that males are weaker than females.

In complex modern societies at least, males continue to decrease in relative numbers throughout all the later ages of life. At puberty they enjoy only a 2 per cent advantage over females, in contrast to the $5^1/2$ per cent at birth, and at maturity the ratio is about equal. At later ages females make rapid proportionate gains and pull ahead of males in absolute numbers. In the early seventies females outnumber males by 6 per cent, after seventy-five by 18 per cent, and after ninety by 50 per cent. As a corollary to the figures it may be noted that widows far outnumber widowers in the American population. In any event, the disparities in the older age groups, unlike those discussed in the preceding paragraph, can be attributed to a variety of causes, some cultural and some biological. One could argue, for example, that the pressures of a competitive society afflict men to a much greater degree than women and take a correspondingly higher toll.

It is possible to conceive of a society in which cultural arrangements were such that competition disappeared. Would the differential death rate continue in such a society? No one knows. Comparable statistics for other societies might shed some light on this question, but these are not available. It is possible, in short, that the situation in our own society is due wholly to the operation of sociocultural factors associated particularly with its economic structure. But it is not very probable. It would seem, on the contrary, that some biological inequality exists between the sexes, in the chromosomes themselves, and that no matter what the cultural arrangements may be, males are more susceptible than females to disease and early death.[7]

"The Mysterious Mortality Seesaw"

The situation we have just described is one that, as we have indicated, can be explained by an appeal to both biological and cultural factors; that is, although the evidence for biological inequality would seem to be strong, it is at least possible to argue that the increasing disparities in the sex ratio throughout life are attributable to the peculiar kind of culture characterizing our society. It is an argument that cannot be wholly or satisfactorily refuted in the absence of comparable statistics from other societies. There is another kind of evidence that males are the weaker sex, however, which is even more difficult to explain by recourse to culture. Mr. Scheinfeld calls it the mysterious mortality seesaw.

It happens that in certain countries of the world, Chile for example, standards of sanitation, hygiene, and medical care are relatively low. In these countries the infant mortality rate, as might be expected, is relatively high. In countries on the other end of the scale, New Zealand for example, standards are high and the infant mortality rate is relatively low. So far the relationship is precisely what we should expect.

When we examine the proportion of male deaths to female deaths in both of these situations, however, we confront a surprising fact. In countries where the infant mortality rate is high, about as many male babies die as female babies. In countries where the infant mortality rate is low, on the other hand, a great many more male babies die than female babies. In other words, in countries where many babies die, they die in roughly equal ratios with respect to sex, with males only slightly disadvantaged. In countries where few babies die, male deaths are much more frequent than female. As standards of sanitation, hygiene, and medical practice improve, both sexes gain in that there are fewer deaths, but the females exhibit disproportionate gains.

If one takes a single country, such as the United States, the situation is the same. In our own country the infant mortality rate has been decreasing steadily and satisfactorily during most of the years of the present century, and while this has been happening the excess of male deaths over female deaths has continued to increase. In these situations cultural factors are indeed operating—in the reduction of the infant mortality rate—but they are operating in one respect to bring about an inexplicable result. One can only conclude in the absence of plausible alternatives that some unknown

---

[7] For additional discussion of sex differences in susceptibility to disease, see Hamburg and Lunde, *op. cit.*, pp. 19–20.

biological factor is at work. In any event we have here additional evidence that the male is weaker than the female.

Life Expectancy

One of the most encouraging facts about the twentieth century, in the realm of vital statistics, is the very substantial gains made in life expectancy. People living today in countries like our own have a much greater chance of reaching old age than did people living in any previous period of history. Since the increase in life expectancy is so spectacular, it is easily susceptible to misinterpretation, and we need therefore to introduce the subject with a few precautionary remarks.

The increase in life expectancy does not mean, as many erroneously assume, that the life span of the species has increased in any substantial way in recent decades or that the Biblical reference to three score years and ten is now outmoded. It is the life expectancy that has increased, not the life span. People are not now living to greater ages than they did, say, in the Roman Empire, or in any other period of history, but more of them are living out the span. Most of the increase in life expectancy is due to the decrease in infant mortality, but medical science is also keeping more people alive at every age—except the last, the age at which they die. In other words, more of us than ever before can expect to live to the age of seventy-five, but the life span of the species has not increased.

What now is the situation concerning life expectancy for the two sexes? In the United States, at least, we find a startling fact. Consider the following figures:

Life Expectancy at Birth*

Year	Males	Females	Difference
1900	48	51	3 years
1972	67	74	7 years

*These figures are rounded off and apply only to whites. SOURCES: *Statistical Bulletin of the Metropolitan Life Insurance Company*, vol. 42, August, 1961, pp. 6–8, and World Health Organization, as reported in *The New York Times*, July 6, 1972, p. 16. As a matter of fact, in the ten-year period from 1958 to 1968, life expectancy at birth for males dropped from 66.7 years to 66.6 years and for females life expectancy rose from 73 years to 74.1 years.

As these statistics dramatically indicate, life expectancy has increased for white Americans and for both sexes, but it has increased proportionately more for the female than for the male. Here, again, it is possible to imagine cultural factors that may account for the disparity, but such imagination now has to sustain a bit of strain. It is much more likely that some biological factor is responsible and that in the phenomenon of life expectancy we have additional evidence that the male is the weaker sex.

3. The Stronger Sex

In one sphere, however, the superiority of the male is not in serious question. This is the sphere of muscular strength. The male is physically stronger than the female; only he, for example, can perpetrate the crime of rape—or open the lid on a pickle jar. Females have to accomplish by subtler means what males can accomplish by a display of physical force. The disparity here is obvious and indeed universal in the animal kingdom. It becomes especially noticeable in the field of athletics. There are few athletic activities in which women excel men. Whatever improvements may have been noted in the talents of feminine baseball players, for example, it is impossible to imagine a team of women in the major leagues or a woman on a major-league team. As a matter of fact, the elbow joint of the female has a different angle in relation to the trunk than that of the male, and it is therefore anatomically impossible for the female to duplicate the throwing pattern of the male.

One might suppose that the situation would be altered in cases where skill takes precedence over strength. But even in these activities, where strength is involved at all, the superiority remains on the masculine side. Consider tennis. Here is an activity in which timing and dexterity might seem to count for more than muscle. It is true that the national singles woman champion can beat all but a small number of men who play tennis. But she is no match for the national singles man champion. Whereas some women, in other words, may be better than the majority of men in a given sport, they are rarely as good as the best men in that sport.

With respect to track and field and swimming pool the disparities are huge. No one would expect a woman to put the shot or to throw the javelin the same distances as men, and the statistics clearly indicate the difference in the records. No woman has vaulted 17 feet or run a mile in four minutes. The woman who holds the world record for the 100-meter dash or the 100-meter backstroke could not qualify for Olympic competition if the sexes were not separated. If men are undeniably the weaker sex in the respects treated above, they are just as undeniably the stronger when it is muscles that are being compared. If no amount of training, begun no matter how early, can make the female equal to the male in track and field and pool, then the explanation of such disparities as exist must be biological rather than cultural.

More and more women, of course, are competing in sports formerly reserved for men. Thus, in the United States we have women jockeys, racing-car drivers, airplane stunt pilots, parachutists, rifle shooters, and cross-country runners. In the Boston Marathon of 1972 the first woman to finish came out ahead of 200 men, and in the same year a woman sharpshooter won the intercollegiate marksmanship title. We see women rowing boats in college regattas, an all-girl little league in Detroit, a women's professional football league with teams in Detroit, Cleveland, Pittsburgh, and New York, and women skaters and skiers and swimmers and hockey players indulging in strenuous competition among themselves. Similarly, women hold world records in saltwater and freshwater fishing (for catching largest striped marlin and silver salmon, for example), and women have served as coxswains on varsity crews. It remains true, however, that wherever strength is a factor, all comparisons melt in favor of the male.

4. Sex and Intelligence

Here we walk on dangerous ground. Who would want to claim, and who concede, that one sex is more intelligent than the other? On this question the psychologists in general and the intelligence testers in particular have exhibited a curious but possibly understandable reticence. Here all the tests are inconclusive, and no one obviously wants to say more than he can support. One reason the tests are inconclusive is that they have been constructed to meet a bisexual need. In order that they may be administered to both boys and girls in the elementary schools, questions on which the sexes tend consistently to make different scores are usually omitted. It appears, however, that in some respects boys are superior to girls—in mathematical or mechanical reasoning, in speed and coordination of motor activities—and in other respects girls are superior to boys—in color perception, manual dexterity, memory, and verbal facility. Some writers have claimed that although both sexes range themselves in the same fashion on the normal probability curve, the curve is somewhat flatter for boys than for girls, with the result that the average intelligence of girls is higher and that there are more boys in proportion at the extremities. Thus, it is contended that there is a point on the curve, where the intelligence quotient reaches the level of genius, to the right of which there are many more boys than girls and, correspondingly, a point on the other end of the curve, where the intelligence quotient sinks to the level of idiot, to the left of which there are also many more boys than girls.

This, so far, is about all that can be said about the intelligence of the two sexes. Other kinds of tests, such as college-entrance examinations, college boards, regents examinations, and the like are almost useless for the purpose of comparing intelligence because, in the first place, they test knowledge rather than intelligence and, in the second, they are administered at a time when the culture has already encouraged boys to apply themselves to one set of problems and girls to an entirely different set. Thus, it is no surprise to learn that on most of these tests boys excel in mathematics and physics and girls in English composition. Since it is impossible in the first instance to devise a culture-free intelligence test— that is, one which measures intelligence independently of cultural influences—it is impossible in the second to discover from the tests we have whether boys are more or less intelligent than girls. In other words, we can arrive at no valid generalization concerning the differential intelligence of the two sexes, nor even assert that there is a difference.[8] All we can do is to agree with Dr. Johnson who, when asked which was more intelligent, man or woman, replied, "Which man and which woman?"

5. Achievement and Genius

Genius, as measured by actual achievement, is a rare thing in history. It seems impossible to doubt that it is even rarer among females than among males. Men of genuine distinction appear in positive profusion in comparison with women of distinction. Arguments contending for the superiority of men in this respect take some such form as the following:

If we survey the course of Western civilization, we find few and sometimes no women in recognized fields of endeavor. Where, for example, is there a woman soldier comparable to an Alexander, a Caesar, a Napoleon; a woman statesman comparable to a Washington, a Jefferson, or a Lincoln; a woman diplomat comparable to Metternich or a Talleyrand? In these fields, of course, the questions answer themselves. War and politics and diplomacy have not been feminine activities, and it is useless to expect female achievement in fields in which women have not participated. This answer, however, has only a superficial cogency. One might go on from there and ask why women have not participated, why they have tolerated, in effect, their own exclusion.

Or where again, turning to other fields, is the woman philosopher comparable to a Plato, an Aristotle, a Spinoza, or a Kant? The texts in the history of philosophy contain few feminine names. Where is the female physicist who can compare with Archimedes or Newton or Einstein? Have women made significant contributions to mathematics, astronomy, chemistry, and biology? Yes, of course, but again there is little profit in the comparison. And where are their contributions to medicine? Women

---

[8] For a comprehensive survey of the literature, see the annotated bibliography compiled by Roberta M. Oetzel in Eleanor E. Maccoby (ed.), *op. cit.*, pp. 223–321. See especially Maccoby's own chapter, "Sex Differences in Intellectual Functioning," pp. 25–55.

doctors we have had, but few of them famous, few distinguished, none really eminent in the history of the profession. That few women have achieved brilliant success in science is perhaps understandable, but how can we explain a similar failure in medicine and surgery? Women are gifted with manual dexterity, as we have seen, and they are frequently credited with compassionate interest in the welfare of others. Why then have they not become great physicians and surgeons?

Possibly some fields are more congenial to women than these. But when we consider the arts, the situation remains the same. In the history of music there is no woman composer of the rank of Beethoven or Bach or Brahms or Wagner. Indeed, as in the case of philosophy, it is difficult to name a woman composer. Or call the roll of the great painters. Where is the woman whom one can place with a Rembrandt, a Michelangelo, a Raphael, a Titian, a Leonardo? And speaking of Leonardo, where is the universal feminine genius with accomplishments such as his? Rosa Bonheur painted a picture entitled *The Horse Fair*, which hangs in the Metropolitan Museum of Art in New York, but who would seriously take a census of paintings of men and women in that museum? The history of the plastic arts is similar; from Praxiteles to Rodin few feminine names appear. The great architects, in all ages and societies, have been men. One does not somehow expect women to build bridges, but why have they not written symphonies and painted pictures? In most periods of our history music and art were open to the exercise of feminine talent.

Let us look at literature. Outstanding things have been accomplished by women in poetry, the novel, the short story, and the drama, and their numbers are increasing. But no woman has the rank of the Greek dramatists, or of Dante, Milton, Shakespeare, and Goethe. There are few genuinely distinguished feminine historians. There have been women writers in all of the centuries of Western civilization, and at no time did literary activity seriously violate the norms for women, and yet the differential results are apparent.

In certain other fields, too, feminine representation is small or nonexistent. One of them is jurisprudence. Another is chess. Of some ninety-eight grandmasters in the world, those "suzerains of the sixty-four squares," none is a woman.[9] Still another is invention. An examination of the patent office files would indicate that the overwhelming majority of

---

[9] For an enlightening discussion of this subject, see Collene Taylor Sen, "Women and Chess," *Ms.*, December, 1972, pp. 88–91, 107. Ms. Sen encourages women players to remember that the queen is the most powerful piece on the board and occupies a position to which every pawn aspires.

inventors have been men. As another example, the comic strips in our newspapers are almost universally masculine products, and few people have ever seen a political cartoon drawn by a woman. We may conclude with the observation that men have excelled even in some of the activities we ordinarily associate with women. Although superior cookbooks are frequently written by women, cooking is a masculine profession, the cooks in the world's leading restaurants and hotels are men, and the great culinary artists—those who, like Escoffier and Savarin and Oscar of the Waldorf, have reached the pinnacle—have been men.

In most fields of human endeavor, in fact, men, in the judgment of both sexes, have accomplished more than women. In many fields, some of them surprising, women have no representation. In others they participate, but their level of achievement, again by mutual judgment, is inferior to that of men. As long as a century ago the gentle Charles Darwin wrote in his *Descent of Man,* "If two lists were made of the most eminent men and women in poetry, painting, sculpture, music (inclusive both of composition and performance), history, science, and philosophy, with half-a-dozen names under each subject, the two lists would not bear comparison."[10] The facts, in short, are not in question, either in Darwin's day or ours. What is the explanation?

One explanation, somewhat psychoanalytic in character, would attribute the superior creative achievements of the male to a kind of compensation, or overcompensation, for his inability to create something else, namely a human life. Thus, Dr. Karen Horney asks, "Is not the tremendous strength in men of the impulse to creative work in every field precisely due to their feeling of playing a relatively small part in the creation of living beings?"[11] This suggestion is seconded by Ashley Montagu, who interprets the male's drive to achievement, in part at least, to "an unconsciously motivated attempt to compensate for the lack of biological creativity," and who says further, "I think it probable that men will continue to show a higher frequency of achievement, *not* because they are naturally superior, but because they are overcompensating for a natural inferiority—the inferiority of not being able to have babies."[12] In answer to

[10] Modern Library Edition, p. 873.

[11] "The Flight from Womanhood: The Masculinity-Complex in Women," *International Journal of Psychoanalysis,* vol. 7, October, 1926, p. 330. Quoted by Scheinfeld, *op. cit.,* p. 322.

[12] Ashley Montagu, *The Natural Superiority of Women,* The Macmillan Company, New York, 1953, pp. 50–51. This author says that the use by men of such language as "to conceive an idea," "to give birth to an idea," "brain child," "to be pregnant with ideas," and other obstetrical expressions may be "an unconscious desire to imitate the biological creativity of the female."

this we need only remind those who favor this view that men too contribute to the process of procreation and that their contribution is not altogether a negligible one. Biological engineering, of course, may render it unnecessary sometime in the future.

A more reasonable explanation comes from Mirra Komarovsky, a woman and a sociologist. Miss Komarovsky first concedes that the situation appears to be as we have described it in these pages and then goes on to suggest a factor possibly associated with it:

> Where are the women geniuses? When it comes to truly great cultural innovations, the record of women is unimpressive. While for some this slender yield constitutes prima facie evidence of women's limited capacity for creative achievement, the inference is by no means conclusive. We are reminded that many male geniuses were not deterred by poverty, discouragement, and even persecution and that, consequently, women who had it in them would have also surmounted environmental handicaps. But the environment that counts is not merely the external one of favorable laws and opportunities. It is the inner environment, the self-image and the level of aspirations, which is at the root of motivation. This self-image, subtly molded by society, has been, and still is, inimical to the full development of whatever creativity women may possess.[13]

Miss Komarovsky goes on to suggest that the fierce concentration essential to creativity cannot thrive on "self-doubt" and that, whatever the external constraints or handicaps imposed by society, the internal skepticism suffices to explain why women have not attained the highest reaches of accomplishment. "The surprising thing is not the absence of women geniuses but the great number of highly competent women in the arts and in professions"[14]—a number, incidentally, that includes herself.

The self-image explanation receives support from studies conducted long after Miss Komarovsky's. Matina Horner, for example, concluded after an inquiry into the attitudes of undergraduate women at the University of Michigan that they confronted a dilemma it was impossible to solve:

> . . . consciously or unconsciously the girl equates intellectual achievement with loss of femininity. A bright woman is caught in a double bind. In testing and other achievement-oriented situations she worries not only about failure, but also about success. If she fails, she is not living up to her own standards of performance; if she succeeds she is not living up to societal expectations about

---

[13] *Women in the Modern World*, Little, Brown and Company, Boston, 1953, pp. 29–30.
[14] *Ibid.*, p. 30.

the female role. Men in our society do not experience this kind of ambivalence, because they are not only permitted but actively encouraged to do
well.[15]

To use our own concepts, society ascribes to women statuses to which
contradictory norms are attached, and the resulting conflict may preclude
the kind of creativity that men, who experience no such conflict, are able to
exhibit. It is difficult to accomplish what society does not encourage. If the
norms are such that women are prevented from launching certain kinds of
careers, or discouraged in the pursuit of them, then it is easy to understand
an absence of participation. And even when the norms are relaxed, the
basic and pervasive ideologies may still be inimical. In spite of increasing
numbers of women in the labor force of modern industrial societies, the
feeling persists that woman's place is in the home. If the Women's
Liberation Movement can change these norms and these ideologies, it will
have accomplished one of its major goals.

6. The Second Sex

There is a plethora of books about women. Most of them enjoy a brief hour
of discussion and debate and then are read no more. One of the more
durable, however, was written by the French philosopher and novelist
Simone de Beauvoir, and entitled *The Second Sex*.[16] The authors of most of
these books complain about sexual discrimination. Mlle de Beauvoir has a
more fundamental complaint. Her book is devoted to the single thesis that
it is degrading to be a woman. In all societies it is woman who has been
subject and slave; man who has been ruler and master. Woman is vassal,
receptacle, utensil. She is conquered, subdued, vanquished, in sexual
encounter as in life. Man takes, woman gives; man acts, woman waits.
("Motionless, the egg waits: in contrast the sperm—free, slender, agile—

[15] Matina Horner, "Fail: Bright Women," *Psychology Today*, November, 1969, pp. 36–37.
Reprinted in Judith Hole and Ellen Levine, *Rebirth of Feminism*, Quadrangle Books, New York,
1971. This may be another reason for questioning the merits of coeducation. As Margaret
Mead writes in her autobiography, "As long as I was in high school, the greater maturity of
adolescent girls had not struck me. But in the setting of this coeducational college [DePauw] it
became perfectly clear both that bright girls could do better than bright boys. and that they
would suffer for it.

   "This made me feel that coeducation was thoroughly unattractive. I neither wanted to do
bad work in order to make myself attractive to boys nor did I want them to dislike me for doing
good work. It seemed to me that it would be much simpler to go to a girl's college where one
could work as hard as one pleased." *Blackberry Winter*, William Morrow & Company, Inc.,
New York, 1972, pp. 99–100.
[16] Translated by H. M. Parshley, Alfred A. Knopf, Inc., New York, 1953.

typifies the impatience and the restlessness of existence.") Man is always the One; woman the Other. The traveler is the One when he is at home, the Other when he is abroad. Woman is always, in this sense, abroad and never at home, always destined to wander in the world of men and never in a world of her own. There is no genuine duality in the two sexes. Woman is always the Other, never the One; she is condemned to an eternal alterity.

"Blessed be God . . . that He did not make me a woman." So runs the Hebrew prayer which, in its version for women, says "Blessed be the Lord who created me according to His will." Among the blessings for which Plato thanked the gods was first that he had been born free and not a slave and second that he was a man and not a woman. Aristotle maintained that "the female is a female by virtue of a certain lack of qualities," and attributed to her a "natural defectiveness." Indeed, for this greatest of Greek philosophers woman was a mere receptacle, the passive principle; the efficient cause of a child was its father, who supplied the active principle. The Roman law limited the rights of women on the ground of "the imbecility, the instability of the sex." The Christian attitude toward women was no better; in fact, by any comparative standard it was worse. Mlle de Beauvoir remarks with bitterness that "doubtless there is in the Gospel a breath of charity that extends to women as to lepers," and then goes on to quote some of the more infamous sayings of the early church fathers on the subject.

St. Paul, for example, drawing his views from both Testaments, concluded that "the man is not of the woman; but the woman of the man. Neither was the man created for the woman; but the woman for the man." And again: "For the husband is the head of the wife, even as Christ is the head of the church . . . Therefore as the church is subject unto Christ, so let the wives be to their own husbands in everything." The author neglects to quote perhaps the most famous passage of all, the passage in the Epistle to the Corinthians in which St. Paul's contempt for the flesh could hardly be more clear: "It is good for a man not to touch a woman. Nevertheless, to avoid fornication, let every man have his own wife, and let every woman have her own husband . . . I say therefore to the unmarried and widows, It is good for them if they abide even as I. But if they cannot contain, let them marry: for it is better to marry than to burn." Paul's sentiments were echoed again and again, by John Chrysostom, for example, who asserted that "among all savage beasts none is found so harmful as woman," and by Tertullian, who referred to her as "the devil's doorway." For St. Thomas Aquinas woman was "an imperfect man" and "an incidental being." Indeed, both the Christian and the Jewish views of women in general are exceedingly dim. The distrust of sex in the former in particular is so great that, as Mlle de Beauvoir sagaciously observes, a religion that does not hesitate to condemn its god to an ignominious death protects him neverthe-less from a carnal origin.

It would be idle to extend these observations except to say that they appear in similar form in nonliterate and non-Western societies as well. The Chippewa Indian chief says that women are created for work. "One of them can draw or carry as much as two men" and in addition they "pitch our tents, make our clothes, mend them, and keep us warm at night." According to Buddhist teaching women are a sinful lot. Their only function is to tempt men and the only way they can expiate this sin is to serve them. In Islamic theology women are regarded as the principal source of evil in the world. And in the Norse sagas women are witches and mischief-makers, who render swords unfit for battle. From the earliest nomads to the most recent suburbanites, in short, women have been regarded as inferior beings. They have been consigned to subordinate statuses, and deprived of the equal application of the norms.

Many explanations have been offered for the almost universal preva-lence of this state of affairs. One contributing factor, no doubt, is the male identification of women with sex and of sex, in turn, with sin. In the dualism between the spirit and the flesh we tend, like Paul, to contemn the flesh. Women become the incarnation of sex, and sex serves not to help us transcend ourselves but only to perpetuate our species. Woman is the temptress, the seductress, the sinner; it is Eve who bade man eat the apple and it is she, in consequence, who is the author of his misfortunes. A society in which sex is sinful, an ideology that has deep roots in our own society, is one in which women are likely to be subjugated. Or so at least is one explanation.

Mlle de Beauvoir prefers another. The exclusion of women from warfare seems to her to have something to do with the situation: "For it is not in giving life but in risking life that man is raised above the animal; that is why superiority has been accorded in humanity not to the sex that brings forth but to that which kills." In the female, therefore, life serves no purpose but repetition; it is the male in whom life exists. Man controls the instant; woman surrenders to it. This, at least, is Mlle de Beauvoir's conclusion.

Men have made the mores, they have created the religions and philosophies of the world, they occupy the center of the great stage. Women, on the contrary, Mlle de Beauvoir goes on to note, hover dimly in the wings; they are marginal people destined forever to remain on the fringes of history. Whether as nymph, dryad, siren, undine, fairy, sorcer-ess, sibyl, prophetess, vampire, or witch, woman is a dangerous predator. Ashtar, Astarte, and Cybele were cruel, capricious, and powerful, but the mother of God in Christianity kneels before him and accepts her inferiority. Thus the cult of the Virgin is the supreme masculine victory. And yet, the notion that women are mysterious—and consequently dangerous—is the greatest myth of all. It is a mystery that conceals nothing. There is no such thing as a masculine mystery; men are not mysterious—and for a simple reason. Only slaves, not masters, are ever mysterious, and this kind of mystery therefore is only a defense, itself deficient, against inferiority.

However justified her bitterness may be, Mlle de Beauvoir's arguments may lose some of their cogency with the turn of contemporary events. There has never been equality between the sexes, and there is no equality now, but discrimination on the ground of sex receives less and less support in the folkways, mores, and laws of the more civilized societies. The story of the late twentieth century, at least, is one of the constant narrowing of the gap between the privileges of the sexes. A double standard, unfortunately, continues to exist, but the two standards are now closer together than in earlier periods of history. In the nineteenth century, for example, women could not vote, and they relinquished all control of their own property when they entered the marriage relationship. In France a woman was guilty of adultery no matter where it was committed; a man was guilty only if it occurred in the house he shared with his wife. In New York State a wife seeking divorce could be denied alimony if she was known to have committed a single act of adultery, even though it was similarly known that her husband had been keeping a mistress for many years. The norms change and discrimination recedes. In the seventies of this century, in fact, with the rise of "affirmative action programs" and sexual quota systems, females often find themselves in a favorable position with respect to many elections and appointments, and we begin to see the phenomenon of reverse discrimination.

7. Women's Liberation

A woman problem nevertheless remains. This in itself is a curious expression when it is recognized that we never similarly speak of a man problem. Books, like some of those we have utilized in this chapter, are written about women. There are few books on the subject of man as a sex. Indeed, Simone de Beauvoir herself is uncomfortably conscious of this fact and finds it necessary to say so in her introduction. If there is a woman problem, it exists because biology places certain limitations upon cultural aspirations. To reconcile two careers—one based upon reproductive capacity and the other upon cultural creativity—is the problem for which society has so far found no satisfactory solution. Women and men alike, as we have seen, occupy many different statuses, but for women the norms attached to these statuses pull them more frequently in two different directions and leave them in conflict, caught between contradictory demands. A woman can never forget her sex. As Margaret Mead has written:

A woman's life is punctuated by a series of specific events: the beginning of physical maturity at menarche, the end of virginity, pregnancy and birth, and, finally, the menopause, when her productive period as a woman is definitely over, however zestful she may still be as an individual. Each of these events—because once passed they can never be retraced—is momentous for a woman, whereas a man's ability to command an army or discover a new drug is less tied to the way his body functions sexually. So we can say—at least as far as human beings have thus far developed during the course of civilization—that sex in its whole meaning, from courtship through parenthood, means more to women than it does to men, although single sexual acts may have more urgency for men than for women.[17]

Each of these momentous events, as Miss Mead calls them, punctuates the life of a woman, reminds her that she is a female, and interferes with the single-minded dedication that a man can own and exercise in his career. As Lord Byron, in a more romantic vein, expressed it:

Man's love is of man's life a thing apart;
'Tis woman's whole existence.

The poet's sentiment, however, would be excoriated by the Women's Liberation Movement, a social force that has played so prominent a role in the nineteen-sixties and seventies in the United States. It is a story of anguished and scornful protest against the oppression of women by men, a protest that encompasses every aspect of life and attempts to erase every classification based on sex. The leaders of the movement insist that the only difference between men and women is that the former cannot serve as human incubators or as wet nurses and the latter cannot serve as sperm donors. All other differentiations are spurious, artificial, and destructive of the dignity of women. Unfortunately, an entire book would be required to discuss this subject, but a few observations may be in order.[18]

Let us consider the following indictments:

The history of mankind is a history of repeated injuries and usurpations on the part of man toward women, having in direct object the establishment of an absolute tyranny over her. To prove this, let facts be submitted to a candid world.

---

[17] "Introduction," in A. M. Krich (ed.), *Women*, Dell Publishing, Inc., New York, 1953, p. 12.
[18] An excellent book is available. See Judith Hole and Ellen Levine, *op. cit.* The movement, incidentally, is not a unified association. It includes many different groups, with different degrees of organization, and with different ideologies ranging from moderate to radical.

He has compelled her to submit to laws, in the formation of which she had no voice.

He has withheld from her rights which are given to the most ignorant and degraded men.

He has made her, if married, in the eye of the law, civilly dead.

In the covenant of marriage, she is compelled to promise obedience to her husband, he becoming, to all intents and purposes, her master.

He has monopolized nearly all the profitable employments, and from those she is permitted to follow, she receives but a scanty remuneration. He closes against her all the avenues to wealth and distinction which he considers most honorable to himself.

He has created a false public sentiment by giving to the world a different code of morals for men and women, by which moral delinquencies which exclude women from society, are not only tolerated, but deemed of little account in man.

He has endeavored, in every way that he could, to destroy her confidence in her own powers, to lessen her self-respect, and to make her willing to lead a dependent and abject life.

These words were written not in the 1970s but in 1848. They are taken, highly abbreviated, from a Declaration of Sentiments approved by a convention of some three hundred women which met at Seneca Falls, New York, on July 19 and 20 of that year.[19] A number of changes have occurred since then. The Nineteenth Amendment to the Constitution, passed in 1920, gave women the vote; more recent statutes have erased blatant forms of discrimination in both public and private employment; and, after prolonged debate, an Equal Rights Amendment has been passed by the Congress of the United States.

There is little doubt, however, that women continue to suffer discrimination in Western societies and that the bold and brave aspirations of the Seneca pronouncements have not been satisfied. Inequalities persist. In 1955, for example, the median wage of working women in the United States was nearly 64 per cent of that of working men. By 1970 the figure had dropped to 59.4 per cent.[20] Women encounter serious obstacles in their efforts to enter many occupations and professions; they fail to survive the race for promotion in business, advertising, the arts, and higher education; and they are members, in effect, of a disprivileged majority. If we may be permitted an ethical judgment, discrimination on the grounds of sex is intolerable, as is discrimination on the grounds of any other adventitious

[19] The Declaration of Sentiments and accompanying Resolutions are reprinted in full in Hole and Levine, pp. 431–435.
[20] According to a study by the Department of Labor as reported in *The New York Times* of February 11, 1972.

characteristic, and the movement deserves much credit for the force with which it has brought discrimination to public attention.

Curiously enough, the charge of sexism or of male chauvinism, leveled by women liberationists against men, sometimes applies also to women. That is, women themselves are often prejudiced against women and resent their successes in the world outside the home. Few women feel comfortable working for a woman "boss" and do not hesitate to say so on questionnaires. Few people of either sex prefer female doctors to male doctors. And most parents-to-be both hope that their firstborn child will be a boy. Female prejudice against females is a phenomenon that has attracted insufficient attention. In one study a psychologist gave college women a set of professional articles whose merit they were asked to judge. Attached to one set was a male name, John T. McKay, to the other a female name, Joan T. McKay. They were, of course, the same articles. How does one explain the fact that the women subjects uniformly gave the male author the superior rating?[21]

We have previously remarked that the Women's Liberation Movement exhibits a wide variety of ideologies. It is unfortunately necessary to say that the more radical of these ideologies cross the boundary that separates sense from nonsense. One radical claim is that marriage is nothing but legalized rape, since the wife is required to have sexual relations with her husband whether she likes it or not. Another claim is that the wife is her husband's prisoner because she has to live with him at the location of his choice. Another is that a wife is nothing but a slave because her husband receives more household services from her without pay than he could possibly receive from a paid domestic servant. Another is that every treatment of women as "sex objects," from beauty contests to magazine centerfolds, is contemptible. Rape victim, prisoner, slave, sex object—these are strong words. We learn finally that the English language itself is full of sexist locutions, that a book on sociology carrying the title *Man and Society* is to be condemned, and that the greatest sexist insult of all is that the word "menstruation" contains the three letters "m-e-n." For the radical liberationists the dictionary is the most prejudiced book in the library.

Complaints like these are an affront to intelligence. The claim that marriage is legalized rape has a Victorian aroma about it, suggesting a time when it was denied that women have sexual desires and needs. In modern societies wives too have a right to the sexual attention of their husbands, and the failure to consummate a marriage is a ground for annulment by both sexes. The claim that the husband chooses the place of residence has

[21] Philip Goldberg, "Are Women Prejudiced Against Women?" *Transaction*, April, 1968, pp. 28–30.

validity only when he supports the family. If the wife were the sole support, the situation would be reversed. The claim that the wife is a slave to household duties for which the husband would otherwise have to pay tumbles to the ground for the same reason. The husband contributes to her a household that is at least equal in every amenity to that which he provides for himself. She is not, after all, consigned to slave quarters or even, in the upper class, to the maid's room. The best answer to all of these complaints, however, is that the marital state in the kinds of societies we are talking about is one that the women enters quite voluntarily. No one requires a woman to enter it and accept its responsibilities.

The notion that women should not be regarded as sex objects by men or (the suppressed contrary) that men should not be regarded as sex objects by women flies in the face of nature. Adult females of all species, animal and human, are sex objects to males of the same species, and vice versa—except, of course, in the case of homosexual preferences. If this were not the fact of the matter, species would not reproduce themselves. It may be, as a young and enthusiastic women's liberationist maintained, that there is no need for the human species to reproduce itself, but that is another—and highly philosophical—proposition!

As for the dictionary, the notion that the word "man" in such a title as *Man and Society* betrays a sexist prejudice founders on the fact that "man" in this context is the name of a species and not of a sex. As for "menstruate," the connection is to *mensis*, meaning month, and only philological ignorance would associate it with men. We can only say that no one who reads William Shakespeare with awe and admiration would permit his language to be womanhandled by the Amazons of the feminist Left!

In spite of important and even impressive achievements, the Women's Liberation Movement has sometimes indulged in reverse sexism, and indeed some of its more militant and stentorian members are man-haters in every sense of the term. Some would like to do away with the male sex altogether, look forward eagerly to the time when parthenogenesis will make that possible, and in the meantime sing the praises of Sappho of Lesbos. Too many of the spokeswomen of the movement have ceased to regard men as people and regard them only as oppressors. It is doubtful, however, as Plato might have written in the *Protagoras*, that when Zeus set about to distribute the virtues among the members of the human race, he greatly favored one of the sexes over the other. On this subject we are glad to agree with Jessie Bernard, a distinguished sociologist who otherwise applauds the Feminist Revolution, when she expresses the opinion that "sexism in women is as contrary to the public interest as it is in men."[22]

---

[22] *Women and the Public Interest*, Aldine·Atherton, Chicago, 1971, p. 37.

Finally, it is interesting to note that the Women's Liberation Movement has also attracted a number of women critics. One writer, for example, contends in opposition to the complaint previously discussed that in marriage it is obviously the male who is the slave.[23] It is the man who is forced to support the woman and to contribute to her support even if and after the marriage fails. In the meantime she lives a life of domestic indolence. She may work or not as she chooses, whereas the male has no such alternative. As for housework, it is now so easy in contemporary technological societies, with their ingenious machines, that any woman could do it in two hours a day. She contends in addition that the stupidity of women is so "overwhelming" that anyone who meets it will be contaminated by it. She asserts that the consignment of children to day-care centers is an act of cruelty, perpetrated upon the children by both misguided parents. And she maintains that the Women's Liberation Movement is an aid and comfort to the male ego. It gives him the prestige of a tyrant, a status he could hardly achieve on his own!

Some of these views are as flamboyant as those on the other side. It is unnecessary to do more than mention them. We should like to comment on only one issue, the issue of slavery. Surely it is time to dismiss the notion and to do it for both sexes. Slavery means involuntary, not voluntary, servitude, and "servitude" is a poor synonym for the mature assumption of responsibilities in return for very real rewards.

8. The Sexual Division of Labor

We do not know in detail what Adam and Eve did in Paradise before they ate the forbidden fruit. We do not know what they did after they left the Garden. It is possible that each of them pursued precisely the same designs. One may surmise, however, that when Eve's pregnancy had advanced to the fifth or sixth month, she found it a little difficult to move around. It is easy to imagine that she was then no longer capable of gathering her own food or of protecting herself against the inclemency of the elements and the depredations of animal enemies. At this point she may have asked Adam for some kind of a contract. She would cook the food if Adam would bring it home, she would bear the child and look after it if Adam would stay around and protect them, and she would even make his clothing if he would procure the materials for them both. There were doubtless other items in the contract, some in fine print, but these must have been its essential provisions. Taking it all in all we do not know whether Adam or Eve got the

[23] Esther Vilar, *The Manipulated Man*, Farrar, Straus & Giroux, Inc., New York, 1973.

worst of it, but it was a bargain that has remained in force pretty much in its pristine form right up to the present time.

Now we cannot, of course, find any such history in the Book of Genesis. It is highly improbable, furthermore, that the sexual division of labor was ever determined in a deliberate way. There is such a division in all societies, however, and in all of them it is fairly uniform. The notion that sex roles, especially vocational ones, are reversed in some societies is entertained only by a minority of anthropologists. Because of the fact that it is women who must bear and nurse the babies, the sexual division of labor has a firm biological base. Cultural differences in sex statuses can vary only within the limits of physiological capacities, and among these the most important are the reproductive function of the female and the physical strength of the male. Where there seem to be exceptions they prove, upon further examination, to confirm the rule.

George Peter Murdock once studied 224 nonliterate societies in an effort to discover regularities in the sexual division of labor.[24] In these societies warfare, metalworking, hunting and trapping, fishing, and trade are predominantly male activities. Cooking, the manufacture and repair of clothing, pottery making, and fire making and tending are predominantly female activities. Agriculture, which includes the preparation, planting, and cultivation of the soil, is an activity shared almost equally by the two sexes.

In literate societies we similarly find a sexual division of labor, although changes, always within biological limits, continue to occur. The old-fashioned bookkeeper, seated on his high stool and poring over his ledgers with the aid of spectacles, eyeshade, and cuff protectors, has long since given way to the pert little clerk, and she in turn is vanishing with the advent of the electronic billing machine which can manage the whole process in the twinkling of a transistor. But the sexual division of labor remains. Few women can truthfully hum the ditty, "I've Been Working on the Railroad," none serves as a university president, none commands an ocean liner, none sits on the Supreme Court of the United States, and few work as house painters, plumbers, electricians, carpenters, bricklayers, masons, pharmacists, or engineers. Strange as it may seem, women suffer a rather severe disadvantage in a field where it might be least expected, that is, in the world of the university and its faculties. Women professors, especially in the higher ranks, are fairly rare even in an environment where sexual equality is accepted as a principle. The decade of the seventies, however, began to show some reverse discrimination in this respect. As for men, few of them are in elementary- or nursery-school teaching, few are

---

[24] "Comparative Data on Division of Labor by Sex," *Social Forces*, vol. 15, May, 1937.

nurses or dental assistants, and few serve as stewards on the airlines. Men cut the hair of both men and women, but few women—commercially at least—cut the hair of men.

On the other hand, the number of women heads of state is increasing, a list that could begin, for example, with India, Ceylon, and Israel. It is conceivable that in the lifetime of the reader of this book a woman will become Prime Minister of Great Britain. And if Eleanor Roosevelt had ever run for the Presidency of the United States, she would have had the strong and enthusiastic support of the author of this book, among many millions of others.

It may be that the Women's Liberation Movement will be successful in eliminating all divisions of labor based on sex, except those related to purely physiological capacities. On the other hand, if we escape the provincialisms of our own culture, we have to remark that a sexual division of labor is one of the constants of human societies. Whether it will continue to be so in the future is a question that has to be addressed to prophecy and not to sociology.

9. Voluntary Associations

In view of the growing equality between the sexes in our own society, it is somewhat surprising to observe the large number of voluntary associations limited in membership to one sex or the other. Thus, we have the "Cubs" and the "Brownies," the Boy Scouts and the Girl Scouts, the YMCA and the YWCA, men's colleges and women's colleges, and so on through many adult groups in which men and women do approximately the same things but do them in separate associations. In many cases the men's association has a women's "auxiliary" connected with it. The reverse phenomenon, interestingly enough, appears not to exist; that is, it would be difficult, if not impossible, to find a men's auxiliary to a women's association.[25] In very many cases too there are lodges, associations, and "societies" for one sex only and corresponding groups for the other sex. In this latter category we find, for example, the League of Women Voters and Rotary International.

In other words, in spite of a decreasing emphasis upon sexual criteria in many of the occupational statuses of our society, single-sex groups persist. Even in those informal groupings of people that spring up now and again in society there is a tendency for the sexes to segregate themselves,

[25] I am indebted to Lionel Tiger for this observation. See his *Men in Groups, op. cit.*, p. 140.

often quite unwittingly and without intent. The reader may have noticed that at gatherings which are initially mixed the men tend after a while to drift toward one end of the room, the women toward the other, the former to talk politics, business, and sports, the latter housekeeping, children, and clothes.

The extent of sexual segregation, in both organized and unorganized groups, has not been systematically studied by sociologists for the United States as a whole, but it is apparent that it is a fairly common practice. W. Lloyd Warner and his associates found, for example, that in Newburyport the number of single-sex associations far exceeded those for which both of the sexes were eligible. One rather suspects, in the absence of contrary evidence, that the same situation would be found in most human societies, including those that are referred to as modern and industrial.

Lionel Tiger has advanced the thesis that the propensity of males to associate with one another in groups may be due to what he calls "the male bond," which in turn may have its source in the evolutionary history of the race. Men need the company of men—in a nonerotic sense—for hunting, fishing, war, government, and even recreation at the neighborhood bar or pub. They need associations, from the primitive secret society to the contemporary fraternal order, from which women are systematically excluded. It is this male bond, Tiger thinks, which could serve as an intervening variable in the relationship between biological and social processes. Whatever one thinks of this theory, the separation of the sexes is both a cultural and a social phenomenon; that is, culturally speaking, men and women occupy different statuses and conform to different norms, not only in nonliterate societies but in all societies. This separation is also, as we have seen, a social phenomenon because in all societies there are groups limited to one or the other sex.

Whatever cultural changes may occur in the future, one may say with safety that sexual differentiation is destined to last as long as human societies endure. Those who would erase it completely are in a tiny minority. The majority are attuned to the voice that once rang out in the French parliament: *Vive la différence!* Long live the difference between the sexes, whatever the problems the difference may produce. There is joy and anger between the sexes, affection and hostility, and love and war. But there is never indifference. Let Aristophanes tell us that men cannot live without women—nor with them—and attend to all the authors since, both men and women, who have written new episodes in the perennial contest. The sociologist is content to suggest that here at least we have one of the most important of all kinds of social differentiation and one that will continue to warrant discussion until the end of time.

10. A Note on Age Differentiation

If all societies differentiate their members on the ground of sex, so do they also in terms of age. In none of them do the same norms apply to the very young or the very old as apply to the adult members of the group. Here again we have a kind of social differentiation based upon biological factors and one that distributes privileges and responsibilities, rights and duties, in terms of separate statuses. Age statuses, like sex statuses, are ascribed of course, and not achieved. Their existence is so clear that they require neither an extended discussion nor a chapter of their own. They may, however, merit a paragraph of attention.

The reader himself can immediately think of many instances of age stratification, or age grading, in our own society. Thus, one has to have attained a certain age in order to go to school, to join a church, to be confirmed, to be considered responsible in a court of law, to sign a valid contract, to be guilty of a crime, to vote, to marry, to earn a commission in the armed services, to sit in Congress, and so on through an entire roster of abilities and disabilities. We expect people to conform to the norms attached to their age statuses and are therefore surprised and sometimes shocked by deviations therefrom. When an old man marries a young woman, for example, or vice versa, we tend to respond with some discomfort. The situation is news; it may become a scandal; it is an item for the tabloids.

A similar situation obtains in less obvious instances. We do not expect college freshmen to be in their fifties, their professors in their teens. We should not particularly like having a "boss" considerably younger than ourselves, and certain ages are right for certain activities and wrong for others. A certain vulgarity attaches to an attempt by an older person, whether man or woman, to usurp the prerogatives of youth. A norm is thereby violated. Furthermore, we expect people to occupy certain statuses at definite stages in their lives, and there are regular status successions, as we observed in an earlier chapter, that run through the associations of society. If the first of life is a period of status achievement, the last is one of status relinquishment. Seniority is a factor in all associational life, whether in business, the Army, the university, or elsewhere.

Finally, people who associate with one another informally also tend to segregate themselves in terms of age. For the very young, of course, a difference of a year or two is a very large difference indeed and the high-school senior hardly deigns to look—even down—upon the high-school freshman. Later on, differences in age of ten years or more may seem very little. Outside of families, of course, intimacies rarely develop among people of different generations, and when they do they are usually different relationships from those that exist between contemporaries. The factor of age, in short, is seldom ignored in social intercourse. Neither can it be ignored in sociology. Like sex differentiation, it is one of the ties that bind people together as well as one of the barriers that keep them apart.[26]

11. Summary

In this chapter we have emphasized that one of the most important—and certainly universal—kinds of differentiation in any society is that based upon difference in sex. In no society do males and females do the same things, occupy the same statuses, share identical interests, or conform to the same norms. All societies canalize the conduct of the sexes in different directions, just as they signalize the difference by a distinction in dress. Since the norms surrounding sex statuses are susceptible to considerable variation, some writers, especially in our own century, have speculated that cultural rather than biological factors are by far the more responsible. They thus extend the principle of cultural relativity to encompass also the range of sexual differentiation.

Other writers, however, have been skeptical of this extremely cultural interpretation of sex differences. They note first of all that sexual differentiation is basically a biological and not a cultural fact, that it is rooted in the physiology of two separate and distinct kinds of organisms. Males are males, and females are females, except in an insignificant minority of cases of interest only to the medical profession.

While avoiding, we hope, a dogmatic approach to this problem, we questioned nevertheless the notion that dominance between the sexes is culturally determined. We introduced certain kinds of evidence that seem difficult if not impossible to explain by recourse to cultural factors alone—differences in rate of development, susceptibility to disease, expectation of life, and muscular strength. We discussed in addition, though inconclusively to be sure, the problem of sex and intelligence and the relationship of sex to achievement and genius.

We emphasized, on the other hand, that in every era of Western civilization, and in other civilizations as well, women have suffered disabilities in comparison with men. We saw that this situation might be related in some way to the view of sexual activity that has obtained in Western ideologies. We mentioned "the woman problem," the flood of books about it in European and American society, and the effort of the Women's

---

[26] Simone de Beauvoir, author of *The Second Sex*, has more recently written a large and important book on age: *The Coming of Age*, G. P. Putnam's Sons, New York, 1972. For a comprehensive sociological treatment of the subject, see Matilda White Riley (with others), *Aging and Society*, 3 vols., Russell Sage Foundation, New York, 1968–1972.

Liberation Movement to gain for women the equality that they have long been denied. In the last sections of the chapter we discussed the sexual division of labor, again a characteristic of all societies, and single-sex associations, and we concluded with an incidental note on age differentiation.

In this chapter, as in others in this part of the book, we can often merely indicate the importance of certain kinds of social differentiation and mention some of their ramifications. But we cannot give detailed treatment to them all or solve the problems they frequently involve. This has clearly been the case with respect to sex differentiation. From this subject, however, it is an easy transition to the family, which is the subject of the following chapter.

Chapter 15

THE FAMILY

F ALL OF THE GROUPS that affect the lives of individuals in society none touches them so intimately or so continuously as does the family. From the moment of birth, when the young parents gaze with adoration upon their very own creation, to the moment of death, when sons and daughters are summoned to the bedside of a passing patriarch, the family exerts a constant influence. The family is the first group we encounter in our inchoate experience, and it is the group with which, in one form or another, we shall have the most enduring relationship. Every one of us, with statistically small exceptions, grows up in a family and every one of us too, with perhaps a few more exceptions, will be a member of a family for the larger part of his life.

The family, almost without question, is the most important of any of the groups that human experience offers. Other groups we join for longer or shorter periods of time, for the satisfaction of this interest or that. The family, on the contrary, is with us always. Or rather more precisely, we are with it, an identifiable member of some family and an essential unit in its organization. It is the family, in addition, that gives us our principal identity and even our very name, which is the label of this identity, in the larger society of which we are a part.

The study of the family, curiously enough,

is not an easy study. In spite of our personal experience with it, or perhaps because of this, most of us are ill equipped to view the family as a social phenomenon. It is too close to us, our contact with it is too intimate, to permit us to view it with objectivity. It is worthy of comment that of all forms of human association the family was perhaps the last to receive its share of scientific attention and research. As someone has noted, the only three really unprejudiced observers of the human scene are Adam, the baby, and the man from Mars. Adam knew only one kind of family, the family in which he was a father; the baby knows only one, the family in which he is a child; and the man from Mars in all probability does not exist. Anything a sociologist has to say about the family, therefore, is inevitably tempered by his own experience with it. Although of doubtful significance, it is at least of incidental interest to note that two outstanding books on the family in American sociology were written respectively by a man who was divorced and by one who never married.

In any event, the family is a large area of specialization within the field of sociology and there are many excellent textbooks on the subject. With these textbooks we shall make no attempt to compete. They customarily treat many aspects of family life, particularly those dealing with interpersonal and intrafamily relations, that cannot concern us here. We shall not, for example, offer advice on the age at which people should marry, on how to choose a husband or a wife, how to get along with a difficult mate, how many children to beget, whether to spank or not to spank them after they are begotten, what to do about a mother-in-law problem, how to avoid a divorce, and so on through a myriad of similar questions. Our discussion will be confined to the family as a social phenomenon and will move along on a sociological level. We are interested in the family both as an association and as an institution, but we offer no counsel on how to be happy though married.

1. The Universality of the Family

The family is the most permanent and the most pervasive of all social institutions. There is no human society in which some form of the family does not appear nor, so far as we know, has there ever been such a society. All societies both large and small, primitive and civilized, ancient and modern, have institutionalized the process of procreation of the species and the rearing of the young. As in the case of most social institutions, it is idle to inquire into origins. No one knows, or can know, how or when the family began, if indeed the concept of beginning has any meaning in this connection. It is safe to surmise, however, that the family in some form will always be with us, that as far into the future as the mind can imagine, the family will continue to be a central and indeed a nuclear component of society. There may be no families in utopia, and none in paradise, but the planet we know best will probably always contain them.

It is true that some of our more speculative writers have constructed, in their fancy, societies so "advanced" that the family as we know it does not exist. In *Brave New World*, for example, Aldous Huxley portrays a situation, supposedly a scientific millennium, in which sex is wholly separated from reproduction and in which babies are manufactured in test tubes. They are manufactured, furthermore, for certain specific purposes and are divided at birth into three classes: alpha babies, beta babies, and gamma babies. The alphas are the *crème de la crème* of this artificial society, destined at birth to become the philosopher kings who someday will rule the rest. The gammas are the drones, ticketed from the beginning for the menial tasks that not even Huxley's invention can remove from daily life. They are steadily conditioned to their fates by loudspeakers assailing them, during their stay in the nursery-laboratory, with the words, "You are a gamma baby; you are a gamma baby," thus banishing all desire, all ambition, and all hope. The betas, of course, are in the middle, conditioned for relatively normal lives even in an abnormal society, but never permitted to make a political decision, a privilege reserved to the alphas. No one knows whether it would be possible to live in this "brave new world," and the novelist himself has doubts, as the plot of his book makes clear, but it is unlikely in any event that such a society will ever appear on earth. Huxley's society is as improbable as the one described much earlier in our history by Plato in *The Republic*. The family, so far as we know, is a cultural universal, one of the constants of human life.

2. The Biological Basis of the Family

Throughout this book we have been interested in the role of biological conditions in the explanation of sociocultural phenomena, and it is not inappropriate, therefore, that the question should arise again in connection with the family. A superficial glance at the question would indicate that the family is indeed to be explained in terms of biological factors—the existence of two sexes and the sexual character of reproduction in the human species. The family appears as a "natural" answer to the human sexual drive, and it would seem to be a phenomenon solidly based in the biology of the human organism.

A little reflection, however, will suggest on the contrary that biological factors do not explain the family. The sexual need, after all, can be satisfied outside of the marital relationship, and is so satisfied in all human societies. It is even possible to beget and to rear children outside of a marital and family relationship, although it is inconvenient to do so. Even if the biological factor could explain marriage and the family, it could hardly explain the wide range of variation in these institutions that different societies have exhibited. Sex, as someone has observed, can explain mating but not marriage.

There is another biological factor, related to but different from the sexual, to which importance has been attributed by several writers, although its actual operation and influence remain in the realm of speculation. These writers observe that the long period of pregnancy and subsequent lactation renders the human female relatively unfit in a biological world in which only the fittest survive. During this period, therefore, it is the function of the male to protect her, and later their joint offspring, and to supply them with food that they are physiologically incapable of getting for themselves. This, at least, is one answer to the rather baffling question of why the male continues to attach himself to the female after conception and especially during a period when she can no longer satisfy his sexual needs. The temporary but repeated disabilities of the female and the prolonged infancy of the child in the human species are thus used as arguments to support a biological base for the family.

These arguments have a degree of plausibility and would seem to answer the question from the point of view of the female. Unfortunately, however, no one has yet been able to find in the male any biological need or physiological propensity to perform these services. The females of other species suffer similar disabilities, but similar results do not ensue. If the human male accepts these responsibilities, as he does in all human societies, the reason must be that he is induced to do so by sanctions of one kind or another, and these sanctions, of course, have their source in society and not in the organism. In other words, even in this respect the biological explanation would seem to be insufficient. Indeed, it gives a kind of curious support to the facetious comment that all women should marry, and no men.

On this interesting question the distinguished anthropologist Ralph Linton had yet another answer:

> At the foundation of every variant of the conjugal family lies an assumption of continuity in the mated relationship. Even in those societies which impose no formal strictures on the separation of mates, the role of the conjugal group is based on an anticipation of permanence, and the average individual establishes an enduring partnership with someone of the opposite sex at least by middle age. This continuity of mating has a physiological basis in certain characteristics which man shares with most of the sub-human primates. The primate order is characterized by the absence of any clearly defined rutting

season and by constant sexual activity and interest on the part of the male. It is also characterized by marked differences in the size and vigor of males and females, with consequent patterns of male dominance. There are a few exceptions to the second generalization, but it holds for most primate species, including our own. The combination of male dominance and of constant male interest in females as sexual objects operates to give matings stability and presumably did so even before our ancestors had achieved full human status. Even the earliest men were able to keep particular women to themselves and to prevent these women from bestowing their favors on other men, at least as long as their husbands were present.

Very early in human history these physiological factors must have been reinforced by psychological ones. Although man is the most flexible and the most easily conditioned of all the primates, he has an acute need for security in his personal relationships and a desire for congenial companionship and perfected response. These needs, although less immediately compulsive than the physiological tensions of sex, are far more continuous in their operations. Relationships which will satisfy them cannot be established between any and all individuals and can only be established through long-continued association. When one had found a partner who could satisfy both these needs and the sexual ones, such a partner was to be valued and retained even though sexual curiosity might lead to occasional unfaithfulness.[1]

According to this argument three factors, namely, (1) the absence of a rutting season (oestrous cycle) in the human species, (2) the physical dominance of the male over the female, and finally (3) the need for continuous intimacy with another human being, gave permanence to human matings before the operation of any purely social or cultural factors, and such cultural phenomena as the sexual division of labor depend upon a prior permanence in the relationships between the sexes. Marriage thus appears as a kind of *quid pro quo* arrangement in which the male offers protection and support in return for exclusive sexual partnership and continuous intimate association.

Several observations impair, in part at least, the cogency of this argument. The first of these is that the physical dominance of the male over the female has very little to do with his ability to deny her to others. Only his physical superiority over male challengers could have this result. On biological grounds there is little reason to suppose that the human situation would differ in any significant respect from that of other species, like seals for example, in which males are in physical competition with one another for females. The absence of an oestrous cycle would merely make the

[1] Ralph Linton, "The Natural History of the Family," in Ruth Nanda Anshen (ed.), *The Family: Its Function and Destiny*, Harper & Row, Publishers, New York, 1949, pp. 21–22.

competition continuous. The second observation is that the physical dominance of the male over the female would, however, permit him to ignore or to refuse her demands for protection and support. He might possibly be able to force her to submit to him alone, but she cannot, in turn, force him to feed her.

Finally, although the male may have "an acute need for security in his personal relationships," he has no such need for security in his sexual relationships. The historical prominence of prostitution testifies to the contrary. It is conceivable, in addition, that the need for security in personal relationships could be satisfied in other ways, by male companions for example rather than by wives. The theory merits, nevertheless, the most careful reflection. It says as much for the role of biological factors as one can reasonably claim.

For a full explanation of the family, however, it is clear that we have to turn to society and to culture. If there were no such phenomenon in the human species as bisexual reproduction, it is doubtful that the family would ever have come into existence; this much we may concede to biology. But this is a necessary and not a sufficient condition, for bisexual reproduction is possible without the family. The sufficient conditions lie in society itself. As we shall see, the family performs a number of functions that no other group can perform as well.

3. A Note on Nomenclature

Before proceeding further it seems desirable to clarify the words we use in talking about the family. In an earlier chapter we distinguished between institutions and associations. We said there that an institution is a standardized procedure; an association, a group organized for the pursuit of a particular interest or goal. Stated quite briefly, an institution is an organized way of doing something, an association the organized group that does it.

In these terms it is clear, therefore, that *the family* is an institution, *a family* an association. *The* family is a standardized, formalized, and regularized procedure for the procreation and rearing of children; *a* family is a group that carries on these activities—your family, my family, any family. The distinction satisfies, furthermore, the simple tests that we set up in the earlier chapter as a means of avoiding confusion between the terms *association* and *institution*. We can all belong to *a* family, and most of us do; but none of us can belong to *the* family. A family, in addition, always has a location, an address, but the question of locus makes no sense with respect to *the* family. *The* family, finally, is one of the most durable of all social institutions; *a* family, on the contrary, is one of the most temporary of human associations, so temporary indeed that it cannot survive the lifetimes of its individual members. Our sociological distinction, in short, is clear in logic even if it cannot always be maintained in ordinary speech.

It is necessary next to introduce a second distinction. A family, one might say, is a family, and that is that. Actually, however, a family can be two quite different things depending upon the vantage from which we view it. Thus, the family in which we are a child is one phenomenon; the family in which we are a parent is quite another.[2] The first of these families is called the *family of orientation*, the second the *family of procreation*.

All but a very few of us, an insignificant number in our own country, belong to or have belonged to a family of orientation. The vast majority of us will someday belong to a family of procreation. The first of these is almost an entire community; indeed, to its youngest members it is a community. The second is an association, consciously formed and intentionally (and sometimes unintentionally) increased. Since the family of orientation and the family of procreation are two different phenomena, they cannot be placed in the same category in our classification of groups.[3] The first of these is a social group, the second an associational group. The family of procreation, in short, is an organized group. It conforms to all of the criteria of such a group, and its organization is regulated by the laws of the state.

As a final distinction between these two types of family we may note that the first, the family of orientation, is an involuntary group. We become a member of such a family without the exercise of choice in an initiation ceremony of which we are quite unconscious. The family of procreation, on the contrary, is in our society a voluntary group, a relationship into which we voluntarily enter but one from which, on the other hand, we may not voluntarily withdraw. It follows as a corollary that our status as a member of a family of procreation is achieved. In other societies, of course, those in which the marriages of children are arranged far in advance (sometimes even in infancy) by their parents, the family of procreation is also an involuntary group. In some of these societies a young couple may never see each other before their nuptial day. Our own society, in sharp contrast, respects the freedom of mate selection, discourages outside interference even by parents, and guarantees the voluntary character of the marital arrangement.

---

[2] The expression "the family" in this sentence means a particular family, an association, not *the* family, an institution. Here is an illustration of the fact that the English language is sometimes an awkward instrument and can cloud distinctions that are otherwise clear both in logic and in sociology.

[3] See Chapter 10.

4. Variations in Family Forms

The bewildering variety of family forms to be observed in societies throughout the world, and throughout the course of history, is a cultural phenomenon of considerable interest. It would be easy to devote the rest of this chapter in its entirety to a description, exotic and entertaining, of marital customs quite foreign to our own experience. These, however, belong more appropriately to anthropology, and we shall therefore confine the present discussion to a brief explanation of some of the more important variations.

Mater, of course, is the Latin word for "mother" and *pater* for "father," and these words provide the prefixes for the labels of a number of different family forms and types. Some societies, for example, are *matrilocal* in their marriage customs, others *patrilocal*. In the former case the young married couple takes up residence at the home (tribe, village) of the bride's parents, in the latter of the bridegroom's. Our own culture is patrilocal in that it gives to the husband and not the wife the right to choose the place of residence after marriage. If she refuses to accompany him to a new location, assuming that he is the sole or principal source of her support, it is she, not he, who will ordinarily be guilty of desertion.

Similarly, in a *matrilineal* society descent is traced through the female line, and in a *patrilineal* society through the male line. It is not uncommon on the other hand to trace descent in both ways, and we customarily do so in our own society. Again, *matronymic* and *patronymic* mean, respectively, taking the name of the mother or the father. Our own society, of course, is patronymic, but this is a custom, whether or not we have ever given it a moment's reflection, that is far from universal. There are even exceptions in our own society.

In the nineteenth century an advocate of women's rights named Lucy Stone insisted that women retain their own names after marriage. Although married to Henry Brown Blackwell, she refused to adopt her husband's name and was known as Mrs. Stone. Her followers were known as "Lucy Stoners." The custom continues today among many married women, especially writers, artists, actresses, and entertainers. Parents frequently make the mother's maiden name a part of their son's name and sometimes, though rarely, a husband will add a part of his wife's name to his own. Occasionally too a man will take the name of his maternal grandfather rather than that of his father, especially when the grandfather was famous. But these are the exceptions that prove the rule that our society is patronymic.

We have, finally, terms which pertain to government. *Matriarchy* means government by women and *patriarchy* government by men. Anthropologists now entertain a vigorous skepticism concerning the incidence of matriarchal societies. In spite of such apparent exceptions as Catherine of Russia, Elizabeth I of England, a few other queens here and there in history, and the Amazons of ancient legend, it is doubtful that the women of any society, primitive or civilized, have actually made the *political* decisions in any firmly institutionalized fashion. That they may have *influenced* such decisions, and other decisions as well, has never been denied, and it will certainly not be denied by the author of this book.

Sometimes the word "matriarchy" is used in a sense that has no reference to government. It may mean merely that society is matronymic, matrilineal, or matrilocal, that the maternal line is emphasized in descent and inheritance, and that the mother (or her brother) exercises domestic authority. In this sense of the word it is clear that matriarchies do exist. In this connection another distinction assumes significance—the distinction between the *conjugal family* on the one hand and the *consanguine family* on the other. The conjugal family is comprised of parents and their children, the group we usually think of as the family in our own society. A consanguine family is made up of either parent and his or her blood relatives. One conjugal family thus represents the societal union of two consanguine families.

The point of this distinction is that some societies, those that are matriarchal in the second sense, place a greater stress upon the consanguine family than they do upon the conjugal. In these societies there is frequently a sharp separation between the concepts of "biological father" and "social father," for a man owes his primary family obligation, not to his own children, but to his sister's children. His own children, in turn, become the primary domestic responsibility of his wife's brother. In these societies, in addition, the bond between brother and sister is often stronger than that between husband and wife. In Egyptian poetry the words brother and sister mean lover and beloved and in the greatest of Greek tragedies it was Antigone's brother, not her husband, for whom she made her heroic sacrifice. This system may appear to the American student to be exceedingly curious and possibly reprehensible. It must be conceded, however, that it possesses certain advantages over our own. In the first place biological paternity, which is always difficult to prove, loses its importance, and all children have legitimate status as belonging to the mother and her consanguine family. In the second place quarrels and confusions concerning the inheritance of title, status, or property are more easily avoided. And finally, divorce or separation of the conjugal pair can never interfere with the care of children, which is guaranteed in any event by the mother's brother and her consanguine family. In the patriarchal system, of course, it is the father's family that assumes the greater importance. In the old

Chinese family system, for example, a son's wife entered his father's household, where she occupied a status little superior to that of a domestic servant until she produced a male child.

The number of spouses an individual may have at one time is also subject to societal variation. The two major forms of marriage, of a limited number of mathematical possibilities, are monogamy and polygamy. *Monogamy*, of course, means singular marriage, the marriage of one man to one woman, and it is now the prevailing form throughout the world. *Polygamy* means plural marriage and, although it has become less common in the twentieth century, it can still be found in a number of societies. It has several forms, including polygyny (one man, two or more wives) and polyandry (one woman, two or more husbands), of which the first is much more frequent. There is another form of plural marriage in which several men, usually brothers, are married to several women, usually sisters, but this is relatively rare. And finally, there is the form, typified best perhaps by celebrities in the entertainment world, in which several men marry several women, but only one at a time, and constituting therefore a form, still nameless, that might be called serial polygamy.

In the nineteenth century it was believed that all institutions passed through regular historical stages and that the family was no exception to this evolutionary process. The earliest stages, according to this view, were characterized by a primitive promiscuity, which was followed, in gradual succession, by various kinds of plural marriage, including both polygyny and polyandry, until finally the monogamous family of Victorian England was achieved. This, in turn, was thought to be the apex of civilization, the "highest" form of marriage to be imagined.

The theory, however, could not sustain an accumulation of contradictory facts, facts that opened to question the entire evolutionary hypothesis. These facts indicated that there is no regular progression of family forms in this sense and particularly that some of the most "primitive" societies (that is, primitive by other criteria) have genuine monogamous arrangements, whereas some of the more "advanced" are polygamous or even promiscuous. The theory depended in addition upon an erroneous identification of sex expression with family forms. It is not inconceivable that a society which insists upon a strict monogamy can at the same time tolerate a sexual promiscuity and even support the latter in a system of prostitution—which, like the family, is a social institution. The theory of an historical evolution of family forms, in short, is no longer tenable.

If societies vary in the number of persons one is permitted to marry, they vary also in their prescriptions and proscriptions with respect to marital selection. These variations conform to norms that are summarized in the labels *endogamy* and *exogamy*. Endogamy means marriage within a certain group, exogamy marriage without. Thus, a tribe that is divided into moieties or clans may require that persons marry inside their own tribe (an endogamous restriction) but outside their own clan (an exogamous restriction).

All societies, with minor and very special exceptions, require that persons marry outside their own immediate families, and the nearly universal prohibition of incest is accordingly an exogamous rule. As we have indicated earlier in this book, marriages between fathers and daughters, and mothers and sons, are universally tabooed, and brother-sister marriages are permitted only in the rarest of circumstances—in cases so few indeed as to constitute notable exceptions to an otherwise universal norm. Incest, however, is not always defined in the same way. The marriage of first cousins is permitted in some societies and prohibited in others. Hamlet bitterly accused his mother of incest when she married his uncle, but in some societies a man is required to marry his deceased brother's wife.[4]

With the exception of the incest taboo, endogamous rules are more common than exogamous ones. In all societies people are required, or at the very least encouraged, to marry within certain groups and these endogamous norms define the difference between an "acceptable" and an "unacceptable" marriage. One may be expected, for example, to marry within his own tribe, his own village, his own nationality or region, his own religion, or his own social class. As a matter of fact, most of the world's religions attempt to enforce a strict endogamy among their members. Marriage above (*hypergamy*) or below (*hypogamy*) one's social class or caste falls under similar proscriptions, as does marriage outside of one's ethnic or racial group. In our own society marriages of people of widely different ages, though entirely legal, also tend to excite an endogamous disapproval.

It is impossible in a short discussion to exhaust the range of cultural variation in marital and family arrangements throughout the world. Among many other differences we may briefly refer to differences in the ages at which marriages are contracted, in method of betrothal (by abduction, purchase, parental contract, or partnership agreement), in courtship practices, in duration of courtship, in wedding ceremonies, in ease of divorce, in rules regarding remarriage after divorce or the death of one's spouse, in the treatment of and response to conjugal relatives ("in-laws"),[5] in brother-

---

[4] This custom is called the *levirate*. It was practiced by the ancient Hebrews, but not limited to them. Similarly, the custom by which a woman is required to marry her deceased sister's husband is called the *sororate*.

[5] Some of the strongest taboos are encountered in this area. In some societies a man may never have any contact or communication with his mother-in-law. In our own society mothers-in-law are targets for comedians.

sister relations and responsibilities, and in other practices numerous enough to fill a shelf of volumes. Differences like these obtain even in a single society when it is sufficiently large and complex to contain diverse ethnic, regional, class, and religious groups. The Mormons, for example, practiced polygyny in Utah until the last decade of the nineteenth century, when it was abandoned as a condition of statehood. Cultural variations, in short, are endless.

5. The Functions of the Family

The family owes its existence as a social institution to a number of functions that it performs both for society and for the individual. There is no standard list of these functions in the literature, and indeed they are somewhat difficult to delineate with precision. The reason for this is that from one point of view they are all interdependent and a logical division into separate categories may thus do violence to the actual situation. On the other hand they are all independent of one another in the sense that no necessary connection exists between them and all of them could, in case of necessity, be performed by other social institutions. Some of them, in fact, are performed in conjunction with other institutions. Nevertheless, taking all the functions of the family together, there is no other institution that can perform them so well, no other that can so efficiently satisfy the needs of society, and it is for this reason that the family achieves its universality in history and its very great importance in the life of the individual.

The first of these functions is replacement of the species. The survival of society requires a continuous replenishment of its members. There is no logical reason why this process cannot be left to biological impulse, as it is in the lower orders of animals, but haphazard reproduction would almost certainly lead to confusion. For the sake of order, if for no other reason, the process of reproduction is institutionalized in the family, where it assumes a regularity and a stability that all societies recognize as desirable.

Promiscuous parenthood is almost everywhere deplored, even in the most "primitive" of societies, and it is the family, in consequence, that introduces a legitimacy into the act of reproduction. It is worthy of emphasis that although freedom of sex expression is frequently permitted, freedom of conception falls under an almost universal prohibition. The family, in short, institutionalizes the process of reproduction and introduces an order and a stability into this most important of societal activities. All societies surround this function with stringent norms and support them with strong sanctions. It is conceivable that replacement of the species could be accomplished in other ways, as Plato seriously and Huxley cynically envisioned, but no actual society has ever institutionalized an alternative. The biological relationship between parents and children, although it cannot by itself explain the family, nevertheless gives an impetus to permanence in their social relationship as well. In so doing it satisfies one of society's most importunate needs.

From the point of view of the individual, of course, the family of orientation satisfies a correlative, if unconscious, need. It is the family that gives him life and a chance to survive. Children conceived in promiscuous unions frequently perish by abortion, and children born of such unions often become the victims of infanticide. It is the family, in short, to which we owe our life, and this is an assertion that applies to all but a statistically insignificant minority in the entire population of the world.

A second function of the family is to regulate and control the sexual impulse. This function too the family performs, however imperfectly, in all societies. If sex alone cannot explain the family, as we have previously asserted, it is nevertheless true that here we have the most intimate association between a biological reality and a social design. It should not be necessary, in this age of candor, to stress the insistency of the sexual need. It is a phenomenon, however, that merits more than a moment's reflection.

Whether we consider the entire animal kingdom, or only the human part of it, the sheer power of the sexual drive must awe the thoughtful mind. Let us attend, for example, to Plato. In the beginning of *The Republic* Cephalus, the father of Polemarchus, is asked by Socrates how it feels to arrive at what the poets call "the threshold of old age." Cephalus replies that he would say, with Sophocles, "Most gladly have I escaped the thing of which you speak; I feel as if I had escaped from a mad and furious master." Indeed, Cephalus now views not only with equanimity but with enjoyment the repose that has come to him since the passions have relaxed their hold.

When we think about this "mad and furious master," we begin to wonder, not why there are deviations from the sexual codes, but how there could ever be any conformity, how there could in fact be a norm from which to deviate. Somehow, some time, society had to take this powerful force into account, to construct a code of sexual conduct, to "write" prescriptions and proscriptions on sexual activity, and to surround the sexual impulse with commandment and taboo. No one knows exactly how this happened, and no one can trace its history. Whenever people live in groups, as of course they always do, whether in roving bands or in settled communities, something has to be done about this ineluctable biological force, the force without which the race would disappear.

The task was somehow accomplished. Codes were constructed and supplied with sanctions; the mores brought this imperious drive under at least a semblance of social control. And the institution that played a central role in the process, was, of course, the family. Marriage is society's way of regularizing a sexual relationship. The family obviates the chaos that would otherwise be the inevitable accompaniment of an urge so ineluctable, a drive so demanding. A family, initiated in an established manner by marriage, thus serves as a sanctioned locus for the satisfaction of the sexual impulse and reduces the disorder that would otherwise prevail.

Note again, however, that it is not the biological factor of sex alone that requires the family. On the contrary, sex as a physiological function requires only expression and release. It is society, in an effort to cope with sex, that "invents" the institution of the family in order to provide the appropriate controls. Order and stability are social conveniences, not biological necessities.

Reduction of the chaos that would ensue from sexual anomy may seem like a purely negative function for the family to perform. Social order, however, is never a negative achievement. As we have emphasized in the preceding section of this book, all of the norms contribute to the same goal; all of them contribute structure to society. They are, in a sense, synonymous with its structure. It would be difficult therefore to exaggerate the importance of the family in performing for society this important function.

If the family serves society as a means of sexual control, it serves the individual, correlatively, as a locus of sexual activity. George Bernard Shaw once remarked that marriage combines a maximum of temptation with a maximum of opportunity. Although the first part of his assertion may possibly be open to question, on the ground that familiarity often breeds contempt, there is no question that marriage does provide a maximum opportunity for sexual satisfaction. It offers much more, of course, than the satisfaction of a moment; it offers a satisfaction that can endure for many years and become what a distinguished sociologist, Florian Znaniecki, called a lifelong erotic relationship. The significance of this service can be grasped most readily by considering how precarious the sexual situation would be for the individual if there were no such institution as marriage. It is in the family that an appropriate recognition is given to the importance of sex in the life of the individual.

It is interesting to observe that it took our Western civilization many centuries to learn that sex has a value and a purpose beyond that of reproduction. In the early Christian tradition, as we saw in the preceding chapter, there was a clear dualism between the soul and the body, and bodily functions were regarded as somehow unclean and as contaminating the soul. Sexual asceticism was therefore encouraged, and St. Paul's famous words—"It is better to marry than to burn"—carried their oppressive weight into succeeding centuries. Both Calvin and Luther, as the distinguished theologian Reinhold Niebuhr reminds us, accepted uncritically the Pauline opinion; and Luther, though he personally rejoiced in marriage as a source of grace, nevertheless permitted himself also to describe it as "a hospital for sick souls."[6]

As a consequence of views like these, sexual relations even in marriage were regarded as sinful unless conducted for the purpose intended by "nature" namely, procreation. On this question there remains a division between Catholicism and Protestantism in our own society, the latter now having the more liberal view. Indeed, Niebuhr, the Protestant theologian, argues that the Pauline proscriptions negate the important fact that a sexual partnership is also a comradeship and that sex has its own incomparable contribution to make to marital happiness and stability.

One final observation detains us. Although clearly never planned for the purpose, the family may serve to sanction the sexual claims of women that they would be unable to assert for themselves in a purely biological world. We do not mean to imply that women are devoid of offensive sexual weapons—their sheer physical attraction, for example—but only that sex is a right which they could not demand if there were no such institution as marriage. Marriage recognizes the reciprocal obligations of both sexes and sanctions a claim to expression on the part of the female. The failure to consummate a marriage by having sex relations constitutes a ground for annulment for either spouse; each has a right to sex relations with the other. But it is a right that, in the absence of marriage, a male could assert by force and a female could not. The institution of marriage, in short, gives societal recognition to the sexual needs of the female. This right, of course, is a purely social fact; it has no existence among the lower orders of animals. Marriage thus creates and confers upon the female a right she would otherwise be unable to assert for herself.[7]

To summarize this second function of marriage and the family we may say that for society these institutions are mechanisms of sexual control, for the individual avenues of sexual opportunity. Although our discussion has involved an emphasis upon biological need, it shows that the satisfaction of this need is overlaid by social sanction and social control. It indicates once again that even a basic physiological function finds expression on the human level only in terms of culture and of cultural norms. And it provides a vital illustration, in a literally vital sphere, of the manner in which the

---

[6] Reinhold Niebuhr, *The Self and the Dramas of History*, Charles Scribner's Sons, New York, 1955, pp. 107–108.

[7] If this right is a purely social fact it is also, in a sense, a recent social fact. When it is denied that females have sexual needs, as it was in an earlier intellectual climate, then marriage serves no such purpose. Then it serves instead merely to confer legitimacy upon a woman's offspring and to entitle her to economic support.

norms contribute structure to society, stability to social relationships, and regularity to the lives of individuals.

The third function of the family serves both society and the individual in essentially the same way. We may summarize it in a single word—maintenance. The family maintains the child for the society into which he is born. Maintenance could, of course, be institutionalized in quite different ways. Children could be maintained, for example, by the state or by the church, by hospitals or asylums, or even by the Army. It is doubtful, however, that any of these alternatives would work so well. Although the state, say, might in many instances be better able than the family to provide for the material needs of children, the family combines an intimate, personal response with social care, and it is a combination that no other institution can successfully challenge.

In this connection it is worth noting that the human child has an extraordinarily long period of dependence upon adults. In most species the young go their separate ways as soon as they reach sexual maturity. In the human species, on the contrary, puberty and maturity are two quite different concepts, and the former precedes the latter by a significant number of years. If we use twelve to fourteen as the age of puberty, and eighteen to twenty-one as the age of maturity, that is, the age when society permits a person to exercise the prerogatives of adult status, then we can see that one process takes half again as long as the other.

It is the second process, of course, that is a matter of societal definition. And it is the second process, too, that increases the importance of the human family. From birth to maturity, the individual requires the physical maintenance and economic support that no other institution of society can so efficiently offer. As society becomes more complex, the period of dependency is prolonged.

From the point of view of the individual the situation is the same. The infant requires care in order to survive. The young child needs protection—if not, as in more primitive societies, against the inclemency of the elements and the hazards of predatory animals and poisonous plants, at least against the dangers of traffic and household machines. The adolescent, in turn, requires more, not less, economic support in order to compete effectively with his peers for vocational preferment and professional success. In this sphere indeed our complicated urban society exhibits a sharp contrast with simpler rural societies. In the latter, children tend to be economic assets; in the former, economic liabilities. The subsistence obligation is one, furthermore, from which the family is never relieved. As someone has facetiously remarked, home is a place where, if you go there, they have to take you in. It would be difficult in any event, whether seriously or facetiously, to overestimate the importance of the maintenance function of the family.

A fourth function of the family is its service as an instrument of culture transmission. When, in our nonsociological moments, we think of culture we tend to think of it as something that is contained in books and consciously taught. In this sense culture is transmitted by the institution of education through the operation of such associations as schools, libraries, and museums. A moment's reflection, however, will disclose that a very considerable part of culture, even in a society whose members are literate, is of a nonliterate of nonliterary variety and that this part of culture too is transmitted from one generation to the next. It is also clear that the family is instrumental in performing this service and that during the earliest years of an individual's life it is the only agency engaged in this activity.[8] The human family thus guarantees not only the biological continuity of the species but also the cultural continuity of the society of which it is a part.

Let us pause a moment to emphasize the importance of the family as a vehicle of culture transmission. Its importance is especially great in the transmission of ideas and ideologies and, above all, of the mores; indeed, the family is the initial source of all of our moral ideas. It is our families, represented primarily by our parents, who teach us what is right and what is wrong, what is good and what is bad, what to desire and what to disdain, how to win and how to lose, what to keep and what to share, what to learn and what to ignore, when to surrender and when to stand firm, and so on through an entire catalogue of attitudes and ideas. In our own society there comes inevitably, for most of us, a time of transition, when we leave our family of orientation and begin to make our own decisions and solve our own problems. But we can never emancipate ourselves completely from that part of our culture which we have absorbed during our early life in a family.

We may emphasize again, as we did in an earlier chapter, that the things we have absorbed have come from a particular family and not from an entire society. Each family, like every other group, has its own subculture, its own rites and symbols and ceremonies, its own ways of doing things. A family represents to its children the culture of the larger society of which it is a part, but it is also true that in small and often subtle ways it differs from that society and has a miniature culture of its own. Certain ideas, certain ways of doing things, certain possessions typify a particular family just as certain ideas and norms and materiel characterize a larger and more comprehensive society. The ideas are seldom of earth-shaking importance; they concern for the most part the trivialities of daily living, but they are nevertheless important to those who share them. A family's traditions may consist of special turns of phrase, favored drives and

---

[8] Some culture, of course, as we have previously remarked, is transmitted by "peer groups."

picnic places, a schedule for workdays and another for holidays, and so on through all of the history and legend of family life and containing all of the sentiment we usually associate with home.

Sometimes these traditions and norms may differ from those in the surrounding society in nonessential or unimportant ways. The writer knows a family, for example, in which several words are always deliberately mispronounced as a reminder to its members of a happy occasion when one of the children first stuttered over them. Each family, in short, has its own folkways, the ways of the family, and these are intimate and dear to the family members. And finally, of course, a family has its own unique and often irreplaceable possessions—its house and its furniture, its ornaments and its heirlooms, its prizes and trophies. All of these things, and countless more, contribute solidarity and cohesion to this small group and give it a meaning for its members that cannot be duplicated in any other association in society.

If the family serves society as an instrument of culture transmission, it serves the individual, correlatively, as an instrument of socialization. A family prepares its children for participation in a larger world and acquaints them with a larger culture. With a curious and almost unique mixture of love and authority it introduces the child to an equality of rights and an inequality of privileges—a situation that, however paradoxical it may appear, seems in some degree to characterize all societies and all social groups. Some of our statuses, in effect, produce relations that are equalitarian, others produce relations that are stratified, and the family itself exemplifies the contrast. In this connection Kingsley Davis makes the following observation:

> The family furnishes both kinds of relationship—the authoritarian (as between parent and child) and the equalitarian (as between siblings)—within which socialization can take place. In this it differs from play groups and cliques, which are almost purely equalitarian. Each type of relationship supplies a unique and necessary element in socialization; and the fact that the family provides them both in a small circle gives it a special completeness in performing this function.[9]

And Reinhold Niebuhr, the theologian we quoted earlier, remarks: "The family is indeed the embryo of all social integration. Love and power are more coordinate in its organization than in any other."[10] Ideas of love and

---

[9] *Human Society*, The Macmillan Company, New York, 1949, p. 406.
[10] Niebuhr, *op. cit.*, p. 191. Neibuhr adds: "One might sentimentally define our whole social problem as an effort to reconstitute the coordination of love and power in the larger communities which obtained in the family."

authority, generosity and property, are only four of the many notions essential for socialization, and the structure of the family gives it an especial competence in teaching them to its younger members. It is the family in short that transforms the infant barbarian into the civilized adult, even when it cannot claim complete or universal success in the process.

We arrive at a final pair of functions that the family performs—status ascription for society and societal identification for the individual. We have already discussed the importance of status relations in a society so large and so complex that its members are unable to know one another personally and whose interactions, to a very significant degree, must perforce proceed in terms of the statuses they occupy. We have suggested in addition that some statuses are ascribed and others achieved. Here we are interested in the ascribed statuses. Two of these, age and sex, are biological ascriptions. Others, however, are social ascriptions, and it is the family that serves almost exculsively as the conferring agency or institution.

Society at large recognizes us first of all by our names, and our names, of course, come directly from our family, which serves, therefore, as the source of our societal identification. It is not too much to say that when the society asks who we are it is the family that provides the answer. Numerous statuses are initially ascribed by our families. Our ethnic status, our nationality status, our religious status, our residential status, our class status—sometimes our political status and our educational status as well—are all conferred upon us by our families and, although most of these may later be changed, it is in terms of these statuses that we first gain social recognition. In some societies, not excepting to some extent our own, occupational statuses are similarly the results of familial ascription. And again, wherever statuses are inherited, as in the case of royalty and nobility, it is the family that serves as the controlling mechanism. As simple and as obvious as this function may be, it nevertheless requires specific acknowledgment. Status ascription and societal identification are two facets of what is in effect the same process seen from two different points of view, and the importance of the family in this respect can hardly be exaggerated.

The five functions of the family that we have just discussed may be briefly summarized as follows, even though the separation into two columns is somewhat artificial:

Functions of the family

For society	*For the individual*
Continuation of the species	Life and survival
Sexual control	Sexual opportunity
Maintenance	Protection and support
Culture transmission	Socialization
Status ascription	Societal identification

Although the family may perform other, and subsidiary, functions, these five are the important ones and these, moreover, are performed by the family in all societies in independence of the cultural variations that otherwise characterize them. Every one of them could, conceivably, be accomplished in other ways, some of them are shared by other institutions, and some of them, finally, are accomplished by the family with something less than complete success. But—taking them all together—it is difficult to imagine an alternative arrangement that could so well serve these societal and individual needs. The family doubtless operates imperfectly, as do all other human institutions, but in the performance of all five of these functions it has no peer, or near competitor.

6. The Family as a Primary Group

Earlier in this book we introduced the concept of the primary group, a group in which personal rather than status relations prevail. It is clear that the family is the primary group par excellence and, indeed, generally the most important primary group that we ever experience. It is also the most enduring of all the primary groups that claim us as members. For these reasons this aspect of the family merits perhaps a paragraph or two of elaboration.

Most of our primary groups are highly transitory. We have different companions, different colleagues, and different circles of friends at different periods of our lives. By the time we enter college, for example, most of us have difficulty remembering who our best friend was when we were in the fourth grade of the elementary school, or even in our freshman year at high school. Sometimes, of course, these early friendships continue for a considerable time, and even on into adult life. But more frequently they disappear with changing circumstances. The friends with whom one has been most intimate before marriage, for example, tend to drop away, and husbands and wives make new friends together. Similarly, the ties that bind us to our college friends and roommates are replaced later on by others from our business and professional worlds. The process is an inevitable one, as inevitable as the process of life itself.

There is one group, however, that we carry with us through the whole of our lives, the group consisting of our mother and father, our brothers and sisters—the group, in short, that is our family. It is true that in a society in which people are as mobile as they are in ours we may cease to live in the same city as our parents or even in the same region of the country. But the ties remain in spite of the distances between us. The family is not only primary of course; it is also, as we have emphasized, persistent. All other primary groups—and we are members of a respectably large number of them during the course of a lifetime—are relatively transitory, their composition changing with our external circumstances. But the family remains. So long as parents live, their children retain with them a relationship that is unique. Where there are exceptions, as there are to nearly every observation, they are regarded as unfortunate and abnormal.

The distinguished American sociologist W. I. Thomas was always impressed with the importance of sex in society and indeed developed an appreciation of its role at least as early as did Sigmund Freud and in independence of the great Austrian whose name is now linked with this phenomenon. Toward the end of his life, however, Thomas often speculated about another factor, one somewhat subdued and even concealed in the Freudian emphasis. As important as sex may be, it is altogether possible, as Thomas once reflected,[11] that intimacy is even more important and that only an understanding of the latter can disclose the ultimate nature of interpersonal relations.

Thomas never wrote on this subject as such, but his notion is a suggestive and possibly even a seminal one. It is a notion, furthermore, that is related to the "four wishes" introduced into the literature by Thomas and Znaniecki. These wishes, it will be recalled, are the wish for recognition, response, security, and new experience. The wish for recognition is satisfied in the larger society where one comes to be known for his work, his affiliations, and his achievements. The wish for response, however, is satisfied only in the primary groups and, among these, especially in the family. It is in this group that an individual is appreciated and indeed responded to not for what he has done, or can do, but what he basically and fundamentally *is*. Here the individual himself is important. His statuses, which govern his activities in the larger society, recede into relative insignificance and here, in his family, he receives a response as a person. Here is a group those members care not about this or that aspect of his activities, to the exclusion of the rest, but about his entire being. This is not the only group society about which this can be said—friendship groups, for example, provide another illustration—but the family is the most persistent and definite locus of this kind of intimate, personal evaluation. It is the family, in short, in which we first know triumph and failure, joy and sorrow, hope and despair.

7. Family, Church, and State

It is apparent that the family as an institution is related in a number of involved and interesting ways to other institutions in society. Among these other institutions we may note particularly education, business, religion, and government, the last two of which merit some attention here. The family is in no sense an independent institution. Our own Western history

---

[11] In private conversation with the author.

has exhibited a constant competition between church and state for the control of the family, and it is a struggle that has by no means reached a conclusion as we approach the twenty-first century. In countries where there is an established church, like Spain and Israel for example, the state itself enforces religious norms, among which endogamous rules are perhaps the most important. In countries where there is a separation between church and state, some *modus vivendi* is worked out which, in the case of the United States, has given a position of clear superiority to the state.

The state in fact exercises a rather stringent control over the family. It prescribes the form of the marriage contract, decides the age at which individuals may marry, sets endogamous limits upon marital choices, treats certain violations of the contract (bigamy, for example) as criminal offenses, defines the obligations that family members have to one another, sometimes tries (usually unsuccessfully) to prohibit contraception, registers the birth of children, legislates rules for the inheritance of family property, determines when, and under what circumstances, family membership suffices to confer citizenship status upon an individual, and articulates the conditions under which the initial contract may be dissolved. Indeed, these are only a few of the controls exercised by the state over the family, and family law is a subject about which entire books have been written.

Whether or not the state should exercise this degree of detailed control over marriage and the family is a matter for moral, political, and social debate. It has been argued, for example, that the care and protection of children afford the only grounds on which the state may reasonably claim to govern the marriage contract and that the state, accordingly, whould have nothing to do with marriages before children arrive or after they have departed from the family domicile. Questions like these, however, are normative in intent and conclusion and are therefore concerns of social policy rather than of sociology.

We may observe in any event that the United States presents an unusual situation with respect to marital and family law. There is no such law on the national level but instead fifty different sets of law, one for each state in the Union. Although certain similar principles underlie them all, they nevertheless differ in detail and thus frequently give rise to confusions and contradictions. An extreme case of such confusion once resulted in a decision by a court that a woman was married to a man but that he, in turn, was not married to her.[12] Divorces, similarly, have been granted in some

---

[12] This situation occurred in the following way. The Commonwealth of Massachusetts has a law which forbids the remarriage of the "guilty party" in a divorce for a period of two years after the decree is granted. A man falling into this category married a woman in the state of Rhode Island before the two years had elapsed. The divorce of course was valid in Massachusets, and the remarriage in Rhode Island. When the pair returned to Massachusetts, however, they found themselves in trouble and the decision referred to above was made by the Massachusetts Supreme Court. Ray E. Baber, *Marriage and the Family*, 2d ed., McGraw-Hill Book Company, New York, 1953, p. 523.

states and refused recognition in others, and this is a sphere so full of confusion that lawyers and sociologists alike despair of any reasonable solution in the foreseeable future. Indeed, the attitude of the state in general toward divorce is so illogical as to be ludicrous. Although there are many differences in detail in the several states, in all of them divorce is an adversary proceeding based upon an assumption that one of the parties is innocent and wants the divorce and that the other is guilty and does not. This assumption, needless to say, frequently contradicts the facts. It results in the anomaly that Professor Baber expressed as follows:

> If only one person wants the divorce and can convince the court of the cause, it is granted, but if both want the divorce and agree to it, *even for exactly the same cause,* it becomes collusion and technically cannot be granted. Therefore, if a marriage becomes intolerable to either husband or wife, it may be dissolved; but if it becomes intolerable to both, the state rules that in the interests of society it must be maintained.[13]

The situation in the United Kingdom is no less capricious and cruel. As Brigid Brophy, the Irish novelist, has written from London:

> We have legislated ourselves a divorce system of notable irrationality. We insist that marriage, because it is by implication a reciprocal contract, cannot be dissolved by unilateral declaration. Then we insist that neither can it be dissolved by bilateral agreement. Indeed, there are commonly only two circumstances in which we will allow ourselves to be granted a divorce at all. Either we must be lucky enough to have married someone who will commit a 'matrimonial offence' by adultery, desertion, or being cruel to us: or we must commit one of those acts ourselves and at the same time have the good fortune to be married to someone who doesn't love us enough to forgive us but doesn't hate us enough to refrain through spite from suing.[14]

One of her own suggestions is that both marriage and divorce, like such *rites de passage* as confirmation and bar mitzvah, be left to the church, for those who have a church, and not be imposed at all upon the nonreligious.

The divorce laws of the various states in the United States and countries of the world are so various that we cannot begin to exhaust the subject here, or even properly to introduce it. It will suffice to say that both marriage and divorce are subject to rigorous regulation by both church and state and are seldom a matter for purely individual determination. As we have just seen, the marital pair is not even considered competent, in the legal sense, to judge whether or not they should remain as husband and

---

[13]Baber, *op. cit.*, p. 479. Beginning on January 1, 1970, however, divorce ceased to be an adversary proceeding under California law, and mutual incompatibility became one of the accepted grounds, the other being insanity.

[14]"Divorce," *The Listener*, Vol. 81, No. 2088, 3 April 1969, p. 441.

wife. The other institutions of society, presuming to represent the interests of society itself, always interpose their views, their principles, and their attempted controls. The extent of the interest displayed by church and state in the family at least provides a further index, if any more be needed, of the importance of the family in society.

8. Summary

In this chapter we have discussed the association and institution of the family. We have noted that the family is pervasive and universal, that as far into the past as records can reach there is no societal instance of its nonoccurrence. The very universality of this institution induced us to inquire whether it might have a biological base and might, in consequence, be a biological phenomenon. We answered this second question in the negative, suggesting again, as so often in this book, that biological factors were necessary, but not sufficient, to explain the family. Though rooted in the sexual character of the species, the family is a social and cultural phenomenon.

In the next section of the chapter we noted again the difference between an association and an institution, emphasizing that *a* family belongs in the former category and *the* family in the latter. We distinguished also between two kinds of families: the family of orientation, an involuntary group with some of the characteristics of a community; and the family of procreation, a voluntary association. We introduced in addition such words as "matrilocal" and "patrilocal," "matrilineal" and "patrilineal," "matronymic" and "patronymic," and "matriarchal" and "patriarchal," and suggested that in some societies there is a greater emphasis upon the consanguine family than upon the conjugal. Such other words as "monogamy" and "polygamy," "polygyny" and "polyandry," "endogamy" and "exogamy" also entered the discussion, and we observed in particular the importance of endogamous and exogamous norms.

The central section of the chapter was devoted to the functions of the family. We need not recapitulate them here but will say again that, taking them all in all, no other institution can perform them so well. We ended the chapter with a few brief paragraphs first on the family as a primary group and second on the relations of the family with such other institutions as church and state. On this latter subject alone volumes can be written in expansion of these remarks.

The subject of the family indeed is so vast in its scope and so extensive in its implications that no book can do it justice—much less a single chapter. We hope only that we have been successful in suggesting its overwhelming importance as a sector of sociology. What the future of the family may be, in our own or other societies, we shall make no effort to say. It is conceivable that the family could someday disappear and be replaced either in whole or in part by other institutions, performing similar functions in a superior fashion. But it is not very likely. As Ralph Linton wrote:

> The ancient trinity of father, mother, and child has survived more vicissitudes than any other human relationship. It is the bedrock underlying all other family structures. Although more elaborate family patterns can be broken from without or may even collapse of their own weight, the rock remains. In the Götterdämmerung which over-wise science and over-foolish statesmanship are preparing for us, the last man will spend his last hours searching for his wife and child.[15]

[15] Linton, *op. cit.*, p. 38.

Chapter 16

CITY AND SUBURB

HE SOUND of a siren pierces the city night, its voice rising to a scream and then subsiding again to a whine. It could be a prowl car on its way to the scene of a crime, or an ambulance on an errand of mercy. In the square itself the neon tubes of the store signs and the "spectaculars" above the street awe the bystander with their dancing colors, and around the central building a ribbon of light spells out the news of the moment. On the sidewalks the crowd, wandering who knows where, moves endlessly through the evening hours, north and south and east and west, like a sluggish river with opposing and contrary currents. It thins a little in the early morning hours, but its pedestrian pace never stops, because the city never sleeps.

A few feet below the city's surface the subway passes with a roar that momentarily dominates the babble of the auctioneer as he sells a two-dollar watch for the low, low price of eight ninety-five. From the taxi-dance hall, down a flight of narrow stairs, strident rhythms escape to the street, enticing the listless male to a meretricious companionship. On the corner a barker, cardboard poster in his cap, offers the sight-seeing tour to Chinatown, where the tourist can see a joss house that exists only for him. There is no stillness here, as the neons ripple in the night, the dust swirls in miniature hurricanes, and the buildings shimmer in the artificial light. The sky above is clear, but no one sees it. No star competes with the manufactured illumination, and tomorrow not even the sun will extinguish all of the electric bulbs.

This is the city. Look at it and listen to it. The blue exhaust of the buses, the impatient horns of the taxis, the quieter but insistent hum of rubber on asphalt, the rumble of trucks, the rattle of garbage cans, the push and jostle of the people, the cheesecake on the newsstands, the early morning editions on the sidewalks, the purveyors of pornography and of parlor tricks, the shrill whistle of the policeman as the red light changes to green, the burnt fragrance of roasting chestnuts, the sticky strains from the beggar's accordion, the synthetic orange juice, the drugstores stuffed with toys and cigarettes and powders and pastes, the photographers' booths, the juke boxes blaring, the pinball machines clattering, the sharper notes of the shooting gallery, the bookstores with their remaindered volumes, everywhere the bars and grills, the prostitutes working now in pairs, the sailors from every sea, the cheap hotels whose honeycombs keep particular but no universal secrets. Radios and television sets for sale, all at substantial discounts. Movie marquees in continuous procession, each one crowded by its neighbor. Hamburger stands and open-front restaurants. The clothing store going out of business, as it did last night and will again tomorrow night. And always the crowd flowing relentlessly from one decade to the next.

Not far from the raucous square there stands an opera house that throbs with the pageantry of centuries, a museum that contains the treasures of all times, a coliseum that exhibits the wares of every country and clime, a stock exchange where nervous men buy iron and steel and oils and chemicals (and promises to pay), a bank that lends its money to foreign governments, a cathedral whose spires strive for the firmament but fail to surmount the surrounding skyscrapers, a university where learned men seek new knowledge and disseminate it to the next generation, a library whose volumes store the wisdom and folly of all ages and all civilizations, and a "garden" where spectators of every race and religion watch the sporting events of the day and see, in season, the horse show and the circus.

The crowd has no name and no identity, no purpose and no destination. But without it the opera house, the museum, the coliseum, the stock exchange, the cathedral, and the university would not exist. Without it the city itself would cease to be.

This is the paradox of the city. It has everything that is tawdry and everything that is sublime. It holds both hope and despair. It encompasses millions of people, and it can be the loneliest place on earth. Its noise is sometimes deafening, but it produces the ideas that change the world. It is the vital center of every civilized society, and it is so lacking in essential resources that it can subsist only with the support of its countryside. It is the magnet that draws the ambitious from thousands of miles away and the goad that drives them back again to the peace of the country. The banker lives there and so does the beggar, the diplomat and the derelict, the actor and the accountant, the censor and the clown, the Philistine and the philosopher. Its structure contains every status and its groups every norm. It is both a place and a state of mind.

The history of every civilization is the history, not of its countryside, but of its cities and towns. Civilization means the city, and the city means civilization. Man originally built the city, and the city, in turn, civilized him. He became a citizen when he became a member of a city-state, and with the rise of the world-city, as Spengler tells us, "there were no longer noblesse and bourgeoisie, freemen and slaves, Hellenes and Barbarians, believers and unbelievers, *but only cosmopolitans and provincials.* All other contrasts pale before this one, which dominates all events, all habits of life, all views of the world."[1] City and country, the town and the land, the capital and the province—this, despite Spengler's exaggeration, is one of the most important of all kinds of social differentiation. The city man and the countryman do indeed adhere to two different views of the world, have different rounds of activity, sustain in different ways the progression of the seasons, indulge in different kinds of work and play, and spend their span of life in different surroundings. It is this important kind of differentiation to which we wish to devote the present chapter.

1. The Growth of Cities

Most of the world has been rural most of the time. Until quite recently in fact, in the long scale of history, the percentage of the world's population that lived in cities was small indeed. Before 1800, moreover, the cities themselves were small. Those who live within the city limits of New York, Chicago, Los Angeles, Philadelphia, or Detroit can greet with satisfaction or annoyance, depending upon their mood, the fact that these five places together accommodate more than 10 per cent of the total American population. Those who live in New York City and its suburbs can greet with similar ambivalence the information that one out of ten Americans lives within commuting distance of Times Square. For that matter, New York and London together contain 1 per cent of the entire population of the world.[2] Statements like these can be made for the first time in the history of the world in our own twentieth century. In no other period has a

[1] Oswald Spengler, *The Decline of the West*, trans. by Charles Francis Atkinson, Alfred A. Knopf, Inc., New York, 1939, vol. 2, p. 99.
[2] In 1/20,000 of the earth's inhabitable land.

comparable phenomenon occurred. The metropolitan community, in short, is a new experience in human living arrangements and one to which, it may be, we have not altogether learned to adjust.

The city is culture par excellence; it is the epitome of culture. It is mankind's greatest work of art—and of artifice—because it contains all others. Agriculture too, of course, is a form of culture (literally, "field culture"), but the country uses culture as a tool to work a natural substance—the earth. In the city, on the contrary, both the tools and the objects to which they are applied are almost invariably cultural. A natural environment surrounds the countryman and he governs his life by nature's vicissitudes. But culture, a manufactured environment, surrounds the city man. It is an environment of bricks and steel and mortar and cement, of bridges and tunnels, of sidewalks and streets, of monuments and buildings, of elevators and subway platforms. In the city everything is culture—even the parks, which are planned and tended by a department of the municipal government. Nature frequently intervenes, of course, with rain and snow and flood and hurricane, with searing heat and heartless cold; but for the most part man adapts himself to conditions of his own creation. The city is his, his own product and his own achievement.

How then do cities grow, and why? How do we account for this relatively new phenomenon in human society? What is the history of cities? Although our answers to these questions cannot be complete, or even as comprehensive as we should like, we shall attempt to answer them in order.

For the first time in this book we can have an answer to the question of social origins. No one knows when men first lived in families, or worshiped a God, or constructed a government, but cities appeared in a past not so remote as to be lost in time, in fact no longer than seven to eight thousand years ago. The earliest evidence, of course, is archeological, and this is fragmentary and uncertain. It is uncertain in the sense that, as Kingsley Davis cautions, archeological enthusiasm tends to call a city any digging that discloses a street and a public building or two.[3] But it is satisfactory in proving that settlements existed in this remote period and that people were not distributed evenly over the land.

The reasons for the rise of settlements seem simple. From the very beginning cities depended, as they still do, upon a surplus of foodstuffs grown on the land. So long as each family or unit produces only enough food for its own needs and proceeds to consume it all, cities are impossible. As soon as there is a surplus, however, the rise of cities enters the realm of the possible. It has truly been said that whoever can make two grains of

[3] Kingsley Davis, "The Origin and Growth of Urbanization in the World," *American Journal of Sociology,* vol. 60, March, 1955, p. 429.

wheat grow where one grew before has contributed to the growth of cities. A necessary condition for the rise of cities, in short, is a surplus agriculture, an agriculture of abundance.[4]

Thousands of years ago agriculture took great forward strides because of new inventions—inventions as important in their time as those that later ushered in the Industrial Revolution. Among these inventions we may name the ox-drawn plow, the wheeled cart, new ways of working and using metals, irrigation, the sailboat—all technological inventions—and the domestication of new plants—an agricultural invention. All these combined with favorable geographic conditions, affecting particularly soil and climate, to bring about a productive agricultural economy and, in Kingsley Davis's words, "to make possible the *sine qua non* of urban existence, the concentration in one place of people who do not grow their own food."[5]

Abundance, however, does not in itself suffice to explain a settlement. Nor is there any evidence that a village ever grew into a city by a mere increase in population. It is conceivable, for example, that an expanded food supply would simply induce the growers to multiply, in accordance with Malthusian principles, to the point where the surplus would become a scarcity again, the people remaining evenly distributed over the land. In order for settlements, and subsequently cities, to arise, another factor was needed:

> The rise of towns and cities therefore required, in addition to highly favorable agricultural conditions, a form of social organization in which certain strata could appropriate for themselves part of the produce grown by the cultivators. Such strata—religious and governing officials, traders, and artisans—could live in towns, because their power over goods did not depend on their presence on the land as such. They could thus realize the advantages of town living, which gave them additional power over the cultivators.[6]

Even in this early period, in short, we have a power situation between those in the towns and those on the land, with the former destined to dominate, as they have since done throughout human history. Agriculture thus makes

---

[4] This almost universally accepted theory of the growth of cities has been disputed by Jane Jacobs, who believes that settlements came first and agriculture, as a form of urban new work, second. See her book *The Economy of Cities*, Random House, New York, 1969. It is difficult, however, to see how one can have a settlement, as contrasted with a roving band, without some fairly reliable source of food, and this would indicate agriculture rather than hunting and gathering. Furthermore, without a surplus all men would be destined to be farmers and fisherman, hunters and gatherers, and no urban occupations and pursuits like barter, trade, and commerce could arise.

[5] Davis, *op. cit.*, p. 430.

[6] *Ibid.*

the city possible, but culture itself—especially in the form of social organization—makes it probable, and indeed brings it into being.

The power situation introduces another hypothesis into the sociological problem of the growth of cities. Warfare has so far been one of the constants of social life. With the development of metallurgy at the end of the Neolithic period, those who had metal weapons gained an advantage over those possessing only crude stone axes and thus managed to conquer them. This situation is described as follows by Egon Bergel, recounting a theory advanced by Margaret A. Murray:

> Neolithic peasants who did not know how to make weapons from copper, bronze, or iron were easy prey to invaders armed with metal weapons. The aggressors frightened their more primitive victims, to whom they appeared as gods or demigods, into subjugation. The conquerors then moved into the territory of the peasants, who became their serfs. The overlords, to secure their rule, selected settlement places such as islands, or, preferably, hilltops, which dominated the countryside so that both attack and defense were facilitated. In brief, it is postulated that the first cities were permanent army camps established in the area of a vanquished population.[7]

Men who possess an advantage in arms are not ordinarily reluctant to use it. If cities started peacefully in a differentiation between traders and farmers, it is not unreasonable to suppose that they also began militarily in a differentiation between conquerors and conquered.

Another early division of labor was that between soldiers and farmers, and this factor also doubtless played a role in urban development. H. G. Creel offers the following description of this process:

> A ruling, fighting class gradually separated itself out from the general neolithic population. As fighting became more common, and neolithic and early bronze-using people began to make raids on each other, it was necessary that some of the men of each village should specialize on defense and on fighting. Perhaps whole settlements sometimes found that is was easier to set up as warriors, and let the people around them work for them, than to labor in the fields. The chiefs and their groups of warriors, no doubt, provided the farmers with "protection" whether they wanted it or not, and in return for that service they took a share of the peasant's crop. The size of that share was fixed by the warriors, since they had the power to fix it, and the peasants were helpless.[8]

[7] Egon Ernest Bergel, *Urban Sociology*, McGraw-Hill Book Company, Inc., New York, 1955, p. 18. See also Margaret A. Murray, *The Splendor That Was Egypt*, Philosophical Library, Inc., New York, 1949.
[8] H. G. Creel, *The Birth of China*, Reynal & Hitchcock, Inc., New York, 1937, pp. 278–279. Quoted in Bergel, *op. cit.*, p. 19.

The pursuit of agriculture, in short, was seldom pacific in ancient times, and processes that may have resulted in settlements in any event were given an additional impetus by military activity. The tendency of human groups to covet their neighbors' property and to appropriate it for themselves wherever possible cannot be neglected in any explanation of the rise of settlements. If early cities were army camps, later ones became fortresses, and the military factor continued to play an important role.[9]

The earliest cities, whatever the basis of their organization, were nevertheless small and scarce, and the trends that brought them into being did not exhibit any great acceleration in ancient times. Davis offers the following reasons, largely technological, for the slow rate of urbanization:

> Argriculture was so cumbersome, static, and labor-intensive that it took many cultivators to support one man in the city. The oxdrawn plow, the wooden plowshare, inundation irrigation, stone hoes, sickles, and axes were instruments of production, to be sure, but clumsy ones. Not until iron came into use in Asia Minor about 1300 B.C. could general improvement in agriculture be achieved. The static character of agriculture and of the economy generally was fostered perhaps by the insulation of the religiopolitical officials from the practical arts and the reduction of the peasant to virtually the status of a beast of burden. The technology of transport was as labor-intensive as that of agriculture. The only means of conveying bulky goods for mass consumption was by boat, and, though sails had been invented, the sailboat was so inefficient that rowing was still necessary. The oxcart, with its solid wheels and rigidly attached axle, the pack animal, and the human burden-bearer were all short-distance means of transport, the only exception being the camel caravan. Long-distance transport was reserved largely for goods which had high value and small bulk—i.e., goods for the elite—which could not maintain a large urban population. The size of the early cities was therefore limited by the amount of food, fibers, and other bulky materials that could be obtained from the immediate hinterland by labor-intensive methods, a severe limitation which the Greek cities of a later period, small as they remained, nevertheless had to escape before they could attain their full size.[10]

To these reasons Davis adds certain political and military limitations, including among the former the existence of a large number of tribal societies and the local autonomy retained even in the early empires, and, among the latter, the danger of revolt on the one hand and of invasion on the other.[11]

[9] A concentration of people, once a military advantage for both offense and defense, may of course in the atomic age be a military disadvantage.
[10] Davis, *op. cit.*, p. 431.
[11] "It is symptomatic of the weakness of the early cities that they were constantly threatened and frequently conquered not only by neighboring towns but also by nonurban barbarians. Each wave of barbarians tended to rebuild the urban centers and to become agricultural and sedentary, only to be eventually overwhelmed in turn by new invaders." *Ibid.*

Finally, urban growth was further hindered by such factors as primitive sanitation facilities, the tie of the peasant to his land, the absence of manufacturing, and the traditionalism of all classes. The early cities, in short, were small indeed in terms of contemporary comparisons. It is unlikely that even the largest concentrations of Mesopotamia, India, Egypt, Persia, and Greece ever numbered more than 200,000 inhabitants, no more than 1 or 2 per cent of the total population.[12] The engineering talents and administrative ingenuity of the Romans enabled them to escape some of these limitations, and Rome therefore became the largest city in the ancient world.[13]

Not even Rome, however, was immune from progressive waves of invasion, and the city of the Caesars declined in the early medieval period. Not until the nineteenth century, in London, was the world to see again a city of the size and munificence of imperial Rome. The relative absence of cities in the medieval period and the general retardation of urban growth in the first ten centuries of the Christian era are phenomena that invite speculation. The paucity of new developments in agricultural techniques, the failure of technological development in general, the feudal and manorial systems, the predatory activities of numerous Northern and Western tribes, the political autonomy of the separate city-states, the primitive transportation facilities, and the otherworldly orientation of the Middle Ages all doubtless played a role. For a thousand years the cloister and the castle took precedence over the city. Not until the Industrial Revolution did cities of any size or consequence arise, and the cities we know today are in truth a new phenomenon in history.[14]

It is unnecessary to trace the history of cities from Renaissance times to the present. Certain purely statistical statements, however, will afford some indication of the rapid rate of urbanization since the beginning of the nineteenth century. In the year 1800 there was not a single city in the world with a population of 1 million and there were fewer than twenty-five with as many as 100,000 inhabitants. In 1950—only 150 years later—there were forty-six metropolitan areas with a population of 1 million or more and 700 with more than 100,000. In 1962 no fewer than 112 metropolitan areas in the world had a population of 1 million or more and 31 of these had more than 2 million. In 1972 the city of Tokyo alone had 10 million people,

[12] Davis estimates that from fifty to ninety farmers were required to support one man in the city.

[13] Estimates of the size of ancient Rome vary from 250,000 to almost a million. By the year A.D. 800, however, the population had declined to some 20,000.

[14] Population estimates of early modern cities are interesting for comparative purposes: Florence (1338), 90,000; Venice (1422) 190,000; Antwerp (sixteenth century), 200,000; London (1377), 30,000; Nuremberg (1450), 20,165; Frankfort (1440), 8,719. See Davis, *op. cit.*, p. 432. See also Henri Pirenne, *Medieval Cities*, Princeton University Press, Princeton, N.J., 1939.

London 9 and New York a little less than 9 million. In 1970 the New York metropolitan area contained more than 15 million people and by 1985 this figure is expected to rise to 22 million.[15]

The percentage of the world's population living in cities has grown much more rapidly than the population itself. In the year 1800 about 15.6 million people lived in cities of 100,000 or more. By 1950 the comparable figure was 313.7 million, or twenty times as many. This growth seems to be characteristic of the entire world, although the highest degree of urbanization is still to be found in Northern Europe and those regions that Northern Europeans have settled. Asia and Africa remain the least urbanized of the world's larger regions. There is clearly a correlation between urbanization and industrialization. But industrialization continues to spread and cities continue to increase in number and size. The increase is so rapid in fact that before another century has passed most of the world's inhabitants will be living an urban existence.[16]

2. A Note on Definition

The words "urbanization" and "urbanism" sometimes cause confusion, and indeed it is instructive, but hardly encouraging, to note that distinguished books in the field of urban sociology use them in exactly opposite senses. It is best, perhaps, to follow Bergel, who refers to urbanization as a process and urbanism as a condition; that is, urbanization is the process in which rural areas become transformed into urban areas, the process in which the country becomes "citified," the process by which cities rise and grow; and urbanism is the condition that results from this process. This distinction has the merits of grammatical correctness and logical clarity.

Urbanism, however, is more than a statistical concept, and it cannot be correlated simply with the percentage of people in a given national state who live in cities. Thus, the percentage of the population living in cities in Chile is higher than in Canada, but every other index of urbanism would suggest that the former is less urban in its total character than the latter.[17] Neither is the size of the principal city of a nation a reliable index. Ireland, for example, would ordinarily be regarded as a more urban nation than Mexico although Mexico City is six times as large as Dublin.[18] Scotland may well be the most urbanized of all countries. Most of its population lives in Glasgow and Edinburgh, and the narrow band between, but the moors of

---

[15] Raymond Vernon, *Metropolis 1985*, Harvard University Press, Cambridge, Mass., 1960.
[16] See Homer Hoyt, *World Urbanization*, Urban Land Institute, Washington, D.C., 1962.
[17] Kingsley Davis, *Human Society*, The Macmillan Company, New York, 1949, p. 318.
[18] Bergel, *op.cit.*, p. 11.

the Highlands and the Hebrides preserve for it a rural flavor. Considerations like these suggest that purely statistical comparisons, useful as they are, have certain limitations in articulating the nature of a sociological phenomenon.

As we have already briefly suggested, the life of the man or woman living in the farmhouse on the hill or in the valley differs in many important respects from the life of their counterparts whose address is Apartment 1401 on the fourteenth floor of a residential skyscraper. Some of these differences we want to consider in detail in the following sections. It is desirable, however, to introduce our comparisons with several cautions.

In the first place the words "rural" and "urban" represent a continuum that, like other sociological classifications, cannot be graduated with precision; that is, we are dealing with a gradient rather than with a set of separate categories. Villages shade imperceptibly into towns, towns into cities, and cities into metropolitan regions.

Secondly, we find it impossible to rely upon a census for our differentiations. A city of more than 200,000 population, like Des Moines, Iowa, for example, is more rural in many of its characteristics than a suburb like Rye, New York, with a population of around 15,000. The successful novelist living in voluntary isolation in his remodeled farmhouse in southern Vermont, or on the Florida keys, is almost certainly as urban in his attitudes as the residents of the city of Chicago. The more than 840,000 people who read *The New York Times* every day, wherever they may live, are at least as urban in their tastes and customs as the 840,000 people who live in San Antonio, Texas.

Urbanism, in short, depends upon the existence of cities, but it does not require physical residence within their limits, nor even a geographic proximity. In the following sections of this chapter, therefore, we shall be interested in city and country not as demographic but as sociological phenomena.[19]

3. Homogeneity and Heterogeneity

The countryside presents a sameness to those who dwell on the land. The city alters its attractions with every passing block. Soil and cement are two

---

[19] Important contributions to the sociology of urbanism have been made by such outstanding sociologists as Georg Simmel, Max Weber, Robert E. Park, Louis Wirth, and Kingsley Davis, to the last of whom we have already referred. Wirth's paper, "Urbanism as a Way of Life," which was first published in the *American Journal of Sociology* in 1938 (vol. XLIV, pp. 1–24), is regarded as a classic treatment of the subject. At least as important, however, are works written by two men who did not wear the badge stamped "sociologist," one of them the German Oswald Spengler and the other the American Lewis Mumford.

different environments, and of the two the cement has more shapes. The countryman's corner of earth imposes upon him a more homogeneous round of activity than his cousin in the city pursues. He responds more directly to the hours of daylight and the hours of night, and follows in greater harmony the progression of the seasons. The earth itself gives him a predominant mode of occupation and determines his time to work and his time to sleep. The countryman pursues his span of life in intimate relationship with the physical forces that make the day and the year, the weather and the wind. The city man, on the contrary, performs his tasks in independence of the wind's vicissitudes and the season's change.

If the dominant occupation on the land is agriculture, an occupation that most other activities serve in some measure or other, the city in contrast offers an almost limitless range of ways to make a living. Indeed, it is impossible to describe the diversity and the heterogeneity of occupational life in the city. Here can be found every trade known to man, every skill and every talent, every kind of research and every kind of inquiry. If we pick up the "employment opportunities" section of a large metropolitan newspaper, the chances are very great that we shall find advertised there a job so remote from our own experience that we have never heard of it before. Umpires and diamond cutters, electronic engineers and brokers, detectives and psychoanalysts, and many more without number have their principal abode in the city. Trade and finance and commerce and industry and research all thrive in the city as they cannot in the country. The city is the locus of occupational variety, and it is in the occupational sphere above all that it exhibits its versatility and heterogeneity.

This situation, however, contains a paradox. For in the country, where there is a dominant mode of occupation, the farmer cannot be a specialist. He has to know how to cultivate different kinds of crops and to tend different kinds of animals, how to mend a fence and repair a tractor, to dig a well and fix a windmill, and to operate as general handy man around his house and barn. In the city, on the contrary, each man is a specialist, performing day after day, and in all seasons, essentially the same job. Occupational heterogeneity, in short, stimulates specialization whereas occupational homogeneity, on the other hand, requires skills of a more general and unspecialized kind. The farmer and his wife can do things that leave the city man and woman in wonderment, and although this observation is also true in reverse, the "doing" of the urbanite is of a different kind. The paradox, if such it be, only emphasizes the contrast between two different modes of life.

The countryman, far more than his acquaintance in the city, has a common task, a common earth, and a common hope. He responds to one environment and to one culture. The city man, on the contrary, reacts to different environments and to many groups—each, it may be, with a different culture.

The heterogeneity of the city, of course, extends far beyond its occupational diversity. There is heterogeneity in patterns of recreation, in education,[20] in wholesale and retail trade, in religion, in political opinion, in ethnic origin, in modes of transportation, in styles of living, and styles of thought. There is heterogeneity in the goals that men pursue and the paths they follow to their different destinations.

And yet it must be recognized that contrasts once sharp are now softening, that twentieth-century developments in agricultural technology, in transportation, and in communications are diminishing the differences between the city and the country, making the former more homogeneous with respect to certain kinds of conformity and the latter more heterogeneous with respect to certain kinds of stimulation. The American farmer in particular was always a pioneer, not a peasant, and his periods of prosperity have frequently made him a citizen of the nation, if not of the world. An Iowa farmer and a Russian dictator once became good friends.

In traveling the endless prairies of the Middle West, for example, one cannot help noting the splendor of the rich, black loam and the stateliness of the farm dwellings.[21] In one of the fields the traveler sees an airplane—a vehicle that transports its owner and his family to Florida once or twice a season, to California on occasion, and to farm conventions far and wide. The man who owns it is a college graduate, and he has an advanced degree in veterinary medicine, genetics, dairy production, or the chemistry of the soil. In August his fields are high with hybrid corn, and the television set in his living room gives him more of the world and of an urban civilization than his rural ancestors could ever have conceived.

Finally, mass production, specialized techniques, and mechanization have come to agriculture too. We now have "factories in the fields," enterprises of vast acreage, and fantastic machinery preparing the soil and seeding it, picking cotton, and harvesting wheat and corn. The twentieth century has brought with it a new technological revolution in agriculture, and the social consequences cannot be predicted in detail. Two consequences, however, are probable. It will contribute an additional stimulus to the growth of cities and further diminish the population in rural areas. And then, when the land has no more people to offer, cities will have to provide their own sources of population if they continue to grow..

[20] In New York City, for example, there are specialized high schools devoted to commerce, to needle trades, to food trades, to machine and metal trades, to aviation trades, to music and art, to printing, to industrial art, and to the performing arts.
[21] To say nothing of barns.

4. Primary and Secondary Groups

We have previously observed that, even under the best of circumstances, there are only a relatively few persons with whom a given individual in society has intimate and personal relations—that is, primary relationships. No man, no matter how gifted or prominent or wealthy or popular, has more than a few dozen others whom he admits to his primary social circle. In this respect the city man and the countryman are at one.

The difference between them appears in a striking fashion, however, in their secondary relationships. The relationships the urban dweller has with others are to a very large extent status relationships and not personal relationships. He may go from one end of the metropolitan region to another, by taxi, bus, and subway, interact with a hundred people during the course of a day, and know few or none of them personally. He interacts with them on the contrary in accordance with the norms attached to their statuses and to his. This predominance of secondary contacts, secondary groups, and status relationships over the primary and personal—in number though not, of course, in intensity or warmth—is one of the significant characteristics of city life.

The man who dwells on the land, and who works it, tends to a far greater extent to know personally the people with whom he comes in contact during the course of a day, a week, or a season. He knows his neighbors, and they talk together after the manner of men who have common problems and common tasks. In the city, on the other hand, the salesman may know nothing of the life of the hackie in whose cab he rides, and the cab driver in turn knows nothing of the policeman who waves him on his way, nor the policeman of the night-club comedian to whom he gives a parking ticket, nor the comedian of the accountant who helps him with his income tax.

It is not only the relationships themselves but the groups of which we are members that exhibit this contrast. Group life in the country tends to display few of the organizational rigidities that characterize group life in the city. For the farmer, organized and unorganized groups are generally the same; he knows the members of the former as well as he does the members of the latter. They are the same people, his neighbors and friends, whether he meets them in the fields, in church, at the grange hall, at a community festival, or at a ball game. The city man, for example the broker at his telephone, may interact all day with customers all over the country, with people he may know only by name, and with whom he carries on transactions of considerable size and financial importance. Similar observations can be made about the clerk at his counter, the ticket seller in his booth, the policeman at the intersection, the teller in his cage, the chef in his kitchen, the doctor in his ward, the hotel clerk at his desk, the dispatcher at the terminal, and the toll taker at the bridge. All of their activities, highly organized as they must be, and representing hundreds of highly organized associations, involve secondary rather than primary contacts, status rather than personal relationships. And the associations that contain these statuses are the locus of the city man's life, the place where he earns his living, the nodal points in the web of his society.

Before turning to these associations, however, we should reject the implication that there are no primary groups in the city apart from families and friends. If a man lives in the same neighborhood for any length of time he will come to know his newsdealer, the clerk at the cigar store, the pharmacist, the grocer, the butcher, the cashier at the restaurant, the bartender at his favorite tavern, the doorman in his apartment house, the building superintendent, and many others. These will be segmentel relationships, to be sure, relationships initiated and maintained through status and location rather than through personal regard. But these too may ripen after a while and take on a genuine warmth even in the absence of intimacy. The city seems unfriendly only to the visitor, the tourist, and the stranger, people who seek its superficial pleasures and never see the quiet neighborhoods, far from the milling crowd. As a matter of fact, the crowd on Times Square, to which we have previously referred, is composed overwhelmingly of "foreigners," people who come to visit and not to stay. As still another paradox we may note that only in the city is privacy possible, that the country offers not privacy but only isolation. Involuntary privacy can turn into loneliness, and we have already remarked that the city can be the loneliest place on earth, expecially for its unattached inhabitants; but voluntary privacy, a virtue that is consciously sought, can almost never be achieved in a rural or small-town environment.

There are those, on the other hand, who believe that the pace of the city is too rapid and that peace of mind can be won only in the country. The city to them is a chattering chaos, the cause of ulcers and neuroses, from which the sensible man will escape as soon as he can. Where in this ominous press of people can we find the tranquillity, the peace of mind, that we can enjoy in the country lane, in the west pasture of the farm, around the stove in the country store, in farmhouse kitchen and village church? Where in the city can we contemplate the mists that hover over the distant ridge, the starlit sky of a summer night, the bracing air of a clear October morning? The city too has its poets, however, who would reply that it also knows its areas of silence and its hours of peace.[22]

---

[22] Ronald Blythe has written an enchanting book on contemporary village life in Suffolk. See his *Akenfield: Portrait of an English Village*, Dell Publishing Co., Inc., New York, 1970.

There is no question, in any event, that the city is the locus of an amazing number and variety of voluntary associations. This characteristic is a corollary of the predominance of status relations and of the sheer number of people congregated in one place. No matter what a person's interest may be, no matter how trivial or esoteric or profound, he is almost certain to find others in the city who share it and who, in all probability, have formed an association to pursue it. In a small town there may be only one or two persons who have an enthusiasm, say, for stamp collecting. In New York City 50,000 people will pay admission to an exhibition of stamps on a single day. Whether the interest be stamps, foreign automobiles, tropical fish, flowers, dogs, the scientific study of religion, atomic fission, space travel, curling, the single tax, the works of Robert Browning, or almost anything else that fascinates the human mind, there will be an association in the city to satisfy it; and if no association happens to exist for a particular purpose, it is usually easy enough to find others who are interested and to initiate one. No one can speak with confidence about the durability or the mortality of these associations, but there is no doubt that they exist in profusion.

We may note also in this connection that the associations represented in the city tend in large measure to be horizontal rather than vertical in their membership; that is, factors of location and residence diminish in importance, and the interest is everything. In the country and in the small town people organize and belong to associations because they live in a particular place and share a common problem or pursuit. In the city and the metropolis the members of an association may live anywhere, even on the other side of a continent. The rural association, in short, tends to be a locality group, the metropolitan association a stratum.

It is not improbable, to choose only one example, that a professor of philosophy at New York University has closer relations, both personal and associational, with his colleagues at the University of Minnesota, the University of California, and the University of Illinois than he does with the professors of Spanish whose offices may be in the same building, on the floor below. He may see the latter more frequently—even that is doubtful—but the former are his closer friends. When this situation is multiplied by the number of occupational, professional, and other interest groups that obtain in a society, it is easy to see the importance in the city of horizontal groups as contrasted with the vertical groups that predominate in the village and town.[23]

---

[23] We do not mean to imply that vertical groups do not arise in the city. It is quite common, on the contrary, for the tenants in an apartment house to organize in order to induce the landlord to lower his rents or to remodel the lobby, and so also for other locality groups.

5. Formal and Informal Social Control

Social control in the city presents a striking contrast to its counterpart in the country. In the former situation it tends to be secondary and formal; in the latter primary and informal. The gossip that keeps the individual member of a small community "in line" and that operates as a potent sanction inducing conformity to the norms has little role or relevance in the city. Social pressures of this kind work steadily and inexorably in primary groups. Ostracism for nonconformity is much more serious when the nonconformist has no other groups to which he can readily turn. Many stories tell with poignance of the frightful weapon that gossip can be—how, with an efficacy that is often cruel, it punishes its sometimes innocent victims. We need not elaborate upon the function of gossip as a means of social control. It is the instrument, in the small community, that permits the prompt application of sanctions to those who fail to conform to the norms.

It is apparent that gossip can have no such function in the metropolis. The primary groupings in which it operates so effectively in the village have no definite locus in the city; they exist, but not at a given place. An individual can easily withdraw from them, or otherwise avoid them. If the city provides privacy, it also furnishes anonymity to those who desire it. One may escape the primary social controls altogether at the price of dispensing with group affiliations, both formal and informal. On the other hand, the formal social controls—the law and the police—are very much more in evidence in the city than they are in the rural community. No one is immune from the parking regulation, none from the traffic ticket. The sanctions of the law press upon all alike who are tempted to stray from its requirements, and they are applied, if not with complete impartiality, at least with impersonality.

At the same time it is apparent that the city exhibits more tolerance for certain kinds of conduct and behavior, and for individual idiosyncrasy, than does the small community. The reason is simple. The city is a place of contrasts; its very heterogeneity suggests that there will be many different sets of norms; the citizens themselves are exposed to variegated cultures and to diversified ways of working and worshiping. The city man sees the foreign-language newspapers on the stalls and in the subway, notices that the Sabbath is celebrated on one day of the week by one group and on another day by others, and notices too that every step on the spectrum of political opinion has its advocates. He is accustomed to differences, and learns to tolerate them. The strange and the unfamiliar, whether it gives him pleasure or pain, at least is not surprising. The city has taught him to expect it and to live with it. The countryman, on the other hand, is likely to greet the unfamiliar with suspicion and even with hostility. It poses a threat to his way of life and may call into question traditions and beliefs to which he has always been deeply, if unconsciously, committed. Exposure to social differentiation itself induces tolerance and sometimes even understanding, and it is in the city that differentiation reaches its extreme. As the German proverb has it, city air makes for freedom—*Stadtluft macht frei.*

6. Social Mobility

The society of the city, in contrast to that of the country, is a fluid one. Its social strata may be more apparent, the lines more clearly drawn, but the individual can move more freely up—and down—the scale.

Cities differ, of course, in this characteristic, depending upon the rigidity of the class structure of the larger society of which they are a part. But where there is any mobility at all it is certain to be accelerated in the city. It may be recalled that cities grow in the first place because of migration from the country and that geographic mobility is itself a stimulus and an aid to social mobility.

Social mobility has a particular application to American cities. The penniless immigrant who becomes a millionaire, the impoverished graduate student who later achieves the presidency of a college or university, the clerk in the corporation who later becomes chairman of the board—these and many similar instances are phenomena of the city. There are more "escalators" there and more people riding them. The division of labor, and the differential evaluation of occupational endeavor, which gives rise to social class in the first place, paradoxically makes possible a greater individual mobility than a less highly differentiated situation can offer. This is doubtless one of the reasons why the city, as we have observed, attracts the able and the ambitious from the hinterland.[24]

The able and the ambitious, in turn, generate the ideas that move the world. It is the man of the metropolis who writes the poems and the novels that will represent his age and generation, and it is the man of the metropolis too who paints the pictures, composes the music, and builds the towers that will endure as tokens of his time and place. It is the city man who discovers new truths about the universe and it is he who integrates them into new systems of philosophy. The city man is the creative man—the creator of a civilization. The reason that this is so is not only that the city attracts the man of genius. It also furnishes the soil, as it were, in which his genius can flower. It provides him with the stimulus of those who pursue a similar destiny. Character, as Goethe said, is built in solitude,

[24] The following chapter discusses the question of social class in detail.

talent in the stream of the world. And the stream flows nowhere more swiftly than in the teeming city.

7. Specialization and Localization

In the country almost all activities are subsidiary to one dominant concern—agriculture. One may roam far and wide over the land, with its sprinkling of villages and towns, and see everywhere, in spite of regional variations in the crops, essentially the same modes of work. In the city the sameness disappears, and we meet again the endless diversity to which we have repeatedly referred. Diversity makes for specialization, and the specialization we now want to mention is of two kinds.

In the first place, cities themselves tend to be specialized, so that different cities emphasize different functions and activities. In the United States, for example, we associate Detroit with automobiles, Pittsburgh with steel, Hartford with insurance, Hollywood with motion pictures, Washington with government, Miami with recreation, Norfolk with the Navy, Gloucester with fishing, Oak Ridge with atomic energy, Atlantic City with conventions, Scranton with mining, Oklahoma City with oil, Houston with space exploration, and Louisville with the Kentucky Derby. Chicago, of course, is "hog butcher for the world." Princeton, Cambridge, New Haven, Ann Arbor, Iowa City, and Charlottesville—to mention only a few—are university cities, and consequently centers of learning and research. Each city, except the very largest, tends to have its own special reason for being and comes to be associated with its own dominant activity.

It is interesting to note in this connection that in the United States "government cities" are not always the largest. Thus, on the national level Washington, D.C., is smaller by far than New York, and on the state level Springfield, Albany, Sacramento, and Jefferson City are small towns in comparison with Chicago, New York, San Francisco, and St. Louis.

In the second place certain areas within the city become specialized and as a result certain groups and certain activities are localized there. In New York City, for example, the financial district is at the southern tip of Manhattan Island. Wall Street, a short, narrow canyon with a graveyard at one end and a river at the other, symbolizes finance for the entire country. An area farther north contains the buildings in which all three levels of governmental activity are carried on—city, state, and Federal. The fashionable shopping district, of course, is on Fifth Avenue. Surrounding Carnegie Hall, on 57th Street, are the studios and music shops. The radio and television industry is focused at Rockefeller Center, and the garment workers fill the congested blocks between 34th and 42nd Street on Seventh Avenue. Opera, symphony, and ballet are found at Lincoln Center. The theater district of course, is Broadway, although most of the theaters are located just off this famous (or notorious) thoroughfare. Art, higher education, wholesale flowers, secondhand sewing machines, retail radios, linens, textile imports, retail hardware, diamonds, and other interests and commodities too numerous to mention all have their own special areas. And Madison Avenue, as the center of the advertising business, means the street of the "hucksters" wherever advertisements are read. So also was it in ancient Rome, where the streets often received their names from those who plied their trades upon them—the Vicus Vitrarius for the glassblowers, the Vicus Lorarius for the harnessmakers and the Vicus Sandalarius for the sandalmakers.

Residential localization also characterizes the city, and this localization proceeds in terms of several variables, especially ethnic groups, nationality, and social class. Taking the first two together, every large American city has districts in which people of Negro, German, Spanish, Italian, Irish, Polish, Greek, Puerto Rican, and Russian ancestry congregate and live. Sociologists have noticed regular stages of succession in these groups, the groups following one another in turn into certain areas and regions. To the New Yorker, for example, Harlem means the home of the Negro populace (although there are other Negro localities as well), Yorkville of the German, Greenwich Village of the Italian, and so on.

Similarly, there are the neighborhoods of the wealthy and the neighborhoods of the poor, the two often in close geographic proximity. But neighborhoods often change their character; and even the costliest residential districts may ultimately lose their exclusiveness as time brings new developments. Thus, Riverside Drive, once the residence of the rich, has long since succumbed, its mansions now rooming houses, and Park Avenue, nationally famous as a luxury address, is currently suffering the encroachment of commerce. In the meantime new "most desirable" locations come into being—for example, along the East River in midtown Manhattan. In London too, Soho and Kensington, Paddington and Bloomsbury, Mayfair and Chelsea, are districts of different kinds. These differentiations provide a fruitful source of data and investigation for the sociologist, the city planner, and the urban architect.

Still another kind of change occurs in the larger cities, a change which may be called the depletion of the middle class. New York City, for example, and expecially Manhattan Island, is a place in which, by and large, the extremes of the income scale are represented in greater numbers than the normal curve of probability would indicate. It is a matter of serious concern that only the rich and the poor continue to live there; those of middle-class means escape to the suburbs, where they attempt to recapture the values of small-town living and spend their free time painting, repairing, changing storm windows to screens and back again, and fighting a losing battle against the crab grass in their lawns.

This outward migration of the middle class creates a financial problem for the central city. The large number of persons who then commute and earn their living there receive most of the benefits of the city's services— police department, fire department, transportation, sanitation, and so on—without contributing to their maintenance in the form of taxes. The costs of these services increase in direct proportion to the number of commuters and thus intensify the problem. The problem of cities, the pollution of their atmosphere, the litter of their streets, the congestion of their traffic, the tension of their ethnic groups, their invitation to crime— perhaps their ultimate ungovernability—escape in their seriousness any treatment here.

If the preceding pages have painted too roseate a picture of the city, however, we ought to take a brief look at the South Bronx where, as a writer for *The New York Times* has poignantly put it, "civilization has virtually disappeared." The South Bronx is a region of New York City. Four hundred thousand people live there; 40 per cent of them are on welfare, and 30 per cent of them are unemployed. Twenty thousand of them are drug addicts, and ninety-five hundred of them are members of rampaging gangs, preying upon the rest. The fire hydrants have been pried open, even in the cold of winter, because for eighty thousand residents they are the only source of water; 50 per cent of the tenements are without heat 50 per cent of the time. Packs of wild dogs roam the streets. Stores close at sunset, and in many of them business is conducted through bulletproof glass. The residents, formerly afraid to go out at night, are now afraid to go out in the daytime. Looting is rampant. Fires are everywhere, and the firemen who attempt to quench them are attacked with chains, knives, and bricks. It is a place of rage, of vandalism, and of mindless violence. What is the solution to this "necropolis, this city of death?" Sadly, no one knows.[25]

8. The Suburb—Way Station to Utopia

There was a time in America, an earlier and quieter time, when the suburb meant to those who lived there, and who viewed it with affection, a paradise on earth. They saw it as a place inhabited by happy people, who lived in large houses set at generous intervals on tree-lined streets and surrounded by lawns and flower gardens. It meant a village square with its white church steeples and independent stores, its corners free of parking lots and filling

[25] These facts are from a four-part article written by Martin Tolchin, *The New York Times*, January 15, 16, 17, and 18, 1973.

stations. On one side of the square, or possibly a block or two away, stood the railroad station, the starting gate for the trip to the city undertaken every weekday morning on the 7:28, the 7:49, or the 8:07, depending upon one's position in the world, and in the evening the finish line where those who arrived there gained the peace and contentment, the rest and the restoration, that would enable them to face the journey on the following day, and so on through the years.

It was a place where children played in spacious yards instead of on city streets, where they attended schools whose pupils were of their own class and kind and whose teachers were dedicated to their calling, and therefore to the children. It is still for the sake of the children that young urban couples are willing to leave the excitement of the city, the convenience of closeness to store and office and restaurant and theater, borrow a down payment and mortgage their future for the split-level in the suburb. The prevalence of children, of course, gives a special character to the suburb, and it is the shaded suburban street that rings with their voices and with the bell, too, of the ice-cream truck as it finds its rich market in the summertime. Other suburban sounds have nostalgic echoes for the residents, many of whom have come from smaller and even quieter places on the American prairie—the tintinnabulations of the scissors grinder, for example, as he moves through the streets of the town. These are the memories that people yet retain who grew up in James Thurber's Ohio, Carl Sandburg's Illinois, and other places both south and west. For the suburbs of all the large cities are full of displaced persons from the smaller towns who came to the city to seek their fortunes and who succeeded well enough to remove their families from the city streets.

If there is a prevalence of children in the suburb, so also, during the day, is there a preponderance of women. From the time the last commuter train leaves in the morning until it returns to the station at night, the suburban streets and supermarkets are noticeably populated by one of the sexes and not the other. If the women own the suburb during the day, what is it that they do with it? Many of them spend their time—when they are not chauffeuring husbands to stations, children to schools, and dogs to veterinary clinics—participating with other women in this or that voluntary association dedicated to the good of the community. There are the Parent-Teachers Association, the Home and School Association, the Boy Scouts and the Girl Scouts, the League of Women Voters, the Recreation Commission, the Ambulance Corps, the Drama League, the many church societies, the local chapters of national charities, and so on—all contributing to the high degree of organized activity that obtains in the life of the suburban woman. Above all else, the suburban woman is busy. She is, of course, almost always a wife and mother, and possesses all of the duties, obligations, and responsibilities that these statuses require. She is business manager of a household, an enterprise that has considerable scope in suburbia. She frequently handles the household accounts, pays the bills, figures the income tax, does the marketing, plans the menus, prepares the meals, dresses the children, and performs all the other chores that the domestic enterprise demands. She is never actually at work, of course, in the pages of the popular magazines. There she is always the tall, tanned matron alighting from her station wagon, her poodles on leash, a picture of sophistication and success. Few would deny that in the American society at least the suburb is the locus of the successful woman, nor that the suburb represents perhaps the only genuine matriarchy in the history of human society.

It is easy to describe the advantages of the suburban mode of life for women and children, but what about the man in the house? One can say, first of all, that he endures the daily tortures of transit precisely because of the women and children and that this, therefore, is one of his major services to the welfare of his family. Certainly no one commutes for the pleasure of it[26] or for the enjoyment of the scenery along the way. But commuting has compensations for the commuter too. He also may be partial to grass and trees, prefer green lawns to asphalt pavements, and capacious houses to cramped apartments. His house gives him room to move around in, a basement to putter in, a garage in which to keep his car, and an attic in which to reminisce. He is nearer the golf course now, and for his domestic pleasure there is the charcoal grill in the yard and possibly also a swimming pool. Furthermore, he is a citizen in a community, not a cipher in a city. He has a voice on how taxes will be levied and spent, how the schools will be built and administered, and how the zoning ordinances will be written. He is a neighbor and has neighbors in the sense in which the word is meaningless in town. He knows the policeman at the intersection, the principal in the elementary school, the tax assessor in the borough hall—and for all he has a friendly greeting. For the man in the family, as well as for its other members, the suburb offers an attractive way of life, one that enables him to be both a "local" and a "cosmopolitan" and one that gives him, at one and the same time, the advantages of both city and country living.

This, in any event, is the suburban idyll and the suburban ideal. It is a

---

[26] One exception has been found—a commuter on the Long Island Railroad, which carries 80,000 passengers a day. This man explains:"At home every time I sit down the wife and kids are at me for something. All day at the office I'm either dictating, on the phone, or in conference. I'd be dead if it weren't for peace aboard the Long Island," Quoted in Edward Higbee, *The Squeeze: Cities without Space,* William Morrow and Company, Inc., New York, 1960, p. 11.

pleasant picture. It is also full of stereotypes. The suburban style of life looks utopian indeed when compared with other styles of life in a complex and crowded society. It promises so much that we have called it a way station to utopia. Unfortunately, it is only a way station. The utopia visualized at the end of the line is still far away, and indeed unattainable. The suburb of today—the automobile suburb—is not the suburb of a generation ago—the railroad suburb—and the suburb of tomorrow will be even less like it. For the sad truth is that the suburb as we have known it is destined to disappear. Let us examine the situation in more realistic terms.

In the first place, the picture drawn in the preceding paragraphs is biased in that it portrays a class phenomenon and not a geographic or ecological or "sub-urban" phenomenon at all. Stated alternatively, the settlements that lie on the rims of cities may or may not be suburban in any sociological sense of the word. The suburbia described above exists, of course, but it exists only in upper-middle class and upper-class localities. The description conceals the fact that there are lower-class suburbs too, where living conditions are clearly less attractive.[27] Most of us—including most sociologists—have a tendency, when we think of the suburbs of New York City, for example, to think of places like Rye and Scarsdale, Stamford and Montclair, Mamaroneck and Manhasset, Tenafly and Ridgewood—to all of which our stereotype applies. We do not think of Yonkers and Secaucus and Weehawken and Hoboken and Union City—to all of which it does not. Furthermore, Riverdale, which is in the Bronx and is therefore no suburb at all, is more suburban in terms of our stereotype than Fort Lee, New Jersey, which, since it is not only outside the city limits but even outside the state, is suburban in fact. Some suburbs in short conform to the stereotype and some do not, and this in some independence of their geographical location. The suburb, as most people conceive of it, is a sociological and not a geographic concept. A more important question, however, is whether the "successful" suburbs can continue to offer the suburban way of life, and this is a question that invites increasing skepticism.

The suburban style, as we have described it, is not only a class phenomenon. It has to do in addition with the factor of size. When we think of quiet, tree-shaded streets we think also of the abbreviated business or commercial districts that accompany them and occupy no more than the four sides of a village square, or three or four blocks of the main street of the town. We think in terms of a village or a borough or a small community. No one calls Newark a suburb, or Bridgeport, or Camden, or Wilmington, or Gary, or East St. Louis, or Oakland. One could, of course, devise a

[27] See Bennett M. Berger, *Working-Class Suburb: A Study of Auto Workers in Suburbia*, University of California Press, Berkeley, Calif., 1960.

quantitative measure that would provide an arbitrary answer to this question. When the number of adult male residents who commute to the central city, for example, is larger than 60 per cent, say, of all adult male residents, we could agree to call it a suburb, and when this number falls below 60 per cent we could call it something else. One could raise the additional question whether one needs to commute to a central city or only to another suburb—a phenomenon of increasing significance, incidentally—in order to be counted as a commuter. In the stereotype, on the other hand, all of the adult male members of the community commute except, of course, the ministers, the police, and that minimum number needed to man the few suburban business establishments, all dealing with local services. As suburbs grow in size, therefore, and as the demand for local goods and services increases, and as the number of commercial and possibly industrial and professional statuses also increases, so also must the number of commuters suffer a proportionate decline. As the suburb grows in size, in short, so also does it to that degree cease to be a suburb.[28]

Distance also requires some consideration. As the near-suburbs fill up with people, as they become, in effect, more urban and less suburban, so also must the suburb seeker move always farther away to escape the apartment houses that pursue him. And pursue him they do. An increasing proportion of new dwelling units authorized in suburban areas are apartment houses. As this process continues, the outward mover will ultimately find himself in something called exurbia, a region so far out that its inhabitants no longer commute every day and where only those who do not have to do so can therefore afford to live.

There is obviously a limit, however, to the process of moving outward. When the distance becomes so great that the time and cost cancel out the advantages for which the trip is made, when the journey in short becomes unprofitable, then it will no longer be taken. As the intervening space fills up, the suburb will disappear in a thicket of new apartment buildings, and there will no longer be any architectural distinction between the central city at the core and the suburb at the periphery.

There is another barrier to the continuous geographic expansion of the periphery, and this perhaps is the most impressive of all. It is a factor that is even now causing the death of the suburb and the suburban way of life—and that, of course, is the growth of population. When the suburbs of one city spread out to meet the suburbs of the next city and when all the

---

[28] The census of 1970 produced the interesting facts that the suburbs have a larger population than the cities they surround, that they provide more jobs than do the central cities, and that only one in four suburbanites commutes to a city job, the other three remaining to work in the suburbs themselves.

interstices are filled with people and highways and factories and houses and stores, then we no longer have suburbs at all but rather one vast and single conurbation, the newest social phenomenon which may be called the continental city. It is a phenomenon whose appearance was unsuspected even by Spengler, to whom the rise of the great city was the tocsin of disintegration and of cultural decay. It will be the final victory of the city over the suburb.

The suburb, in short, is going to die because it is becoming increasingly urban. In many regions of the country it is being absorbed by the continental city that stretches continuously now on the Eastern Seaboard, for example, from Portsmouth, New Hampshire, to Norfolk, Virginia. In this new kind of city, sprawling over the boundaries of ten archaic political arrangements we call states, there live at the moment of writing these lines some 32 million people. The city population of the region—"city" meaning, in the old sense, a center of at least 50,000 population—decreased 2.8 per cent during the decade 1950 to 1960, but the suburban population increased in the same period by 44.2 per cent. This process is taking place in other parts of the country as well: the Albany-to-Syracuse area; Pittsburgh to Youngstown, Ohio; Detroit and cities to the west and north; Chicago, with Milwaukee to the north and South Bend to the east; Miami and north; the Dallas-Fort Worth complex in Texas; San Francisco and the peninsula to the south and to Sacramento on the east; Portland to Seattle in the Northwest; and finally Los Angeles, which is no city at all but only a colony of suburbs. Every year more than a million acres of crop land are taken out of production in order to support this process of "human glaciation," and in the last fifteen years an area equal to one-twentieth of all the productive cropland in the United States has been sacrificed to the growth of these continental cities. The New York metropolitan area alone, at the present rate of population increase, will occupy all the land within a fifty-mile radius of Times Square by 1985 and will exhaust a surface area of some 7,000 square miles, roughly six times the area of the state of Rhode Island. It will be an area more densely populated than either India or China and it will be an area, whether or not the central city in its old form survives, that will be wholly urban.

These facts may or may not be frightening. But it is clear that they mark the end of the suburb as we have known it. Already we hear the expression "suburban sprawl," already—in spite of stringent zoning procedures—the suburbs are sustaining an invasion of apartment houses, and already we are having to cope with suburban slums and suburban crime. So long as there are income differentials, of course, there will be different styles of living. There will be rich and poor in various ecological arrangements throughout the new urban spread. It is even conceivable that some of the suburbs will be able—though not without difficulty—to retain their characteristic flavor and atmosphere for some time to come. But their ultimate fate is certain. The present rate of population growth in the United States will transform them into sociological fossils—relics of a pleasant but rapidly receding past. And so we say again, changing the tense as we conclude, that the suburb was a way station to utopia, and no one found a way to follow the track to its destination.

9. Summary

In this chapter we have introduced the student to one of the most widespread kinds of social differentiation, that between the city and the country. It is a differentiation to be found in all human societies except the most primitive, and in most of human history. Soil and cement, the land and the pavement, the lane and the street—these are symbols of two different ways of life, two different cultures. There is, in this complex, a third culture, the suburb—but this, as we have seen has taken different forms in recent decades and is at the moment in danger of extinction. In any event, the juxtaposition of these three groupings, like other juxtapositions in society, is constantly changing, and presents always new facets for wonder and discernment.

Chapter 17

CLASS AND CASTE

OUR DISCUSSION of some of the more important groupings that appear in complex societies has thus far been concerned primarily with social differentiation, that is, with the way various groups and statuses can be marked off and distinguished from others. Thus, a neighborhood is one kind of group, a community another, and a family still another. Similarly, we have noticed that the status of plumber is one kind of status, the status of physician another, and so on. When we introduce considerations of level or rank, however, we have another way of differentiating, and this is the way of social stratification. Society is composed not only of different groups but also of different strata, an observation which means that groups are evaluated as "higher" or "lower" than other groups. Our knowledge of the structure of any society will be incomplete unless we arrive at some understanding of this stratified arrangement that results in class and caste, the subject of our present chapter. Within the limits of a single chapter it is impossible of course to survey even a representative selection of class structures in historical and contemporary societies. In most of what follows, therefore, we shall confine our illustrations to an earlier period in the American society and, accordingly, to class, for the most part, rather than caste.

1. The Universality of Class

Class is almost, but not quite, a universal phenomenon in human society. It is a phenomenon that is absent only in the smallest, the simplest, and the most primitive of societies. All societies of any size have a class structure, not excepting the Union of Soviet Socialist Republics or the United States of America. If small and primitive societies do not have a class structure and if large and civilized societies do have, we wonder when and how and why this phenomenon came into existence. Questions of origin are always difficult in sociology and perhaps ultimately unanswerable. They are clearly unanswerable if we ask them in an historical frame of reference and seek the sources of stratification in a period before the invention of writing, that is, before the beginning of the historical record. We may however indulge in a modicum of speculation on this subject.

We should be relatively safe in assuming that social stratification has something to do with two factors—the size of the society and the division of labor. Since the division of labor, in terms other than age and sex, is itself a function of size, the latter factor is probably of basic importance. We have noticed that as societies grow larger different groups form within them. People no longer interact with everyone else, as in a small tribe or village, but interact instead with some members of their society and not with others. This would seem initially to be a matter of sheer size of community and of the physical distance between people, which necessarily increases as the number of people increases. But this would be only one of the conditions necessary for the origin of class. Another necessary condition would be a division of labor.

Class is related to status, and different statuses arise in a society as people do different things, engage in different activities, and pursue different vocations. These different occupational statuses then come to be ranked with respect to one another in terms of the contributions the individuals who occupy them make to the welfare of the tribe or the community. It is easy to suppose, therefore, that in a society where all of the adult males do the same things in the same traditional ways and on the same traditional occasions, their statuses are relatively undifferentiated and, accordingly, unstratified. When all of the men both make arrows and shoot arrows, there are no differences of rank between them. It may happen, however, that the arrows that some of the men make are superior to those that others make. It may happen in addition that those who do make superior arrows are encouraged to spend their time making them and are no longer required to go out and shoot them. The game that is killed by the hunters is then exchanged for the arrows made by the arrow makers.

In this way two different statuses would arise in the society, the status of hunter on the one hand and the status of arrow maker on the other. The stratification of these two statuses could be in either direction; that is, in a situation where game is scarce and hunters require skill, it is likely that the status of hunter would outrank the status of arrow maker. In the reverse situation, where game is plentiful and easy to get, it is likely that the status of arrow maker would receive the higher evaluation, especially if arrow making involves some technical or artistic virtuosity. In other words, as soon as there are several statuses in a society, it is almost inevitable that they will be differentially evaluated. Some will be considered more important than others. And thus we have the beginnings of stratification.[1]

In his illuminating discussion of this subject, Kingsley Davis suggests that stratification results when some activities are judged to be of more service to a society than are others.[2] Some statuses, in other words, have a functional importance in the community and others do not. Some are easy to fill and some are difficult. Some require a rare combination of talents or great achievement, others a long period of learning or training. Indeed, there are many possibilities in this respect and it would be an extensive task to discover their combinations in all the societies of the world. The hewing of wood and the carrying of water, though quite important, are not difficult; consequently such occupational statuses would not be accorded a very high rank. The practice of witchcraft, on the other hand, is believed to involve a knowledge of secret lore and possible also a visitation from the deities, and so it receives a relatively high evaluation. The achievement of pole vaulting 18 feet, though quite difficult, is not considered to have much functional importance in our society; thus little prestige attaches to the status of pole vaulter. Modern medicine, on the other hand, as Kingsley Davis says, "is within the mental capacity of most individuals, but a medical education is so burdensome and expensive that virtually none would undertake it if the

---

[1] It is not necessary to suppose that these statuses would always be occupational in a narrow sense. It may happen that an individual, through some courageous action in time of war or other disaster, distinguishes himself as a hero, and thus comes to occupy a special status in society.

[2] Kingsley Davis, *Human Society*. The Macmillan Company, New York, 1949, pp. 366-370. The fourteenth chapter of this book, in its entirety, offers an outstanding treatment of this subject. To the observation above Davis adds a significant qualification: "Actually a society does not need to reward positions in proportion to their functional importance. It merely needs to give sufficient reward to insure that they will be filled competently. In other words, it must see that less essential positions do not compete successfully with more essential ones. If a position is easily filled, it need not be heavily rewarded even though important. On the other hand, if it is important but hard to fill, the reward must be high enough to get it filled anyway. If it is unimportant and hard to fill, it will possibly be dropped altogether. Functional importance is therefore a necessary but not a sufficient cause of high rank being assigned to a position." p. 368.

position of the M.D. did not carry a reward commensurate with the sacrifice."[3] The healing arts in all societies, primitive and civilized, are so closely linked with survival that their functional importance is great, and accordingly the status of medicine man, both primitive and civilized, carries with it a high prestige.[4]

It is not necessary that these evaluations be "rational" in any sense of the word. Some societies have evaluated very highly accomplishments and activities that we, in our society, would view with indifference and even with distaste. On the other hand, some of us in our society place great value on activities that would hardly excite the approval or even the interest of the more "primitive." The reasons for the differential evaluation of different activities are basically ideological in character, and in order to understand them it is usually necessary to understand an entire culture. Nevertheless, certain statuses, or clusters of statuses, come to be evaluated positively in all societies, and among these we find the status of chief (ruler), medicine man (doctor), shaman (priest), sage (professor), and so on. It is these clusters of statuses that begin to form a foundation for the class structure of a society and to constitute its strata.

But the stratification of statuses does not of itself produce a class structure. Class is a group phenomenon and depends upon the juxtaposition of groups in some order of rank. We need therefore to invoke another condition of class before we can assign sufficient reason to this phenomenon, and this final condition is the extension of the prestige of the status to the family of the person occupying it; that is, the prestige conferred upon certain statuses must be enjoyed not only by their occupants but also by their families and their descendants.

Societies regard the unity of the family as a matter of extreme importance, since societal survival depends, to some degree at least, upon a family system. The occupational prestige accorded to the status of an adult male in a patriarchal society, therefore, comes to be accorded also to his wife and to all of their children. To wives is ascribed the status of their

---

[3] *Ibid.* p. 369.
[4] The Davis-Moore thesis, as it came to be called, led to a famous debate in American sociology. See Kingsley Davis and Wilbert E. Moore, "Some Principles of Stratification," *American Sociological Review*, vol. 10, pp. 242–249; Kingsley Davis, "Reply" to Tumin, same journal, vol. 18, August, 1953, pp. 394–397; Wilbert E. Moore, "Comment," same issue, p. 397; Melvin M. Tumin, "Some Principles of Stratification: A Critical Analysis,"*American Sociological Review*, vol. 18, August, 1953, pp. 387–394; and Tumin's "Reply to Kingsley Davis," same journal, vol. 18, December, 1953, pp. 672–673. For treatments of the theoretical issues involved, see also Milton M. Gordon, *Social Class in American Sociology*, The Duke University Press, Durham, N. C., 1958; Harold M. Hodges, *Social Stratification*, Schenkman Publishing Co., Cambridge, Mass. 1964; and Gerhard Lenski, *Power and Privilege*, McGraw-Hill Book Company, New York, 1966.

husbands, to children the status of their parents. In this way the stratification of statuses comes to be a family and, therefore, a group phenomenon. Later on this status ascribed to the family becomes hereditary, and ultimately it exceeds occupational status in importance. What is first a function of occupational status thus tends to become a hereditary function of family membership. At a given time in the life of a society, therefore, family status based upon ancient occupational prerogatives and prestige may take precedence over present occupational status in determining an individual's position in the class structure.

We find sometimes, and especially in relatively static societies, a new support and sanction for a class structure—the sanction of religion. It comes to be assumed—and these assumptions of course form a part of the ideological culture of a society—that the class structure is ordained by God and may not be tampered with by mortal men without interfering with the divine plan. When this ideological support is introduced, class strata become even more clearly and definitely articulated than before, and the result is often a relatively permanent, and therefore closed, class system. The following medieval jingle illustrates this situation:

> God hath shapen lives three,
> Boor and priest and knight they be.[5]

Here we have three distinct classes, three "estates" as they are frequently called, which are presumably established not by the normal operation of social forces but by the God of the universe. It is easy to understand how religious support could introduce great rigidity into a class structure, and this illustration shows once again the importance of the ideological components of culture.[6] In the medieval situation, furthermore, there was little reason to try to alter the structure. The eyes of medieval men were focused not on this world but on the next, the City of God, and whatever inequalities existed on earth would be adjusted in the life to come.

It is obviously impossible in a brief discussion to outline a complete theory of social class and to marshal the evidence to support it. The preceding observations, therefore, are to be construed merely as suggestions that may shed some light upon the preliminary processes of class formation. In summary, we may say that the development of a class

[5] To which there was also, incidentally, a medieval rebuttal: When Adam delved and Eve span, who was then the gentleman?

[6] Egon Bergel argues with cogency that a caste system cannot be sustained without the support of religion. See his scholarly discussion in *Social Stratification*, McGraw-Hill Book Company, New York, 1962, pp. 35–67.

structure in any society requires, first, a size beyond the possibility of "facial recognition" and, second, a division of labor (on grounds other than age and sex). These factors, however, though necessary, are not sufficient to explain social stratification, and so two further conditions are required: a differential evaluation of statuses and the extension of these evaluations from individuals to families. The family factor, by enabling evaluations to carry through from one generation to the next, introduces stability into the structure, and additional sanctions like religion introduce rigidity. Despite endless variation in detail, it seems reasonable to suppose that in some such manner as this classes are formed and perpetuated in human societies.

2. Open and Closed Class Systems

Before we introduce illustrations of class structures in our own society, let us first distinguish between class and caste, or—to use synonymous expressions—between "open" and "closed" class systems. It is apparent even without discussion that class structures vary in their rigidity from one society to another, and from one period to another in the same society. A class structure may be barely perceptible in a small community where all or most of the social relations are primary. On the other hand, as we have said, class is a phenomenon that appears in all complex societies. From a descriptive point of view it is possible to discern two kinds of class systems, which differ in degree. These are open class systems and closed class systems, the two representing a continuum.

An open class system is one in which vertical social mobility is possible. This means that there are no restrictions, or at the most only very mild restrictions, on the upward and downward movement of individuals with respect to the several strata. In the polar case there would be no restrictions whatever; class status would be completely achieved by every individual and never ascribed except at the very beginning of life. A closed class system, on the other hand, is one in which vertical social mobility is considerably restricted and perhaps, at one or more points on the scale, even prohibited. In the polar case class status would always be ascribed to the individual and never achieved by him. His class status would continue to be that of his family and he would be required in addition to choose his marriage partner from his own class.

The family, in other words, assumes a greater importance in the closed class system, the individual in the open class system. A society that has the former is likely to lay greater stress upon the family; a society that has the latter tends, on the contrary, to emphasize individual achievement. Whenever we find a relatively closed class structure, therefore, we know also that the family in such a society is an extremely important social phenomenon and one whose significance does not diminish with the adulthood of its members.

Although the terminology is not yet standardized in the literature of sociology, we regard a closed class system and a caste system as synonymous. In other words, when the structure is completely closed at one or more points we have a caste structure. The number of points at which it is closed, of course, may vary. In the old caste system of India, now disintegrating, the separate castes were clearly articulated and there were impassable hereditary barriers at every point. Thus caste systems may vary according to the number of barriers to vertical social mobility that a society exhibits, and this number, in turn, is derived from the number of castes that the society contains. A completely open class system and a completely closed class system, of course, are limiting cases, polar opposites as it were, and it is doubtful if these extremes are represented by any society. In all actual societies there are some barriers to vertical social mobility, no matter how permeable they may be, and in all actual societies too there is some vertical mobility, even though it may not be encouraged.

3. Class in American Communities

When we look at so territorially vast a society as our own, a society composed of so many heterogeneous groupings of people, the problem of illuminating its class structure—if indeed it has only one class structure—takes on considerable complexity. Before discussing the possibility of a general class structure, let us first take a look at some particular class structures discoverable in different American communities of a generation or two ago. This latter problem, an easier one, has received detailed attention from sociologists and social anthropologists. In this section, therefore, with a roving camera eye as it were, we shall have a look at the class structures of several American communities, imaginary and real, of different sizes, at different times, and in different parts of the country.

Zenith

In Zenith, a fictional city of some 100,000 population, there lived a forty-six-year-old "realtor" named George F. Babbitt. Babbitt, a graduate of the state university, lived in a good residential section named Floral Heights and had a wife named Myra, and three children, Ted, Verona, and Tinka. He was a successful businessman and belonged to a number of lodges and clubs, as did every "decent" male citizen of Zenith. He did not, however, associate on equal terms with everyone in the city. Indeed, he aspired to associate with Charles McKelvey.

McKelvey, a college classmate, had gone on to become a power in the community as the owner of a successful construction company and as a politician with influence in the state legislature. McKelvey, in the words of his creator, was "baronial." "He was a peer in the rapidly crystallizing American aristocracy, inferior only to the haughty Old Families. (In Zenith, an Old Family is one which came to town before 1840.)" Babbitt and McKelvey met at the reunion dinner of their university class and Babbitt, after hinting that he could give McKelvey a tip on a real-estate development, hoped somewhat tentatively that the McKelveys might come to the Babbitt house for dinner. The rest of the story has to be told in the words of Sinclair Lewis himself, who caught the flavor of social class in an acute and penetrating manner:

> The Babbitts invited the McKelveys to dinner, in early December, and the McKelveys not only accepted but, after changing the date once or twice, actually came . . .
>
> The McKelveys were less than fifteen minutes late.
>
> Babbitt hoped that the Doppelbraus [his neighbors] would see the McKelvey's limousine, and their uniformed chauffeur, waiting in front.
>
> The dinner was well cooked and incredibly plentiful, and Mrs. Babbitt had brought out her grandmother's silver candlesticks. Babbitt worked hard. He was good. He told none of the jokes he wanted to tell. He listened to the others. He started Maxwell off with a resounding, "Let's hear about your trip to the Yellowstone." He was laudatory, extremely laudatory. He found opportunities to remark that Dr. Angus was a benefactor to humanity, Maxwell and Howard Littlefield profound scholars, Charles McKelvey an inspiration to ambitious youth, and Mrs. McKelvey an adornment to the social circles of Zenith, Washington, New York, Paris, and numbers of other places.
>
> But he could not stir them. It was a dinner without a soul. For no reason that was clear to Babbitt, heaviness was over them and they spoke laboriously and unwillingly.
>
> He concentrated on Lucille McKelvey, carefully not looking at her blanched lovely shoulder and the tawny silken band which supported her frock.
>
> "I suppose you'll be going to Europe pretty soon again won't you?" he invited.
>
> "I'd like awfully to run over to Rome for a few weeks."
>
> "I suppose you see a lot of pictures and music and curios and everything there."
>
> "No, what I really go for is: there's a little *trattoria* on the Via della Scrofa where you get the best *fettuccine* in the world."
>
> "Oh, I—Yes. That must be nice to try that. Yes."
>
> At a quarter to ten McKelvey discovered with profound regret that his wife had a headache. He said blithely, as Babbitt helped him with his coat,

"We must lunch together some time, and talk over the old days."

When the others had labored out, at half-past ten, Babbitt turned to his wife, pleading, "Charley said he had a corking time and we must lunch—said they wanted to have us up to the house for dinner before long."

She achieved, "Oh, it's just been one of those quiet evenings that are often so much more enjoyable than noisy parties where everybody talks at once and doesn't really settle down to—nice quiet enjoyment."

But from his cot on the sleeping-porch, he heard her weeping, slowly, without hope.

For a month they watched the social columns, and waited for a return dinner-invitation.

The invitation never came, of course, and after a while "they did not speak of the McKelveys again."[7]

This, however, is only half of the story. Let us turn a few pages more:

It was a shame, at this worried time, to have to think about the Overbrooks.

Ed Overbrook was a classmate of Babbitt who had been a failure. He had a large family and a feeble insurance business out in the suburb of Dorchester. He was gray and thin and unimportant. He had always been gray and thin and unimportant. He was the person whom, in any group, you forgot to introduce, then introduced with extra enthusiasm. He had admired Babbitt's good-fellowship in college, had admired ever since his power in real estate, his beautiful house and wonderful clothes. It pleased Babbitt, though it bothered him with a sense of responsibility. At the class-dinner he had seen poor Overbrook, in a shiny blue serge business-suit, being diffident in a corner with three other failures. He had gone over and been cordial: "Why, hello, young Ed! I hear you're writing all the insurance in Dorchester now. Bully work!"

They recalled the good old days when Overbrook used to write poetry. Overbrook embarrassed him by blurting, "Say Georgie, I hate to think of how we been drifting apart. I wish you and Mrs. Babbitt would come to dinner some night."

Babbitt boomed, "Fine! Sure! Just let me know. And the wife and I want to have you at the house." He forgot it, but unfortunately Ed Overbrook did not. Repeatedly he telephoned to Babbitt, inviting him to dinner. "Might as well go and get it over," Babbitt groaned to his wife . . .

He accepted Overbrook's next plaintive invitation, for an evening two weeks off. A dinner two weeks off, even a family dinner, never seems so appalling, till the two weeks have astoundingly disappeared and one comes dismayed to the ambushed hour. They had to change the date, because of their own dinner to the McKelveys, but at last they gloomily drove out to the Overbrooks' house in Dorchester.

It was miserable from the beginning. The Overbrooks had dinner at

[7] From *Babbitt*, by Sinclair Lewis, copyright, 1922, by Harcourt, Brace and Company, Inc.; renewed, 1950, by Sinclair Lewis. Reprinted by permission of the publishers. With omissions.

six-thirty, while the Babbitts never dined before seven. Babbitt permitted himself to be ten minutes late. "Let's make it as short as possible. I think we'll duck out quick. I'll say I have to be at the office extra early tomorrow," he planned . . .

Babbitt tried to be jovial; he worked at it; but he could find nothing to interest him in Overbrook's timorousness, the blankness of the other guests, or the drained stupidity of Mrs. Overbrook, with her spectacles, drab skin, and tight-drawn hair. He told his best Irish story, but it sank like a soggy cake. Most bleary moment of all was when Mrs. Overbrook, peering out of her fog of nursing eight children and cooking and scrubbing, tried to be conversational.

"I suppose you go to Chicago and New York right along, Mr. Babbitt," she prodded.

"Well, I get to Chicago fairly often."

"It must be awfully interesting. I suppose you take in all the theaters."

"Well, to tell the truth, Mrs. Overbrook, thing that hits me best is a great big beefsteak at a Dutch restaurant in the Loop!"

They had nothing more to say. Babbitt was sorry, but there was no hope; the dinner was a failure. At ten, rousing out of the stupor of meaningless talk, he said as cheerfully as he could, "'Fraid we got to be starting, Ed. I've got a fellow coming to see me early to-morrow." As Overbrook helped him with his coat, Babbitt said, "Nice to rub up on the old days! We must have lunch together."

Mrs. Babbitt sighed, on their drive home, "It was pretty terrible. But how Mr. Overbrook does admire you!"

"Yep. Poor cuss! Seems to think I'm a little tin archangel, and the best-looking man in Zenith."

"Well, you're certainly not that but— Oh, Georgie, you don't suppose we have to invite them to dinner at our house now, do we?"

"Ouch! Gaw, I hope not!"

"See here, now, George! You didn't say anything about it to Mr. Overbrook, did you?"

"No! Gee! No! Honest, I didn't! Just made a bluff about having him to lunch some time."

For a week they worried, "We really ought to invite Ed and his wife, poor devils!" But as they never saw the Overbrooks, they forgot them, and after a month or two they said, "That really was the best way, just to let it slide. It wouldn't be kind to *them* to have them here. They'd feel so out of place and hard-up in our home."

They did not speak of the Overbrooks again.[8]

Middletown

Zenith appears only in the novels of Sinclair Lewis, but Middletown can be found in the state of Indiana. As its name implies, it is an average,

[8] Ibid., with omissions.

middle-class, middle-sized American city.[9] It was studied, first in 1925 and then again in 1935, by two sociologists, Robert S. Lynd and Helen Merrell Lynd, and the two books they published on it, *Middletown* and *Middletown in Transition*,[10] are among the most famous community studies in sociology. We shall not be interested here in what the Lynds say about the city in general, except to note that there is hardly a detail of life which escapes their trained attention and that seldom, if ever, has a city been so throughly analyzed, dissected, and described from a sociological point of view. The two Middletown books became best sellers, and they stand today as contributions not only to American sociology but also to American literature.

We have already suggested that no examination of any community of significant size can fail to disclose the phenomenon of social class. People in Middletown simply do not associate on equal terms with one another. Like the citizens of Zenith, to whom we have just been introduced, they have different incomes, they work and play and eat and drink with different people, they follow different occupational pursuits, and they have different styles of living. The Lynds found it convenient for their purposes to divide the people of Middletown into two classes, the business class and the working class. The working class earns a living by working with *things*, the business class by working with *people*. The working class makes things and sells its services for a wage; the business class, on the other hand, deals with people, with hiring and firing and using and even manipulating them, and deals in addition with such abstractions as credits, contracts, sales, education, management, and government.

Although this division has the virtue of simplicity, it blurs the position of many people in ways of which the Lynds are well aware. They comment on this problem in the following passage:

> Were a minute structural diagram the aim of this study, it would be necessary to decipher in much greater detail the multitude of overlapping groupings observable in Middletown. Since what is sought, however, is an understanding of the major functional characteristics of this changing culture, it is important that significant outlines be not lost in detail, and the groups in the city which exhibit the dominant characteristics most clearly must, therefore, form the foci of the report. While an effort will be made to make clear at certain points variant behavior within these two groups, *it is after all this division into working class and business class that constitutes the outstanding cleavage in Middletown*. The mere fact of being born upon one or the other side of the watershed roughly formed by these two groups is the most

---

[9] Its population in 1920 was some 35,000.

[10] Both published by Harcourt, Brace and Company, the first in 1929, the second in 1937.

significant single cultural factor tending to influence what one does all day long throughout one's life; whom one marries; when one gets up in the morning; whether one belongs to the Holy Roller or Presbyterian church; or drives a Ford or a Buick; whether or not one's daughter makes the desirable high school Violet Club; or one's wife meets with the Sew We Do Club or with the Art Students' League; whether one belongs to the Odd Fellows or to the Masonic Shrine; whether one sits about evenings with one's necktie off; and so on indefinitely throughout the daily comings and goings of a Middletown man, woman, or child. [Italics added][11]

In *Middletown in Transition* the Lynds alter to some extent their simple two-class scheme, but in their second look at the city they continue to emphasize "the long arm of the job":

One's job is the watershed down which the rest of one's life tends to flow in Middletown. Who one is, whom one knows, how one lives, what one aspires to be,—these and many other urgent realities of living are patterned for one by what one does to get a living and the amount of living this allows one to buy.[12]

But there were changes in the ten-year period, not the least unimportant of which was the Depression of the 1930s. Furthermore, *Middletown* was criticized by some because the Lynds had paid insufficient attention to the phenomenon of the "X" family. In their second study, therefore, they described what they were moved to call the "reigning royal family," a family whose power and influence were characterized by a "lesser citizen" as follows:

If I'm out of work I go to the X plant; if I need money I go to the X bank, and if they don't like me I don't get it; my children go to the X college; when I get sick I go to the X hospital; I buy a building lot or house in an X subdivision; my wife goes downtown to buy clothes at the X department store; if my dog stays away he is put in the X pound; I buy X milk; I drink X beer, vote for X political parties, and get help from X charities; my boy goes to the X Y.M.C.A. and my girl to their Y.W.C.A.; I listen to the word of God in X-subsidized churches; if I'm a Mason I go to the X Masonic Temple; I read the news from the X morning newspaper; and, if I am rich enough, I travel via the X airport.[13]

Here we have a class phenomenon of a different order, a family that belongs neither to the working class nor to the business class but one that

[11] *Middletown*, pp. 23–24.
[12] *Middletown in Transition*, p. 7.
[13] *Ibid.*, p. 74.

exercises power over them both. The power extends into every sphere of the city's life—its business, its education, its medical care, its politics, its leisure, its housing and real estate, its philanthropy, its journalism, its religion. Here we see a new dimension of the class structure of Middletown—class not only as a distinction in "life styles" but class as a phenomenon of power. "First-generation wealth," as the Lynds suggest, becomes "second-generation power,"[14] and this is a phenomenon that exercises far-reaching effects upon the stratification of the city in general. It is a phenomenon to which we shall return in a later section of this chapter.

Plainville

Let us move our camera now to a small village somewhere in the Middle West, a village studied first by James West.[15] The population of Plainville in 1939 was 275, and one of the reasons why it was selected for study was that it was presumed to be as devoid of class stratification as a community could possibly be. Indeed, the normal response of the inhabitants to questions concerning social class was as follows: "We're all just one plain old class of common average working people here. You don't find no very rich people here, and no very poor people, like you find lots of places."[16] With this sentiment all local citizens were in agreement. Nevertheless, West learned very soon after his arrival that he would have to deal with "a discrimination system of enormous complexity":

> Friends began to warn and instruct me about whom I should or should not visit and be seen with, if I wanted to gain correct information and maintain the respect of "worth-while" people. Judgments of neighbor on neighbor, and all evaluations of individuals, appeared to be repeating patterns of great uniformity, despite the wariness with which they were phrased.[17]

We do not need to follow Mr. West's study in detail. It will suffice to say that he did indeed find a clearly articulated social class structure in his small community:

> . . . [This structure] provides for every person living there a master pattern for arranging according to relative rank every other individual, and every family, clique, lodge, club, church, and other organization or association in Plainville society. . . . It provides also a set of patterns for expected behavior according

[14] *Ibid.*, p. 100.
[15] James West, *Plainville, U. S. A.*, Columbia Universtiy Press, New York, 1945.
[16] *Ibid.*, p. viii.
[17] *Ibid.*, p. xii.

to class, and a way of judging all norms and deviations from these norms in individual behavior.[18]

Plainville, in short, exhibits two distinct social classes, with minor gradations on each side of the dividing line. Each class contains roughly half of the population. The upper class is made up of "good, honest, self-respecting, average, everyday, working people," and when this entire expression is used, as the author notes, there is no doubt where the people belong. The members of this class, significantly, take pride in being "plain" and "average," and in this society, with its strong equalitarian and democratic tradition, these are honorific adjectives. The members of the lower class are not described in the same way. The top third of this class is "respectable," and decent, but poor; the middle third is no longer "respectable," and the lowest third is comprised of "people who live like animals."

What, now, are the criteria by which these two classes in Plainville are distinguished? West discovered that there are six: place of residence (prairie people versus hill people), technology (modern methods of agriculture versus "patch-farming," hunting, fishing, trapping, and wood chopping), lineage, wealth, "morals," and "manners." The last two of these would seem to be the most important, and it is interesting to note that the last one, "manners," includes knowledge. The people in the lower class "just don't *know* any better." And "the people who live like animals," of course, know the least of all. "They don't know how to act." Religion and membership in certain voluntary associations, like the Masons, for example, also serve as distinguishing factors in class identification. The people in the upper class belong to the Methodist, Baptist, or Christian church, in the lower class to the Holiness church or to none at all.

Three of West's observations invite special attention because they afford an insight into the nature of class structures in general. The first of these concerns the great disparity between the ideal culture pattern and the real culture pattern. In the ideal culture pattern of Plainville, as in most other American communities, there is no such thing as a class structure; all men are created equal and remain equal; every man is as good as every other man and possibly a little bit better. In the real culture pattern, in direct contrast, there is a very clear class structure and one that touches the lives of Plainville citizens at almost every point. The second finding of importance is that a class structure of such complexity exists in a community of only 275 persons, one in which it is almost possible for every inhabitant to know personally every other inhabitant.

[18] *Ibid.*, p. 115.

The third observation concerns the difficulty of crossing the line that separates the two classes from each other. "Practically, the two main classes are rigidly exclusive systems into which people are born. Movement across the line separating the upper class from the lower class is virtually impossible, without leaving the community."[19] Indeed, West found only three cases in which people who lived in Plainville managed to change their class status, two in the "ascending" direction and one in the "descending." The former were men of lower-class origin who became, respectively, a rural mail carrier and a county official; the latter was a man of upper-class origin who married a "back-woods girl," moved to the hills, and conformed to the lower-class pattern of relatively shiftless living. West does not hesitate to say, in fact, that—difficult as it is to move from the lower class to the upper class—it is still more difficult to move from the upper to the lower. Since people in the upper class already "know how to act," they can shift positions only by a deliberate, persistent, and permanent refusal to conform in a situation where temporary transgressions are always forgiven.[20]

Clyde (Yankee City)

Clyde, Massachusetts, the locale of John P. Marquand's novel, *Point of No Return*, and Yankee City, the scene of W. Lloyd Warner's sociological studies, are the same city—Newburyport, Massachusetts.[21] We thus have two different approaches to the same phenomenon, the class structure of Newburyport, one in fiction and one in social science. We shall not pause here to remark upon the respective merits of the two approaches except to say that, though there are advantages and disadvantages attached to each, the novelist can sometimes give us insights that are denied to the investigator who uses more formal methods.

In Yankee City Warner and Lunt discovered six separate social classes—upper-upper, lower-upper, upper-middle, lower-middle, upper-lower, and lower-lower. By classes they mean "two or more orders of people who are believed to be, and are accordingly ranked by the members

[19] *Ibid.,* p. 135. The author goes on to say: "It is not easy even by way of migration, because local manner, training, viewpoints, and the initial contacts of migrating Plainvillers with the outside world are pretty apt to place them in a first job or social setting from which no very great 'rise' is likely."
[20] A more recent study of Plainville comes to somewhat different conclusions. See Art Gallagher, Jr., *Plainville Fifteen Years Later* [Foreword by Carl Withers (James West)], Columbia University Press, New York, 1961.
[21] *Point of No Return* was published in 1949 by Little, Brown and Company, Boston. "Yankee City" is the "shorthand" title of a four-volume work by Warner and others, of which the first volume, *The Social Life of a Modern Community,* by W. Lloyd Warner and Paul S. Lunt, was published in 1941 by the Yale University Press, New Haven, Conn.

of the community, in socially superior and inferior positions."[22] As to the criteria in terms of which the people are ranked in this way the authors have the following to say:

> In these interviews certain facts became clear which might be summarized by saying a person needed specific characteristics associated with his "station in life" and he needed to go with the "right kind" of people for the informants to be certain of his ranking. If a man's education, occupation, wealth, income, family, intimate friends, clubs and fraternities, as well as his manners, speech, and general outward behavior were known, it was not difficult for his fellow citizens to give a fairly exact estimate of his status. If only his social participation in family, clique and association were known, he could be placed to the satisfaction of all the better informants by the process of identifying his social place with that of the others who were like him.[23]

The authors believe that the distinction between their six classes are clear, with the exception of the line between the lower-middle and the upper-lower classes.

The upper-upper class is comprised of "old families." In most cases their ancestors arrived in Newburyport before the Revolutionary War and acquired their wealth in the shipping and whaling industries. The old families may or may not live on Hill Street, but they live in the Hill Street section of town and they are invariably referred to as "Hill Streeters." Indeed, in Newburyport, as in other American communities, there is always an ecological correlate of class, always, as it were, a "right" and a "wrong" side of the tracks. The lower-upper class is made up of later arrivals, people who would qualify for the highest class except for the fact that they are not "old families." They frequently have larger incomes, larger houses, and more expensive automobiles than those in the upper-upper class.

The upper-middle class is comprised of merchants and professional men and their families, some well-to-do, who because of the location of their houses, the associations to which they belong, and their general activities do not qualify for high class status. The lower-middle and upper-lower classes, not easily distinguishable, live in their own sections of town, work in the stores and factories of Newburyport, and have different interests and tastes from those "above" them. Many of these families, curiously enough, can also trace their ancestry back to the halcyon days of whales and of ships, of rumrunning and the slave trade. At the very bottom, the lower-lower class, we find the Riverbrookers. They are at the bottom

---

[22] Warner and Lunt, *ibid.*, p. 82.
[23] *Ibid.*, pp. 83–84.

because of where they live, down where the river runs into the sea, and because, like the "people who live like animals" in Plainville, their "morals" are not what the rest of the community thinks they should be.

The entire first volume of the Yankee City studies is devoted to a discussion of the differences between these six classes. There are differences in income, in kinship or "family," in place of residence, in associational membership, in ethnic-group affiliation (a complicating factor in Newburyport), in marriage and courtship patterns, in the expenditure of income, in religion, in reading habits, in education, and so on through a large number of characteristics. No single criterion suffices to discriminate between the classes in any consistent way. The highest income in the lower-lower class, for example, is twice that of the lowest income in the upper-upper class. But when all of these criteria are taken together they add up to something that might be called a "life style," and this, according to the investigators, is what in the last analysis distinguishes the six classes from one another.

This study of the class structure of Newburyport has been subjected to numerous and sometimes to severe criticisms. We do not need to examine these controversies in detail. In a later section we shall have something to say about the deficiencies of all attempts to infer something about the class structure of a total society from an investigation of local and limited communities. Here we should like to say only that the class structure, even in a relatively stable community like Newburyport, is probably not so clearly articulated as the authors have maintained and that, in particular, the conclusion that there are six classes in the city, not five or seven or some other number, should be treated with extreme caution. Nevertheless, the authors are to be congratulated for their painstaking research and for their demonstration that the top class, the upper-upper class, is almost completely closed.

This last phenomenon, in fact, is also emphasized in Marquand's novel dealing with the same community. Charles Gray, a young New York banker, has an opportunity in the course of his business to return to his native Clyde and to reminisce about the events of his youth. Charles had been in love with Jessica Lovell and she with him, but strong ancestral forces kept them apart in a community where everybody knew who everybody else was and where members of the different strata did not mingle on terms of equality with one another. Jessica was a Lovell who lived on Johnson Street, and Charles was a Gray who lived on Spruce Street. Between Johnson Street and Spruce Street lay a canyon—a social canyon to be sure—that was wide and deep and, so long as one lived in Clyde, uncrossable.

Both the Lovells and the Grays were "old families" in town, dating their residence back many generations, but Jessica's ancestors were shipowners, Charles's only ship captains. When Mrs. Sarah Hewitt came to call on Charles's mother it was an act of *noblesse oblige*, the shipowner's wife calling on the ship captain's wife, even though there had been no shipping and no ships in Clyde since the end of the preceding century. Jessica's father was not really wealthy, like Mr. Stanley who owned the mill, but his money, unlike Mr. Stanley's was "old" and "dignified." He served on the library board and on the Clyde Fund and he belonged to the Clyde Historical Society and the Tuesday Club, associations that Charles's father was never invited to join. Everyone in town knew that John Gray liked to play poker and drink beer on Saturday afternoons with the boys in the Pine Street Fire Company.

The sons of the Johnson Streeters went to Harvard; indeed on Johnson Street there was never any question as to the choice of a college. Charles, on the other hand, had gone to Dartmouth. Since Charles, as the anthropologist frequently remarks, is a "mobile" person, he works only a short time in the accounting department of Mr. Stanley's factory and then joins the bond department of E. P. Rush & Company in Boston. Once again, however, he has no future. The first day he realizes that "it might be just as well if he did not talk much about Dartmouth," and indeed he very soon becomes aware of the fact that he will never be made a partner in the company, that only Harvard men ever become partners in the company. Still mobile, not yet having reached the "point of no return," he later turns his back on Clyde and its tight little social structure, and also on Boston and its tight little social structure, and leaves for New York City, where he pursues a career in the Stuyvesant Bank.

Sociologists and novelists have studied and written about many other communities, but few of them carry the wealth of statistical data that distinguishes the study by Warner and Lunt or the wealth of insights that distinguishes the work of Marquand. The point we have to make is that all communities are like Clyde. Some of them may have more classes, some fewer; in some the criteria of class may be different than in others; some may be more rigid and some less rigid—but in all of them we can find a class structure if we know where to look for it. In no community of any size, anywhere in the world, do people associate with one another on strictly even terms. There is always deference and sometimes obedience on the one hand and condescension and sometimes command on the other. The society that makes possible the multifarious relationships that people have with one another also limits these relationships and confines them within certain patterns of stratification.

4. The Criteria of Class

Among the various criteria that appear to be related to class status in our own complex society we may briefly discuss the following: (1) wealth, property, or income; (2) family or kinship; (3) location of residence; (4) duration of residence; (5) occupation; (6) education; and (7) religion. Although it is necessary to discuss these criteria one at a time, we should like to emphasize once again that no single criterion, taken by itself, embraces the whole of the phenomenon of class and that the class structure delineated in terms of any of these criteria would not necessarily coincide with that delineated by any of the others.

Wealth, Property, Income

No one can with confidence assign first place in importance to any one of these criteria. Few would doubt, however, the importance of wealth, not only in itself but for what it enables its owner to do. Wealth multiplies his living choices, his life chances, and his opportunities. It does not, as such, determine his life style but it provides a wider range of possibilities from which to choose. Its very possession confers prestige upon its owner and his family and, in spite of inheritance taxes, it can be transmitted from generation to generation. In addition, high income serves as a symbol of success in a society in which monetary emoluments are attached to so many activities.

As important as this criterion is, however, it does not suffice, even in our own monetary society. We have already indicated that some incomes in the lowest class in Newburyport are higher than some incomes in the highest class. If income does not affect life style, it has nothing to do with class position. The death of a derelict frequently discloses the possession of untold wealth. Within recent years a Boston fruit dealer, unknown on Beacon Street, gave more than a million dollars to the Boston Public Library, and a retired mathematics professor, whose friends at his death wondered if there would be enough money to bury him, left a million dollars to the University of Illinois. These cases suggest that it is not money itself but rather the manner in which it is used that has relevance to class.

An additional observation merits a modicum of attention. Wealth itself may in some cases be less important than the manner in which it was acquired. Is the money "old" and "dignified" or new and ostentatious? Is it inherited or earned? For reasons that contradict the Protestant ethic[24] inherited wealth frequently confers a higher prestige than earned wealth—primarily, one supposes, because those who have inherited it know how to

[24] For a discussion of the Protestant ethic see Chapter 20.

use it whereas those who have earned it do not. Furthermore, different ways of earning it are subject to different evaluations. One cannot, of course, earn it in criminal enterprises, or in ways that, whether or not they violate the law, clearly do not conform to the mores of the society. But even if wealth is earned in legal and ethical ways, there are additional differences to be noted. Money acquired in laxatives, depilatories, cosmetics, gadgets, patent medicines, motion pictures, or retail trade may not have the "rank" attributed to money acquired in steel, railroads, lumber, shipping, finance, or heavy industry. This consideration, however, brings us close to the occupational factor, which is a different criterion.

Finally we may note that wealth, property, and income do not receive the same evaluation in all societies. It is true that property usually carries some kind of prestige, even in the most primitive societies, but in some societies it is more or less important than in others. It is difficult to set down any general principle on the relative importance of wealth, for different societies emphasize different criteria. On the whole, however, we should say that wealth, in our society as perhaps in others, is one of the most important of the criteria of class status and one that cannot be ignored. On the other hand, it is not a simple criterion but rather a relatively complicated one, and if we use it as a single criterion of class we can easily arrive at erroneous inferences.

Family or Kinship

When statuses are differentially evaluated the evaluation frequently applies not only to the individual who occupies the status but also to the members of his family. Class status in general is a family rather than an individual phenomenon. It also comes to be a hereditary one; that is, class status, once attained, tends to endure through several generations. When this happens family or kin becomes an important criterion of class position.

In this country we have the expression "three generations from shirt sleeves to shirt sleeves," which implies that ascent and descent in the class scale can be quite rapid. But kinship is not to be minimized as a factor in class status even in the United States. The class status of children is initially ascribed, not achieved, and it frequently continues to be identical with the class status of parents, even in open class societies. As we have seen in the case of Plainville, it is extremely difficult for a man to lose "prairie" status even if he moves back into the hills and marries a "hill" girl.[25] The sons and daughters of "proper Bostonians" tend to remain "proper Bostonians" through several and, in some cases, many generations. When class

---

[25] But his children, in this situation, will be "hill" children in spite of the prairie status of their paternal grandparents.

endogamy—that is, marriage within one's own stratum—is encouraged and customarily practiced, class status can be perpetuated over relatively long periods. In some societies it is symbolized by titles of rank and perpetuated by a hereditary nobility. The importance of family or kin as a criterion of class is not the same in all societies, but it is a criterion that plays some part in the total picture. In the United States, for example, one need only mention the Adams and the Lowell families in Massachusetts and the Byrd and the Randolph families in Virginia.

Location of Residence

We have suggested that there is always an ecological correlate of class status, always a "hill" and a "prairie," a Beacon Street and a South Boston, a Park Avenue and a lower East Side, a North Shore and a Halstead Street, and so on. This ecological factor, of course, is not purely geographic. Hill Streeters in Newburyport do not all live on Hill Street, and not all of the residents of Hill Street are Hill Streeters. Nevertheless, in the absence of other criteria sheer location of residence can usually serve as an index of class position.

People strive to move into the sections of town that are considered desirable from this point of view, but again these are not necessarily the same sections generation after generation. In some of his later studies Lloyd Warner has suggested that only the very oldest families can afford to remain in mansions now encroached upon by the central business district without losing prestige. In every community these mansions may be found in this location, but in most cases they have long since been cut up, first into apartments and then into single rooms for transient occupancy.

Duration of Residence

No one can expect to achieve the highest class status automatically by acquiring substantial property and establishing residence in the "best" section unless he is also a member of an "old" family. Sometimes it takes half a lifetime to be accepted into the upper stratum of a community, sometimes it is necessary to have been born there, and for the greatest prestige in this sense it may even be necessary to claim several generations of ancestors who were born there. This can be illustrated all the way from Boston to San Francisco. The medical director of a famous hospital in the former city once lamented that, no matter how distinguished his career, he could never really be a Bostonian because he had not been born in Boston. This regret was assuaged for him, however, by the fact that his children were Bostonians—a comment expressed without a trace of humor. Duration of residence as we have noticed, is also one of the marks that distinguish the lower-upper from the upper-upper class in Newburyport.

The stranger is always classless and so, for varying periods of time, is the newcomer, whether he comes newly to Boston or San Francisco or Richmond or Seattle or Atlanta or to any of a thousand communities.

It is not easy to say why prestige is attached to duration of residence, but it is a phenomenon that occurs in all groups. The new recruit on the baseball team, the new man in the office, the new arrival in the community, the freshman or transfer student at the university, even the newcomer to the concentration camp—all these have to prove themselves before they win acceptance into the group, and few of them enjoy initial prestige. A probable explanation is that all groups, organized or not, jealously guard their norms, and acceptance is therefore withheld until the newcomer indicates his willingness to conform to them. Since it takes time to learn them the process is never an immediate one and seldom a rapid one. Conversely, only the old members are permitted to experiment with the norms and to recommend changes in them.

Occupation

It is clear from many studies that what people do for a living has a great deal—perhaps most of all—to do with their class position. Those who have high rank or status in their occupational associations will also, with some exceptions, have high-ranking status in their communities. High political and diplomatic officials, kings, presidents, and other kinds of rulers, ecclesiastical dignitaries, university presidents, corporation executives, and professional men in law, medicine, engineering, military service, religion, and education are usually accorded a high class position in independence of their kin and income. A bishop of the Episcopal Church, for example, may have only a small income, relatively speaking, but the status of bishop confers the prestige that supports a high rank on the class scale. The same observation applies to lawyers, doctors, professors, ministers, generals, admirals, and so on. If we could examine the incomes of all professional men, we would find great disparities indeed, and these disparities would be greater than the disparities in class position. On the other hand, the incomes of entertainers and professional athletes sometimes reach astronomical proportions—or so it seems to the rest of us—without contributing very much to the enhancement of their class positions.

Evaluations of occupational statuses vary widely from society to society and from time to time in the same society. Generals and admirals, for example, have historically been accorded higher status in Germany than in the United States, where their prestige increases in time of war and decreases in time of peace. Immediately after a war, when their prestige is high, officers whose training on the whole may be somewhat limited are frequently chosen for important posts in the diplomatic service or in university administration. As another example, the status of university professor has never been evaluated as highly in the United States as it has in European countries. The differential evaluation of occupational statuses offers a number of clues to the ideologies that prevail in different cultures.

Education
We have just noted that the status of university professor carries different degrees of prestige in different societies. The same observation applies to the possession of knowledge in general and to education. In all societies learning, whether sacred or secular, distinguishes those who have it from those who do not. This is true both because its acquisition requires effort and because its possession permits the performance of tasks that would otherwise be impossible.

In certain societies, however, this factor confers more prestige than in others. In the old Chinese society, for example, the Confucian scholar, the man who could read and interpret the ancient books, had a station that others could not approach. Knowledge of sacred, secret, or esoteric writings almost always adds stature to station. In some societies, however, not secret knowledge but technological knowledge has this effect, and here technicians, inventors, and engineers rank high. With respect to education in general, one may say that the mere possession of a Bachelor of Arts degree distinguishes those who have it from those who do not, and that this group has many of the characteristics of a stratum.

In the United Kingdom there is another curiously persistent criterion of class status, and that is accent. It is, of course, related to education but not always or necessarily identical with it. Those who speak with the cultivated accents of the announcers and interviewers of the British Broadcasting Corporation and the graduates of Oxford and Cambridge universities are clearly of one class and those who speak the Cockney of the London streets are clearly of another. Accent in fact is a great barrier reef in Britain, and the diffusion of the "telly," as "TV" is called there, has done little to soften or ameliorate it. In the United States, in interesting contrast, conformity to grammatical rules has class significance—no upper-class or middle-class person would use the word "ain't" except in joking circumstances—but accent as such has no class connotations.

Religion
We should not like to emphasize overmuch the importance of religion as a criterion of class status, but candid investigation of this matter in societies where there is a variety of sects discloses that it may not be altogether ignored. There is no doubt, for example, that in our own society membership in a Unitarian or an Episcopal church generally carries more prestige

than membership in, say, the Jehovah's Witnesses, the Holy Rollers, or the Church of God. It is possible that in the United States as a whole Congregationalists and Presbyterians rank a little higher than Methodists, who, in turn, rank a little higher than Baptists, who, in turn, rank higher than the sects mentioned in the preceding sentence. It is doubtful whether an Irish Catholic can ever be a "proper Bostonian," even if he is a multimillionaire. Evaluations of religious status change, of course, as we move from one community to another, from one region to another, and from one country to another, but there is little question that we have here a factor not wholly unrelated to class. And what we have said about religious affiliation also applies to various other associational affiliations, both voluntary and involuntary, that the members of a society may have.

5. Class and Higher Education in the United States

One of the striking features of contemporary American society, in contrast to most other societies, is the large number of the young who flock to the colleges and universities, a proportion that in the appropriate age groups is approaching 50 per cent. Some of them go in order to acquire the knowledge and technical skill that will enable them to pursue one of the professions. Others—a small minority one supposes—are afflicted with a zeal for learning and pursue knowledge as an end in itself. The vast majority, however, attend for neither of these reasons but rather because the B.A. degree has become a ticket of admission to a well-paying job in the world outside. It has in fact a rather considerable monetary value over the course of a lifetime and confers a distinct advantage upon those who have it in comparison with those who do not. For this reason, in a society that places so much ideological emphasis upon equality, a college education, once a privilege, is now deemed to be a right, a right to be freely extended to all and with no relation to intellectual capacities or interests. Indeed, many listen sympathetically to demands for open admissions and for the abolition of grades so that, again in the name of equal opportunity, the B. A. degree will be accessible to all.

    The wisdom of this policy, of course, is not a matter for discussion in these pages. We are, however, interested in consequences. One consequence is the prolongation of infancy, or at least of financial dependency, to an age greater than that in any society in history and a widening gap between sexual and social maturity, the former biologically and the latter culturally defined. A second consequence is that we may be drawing a new class line across the structure of American society, a line marked by the B.A. degree. If earlier societies were divided into lords and serfs, or nobles and commoners, or, as in Middletown, into the working class and the business class, the new one could use, as its class demarcation, the college degree. Those who have it will begin their careers at one place in the occupational hierarchy and move upward so far as their talents or good fortune permit; those without it will begin at another place and also move upward but only to the point where they reach an uncrossable line. The same line, in short, becomes a floor for half the population and a ceiling for the other half. Thus the society as a whole could conceivably come to resemble the structure of the armed services, with their distinction between officers and enlisted men. There is a possibility in fact—although this is speculation—that we shall have a polarized society composed of two large classes drawing always farther apart and with decreasing social interaction between them.

We can now complete the circle and suggest, less speculatively, that here we have another reason for attending college, namely, the class status it confers in this particular society, and a status otherwise denied. It is a reason again that has nothing to do with education itself. It is, in short, a class-induced phenomenon.

6. Commensalism as a Symptom of Class

Throughout this discussion we have emphasized that in no society can any single factor be used as a sole criterion of class status. Nor can we say that in general in human societies some criteria are more important than others. Some combination is always involved, but the combination exhibits subtle differences from society to society. It is obvious that the various criteria are related to one another and that people who rank high in several of them tend, more frequently than not, to rank high also in the others, although here again the criterion of kinship seems to be an exception. When we take them all into consideration—that is, if we know a person's standing with regard to wealth, property, or income; his family; his occupation; the location and duration of his residence; his education; and his religion— then we can make a good and usually an accurate guess about his social class.

All of these criteria together tend to make up what some sociologists have called a life style, or manner of living. And there is one almost infallible sympton of a shared life style that enables persons otherwise unknown to one another to recognize that they belong essentially to the same class. This symptom has to do with the culture of eating and might therefore be called, somewhat jocosely, the alimentary index. We shall call it "commensalism," that is, sharing a common table. In any event, it is well illustrated by the German proverb *"Am Tische scheiden sich die Klassen."* (At the table the classes are distinguished.)

We observed earlier in this chapter how difficult it was for the Babbitts to dine with the McKelveys and how difficult also for them to dine with the Overbrooks. It is interesting to note that Sinclair Lewis, with the insight of an artist, chose the table as the symbol of class distinctions in Zenith. This is a sound sociological insight too. In few human activities are class distinctions so readily apparent as in the culture of the table. It is a common but nevertheless a curious observation that persons will have sexual intercourse with, and permit their children to be suckled by, people with whom they would under no circumstances share a common table. The question of who eats with whom, therefore, will almost invariably disclose the strata of a society.

7. A Critique of Class Analysis

As intimated above, one criticism of community studies of class has considerable cogency, and we should like to give it a brief examination. It is argued that if we are interested in the class structure of an entire society we may be misled if we look for it on the local community level. Such studies as we have included in this chapter may not, therefore, be the proper locus for inferences concerning the class structure of American society in general. Indeed, the question whether there is a generalized class structure in the United States and the question whether there are class structures in particular American communities like Zenith, Middletown, Plainville, Newburyport, and so on are two different questions. It is conceivable that one could answer the first question in the negative and the second in the affirmative, and there is some warrant for the suggestion that this is indeed the case.

Inferences from the class structure of particular communities to the class structure of the society at large are based upon two assumptions, both of which are questionable. The first of these assumptions is that the class structure in one American community is comparable or even coincidental with that in another. The second assumption is that a particular American community is the American society in microcosm, that is, that the phenomenon found in a community is representative of the society at large.

The difficulty with the first assumption is that there may be no "carry-over" from one community to another. It is clear, for example, that the upper class in Plainville is not the upper class in Zenith, and so on for all of the other communities mentioned. The McKelveys do not like to dine with the Babbitts, but they would not like to dine with the Lovells of Clyde either. Nor is it likely that they would be invited—and vice versa. The class structures we have been talking about, in other words, are not only local community phenomena but phenomena that to a considerable extent are *limited* to the local community. We cannot infer from them, for example, that the entire American society consists of two classes, hill people and prairie people, or a working class and a business class, or the six classes that Warner and his associates discovered in Newburyport. Such inferences result from a confusion largely engendered by the application of anthropological methods to the study of complex societies and, specifically, by the anthropological assumption that a local community in the United States is a phenomenon comparable to a primitive tribe.

There would be warrant for inferences like these if every American lived his entire life in the community in which he was born, if no one ever moved from one town to another or from the country to the city. The extreme geographical mobility of the American people, however, to say nothing of the influence of mass communications, prevents the rigidification of a class structure and contributes to the fluidity of the society. One might suggest that horizontal social mobility (that is, moving from group to group) inevitably results in vertical social mobility (that is, moving from class to class), or at least that the former facilitates the latter. In this connection, incidentally, John P. Marquand noted that Charles Gray might have been successful in his suit for the hand of Jessica Lovell if, given identical circumstances in other respects, he had come from any place other than Clyde.

The second assumption, that a local community is the entire society in microcosm and that therefore a local class structure represents the class structure of the larger society of which it is a part, is even more questionable. Many Americans who are highly mobile, for occupational or other reasons, may not identify themselves with a local community at all. In the second place, a local community like Zenith or Middletown or Plainville or Newburyport is wholly devoid of certain occupational statuses. In none of them are we likely to find a ballet dancer, an opera singer, a concert pianist, a university president, an atomic physicist, an ambassador, an international banker, a Cabinet member, a delegate to the United Nations, a governor, a bishop, an admiral, a high labor-union official, the publisher of a national magazine, a justice of a Federal court, a political philosopher, a syndicated columnist, a Nobel Prize winner, a diamond cutter, a major-league umpire, a motion-picture actress, or an astronaut. There are probably more unrepresented than represented statuses. For this reason, if for no other, the local community picture is incomplete.

In this connection there is another phenomenon to which the German sociologist Karl Mannheim invited our attention, the phenomenon of the *"freischwebende Intelligenz"* or, literally, "free-swinging intelligentsia." In all complex societies there are certain groups of people, including artists, writers, scholars, and so on who are "classless" in the sense that they can associate with anyone high or low on a particular scale and can remain unattached to the strata of a local community. The differentiation between "town and gown," that is, between townspeople and faculties, in all university communities in Western history is another illustration of this phenomenon. The ties attaching faculty members to their fields of learning are stronger than those attaching them to their localities. They are consequently highly mobile and do not strive to conform to the class criteria operating in the communities in which they teach.

An associate professor of English in a large Middle Western university, for example, may not have the slightest desire to join the local country club or Rotary Club, associations that are symbols of class prestige to doctors, lawyers, and businessmen. He will almost certainly be more interested in his membership in the Modern Language Association, the Princeton Alumni Association, and the American Civil Liberties Union, all of which are national rather than local associations. There are individuals other than college professors, of course, whose community ties are tenuous, people who gain their recognition in other than local associations. Junior and senior executives of large corporations and of labor unions fit increasingly into this category. There is a significant differentiation, in short, between "locals" on the one hand and "cosmopolitans" on the other—to use the labels first suggested by Oswald Spengler. Studies of class in American society done in the anthropological manner cannot give this kind of differentiation the emphasis it requires. Whatever the validity of their descriptions, therefore, we cannot extend their generalizations beyond the city limits.[26]

There is finally a third and most important reason why these community studies do not exhaust the phenomenon of stratification in the American society and why it is unsafe to infer the class structure of the society in general from the class structures of particular cities and towns. The reason is that in the society as a whole, class is not only a prestige phenomenon but also a power phenomenon. And as a power phenomenon it has political consequences that community studies do not ordinarily disclose. There is an overlap, of course, between class as prestige and class as power, but as we have seen they are two different things.

The steel-company executive who commutes once or twice a week to New York from Pittsburgh in his private plane, the labor leader who exercises a vast authority from his Washington office, the holder of multiple directorships who attends the board meetings of many corporations, the

[26] We may note, for example, that in the society as a whole, as contrasted with the local community, the criteria of kinship and duration of residence lose almost all of their importance.

financier who underwrites and reinsures loans to foreign governments, the political boss who rules a city—these are men of power. They may have the prestige we have been talking about, but they do not need it and may even disdain it. In comparison with this stratum the upper-upper class in Newburyport pales into insignificance. Indeed, the class theory of Karl Marx, which cannot be treated at all in a brief chapter, is built upon power and exploitation rather than repute and prestige.

8. Summary

Additional aspects of the subject of class and caste could easily double the length of this chapter. It is beyond the scope of this work to inquire, for example, into those societies, not excepting our own, that are stratified in terms of caste as well as in terms of class. To appease the reader's curiosity we shall say only that there are two authentic instances of caste in our contemporary American society. There is a caste line between blacks and whites in the entire society and one between officers and enlisted men in the armed services. The first of these examples is treated in a separate chapter; the second some readers of this book may, unhappily, discover for themselves. The second, it should be added, is a cultural survival that no longer possesses all of the characteristics of caste.

In summary then, and in full consciousness of unexplored territory, we may claim to have provided only a rudimentary discussion of the subject of social class. We began with the observation that although human groups are differentiated in various ways from one another, they are also stratified, that is, ranked as higher and lower. We observed further that stratification appears in all societies except those that are exceedingly small and simple. We ventured next to suggest that the difference between class and caste, both of which are forms of stratification, is a difference of degree—that is, that a caste system is a class system which is closed at one or more points on the scale.

We then introduced the reader to some of the famous studies of class in American society, studies both literary and sociological. In our survey of Zenith, Middletown, Plainville, Newburyport, and Clyde we noticed that people do not freely and easily associate with all of the other members of their communities, that they fall in fact into several strata. Among the criteria that articulate these strata we detected (1) property, wealth, income; (2) kinship; (3) occupation; (4) location of residence; (5) duration of residence; (6) education; and (7) religion. We noticed too that there is a useful index of the way these criteria operate in combination, and this we called "commensalism." Members of the same classes or castes eat together frequently without embarrassment; those of different strata do not.

In the concluding section of the chapter we suggested that there are several serious limitations in the community approach to class and that we cannot infer a generalized class structure in American society from the class structures of particular communities. Three reasons for this are that (1) the strata of one community do not necessarily coincide with the strata of another, (2) many of the most mobile members of the population lack local community attachments but nevertheless occupy important and highly evaluated statuses in the society at large, and (3) in the larger society class is not only a prestige phenomenon but also a power phenomenon, and prestige and power, although related, are two different things.

The last word, however, has clearly not been said on this interesting and indeed intriguing subject. Problems of class and caste, and of social stratification in general, will continue to engage the best attention and effort of sociologists in the decades to come. Only after much more research, and after refinement of concepts too, will it be possible to arrive at safe conclusions. In the meantime we may say again that class is a phenomenon that characterizes every society of any size throughout the recorded history of the human race.

Chapter 18

COLOR AND CREED

HE COMPLEX societies of the modern world
contain many different kinds of people, and that,
of course, is what makes them complex.
Throughout this book we have steadily
emphasized the prevalence of differences and we
are all aware of their importance.
They create a situation that has its
merits and virtues as well as its perils
and problems. In this chapter we
shall be concerned with one of the
problems. But before we begin let
us briefly consider one of the virtues.
Imagine, for example, the
monotony of living in a society in which all of
the people were alike. It is ridiculous, of
course, to suppose that they could all be of the
same age or of one sex. The facts of biology
prohibit a notion so fanciful. But suppose
we had a society composed exclusively
of Mohammedan shepherds, Chinese
farmers, Polish mathematicians,
Lutheran stockbrokers, Catholic
physicians, Episcopal economists,
Jewish philanthropists, Venetian
gondoliers, Swiss musicians, Irish
policemen, English diplomats, French
philosophers, or American inventors. This
notion is as fanciful as the first one, but for
sociological rather than biological
reasons. Even if such a society were
possible it would clearly seem, to most
of us, to be deplorable. One of our
oldest saws says that variety is the spice
of life. It is also the spice of society.
There are those, of course, who prefer
their fare less highly seasoned than
others. And some in society would

prefer less differentiation, perhaps, than would others. Those who might concede the biological necessity of different ages and sexes and the sociological necessity of different occupations might still prefer that all of us were of one color and one creed, one complexion and one belief, one race and one religion. This is indeed the situation that obtains in the smaller and simpler societies. But it does not obtain in the so-called civilized societies like our own. Differentiation, in fact, is one of the prices we pay for civilization; it is one of the costs of complexity. We are now of different colors and different creeds, and these colors and creeds have consequences that we wish to explore in this chapter.

1. Consciousness of Kind and Consciousness of Difference

Earlier in this book we used the criterion of "consciousness of kind" in order to distinguish societal groups from those that are merely statistical. We noted that this concept was introduced into the literature of sociology by Franklin H. Giddings and noted in addition that it was one of high analytical utility. Indeed, consciousness of kind is perhaps the most important factor in the explanation both of group membership and of social interaction. It is the similarities that people recognize in one another that induce them to seek one another out and to form groups, either consciously for the purpose of social interaction or unconsciously because others, who are different, consider them alike and react to them as belonging together. It is consciousness of kind that helps to determine the flow of people into this group or that one, encourages this man to meet with that man, and ultimately fixes the juxtaposition of people in an entire society. It is not too much to say that we have social groups in the first place because certain people are similar, because they possess traits or interests in common, and because they are conscious of what they share.

If we are like some other people, however, it follows inevitably that we are also unlike some. Our coin, in short, has two faces, and consciousness of kind means also consciousness of difference. If consciousness of kind encourages a man to greet his neighbor, consciousness of difference cautions him against the stranger. If the first stimulates social intercourse, the second inhibits it. If the first builds roads and paves them, the second raises a barricade and blocks the stream of traffic. The first includes, the second excludes; the first invites, the second contemns; the first leads often to unity and to group formation, the second to disunity and to group decay. When we recognize that some people are different from us, we are ordinarily less ready to admit them into the small circle of our intimates and to ascribe to them the virtues that distinguish "people like us"; we are more likely, in fact, to assign the sins of society to "people like them."

Once more we have the story of the "we" and the "they," the in-group and the out-group. We are the privileged, the elect, the right; they are the disprivileged, the remainder, the wrong. We, "we happy few," are quite sufficient unto ourselves; we need no help or sustenance from them, the unhappy many. And they, of course, have the same notions about us. They too, to themselves, are an in-group and from it *we* are excluded. They too assert their exclusiveness, their righteousness, their obvious superiority. And so our in-group is set against their in-group. We are we and they are they—and this endeth the lesson. Let them keep to their places and we shall keep to ours. In fact, if we are stronger than they, we will *make* them keep to their places.

Of course we do not really know all of those others. We have met indeed only some of them; most we have never seen. But we have them stereotyped: "Why, my brother-in-law was telling me that a friend of his, works down at the office with him, had an aunt whose neighbor's sister once had a most unpleasant experience with one of them. Just what you'd expect. I've heard other stories too, I know what *they're* like. I had a run-in with one of them myself a couple of years ago, and got a pretty good notion. And look at the way some of them live! You'd think they'd at least have a little decency. Not that I'm prejudiced against them, you understand. Give them their due I always say, but don't let them go where they're not wanted either. You'd think they'd know without being told. But some people never understand. Maybe you can't expect them to."

All of us, unfortunately, have heard sentiments like these. They are a frequent accompaniment to the process of living in a heterogeneous society. With people in other groups we are in contact at many points and in many public places. But contact does not always mean communication, and communication does not necessarily mean understanding. Our selves are shuttered off—eager to open, perhaps, to the familiar, the recognized, and the known, but ready to close again at the first sign of the foreign, the exotic, the strange.

As we become members of some groups, so do we, in the same process, exclude ourselves from others. As certain statuses are ascribed to us, so also are certain others denied. One might suggest in fact that status denial is a necessary consequence of status ascription. And so we arrive at a society made up of different groups, in always-changing juxtaposition with one another, their members moving in and out of them, qualifying themselves for some and at the same time disqualifying themselves from others. We cannot "associate" without at the same time "dissociating." Association and dissociation are two consequences of the same act, two facets of the same fact. As soon as we join with some people we separate ourselves from others. We are always conscious of our kind and conscious too of those who are not our kind. And furthermore, it is always *they* who are different—*we* are always ourselves.

If no man is an island, neither is any group. Societal groups inevitably come into contact with one another, and when there is contact there is a setting for conflict. We thus live in a world in which tensions rise and subside, and rise again. It is a world that contains blacks and whites, Catholics and Protestants, Jews and Gentiles, Hindus and Moslems, Frenchmen and Germans, Israelis and Arabs, Russians and Americans, Montagues and Capulets, Hatfields and McCoys, Greeks and barbarians, playwrights and critics, authors and publishers, residents and commuters, landlords and tenants, upstaters and downstaters, farmers and city dwellers, "natives" and "summer people," and so on through an endless list. Different traits and different ideas and different purposes create different groups, and the fact of differentiation is one that can neither be denied nor sensibly deplored. But differentiation does not in itself mean conflict and differentiation does not by itself produce prejudice. At what point does prejudice arise? This is one of the most vexing of all sociological problems. It is a problem that has many answers and, to date, no solutions. We shall consider it in some detail.

2. Pride and Prejudice

Let us concede at the outset that any preference is a kind of prejudice. If preferences are normal, so also are prejudices. If we have to face stark facts in the universe of nature, we have to face similar facts in the universe of society. The rain that ruins a picnic saves a crop. The heat that makes us miserable increases the yield of corn. We are taught to take the bitter with the sweet, and so also it almost has to be in human relations. Prejudice is the price we pay for preference, and for pride.

It is unreasonable to ask us both to take pride in our own groups and their accomplishments and at the same time to refrain from considering them superior. It is the superiority in which we take the pride. And if our groups are superior they must be superior to something that is inferior, or language has no meaning. What is a virtue, in other words, becomes in reverse a vice. The same attitude that is commended in one situation is condemned in another and for precisely the same reason. Pride means prejudice. It is impossible to have one without the other. It is impossible for us to praise our own country, for example, or to take comfort in our own religion without at the same time being thankful that we have this country, or this religion, and not some other one. We are glad that we are Americans, for example, not sorry; and we are encouraged—even taught—to be glad. If patriotism is a virtue, can prejudice be a vice?

Prejudice in favor of one's own group would seem to be a normal phenomenon in the human species. Prejudice, in short, can mean merely preference or preferment, and need not be anti-anything. To be prejudiced may mean only that we favor our own groups, our own associates and companions. If one is white and Anglo-Saxon and Protestant—a Wasp in short—he need not be anti-Semitic or anti-Negro even if he associates for the most part with other white Anglo-Saxon Protestants. Nor if one is black or Jewish need he for the same reason be anti-Wasp. Prejudice can be for, rather than against. In these cases one begins to wonder whether prejudice is the right word. In any event it is clear that one way to eradicate prejudice or preferment is to eliminate at the same time such virtues as group loyalty, group pride, and patriotism. Whatever is responsible for the one is responsible for the other.

There is one other way to eradicate prejudice, a way that reaches absurdity in practice but that illustrates a principle in theory. This way is simply to abolish all societal groups in which a consciousness of difference is exhibited. Abolish them so completely that no one will ever be able to identify a given individual as a member of this group instead of that, of that group instead of this. The price for this solution, however, would be more than most of us would want to pay. It has been suggested in fact that if there is any tension, for example, between Protestants, Catholics, and Jews, there is one sure, if radical, way not only of easing it but of curing it altogether. All people have to do is to stop being Protestants, Catholics, and Jews. The degree to which we do not want to do this, the degree to which we insist upon having several religions instead of one, is precisely the degree to which we will attract the prejudices of others and will prejudge them in return. Distinction involves separation, and separation inevitably invites suspicion. So long as people want to be different they must pay a certain price for their desire.

As sociologists we can once again observe how the in-group–out-group principle operates. The reader will remember this distinction from our earlier discussion. The in-group is the "we" group, the one to which we belong. The out-group is the "they" group and is made up of everyone else. We noted two corollaries of this distinction—(1) that in-groups stereotype out-groups and (2) that any threat from an out-group, real or imagined, intensifies the cohesion of the in-group.

Let us attend for a moment to the second of these corollaries. If an out-group can intensify cohesion it can also, sometimes, create cohesion, that is, create an in-group where one would not otherwise exist. Some groups, in other words, would fly apart if they were not poised in juxtaposition to (or in opposition to) some other group, and it is the juxtaposition in fact that may give it sustenance and endurance. Remove the out-group, and the in-group may no longer be able to justify itself.

If we now apply this principle to the problem of religious groups, we can understand the argument that the Jews, for example, should welcome *some* anti-Semitism because without it their continued existence might be jeopardized. A rabbi in São Paulo, Brazil, has commented in fact that there is so little anti-Semitism there that it is difficult for him to keep his synagogue alive. We are not suggesting that groups can exist only when there are opposing groups. Many other variables enter into this equation, including the size of the groups and, more especially perhaps, their majority or minority status. But the degree to which religious sectarianism thrives upon intolerance and starves with increasing tolerance is a question that merits sustained sociological inquiry.

There is little chance, however, that societal groups will disappear. They represent the differences between men, and the differences between men are legion. Men will disagree upon the slightest provocation, and their different groups emphasize the degree of their differences. It is something of a paradox, on the other hand, that when groups are too different no tension arises between them. Differences in interest, function, or purpose raise no issues and invite no conflicts. Thus, the United States Steel Corporation is not in conflict with the St. Louis Cardinals, nor the St. Louis Cardinals with the University of Pennsylvania, nor the University of Pennsylvania with the Principality of Monaco. As groups become more alike, so also do they become aware of their differences. And the more aware of their differences, the more zealous they become in their adherence to them. The more zealous they become, the more the tensions take hold. When there are no large differences between men, the importance of the small ones will be magnified; thus the more similar groups become, the more they tend to exaggerate the differences that divide them. This paradox explains why civil strife is often the bloodiest of all and why enmity between brothers is sometimes so intense. Finally, there is frequently more bitterness between two factions of the same political or religious sect than between the sect and all its enemies—provided that these common enemies are not at the moment threatening the sect as a whole and thus contributing to its cohesion.

We are now viewing from another side the principle of the in-group–out-group relationship. Let us utilize once again an illustration from an earlier discussion. As Englishmen you and I, of course, are quite superior to foreigners, those benighted people who live in other countries. But as Londoners we are superior also, of course, to all those Englishmen who live in the provinces. As educated men we are superior in addition to all of those who are uneducated even though they have the good taste to live in London. As intellectuals we are naturally superior to lawyers, doctors, dentists, ministers, veterinarians, sea captains and such, even though these types also live in London and are educated men. As scientists we quite naturally think our work is more important than that of literary critics and other intellectuals and wonder how they can spend their lives on matters that, however interesting, can never be more than trivial. But then as physicists we are naturally doing more important work than those who conduct investigations in such inexact sciences as bacteriology, neurology, and meteorology. And as atomic physicists there is scarcely any doubt that we are superior to those who study light, motion, heat, and other unimportant problems. As a matter of fact, though I hate to say this, my work exceeds yours in importance because my cyclotron is very much more powerful than yours. . . . Here again we have an entirely imaginary monologue. But we can hardly doubt that all men sometimes have thoughts like these, no matter what the in-group variables they employ.

If differences in color and creed seem more serious than those between physicists and literary critics, it is because the former represent affiliations from which it is difficult or impossible to resign. Involuntary group memberships and the ascribed statuses that accompany them in a given society are relatively fixed. They can sometimes be changed, through subterfuge or some other means, but in general it is quite difficult to withdraw from certain kinds of statuses and certain kinds of groups. It is difficult, for example, to stop being black and to start being white, and it is similarly difficult to reverse the status in the other direction. It is difficult, for the same reason, to stop being a Jew, even though one embraces another religion, and it difficult to become a Jew even if one is converted to the Jewish faith. It is not even easy to stop being a Catholic. As a perceptive sociologist, Everett Hughes, has observed, the culture of French Canada, for example, is so Catholic that even the freethinkers are Catholic. And indeed, a Protestant atheist is different from a Jewish atheist.

Similar observations apply to the fact of national origin. It is clearly possible, of course, for a native of Poland to become an American. The sociological and psychological factors involved in this process have been analyzed in many books, most notably by William I. Thomas and Florian Znaniecki in *The Polish Peasant in Europe and America*. But however American a man may become, he does not wholly cease to be a Pole so long as he retains anything of the Polish language and literature, custom and tradition. The process of assimilation is one that the individual can seldom complete, and it usually requires at least two generations. National origin, an ascribed status, thus separates group from group and individual from individual when they live together in the same society. This situation obtains especially in the United States where everybody—excepting only the Indians—has a non-American ancestry. Involuntary group memberships and ascribed statuses thus create a problem.

Still another kind of problem arises that might be called the problem of the native and the stranger (or who got here first?). Wherever they meet, anywhere in the world, the native and the stranger entertain for each other a mutual suspicion. The two groups do not know each other's norms, each distrusts the other's ways of doing things, and each regards the other's customs as queer and quite possibly as absurd. There may even be an additional source of hostility. The native may suspect that the stranger has designs on his location and will one day displace him from it. Even when the stranger is welcome his hosts may take some time to accept him. It is for this reason that visitors are usually received more hospitably than those who aspire to become inhabitants. Finally, those who come first to an unoccupied region may try to exclude those who want to come later, even though in this situation no one is a native.

In these paragraphs we have been saying that prejudice is a normal phenomenon, that in one sense it is little more than a form of preference, and that prejudice "for" entails almost inevitably prejudice "against." It is doubtful if there is such a thing on earth as a wholly unprejudiced person. Such a person would be devoid of conviction, devoid of opinion, devoid of preferences—in short, a cipher. Even those who take pride in being, as they think, unprejudiced are prejudiced against the prejudiced.

It appears that we are rapidly reaching the conclusion that some prejudices are "good" and others "bad." Those who are prejudiced against "us" can reach exactly the same conclusion. It can be seen that the problem of prejudice is thus, in a sense, insoluble. And, as the case of patriotism suggests, prejudice may be a virtue as well as a vice.

3. Discrimination

Prejudice is one thing. Discrimination is something else. Prejudice is a matter of belief. Discrimination is a matter of behavior. Prejudice can be "for" as well as "against." Discrimination is always "against."[1] To discriminate means to deny to an individual or a group a privilege or an opportunity or a pleasure that is thereupon reserved for one's own group. The denial, furthermore, is made on irrelevant grounds, for reasons that have nothing to do with the qualifications of the person in question.

Thus, a man who possesses all of the qualifications for admission to a law partnership may be denied admission because he is a Jew. A man who possesses all of the qualifications for employment as a chemist may be denied employment because he is a Negro. In the first case it is difficult to

---

[1] Even in this respect we encounter a semantic problem. Discrimination is not always an unpleasant word. Sometimes it has a favorable connotation and sometimes discriminations are "nice." To discriminate in this sense means to make fine distinctions, to recognize small differences, to distinguish accurately. In this sense, of course, discrimination is a sign of intelligence, and a discriminating taste is a virtue altogether to be admired. It is hardly necessary to say that we are not using the word in this sense in this chapter.

see the relationship between the Jewishness and the practice of law. In the second it would require an abnormal imagination to conclude that the color of a chemist's skin interferes with his ability to do quantitative or qualitative analysis of organic or inorganic compounds. An abnormal imagination, however, frequently comes into play in situations of this kind.

It is necessary, of course, to distinguish between discrimination and simple exclusion. We have seen in an earlier chapter that all associations, of whatever kind, have tests of membership, sets of criteria in terms of which members are selected, rules of eligibility. The Roman Catholic priesthood is thus not open to infidels, registered Democrats may not vote in Republican primaries, convicted criminals are denied some of the rights of citizenship, and neither of the writer's daughters has much chance of becoming the Queen of England. These exclusions are legitimate because the qualifications are clearly related to the situation involved. All associations, in other words, have tests of membership that are related to the purposes for which the groups are formed and the interests they exist to satisfy. When the tests have no conceivable relationship to these purposes or interests, when persons otherwise qualified are denied admission, when exclusions occur for reasons that have nothing to do with the case, then we see the processes of discrimination at work.[2]

The practice of discrimination covers a wide spectrum. Its victims may be anyone, or any group. It can appear in any society. In the United States, for example, it has several persistent forms—against Puerto Ricans in New York, against French Canadians in New England, against Chinese and Japanese on the West Coast, against Mexicans in the Southwest, against Negroes in the South, and against Jews without respect to region. One might amend this sentence to say that these minority groups suffer discrimination everywhere in the United States but that in the case of most of them the problem is more serious in some regions than in others. One cannot, of course, without writing an extensive treatise, discuss each of these groups in detail, nor indeed is it necessary to do so. Since we are interested in an analysis of the phenomenon as such we need only one case for illustration. In what follows therefore we shall confine our attention to the plight of the Negro not in South Africa, and Rhodesia, where it appears

---

[2] Questions sometimes arise as to the relevance of the test. A controversy once developed in New York concerning the selection of probation officers for the children's division of the Domestic Relations Court. The law requires that whenever it is practical, children be placed under the supervision of a probation officer of their own religion. Since fewer Jewish children come before the court than Catholic or Protestant children, the result is that fewer Jewish probation officers, otherwise qualified, are hired. Is the religion of the probation officer relevant in this situation? Or does the method of selection violate the constitutional provision that prohibits the imposition of religious tests for public employment?

to be steadily deteriorating, but in the United States, where it appears to show a slow but often encouraging improvement.

Improvement, however, is always relative. Let us examine a number of areas in which discrimination deprives the black citizen of equal opportunity. In the area of education, first of all, no one would claim that the black has ever enjoyed benefits comparable to those of his white neighbor, either in the North or the South. Black schools, segregated as they have been, have had few resources in comparison with their white counterparts. Black colleges and universities have not been able to achieve or to maintain the level of competence characterized by American higher education in general. The proportion of black faculty members with the Ph.D. degree, for example, is less than half that of the average faculty in the United States. For that matter, few blacks serve on the faculties of American colleges and universities—except Negro colleges and universities. By 1970, however, because of affirmative action programs designed to compensate for past discrimination, they were in demand almost everywhere in higher education. Indeed, to be both black and female was to have a double advantage. Quota systems, once condemned, were reinstated (under other names) so that the number of blacks on university faculties and in professional schools would bear some relationship to the number of blacks in the population; universities receiving federal assistance were required to take positive steps in that direction. The number of black students attending college increased by some 200 per cent during the decade from 1960 to 1970, and more than half of them were in colleges predominantly white.

The new influx of black students, however, produced problems of its own. The more militant among them reversed the field, as it were, and began to demand black dormitories, black quadrangles, black student unions, black cultural centers, black recreational facilities, and black courses for blacks only. These actions, which appeared in other pockets of the society as well, raised the threat of black separatism and offered proof of the unfortunate fact that no race is entirely free of racism.

The story in the lower schools reached a turning point on May 17, 1954, when the justices of the Supreme Court of the United States, in *Brown v. Board of Education*, unanimously decided as follows: "We conclude that in the field of public education the doctrine of 'separate but equal' has no place. Separate educational facilities are inherently unequal. Therefore, we hold that the plaintiffs and others similarly situated for whom the actions have been brought are, by reason of the segregation complained of, deprived of the equal protection of the laws guaranteed by the Fourteenth Amendment." The Court demanded that desegregation proceed "with all deliberate speed," but there has been more deliberation than speed, and in addition the decision aroused a bitter opposition in some of the states, both North and South, which twenty years later had not subsided.

Discrimination has produced in the area of housing an almost universal segregation, with its inevitable accompaniment of the black ghetto. Urban redevelopment has only begun to attack the problem and the situation is no better in the North than in the South, partly because of the continued high rate of black migration to the North. Philadelphia, Pittsburgh, Cleveland, Detroit, and Chicago all have their black slums, and Harlem is a disgrace to one of the great cities of the world.

In economic affairs the dismal picture repeats itself. Blacks suffer discrimination in employment, in union membership and preferment, in promotional opportunities, in income, in working conditions, and so on through the fabric of occupational and professional life. Blacks are always overrepresented in the unemployment statistics, partly because they hold in higher proportions the unskilled jobs of the economy. They are over-represented in the morbidity and mortality statistics too, in some of which their rates are twice as high as the corresponding rates for whites. With regard to religion it is unnecessary to say more than that, whatever the denomination, there is almost complete segregation.

The discrimination that resulted in the suppression of civil rights was perhaps the most serious of all. In 1960, for example, some 14,000 blacks lived in an Alabama county, of whom 1,000 were registered to vote. In the same county 2,818 eligible whites lived, of whom 3,310 were registered to vote—a 117 per cent registration! In a number of counties no blacks at all were permitted to vote, and one technical device after another was introduced in order to give a semblance of legality to the exclusion. To qualify for registration, for example, blacks were required to recite the Constitution of the United States and were then disqualified if they omitted the punctuation. Sometimes two days were consumed in testing the literacy of a single black person, while others waited in a long line, and sometimes the registrars did not deign to notice them at all. Concerted action, however, has in more recent years resulted in notable improvements. No fewer than six major civil rights bills were passed by Congress during the years from 1957 to 1970, two of which were addressed specifically to voting rights.

Discriminatory practices are sometimes ludicrous as well as cruel. In one state, for example, a bill was introduced in the legislature requiring that textbooks for use in black schools be stored in separate warehouses from those used in white schools. In the same state a bill requiring the reading of the Constitution of the United States in the public schools was defeated when a legislator pointed out that the Constitution includes the Fourteenth Amendment. A soft-drink vending machine once in use in this country had separate coin slots marked "White" and "Colored." There was also a cemetery for dogs in which black dogs could be buried if they were owned by white people but not white dogs if they were owned by black people. Finally, one remembers with poignancy that during World War II a contingent of German prisoners was being transferred from one place to another by rail. The military train stopped at a small station for lunch. The German prisoners were fed in the station restaurant. The American soldiers who were in charge of them went hungry because they were black and the nearest restaurant "for colored" was too far away.

This, and much more, is discrimination. Many books have been dedicated to an effort to explain it and many theories have been advanced. None is wholly satisfactory. Before we look at some of these efforts let us consider suggestions that seem unsound or useless, either as causes or as cures.

4. Misleading Trails

In the ensuing discussion of misleading trails we shall put prejudice and discrimination together again and view the latter as an overt expression of the former.

(1) The first of these misleading trails is the denial that races exist. This is the solution offered by many writers whose motives are among the most meritorious of all. If there is no such thing as a race, they argue, there can obviously be no such thing as race prejudice either. Those who appear to be prejudiced, therefore, are indulging themselves in what is at best a superstition and at worst a delusion. They have, at the very least, lost touch with reality because in reality there is nothing to be prejudiced against.

However admirable this sentiment may be, the fact is false. The trouble with this strategy is that everybody knows that races do exist, and denial therefore only does a disservice to the truth. Despite the disclaimers of those who support this idealistic solution, everybody realizes that there are differences between, say, an Ethiopian, a Navajo, a Chinese, and a Swede. The strategy, in consequence, does harm where it is intended to do good. It increases the suspicion the unlearned already entertain for the learned, brings scientific inquiry into disrepute, and fails altogether to solve the problem. As a matter of fact it solves neither the social nor the sociological problem; that is, it neither supplies a cure nor suggests a cause. It merely induces the layman to lend credence to the German proverb *Je verlehrter, desto verkehrter.* (The more learned they are the crazier they are.)

(2) A second device frequently employed is the denial, not that races exist, but that their differences are important. It is quite valid, of course, to

deny that the discernible differences between races are relevant to certain other characteristics. There is no evidence, for example, that skin color is in any way related to cultural accomplishment, nor is there any known connection between stature and intelligence. But we refer here to something else—the attempt to convince those who think that racial differences are important that they are, in fact, not important. If some people think they are important, they *are* important, no matter what other people may say. No amount of emphasis upon the insignificance or irrelevance of racial characteristics could have induced the Governor of Georgia to attend the funeral of Martin Luther King, Jr., in 1968.

The strategy suggested by this device can succeed only with those who are accustomed to accepting scientific evidence. Scientific evidence that segregation does harm to both races, the white as well as the black, is either rejected or denounced as irrelevant by those who wish to preserve the patterns of the past, the norms they have been taught to respect, the conduct they believe is proper. Their answer can always be that, although race differences may not be important to *you*, they are important to *me*, and I'll thank you therefore not to interfere.

(3) Our third misleading trail belongs in the category of erroneous assumptions rather than of mistaken strategies. It concerns the fact that in recent years problems of prejudice have been identified with—and labeled as—minority-group problems. The relationship of majorities to minorities is indeed relevant to prejudice but it is incorrect to conclude that the victims of prejudice are always members of minority groups. Many minority groups are not discriminated against at all and some majority groups have attracted vicious persecution. Doctors of philosophy, millionaires, and residents of the city of St. Louis, Missouri, for example, are all minorities in the American population, but they hardly suffer discrimination on that account.

It is recorded, of course, that it is easier for a camel to go through the eye of a needle than for a rich man to enter the gates of heaven, but if this is an example of prejudice on high, it is one that seems not to operate on earth. The poor we have always with us, and always in majority numbers. As serfs they have been discriminated against by the nobility, as peons they have been pressed into servitude, and as workers they have been oppressed by employers. Conquerors, similarly, have discriminated against a larger number of the conquered, and imperialists have not often outnumbered the natives whom they have exploited. The problem of prejudice and discrimination, in short, is not an inevitable accompaniment of a majority-minority relationship nor is it, strictly speaking, a "minority-group problem." We are—all of us—members of some minorities, but we do not all suffer discrimination for this reason.

(4) A fourth trail that can lead to a dead end involves a fallacy that is

obvious in logic but not so clear, perhaps, in sociology. We tend to assume that in order to understand prejudice we need to study the group against which the prejudice is expressed. Thus, in order to understand anti-Negro prejudice we spend vast amounts of money and energy studying Negroes and in order to understand anti-Semitism we similarly study Jews. We tend to assume in addition that black sociologists are authorities on the Negro problem and Jewish sociologists are experts on Jewish relations. We have here a nest of false assumptions, however plausible they may appear prior to examination. Thus, for some reason, we assume that if Group A is prejudiced against Group B there must be something in Group B to account for the fact. The assumption can, of course, be correct. But upon reflection it seems much more likely that the cause of the prejudice is to be found in Group A. It is this group, after all, that owns the prejudice and that does the discriminating.

Actually it seems obvious, when openly stated, that in order to study prejudice we should study the subjects of prejudice at least as intensively as we do the objects. It was a stroke of good fortune when the Carnegie Corporation induced Gunnar Myrdal to undertake a comprehensive study of the Negro problem in the United States. As a result of his study he concluded that "the Negro problem" is not a Negro problem at all but rather a white problem. But no one yet has offered to subsidize a study of the person in whom anti-Negro prejudice is vocal and anti-Negro discrimination direct. What makes this man so vehement, so dogmatic, so passionate in his prejudice? This is the question that requires an answer.

(5) As a corollary to the preceding observation, however, we have to note as a fifth point that groups that are discriminated against are not always free of the faults of the groups that discriminate. Group B, which is discriminated against by Group A, may in turn discriminate against Group C, and C, in turn, against D, and so on through an entire "pecking order" of groups. The members of all groups prefer themselves to others, and any strategy for reducing prejudice that ignores this simple fact is sure to invite failure.

Recognition that any group may be the subject as well as the object of prejudice, and sometimes both at the same time, may give us an insight into the problem. It may also interpose practical difficulties into a solution. Group A, for example, may believe[3] that Group B would discriminate against it if it were in a position to do so. Group A will therefore discriminate against Group B in an effort to prevent it from arriving at such a position. The situation here, with groups poised in mutual suspicion,

[3] The reader will condone the elision on the ground of convenience. Groups, of course, do not believe, nor do they think. It is their members who believe and think.

presents a picture not unlike that of an armaments race. Both groups discriminate because they both fear discrimination. Fear is thus a kind of sand in the gears of society.

5. Once More, the Laws and the Mores

Our sixth and final misconception requires a section of its own. This is the view, widely accepted, that in order to solve the problem of discrimination it is necessary only to "pass a law." The hope that either a legislative act or a judicial decision can solve this social problem, or any social problem, is one of the more prevalent delusions of the human mind. We need not expose its fallacy here. We have, in fact, already done so in an earlier chapter, where we discussed the relationship between the mores and the laws and stressed the futility of expecting the laws to cure a social malady.

Laws are impotent when confronted by contrary mores, as was recognized by Tacitus and by every serious social thinker since. Indeed passing a law under these circumstances frequently has an effect contrary to that intended. It comes to be more honored in the breach than in the observance, as Shakespeare put it in one of his immortal contributions to the language. The fact that it is on the books sometimes has two consequences, the second of which is unanticipated; that is, it appeases the conscience of the community on the one hand and offers impunity to individual violation on the other. In any event, the community then no longer concerns itself with the issue. The sociologist, in short, can be quite definite in his assertion that, as a matter of prinicple, laws cannot solve a social problem and are powerless by themselves to "improve" society.

It would be erroneous, however, to conclude from this direct and even dogmatic assertion that the resources of the state, or of the state's judiciary, should not be employed to enforce the peace between different groups and to abolish the discriminatory practices that one group visits upon another. In some respects and in some situations a law can be both useful and influential. A law, in a sense, serves notice that *this* is the will of the community. In situations where the mores lack definition, a law can introduce a concrete clarity and indicate what is henceforth the proper conduct. In situations where the community is divided, as on the segregation issue in the United States, the law can hasten a process—not without some intensified opposition—that has come to be inevitable in any event. Even more important, perhaps, the law can operate as an instrument of education, lending dignity and rectitude to a course of conduct that might not otherwise be openly approved or candidly pursued.

Wherever "law-abidingness" is itself a value, as it is in civilized societies, the social potency of the law is great indeed. It is for this reason that there is no inconsistency in asking on the one hand, What are laws without mores? and in recognizing on the other hand the societal efficacy of legislative acts, judicial decisions, constitutional amendments, and "fair employment practices commissions." Law by itself is helpless. In the total fabric of norm and ideology, however, it plays a heavy and substantial role. If it is not the creator it can at least serve as the buttress of morality.

　　The problem of the laws and the mores can be approached in yet another way—by emphasizing once again the distinction between prejudice and discrimination. Prejudice is an attitude of the mind and as such is quite beyond the reach of the law, the policeman's club, the robed decision. No force on earth can induce a courageous man to change his mind on what is to him a matter of principle. The Supreme Court of the United States can help to end segregation, but no decision of that Court, however unanimous, can force the Governor of Mississippi, for example, to like integration. It would be sheer folly to pass a law prohibiting people from disliking Jews, Negroes, Catholics, or Protestants, just as it would be silly, for the same reason, to require them by law to prefer football to basketball. But it is neither folly nor foolishness to enlist the sanction of the law and the sovereignty of the state to assure that all children, whatever their color, enjoy the same privileges in school and all men the same rights in society. Acts, in short, are susceptible to legal treatment; attitudes are not. Discrimination can be abolished by law, and by legally sanctioned force if necessary, but neither law nor force can sweeten hospitality nor encourage kindness.

6. A Note on Attitudes and Actions

We shall not in this chapter undertake to survey the voluminous literature on racial and ethnic attitudes. The omission is explained by two considerations. The first of these is that the subject of attitudes (and attitude testing) as such, a field in which recent years have brought notable advances, belongs primarily to social psychology rather than to sociology. The second is the large disparity that has been shown to exist between attitudes on the one hand and actual responses on the other or, stated differently, between private and public attitudes. It is seldom safe to predict what a man will do by asking him what he intends to do. The course of action a man describes for himself in a hypothetical situation may not correspond at all with his future action in a real situation. Many Southerners who must in public support discriminatory practices against the Negro may in private believe in and even exhibit a much more favorable sentiment. Many Northerners who swear in public that they are wholly devoid of prejudice and are in fact "liberal" on the race question may in private exhibit an attitude that ranges from indifference to hostility.

The disparity between attitudes and actions was once demonstrated by Richard T. LaPiere in what has come to be a classic experiment in the history of sociology.[4] Professor LaPiere traveled up and down the Pacific Coast with a Chinese couple, who were refused lodging only once. Upon their return to Stanford University he wrote to the proprietors of the inns and hotels where they had stopped and inquired whether they would accept Chinese guests. Most of them replied that they would not.

We should not conclude from this stark illustration that attitudes and actions have no relation to each other. They may, in fact, correspond quite closely, and frequently they reinforce each other. The person who has no prejudices will hardly be tempted to practice discrimination. As discrimination decreases, so also will prejudices soften. From this fact those who seek a solution can find some solace. We return to it below when we discuss the principle of circular causation.

7. Indoctrination

Having warned against several misleading trails, we now want to take a positive approach and indicate some of the more likely sources of prejudice. One of these sources is indoctrination, the process by which an individual absorbs the culture that surrounds him. When prejudice is a part of the folkways, for example, he will take it in and make it a part of him in precisely the same manner in which he makes all the other components of culture a part of him. If a white child grows up in a group in which anti-Negro sentiments are steadily expressed and anti-Negro discrimination steadily practiced, it is too much to expect of him that he will easily rid himself of his feelings. One might as well expect an orthodox Jew to take gustatory pleasure in a pork roast or an orthodox Catholic to eat meat on Good Friday.

It does little good, for example, for the Northern reformer to assault the sensibilities of the Southern white on the race question, no matter how immoral or subversive he may regard the latter's views. The Southerner may have come by his opinions quite honestly, as it were, and it is altogether too much to expect that a single individual will rebel against his friends and relatives—his parents, his grandparents, and his ancestors—for a theoretical justice that appears to him to involve an erroneous assumption. He may, of course, feel intellectually or religiously or ethically

[4] "Attitudes versus Actions," *Social Forces*, vol. 13, 1934, pp. 230–237.

uncomfortable in his position, and logically uncomfortable as well if he tries to make sense of it; but if it is one he shares with nearly everyone he knows, his prejudice can hardly be called abnormal or pathological or even unusual. It is simply a part of the culture of the groups to which he happens to belong.

The notion that the Negro is an inferior being may be just as much a part of the Southerner's ideology as the notion that there is only one God, or that the United States of America is the greatest country on earth, or that Georgia is the most beautiful state in the Union, or that Robert E. Lee is the greatest military figure in history, or that the Southern woman is an especially superior, if somewhat delicate, creature. Prejudice against any people may take this cultural form, and once it has crystallized in the ideologies of several generations it is difficult to eradicate.

It should not be necessary to emphasize, in discussing this point, that prejudice is not innate. One does not acquire a dislike or a distrust of another group of people in the process of being born, nor does one acquire in this way the urge to discriminate. Babies are wholly free from prejudice, as they are free from every other idea, good or bad, that they will later acquire simply as a matter of belonging to certain social groups. Prejudice is learned, just as culture in general is learned. Indoctrination and habituation, responsible as they are for inducing conformity to the norms, are thus responsible also for inculcating patterns of prejudice and of discrimination, when these too are a part of the culture.

To remove this kind of prejudice it is quite useless to attack the individual. It is necessary instead to change the norms that guide the discriminatory practice. It is in this respect that legislation and judicial decision can be especially effective. They can indicate that in the larger society the norm no longer possesses the appropriate sanction and that the majesty and dignity of the law, in fact, are on the other side. By slow degrees the norm can thus be changed.

8. Frustration

Prejudice, however, is not always a matter of mere conformity. Sometimes it results from personal frustration.

The experience of failure in the face of another's success is a common and, one might say, even a normal cause of frustration; and frustration frequently expresses itself in aggression. It is not too difficult to understand how, in a period of economic crisis or severe depression, a black father desperately seeking work in order to support his family would look with disfavor upon Wasps or Jews who manage to hold on to their jobs after he has been dismissed. Similarly, one who loses an honor of some kind, a promotion, an increase in salary, a job, or a business deal to a competitor who can be identified with some other ethnic or religious group, especially one against which there is already some prejudice or discrimination in the society, is more than ready to ease his frustration by accusing the winner of trickery, dishonesty, deceit, and mendacity. He goes further. He then attaches these unpleasant characteristics to the entire group to which the latter belongs. The successful man, the confident man, the serene man, on the other hand, does not need to discriminate. In this connection the late American novelist Elliot Paul had a pertinent anecdote. He once asked a French hotelkeeper why it is that—unlike the Germans, the Americans, and the English—the French seem singularly free of anti-Semitism. "Why, Monsieur," she replied, "we have no need to discriminate against the Jews. You see, the French also are intelligent."

It is always easy to blame others for the faults perceived in ourselves, and what could be more convenient than to blame those who already occupy a disprivileged position. This is an especially convenient device when they have no way to retaliate. There is no malady of society, whether it be poverty, war, depression, "radicalism," corruption in government, crop failure, or international tension that has not been blamed on some ill-fated ethnic or religious group. A scapegoat is needed, someone to blame, someone on whom to project one's own responsibility and guilt. Aggression follows frustration as blame follows failure. When this happens to groups it begins to explain some of the tension, the unpleasantness and hostility, that exists between them. In this way did the medieval Christian blame the Jews for everything from the plague to the poisoned well, and in this way too did the Nazi blame them for every catastrophe in German history. In this way indeed a similar plight can befall any group in society.

9. The Vicious Circle

Sensitive students of prejudice, sociologists like Myrdal and MacIver, have noticed an interesting phenomenon in connection with its causation. They have discovered that prejudice itself is one of the causes of prejudice. Ordinarily an assertion of this kind means nothing and serves only to illustrate the fallacy of circular reasoning. Certainly we learn nothing new when we learn that opium puts us to sleep because of its "dormitive property," or that the disintegration of social relationships is one of the "causes" of war, or that the law is the "cause" of crime, and so on through innumerable examples. We know in addition that naming something is not equivalent to explaining it, that a cause cannot be included in the definition of the effect, and that a phenomenon cannot be explained by itself. Nevertheless, it makes sociological sense to say that prejudice is one of the causes of prejudice, and we want to explore this situation in order to see how it can be so.

Let us appeal to Robert M. MacIver both for an explanation of the principle and for an illustration of it. First the explanation:

> We now turn to patterns of causation in which a series of conditions or forces sustain, confirm, and generate one another. Each of the conditions so interacts with the other conditions as to promote and perpetuate them and thus the whole system they together constitute. These patterns exhibit something more than the interdependence of factors that obtains in every established system. To take the simplest possible case, if you begin with condition *a* it sets in motion condition *b*, and *b* in turn keeps *a* going. The system, in other words, embodies the principle of circularity.[5]

And now for the illustration:

> A rumor spreads through a community that a particular bank is insolvent. There is a run on the bank. Since no bank can immediately liquidate its resources—apart from outside help—so as to honor all the claims upon it, the bank closes down. The rumor is self-confirming.[6]

In precisely the same way, the view that blacks, for example, are inferior contributes to their inferiority and the assertion is a factor that helps to produce its own confirmation. Let us see how this can happen.

Northerners used to be informed by their Southern friends that they do not "really know" the Negro. Actually, they will say, the black man clearly belongs in the station to which he is consigned. He is an inferior, dirty, shiftless, stupid, uneducated, and immoral creature, fit only for the menial tasks of society and those only under close supervision. They failed to realize, however, that the degree to which all this is true is caused, in part at least, by their belief that it is true. Why is the black inferior? Because he is ignorant. Why, then, don't you educate him? Because he is inferior. And so the vicious circle turns. Discrimination means unequal treatment, which results in poverty, which in turn means poor education, which means inferiority, which breeds discrimination. The circle may be large or small; the effect is the same. Prejudice ultimately becomes one of the causes of prejudice, and discrimination causes discrimination. This situation was

[5] Robert M. MacIver, *The More Perfect Union*, The Macmillan Company, New York, 1948, p. 61.

[6] *Ibid.*, p. 62. Professor MacIver calls this "the self-fulfilling postulate." Robert K. Merton, using the same example, calls it "the self-fulfilling prophecy"; see his article with that title in *The Antioch Review*, Summer, 1948, pp. 193–210. It is related too to what is called the "labelling" process in society.

described with dramatic force in an observation attributed to George Bernard Shaw. In America, he is reputed to have said, they force the Negro to shine their shoes for them—and then look down on him because he is a bootblack.

But if the circle can turn in one direction it can also, happily, turn in the other. If discrimination is one of the causes of discrimination, so also can tolerance serve as a cause of tolerance, and fair play can breed fair play. If one of the variables in the circle is altered in a favorable way, others too will change, and ultimately favorable consequences will follow. A higher income for the Negro, for example, will mean a higher standard of living, which in turn will mean a better education, which will make a still higher income possible, with prejudice decreasing all along the line. If segregation increases prejudice, so also does desegregation decrease it. As discrimination in general disappears, so also will prejudice subside. The circle can be beneficent as well as vicious.

We have maintained in this and in preceding sections of this chapter that prejudice, far from being pathological, is in fact a normal human tendency, a corollary of the distinctions we make between groups, our own and others. Its incidence can be wholly normal in an individual, however one may wish to characterize the group or society in which it finds expression. When we concede that something is normal, however, and normally learned, we do not have to concede in addition that it is socially acceptable in the larger society, or in the world in which all of us, of all sizes and shapes and colors and races, are destined to spend our lives. Prejudice may be normal, but when it issues in discrimination it is hardly ennobling. It contradicts in fact the ideologies of most religions and of every humanitarian ethic. Just as it is necessary in all societies to control and often to overcome some of our normal human tendencies if we want to enjoy the company of our associates, so also we may have to distinguish after a while between "good" prejudices and "bad" prejudices, between those that have some rationale and those that have none. There is a difference after all between courtesy and cruelty, and there would seem to be no warrant either in ethics or in sociology for using color of skin as an excuse to be cruel.

It is interesting to observe, finally, that sophistication has an important role to play in the dissipation of prejudice. In the history of human societies intellectual sophistication and common morality have often been opposed. Some of the greatest philosophers in Western history, like Spinoza in the seventeenth century and Bertrand Russell in our own, have suffered excommunication and imprisonment for the crime of inquiring into the religious and moral premises of their societies. Socrates himself, one of the most sophisticated of mortals, drank the hemlock because, according to his accusers, he had corrupted the morals of the youth committed to his care. Here, however, on the issue of prejudice, we find sophistication and morality on the same side of the argument. Sophistication is essential if one is to surmount the normal prejudice and support the moral good, a good that ignorance and innocence would otherwise leave unattended. Everywhere in the world the literate and articulate voices are enlisted on the side of decency and fair play.

10. The True Believer

So far in this chapter we have emphasized color rather more than creed, but before we conclude this discussion we should like to give brief attention to the significance of belief and the manner in which differences in ideological commitment separate man from man and group from group. We have previously stressed the importance of ideologies in society and have shown how they operate as norms, giving guidance to conduct and moral sanction to belief. Among these ideologies, political and religious convictions tend to be especially intense, and perhaps the latter are the most pervasive and most intimately personal of all.

Adherence to religious beliefs has an emotional tone, and the tone causes trouble and dissension between groups and encourages their members to entertain a mutual prejudice. In a society in which only one religion flourished, religion would hardly be a source of suspicion. In a society where many religions exist side by side, each claiming to represent the truth, conflict is almost inevitable.

Religion, of course, is not always a barrier to social interaction. In an ideal society it would never be. But we do not, unfortunately, live in an ideal society, and the society we do live in has no ideal inhabitants. We are asked to believe that there is only one true faith—our own. If this is indeed the case then those who differ from us must be wrong. Since they have precisely the same opinion about us, a conflict situation exists. Each group views the others with apprehension and insists upon the truth of its own belief. Creeds are precious things, but only ours is believable; yours is simply the measure of your stupidity. There is only one true faith and only one group, therefore, of true believers.[7] Sometimes, as apprehension grows, we can almost hear a process of reasoning that runs like this: When you are in power it is your duty to tolerate me because I am right; but when I am in power it is my duty to persecute you because you are wrong.

Such is the strength of creeds, such the ideas that devotion can

---

[7] See Eric Hoffer, *The True Believer*, Harper & Row, Publishers, New York, 1951. This brilliant book was written by a longshoreman on the Pacific Coast who was blind until his fifteenth year and who had no schooling at all.

support, and such the passions that ideas can arouse. As we suggested earlier, men are exiled for their ideas even more readily than for their deeds. The man who is wrong is not only wrong; he is also dangerous. He is a threat to us and to the existence of our group. He should therefore be exterminated or, at the very least, persecuted for his queer and unacceptable notions.

This almost universal attitude has written a sad chapter in the history of humanity. The true believer is the fanatic; his contrary is not the false believer but the skeptic. As a matter of fact, the intensity of a belief often creates more havoc than the belief itself, and few beliefs are held more intensely than those related to religion. No religion can tolerate an adverse idea—excepting only perhaps Confucianism, which is not, strictly speaking, a religion at all but rather a system of ethics. The true believer is the man who, as George Santayana defined him, "redoubles his effort after he has forgotten his aim."

Fanaticism, of course, is destructive of intergroup harmony. Strong attachments, however admirable to the in-group, attract hostility from the out-group, and intensity of belief is itself conducive to intolerance. This is the reason, sociologically speaking, for the tension that obtains between the different religions. What is sacred to one group is profane to another; what is clean to one is unclean to another; what is proper to one is improper to another; and what is true for one is false for the other. And so we have the great insoluble, the great surd that prevents a rational solution to the social equation and throws the relations of one religion to another into discord. The man of unswerving principle wins the plaudits of the crowd. The fanatic wins its jeers. But they are often the same man.

11. Summary and Conclusion

We have concluded our discussion of color and creed, two of the criteria in terms of which complex societies are differentiated. Our treatment has been intentionally more analytic than descriptive. We began by asking what factors were involved in the etiology of prejudice and traced them first of all to a social universal that on the one hand means consciousness of kind and on the other consciousness of difference. So long as society exists we shall be conscious of similarities with some people and dissimilarities with others. This is the consciousness that results in group formation and that encourages group pride. But pride, as a preference, is a form of prejudice, and thus we discovered that prejudice is inherent in societal life.

When prejudice is expressed in conduct, however, it becomes discrimination; and discrimination is more than a mere preference. It implies action, ranging from discourtesy to cruelty, and we included for illustration a brief description of discrimination against the Negro in the United States. We suggested next a number of misleading directions in which the causes of discrimination are sometimes sought, discoursed again on the mores and the laws, and mentioned indoctrination and frustration as two of the factors involved in producing prejudice and discrimination. Concluding sections dealt with the vicious circle and the true believer. Throughout we emphasized that prejudice in favor of our own groups is normal and that a degree of sociological sophistication, so to speak, helps to prevent our turning it outward, and against other groups.

If the general tenor of the chapter seems pessimistic, our final word is a hopeful one. Discrimination on the ground of color, at least, is destined ultimately to fail. It violates the canons of courtesy, contradicts the American creed, and flouts the ethical precepts of the world's great religions. As the great Negro leader Walter White pointed out:

> The basic principle of human equality, which is written into every important document of state, from the Declaration of Independence through the Emancipation Proclamation to the Charter of the United Nations, acts as a force of compulsion on the American conscience. Even when the average American neglects or fails to live up to these pronouncements, he suffers from a sense of guilt.[8]

He knows, in short, that he is opposing the basic political philosophy of his own country, a philosophy for which in other circumstances he professes a proud respect. And he knows too that he is opposing his religion. According to an ancient Hebrew legend:

> . . . the Lord took dust from the four corners of the earth in equal measure. Some of the dust was red, and some black, some white, and some as yellow as sand. These he mixed with water from all the oceans and the seas, to indicate that all races of mankind shall be included in the First Man, and none shall be included as superior to the other.

The average American may not know this text. But he cannot honestly forget a Rule that admonishes him to do unto others as he would have them do unto him.

---

[8] Walter White, *How Far the Promised Land,* The Viking Press, Inc., New York, 1955, pp. 26–27.

Chapter 19

SOCIETY AND THE INDIVIDUAL

OTHING ILLUSTRATES with so
much clarity the complexity
of modern societies as does
the multiplicity of their
associations. In an earlier chapter
we discussed the nature and formal
characteristics of associations
and institutions from the point of view
of social organization. In this
chapter we want to emphasize
the importance of these large
associations, not only in the life
of the individual, but in the profile
of a society. A society, as
we have suggested, consists of
an infinite number of groups,
some organized, some
unorganized. All of them
together exhibit a panorama
of collocations and aggregations,
of settlements and strata. Most
of the groupings we have so far
discussed in some detail
are unorganized—men and women,
city and country, class and
caste, and color and creed. We now
turn our attention to another kind of
differentiation, differentiation by
association, and the groupings we
discuss here are organized. In
associations we can discern a large
part of the lives of a society's members
and in them too the character of a
society itself. If the reader will
reflect a moment, he will realize
that much of his time is devoted to
participation, sometimes active

and sometimes relatively passive, in associations of one kind or another. These associations outline his obligations, dictate his duties, invite his loyalties, define his activities, and reward him with their perquisites and privileges. It is true, of course, that each of us is frequently during the course of a day a member only of a multitude—strollers on the sidewalk, visitors to a shrine, spectators in a stadium, customers in a store, and passengers in a bus or train. In these situations we conform to community norms, norms that apply to all of us alike and guide us through the maze of social relationships involved. It is true that at all times we are members, often involuntarily and by ascription, of many groupings of a statistical, societal, and social character[1]—age group, sex group, ethnic group, nationality group, social-class group, and so on. But a description of our group affiliations would be incomplete if we did not direct some attention to our associational groups, the groups which have a definite organization, including their own norms and statuses, and in which we are formally enrolled as members.

If the reader will continue his reflection, he will note how much of a man's life in a modern society is devoted to his school and college, his job, his union, his government, and his church. All of these make comprehensive demands upon him, and all of them involve associations. All of them represent highly organized endeavors in themselves and contribute in addition to the organization of the society of which they are a part. A college, a business, a union, and a church are only a few of the associations in which men and women have formal membership. There are many, many more.

It would be an instructive exercise, for example, simply to count the number of associations mentioned in a single issue of a single newspaper—say, a daily edition of *The New York Times*. The total, we may be sure, would run into several thousands. And we may be sure in addition that the number of associations would exceed the number of individuals, for nearly every person named is identified by at least one and usually by a number of his associational affiliations.

Even more significant, the stories deemed the most newsworthy concern for the most part associations themselves, and not individuals in their private capacities. We may want to know what kind of day a particular player had in the field or at bat, but we are even more interested in the scores of the games. We may note with casual interest that someone succeeded someone else as a vice president of Pan American Airlines, but our interest in the price of the company's stock can easily be more than casual. We are ordinarily more interested in the decisions of the Supreme

[1] In terms of the classification of groups in Chapter 10.

Court than in the names of the persons who initiated the litigation or even in the sometimes separate decisions of the individual justices. And we care much more about the rising tensions between two foreign countries than about the names of the officials who delivered the reciprocal notes of protest.

These observations have nothing to do with the frequent denial of the importance of the individual in a so-called mass society. This is another problem, one that agitates particularly those sociologists who worry about alienation, the inability of the individual in a mass society to discover and to retain his own identity. It is a problem to which we shall return at the end of the chapter. All we mean to emphasize at this point is the incredible number and variety of associations in contemporary society, the fact that almost every member of such a society has his own associational affiliations, and the very great importance, especially in the twentieth century, of these formally organized groupings of people.

1. The Institution of Government

It is always difficult to know how much to include about specific associations and institutions in a book on sociology, for at this level of discussion we come close to the concerns of other social sciences. It seems unnecessary and even gratuitous, for example, to write an extended discourse on political science or economics or religion or education, not only because justice cannot be done to these subjects in a single chapter, but also because each of them has an extensive literature of its own. Furthermore, in the field of sociology itself serious treatises have been written on institutions in general and on contemporary American institutions in particular. The place of associations in modern society is so imposing, however, that we need at least one illustration. From the range of possible choices we shall select one of the most important of all institutions, the institution of government, and attempt to exhibit the role of associations in a complex institutional process. We choose government also because only some of us are members of labor unions, or of trade associations, or of bar associations, or of churches, or of learned societies, but we are all members of a modern state.

There are those indeed who would say that among human institutions government has a certain primacy—and therefore the first claim upon our attention. In the first place, a political state is an association in which membership is compulsory and exclusive. The status of citizenship, for most of us, is ascribed rather than achieved. The process of achieving a new citizenship is always difficult, always circumscribed by condition and qualification. Although most of us are free to join an almost infinite number of other associations, we can be members, usually, of only one state, citizens of only one nation. The state, in its turn, embraces in our time a larger variety of interests than any other association, interests that touch the lives of its members at many points. Finally government has a monopoly of the legitimate use of force in society. It alone can legitimately employ the negative sanctions that deprive its members of their freedom, their property, and their lives.

In the preceding paragraphs we have used two concepts, "government" and "the state," and it seems desirable to distinguish between them. A state is a politically organized society; a government is the association through which the politically organized society functions and works. A government is thus the instrumentality of the state, the agency by means of which the state is able to carry on its activities at a given time. Perhaps an analogy or two will help. The stockholders in a corporation are all members of it and their membership is signalized by their shares. They do not, however, "run" or manage the corporation from day to day. They assign these duties to a board of trustees, a president or general manager, and others whom they employ. These others then serve as the instrumentality through which the policies of the stockholders are executed. The stockholders in this analogy would be comparable to a state; the management in turn is comparable to a government. Similarly, the whole body of believers in a particular religion would constitute, in political terms, a state. The priests and bishops, and indeed the total "management" hierarchy, would comprise, again in political terms, a government.[2] A government, in short, is less inclusive than a state. The whole body of citizens, all together, constitute a state, but they are not all part of the government. The government is made up of those officials, elected and appointed, who write, administer, enforce, and interpret the laws.

The political system of England illustrates this distinction with greater clarity than does that of the United States. The Queen of England is the chief of state; the Prime Minister is the head of the government. The President of the United States, on the other hand, is both chief of state and head of the government. It is for this reason that when the British Prime Minister visits the President of the United States, protocol recognized on both sides requires that the latter take precedence. The President, in short, occupies two statuses, the Prime Minister, in this respect, only one. But both a state and a government are associations. The first is the body politic, comprising all citizens; the second is its agent and instrumentality. A state is synonymous with civil society and it is an enduring association; a government, on the other hand, changes many of its members with each election.

[2] These analogies of course, like most analogies, are imperfect.

We have also used in the preceding paragraphs both of our sociological concepts—"association" and "institution." We did so deliberately because the same phenomenon can be viewed and investigated from both of these sociological vantages. An association, the reader will recall, is an organized group, an institution an organized way of doing something. Thus *a* government is an association; government an institution. We may ask our immediate question, therefore, in two ways: How did some men come to govern others, and form associations for doing so? and, How did the process of governing become instutionalized, so that everywhere in the world, wherever government appears, it exhibits a set of common characteristics?

Unfortunately, there is no simple or easy answer to these questions. The problem of government has attracted the attention of leading thinkers in all ages, and even now there is no universally accepted theory regarding the origin and basic nature of this fascinating phenomenon. The history of political thought is almost as old as the history of thought in general, and we would not presume, in these few pages, to add anything of profound significance to this enduring inquiry. Political science and sociology, however, touch each other at many points. All associations, governments included, have their source and origin in society, and all institutions, government included, consist of an elaborate set of established norms. A government, however comprehensive and pervasive, is only one of the associations of society; and government, however necessary, is only one of the aspects of culture. A government, like other associations, rises out of the matrix of a human community; it is one of the agencies of society. Its character and temper will be determined by the culture of the society it serves and especially by that society's ideologies. Its force and efficacy will depend upon the juxtaposition of groups in their ever-changing conflicts and relationships, its power upon the size and resources of its community, its authority upon the philosophy that prevails in this community, its functions upon the desires of the people, and its limits upon the constraints they impose.

2. The Origin of Government

How then, and why, do governments arise among men? To answer this question, as we have intimated, would require us to rehearse the entire history of political theory. Here we can only mention several of the major theories. The first of these, held in earlier times but now perhaps less popular, attributes the origin of government to a divine plan. This theory would invest king and chieftain with sacred attributes, make them earthly representatives and even descendants of the gods on high, and have them derive their authority from the powers that rule the universe. "Earthly power doth then show likest God's," and the government of society reflects the government of heaven.

A second theory proposes that the answer is to be found in force, the ability of the strong or the cunning to assume the mastery of the weak and the honest, dispensing justice then to suit themselves. Since, however, as Thomas Hobbes pointed out long ago, one man is not much stronger than another—or, he might have added, much smarter—even the strongest and cleverest would have had to unite with others and to form associations for their mutual advantage and aggrandizement. Variants of this theory lodge the force in a conquering army or, as in the Marxian approach, a dominant class. The trouble with this theory is that before a group can exercise control over others, especially since it represents a minority, it has to have some form of organization, some allocation of authority among its own members—in short, the group has to be an association that already has a government. Every association in society in fact has its own government, and the theory cannot, therefore, be used to explain the origin of government. Robert M. MacIver comments on this theory as follows:

> The notion that force is the creator of government is one of those part-truths that beget total errors. . . . Force alone never holds a group together. A group may dominate by force the rest of the community, but the initial group, already subject to government before it can dominate, is not cemented by force. Conquerors may forcibly impose their will on the conquered, but the conquerors were themselves first united by something other than force. Nor is one group able to maintain for long its rule over another unless it gives the subject group other grounds for acquiescence than the force at its command. To say that in the struggle of groups the more powerful wins is to say nothing, for the power of a group is no simple function of the force it disposes; it depends no less on its solidarity, its organizing ability, its leadership, its resources and its resourcefulness, its tenacity of purpose, and other things.[3]

The effective exercise of force, in other words, depends upon a prior structure of authority, and this structure is itself a form of government.

Still another theory, advanced by Thomas Hobbes and developed further by Jean Jacques Rousseau, prevailed for roughly two centuries, from the seventeenth to the nineteenth. According to this theory men lived originally in a "state of nature," wholly free of government. The state of nature, however, was a remarkably inconvenient and even a dangerous arrangement. The trouble lay in man himself who, in the view of Hobbes, is

---

[3] Robert M. MacIver, *The Web of Government*, The Macmillan Company, New York, 1947, pp. 15–16.

a quarrelsome and unreliable animal. In the famous words of this philosopher, the life of man is "poor, solitary, nasty, brutish, and short," and
the initial state of society was a war of all against all (*bellum omnium contra
omnes*). The only solution for this intolerable condition was government.
Men therefore had to get together and form a contract in which they
surrendered some of their "natural liberties" in return for the security of a
civil society and its government. This view, called the "social-contract"
theory, implies that the origin of government is to be found in a deliberate,
rational act of men who could not otherwise get along together.

From our twentieth-century point of vantage it seems curious that this
theory, depending as it does upon an erroneous initial premise, could have
enjoyed so long a life and so deep a lodgement in the history of political
thought. The false premise, of course, concerns the "state of nature" in
which Hobbes presumed that men originally lived. It is difficult if not
impossible for contemporary sociology to ascribe any meaning to this state
of nature. A human society wholly devoid of culture is inconceivable.
Anomy, as we have seen in another chapter, is a limiting case, useful
sometimes for analytical purposes, but not a social reality. In a total absence
of norms men would be unable to get together for any purpose at all, and
would certainly be unable to get together for the complicated purpose of
forming a civil society. But even if we grant this impossible assumption,
anomy does not by compact transform itself into society, nor anarchy into
government. The process is a gradual one, one in which, as we have said,
precedent slowly transforms itself into custom, and custom into institution.

The theory furthermore requires us to assume that at some specific
time, some lost date in history—was it a morning in November, or an
afternoon in May?—men suddenly decided, without prior conference or
negotiation, to confer and negotiate. Hobbes was a stimulating and original
thinker, not only in political theory but in philosophy in general, and it was
altogether appropriate and even ingenious for him to question the Aristotelian doctrine that man is a social animal. But this time the ancient was right
and the modern was wrong. As MacIver has written:

> It was necessary to go back to the rejected insight of Aristotle, that man is a
> social animal. As soon as we appreciate this truth we perceive the defect of all
> doctrines that explain government by any formula of contract or of subjuga-
> tion, of leadership or of class struggle. Government is a phenomenon that
> emerges within the social life, inherent in the nature of social order. Man's
> social nature is a complex system of responses and of needs. In the relation of
> man to man everywhere there is the seed of government. It takes different
> institutional shapes according to the interplay of these relations. Sometimes,
> in the simplest communities, it has no ministers or agents, but is sufficiently
> maintained by the spontaneous reaction to the prevailing folk-myths. Always
> it is guarded by these myths, however elaborate the machinery through which

it operates. Wherever man lives on the earth, at whatever level of existence, there is social order, and always permeating it is government of some sort. Government is an aspect of society.[4]

Order of some kind, in short, precedes government, and society precedes its own *political* organization. The origin of a civil society, therefore, and of government, must be sought in another place.

MacIver goes on to discover the origin of government in the family. The family, whatever its relationship to the other institutions of society, already exhibits a structure and a rule. It is in the family that men and women surrender certain idiosyncrasies in order to retain and enjoy certain others. The same necessities that create the human family also create the regulation of familial—and especially of sexual—relationships. Order is established first in the family—otherwise there would be no family, but only two sexes of older and younger ages—and from the family it expands to a group of families, to close kin at first, and then to an entire tribe. Kin loses its significance as other relations increase in number and intensity; and as these relations come to be exemplified in nonfamilial associations, associations built on other interests, government itself comes into being on a small and relatively undifferentiated scale. But always there is order, even in the midst of conflict. There is an important sense indeed in which conflict is even a stimulus to order. For the contenders require some kind of organization among themselves, however primitive, in order to pursue their goal.

Government, in short, is the institutionalized end product of a process as old as history, as old in fact as society itself. Wherever there is society there is order, and when the processes of sustaining this order become institutionalized, as they do in all societies of any size, government is the result. Just as the dissemination of news precedes the institution of journalism, just as barter and trade precede the institution of business, and just as wonder and worship precede the institution of religion, so order precedes the institution of government. The norms come first; the institutions follow. But the institution in effect is already contained in the norms and needs only specific functionaries, specific statuses, and a specific association in order to become explicit.

3. The Functions of Government

If an institution is an organized procedure, and if government is an institution, what then is it that government does? What are the functions that become institutionalized as government? Fortunately, there is wide-

---

[4] *Ibid.*, pp. 20–21.

spread agreement on the basic functions of government, although much less agreement on its subsidiary functions. In this section we attend to the former, the basic functions, and ignore the secondary issues, which arouse a politically intense but sociologically irrelevant controversy.

Earlier in this book we observed, and went on to emphasize, that every norm in society is supported and sustained by an appropriate sanction. We proceeded to list the various factors, in addition to punishment and reward, that induce individuals to conform to the norms of their society. We indicated that the sanctions supporting the laws are different from those supporting the folkways and the mores and are applied in a different fashion. We now need to stress this difference in order to understand the functions of government.

The plain truth of the matter is that the informal sanctions of ridicule and ostracism do not always work. What happens when an individual, for whatever reason, violates with an apparent persistence the norms of his society? What happens when, in his contrary actions, he challenges their validity, disregards their intent, or insists that they do not apply to him? The answer is that some of these norms are transformed into laws and are then *enforced* by the government of the community, an association specifically designed for that purpose. No society can long endure individual caprice in matters deemed essential to its welfare. None can permit its members freely to indulge in premeditated murder, in reckless homicide, in assault and rape, in forgery and theft. Nor can any society allow the victims of these violations to exact retribution in their own name and on their own account, even if they are capable of doing so, or to punish the perpetrators themselves with whatever means they may have at their disposal. Such a situation would throw the whole society into cataclysm and into chaos. No man would be safe from his neighbor's depredations, either in his person or in his property, and the fundamental order that characterizes society would be destroyed. A society, in short, must protect itself from the irresponsible few who would do it harm, and it must do so in the name of all of its members.

The first function of government, therefore, is to ensure conformity to certain norms—specifically, the laws—by the use of force. Without force as an ultimate sanction the individual violator could not finally be suppressed and would threaten the existence of the entire society. It is this ultimate purpose that government is designed to accomplish. Force is thus, as has been said, the *ultima ratio* of society, and its legitimate use the first function of government. It is government, in fact, that *confers* legitimacy upon the use of force in any civilized society.

Societies exhibit not only deviant individuals but also dissident groups. As these groups organize they too can constitute a threat to order and stability and may finally endanger the peace of the whole. Again there must be some agency to draw the line, to say this far and no further, and to defend the majority against disruption by minorities. Groups in short are often in conflict with one another, and these conflicts sometimes involve not only differences of opinion but also oppositions of power. Somewhere contrary contentions must be adjudicated, somewhere the tendency to violence must be checked, somewhere a *modus operandi* must be found. The conflicting interests of powerful groups, inevitable in a complex society, would destroy a society unless subjected to ultimate control by an agency of the society itself.[5] A society, in short, cannot permit its various and multifarious groups to advance their own causes through the use of force, to use force against the groups that oppose them, and to settle issues solely in terms of a superiority of power. Only one agency or association in society, one representing (however well or ill) the entire society, can be given the right to the use of force. It must have a monopoly of this ultimate instrument of social control. And this is the function of government.

Secondly, all civil societies are surrounded by others with which they have sometimes friendly but sometimes hostile relations. Every society, therefore, must have some agency that will be responsible for protecting it from invasion. This too is a function that can be performed effectively only by a total coordination of effort and by one central agency, and this, in consequence, becomes a function of government.

Modern governments, of course, perform many more functions than these. A government like our own is intimately engaged in business, education, insurance, welfare, conservation, price regulation, mail delivery, the determination of interest rates, tariffs and trade, the prevention of economic monopoly, international organization, and many other affairs. The range of government activity and enterprise, as we have suggested, is a perennial problem in political philosophy and one that incites an argument wherever politics are discussed.

The basic functions of government, then, the functions for which government exists, are to preserve the internal order and to guard against external danger. Whatever else government may do, these are its prime purposes, to which all others are subsidiary and secondary. It is for these services that men relinquish the sovereignty that resides in their persons and delegate the power that resides in their majorities to a single agency, where it becomes institutionalized as government. They surrender the right to use force against friend and foe alike in return for the personal security that government can guarantee.

[5] It should not be supposed that conflict is always dysfunctional in the life of a society and its associations. See the thoughtful and important study by Lewis A. Coser, *The Functions of Social Conflict*, The Free Press of Glencoe, New York, 1956.

4. Associations and the Governmental Process

We turn now to the associational aspect of government. As we have emphasized, wherever there is an institution there is at least one association. The institution of government therefore has an association, a government, to carry on its activities. It is an association of great size and complexity, more comprehensive in its functions than other associations, and more highly organized. It is, moreover, an association composed of an almost incredible number of subsidiary and dependent associations.

Thus, in the government of the United States, the Congress is an association, and so are its two parts, the Senate and the House of Representatives. Every committee of the Senate and every committee of the House is also an association. The Executive Department, headed by the President, is an association, and so also are all of the administrative departments represented in the Cabinet. The Department of Defense is an association and so also are the Army, the Navy, the Air Force, and (under the Navy) the Marine Corps, and (under the Treasury in time of peace) the Coast Guard. Every battalion, regiment, company, and platoon, every naval installation and naval ship, every unit and every command is an association. The Supreme Court of the United States is an association and so is every lower court. Every "alphabetical agency" of the government is an association. And so also the Federal Trade Commission, the Federal Reserve Board, the Federal Communications Commission, the Interstate Commerce Commission, the National Science Foundation, and the Bureau of the Budget. Indeed, the government of the United States is so complicated a collocation of subsidiary associations that the introductory course in American government on the college level is devoted almost entirely to their history, their description, and their identification.

If the study of government agencies, bureaus, departments, and divisions belongs almost exclusively to political science, so also, for the most part, does the study of political parties (which also are associations). But these two kinds of phenomena by no means exhaust the governmental process. An infinite number of nongovernmental associations are also involved. Indeed, the policies pursued by official government associations, and advocated by political parties, depend upon these other associations. Fortunately, the subject has received the comprehensive attention of a political scientist, David B. Truman, and the following discussion is indebted to his distinguished book.[6]

We are all familiar, of course, with the existence of associations commonly called pressure groups, interest groups, and lobbies. The trouble with these words is that they are largely epithets with more emotional than

---

[6] David B. Truman, *The Governmental Process*, Alfred A. Knopf, Inc., New York, 1951.

rational content. Pressure groups and lobbies in particular are always advancing causes that, in our opinion, will benefit small privileged classes to the detriment of the common welfare. When they advance causes that we ourselves support we no longer call them pressure groups. Now they become enlightened organizations whose work ameliorates the condition of mankind, disseminates wisdom throughout the populace, and increases the wealth, welfare, and happiness of the human race. It all depends upon where we stand. Actually, as a moment's reflection will disclose, the conflicting interests of the millions of people whom a government serves can find expression only in their various associations, organized for the specific purpose of promoting policies.

This fact becomes even more apparent, on an abstract level, when we soberly recognize how little influence a single individual can exert upon his government. In a society large enough and complex enough to need a government in the first place, the voice of one man can hardly be heard in the din of the multitude, and he is therefore required to associate with others in the pursuit of a common cause. The "unorganized" individual is impotent in the political or in any other social process. The organized group, on the other hand, as we have previously suggested, can be one of the most potent forces on earth. Wherever the power of this group is directed, whether to politics, religion, education, business, or labor, it is a force for the society to reckon with—and for the social scientist to study and understand. Organized interest groups are not confined, therefore, to politics; they embrace all the concerns of society. But it is in the realm of government, perhaps, that their actions and activities can most easily be discerned.

Certainly it is unrealistic to suppose that government is somehow an institution carried on in purely formal or legal terms by an executive, a legislature, and a judiciary. Government, on the contrary, is a product of the activities of organized groups throughout the society. As a matter of fact—though oppression sometimes conceals it—neither absolute monarch nor authoritarian dictator is immune from, or impervious to, the influence of associations. It is for this reason that totalitarian governments try to restrict the freedom of association and to suppress all associations that might possibly pose a threat to their existence. The absence of independent labor unions, for example, or of associations of artists and writers, is an index of this kind of government. So also, *a fortiori*, is the absence of opposing political parties.

We may sometimes wonder if the voice of the individual, the single citizen, is not lost in the conflict and counterpoise of associations and whether the ultimate result of their eternally changing juxtapositions does not somehow reduce him to a cipher in the vital processes of society. The question is a good one, and it has a reasonable answer. We have previously remarked upon the fact that individuals often occupy two or more statuses whose norms push and pull them in different directions. This is the phenomenon that sociologists have come to call "role strain," and it is a phenomenon that afflicts us all. Sometimes persons caught in these situations face unfortunate and even insoluble problems. The norms of family membership, as we have suggested, sometimes conflict with the norms of peer-group membership, the norms of religion with those of nationality, and sometimes we decline on grounds of conscience to obey the law. But seen in the perspective of society itself the situation has its saving grace.

This saving grace arises from the fact that many associations compete for our time and attention, and the decisions we make with regard to them will have an influence upon the direction of policy. The voluntary associations of a free society offer us alternatives, and in choosing between them we can have something personally to do with the process of government. Sometimes—and here again the role strain is apparent—our choices are difficult and even painful. The League of Women Voters, for example, espouses in a majority vote a bill providing for the sterilization of the mentally unfit, a bill opposed by the Catholic church. What does a member do who happens to be a Catholic? Or, to take a more poignant example, what does the student do who is called upon to fight in what he regards as an unjust war?

Not all role conflicts are as serious as these, and not all of them present the individual with a genuine moral dilemma. A classic and amusing case is that of Pooh-Bah in *The Mikado*. When Ko-Ko conferred with him about the amount of money to be spent on his marriage, Pooh-Bah replied as follows: "Speaking as your Private Secretary, I should say that, as the city will have to pay for it, do it well. . . . But . . . you will understand that as Chancellor of the Exchequer I am bound to see that due economy is observed." One could hardly find a more luminous illustration of status contradiction.

The point we wish to make, however, is that in influencing the policies of his own associations the individual is also exerting an influence, however small, upon the process of government. It is in the internal politics of nongovernmental associations, the juxtapositions of their majorities and minorities, that the voice of the individual can be heard. Here also we find the leavening effects of overlapping membership. Here we find a dynamic situation in which each individual, because of his various interests and group affiliations, exerts his own influence upon the associations of which he is a member and in turn upon the government that rules him and the society in which he lives.

It may be true of course that an individual in a complex society has only that degree of influence which he is able to exert through the organized groups of which he is a member. But he is a member of many groups, and stands on the fringe of many others, groups whose policies may lie at different and even distant points on the political spectrum. As he moves in and out of these associations, relinquishing membership in some and adhering in turn to others, his changing affiliations and allegiances will ultimately have something to do with the policies his government pursues. So long as the society of which he is a part preserves the voluntary character of associations, so also to that degree will it help to guarantee the worth and weight of the individual in the political process.

5. The Power Elite

This view of the process of government, however, enjoys rather less than a consensus, and we would perhaps be remiss if we did not mention an opposing view. The process of government is seen by some sociologists not as a matter of voluntary associations and the freely and frequently changing juxtapositions of their members, but rather as a function of a power elite of which the ordinary individual is a hapless and helpless victim. This, for example, is the thesis of a furious, exciting, and somewhat impressionistic book by the late C. Wright Mills, a book that captured the imagination of a generation of students and gave, almost at one stroke, a new direction and dimension to political sociology.[7] It was a book written with deep misgiving, with indignation unconcealed, and with a sense of very real frustration.

Mills himself, in the language of Spengler, was a "cosmopolitan" rather than a "local," but his strictures in this book were focussed upon the United States. Eschewing most of the proper (and sometimes incapacitating) cautions of the scholar, he argued that the American society, nostalgically thought to be a participatory democracy, had actually fallen under the control of three interlocking hierarchies—the military, the industrial, and the political. To make matters worse there is an easy interchange between the three hierarchies. Military men are rewarded with political power and, upon retirement, with seats on corporate boards of directors; business men win military contracts and political appointments; and politicians enjoy the exercise of power that control over men and money can provide. These are the men—"warlords," "commissars," and members of the political "directorate" in Mills' colorful language—who make the "big" decisions and who constitute the power elite.

[7] *The Power Elite*, Oxford University Press, New York, 1956.

We see in these hierarchies not only an interchange of statuses but also an establishment, in which the top men in all three of them come from the same kinds of families, enjoy the benefits of a superior education at prestigious schools and universities, and rely upon one another for preferment. Although these men are not Florentine conspirators in any Machiavellian sense (Mills carefully avoids a conspiratorial theory of politics[8]), they nevertheless understand one another, share a common set of political premises, and use their establishment positions to rule the society. As an intellectual, and therefore member of a powerless elite, Mills could not contain his scorn and contempt for a societal arrangement of this kind. He railed against "monstrous decisions" made in an "undemocratically impudent manner," at the "public mindlessness" that permits these proceedings, at the "organized irresponsibility" it encourages, and at the "higher immorality" that results. With the moral fervor of a revivalist he denounced the power elite as an evil phenomenon and exhausted his career, and even his life, in its condemnation.

There is only one flaw in this influential thesis. And that—a fatal one—is that it does not happen to be true. This at least is the contention of one of Mills' critics, the late Arnold M. Rose.[9] For Rose the thesis of the power elite is so fanciful as to be "a caricature of American society." Elites of course exist, in the American society as in all others. For that matter, the power structure is always pyramidal, and it is only naive to suppose that it can ever be anything else. There are always fewer captains than corporals, and this is a generalization that the nature of social organization itself imposes upon the political process. It will not do, however, to substitute a power elite, however constituted, for a public and its voluntary associations, especially in a democracy which, whatever its imperfections, means a government that must always be responsive to the will of the governed.

None of the elites to which Mills devoted his attention—neither the economic, the military, nor the political—has been able to coordinate its actions and decisions. As a matter of fact, the history of federal legislation since the administration of Franklin D. Roosevelt has been consistently on the side of labor, social welfare, social security, medical care, and civil rights, in spite of the frequent opposition of the economic community. Furthermore, there is not one economic community but several, and here too one finds interests in opposition. Nor is there a single political "directorate." The differences between the two major political parties seem

---

[8] The conspiratorial theory, incidentally, always proves itself. If evidence of a conspiracy is found, then the case is made. If it is not found, this only "proves" that the conspiracy is more deep-seated and secret than was at first supposed.

[9] *The Power Structure*, Oxford University Press, New York, 1967.

small and sometimes indiscernible, especially to foreign observers, but differences there are. Each of the parties in addition has its own conservative and liberal wings, in constant political competition. Mills also ignores the increasing restraints that government imposes upon business through its authority to tax, to license, to set rates in interstate commerce, to determine minimum wages, to insist upon accuracy in labelling and in the indication of interest charges on installment purchases and loans, and to regulate the securities markets, among many others.

Finally for Rose, who was once himself a member of the Minnesota legislature, it is unnecessary to go even a short distance behind the scenes and discover a power elite. The flow of power in American society can best be observed in its visible government—in its nominating conventions, its election campaigns, in the votes of its legislators (who must after all give some satisfaction to their constituents), in administrative decisions, and in all the voluntary associations whose activities affect these outcomes.

There may of course be too much optimism in this picture, and too much pessimism in the scenes that Mills portrays. Of the two books, the one by Mills is the more exciting, the one by Rose the more impressive in its evidence. This is not the place in any case to settle the debate between the "elitists" on the one hand and the "pluralists" on the other. If Rose and the many members of his school are right, however, we can appreciate once more the importance of associations in the political process of a democratic society.

A final note on voluntary associations, having nothing to do with the power elite, concerns perhaps a more profound problem, one of the problems of modern industrial societies. It was Emile Durkheim who both perceived it and who tried to supply an answer. What is the source, the explanation, of the moral order of society? Auguste Comte had believed that some kind of moral consensus is an essential prerequisite for the social order. Durkheim, on the contrary, advanced the view that the existence of society is the basic condition of moral integration. Morality has its source in society. This thesis, however, presents a difficulty in that the increasing division of labor in modern industrial societies (Durkheim was writing in the last decade of the nineteenth century), where the mechanical solidarity formerly provided by a collective consciousness has disappeared, would seem to lead to a disintegration of common values and ultimately to anomy. For Durkheim, however, it was the division of labor itself that contributed what he called the organic solidarity of the industrial society. The more individuals do different kinds of work the more—rather than less—dependent they become on one another, and thus the division of labor serves as a cohesive factor. The fear that the division of labor results in fragmentation is therefore unfounded.

In order to achieve moral integration, however, something else is necessary, or at least helpful, and this is occupational associations or, as Durkheim called them, "corporations," which of course has nothing to do with the comtemporary meaning of the word. The growth of these occupational associations is especially important in industrial societies where work assumes an ascendancy over other interests—military and religious for example—and becomes an end in itself. It is these associations then that take on a regulatory function in society and become in turn one of the sources and supports of moral integration. Durkheim's "corporations" did not develop in the manner that he anticipated, but it is interesting nevertheless to recall the emphasis that this great sociologist placed on the role of associations in society.

6. Society and Its Dominant Institutions

Instead of using the institution of government as an example of the role of associations in modern society, we could have chosen any one of a number of other institutions—religion, education, labor, business, or recreation, to mention only five. In each of these cases we would have observed the same sociological processes, the formation of associations to pursue the relevant activities in an organized way and the constant interplay of these associations in a comprehensive procedure. We would have noticed again that this interplay involves at times cooperation and at other times conflict, that cooperation itself involves conflict, and conflict cooperation. It would have been appropriate indeed to devote a chapter to each of these major institutional concerns of a complex society. A detailed study of particular institutions, however, involves a degree of specialization that would be inappropriate in this place. We are interested here in the prinicple and not in the specification, in the rule rather than the detail.

In this section we want to introduce another consideration, one briefly mentioned earlier in the chapter, namely, that the profile of a society can be read in its dominant institutions. When we look at a society at a given point in time, we sometimes find that one or a small group of its institutions and accompanying associations seems more important or at least more prominent than others. Even a superficial glance at our own society in the twentieth century would disclose that government and business, for example, occupy much of the cultural landscape and that what happens in these large institutional complexes has very much to do with the lives of American citizens. If we were to look at ancient Sparta or at nineteenth-century Prussia, we should notice, on the contrary, that the army dominated other associations and indeed owned a place of preeminence among them. In the medieval period, in Western Europe, it was the church that played a featured role in the center of the societal stage. And in the Soviet Union of our own day it is, of course, the political party.

Not all societies, and not all periods of history, exhibit the rather clear-cut pattern of prominence of the examples just mentioned. Not all societies possess integrated cultures of the kind that make such observations possible. Here we meet the general problem of cultural integration, a problem that has attracted the attention of sociologists, anthropologists, and historians alike. Unfortunately, the factors in terms of which some institutions exert more influence than others, the factors involved in the expansion and constriction of this influence, and the resultant changes in the society and its culture are not clearly known at the present time.

Long ago William Graham Sumner talked about the "strain toward consistency" in the mores, and even longer ago Saint-Simon expressed himself on the "universal gravitation" of all historical events toward a unitary social order. It is possible that culture itself tends toward its own integration. Whether or not this proposition is susceptible of proof, it is clear that all of the component parts of a culture may appear to support a single set of norms, a predominant ideology, and a uniform philosophy. When this happens both the culture and the society are integrated, and the associations that arise in the society will reflect this integration.

Actual societies, of course, unless they are very small, seldom exhibit this degree of unity, and historians writing a thousand years after the demise of a particular culture often find more unity than the culture in fact possessed. Time blurs the corners and softens the contours, as erosion smooths and rounds a boulder exposed for centuries to rain and wind. In spite of these admissions, however, societies do have their distinctive characteristics, characteristics that differentiate one from another, and these differential characteristics come to be indicated and signalized by their dominant institutions.

7. The Individual and His Society

We cannot conclude our treatment of the structure of society in general, nor this special subject of social differentiation, without referring finally to the relationship between society and the individual. This is ultimately one of the most profound of all the problems of social philosophy. It is in fact a philosophical rather than a sociological problem, for it involves the question of values. We see ourselves on one side and our society on the other—the person and the group, the individual and the collectivity. What does each owe to the other? In what sense is the single individual a part of a whole that is greater than he? In what sense does the whole exist for the individual? When we say with Aristotle that man is a social animal, what does this assertion ultimately mean? These are difficult questions, and involve another order of inquiry than that in which we have pursued our study of society. The sociologist, nevertheless, cannot remain altogether silent when confronted with these larger issues of human worth and human destiny.

The reason he cannot remain silent is that sociology itself, simply because of the kind of quest it is, seems on the surface to give one kind of answer to them. The reader of this book will have noticed by this time that we have said very little about the individual—the living, breathing, working, playing, resting, praying, sometimes sweating, sometimes swearing person who, with millions like him, constitutes this thing we call society. In the beginning of this book we said that the individual, from the historical point of view, was the concern of biography and, from the scientific point of view, the concern of psychology. The entire tenor of our discussion has been focused not upon the individual but upon the structure of the society in which he lives. We have stressed the culture that surrounds and encompasses him, the norms to which he conforms, the statuses that he occupies, and the groups of which he is a member. We have doubtless given the impression that every man is a creature of cultural circumstance, impotent in the face of the larger structures within which he carries on his life, a cipher in a total complex that he is unable to control or fully comprehend. Our theme has found its locus, not in the individual, but in the status, the norm, the group, and the institution. Where, we may now ask, does the individual belong in this system of sociology? What is his role and responsibility to himself and to his society? Is the individual lost in society, or is it only in society that he can find himself?

The burden and emphasis of our essay on society would seem to support the social point of view. Everywhere and all the time we are members of groups. The isolated individual does not exist, if by isolation we mean a total and permanent separation from society. The language we speak, the clothes we wear, the foods that sustain us, the games we play, the goals we seek, and the ideals we cherish are all derived from our culture and, as we have seen, the culture of our own society differs in many respects from the culture of every other. Society surrounds us in our infancy and follows us to our resting place. We depend upon society and its processes not only for our livelihood but for our very lives. Where, in this welter of processes, in this structure of norms and statuses and groups, is there room for the person, what guarantees his integrity as an individual, what confers upon him the irrepressible and unrepeatable character of his own personality?

The answer is that society does this too. As we have suggested, we need culture in order to become human and so also do we need society in order to become a person. Society is no great engine of which we are merely a mechanical part, nor is it a giant organism in which we are only a microscopic cell. Society on the contrary is a reality of its own kind, itself unique, and different from every other natural object. From it we receive the gift of individuality and in it we express our personality. It is in "the vast intrinsic traffic of society," joining first this group and then that group, conforming first to this norm and then that one, that we reach full stature as human beings and realize the meaning of our selves. Society gives us choices, inviting us to accept or decline, and in our selections we become ever more completely what we are.

And finally, even in society we are always, in some sense, alone. There is always a part of us that we never share, a thought that is uncommunicated, a dream that stays in its private chamber. For it has also been written that "the heart knoweth its own bitterness and a stranger intermeddleth not with its joy."

SOCIAL CHANGE

Chapter 20

THE PROBLEM OF SOCIAL CHANGE

W HEN ADLAI E. STEVENSON, then Governor of Illinois, accepted the Democratic nomination for the office of President of the United States in Chicago in 1952, he said that "candor and confession are good for the political soul." They are no less good for the sociological soul. It is candor that compels us to confess at the outset that sociology does not possess, as yet, a solution to the vast and complex problem of social change, a problem that, in a sense, is the *ultima ratio* of the sociological discipline, the ultimate reason for its existence. As we suggested at the end of our introductory chapter, a cogent theory of the process of history is the final, the acid test of sociological inquiry, and this, at the moment, is a test that sociology cannot pass. Clio, the muse of history, does not readily disclose her secrets, and what these secrets may be is now a matter of speculation rather than of dependable scientific knowledge.

We begin then, hesitantly, by inviting the reader to reflect upon a profound remark made by an ancient Greek philosopher named Heraclitus. Heraclitus said that it is impossible for a man to step into the same river twice. It is impossible for two reasons: the second time it is not the same river and the second time it is not the same man. In the interval of time between the first and the second stepping, no matter how short, both the river and the man have changed. Neither remains the same. This is the central theme of the Heraclitean philosophy—the reality of change, the impermanence of being, the inconstancy of everything but change itself. The opposing philosophy, propounded by Parmenides, asserts on the contrary that change is an illusion, that everything remains the same, and that the only reality is being; and this was the view of all of the members of the Eleatic school.[1]

Permanence and change, being and becoming—each of these has been emphasized by different philosophers in the Western tradition as more important and more pervasive than the other. The author of the Book of Ecclesiastes apparently agreed with Parmenides, for he has written there that there is nothing new under the sun. We confront here indeed a most serious and difficult metaphysical problem, a problem that involves such basic philosophical categories, for example, as time and identity and existence. In this form, of course, it is not a problem for sociology.

The task of sociology is not concluded, however, when it exhibits the structure, the anatomy of society. The order that is society is after all a changing order, and ever since Comte sociologists have encountered two large questions, the question of social statics and the question of social dynamics, what society is and how it changes. There is a sense indeed in which sociologists have asked the first of these questions only to assist them in seeking answers to the second. It is not given to men to pierce the veil that conceals the future from the present and only in certain limited areas examined by the most exact sciences, such as astronomy, is accurate prediction possible. But if we cannot peer into the future of human societies, we want at least to know the factors that have brought present societies into being, the factors that explain their structure and account for their culture.

The sociologist, not satisfied when he has outlined the structure of society, seeks also its causes. He takes seriously the remark of the Roman poet Lucretius, "*Felix qui potuit causas rerum cognoscere.*" (Happy is he who can know the causes of things.) His causal curiosity never rests; nothing stills his desire to know and to understand. The generations pass one after

---

[1] Including Zeno, who "proved" that a flying arrow does not move and that Achilles can never catch the tortoise in a race in which the tortoise has a head start.

another in response to inexorable biological process and, in passing, alter the character of human societies. Nothing social remains the same; nothing social abides. What are the factors that first form societies and then change them in ceaseless flux and flow? The question itself has a kind of splendor. It is the most sublime of all sociological inquiries. We need, therefore, in this final chapter, to introduce the time dimension into our consideration of society.

Unfortunately, this is the most complex and the most difficult of all sociological problems. Societies, like men and women, appear in endless variety. No two of them are alike, either in their totality or in their constituent groups. No two of them have an identical history, no two the same culture. None is a replica of another. All of them serve, in better or worse degree, the needs of their members, but these needs in turn are determined in different measure by their different cultures. In all of them there are recurrences and regularities, but in all of them too there are differences in detail, differences in spirit and meaning, in idea and norm and value. The historical courses of different societies follow no single track; by different routes they arrive at different destinations. The tempo of change itself is different in different periods and in different societies, and even in different parts of the same society. The metronome of history beats now faster, now slower in separate ages and epochs. Where can we begin, amid this welter of difference, to discover the principles that guide and inform the processes of social change?

First of all we have to seek a proper sociological level on which to focus our inquiry. It is obvious that we face here a problem of such imposing magnitude that it requires a sustained attack by scholars in many disciplines—not only by sociologists but by philosophers and historians as well. It is a problem indeed that requires the resources of many more than these. It is a problem to which all of the social sciences have something to contribute, and it would be a species of forensic arrogance to claim it as distinctively or exclusively sociological. Let us therefore carve out, as it were, and subtract from the total problem those issues that, for the purposes of our present discussion at least, are more properly philosophical or historical. We shall do this, however, with an important caution, with the warning in short that these subtracted concerns have an ultimate sociological significance.

1. A Philosophical Problem

Among the many vexing and unanswered questions in this theater of inquiry is the question of social causation itself. What do we mean when we say that events have causes or that ideas and inventions, for example, exert an influence upon human societies? What is a "cause" and what is an "influence"? This is a philosophical or, more specifically, a methodological problem. It seems unfortunately to be in addition an unsolved problem, a problem to which more than two thousand years of philosophical speculation have been able to supply no wholly satisfactory answer, a problem, moreover, that may even elude an ultimate solution. In any event, it is a problem that we shall certainly not attempt to "solve" in these pages, nor even to discuss in detail.

Although everyone "knows" what a cause is, no one can explain the principle of causality, and neither reason nor experience, nor both together, can guarantee the validity of the principle. For, as the skeptical Scottish philosopher David Hume (1711–1776) so penetratingly pointed out, we never experience *causation* but only *succession*. We see one billiard ball strike another and we see the second move and strike a third, but all we have actually seen or sensed is a succession of events and have no evidence that the first event is the cause of the second, the second of the third. And how much more difficult it is in the area of social and historical affairs when, to continue the example, the "billiard balls" are never round, the table is seldom level, and the cue is always crooked. Some contemporary philosophers, unable to answer Hume, would abandon the causal principle altogether and substitute instead a probability principle, but this issue is too complex and too technical to detain our attention here.

If we are unable to answer Hume, however, we nevertheless have to accept, as sociologists, the validity of the category of causation. This assumption, this premise, is a prerequisite of all intellectual inquiry and particularly of scientific inquiry. Unless we assume that events have causes the world of nature dissolves into pure confusion and the world of history into pure caprice. Without this assumption knowledge becomes fortuitous and science impossible. To attribute anything to chance or fortune or fate or luck is to plead ignorance of the causal factors involved, and this neither physicist nor sociologist is permitted to do. The gods on Mount Olympus may be throwing the dice that determine the destinies of human societies, but if this is really the case—and none of us believes that it is—we should have to surrender all of our aspirations to sociological knowledge.

The problem of validating the category of causation continues to be one of philosophic concern. Although sociologists have made important contributions to it,[2] and must necessarily attack it again and again, it still defies a satisfactory solution.

[2] See Robert M. MacIver, *Social Causation*, Ginn and Company, Boston, 1942; Florian Znaniecki, *Cultural Sciences*, The University of Illinois Press, Urbana, Ill., 1952; and Pitirim A. Sorokin, *Socio-Cultural Causality, Time, Space*, The Duke University Press, Durham, N.C., 1943.

2. An Historical Problem[3]

In the first chapter of this book we indicated that sociology is an abstract and not a concrete science. The difficult task of describing and explaining singular and concrete events, therefore, belongs not to sociology but rather to history. Some of the difficulties are amusingly illustrated by Mark Twain. This great American humorist had been asked by the editors of a magazine to discuss the turning point of his life, the event that caused him to become a writer. After thinking this problem over, he decided that the real "cause" was Caesar's crossing of the Rubicon in 49 B.C.:

> This was a stupendously important moment. And all the incidents, big and little, of Caesar's previous life had been leading up to it, stage by stage, link by link. This was the *last* link—merely the last one, and no bigger than the others; but as we gaze back at it through the inflating mists of our imagination, it looks as big as the orbit of Neptune.
>
> You, the reader, have a *personal* interest in that link, and so have I; so has the rest of the human race. It was one of the links in your life-chain, and it was one of the links in mine. We may wait, now, with bated breath, while Caesar reflects. Your fate and mine are involved in his decision.
>
> While he was thus hesitating, the following incident occurred. A person remarked for his noble mien and graceful aspect appeared close at hand, sitting and playing upon a pipe. When not only the shepherds, but a number of soldiers also, flocked to listen to him, and some trumpeters among them, he snatched a trumpet from one of them, ran to the river with it, and, sounding the advance with a piercing blast, crossed to the other side. Upon this, Caesar exclaimed: "Let us go whither the omens of the gods and the iniquity of our enemies call us. *The die is cast.*"
>
> So he crossed—and changed the future of the whole human race, for all time. But the stranger was a link in Caesar's life-chain, too; and a necessary one. We don't know his name, we never hear of him again; he was very casual; he acts like an accident; but he was no accident, he was there by compulsion of *his* life-chain, to blow the electrifying blast that was to make up Caesar's mind for him, and thence go piping down the aisles of history forever.
>
> If the stranger hadn't been there! But he *was*. And Caesar crossed. With such results! Such vast events—each a link in the *human race's* lifechain; each event producing the next one, and that one the next one, and so on: the destruction of the republic; the founding of the empire; the breaking up of the empire; the rise of Christianity upon its ruins; the spread of the religion to other lands—and so on: link by link took its appointed place at its appointed time, the discovery of America being one of them; our Revolution another,

---

[3] Or, more precisely, an historiographical problem, that is, a problem not in history but in the writing of history.

the inflow of English and other immigrants another; their drift westward (my ancestors among them) another; the settlement of certain of them in Missouri, which resulted in *me*. For I was one of the unavoidable results of the crossing of the Rubicon. If the stranger, with his trumpet blast, had stayed away (which he *couldn't*, for he was an appointed link) Caesar would not have crossed. What would have happened, in that case, we can never guess. We only know that the things that did happen would not have happened. They might have been replaced by equally prodigious things, of course, but their nature and results are beyond our guessing. But the matter that interests me personally is that I would not be *here* now, but somewhere else; and probably black—there is no telling. Very well, I am glad he crossed. And very really and thankfully glad too, though I never cared anything about it before.[4]

Before he finished this essay, Mark Twain decided that he had not pushed his analysis back far enough, that the real turning point of his life must be sought not in the events of 49 B.C. at the River Rubicon, but rather in the Garden of Eden. If Eve had not been tempted by the serpent and if Adam had not been tempted by Eve, then the history of the human race would have been different; Mark Twain would not have come to be and certainly he would not have come to be a writer. Indeed, God may have made a mistake in placing Adam and Eve in the Garden. He should have put Martin Luther and Joan of Arc there instead: "By neither sugary persuasions nor by hell fire could Satan have beguiled *them* to eat the apple."[5]

Now obviously no speculation could be more idle—or more delightful—than this. The assertion that a single event, taken at random, is one of the causes, or the cause, of all subsequent events may, in sober fact, be true. But it is not very helpful. And it contributes nothing to an explanation of social and cultural change. Furthermore, it involves the human mind in an infinite regression toward a First Cause, a *Primum Mobile*, and this is a problem in cosmogony, which treats of the origin of the universe, and not a problem in sociology.

It is no part even of historical inquiry to indulge in speculations like these. Historians try to explain, not the lives of single individuals (this is the task of the biographer), but rather those larger events that agitate and change the destinies of societies. They describe the changing situations, the series of happenings that led, for example, to the discovery and subsequent colonization of America, to the Declaration of Independence, the Revolutionary War, the Constitutional Convention of 1787, and so on. They do this similarly for all nations, with the political state frequently the most

---

[4] "The Turning-point of My Life," in *What Is Man? And Other Essays*, Harper & Brothers, New York, 1935.
[5] *Ibid.*

prominent unit of their story. Sometimes they write instead the history of art or literature or religion or science or philosophy. Sometimes they take a phenomenon of great significance, such as the Peloponnesian War, (431–404 B.C.), the decline and fall of the Roman Empire, the rise of Christianity, the Industrial Revolution, the American Civil War, and so on, and tell the story of these events in as complete and as accurate detail as the documents and other data permit.

In all of these efforts they try not only to describe, that is, to tell the story exactly as it happened, but also to explain, that is, to weigh and to estimate as carefully as possible the factors that produced these momentous consequences and made them what they were. This quest too is a causal one. In other words, historians are seldom content merely to report the events of the past; they want, in addition, to explain them, and explanation requires a search for causes. All history that is not simple chronology, that is, merely a catalogue of dated events, is motivated by causal concerns. In this sense all history has sociological significance and sociologists would be helpless without the evidence supplied by their historical colleagues.

But inquiries like these, being concrete, are not themselves sociological in focus and emphasis. We have previously remarked that sociology, a relatively abstract science, examines not historical events themselves but rather patterns of events, patterns that repeat themselves in time and space. We have said, for example, that sociology is interested not in a particular war but in war in general, because war is a recurrent phenomenon in history and because there are certain similarities between the Peloponnesian War of the fifth century B.C. and the Second World War of the twentieth century. Nor is sociology interested in the development of a particular association of capitalistic enterprise, such as General Motors, the United States Steel Corporation, or E. I. du Pont de Nemours and Company, but in capitalism itself as a recurrent and relatively pervasive form of socio-economic organization. The causal inquiries of sociology, in short, are directed to patterns rather than to particulars, to classes of events rather than to the events themselves. In the discussion that follows we shall consequently ignore the causes of particular events. As a concluding caution, however, we invite the reader again to remember that historians and sociologists are colleagues in a great inquiry and that it would be a serious error to contrast too sharply their separate questions and endeavors.

3. The Factors of Sociocultural Change

There is another methodological difference between the historical and the sociological approaches to the problem of social and cultural change, a difference in the direction of inquiry. The historian moves from effects to causes; the sociologist from causes to effects. The historian attempts to discover the multiple causes that produced a particular phenomenon, the sociologist the multiple consequences produced by classes of causes. These classes of causes we may call "factors," and in the following discussion we single out certain factors that social thinkers have emphasized as contributing to the changes that occur in societies and consider them seriatim, that is, one after another, in greater or less detail. Each of them, taken singly or in combination, is associated with a particular theory of social change.

We should say also that few sociologists are so naive as to suppose that any single factor can explain the myriad processes of history or the dark complexities of social change. Social causation is always multiple causation—at least on the larger stage. And yet those theorists who, in an excess of enthusiasm perhaps, have emphasized one factor over others have contributed more to our understanding than the ecumenical theorists who have blandly taken an option on multiple causes. Thus we have learned something from Herbert Spencer's insistence upon natural selection, Henry Thomas Buckle's regard for geography and especially climate, Karl Marx's emphasis upon modes of production, Arthur de Gobineau's stress upon race, Emile Durkheim's respect for society itself, and Max Weber's recognition of the significance of an economic ethic. All of these writers, all distinguished sociologists in the history of the discipline, utilized what we have called "the theoretic bias,"[6] and although every one of them was almost surely wrong, they all gave us glimpses into the social process, glimpses that teach us even when they do not entirely convince.

Finally, it is not always easy to determine when a theory ceases to be sociological (that is, conceived and written in terms of the methodological principles enunciated in our first chapter) and becomes speculative and metaphysical. In the latter category we find the theories of some of the German philosophers of history in the nineteenth century, those like Hegel's for example, in which logic itself becomes a force and a Destiny Idea that threads its sinuous way through history in response to an inevitable and eternal dialectic of thesis, antithesis, and synthesis. Theories of this kind we shall ignore, except for some of the more recent ones, less metaphysical than Hegel's, that attract our attention because of their intrinsic and contemporary interest.

Our procedure will be first to discuss the factor theories of social change and then several theories built in terms of a principle rather than a factor. There are a great many factor theories and some of them are almost too fantastic to win any credence. We shall nevertheless mention a few of

---

[6] Robert Bierstedt, "Sociology and Humane Learning," *American Sociological Review*, vol. 25, no. 1, February, 1960, pp. 3–9.

the more fanciful ones for the sake of completeness. Other factor theories—those emphasizing the geographic factor, the biological factor, and the demographic factor—we have already treated in the second part of this book, and our present discussion of them can accordingly be brief.

4. The Geographic Factor

First of all we discover a variety of theories that attempt to attribute the commotions of societies to cosmic disturbances of one kind or another. Thus, sunspots, those vast atomic eruptions on the face of our own domestic star, have been held by some writers to be responsible for the fluctuations that occur in human societies. These writers suggest that in periods of high sunspot activity some kind of energy communicates itself across the void that separates sun and earth and stimulates the normal restlessness of peoples, encourages them to explore in new directions, and stirs them to new activity.

The notion that the stars, including the sun, somehow guide and control our destinies is a very ancient one, and one that still survives in the pseudoscience of astrology. If the reader believes that the conjunction of constellations on the date of his birth has something to do with the course of his life, then he is free to believe that the stars have something to do with the progressions and changes of human societies. If he regards astrology as a species of superstition, however, he will give short shrift to any astrological theory of social change. There is no doubt that sunspots do exert certain kinds of influences upon terrestrial activities—they affect, for example, the transmission of radio waves—but to explain such a social phenomenon as war in terms of them is to reach the outer edge of speculation.

Geographic theories in general, those in which the emphasis shifts from the sun and its spots to the earth and its climate, were discussed at length in the second chapter, where we suggested that geographic factors are necessary but not sufficient to explain social structure and social change. There is no reason for altering that conclusion here. For no period of human history do we have information of a geographic character that will adequately account for the social changes that occurred. The arguments offered earlier in this book will suffice for the present purpose, and we may even say, this time misquoting Santayana, that although geography does of course explain man's habitat, it cannot by itself explain his history.

5. The Biological Factor

Sometimes race, a biological factor, is elevated to supreme importance and credited—or discredited—with all of the changes that occur in societies. As we pointed out in great detail in the third chapter, and say again here for additional emphasis, there is no evidence whatever that the slight physical differences between the various racial groupings of mankind imply differential intelligence and none that they exert any particular influence, as such, upon the course of history.

We have, of course, been subjected in recent centuries to theories that arrogantly explain social developments in terms of a "master race" or a superior hereditary endowment. The notion that "blood will tell," in groups and societies as well as in individuals, is one that appears over and over again, and we may surmise that even in prehistorical times the peoples of earth attributed their own superiority, of which they were assured, to their supposedly superior physical constitution. As a matter of fact, theories of this kind are so prevalent that one finds them in every society in all parts of the world and in every epoch. We may remark, parenthetically, that only in a sociologically sophisticated society do men discover that racial theories are only a primitive form of ethnocentrism.

The theory that biological or racial differences explain the superiority and inferiority of nations and the changes that occur in them is, in short, one that no present evidence can support. The *belief* that such differences as color of skin, jut of jaw, or slant of eye are important, however, is itself a factor to be reckoned with in any interpretation of society. As we have seen, if men believe that racial differences are significant, then the belief has certain real social consequences, consequences that may not be too different from those that would occur if the situation were actually as it is believed to be. For this reason, of course, racial interpretations require our attention, but in examining them from this point of view, we are dealing not with a biological factor as such but rather with attitudes and ideas. Thus, it is not the situation itself but "the definition of the situation" that becomes a factor in social change.

6. The Demographic Factor

Other theories of social change attribute causal efficacy to demographic developments. This again is a subject to which we have devoted an earlier discussion. Throughout this book, in fact, whether we have been dealing with groups, associations, or entire societies, we have emphasized the importance of size, and of changes in size. Very small societies seldom rise to positions of historical eminence; very large ones exert influences not only upon their neighbors but upon the course of history. An expanding population, in any country, brings many changes in the nation's economy, and a contracting population has effects of a contrary kind. Population pressures, actual or presumed to be actual, have frequently been cited as the cause of wars. Differential fertility in various classes of a population has similarly been cited for the changes that occur in the juxtapositions and transformations of groups and consequently in the structure of a society.

Many other demographic phenomena also influence a society and its institutions. Along with gross size and differential fertility we should include the general age distribution, regional distribution, ethnic composition, sex ratio, differential mortality and morbidity rates, ratio of population to total land area and to arable land area, rural-urban ratios, ratio of population to general technological level of the culture, immigration and emigration, and many others. Some of these are causes of uncertain effects, and all of them are effects of other and still unknown causes. Taking them all together, it is evident that they cannot be discounted in any attempt to solve the problem of social change.

7. Political and Military Factors

Social change for many writers is the story of battles and skirmishes, of victory and defeat, of dynasties and wars. Indeed, history itself is often written almost exclusively in terms of military power, and accordingly we have a military theory of society and of social change. In terms of this theory inventors, philosophers, and scientists become only minor actors upon the stage of society, actors whose function it is to support the soldiers, who are the stars of the drama. In this view too history is to be understood in terms of crucial battles, and the story of these battles is the story of social change.

If the Persians had defeated the Athenians at the Battle of Marathon, if Charles Martel had not repelled the Moors in A.D. 732, if Napoleon's march to Moscow had been successful, or if Hitler had been able to cross the English Channel—to mention only a few of a multitude of examples— then, according to this military theory, the course of civilization would have been different. When interpreted in this way, history can be understood only in terms of the fluctuating fortunes of armies and navies as they clash by land and sea. The conquest of an army becomes the single factor that explains the multifarious changes in the course of a society's development, and the story of society thus becomes a story of conflict and of war, of victory and defeat.

This, of course, is an ancient tale, one as old as the writing of history itself. Revolutions succeed and subside, nations rise and fall in response to military exigencies, and the sum total of these affairs of blood and arms gives direction and significance to human societies. Here again we have a theory whose implications cannot be discussed in detail in a single chapter. We may pause only to suggest that, in so far as it elevates the factor of force to a position of predominance in accounting for social change, it suffers from certain sociological inadequacies. Force is always applied in a social context, not in a vacuum, and the character of this context can seldom be understood in terms of military power alone. By itself the military theory cannot even explain the sociology of war, a phenomenon with which it is most intimately related.

It is difficult, furthermore, to separate the military factor from the political, since revolution and war, in the vast majority of cases known to history, are political phenomena. Indeed, war has been defined as the continuation of diplomacy by other means. It has also been said that history is past politics, politics present history. As we have noted on several occasions, the manner in which men govern themselves—and others—is one of the most important questions one can ask about a society. History was once the story of rulers and of ruling houses, and any changes that occurred in these dynasties, from their domestic arrangements to their territorial conquests, brought changes throughout the societies over which they ruled. The sociological significance of these political and dynastic influences, however, is not yet clear. Pascal once asked a startling question. He wondered whether the entire history of Western civilization would have been different if Cleopatra's nose had been an inch longer than it was. This, however, is a theme for a dramatist, not for a sociologist, and here indeed we have returned to the wonderful nonsense of Mark Twain.

8. The Role of "Great Men"

The political interpretation of social change leads quickly and easily into the so-called "great-man" theory of history, It has been said that history never recovers from the impact of a great man (or woman, shall we say, like Helen of Troy?), and indeed writers like Carlyle and Nietzsche have never tired of praising the "hero" or the "superman" and his role in the collective drama of human life. History in this view is the serialized biographies of great men and it is to be understood not in terms of the movements of nameless masses but in terms of the achievements of genius.

Here we arrive at one of the most intriguing questions of all: Do men make history or does history make the man? It has been noted, for example, that the greatest of the American presidents—Washington and Lincoln, not to mention others—have been war presidents and the question arises whether they would have been equally great if they had lived in different times and circumstances. Or, to take another example, was World War II a precipitation of forces beyond any man's power to influence and control, or can it be understood only in terms of the personalities of Hitler, Mussolini, Hirohito, Chiang Kai-shek, Stalin, Churchill, and Roosevelt?

Would the war have happened, or would it have taken the course it did, if Messerschmitt, Pugliese, Yamamoto, Soong, Karpovich, Smith, and Jones had occupied the seats of political authority during this period?

On this question it would be easy to quote extensively from *War and Peace*, one of the greatest novels ever written. We have time, however, to listen to Tolstoy only long enough to hear him say:

> The higher a man stands on the social ladder, the more people he is connected with and the more power he has over others, the more evident is the predestination and inevitability of his every action.

and:

> A king is history's slave. History, that is, the unconscious, general, hive life of mankind, uses every moment of the life of kings as a tool for its own purposes.

and:

> In historic events, the so-called "great men" are labels giving names to events, and like labels they have but the smallest connection with the event itself.
>
> Every act of theirs, which appears to them an act of their own will, is in an historical sense involuntary and is related to the whole course of history and predestined from eternity.[7]

No one, of course, has any idea how to weigh and to estimate the influence of single individuals in the process of social change. Sociologists in general, in contrast to biographers and most historians, are inclined to agree with Tolstoy and to be extremely chary about attributing major influence to the great and vagrant personalities of men and women. Personality itself is seen to be shaped and formed by patterns of culture and of historical circumstance, and sociologists in consequence tend to interpret changes in societies in terms of deeper-lying phenomena, of which great men are only the surface representations. The question, of course, has been debated endlessly—sometimes in terms of a "devil theory of history"—and all we can do is ask it here and then go on, without waiting for an answer.

Ultimately, of course, all social change occurs because of the actions of men and women. Culture is not self-innovating, ideas are not self-creating, and technology is not self-inventing. Somehow, somewhere, in a society, a

---

[7] *War and Peace*, trans. by Louise Maude and Aylmer Maude, Simon Schuster, Inc., New York, 1942, book 9, sec. 1, pp. 670, 671. On Tolstoy's view of history see also Isaiah Berlin, *The Hedgehog and the Fox*, Simon and Schuster, Inc., New York, 1953.

man breaks however slightly from tradition. He does something in a different way. He finds a short cut. He has a new idea, or makes a new discovery. When that happens, whether he is a "great man" or not, he has disturbed the stream of culture and, like a stone tossed into the waters, its ripples may go on forever. It may affect, after a while, all the compartments of culture and all the sectors of society.

In the foregoing sections of this chapter we have mentioned only a few of the theories of social and cultural change. It would be difficult to make an exhaustive list of such theories. Indeed, history has been interpreted in terms of an astonishing variety of single factors—sunspots, rats, lice, bread, paper, clothing, sex, and other things too numerous—or too fantastic—to mention. Among so many factors, however, three merit special attention. These are the technological, the economic, and ideological. In the pages that follow we consider each of these at some length, not because they are necessarily more cogent than some we have previously mentioned and now neglect, but because they have received a more comprehensive discussion in the sociological literature.

9. The Technological Factor

Many writers on sociology and allied subjects are proponents of the technological theory of social change. Obviously we cannot consider all their separate views, nor indeed can we treat even the basic theory in the detail that its importance warrants. Because of these limitations our discussion is confined to the theory as advanced and developed by a prominent sociologist, William F. Ogburn (1886–1959).

Professor Ogburn first divides culture into two large categories— material culture and nonmaterial culture. He then suggests that, although changes may occur first in either material or nonmaterial culture, they usually occur first in the material culture, and the nonmaterial culture accordingly has to adjust to them. Changes in the material culture are thus causes of changes in the nonmaterial culture, and the latter, though it lags behind, is always in process of adjustment to the former. In this way technological invention becomes the primary factor in explaining cultural change.

When we think of the many changes in patterns of living, and changes too throughout the structure of society, that have come about as a result of inventions like the wheel, the boat, the compass, gunpowder, the printing press, the steam engine, the telephone, the automobile, radio, the airplane, television, and the atomic bomb, we are in a position to appreciate the very great importance of the technological theory. One could indeed fill many books with examples of social and cultural changes that are directly or indirectly induced by changes in material techniques, by new combinations of material-culture traits, by invention.

Ogburn gives us many illustrations of this kind. He suggests, for example, that the invention of the self-starter on automobiles had something to do with the emancipation of women. Without the self-starter, women would have been unable to use the automobile on equal terms with men and thus would have had to remain in the home, where several generations of Victorian men had consigned them. The self-starter gave them freedom of a new kind, and it was only a matter of time before they demanded freedom of other kinds as well.

If the emancipation of women seems like a vast social effect to attribute to a single technological invention, the answer is that other inventions also contributed to this change, especially the invention of labor-saving devices in the home, which were also due to the utilization of electricity. But without these inventions, of which the self-starter was one of the most important, this development, it is contended, would not have occurred.[8] In a similar fashion Ogburn suggests that the invention of the elevator, which made possible the construction of tall apartment buildings, in which it is difficult to rear children, had a depressing effect upon the urban birthrate.[9]

As another example, this time of a more specific and significant social change, let us consider, with Ogburn, the War between the States. The causes of this war, one of the vital episodes in American history, have puzzled historians and sociologists for many years, and interpretations seem to fluctuate with changing fashions. The moral cause, slavery, has been out of fashion for some time, although some historians have begun to reemphasize it. Other interpretations are purely political or purely economic, and the latter have been accepted by many students of the problem. According to this view slavery was an unimportant and surface phenomenon that had nothing essential to do with the war, which was inevitable in any event because the South, with or without slaves, was a dying economy that had lost its place in the sun to the industrial North. The factors are thus seen to be largely economic, and the slavery issue is viewed as merely a catalyst.

Ogburn, however, pushes his explanation back beyond the economic factor to a technological factor. For him the cotton gin—invented, as every schoolboy knows, by Eli Whitney—was an important cause, as he explains in the following passage.

[8] See William F. Ogburn, *The Social Effects of Aviation*, Houghton Mifflin Company, Boston, 1946, p. 5.
[9] William F. Ogburn, *Machines and Tommorrow's World*, rev. ed., Public Affairs Pamphlets, no. 25, 1946, p. 6.

An invention has a succession of effects, attached more or less as the links of a chain follow one another. The cotton gin seems to have increased the number of slaves, making it possible to increase the planting of cotton, which had the effect of stimulating trade with England, the best policy for which was free trade. The economic system of the South, where Cotton was King, then led to conflict with the economic system of the North, based upon a protective tariff favoring infant industries, and ended in the War Between the States.[10]

A technological factor, in short, led to a conflict of economic interest and finally to a conflict of arms.

How are we to evaluate this contention? First of all we have to relieve Professor Ogburn of any charge of dogmatism. He does not say that the cotton gin was *the* cause of the Civil War, nor even that the cotton gin was the sole cause of the increase in cotton production. Indeed, he carefully qualifies his thesis, as all competent scholars must, and notes that other factors also were operating to produce this effect and that other consequences proceeded derivatively from this cause.[11] Nevertheless, his emphasis upon the cotton gin is unmistakable and his preference for the technological explanation is clear.

In the second place, we cannot say what would have happened if the cotton gin had not been invented. The process of history, like the passage of time itself, is irreversible, and we cannot repeat it with one of the variables omitted in order to test its effect and influence. Social forces and factors cannot be put into test tubes, and Bunsen burners cannot alter their composition. We cannot experiment with society or with history. We must be ready, therefore, to concede that this invention did indeed exert an influence and that it had something causally to do with the events that followed.

This very concession, however, has interesting and perhaps unfortunate logical consequences. For if the cotton gin is responsible for the War between the States, it is responsible also for everything associated with that war. By a process of free association, in fact, we can attribute to the cotton

---

[10] William F. Ogburn and Meyer F. Nimkoff, *Sociology*, 2d ed., Houghton Mifflin Company, Boston, 1950, plate 20, facing p. 514. It is interesting, and almost amusing, to contrast this explanation with one written by Arthur Krock, then Washington correspondent of *The New York Times*, which appeared in that newspaper on Sunday, December 14, 1952: "The Dred Scott decision, in which Chief Justice Taney held for the majority that a Negro born a slave could not become free through residence in a free state or territory, furnished the major political issue between Lincoln and Douglas in their contest for a Senate seat from Illinois in 1858, completed the split between the Northern and Southern wings of the Democratic party and led directly to the election of Lincoln as President in 1860 and the War Between the States." Sec. 4, p. 3.

[11] Ogburn and Nimkoff, *op. cit.*, pp. 540–541.

gin almost everything that has occurred in American history since the date of its invention. The trouble with the theory, accordingly, is that it proves too much. Thus, if the cotton gin was the cause of the war, it was also the cause of Lincoln's Gettysburg Address, for without the one we should not have had the other. It is responsible in addition for Stephen Crane's novel *The Red Badge of Courage* (1895), and ultimately for the motion picture based on that novel. The cotton gin, furthermore, is responsible for concessions made to the South during the Nixon administration, for the rise of the Black Panther movement in the late 1960s, for the presidential campaigns of George Wallace, for intermittent race riots in American cities—and for *Gone with the Wind.*

One could obviously stretch out these "effects" of the cotton gin endlessly, or at least to the limit of the human imagination. The theory thus has the defects of its virtues. If it can explain the War between the States it can explain everything else even remotely associated with that war. We can now see why the logical consequences of this theory are unfortunate; a theory that explains too much is as useless as one that explains too little.[12]

The progression from cause (the invention) to effect (the social change) is seldom, however, an easy or automatic process. Although some innovations in technique are so reasonable or so efficient that they are immediately adopted, and the effects follow quickly, most technological changes meet resistance of one kind or another. It is a sad historical fact, as Ogburn points out, that some of the greatest blessings to the human race were resisted for years before they were allowed to prove their benefits. Ogburn discusses these resistances under such headings as intolerance of early imperfections, apprehension of social dislocations, economic costs, habits, conservatism of old people, fear of the new, reverence for the past, and vested interests. Invention, in short, is not enough. Inventions require acceptance before they can change the society in which they appear. We thus meet again the concept of cultural lag.

By "cultural lag" Ogburn means that one part of the culture changes more rapidly than another and that there is always, in consequence, a dislocation between the parts. Indeed many, if not all, social problems can be traced to the fact that the various parts of culture are not in adequate adjustment to one another. It takes a long time, sometimes several centuries, for society to adjust to the shock or the novelty of a new

[12] Ogburn similarly attributes the settling of the Great Plains between the Mississippi and the Rockies to three essential inventions: the six-shooter, barbed wire, and the windmill. The first of these enabled the frontiersman to defeat the Indians, the second transformed the open range into individual farms, and the third made it possible to feed the larger settled population. On this point see also Walter Prescott Webb, *The Great Plains*, Ginn and Company, Boston, 1931, pp. 169–179.

invention, and the pace of inventions may continuously outrun the possibility of such adjustment.

Technological changes in the automobile industry, for example, seem to proceed more rapidly than highway systems can adjust to them. Automotive engineering created cars that could travel 70 miles per hour before highway systems could accommodate this rate of speed. As a matter of fact, the interstate highway and the toll road—roads like the great Indiana, Ohio, New Jersey, and Pennsylvania turnpikes, the Merritt and Wilbur Cross parkways of Connecticut, the Maine Turnpike, and the New York Thruway—are almost obsolete the day they are opened to traffic. The traffic problem indeed seems to be beyond solution. It has been estimated, for example, that if all the automobiles in the United States were to take to the road at one time they would fill every highway, superhighway, and street and that there would be thousands of them left over.

The automobile, of course, is only one of many thousands of examples that could be chosen to illustrate the principle of cultural lag. Nearly every technological innovation, from the most insignificant gadget to the atomic bomb, creates problems that are only slowly solved. Indeed, the invention of the bomb has visited upon the world one of its most appalling problems, and no one can predict how great the lag between invention and adjustment will be. It is sometimes recommended, quite seriously, that the government declare a moratorium on scientific development and technological invention, banning all activity in these fields for a period of years in order to give society time to adjust to the technology it now has. Such proposals of course are no more realistic than King Canute's order to the tides of the ocean to cease their rise and fall.

Finally, no one can estimate the social consequences of what can only be referred to as "The Pill." Here is a birth control device so simple and inexpensive that it can be used by almost every woman in the world and a device in addition that appears to have an almost total safety and efficacy. What effect this technological invention will have upon the birthrates of both developed and underdeveloped countries, upon the sexual mores of all peoples, and upon family life in general, can only be surmised. It may or may not be a panacea for one of the world's ills, the ill of overpopulation. It offers dramatic evidence, however, of the importance of technological innovation.

Professor Ogburn, as we have indicated, classifies culture into two great compartments, material culture and nonmaterial culture. Since innovations may appear in either of these compartments, we have four causal possibilities: (1) mechanical inventions may cause social inventions, (2) mechanical inventions may cause other mechanical inventions, (3) social inventions may cause other social inventions, and (4) social inventions may cause mechanical inventions. An example of this last possibility, one doubtless familiar to the reader, is the social invention of the true-false type of college examination, which in turn induced the invention of the mechanical grader that enables testing services and universities to administer thousands of examinations at a single sitting and to grade them with electric dispatch.

If innovation may appear first in either of these compartments, the question arises as to which sequence is the more likely. Ogburn answers this question as follows:

> It is clear that social conditions bring about mechanical inventions and also that mechanical inventions cause changes in social conditions. But it is desirable to know which sequence is the more common. A comprehensive generalization on this point has not been established, but at the present time in the modern world, it appears easier to find illustrations of technology causing changes in social conditions. Hence we are inclined to favor the hypothesis of the greater importance of the sequence of technology causing social changes.[13]

It is this conclusion, temperate as it is, that places Ogburn among the proponents of the technological theory of social change, among those who argue that changes in material techniques are the most important of the factors that are ultimately responsible for social change.

We have to concede that this is a remarkably cogent theory. It is easy to find evidence in support of it and difficult, if not impossible, to disprove it. Among the theories of social change it maintains a high rank and much sociological merit. The only deficiency we have noticed so far is that it tends to prove too much; that is, by a free association of ideas one can link almost every development—literary, religious, economic, industrial, financial, and possibly even philosophical—to changes in the material techniques of society.

If the civilized world differs from the primitive, if our own period of history is unlike the centuries of ancient times, certainly the differences in material culture are the most striking of all the differences. It has frequently been remarked that Socrates, an ancient Greek, would have been less surprised by the world of Leonardo da Vinci than Leonardo, a Renaissance man, would be were he suddenly to arrive in the City of New York today. The Industrial Revolution changed all the contours of society and brought a new civilization into being. And the Industrial Revolution, of course, was a technological revolution. Atomic energy, electronic computation, communication satellites, and automation will have similarly profound and

---

[13] Ogburn and Nimkoff, *op. cit.*, p. 547.

comprehensive consequences in our own century. The facility with which we can make this prediction may induce us to underestimate its importance.

Some additional questions, however, remain. It is apparent that here, as in other theories of social change, we meet the extremely complex problem of an uncaused cause. What, we may ask, caused the Industrial Revolution? What encourages or stimulates a man to invent something, to introduce an innovation into society? To what may we attribute the fact that some inventions are accepted and others rejected? What determines when a society is "ready" for an invention? And how does it happen that when a society is "ready" the same invention will be made simultaneously and independently by different people?

Some of these questions are probably unanswerable. All of them suggest the difficulty of arriving at a definitive evaluation of the technological theory of social and cultural change. What we have here indeed is the old chicken-and-egg problem. What comes first, the idea or the invention? Are the changes to be expected in our own society to be attributed to the technological fact of atomic energy or to Einstein's mathematical idea that energy is equal to the product of mass and the square of the velocity of light—the equation that made the utilization of atomic energy possible? Indeed, Professor Ogburn himself, in his final summary, says that "all social change takes place through the medium of ideas."[14] However convincing the technological theory may appear, therefore, must we not at least supplement it with reference to factors of another kind? The answer would seem to be in the affirmative.

10. The Economic Factor

The economic interpretation of social change, of course, is most closely associated with the name of Karl Marx, the "spiritual" father of a "materialistic" society. Actually, the economic interpretation of society far antedates the life and work of Marx. Like most sociological theories it has an ancient lineage. It can be found in the books of the Chinese sages, Confucius and Mencius; in the sacred books of the East; and in the Christian Bible. One finds it expressed also, and sometimes with great clarity and emphasis, in the writings of the Greek historians and philosophers. Thucydides, for example, stresses the importance of economic factors like wealth, production, and commerce in determining changes in the political and social organization of society and notes particularly the influence of the love of gain. And Plato, in the immortal *Republic*, says, "For indeed any city, however small, is in fact divided into two, one the city of the poor, the other of the rich; these are at war with one another."[15] It is

---

[14] Ogburn and Nimkoff, *op. cit.*, p. 553.
[15] *The Republic*, IV, 423.

hard to imagine how the theory of class conflict based upon economic conditions could be more succinctly stated. Indeed, it has been suggested that it is almost impossible to find an ancient writer who failed to mention, somewhere in the corpus of his work, the importance of the economic factor.

Throughout the history of our Western society many excellent men, including the founding fathers of the United States, have emphasized the role of economic factors. And there is good reason why this should be so. It is a biological truism that one must eat in order to live and it is nearly as obvious, in all but a most insignificant minority of cases, that one must work in order to eat. Factors involved in the production and distribution of food thus become paramount in human life.

One of the most important facts about any of us as individuals is how we earn our living, and one of the most important facts about any society, correspondingly, is how its members produce and distribute their food supply. In most societies people do not have all the food they want and some have more than others; there is an economy of scarcity rather than of abundance, of poor rather than of perfect distribution. If air and water, which are available to all, were as nourishing as bread and meat, there would be no economic problem and, in consequence, no economic interpretation of society and of social change. Since this is not the case, all men have economic problems, and the way in which they attempt to solve them has something to do with the character of their societies. These ways develop into norms—norms of barter, trade, exchange, and property—and any changes in these norms introduce additional changes throughout the fabric of society. Thus, we have here a theory that emphasizes as the prime factor in social change not a change in materiel, as the technological theory does, but a change in the basic norms governing the economic relations that people have with one another.[16]

The economic interpretation of social change has become so familiar to all of us that we need not discuss it in detail. The distinctive features of

[16] A famous American economist, Edwin R. A. Seligman, who was in addition editor-in-chief of the *Encyclopaedia of the Social Sciences*, once expressed this theory as follows: "The existence of man depends upon his ability to sustain himself; the economic life is therefore the fundamental condition of all life. Since human life, however, is the life of man in society, individual existence moves within the framework of the social structure and is modified by it. What the conditions of maintenance are to the individual, the similar relations of production and consumption are to the community. To economic causes, therefore, must be traced in the last instance those transformations in the structure of society which themselves condition the relations of social classes and the various manifestations of social life." *The Economic Interpretation of History*, 2d ed., Columbia University Press, New York, 1917, p. 3. A great American historian, Charles A. Beard, in quoting this passage from Professor Seligman, remarks that it "seems as nearly axiomatic as any proposition in social science can be." *An Economic Interpretation of the Constitution of the United States*, 2d ed., The Macmillan Company, New York, 1939, p. 15n.

Marx's treatment, perhaps, are its clarity and its influence, and we may therefore quote several of his propositions:

> In the social production which men carry on they enter into definite relations that are indispensable and independent of their will; these relations of production correspond to a definite stage of development of their material power of production. The sum total of these relations of production constitutes the economic structure of society—the real foundation, on which rise legal and political superstructures and to which correspond definite forms of social consciousness. The mode of production in material life determines the general character of the social, political and spiritual processes of life. It is not the consciousness of men that determines their existence, but, on the contrary, their social existence determines their consciousness. At a certain stage of their development, the material forces of production in society come in conflict with the existing relations of production, or what is but a legal expression for the same thing—with the property relations within which they had been at work before. From forms of development of the forces of production these relations turn into their fetters. Then comes the period of social revolution. With the change of the economic foundation the entire immense superstructure is more or less rapidly transformed.[17]

And in the *Communist Manifesto* we find these famous lines on the class struggle:

> The history of all hitherto existing society is the history of class struggle. Freeman and slave, patrician and plebeian, lord and serf, guild-master and journeyman, oppressor and oppressed, stood in constant opposition to one another, carried on an uninterrupted, now hidden, now open fight, a fight that each time ended either in a revolutionary reconstitution of society at large, or in the common ruin of the contending classes.

Society is thus conceived to be composed of highly differentiated interest groups pitted against one another for economic advantage, and in this situation class struggle is inevitable. At the time at which Marx was writing, this process had become crystallized. As he put it: "Society as a whole is more and more splitting up into two great hostile camps, into two great classes directly facing each other; Bourgeoisie and Proletariat."[18] The story of the twentieth century was to be one of open conflict between these two classes, a conflict that would result in the inevitable victory of the proletariat—who had nothing to lose but their chains—and the classless society would then become a reality. This, furthermore, was to be the final

[17] *Critique of Political Economy*, trans. by Stone, Chicago, 1904, pp. 11–13.
[18] *The Communist Manifesto*.

revolution in history; men would thenceforth forevermore dwell in a Communist utopia where no one owned anything and everyone owned everything in a total abolition of the institution of property.

It is unnecessary to write an extensive refutation of this theory. In the stark terms in which Marx and his collaborator, Engels, expressed it, it is clearly a vast oversimplification of the process of history. That economic factors are important no one who works for a living would be inclined to deny. But that all other factors are unimportant is too much to believe. Economic factors are surely involved in many historical crises and transitions, but to say that the Crusades, for example, were motivated by economic rather than religious concerns, that the War between the States was fought because of the operation of inexorable economic forces rather than the issue of slavery, that the geographic explorations of the fifteenth century were prompted by greed rather than by curiosity, that the discovery of atomic fission was motivated by economic rather than scientific concerns, that men climbed Mt. Everest or travelled to the moon for economic gain is to claim too much. A great many changes occur in society that are only remotely related to changes in modes of production, and it is surely an exaggeration even to imply that the history of human society is nothing but the record of class conflict.

The sociological theory of Karl Marx is an excessive, dogmatic, and radical variant of economic interpretations that are as old as human thought itself. In Marx, in addition, the theory contains a curious inconsistency. He argues on the one hand that economic factors are all-important and on the other that they will eventually cease to operate. Once the classless society is achieved, modes of production no longer change or, if they do, such changes no longer have any social consequences. An otherwise respectable theory thus becomes subservient to political doctrine, and the political freight becomes too much for the sociological locomotive to haul.

Nevertheless, in less extreme terms, there is no doubt that economic factors do play a significant role in social change. Changes in economic variables have been correlated, in specific and sometimes precise ways, with changes in other variables in society. There are thus correlations between economic conditions and the health of a population, mortality and morbidity rates, marriage and divorce rates, suicide and crime, immigration and emigration, and so on. Alternating periods of prosperity and depression—the business cycle in short—affect these variables, and others, in manifold ways.

Attempts to establish correlations between economic factors and social factors of this kind have met with considerable success, and current and future sociological research will continue to explore in these directions. It has also been possible, in many cases, to associate economic conditions with social unrest and political turmoil, with revolution and war. Indeed, the interrelationships between economic and political phenomena, almost of necessity, are so close that in this field the economic interpretation can appear in its strongest light.

Almost any political phenomenon has its economic conditions and ingredients, and the history of political society cannot be wholly understood without some attention at least to underlying economic factors. Even so noble a document as the Constitution of the United States has been analyzed by an eminent historian, the late Charles A. Beard, in terms of the thrust and counterthrust of economic interests at the time of the conclusion of the American Revolution.[19] For that matter let us listen for a moment to one of the authors of the Constitution, to no less a person than James Madison, later to become the fourth President of the United States. In the famous *Federalist Papers*, written before Karl Marx was born, Madison has the following to say:

> The most common and durable source of factions has been the various and unequal distribution of property. Those who hold and those who are without property have ever formed distinct interests in society. Those who are creditors, and those who are debtors, fall under a like discrimination. A landed interest, a manufacturing interest, a mercantile interest, a moneyed interest, with many lesser interests, grow up of necessity in civilized nations, and divide them into different classes, actuated by different sentiments and views. The regulation of these various and interfering interests forms the principal task of modern legislation, and involves the spirit of party and faction in the necessary and ordinary operations of the government.[20]

And Alexander Hamilton, who well knew the importance of "the pecuniary

---

[19] "The members of the Philadelphia Convention which drafted the Constitution were, with few exceptions, immediately and directly and personally interested in, and derived economic advantages from the establishment of the new system" *An Economic Interpretation of the Constitution of the United States*, p. 324. See also, by the same author, *Economic Origins of Jeffersonian Democracy*, The Macmillan Company, New York, 1927, especially p. 3, where the following passage appears: "The contest over the Constitution was not primarily a war over abstract political ideals, such as state's rights and centralization, but over concrete economic issues and the political division which accompanied it was substantially along the lines of the interests affected—the financiers, public creditors, traders, commercial men, manufacturers, and allied groups, centering mainly in the larger seaboard towns, being chief among the advocates of the Constitution, and the farmers, particularly in the inland regions, and the debtors being chief among its opponents. That other considerations, such as the necessity for stronger national defence, entered into the campaign is, of course, admitted, but with all due allowances, it may be truly said that the Constitution was a product of a struggle between capitalistic and agrarian interests." See also Beard's *The Economic Basis of Politics*, Alfred A. Knopf, Inc., New York, 1934, where he remarks that "political science with economics left out is an unreal and ghostly formalism." p. iii.

[20] *The Federalist*, no. 10.

transactions of mankind,"[21] remarked, "It is an observation, as true as it is trite, that there is nothing men differ so readily about as the payment of money."[22]

Even in the political sphere, however, it is desirable to avoid definitive inferences with respect to the operation of economic factors. Sharp political changes frequently occur without any noticeable changes in economic variables. Modes of production, for example, changed very little during several centuries of European history, but these same centuries were packed with political events of momentous consequence.

The causal influence, furthermore, is not always a one-sided affair. Political decisions also have economic consequences, some of them unanticipated. The waning of the British Empire in the twentieth century is traceable in large measure to the effects of two world wars, but these wars cannot be completely explained by economic issues affecting the relationships between the United Kingdom and Germany. Present political alignments in the United States can be illuminated by reference to the War between the States, whether or not the primary causes of that war are discovered in the operation of economic factors. The notion that the party in power cannot be defeated during periods of prosperity has been disproved in a number of elections. Thus, it is a mistake to conclude that wherever there is a relationship between economic and political phenomena, the former always have causal priority. The situation in society is more complex than that, and simple explanations properly arouse suspicion.

Conclusions about the role of economic factors in society, therefore, have to be hedged with caution. The enthusiasm of the Marxian writers stems from faith in things hoped for rather than from knowledge of things as they are. If in certain areas of human affairs, such as the political, we watch with alertness the operation of economic forces, in others the influence of these factors, when it is present at all, is likely to be attenuated and incapable of explaining the social consequences in which we are interested. Indeed, to explain the history of music or art or philosophy or science or religion in simple economic terms is to indulge in unsupported flights of speculation. Homo sapiens is not only *Homo oeconomicus.* Economic man must eat, but the whole man needs also to love and think and create and understand. There is no reason to assume therefore, in the present state of sociological knowledge, that economic factors have an independent and a universal effect in all the instances of social and cultural change.

[21] *The Federalist,* no. 30.
[22] *The Federalist,* no. 7.

11. The Ideological Factor

There remains yet another important theory of social change to be explored. This theory deals with the role of ideas in society and concerns itself with what may be called the ideological factor. In an earlier chapter we distinguished between ideas and ideologies, defining the latter as ideas that people in a given society have a moral obligation to believe, the ideas supported by the norms of that society, or of smaller groups within it. Here we shall consider ideas and ideologies together and attempt to show that they are powerful motivating forces in social change. What people think, in short, determines in very large measure—in so far as anything is ever determined in society—what they do and what they want. It is not surprising, therefore, that many sociologists should single out changes in ideas as the most important initiating impulses in social change and give to ideological innovations a place of precedence in the solution of this problem.

The most impressive theory of this kind is attached to the name of the great German sociologist Max Weber whose career, as has often been observed, was a constant dialogue with Karl Marx. For Marx, as we have just noted, economic factors were basic, the bottom layer of the cultural pyramid as it were, and social and political organization, art, literature, science, philosophy, and religion were all part of the superstructure, dependent upon this bottom layer. Weber too appreciated the importance of economic factors, but he did not ascribe to them the importance that they have in Marxian theory. He thought that other factors were also important and that among these factors religion or, more broadly, what people believed, should be given consideration.

Weber himself was too careful a scholar to subscribe wholeheartedly to any single-factor theory—a fact that his critics have sometimes overlooked—but the net result of his research was to give a heavy emphasis to the ideological interpretation of social change. In effect, when Weber's own careful qualifications are disregarded, his theory stands in complete contradiction to the Marxian theory. For Marx economic influences were paramount and determined all the rest, including the religious; for Weber, on the other hand, economic phenomena themselves rest upon a broad ideological base, and particularly upon religion. Let us see how he develops this theory in his famous book.[23] In the first place, in the study at hand Weber confines his attention to one particular economic phenomenon, capitalism, and one particular religious phenomenon, Protestantism, and

---

[23] *The Protestant Ethic and the Spirit of Capitalism*, trans. by Talcott Parsons, George Allen & Unwin, Ltd., London, 1930. We shall not follow Weber's argument in detail but rather present a general and somewhat expanded version of it.

refuses to indulge in sweeping generalizations of a more speculative variety. For the Marxian writers the relationship between profit and Protestantism is simple and one-sided. The Protestant Reformation was the result of such economic forces as a German revolt against papal exploitation or the dislocation caused by the influx of gold from the New World. Such assertions are too unsophisticated for Weber. He lends the weight of his scholarship to a different thesis, namely that the modern development of capitalism is attributable to some extent at least to the Protestant Reformation. The profit motive may operate in all civilized societies; greed and the desire for gain may be all but universal. But such psychological factors, if they are presumed to be universal, must also be constant, and they cannot therefore explain a particular phenomenon that appears at a particular time in history, a phenomenon like capitalism. It is Weber's thesis that there is something in Protestantism that helped to create the system of economic norms we know as capitalism and that it was the Protestant Reformation that gave an impetus to the development of a capitalistic economy.

In the second place, Weber develops a new and interesting method by which to study this relationship. The questions arise, What is capitalism? and What is Protestantism? There is no "pure" case of either in history. "The trouble with Christianity," as someone with an uncomfortable wit has said, "is that it has never been tried," and the same might be said of both capitalism and Protestantism. In no society has either of these phenomena existed in its pure form. They exist always as a part of a complicated cultural situation and never as isolated phenomena. In order to surmount this difficulty Weber introduces the notion of an "ideal type." He will study the ideal type of capitalism, capitalism as it would be if it were historically "pure," and similarly the ideal type of Protestantism. The ideal type, in short, is what a phenomenon would be if it always and everywhere conformed to its own definition.

Capitalism, in its market phase, is simply a rational bureaucratic organization devoted to the acquisition of pecuniary profit. And Protestantism? Here Weber is interested not in theological doctrine, but in what he calls the Protestant *Wirtschaftsethik*, the economic ethic of Protestantism. And this economic ethic he finds ideally exemplified in the aphorisms of Benjamin Franklin as they appear especially in his *Autobiography*, his *Advice to a Young Tradesman,* and his *Necessary Hints to Those Who Would Be Rich.* Here we find the maxims that are so familiar to American students, the stock in trade of every schoolroom and of many homes: "Honesty is the best policy," "A penny saved is a penny earned," "Time is money," "Money begets money," "Early to bed and early to rise makes a man healthy, wealthy and wise," and so on. When we add these aphorisms together we find that they are all saying, in effect, that work is a virtue and that it is right and proper and good to earn and to save money.

Now the notion that work is a virtue is something relatively new in the history of Western civilization. It is a Protestant idea. It cannot be found in the Catholic ethic where leisure, not work, is accorded the higher place.[24] It will be remembered that, when the Lord God invited Adam and Eve to depart from Paradise for having eaten of the fruit of the tree of the knowledge of good and evil, he visited condign punishment upon both of them. Eve and her daughters would henceforth bear their children in pain and Adam and his sons would earn their bread by the sweat of their brows. Labor in this ethic, then, is not a virtue but a punishment. One cannot add cubits to one's spiritual stature by work. Work, on the contrary, is the reminder of original sin. How different is the Protestant attitude. In the Protestant ethic work is something to be done for its own sake, something that it is good to do, and—even more important—something that contributes to the glory of God.

This is the attitude that has prevailed in Protestant societies since the Reformation, and all of us in the United States, whether Catholic or Protestant or Jewish, are imbued with this idea. We think that too much leisure is somehow wrong and is not to be encouraged; we must work whether there is anything to do or not. Indeed, most of us, when we speak the truth, feel a little uncomfortable about sleeping too long in the morning and about rising too late. Our conscience disturbs us. There is thought to be a moral deficiency somewhere about doing nothing. We insist that people in our society work—that is, "do something"—even if work for some of them is not a financial necessity.

The first contribution of Protestantism to capitalism, therefore, is a changed attitude toward work. The Protestant ethic now supports gainful enterprise and makes a virtue out of what had formerly been a punitive necessity. This new attitude, whether encouraged officially by Protestant preachers or not, became an intimate part of the ordinary Protestant's belief and practice. The stimulus such an attitude gave to the development of capitalistic enterprise is apparent.[25]

---

[24] Leisure, of course, does not mean idleness, indolence, or sloth. For a Catholic statement of the relationships between leisure, work, and culture, see Josef Pieper, *Leisure the Basis of Culture*, Pantheon Books, a Division of Random House, Inc., New York, 1952. Labor was of course required of the monks in the monasteries, not, however, because it is good in itself but because it induces fatigue and "curbs concupiscence."

[25] Incidentally, only in Protestant cultures does one find the somewhat curious notion that "cleanliness is next to godliness." All of us are familiar with the housewife who is so conscientious about her domestic duties that she dusts and sweeps and scrubs her house whether it needs it or not. Our theory here can suggest why this should be the case. To keep clean requires an effort, and the effort—work—is good for its own sake, even when it is unnecessary. The housewife who keeps the cleanest house, compliments herself, and receives compliments, not only on her efficiency but also on her virtue. She has accomplished something that wins her a *moral* approval. In the Protestant ethic cleanliness is as much a matter of morality as it is a matter of sanitation.

The second contribution of Protestantism that had favorable consequences for capitalism was the concept of the "calling." This concept arises not in Lutheranism but in Calvinism. Calvinism, today known as Presbyterianism, maintains the doctrine of predestination, namely, that every soul is predestined at birth for heaven or for hell and that nothing an individual does in this life can affect his ultimate fate. No one, in addition, knows what his fate will be. There are, nevertheless, certain signs which may reveal that one is among the elect. One of these signs may be that one is successful in his work, or his "calling." Success may be one of the signals by which God indicates to society those who are predestined for ascent into heaven. It is therefore worthwhile to work hard at one's calling, and if this calling is business or the pursuit of private economic gain, this too can help to show that one is marked for a favorable fate. In any case it can contribute to the glory of God since the "calling" is a part of God's plan for the individual.

To the contemporary reader this may not sound like a very comforting doctrine. But so long as it was held by the rising business classes of the sixteenth and seventeenth centuries, it added its share to the economic climate. Capitalistic enterprise, like any other calling, is part of a master plan, predestined from all eternity, and grace may therefore attach itself to those who indulge in it. It is easy to see that in terms of this estimation of a calling one did not have to enter a monastery, make pilgrimages, or devote himself to poverty, chastity, and obedience in order to serve God. One could practice his religion in the market place as well as in the parish church.

The third contribution of the Protestant ethic to capitalism, also a Calvinistic rather than a Lutheran notion, was a new attitude toward the collection of interest on loans. One of the maxims of Benjamin Franklin, quoted above, is that money begets money. The Greek philosopher, Aristotle, on the other hand, had said that money cannot beget money. These two assertions are in direct contradiction. It was the Aristotelian assertion, however, that—through its acceptance and reemphasis by St. Thomas Aquinas—became an official theological doctrine in Catholicism. The Catholic theologians wrote strictures on usury, and usury was a sin subject to plea in the confession box and to expiation and penance. It was also frequently against the law. An abbreviated medieval statute reads as follows:

> But forasmuch as usury is by the word of God utterly prohibited, as a vice most odious and detestable, which thing by no godly teachings and persuasions can sink in to the hearts of divers greedy, uncharitable and covetous persons of this Realm, be it enacted that no person or persons of what Estate, degree, quality or condition so ever he or they be, by any corrupt, colourable or deceitful conveyance, sleight or engine, or by any way or mean, shall lend,

give, set out, deliver or forbear any sum or sums of money to or for any manner of usury, increase, lucre, gain or interest to be had, received or hoped for, over and above the sum or sums so lent, upon pain of forfeiture of the sum or sums so lent, as also of the usury, and also upon pain of imprisonment.

In the medieval period, furthermore, usury did not mean what it means today. Now it means excessive interest, and the collection of interest higher than a certain rate is subject to legal penalties. Then, however, it meant *any* interest at all. Before the Reformation, interest and usury were synonymous terms. Christian moneylenders could not, in consequence, operate openly because such activity fell under theological proscription. As a result the Jews, who suffered no such theological restriction vis-à-vis the Gentiles, became the moneylenders of the time, and this, incidentally, was one of the sources of medieval anti-Semitism.

As one might suspect, there were ways of getting around this prohibition. Mr. A, a fifteenth-century man, lends Mr. B a hundred thalers for a year. He must not charge for the use of the money, for such a charge would be usury. Mr. A and Mr. B, however, have a tacit understanding that the loan will not be repaid on the day it is due but rather three days later. Mr. B then pays Mr. A, in addition to the principal, five to ten thalers as a penalty charge for having been tardy in his repayment.

Despite such circuitous devices, the prohibition on usury discouraged the accumulation of capital, and the accumulation of capital for venture purposes is a necessity of business enterprise. Of course, large amounts of capital did accumulate in certain hands before the Reformation. One need only mention the great houses of the Fuggers and the Welsers and the Florentine banking house of the Medici. For that matter, some of the popes themselves were actively engaged in operations that might accurately be described as speculative banking. But the intellectual climate was not "right" for this kind of operation on an open and universal scale.

This attitude toward interest changed completely and, one might say, "officially" after the advent of Calvinism. In 1545 Calvin wrote a famous letter giving theological sanction to the collection of interest on loans, and a practice which had been prohibited in Catholicism came to be approved in Calvinism.[26] Now money could openly be loaned at interest, now capital could accumulate, now money itself could be "hired" without incurring the displeasure of the deity or placing the soul in jeopardy. And here again it is

---

[26] "For," says Calvin, "if all usury is condemned, tighter fetters are imposed on the conscience than the Lord himself would wish . . . Therefore usury is not wholly forbidden among us, except it be repugnant both to justice and to charity." This letter is reprinted in Franklin Le Van Baumer (ed.), *Main Currents of Western Thought*, Alfred A. Knopf, Inc., New York, 1952, pp. 231–233.

easy to appreciate the stimulus which this new Calvinistic idea gave to the development of capitalism. Here again the Protestant ethic and the spirit of capitalism are in harmony. In the Protestant nations today the notion that it is a "vice most odious and detestable" to charge interest on loans is so unfamiliar that the author of this book would be willing to wager that few of his readers have ever heard of it.

Various other aspects of the Protestant ethic were also favorable to the development of capitalism. Strictures on the use of alcoholic liquors, for example, are generally somewhat less severe in Catholicism than in Protestantism. Indeed, the prohibition movement in the United States was a Protestant movement and the Baptists and the Methodists in particular have frowned upon any indulgence of this sort. One might say, with only a slight exaggeration, that sobriety is more of a Protestant than a Catholic virtue. Here again there is no implication that Catholics drink and Protestant do not. As in the case of usury there are ways of evading both religious and legal proscriptions. But one can see how this difference in attitude contributed to the rational efficiency of capitalistic endeavor. As Charles A. Beard has wryly commented, "Grass may grow and sheep may graze if the peasant lies drunk under the hedge occasionally, but the wheels of mills cannot turn steadily if boiler stokers must have frequent debauches."[27]

A growing literacy, encouraged by the Protestant viewpoint that every man should read his own Bible rather than depend on priestly intercession and authority, together with Luther's translation of the Bible from the Latin to the German, also contributed something to the rational procedures of capitalism. Our intoxicated peasant, mentioned immediately above, does not need to know how to read, but the factory foreman requires the gift of literacy in order to do his job.

Finally, we may notice one more difference between the Protestant and the Catholic ethic that has implications for business enterprise. The Catholic calendar is full of holy days that are lacking in the Protestant calendar. This too is due in part, on the one hand, to the Catholic belief that one needs leisure to honor God with meditation or celebration and, on the other, to the Protestant view that work itself contributes to the glory of God. Work, in short, is more frequently interrupted in the one case than in the other. Many American factories today operate continuously, twenty-four hours a day, seven days a week, with the labor force on different shifts. Too many holidays would make continuous operation of this kind impossible. Capital cannot be employed to its full efficiency in the face of too much vacation time, and the Protestant calendar, coupled with the Protes-

---

[27] "Individualism and Capitalism." *Encyclopaedia of the Social Sciences*, The Macmillan Company, New York, 1930, vol. I, p. 149.

tant attitude toward work, contributed therefore to the efficacy of capitalistic enterprise.

When we consider these various components of the Protestant ethic together—the moral attitude toward work, the concept of the "calling," the distinction between usury and interest, the exaltation of sobriety, the emphasis upon literacy, and the reduction of holidays—and when we note that these components are lacking in the Catholic ethic, we can then appreciate the significance of the Protestant Reformation, and more particularly of Calvinism, in the development of capitalism. Changing ideas introduced changing norms into the economic structure of society. New ideas brought new practices and encouraged the increased production of economic goods. Protestantism and its economic ethic thus served as potent positive forces in the rise of capitalism. In stating this conclusion we want to remind the reader again that, as important as Protestantism may have been, other factors too were at work in this vast historical process.

We may now ask whether this theory is merely a matter of argument, however reasonable and compelling, or whether there is empirical evidence to support it. The answer is that there is very good empirical evidence indeed. If we ask in what countries capitalism has attained its highest development, we find in fact that they are all Protestant countries, England and the United States, for example, in contrast to Italy and Spain. In countries that were both Protestant and Catholic, like Germany, it is clear from the evidence that Weber himself adduces that it is the Protestants who, by and large, became the capitalistic entrepreneurs and who responded to the challenge of the Industrial Revolution. Even persecuted Protestants, like the Huguenots of France, demonstrated their business acumen in the countries that gave them sanctuary, especially in England, Germany, the Netherlands, Switzerland, and the United States. Most striking of all, of course, is the contrast mentioned first. If one compares the industrial and capitalistic developments of Spain and her colonies on the one hand and England and hers on the other, the evidence in support of Weber's theory becomes impressive indeed. After the Reformation Spain declined and England prospered. Mexico, a Catholic country, is still, like Spain, largely unindustrialized, whereas her neighbor to the North is the exemplification of industrial might.

This, then, is the Protestant ethic and this is the manner in which an idea, or a series of related ideas, can influence the structure of an economy or a society and become a factor in social change. We have noted that Weber, a careful and studious sociologist, does not weaken his theory by overstatement. Nor does he indulge in sweeping generalizations about the role of ideas in the entire course of historical development. Among the many ideological interpretations of social change, his theory assumes a very high rank.[28] Sociologists who, like Weber, support the ideological interpretation do not deny that economic, political, geographic, and demographic factors are important in disturbing the tenor of societies as they move through time. But they are convinced, in addition, that what people think, the ideas they have or acquire, their basic philosophies in short, also have much to do with the character of cultures and the changes of societies. It may be indeed, as Shelley said, that "Poets are the unacknowledged legislators of the world."

We have now concluded our examination, in all cases too brief, of various single-factor theories of social change. This is not the place in which to commit ourselves or our readers to any one of them or even to any combination of them. The problem is too large for treatment here and we shall therefore have to be content with the foregoing summary statement and examples. In the next section we want to consider a different kind of theory, a theory that appeals to a principle rather than to a factor.

12. The Idea of Progress

The notion that each succeeding society or each succeeding age in the world's history is somehow "better" or "superior" to the preceding societies and ages is so familiar to Americans in general and to American students in particular that it may come as a surprise to them to learn that this idea is not in fact very old. It was unknown in the history of our own Western civilization until the sixteenth century and in other civilizations the idea did not appear at all. We have somehow come to take it for granted—as a result, one supposes, of the "progressive" spirit in our own society—that things in general are improving all the time, that "every day in every way things are getting better and better." History, in this view, is a continuously rising line on the graph of the cosmos, and the future of every society must always be superior to its past.

The Greeks, however, did not share this view. To them the golden age lay in the remote and distant past and every succeeding age was destined to be inferior. In some of their reflections this idea was inconsistently coupled with another, the idea of eternal recurrence. According to this doctrine everything that has happened will sometime happen again and the course of human history is therefore a series of cycles, each cycle like its predecessor and each following each in rhythmic alternation throughout eternity. In this conception of social change there is no room for a theory of progress.

[28] It is only fair to say that Weber's thesis has been severely criticized; for example, by Brentano in Germany, Tawney in England, Robertson in England, Fanfani in Italy, Beard in the United States, and Samuelsson in Sweden.

Nor do we find the idea of progress in the Middle Ages. The orientation of the medieval mind was otherworldly and what happened in this world and in this society was of little import, scarcely worth the expenditure of curiosity. Attention was focused upon the Day of Judgment, that awesome last day when every man would stand before his Maker and receive the decision that would consign him to torment or to bliss. It is apparent that there is similarly no room here for a theory of progress and no interest in such an idea as it might apply to the course of mundane affairs.

With the coming of the Renaissance, however, social philosophers began to turn their attention to the events of earthly history and to find in them the evidence of progress. We cannot trace the development of this idea in these pages, but the story has been brilliantly told by the late English historian J. B. Bury in a book dedicated to the memories of four outstanding apostles of progress, Saint-Pierre, Condorcet, Comte, and Spencer, the last two of whom were sociologists in name as well as fact.[29] In the nineteenth century the idea of progress received additional support from an unexpected source, the biological theories of Charles Darwin, and it was Herbert Spencer who translated the idea into the language of Darwinian evolution. Social Darwinism then became the doctrine that dominated late nineteenth-century and early twentieth-century thought, and the history of everything from science to art was written in evolutionary terms. Society itself was seen as a continuous development through regular stages, and all societies were presumed to go through these stages with the necessity and inevitability of the evolutionary process. At the turn of the twentieth century it was easy to believe in peace and prosperity and progress. The First World War, however, to say nothing of other events, brought disenchantment, and sociologists began to deny that progress was probable and evolution inevitable. The later advent of nuclear weapons and the continuing and uncontrolled rise in the world's population induced increasing skepticism and anxiety. Furthermore, "progress" was seen to be an ethical or evaluative, rather than a scientific or objective, concept. About anything—whether increasing literacy, decreasing mortality, increasing knowledge, increasing speed of motion, or more powerful detonations—it was always possible to ask, "Is that good?" and the answer, of course, depended upon one's definition of the good.

If progress means development in a desirable direction, then what seems desirable to some may seem undesirable to others. Although several

[29] *The Idea of Progress*, The Macmillan Company, New York, 1932.

attempts were made to define "progress" objectively,[30] the concept had to be abandoned for sociological use. In the process the concept of evolution, in so far as it applied to society or to history, was also abandoned, and indeed it seldom appears in the lexicon of contemporary sociology. There is reason to believe, however, that this second abandonment was perhaps a little hasty and that certain changes do occur in both groups and societies, as they grow or age, which can reasonably be described as evolutionary. It is a possibility at least that merits continued reflection.

In the last few decades various general theories of social change, new philosophies of history, made their appearance. To discuss all of these would require a large volume. Before concluding this book, however, we should like to mention three that have achieved some prominence, the theories of Oswald Spengler, Arnold J. Toynbee, and Pitirim A. Sorokin.

13. Oswald Spengler

Oswald Spengler, once an unknown German schoolmaster, achieved immediate and international fame in 1918 with the publication of the first volume of a two-volume work entitled, in translation, *The Decline of the West*.[31] In this book he denounces all previous writing of history as having been achieved in terms of an erroneous conception of historical time. There is not one linear time, Spengler declares, but as many "times" as there are historical civilizations. Neglecting all primitive societies as "historyless," Spengler discovers eight high civilizations with a similar development and a similar destiny. Each of them had an existence like a great organism—a birth, an adolescence, a maturity, a decline, and a period of decay and disintegration. Spengler refers to the society in its rising phase as a "culture," in its falling as a "civilization." All creative activity occurs in the culture, and when this efflorescence is over the society turns to an elaboration of techniques, becomes a civilization, and inevitably declines. Instead of studying history continuously through a linear time, therefore, Spengler conceives of each of these civilizations as having its own organically separate course of life and devotes his pages to tracing the parallels

---

[30] These attempts were usually couched in technological terms. It might be said, for example, that a 1970 automobile is better—that is, more efficient—than a 1940 model. But even about efficiency it is possible to ask, "Is it good?" There are numerous societies in which the American ideal of efficiency is unimportant and others in which it is meaningless.

[31] Volume 2 was published in 1922. The American edition, translated by Charles Francis Atkinson, was published by Alfred A. Knopf, Inc., New York, 1926 and 1928; a special one-volume edition (also published by Knopf) appeared in 1939.

between them. Caesar and Cromwell, for example, were identical men in different civilizations and in both their appearance was inevitable.

In beautiful but pessimistic prose Spengler announces that our own civilization, one of the eight, has passed its peak and that there is nothing left to anticipate but its inexorable decline. Wars and cities are among the portents of this decay. The implication that societies are like organisms—the biological analogy in short—has appeared in social thought from the earliest times, but no one except Spencer perhaps has ever exploited it with such extravagance. "Cultures are organisms," says Spengler, "and world-history is their collective biography." In his view societies move through cycles with the measured and ineluctable pattern of birth and death. Nothing can stay this cycle, although it may be aborted as in the case of the Mayan civilization of Mexico, which succumbed in mid-carrer to the Spanish conquistadors.

Spengler's thesis, developed with great learning and undeniable literary power, attracted a wide attention at the time of its publication, and its importance may be gauged, in part at least, by the fact that books and articles on the author and his works still find their way into print. However much sociologists may admire the Spenglerian achievement—and there is no question that it merits admiration—they now almost unanimously withhold assent from his mystical and speculative doctrine.

14. Arnold J. Toynbee

Arnold J. Toynbee, the English historian mentioned in the second chapter, is the author of a massive and many volumed project entitled *A Study of History*. The first observation to make about *A Study of History* is that it is not a history of anything at all but rather a work of pure speculative sociology. Where Spengler saw eight "cultures" or civilizations, Toynbee discerns twenty-one. With these twenty-one "cases" before him he attempts to discover in them some common pattern of growth, some key to their development, some principle of social change.

Once again we find it impossible to enter into any detailed discussion of so comprehensive a work, and it is surely unfair to its author to outline only the bare essentials. Nevertheless, we have to indicate that Toynbee constructs his sociological theory in terms of two major concepts, the concepts of "challenge" and "response." Each literate society begins its life, as it were, as a response to a challenge and works out its destiny in a series of responses to successive challenges. The initial challenge, as we have indicated before, is the challenge of the environment. The geographic circumstances of the society must be such as to constitute a challenge; that is, they must not be so easy that no effort is required to adjust to them nor so severe that sheer survival exhausts all energies. When this condition is met the society in a sense is started on its way.

Succeeding challenges are social rather than geographic. They are the challenges of both an internal and an external proletariat. Societies survive some of these challenges and succumb to others. And this, in brief, is the story of their changes, a story of challenge and response, of withdrawal and return, of rally and rout, of disintegration and transfiguration.

The tone of Toynbee's work, in contrast to Spengler's, is optimistic. Some societies can utilize the experiences, the legends, and the religions of earlier societies to which they are affiliated and thus rise to greater heights. The course of history then is cyclical, but each cycle—that is to say, each succeeding civilization—has a little more stature than the one preceding. This interpretation, accordingly, may be called the helical or "circular staircase" theory of history. Another image is that of human beings striving steadily to climb the face of a mountain, the jagged peaks above them, the shadowed canyons below. They fall off in droves but, each time they try, some of them manage to work their way a little closer to the top. Toynbee's optimism is sustained by his religious faith, by his belief that the Anglican religion represents the highest achievement of mankind thus far. Indeed, his recourse to this kind of estimate and this kind of hope has induced an adverse critic to remark that he has buried the philosophy of history in an Anglican churchyard.[32]

Evaluation of Toynbee's thesis would be wholly inappropriate in these pages. His scope is spectacular, his learning is impressive, his concepts are imaginative—and his conclusions are unverified. Neither the pessimism of Spengler nor the optimism of Toynbee can currently be justified by even the best of historical evidence. We are nevertheless indebted to Toynbee for his sociological courage, and students who increase the debt by reading him on their own account will find that it is an exciting debt to owe.

15. Pitirim A. Sorokin

Pitirim A. Sorokin, the distinguished Russian-American sociologist, has also made an assault upon the vast problem of social change in a four-volume work entitled *Social and Cultural Dynamics*.[33] Sorokin sees the course of history as a continuous but irregular fluctuation between two basically different kinds of cultures, the "sensate" on the one hand and the

---

[32] See the critical review by Harry Elmer Barnes, *American Sociological Review*, vol. 12, August, 1947, pp. 480–486. For a collection of critical essays and reviews see M. F. Ashley Montagu (ed.), *Toynbee and History*, Porter Sargent, Publisher, Boston, 1956.
[33] American Book Company, New York, 1937, 1941.

"ideational" on the other. A culture for him is a system of items and traits that possess some kind of unity, that belong together in some kind of "logico-meaningful" integration. Not all collections of cultural items have this unity. Some of them are so heterogeneous that they constitute a mere "congeries," not a system. A system, in contrast, is built out of consistent items and can be represented, on a small scale, by such things as the multiplication table, an internal-combustion engine, the *Dialogues* of Plato, the musical works of Bach, scholastic philosophy, and so on. These systems, in turn, build up into "supersystems" and these supersystems, still consistent within themselves, are ultimately sensate or ideational, with a mixed or transitional culture between them that Sorokin calls "idealistic."

A sensate culture is one in which all expressions—art, literature, religion, law, ethics, social relations, and philosophy—appeal to the senses and satisfy sensual needs and desires. An ideational culture, on the contrary, is one in which these expressions appeal to the soul, the mind, or the spirit. Sensate art, for example, is visual, sensational, and photographic; ideational art is symbolic, religious, and often abstract. Sensate sculpture emphasizes the nude human body in realistic fashion; ideational sculpture clothes the body in religious vestments. Sensate literature emphasizes the degeneracy of unimportant people, whereas ideational literature sings of the sublimity of souls and the sanctity of saints. Sensate philosophy invokes the truth of the senses (empiricism), whereas ideational philosophy relies upon the "truth of faith" (fideism). Sensate psychology is behavioristic; ideational psychology introspective. Sensate music, of course, is rock and jazz; ideational music reaches its height in the sacred choir and in the Gregorian chant. Sensate religion is of the lecture-hall variety and emphasizes social welfare; ideational religion is ritualistic and formal and gives its attention to heaven and to hell. Sensate ethics, law, and social relations are "compulsory" and "contractual" rather than "cooperative" and "familistic."

Sorokin devotes several thousand pages to contrasting these two kinds of culture. They are distinct even in mood and temper, for we find the sensate man saying, "*Carpe diem,*" and, "Eat, drink, and be merry, for tomorrow you may die," whereas the ideational man turns the other cheek and preaches the golden rule. Science and invention, in this theory, are almost wholly sensate accomplishments and are not to be expected in an ideational culture. Religion, on the other hand, falters in a sensate culture. In summary, the contrast between these two kinds of culture can be expressed most briefly by saying that the sensate culture is scientific, the ideational culture religious, and that this basic and fundamental distinction pervades every compartment of art and life and thought.

Now Sorokin does not contend that history ever gives us an example of either type of culture in its pure form. He maintains, nevertheless, that various periods of history approach these polar positions. The medieval period is one of the best illustrations, in Western history, of an ideational culture. Our own twentieth-century civilization, on the contrary, is in an "overripe" sensate phase. The entire course of Western history in the last three thousand years has exhibited constant fluctuation between these two poles, the sensate and the ideational. An excess of sensatism begins to produce an opposite effect; the swing begins again to the ideational pole, and vice versa.

If this process is inevitable, however, it is also irregular. History exhibits not cycles but only fluctuations, and although culture is always moving, as it were, in the sensate or ideational direction, it does not always reach these poles. It cannot, however, move permanently in either of these directions. There are limits at which it must inexorably turn in the opposite direction. This "principle of limits" Sorokin illustrates in a simple but graphic fashion: If you strike a piano key you will get a sound. If you strike it harder you will get a louder sound. But there is a limit to this process. There comes a time when, if you strike the key still harder, you get not a louder sound but a broken piano. And so it is with cultures. There comes a time when increasing sensatism produces an opposite effect and so also for increasing ideationism.

The question arises finally as to the basic motivating force of this perennial fluctuation. What is the dynamic, the nisus, the urge, the push, the cause, or whatever one may wish to call it? For an answer to this question Sorokin appeals to something he calls an immanent self-directing principle of change. Culture changes from ideational to sensate, and from sensate to ideational, because it is its nature to change in this way. An acorn develops into an oak tree and not into some other kind of tree because this is its nature. A human organism cannot help going through the successive stages of birth, growth, maturity, decline, and death because this is the nature of organisms. And so once again we find, in spite of the best intentions, the old and familiar biological analogy. Societies, like organisms, may be destroyed before they complete their natural careers, but in the absence of external destructive factors the inherent, internal, immanent causes carry the society to its ideational or sensate destiny. Societies change because it is their nature to change.

What can we say about so impressive a theory? First of all we have to pay a deserved tribute to Sorokin's industry and to his erudition. But then we have to ask some questions. If we hesitate to accept his theory as it appears in these four ambitious volumes, it is because three major problems continue to plague us.

We notice, for example, that Sorokin's concepts of "ideational" and "sensate," though perhaps adequately defined, are ultimately subjective rather than objective categories. The author's prejudices "show through" his argument. The style of the work discloses that by "ideational" Sorokin means most of the things he likes and by "sensate" most of the things he dislikes. Throughout his pages there runs an easily detectible nostalgia for the Middle Ages, a period when truth was established and certain and when all doubts were stilled by authoritarian utterance. Throughout his pages too there runs an animosity toward most of the things our modern scientific, industrial, and technological civilization has produced.

Such sentiments are defensible, and Sorokin, like other men, has every right to enjoy them and to express them. There was much of value in the medieval "ideational" synthesis and much that is tawdry in our own "sensate" accomplishments. It is even meritorious to be reminded that the solution of the world's problems lies in the universal observance of the golden rule and in the conversion of men's hearts to the principles of altruism and of love. But the sociologist needs to know the social and cultural conditions under which these ethical norms can operate, the conditions that encourage or discourage conformity to them, the reasons why they appear in some societies and not in others, and the factors responsible for their social acceptance and practice. These questions Sorokin leaves unanswered.

Nor does it quite suffice to say, on the sociological level, that cultures become sensate or ideational because it is their nature to do so. And this is the second criticism that Sorokin's thesis cannot well sustain. One does not explain a phenomenon by asserting simply that it behaves in a way that is natural to it, by positing some immanent but unknown causes for its operation. An automobile too moves by "immanent causation," but if we were satisfied with this explanation we would know very little about the mechanics of internal-combustion engines. And similarly for societies. They may change because it is their nature to change, but this answer gives us little knowledge of their dynamics.

And finally, as a third source of skepticism regarding Sorokin's theory, we have to suggest that the ideational culture whose virtues he extols is to some extent at least a creation of his imagination and was never even approximated as an historical phenomenon. This creation is a kind of utopia, an Erewhon that appears nowhere, neither in the medieval nor in any other period. Poverty, cruelty, and ignorance are no more admirable in the thirteenth century than they are in the twentieth, and it is altogether fruitless to deny that these traits also, along with religious sensibility, characterized those distant middle centuries of our era. By taking what is best in the Middle Ages and contrasting it with what is worst in our own society, the earlier age seems utopian indeed. But such a comparison is just as illicit as the contrary one would be. Contrasts of this kind, which can easily be supported by selected historical evidence, unfortunately reveal more about the prejudices of the investigator than they do about the processes of history.

Sorokin has given us, in short, a stimulating piece of work, a major assault upon the most important and difficult of all sociological problems, and an original theory. It may be said in addition that he avoids some of the pitfalls of his predecessors. But newer assaults need still be made upon the all but impregnable arcanum that contains the secret of history.

16. Conclusion

In this chapter we have taken a long, long journey, a journey that has no destination. The problem of social and cultural change remains unsolved. For this, however, we offer no apologies. A more extensive treatment of the subject would require careful distinctions between process and change, between single-factor and multiple-factor theories, and particularly between social change and cultural change, together with an analysis of the category of social causation. Our aim in this introductory treatment has been merely to describe the problem, to suggest its magnitude and magnificence, and to indicate some of the solutions that have been proposed for it. Since the entire chapter has been in the nature of a summary, we need not review these solutions here. It is in this field of inquiry that history, philosophy, and sociology meet, and it may reasonably be hoped that the combined efforts of scholars in these three disciplines will in the future present new and still more stimulating answers.